The United States Government:
A Citizen's Inquiry Into What It Is and Might Be

The United States Government:
A Citizen's Inquiry Into What It Is and Might Be

William B. Ayars

www.ivyhousebooks.com

PUBLISHED BY IVY HOUSE PUBLISHING GROUP
5122 Bur Oak Circle, Raleigh, NC 27612
United States of America
919-782-0281
www.ivyhousebooks.com

ISBN: 1-57197-353-2
Library of Congress Control Number: 2002113542

Printed in the United States of America

This book belongs to the citizens of the United States of America. Therefore it is dedicated to every concerned citizen of this potentially great nation.

CONTENTS

PART III
A DISTANT BEACON

PART IV
CONCERNED CITIZENS SEIZE THE OPPORTUNITY

PART V
THOUGHTS ON A NEW WORLD ORDER

Preface

Neither aiming at originality of principle or sentiment, nor yet copied from any particular and previous writing, it was intended to be an expression of the American mind, and to give to that expression the proper tone and spirit called for by the occasion.

—Jefferson's thinking while writing the Declaration of Independence

"Give me your tired, your poor, your huddled masses, yearning to breathe free." Ancestors of many of today's citizens of the United States of America came, breathed free, and built. Their united blood, sweat, and tears built a strong, proud nation.

This book is about what has happened since then. It is also about what this country could be if citizens were to once again unite, sweat, and build in a common quest for a glorious future.

A black hole is a region in space that contains objects of such incredible density that nothing can escape from their gravity, not even light. The analogy with the government in the Washington, DC is accurate: Everything is sucked into the maw, and not even light can escape. Therefore the only way to bring about constructive change is to create a light outside the government. This light will be a beacon that will provide broad direction for systemic change.

The government exists at the core of a class of elites. Although the elite class in this country consists of around 4 million people, there are 210 million adult citizens outside of and alienated from the government. Under the present system, about all they can do is go on paying for it. Most (if not all) of these people would welcome an opportunity to participate in government like citizens would in a true democracy.

The lack of opportunity in the so-called Land of Opportunity causes feelings of extreme frustration. People are desperately seeking an idea that can unite them in a shared interest in good government. They are thoroughly sick of the deception and fantasy that today's government produces (far more heat than light). Their awareness and suspicion deepens with each passing year.

"An invasion of armies can be resisted, but not an idea whose time has come." The timing is right for the right idea. This book describes in detail the nature and severity of the malaise that infects the US government today. Then it presents an idea that provides a path to freedom for those citizens who are willing to seize the initiative to make it work. The problem is rooted in deception and fantasy, but the solution is rooted in truth and reality.

Institutions such as family, school, church, and government guide people's thoughts and behavior. If these and other institutions are built and maintained through efforts based on the positive side of human nature, citizens' lives will be happy and productive. Today's institutions have been corrupted by big government's constantly expanding intrusions, which are based on the negative side of human nature.

The solution lies in citizens taking the initiative in building their own institutions; people support what they help create. This process is grounded in divine guidance, and in faith in the inherent goodness in people.

"He who has the gold makes the rule." This perversion of the Golden Rule accurately describes Washington, DC. Members of the elite class buy privileges with tainted money. Ordinary citizens are forced to feed the monster with their tax dollars, but this only enables the elite class to further consolidate their privileged position and to continue doing harm to others in their own selfish interest. In a true democracy, citizens make their own laws. When they make them they will make few, and they will obey them.

Paternalistic big government prevents citizens from maturing into fully functioning adults by performing tasks that should properly be done by the people themselves through their own initiative and that would better suit their needs. This means the government does more **to** citizens than it does **for** them. It inhibits people from learning about doing for themselves and therefore restrains their development of self-confidence and control over their destinies. The elite class wants people to remain dependent on government.

In theory, as a child matures, wise parents phase out of nurturing and into enabling behavior. This release gives a child the necessary freedom to move past a primary emphasis on security and toward the risks of full adulthood as a free individual. It also provides the freedom to make mistakes that, under the right conditions, are very effective learning tools. Parents would say to their children, "We don't always love what you do or say, but we will always love **you**." This philosophy enables the preservation into later life of the vital intergenerational bond first developed in childhood, but only when the parents are truly adults.

Properly built and maintained, institutions of government enable this kind of existence to flourish. Participation in such a government then becomes an important behavioral component of the fully functioning adult. But today the elites don't want citizens to realize this truth, and this explains the need for deception and fantasy. Nearly everything to do with government is therefore politicized, even the seeking of truth. This scam can only succeed under two conditions. The first lies in truth that although ultimately desirable is by its nature elusive. The second condition requires that the news media cooperate with the elite class by providing disinformation to the public.

In the early days of this country, citizens were not sure precisely in which direction to take their infant nation; they only knew they did not want a monarchy even remotely resembling the one in England. King George had harassed them for years through overbearing taxation and a host of other abuses.

The American Revolution was still in progress in 1781 when the Articles of Confederation were passed into law. But the former colonists had erred on the opposite side: The articles provided practically no powers for the central government. Even collection of taxes was impractical.

Keenly aware of these difficulties in the summer of 1787, a group of leaders convened in Independence Hall in Philadelphia. They created the Constitution of the United States of America. But they did not tell the citizens that this document was the new supreme law that would govern them; rather, the founding fathers put it out "on offer" for public approval. This offer generated massive discussions, pro and con, among thousands of citizens. Many of them carried copies of the document in their pockets, to facilitate debate on its merits. Through these debates citizens came to realize that if they were to effectively govern themselves, discussion and debate were **vitally important**.

Alexander Hamilton, James Madison, and John Jay combined to write eighty-five papers under the pseudonym Publius. These papers were published in prominent newspapers in 1788, with the intent of convincing citizens of the crucial state of New York to persuade their delegates to the state Constitutional Convention to ratify the proposed US Constitution. The new document represented a radical change from the Articles of Confederation. It gave the national government additional powers, but these were carefully delineated and restricted. The founding fathers intended that the vast bulk of governing would take place among neighbors.

Over the years since that time, politicians' actions based on the negative incentives of human nature have steadily enlarged on and abused these powers. They have stolen the citizens' democracy. Today the nation confronts the need for a second radical change in its government. To respond to this need, this book advocates a transition from today's oligarchy to a future democracy.

The book's message has been supplemented with what are called "Pocket Gofers." The author is Publius II. One of these booklets fits comfortably into the back pocket of a pair of slacks or in a purse. They are intended to function in a way very similar to that performed by copies of the proposed constitution in 1788: to generate discussion and debate on the merits of true democracy at this time for the United States.

The Pocket Gofers address the same topics found in the book, so this resource enables citizens to carry pieces of the book with them for discussion at work, school, clubs, civic organizations, and so on. Others might notice a gofer partially sticking out of a citizen's pocket, will question which one it is, and from there will ensue vitally needed discussion.

This interaction is extremely important, for as long as people don't discuss what is happening in government and the news media refuse to help them, they will be unable to determine truth. **As long as citizens cannot distinguish truth from lies government can go on deceiving them indefinitely**. (Pocket Gofers are available for free on Publius II's web site: www.pocketgofer.info. Anyone can enter the business of selling these guides; a page on the site contains an outline for organizing and operating such a business.

The US Constitution created a republican form of government, in which citizens govern themselves through representatives who swear to determine the public will and act on it. True democracy is devoid of such intermediaries. However, in the late eighteenth century travel and communication were very difficult, so the founding fathers settled for something practical as well as radical. Since that time enormous technological progress has created a very different society. Therefore, this book shares a vision of true or direct democracy, which would be history's first experiment with this concept.

Washington, DC, today is a bloated, overbearing, wasteful, and corrupt oligarchy. Citizens struggle under an oppressive regime of government as officials continue to distract their attention from this grim reality. Therefore the objective is to find a middle ground; citizens would give government more powers than were contained in the Articles of Confederation but far fewer than the elite class has gradually taken from them. In essence, today's needed transition is a replay of the events of 1788 but in an immensely different economic, technological, and political context.

The two major political parties seem to compete furiously for votes. But this is only window dressing; the truth is that they have combined forces to fleece the public. Contained within the following pages is an idea for good government that deviates tremendously from the fluff being handed to citizens by the Republican-Democratic party. For the first time in decades, the voter would have real choices.

There are at least thirty books available that present and discuss the national cultural malaise created by the elite class. The typical author is politically prominent and a member of the elite class. He has experience in or close to government, and along with this, insights into its inner workings. He knows the people are alienated, disgusted, and frustrated with government.

Many will read the book hoping to be led away from gridlock, corruption, and deception. Because the public knows his name, both author and publisher feel certain that the book will sell.

The author quickly bangs something out, he and the publisher make money, and readers come away somewhat assuaged if not happy. They recommend the book to others of like mind. Money is made even if the reader's goal was not seriously addressed. This is hardly surprising, as the author and his elitist friends have no interest in derailing the gravy train they have created.

This book addresses the reader's objective in that it identifies and discusses the problem and then the cause, and finally presents a guide toward a solution that is based on both democracy and original thinking. (It is a guide only, as in democracy citizens make the final decisions concerning how they are governed.)

Best-selling thriller writer Tom Clancy observed, "It is often the writer's task to let people know what is possible and what is not, for as writing is a product of imagination, so is all human progress." The clear first priority is generating widespread discussion. If any reader agrees with everything in this book, that reader is not really thinking and will probably not put much spirit into discussions and debates. Each reader will find at least a few desired aspects of the present government eliminated. But this selectivity is essential because each person appreciates different programs, so in the aggregate these "good" pieces make up the mess in today's national government.

Discussions should be conducted while staying mindful of the long-term potential of good government for the nation's children, grandchildren, and generations to come. If good government can become ingrained in a citizen's psyche, he or she will make efforts to ensure that it stays around for the long term.

Taken as a whole, this movement will enable the Age of Reason to prevail in the society, and not just in the United States. In spite of decades of unpardonable abuses in foreign policy, most people in other countries continue to look to this country for leadership. But there is no future in the type of leadership that the elite class is currently providing. A major systemic change is needed that will enable citizens of the world to take the world society into the third millennium. "Ballots, not bullets" is but a small but vital part of this change.

This book is far from flawless. The search for flaws will provide grist for discussions. The author acknowledges the invaluable support of a loving wife Sylvia, deceased. His wife, Pam, has amply dedicated her love to him, and also her literary and technical expertise to the project. Furthermore, praise and gratitude in generous measure go to President Janet Evans and her capable staff at Ivy House.

The author wishes to offer special recognition of *The Economist* newspaper. Reliance on this vehicle is important because effective criticism of the government in Washington is not available through the American news media. Further acknowledgment goes to Charles Adams's books *For Good and Evil* and *Those Dirty Rotten Taxes,* and to Stanley Meisler's book *The United Nations: The First Fifty Years.*

In his observation at the beginning of this preface, Jefferson looked to the American mind and **spirit** to carry the people through what he knew would be a protracted struggle. It is the author's fervent prayer that this spirit yet burns within the breast of today's citizen of the United States of America.

PART I: TO SET THE STAGE

Human nature will only find itself when it fully realizes that to be human it has to cease to be beastly or brutal.

—Mahatma Gandhi

This book explains the behavior of citizens and public officials in terms of human nature. Nearly every person can recognize him- or herself during a discussion of human nature because its most basic propensities toward behavior are the same for everyone, even if in different degree.

Chapter 1 suggests that a split occurred in human nature back in prehistory; the resulting separate aspects were negative and positive. Although human behavior has changed tremendously over the millennia, human nature has changed very little. It still generates propensities based on either the negative or positive side. If an institutional environment can be developed and maintained that caters to the positive side of innate behavior, the individual citizen's pursuit of happiness will be greatly enhanced.

Chapter 2 presents the evolution of government from the beginning of a need for some form of government. From the pagan era, when priestcraft ruled over people; through the era of conquest and plunder, when kings and empires prevailed; and through the Industrial Revolution (1750–1850), when technology assumed a high profile, some form of remote and often overbearing authority restrained human freedom. Recent experiments with government planning of economic activity also exemplified the apparent need for domineering big government.

Chapter 3 gives a brief history of the United States. From its formal beginning on June 21, 1788, with ratification of the US Constitution, individual freedom was considered of primary importance. Even though incursions into that freedom began almost immediately, active citizens kept government small and relatively harmless for the next 160 years. It was only after the Great Depression and World War II that incursions rapidly accelerated in number and in depth of penetration into society, culminating in today's sad situation.

Chapter One:
The Two Sides of Human Nature

Determined to understand human nature, fascinated by nearly everyone he encountered, [John Adams] devoted large portions of his diary to recording their stories, their views on life, how they stood, talked, their facial expressions, how their minds worked.

—David McCullough

Modern science still cannot definitively prove the existence of heaven and hell, but the passage of millenniums have infused in people a mentality that connects to deeply held religious beliefs concerning them. These two spiritual eventualities generate perceptions of a divide, so people tend to assign good and bad to events and actions. This in turn reinforces their original perceptions.

When very little of modern science was known, priestcraft exerted a strong influence. Certain people were entrusted to explain the many mysteries of life, and through this trust they assumed the mantle of local government. Today's manifestation of this mentality can be experienced, even though science has solved many mysteries. People still tend either to trust or distrust others.

Thomas Jefferson stated:

> *Men by their constitutions are naturally divided into two parties. 1. Those who fear and distrust the people, and wish to draw all powers from them into the hands of the higher classes. 2. Those who identify themselves with the people, have confidence in them, cherish and consider them as the most honest and safe, although not the most wise depository of the public interests. In every country these two parties exist, and in every one where they are free to think, speak, and write, they will declare themselves.*[1]

General Observations

Beginning with apes, humans have evolved over several million years. It was only during the past 10,000 years, when the hunter-gatherer society was gradually replaced by the agrarian society, that cultural influences gained credence. This provides an insight into today's nature-nurture controversy. Human nature does not change from one millennium to the next, but technology-driven human behavior does.

Edward O. Wilson suggested a stream-delta analogy.[2] Genes narrowly define behavior at the upper end, in the early stages of a human life. Then culture largely takes over as a person matures, although genes retain some influence. Primary mental abilities are thus defined by heredity, whereas personality develops through the impact of culture.

Sexual division of labor is mostly cultural; hence the great variety across cultures. Local citizens are influenced by their surroundings, so they make rules to fit both the environmental and the genetic components of human nature. This action maximizes genetic fitness and thus societal efficiency. A framework for building institutions, such as family, belief systems, education, health, and laws, is developed, maintained, and adjusted to reflect technocultural changes.

The biological significance of the sex act is sometimes misinterpreted by today's clergy, quite a few of whom still believe its only purpose is reproduction. Indeed, according to the Christian Bible, God mandated population of the world. But Wilson argued that an important purpose of the act is biological. When the Bible was written, little about biology was understood. Also, humans are the only large animals lacking higher ability for fight-or-flight (no sharp teeth or claws, and slow afoot).

These deficiencies put great emphasis on the brain as a tool for survival of the species. Therefore children require a long maturation period, and so the male is needed to help out. Evolution therefore provided that estrus in the female eventually vanish, so she is available for sex nearly all the time. The conclusion is that bonding is an important part of the biology of sex and parenthood.

Wilson concluded that the Bible disapproved of sex between homosexual people because it did not produce children at a time when it was important for population to increase. Today the situation is different. The purpose served by such activity is clearly bonding, as gays and lesbians need this security as much as do heterosexuals.

Puritan ministers used to rally their flocks by pointing to a constant struggle between passion and reason. More recent thinking is secular; the two can work together. Reason can be balanced by emotion, logic by art, criticism by appreciation, and so on.

In the eighteenth century, David Hume separated reason from divine will.[3] This opened the human psyche to the notions of individualism, initiative, and self-reliance. A belief in predestination could then be replaced by a belief in the exercise of free will. He suggested that in this way virtue comes naturally to men and women. What gives form to life is principles, as these guide the manner of choosing. Society cannot be sure of anything; therefore, the search for truth goes on indefinitely. This further suggests that an open mind and heart and moderation in discussion will lead to a virtuous life.

Rose Wilder Lane argued that life is a struggle.[4] If anyone should emerge from strife he or she would relax and let down his guard. This would be an open invitation for those in positions of leadership to take advantage of the situation. Lane originally wrote *The Discovery of Freedom* in 1942, before the advanced world entered the era of affluence (post–World War II).

Faith is static; it is eternal truth. Faith is security, while science is open to question, and, given full play, will eventually become self-correcting. The pursuit of scientific truth is risky, but it is essential if society is to move forward. People have a choice between life in the cocoon and life on the edge. Because at different times each is needed, the spirit and the mind can complement one another in their functions.

Today science has brought society to a threshold of great potential in biological analysis. Biology is rapidly developing; the human genome project is a shining example. In the future the behavioral sciences will join with and probably prevail over biology to enable people to understand themselves more fully. Then they can engage more effectively in the pursuit of happiness, as mentioned in the Declaration of Independence.

Wilson showed that according to DNA tests there is no difference between the races. This means that beauty and biological race are both skin deep. Any generalized behavioral differences are due to social perceptions that evolved before science. They have as much meaning as people want to infer.

The Economist reported on some recent research at University of California at Santa Barbara:

> *For many years, psychologists have believed (and have found data to support) the idea that, when somebody encounters a stranger, the stranger's characteristics are slotted into three pigeon-holes: sex, age, and race. These pigeon-holes are assumed to be long-established, biologically programmed mental faculties.*
>
> *The sexes and ages of other people are social contexts in which decisions have to be made all the time, so the idea of evolved pigeon-holes . . . makes sense. The reason for skepticism about the third category is that, for most of their evolutionary history, human beings would never have been exposed to individuals of other races. It is therefore hard to see how a specifically racial pigeon-holing system could have arisen.*[5]

Presently there is much discussion about genetic engineering and cloning. In the future these developments may change human nature.

The Negative Side

Jefferson alluded to the widely held PANG assumption, which asserts that People Are No Good. This assumption can and does justify a variety of actions that cater to and reinforce the negative side of human nature. This section will show how the assumption came into being and how aware of it were the forefathers who created the original government of the United States.

Evolution did **not** make culture all-powerful as a determinant of human behavior. Therefore, behavior cannot be shaped in disregard of an individual's genetic heritage and the small society's ongoing efforts to improve genetic fit. These truths, however, do little to deter people in authority from trying to do this.

Humankind originally evolved with innate propensities to think well of others and to be helpful. An explanation why under certain conditions someone deviates from this tendency is in order. Lane provided a strong incentive to search diligently for this explanation.

> *The history of every group of men who ever obeyed a living Authority is a history of revolts against all forms of that Government. Look at any available records of any people, living anywhere at any time in the whole history of the Old World. They revolt against their King, and replace him by another King; they revolt against him, and set up another King. In time . . . against monarchy; they set up another kind of living Authority. For generations or centuries, they revolt and change . . . and set up another kind. When these revolts succeed, they are called revolutions. But they are revolutions only in the sense that a wheel's turning is a revolution. An Old World revolution is only a movement around a motionless center; it never breaks out of the circle. Firm in the center is belief in Authority. Every imaginable kind of living Authority has been tried, and is still being tried on earth now.*[6]

Everyone begins life as an infant, totally dependent on an authority figure. Although this dependency gradually subsides, it often all but vanishes when a mature person acquires a mate, and the role is reversed with the arrival of a child.

But this is theory. Few people realize that in practice there are deviations, and this leads into the explanation for which Lane's quote cries out. It lies in a deviation from the genetic fit that was described previously.

As indicated, people left alone in a village will organize institutions that maximize genetic fit. Place in authority other people who have not lived in the village for any length of time, and the potential for a cultural deviation comes with them. Soon indications become manifest.

Even among the most well-intentioned authorities the temptation is to bring the village back into line with some new rules. These people know they are in authority; because the belief in authority is ingrained, they are derelict in their official duty if they don't do something about the situation.

Unfortunately their actions only increase the divergence and hence further undermine genetic fit. Citizens react against this overbearing authority, but this only exacerbates the situation. This reaction generates another batch of rules, another reaction, and then another batch more oppressive. A vicious cycle is inadvertently and insidiously created. Unless checked, the inevitable result is alienation, mutual contempt and, ultimately, open rebellion. Lane showed that this cycle has repeated itself throughout recorded history.

Jeremy Bentham argued that officials abuse their power by defining villagers' satisfaction in terms of benefits to themselves.[7] At some indeterminate point in the vicious circle they observe restless natives and fall back onto the PANG assumption: "These dumb peasants don't deserve our efforts on their behalf, so we will govern to suit ourselves." This abuse goes unrecognized because people have been indoctrinated to believe that one man is his brother's keeper, and therefore the keepers should keep (read: rule) the kept. The cycle is easily carried forward, as any ordinary citizen who questions it obviously "does not understand what is good for the people." (If she persists, she is silenced in one of several ways.)

Jefferson said, "A departure from principle in one instance becomes a precedent for a second; that second for a third; and so on, till the bulk of the society is reduced to be mere automatons of misery, to have no sensibilities left but for sinning and suffering." Later, Dostoevsky wrote *House of the Dead,* in which he graphically expanded on Jefferson's thinking:

> *Whoever has experienced the power, the unrestrained ability to humiliate another human being . . . automatically loses power over his own sensations. Tyranny is a habit, it has its own organic life, it develops finally into a disease. The habit can kill and coarsen the very best man to the level of a beast. Blood and power intoxicate. . . . The man and the citizen die with the tyrant forever; the return to human dignity, to repentance, to regeneration, becomes almost impossible.*

Hume pointed out that philosophy, religion, reason, and faith could all unite in various ways to subjugate men and women to rules. He referred especially to religion: "Popular rage . . . must be attended with the most pernicious consequences, when it arises from a principle which disclaims all control by human law, reason, or authority." With no room for discussion based on reason, passions will govern behavior. If deemed expedient, public officials will not refrain from twisting even the definition of reason.

Appealing to emotions can rally citizens, and does so in the absence of reason, as Lane implied. Hume went on to state that "when political ends are modest and mundane, politics may be moral. It is only when the end is glory that political violations of moral rules are granted dispensations. Some great movement, an overwhelming purpose, or a noble principle makes everything else shrink out of sight."

Politicians seeking approval for moral violations simply appeal to the public's emotions. A deemphasized role for reason makes this action simple. One sure-fire emotional trigger can lie in a perceived military threat from afar. This gimmick has worked for centuries and is obviously still effective.

Officials spread propaganda about external threats, and they also control internal information, hoping that what citizens don't know will keep them panicked and subjugated. But this action brings forth the same outcome as Hume predicted: It stimulates the rumor mill as a substitute for withheld truth, and eventually mistrust, alienation, and contempt.

Jefferson is widely acclaimed around the world as history's deepest thinker and practitioner of democracy. In 1785 he was in France, serving as a US ambassador. He wrote: "Human nature is the same on every side of the Atlantic, and will be alike influenced by the same causes. The time to guard against corruption and tyranny, is before they shall have gotten hold of us. It is better to keep the wolf out of the fold, than to trust to drawing his teeth and claws after he shall have entered."

Jefferson wrote to Col. Carrington in 1788: "The natural progress of things is for liberty to yield and government to gain ground. As yet our spirits are free." He wrote this after observing universal misery among French citizens under an oppressive government, just before the French Revolution. After returning to the United States in 1792, Jefferson wrote to President George Washington: "These were no longer the votes then of the representatives of the people; and it was impossible to consider their decisions, which had nothing in view but to enrich themselves, as the measures of the fair majority, which ought always to be respected."

The summer of 1787 was long and hot. Delegates to the Constitutional Convention kept all windows and doors closed in Independence Hall because they wanted to present the document to the public for its approval as a whole package. If citizens got hold of parts of it, they might cause such commotion that the document could not be completed. Suspense was at fever pitch on September 17, when the delegates emerged for the last time. Benjamin Franklin was eighty-two years old and suffering from gout and other ailments. He remarked:

> *In these sentiments, Sir, I agree to this Constitution with all its faults, if they are such, because I think a general government necessary for us, and there is no form of government but what may be a blessing to the people if well administered, and believe farther that this is likely to be well administered for a course of years and can only end in despotism, as other forms have done before it, when the people shall become so corrupted as to need despotic government, being incapable of any other.*

Note that Franklin did not say **if** the people should become so corrupted; he said **when**. He thus placed his lot among the several illustrious forefathers who possessed deep insights into human nature.

In 1775, Patrick Henry stated:

> *It is natural to man to indulge in the illusions of hope. We are apt to shut our eyes against a painful truth, and listen to the song of that siren, till she transforms us into beasts. Is this the part of wise men, engaged in a great and ardu-*

ous struggle for liberty? Are we disposed to be of the number of those who, having eyes, see not, and having ears, hear not, the things that so nearly concern their temporal salvation? For my part, whatever anguish of spirit it may cost, I am willing to know the truth; to know the worst and provide for it.

Truth is, or certainly should be, the holy grail. But it is elusive, and therefore subject to abuse by authorities. History shows how thoroughly this lesson has been learned by rulers.

In his farewell address on March 4, 1797, George Washington said: "The unity of government which constitutes you one people is also now dear to you. It is justly so, . . . But as it is easily to foresee that from different causes and from different quarters much pains will be taken, may artifices employed, to weaken in your minds the conviction of this truth." An unknown author said, "Eternal vigilance is the price of liberty."

The Positive Side

This section investigates the ramifications of the flip side of the PANG attitude, discussed previously. The belief here begins with recognition of the PANG: people are stupid, think only in the short term, and so on. Fortunately there exists a superclass of people to rule over them. Then the attitude is reversed in favor of a faith in people. Give them an **opportunity** to install and maintain institutions of their own free choice, and they will respond with an intelligence and wisdom that does not seem to exist in citizens in the absence of this opportunity.

John Adams's thinking reflected this faith in people, as McCullough explained:

Beholding the night sky, "the amazing concave of Heaven sprinkled and glittering with stars," he was "thrown into a kind of transport" and knew such wonders to be the gifts of God, expressions of God's love. But greatest of all, he wrote, was the gift of an inquiring mind. . . . "[A] wonderful provision He has [made] for the gratification of our nobler powers of intelligence and reason. He has given us reason to find out the truth, and the real design and true end of our existence." [8]

Wilson showed that natural Darwinian selection increases genetic diversity through sexual reproduction. In this way genes are mixed, and the result is a better genetic fit in some people than in others. Those with a better fit are generally more active in reproduction. Hence there occurs a gradual improvement in the species over many generations.

Knowledge is combining and will combine with wisdom in the future to provide the ultimate emancipator. With free choice, people will decide which of the elements of human nature to cultivate and which to de-emphasize. Individuals will understand themselves better and make better decisions concerning their destinies. Finally, when genes can be adjusted through genetic engineering, a strong and happy society will emerge.

The Enlightenment (about 1700–1780) forecasted the Age of Reason. Before this period, priests, shamans, and others believed to possess supernatural powers contested for power with kings. Practically nothing of science was known, so rulers relied on passions like superstition and fear to keep the populace in line.

Populations increased and weapons were developed; eventually kings took over from priests. They ruled through conquest and plunder. As science began to make inroads, analysis and reason acquired higher profiles.

Time passed, and colonists in what was to become the United States began to think in terms of a new era, which they called the Age of Reason. Alexander Hamilton and others saw the futility of constant fighting, which had plagued the Old World for centuries. There had to be a better way.

The Industrial Revolution (1750–1850) introduced a new concept called capitalism. It is today the only known nonviolent way to create and accumulate wealth. During the revolution capitalists combined advancing scientific knowledge with workers and machines to move society forward in leaps and bounds.

As new wealth and knowledge diffused through the culture it accelerated a previously established social trend toward secularism. This further moderated the influence of the priesthood but did not erase it.

In terms of human nature, here was an opportunity to redirect the natural aggressive instinct in the male. Weapons and fighting are based more on passions than on reason. This book will demonstrate that in the Age of Reason there will be little need for such negative passions, as thinking and actions based on reason will prevail. Also, if the male is more often home, there will be more sex and bonding. These tend to ameliorate aggression.

Historically, it is surely a strange paradox that although the clergy preach tolerance and world brotherhood, "leaders" have referred to religious beliefs as bases for wreaking massive bloodshed, destruction, and misery. This paradox can be at least partially resolved through the realization that priests have the same problem as government officials in that mundane, daily religion does not create the excitement needed to keep the flock under their influence. Accomplishing this task requires continuing arousal of passions.

Wilson wrote:

> *Overwhelmed by shibboleths, special costumes, and sacred dancing and music accurately keyed to his emotive centers, he is transformed by a religious experience. The votary is ready to reassert allegiance to his tribe and family, perform charities, consecrate his life, leave for the hunt, join the battle, die for God and country. It was true in the past.*[9]

Today the clergy have moved toward the Age of Reason. There is relatively little hellfire and damnation coming from the pulpit, as they answer an evolving

need among individuals for human fellowship. (This book will show how wealth and big government contributed to this evolution.) A logical conclusion is to combine good spiritual nourishment, good sex, and good politics to provide a good society.

Contemporary religion thus assumes a more positive role. With scientific progress and vastly increased knowledge people today can concern themselves with holistic health—the mind, heart, body, and spirit working together in harmony and synergy. With this, the sins of the flesh abate and individuals acquire a morality adapted by each to each.

This morality facilitates the seeking of truth: It needs facilitating lest it be abandoned as a futile quest. In the search for truth the mechanical rabbit on the racetrack always stays slightly ahead of the dogs, but in the seeking society moves ahead. Because truth is elusive, its pursuit must involve constant questioning of dogma, religious and otherwise. But as any institution ages, the status quo gradually looms larger as a guide to its operations. Social gridlock is not a good thing.

Given momentum, the Age of Reason will generate reasoned reflection and an interest in integrity. Without the institutions necessary to provide positive incentives, a deteriorating moral climate will undermine integrity. In the eighteenth century Hume considered integrity the basic political virtue. He saw it as a quality of character, not of particular acts. This quality cemented the individual to standards and pledges regardless of the temptations of immediate advantage.

In a village with a strong genetic fit, altruism will encourage giving of time, talents, and money. Ralph Waldo Emerson said that no one can help others without also helping himself. But another point deserves equal emphasis: such giving must be voluntary to have the desired total impact. The head and the heart should both be involved. Philip Wylie argued that a preoccupation with goods undermines goodness.[10] His point makes it still easier to understand why Mother Teresa won a Nobel Peace Prize.

Jefferson wrote to a young friend:

> *Man was destined for society. His morality, therefore, was to be formed to this object. He was endowed with a sense of right and wrong, merely relative to this. This sense is as much a part of his nature, as the sense of hearing, seeing, feeling; it is the true foundation of morality, . . . The moral sense, or conscience, is as much a part of man as his leg or arm. It is given to all human beings in a stronger or weaker degree, as force of members is given them in a greater or less degree. It may be strengthened by exercise, as may any particular limb of the body. This sense is submitted, indeed, in some degree, to the guidance of reason; but it is a small stock which is required for this: even a less one than what we call common sense. State a moral case to a ploughman and a professor. The former will decide it as well, and often better than the latter, because he has not been led astray by artificial rules.*

Here is another insight into human nature, and a most useful one. Jefferson argued that a man has (with only rare exceptions) the **natural** propensity to live in conjunction with others. If he or she could exist alone there would be no need for morality.

John Locke wrote about natural law during the seventeenth century. In his *Two Treatises of Government* (1690), he attacked the theory of divine right of kings and the nature of the state as conceived by the English philosopher and political theorist Thomas Hobbes. In brief, Locke argued that sovereignty did not reside in the state but with the people. The state is supreme, but only if it is bound by civil and what he called "natural" law. Many of Locke's political ideas, such as those relating to natural rights, property rights, the duty of the government to protect these rights, and the rule of the majority, were later embodied in the US Constitution.

Having experienced misery under King George where the state was not bound by any restraint in its dealings with the colonies, the founding fathers were sensitive to Locke's beliefs when they formulated the Constitution. They felt that the **overriding need was to restrain government** from infringing on the rights of citizens.

Patrick Henry believed the following: "The battle, sir, is not to the strong alone; it is to the vigilant, the active, the brave." His emphasis on vigilance relates to the negative side of human nature: Institutions that elicit behavior related to the positive side may be constructed, but they must be maintained lest they gradually change into those that encourage negative behavior. The founding fathers understood and appreciated this truth. But they also realized that a piece of parchment, however eloquently, intelligently, and wisely constructed, would not guarantee positive behavior in perpetuity. This point is important.

What are natural laws? Locke was not as explicit as was Bastiat in *The Law* (1850):

> *We hold from God the gift which includes all others. This gift is life—physical, intellectual and moral life. . . . Life, faculties, production—in other words, individuality, liberty, property—this is man. And in spite of the cunning of artful political leaders, those three gifts from God precede all human legislation, and are superior to it.*

Note how the Declaration of Independence reflected this philosophy: "That all men are created equal; that they are endowed by their Creator with certain unalienable Rights; that among these are Life, Liberty, and the Pursuit of Happiness."

The US Constitution was designed to protect citizens from the depredations of government, but it also provided a positive incentive toward private enterprise. One reason for this was that a very small central government on a limited budget could not afford to hand out benefits to citizens. There was no incentive for citizens to form groups and demand benefits from government.

Under such a regime, wealthy and middle-class citizens can provide benefits for the masses through productive investment. But when government is not restrained it will grow very large. The wealthy will then use some of their money to buy special favors from government officials, and productive investment will suffer.

The founding fathers exercised rare foresight in this instance. They were guided by three timeless truths: (1) citizens must control themselves through moral self-discipline, or some restraint must stop them from abuse of their liberties; (2) humans naturally seek recognition, influence, and eventually power over others; and (3) man's nature is to work hard toward self-improvement when the way is open for this.

The first truth illustrates both sides of human nature, the second the negative, and the third is positive under the right conditions. Take away the self-control, and government will step in to restrain the citizens. But general laws don't discriminate; they restrain honest people just as they do the dishonest ones. Furthermore, when honest citizens create laws, the result is a proper emphasis on individual morality.

Jefferson stated, "Every man wishes to pursue his occupation and to enjoy the fruits of his labors and the produce of his property in peace and safety and with the least possible expense. When these things are accomplished, all the objects for which government ought to be established are answered."

Incentives that Institutions Can Provide for Individuals

An institution is a formal or semi-formal organization that meets some aspects of the natural need for people to work together. Examples include family, clubs, companies, schools, teams, charities, religious groups, and government agencies. The objective of these institutions is to encourage but not force human behavior based on the positive side of human nature and to discourage the negative.

An institution should have a distant, shared, and unifying goal. It may have a life that lasts well beyond that of its creators. However, because society changes over time, every institution has a limited life. That life can be extended, but only if the people involved in its maintenance remain open to suggestions for change.

People act on their perceptions: They respond to perceived incentives. People naturally tend to perceive good in themselves and in others, but this varies as negative temptations hover nearby and influence perception. These temptations create feelings of insecurity, so properly constructed institutions should be available as resources for needed assistance. On the positive side, institutions also enhance good feelings.

Alexis de Tocqueville toured the United States in 1830.

> *As soon as they have lost the way of relying chiefly on distant hopes, they are naturally led to want to satisfy their least desires at once; and it would seem that as soon as they despair of living forever, they are inclined to act as if they could not live for more than a day. . . .*
>
> *In skeptical ages, therefore, there is always a danger that men will give way to ephemeral and casual desires and that, wholly renouncing whatever cannot be acquired without protracted effort, they may never achieve anything great or calm or lasting.*[11]

Institutions established and maintained by the people who utilize them will nurture distant hopes, primarily through keeping faith in people predominant over skepticism.

Wilson pointed out that today's citizens apparently lack a unifying goal.[12] Major wars are past history (as this book will argue), so society should logically search for a new morality based more closely on a true definition of what it is to be human. Therefore people must look inward at their minds, but when they do this they will discover a need for a "choice that must be made among the ethical premises inherent in man's biological nature." Who is to make this choice?

Local village residents know the territory and can build institutions toward maximizing genetic fit and to minimize the social costs of living together. They will be guided by principles that spring from resolutions of ethical choices through discussion.

People support what they help create. A public-spirited government official will do all that is practical to see that when an institutional landscape is being painted there is a paintbrush in every hand. In practice this will minimize departure from principle. Civic pride will create incentives to contribute.

Once built, institutions will be maintained through debate and constructive criticism encouraged by public officials. This democratic process requires minds that are truly open to change. Thoughts and words must flow freely as hearts and minds unite.

Excellent beginnings toward this objective may be found, first, in the Ten Commandments. These make up a Judeo-Christian concept, but they are nonetheless widely applicable. Discouragement pervades nearly all: No other God; neither make graven images, nor bow down to them; no taking the name of the Lord in vain; no killing; no committing adultery; no stealing; no bearing false witness; and no coveting a neighbor's wife, nor any of his possessions.

These commandments clearly connect with individual morality and self-discipline. A second group of commandments provides what are sometimes called "negative" rights. This is the Bill of Rights, or the first ten amendments to the Constitution. Congress shall make no law restricting freedom of religion, speech, press, or assembly; no soldier shall be quartered in any house; no unreasonable searches or seizures; no conviction without jury; no double punishment; no private property taken for public use without compensation; no excessive bail and no cruel and unusual punishment; rights enumerated here shall not restrict other rights; and no taking by the central government of rights belonging to the states and the people.

Instead of commandments, these are called *principles*. They are not intended to restrain negative behavioral tendencies on the part of individuals; rather the intent is to **restrain people in positions of authority from taking advantage of those positions to infringe on the rights of citizens**. Restraints on the negative behavior of individuals is the proper role of local law, which is based on the principles enshrined in the Constitution. Thus the Ten Commandments can combine with the Bill of Rights to create a free and moral citizen.

Constitutional restraints have been around for a long time. How effective are they? In today's society, prevalent behavior seems to bear few of these marks. Why? The answer lies in overmature, bloated, irrelevant, and stagnant government, and in other institutions. Good men and women refuse to serve because they have learned that these institutions are not amenable to real change. Interest among incumbent officials in continuing without change is so deeply entrenched that an outsider's argument for change has no chance of acceptance. Because of constantly increasing irrelevancy, citizens are frustrated, and they blame elected public officials for not bringing about needed and often promised change. Because no real change is possible, this frustration becomes manifest through complaining, as citizens know that no one will listen to constructive criticism.

The rich do not need to complain, because they have learned how to feed off the system by purchasing privileges from public officials. They do not need to occupy public office to fill their needs. When those institutions that make up the system get sufficiently large, overbearing, and immobile, genetic fit suffers. Concerned citizens become so preoccupied with fighting the system that they see little point in standing for public office even when motivated. This leaves only people who seek power and privilege without earning it outside government. In this way negative incentives influence the behavior of public officials.

An example of such an institution lies in law. The Greek philosopher Plato argued that good people do not need laws to tell them to act responsibly, but bad people will always find a way around law. Much later a German said, "The more laws the less justice." In 1770 Bentham claimed that British common law is actually no law: "Nothing but a large and muddled mass of judicial opinions from which lawyers could draw whatever they liked." Because common law depends so much on precedent, Bentham also claimed that "the body of the law was the same as that administered by the court of judges in the middle of the 12th century."

Law in the United States is derived directly from British common law. There is evidence that today the high and mighty in Washington behave as if there are no laws restraining their activities, even though each year Congress turns out some

7,500 pages of new legislation and the executive branch creates a 75,000-page tidal wave of administrative law aimed at restraining citizens' activities. The unavoidable conclusion is that the government is an institution that is utterly beyond the control of anyone, except possibly top public officials.

Here are some principles that citizens might use to create institutions that meet their needs. One of these is accountability. If a child is not brought to account when he or she is caught with his hand in the cookie jar, he has not learned anything. There is no deterrent to restrain similar behavior in the future. If he is properly and consistently punished for this and other infractions, he may become a moral adult. However, this book will show that if a public official gets near a large enough quantity of public money and no one is looking, he or she will be tempted. In this situation the implications obviously go far beyond that of a missing cookie or a ruined dinner, but the principle is the same.

A second principle is diffusion of power. The negative tendency among people has power always tending to concentrate in one location. The simple rationale is: How can I get anything done without some clout? The answer lies in distribution of power, such that the official must work through several or many citizens to get what he or she wants done. Here is another way to minimize temptation.

A third principle restrains withholding information. Especially in an info-tech society, concentrated information and money mean concentration of power. Citizens should demand free information flow for another reason—without it they cannot discuss issues, formulate ideas, and vote from a full knowledge base.

Because by definition government is force, a fourth principle protects personal freedoms through a minimum of such use. This restraint includes fraud, and deliberately making issues overly complex is a form of fraud.

Another important principle is tolerance. If a paintbrush is placed in every hand, active participation will be encouraged from everyone regardless of skin color, ethnic background, age, gender, and so on. Mutual trust and confidence demands mutual respect as a prerequisite.

The advent of the Age of Reason suggests another principle—the restraint of passions. Whenever passions displace reason they impede effective communication and generate unneeded and undesired conflict.

Finally, individual rights must be accompanied by individual responsibility. This requirement enables personal freedoms to attain their full potential. A society that emphasizes rights without responsibilities will not remain a society for long, because a restraining morality is absent.

When citizens build and maintain institutions they will maximize genetic fit. In the Age of Reason good people will want to serve in elective office. They will help keep the environment geared to freedom of thought, speech, and actions, and they will combine their efforts with those of citizens to move society forward in an orderly, peaceful, and smooth manner.

Natural law was discussed. Its practice ingrains morality as self-discipline restrains a citizen from infringing on another's natural rights. Put another way, a person can do whatever he or she likes, but he may not interfere with the natural rights of others. These restraints are civil rights in respect of others.

A person's natural desire is to improve his or her lot in life. With free choice this can (and often does) involve education leading to self-knowledge, leading in turn to self-discipline, leading finally to an inner integrity and virtue, and honesty in dealing with others.

Seeking truth encourages open dialog with others. This means emphasis on listening as well as effective speaking, because dialog is a two-way street. Effective listening not only brings out ideas that may otherwise never see the light of day; it also creates a climate of mutual trust and confidence. Public officials cannot govern well if they are not good listeners.

There is a place for faith, as science does not reveal all. Furthermore, a fully functioning adult will be encouraged through participation in institutions aimed toward holistic health, where the spirit complements mind, body, and heart. Doubt has a vital role in the maintenance of an institution, because it encourages constructive criticism.

A battle over ideas and recommendations redirects the natural aggression usually found in humans. Tocqueville learned during his visit that people often battled tooth-and-claw over ideas in political meetings and then returned home to a tranquil household. His experience in France showed that, denied this opportunity for intellectual combat, the household all too frequently struggled in marital conflict.

Reflection is an outgrowth of self-discipline. The individual citizen will utilize influence from without in combination with reflection within. This exercise not only generates potentially useful ideas, it also enhances self-knowledge.

Jefferson wrote, "that man is a rational animal, endowed by nature with rights, and with an innate sense of justice; and that he could be restrained from wrong and protected in right, by moderate powers, confined to persons of his own choice, and held to their duties by dependence on his own will."

Notes

1. Thomas Jefferson, *The Life and Selected Writings of Thomas Jefferson*, edited by Koch and Peden. Random House, 1944.
2. Edward O. Wilson, *On Human Nature*. Harvard University Press, 1978.
3. David Hume, *A Treatise of Human Nature.* 1739–40.
4. Rose Wilder Lane, *The Discovery of Freedom*. Fox and Wilkes, 1993.
5. *The Economist*, "Them." December 15, 2001, p. 63.
6. Lane, *Discovery of Freedom*.

7. Jeremy Bentham, *Introduction to the Principles and Morals of Legislation.* 1789.
8. David McCullough, *John Adams.* Simon and Schuster, 2001.
9. Wilson, *On Human Nature.*
10. Philip Wylie, *A Generation of Vipers.* Dalkey Archive Press, 1946.
11. Alexis de Tocqueville, *Democracy in America.* Knopf, 1972.
12. Wilson, *On Human Nature.*

revised through free inquiry. About the same time Sigmund Freud's work and his remarkable ability to promote it stirred people's thinking about themselves. Thus the two theorists combined to demonstrate the potential of free inquiry.

However, people were not used to thinking for themselves, due in large part to the legacy of religious dogma. Their minds were open, but what the typical citizen perceived was tantamount to an intellectual vacuum.

Enter the thinking of Karl Marx. He wrote during the end of the Industrial Revolution, when inexperienced factory managers were exploiting workers. The vacuum was thus filled, but time later proved that Marxian philosophy was flawed.

That said, one might argue that today people's minds are again open to some new thinking. Quite possibly a new vacuum has evolved. But if this is true, the vacuum is currently being filled with drivel, which comes at people through television, deceptive government rhetoric, and an overemphasis on a materialistic imperative (Chapter 4 elaborates).

Thomas Jefferson wrote, "And why subject to coercion? To produce uniformity. But is uniformity of opinion desirable? No more than of face and stature." Uniformity of opinion produces a static society, which rulers heartily endorse. But this type of regime obviously could not persist over the long term before the Industrial Revolution, much less afterward. A change in the right direction would enable the wheel to drive the culture forward; it would stop spinning in the sludge of continuous warfare. To break the cycle systemic change is required, but a power-drunk ruler will not initiate it because to do so would spell the end of his reign.

The Industrial Revolution, Capitalism, and Modern Democracy

A new process with tremendous social impact occurred during the same time period as did development of two new theories. All three are interdependent, so the following discussion will demonstrate this linkage and also explain how it created the societies that exist today in advanced countries. Discussion begins with this statement: capitalism is the only known nonviolent method where a society can create and accumulate wealth.

For democracy and capitalism to flourish there must be free inquiry, which did not exist in a world of monarchies. There must a vibrant private economic sector. Furthermore the *authority* mentality must wane, because otherwise society will send its best and brightest young people into the public sector. This robs the private sector, which creates wealth, of society's most talented and energetic people. The public sector cannot create wealth; it can only spend it. Thus the best people will be motivated through negative incentives (often in spite of good intentions) to spend more, create and expand bureaucracies, and eventually undermine the private sector. The goose that laid the golden egg will sicken and ultimately die. (The most prominent current example is the former Soviet Union.)

Before the Industrial Revolution there was little change over the centuries. There were few inventions because there was practically no incentive to invent. An inventor could not improve his lot in life in a strictly hierarchical society. What science that existed was discouraged. For example, Galileo's reward for his efforts was to stand trial for heresy and be excommunicated. People learned almost exclusively from history, so older people were revered à la Confucius and their opinions became fact.

The Industrial Revolution commenced around 1750 and lasted for roughly 100 years. Although there were machines before this time, they operated on energy derived directly from nature, such as water power. The invention of pressurized steam power opened vast new possibilities to multiply the economic productivity of workers. The muscles and sweat of people and animals gradually became less important.

The agrarian economy phased into a production-oriented economy. Mechanized farming reduced demand for labor, and people streamed into the cities in search of wage labor. These people not only had to adjust to city life, they also had to get used to working for someone other than family or a neighbor. Managers of factories also found themselves in unfamiliar territory, because there was no precedent and hence no known skills that could guide supervision of hundreds of workers. As a result, working conditions were terrible.

Back on the farm, a historically new concept took hold. Up to this time only monarchs and churches owned land; now registration of private ownership and right of inheritance took hold. This provided a positive incentive for farmers to improve their land through drainage and fertilization. Furthermore, with benefit of legal ownership farmers could borrow against their land to purchase better equipment. (The concept of private property was attacked in turn by Marx, Lenin, Stalin, and Hitler, with predictable results.)

Surely the Industrial Revolution would not have continued for 100 years were there not other positive results, and of course there were. Because wage labor was made much more productive with machines, for the first time in history the ordinary worker found money in his pocket that was not needed immediately for the essentials of life. He could save some of this money for a brighter future and spend some of it on luxuries, such as a better diet, a better house, and nice clothes. From management's point of view, surplus wealth was created that could be invested in plant and company expansion. Some of this wealth found its way into banks, stocks, and bonds. This meant that an expanding company strapped for cash could tap into sources outside of internally generated profits. Furthermore, there was financing available for entrepreneurs to start new businesses.

According to Toffler wealth is medium-quality power.[7] Both the carrot and the stick could be used to encourage the horse to pull the wagon. Furthermore, wealth could expand without practical limit. With the aid of financial institutions, such as banks, it could also circulate to where it could be utilized most productively (provided that the market was kept free). Because wealth was no longer confined to king's vaults or squandered on weapons and war, it could enable ordinary people to raise their living standards.

Joseph Schumpeter wrote on creation of new wealth: "The fundamental impulse that sets and keeps the capitalist engine in motion comes from the new consumers' goods, the new methods of production or transportation, the new markets, the new forms of industrial organization that capitalist enterprise creates."[8] Confucius would not have approved of this constructive and dynamic force.

There is nothing as practical as a good theory. Schumpeter also observed: "Queen Elizabeth owned silk stockings. The capitalist achievement does not typically consist in providing more silk stockings for queens but in bringing them within the reach of factory girls in return for steadily decreasing amounts of effort."

The fact that war only destroys and leaves both adversaries poorer was well known. World War II hero Winston Churchill appreciated this fact when he commented on free trade:

> *Both the selling and the buying . . . were profitable to us; that what we sold [was] profit, . . . what we bought, [was] worth our while to buy, and . . . [we] turn[ed] it to advantage. And in this way commerce is utterly different from war, so that the ideas . . . of the one should never be applied to the other; for in trade, like the quality of mercy, are twice blessed, and confer a benefit on both parties.*

Churchill was a student of British history, as Jim Powell demonstrated:

> *Although European countries retained their prohibitive tariffs, England prospered. Cheap food poured into the country, and workers shifted out of agriculture into manufacturing. Then as other countries industrialized, many workers shifted into services. England became the leader of world shipping, commerce, insurance, and finance. From 1846 until the outbreak of World War I, its industrial output soared 290 percent.*[9]

A less obvious result of the Industrial Revolution lies in the notion of democratic leveling. The theory of democracy includes equal opportunity for self-improvement. Alexis de Tocqueville observed:

> *I appreciate that in a democracy so constituted society would not be at all immobile; but the movements inside the body social could be orderly and progressive; one might find less glory there than in an aristocracy, but there would*

> *be less wretchedness; pleasures would be less extreme, but well-being more general; the heights of knowledge might not be scaled, but ignorance would be less common, feelings would be less passionate, and manners gentler; there would be more vices and fewer crimes.*[10]

The young Frenchman examined society in the United States during an 1830 visit, having had previous experience in Europe for use as a basis for comparison. He found citizens fully as interested in money then as today, but at that time it circulated rapidly. Because human nature tends to make children of wealth less industrious, he rarely found successive generations enjoying wealth. Even the poor could perceive opportunities.

Capitalism makes working capital (money) available to entrepreneurs; this is often all an aspiring business owner needs to get off to a good start. To the extent that capitalism exists unfettered, economies will be strong and dynamic.

However, there is a flip side. In mature capitalistic economies dynamism is likely to slow down as crony capitalism gets a start and begins to flourish. Big businesses and other special groups with money develop contacts within government, and they utilize money to buy influence over legislation and administrative law (regulations). Eventually these groups are included in a developing oligarchy.

Crony capitalism soon becomes a mechanism whereby wealth is transferred from the nonrich middle class to the rich. Fettered in this manner, capitalism loses its ability to lift the poor; they lose most in proportion to their wealth. Advanced examples of this phenomenon may be found in several South American countries, where the middle class has been all but bled out of existence.

Members of the elite class need to hide this development from the masses, so they use some of the citizens' own tax money to distribute it and other benefits to them. From here it is but a step to socialism.

Two hundred years of capitalism has conferred another unique benefit on some people. For the first time in history, people are voluntarily working fewer hours and reserving more for leisure. A study indicates that since 1880 a male head of household's nonwork time has increased from 10.5 to 40 hours a week. This healthy development partially explains recent news media hype about a decline in inflation-adjusted wages for workers over the past twenty-five years.

Other conditions have also changed during the past quarter of a century. Welfare recipients are not as likely to report all of their incomes in order to keep qualifying for assistance. Workers are often shareholders today, so they have unearned income supplementing their wages. The conclusion is that capitalism has had a leveling effect, even in spite of the advent of crony capitalism. Aside from a small minority of super-rich the gap in total annual income between the middle class and the poor has been reduced.

An economic study of almost any poor country without capitalism will reveal far greater inequalities of wealth and income between rich and poor. *The Economist* answered critics of capitalism:

> *Their complaint is rather that growth serves the interests only of the rich. . . . inequalities widen and the poor are left out. . . . But a new paper by David Dollar and Art Kraay of the World Bank puts matters straight. Its findings could hardly be clearer. Growth really does help the poor: in fact, it raises their incomes by about as much as it raises the incomes of everybody else. . . . The rich, the poor and the country as a whole are all seeing their incomes rise simultaneously at about the same rate.* [11]

The two researchers used data on eighty countries collected over four decades.

As democracy developed, citizens created local governmental institutions; during the nineteenth century the long arm of government was not so long. Tocqueville observed that when citizens make their own laws they will obey them; crime was not a problem. They used government for disputes only when they could not resolve them by themselves. They found pleasure in participating in government. Government power was acknowledged as necessary, but it was divided among many who exercised it. There was no center of thought, intelligence, action, or power.

The collective wisdom of the mass of citizens was perceived to be better at identifying what is good for them than was a central authority; this was a major departure in thought from the millenniums leading up to the Industrial Revolution. Persuading large numbers of people to be active was often a challenge, but starting a local newspaper was easy; it was part of a local institution aimed at stimulating political dialog.

De Tocqueville noted,

> *Three factors seem to contribute more than all others to the maintenance of a democratic republic in the New World. The first is the federal form adopted by the Americans, which allows the Union to enjoy the power of a great republic and the security of a small one. The second are communal institutions which moderate the despotism of the majority and give the people both a taste for freedom and the skill to be free. The third is the way the judicial power is organized. I have shown how the courts correct the aberrations of democracy and how, though they can never stop the movements of the majority, they do succeed in checking and directing them.*

In a democracy minorities have basic political rights as individuals, which the majority must respect.

The central government itself had no rights, only duties, and only those duties that citizens consented to assign to it. All other rights and duties went to state and local governments and to citizens (the Tenth Amendment to the US

Constitution). Enlightened citizens permitted only a small national government; Tocqueville described Washington as "a sleepy little town."

The Industrial Revolution and capitalism are economic concepts. Democracy is a political concept, which was described by Lewis Lapham as a mentality.[12] Whenever these are interlinked it is worthwhile to investigate how this system affects positive and negative incentives of human nature. The inquiry appears in this book with the benefit of hindsight that was not available to Tocqueville and early leaders in the infant United States. (Chapter 3 will demonstrate that the founding fathers performed admirably well without a thorough knowledge of economics.)

It was Friedrich Hayek in the 1940s who first broke away from looking at the economics of a society in static terms, even though the Industrial Revolution had long before that introduced the notion of dynamism.[13] He saw a market as a "process of discovery" that can "handle complexity." His thinking ventured out beyond economics; he argued that altruism works well in small groups but gets buried in the immense complexity of a large society. This means that for socialism to work as a master plan for organizing a nation's economic activity the political arrangement must include a strong "authority" at the center. That is, people will not cooperate unless the government forces them to do so.

Hayek further argued that a democracy with majority rule cannot work if the minority is suppressed. This is only logical, as reflection reveals that every new idea that has the potential to move any size society forward exists at the beginning in a minority: one thinking and concerned citizen. Such a citizen is not readily identifiable because not every idea is a good one. But when that person is denied a voice, society cannot move forward.

It has been shown in this chapter that strong central government officials value the status quo. Any law or policy they push at the citizens is likely to widen the genetic divergence, which was discussed in Chapter 1.

The benefits of personal political freedom are generally long-term, and the costs may be hard to identify and quantify. The advantages of government-mandated economic leveling are immediately obvious and are proven vote winners. In this way political freedom can be lost through government fakery (more on this in Chapters 9 and 10).

Tocqueville reinforced this conclusion: "But liberty is generally born in stormy weather, growing with difficulty amid civil discords, and only when it is already old does one see the blessings it has brought."

Government Planning of Economic Activity

The spread of capitalism benefits nearly all but simultaneously makes some people feel economically insecure. The combination of more money available and insecurity tends to increase spending on social programs. These become attractive through increased supply (of money) and increased demand (from insecure people). In a society with elections, politicians like these programs for their vote-getting potential.

However, because the distribution of benefits connected with these programs cannot be equal for all, their implementation runs counter to the justice provision in the US Constitution. Also, the concentration of power in the central government that is brought on by the necessary bureaucracies causes public officials to feel the tug of the negative side of human nature. The negative side affects others, too: More free loaders line up for benefits. The end result is a government that can do little besides grow ever larger and overbearing.

Centralized planning of economic activity is commonly known as socialism. Tocqueville compared democracy to socialism in a most incisive manner: "Democracy and socialism have nothing in common but one word: equality. But notice the difference: while democracy seeks equality in liberty, socialism seeks equality in restraint and servitude."

Welfare state capitalism is often a step along the way to socialism. Once such a regime has remained in place for a while, its operatives tend to become entrenched. They wallow in their easy jobs, and so their minds are closed to any new ideas that might endanger the status quo.

Left alone, human nature gradually persuades government officials to transform the regime from one that provides equality of opportunity to one that provides equality of (economic) result. The former is an important part of democracy, whereas the latter requires government planning to forcibly redistribute incomes and wealth from some citizens to others.

Ironically, the very essence of democracy can lead in this direction. In any society human nature will operate to render some individuals better off than others. These people will always be in the minority. Democracy is also majority rule, so sooner or later the majority can act through government to bring about redistribution. An eighteenth-century Scottish historian said, "Democracy cannot last indefinitely; [it] can last only until the majority discover they can vote themselves largess from the public treasury."

Having worked hard and controlled spending to earn high incomes and accumulate wealth, the minority resent this forced taking of the fruits of their efforts. Many of the wealthy will help others anyway, either through setting up foundations or providing local assistance in their communities. Foundations are generally responsive to tax incentives, and local help stems from altruism. The resentment comes from the idea of forcible taxation by government in a presumably free society. Thus political expediency interferes with the natural inclinations of the wealthy to help others and gives them no choice as to whom, when, where, and how they can help.

Often recipients of aid also resent it, as they feel demeaned when they accept help for no work performed. This means a handout is not a hand up. A government guided by a good constitution discourages these activities based on the negative incentives of human nature by guaranteeing protection of private property and the sanctity of contracts. (This means that government will help someone who thinks another party to a contractual agreement is not holding up his or her end and the matter cannot be resolved through negotiation.)

A citizen in a democracy is independent but also weak, in that he or she frequently must depend on others to help get a job done (building a bridge or ship). One cannot force others to help, so voluntary effort is the only practical way. Government policy makers don't know every uniquely different local territory. Therefore policies made from afar aimed at helping people only increase the divergence from a genetic fit.

If the **belief** in the right of an authority to control individual actions prevails, the majority will choose the top person or group to exert this control. Based on his observations in the Old World of the early nineteenth century, Tocqueville made this prediction (in 1787 Benjamin Franklin said much the same thing):

> *It is easy to see the time coming in which men will be less and less able to produce, by each alone, the commonest bare necessities of life. The tasks of government must therefore perpetually increase, and its efforts to cope with them must spread its net ever wider. The more government takes the place of associations, the more will individuals lose the idea of forming associations and need the government to come to their help. That is a vicious circle of cause and effect.*

Government planning can only increase in scope as it struggles to overcome natural expressions of individual freedom. People and government become alienated, and mutual contempt predominates. In the United States in Tocqueville's time a small government saw no need—indeed, lacked the capability—to control the operation of, say, a local quilting bee.

The Roman Empire flourished for centuries, in part because societies of that time evolved far more slowly than they do today. But eventually Emperor Diocletian took over and began to plan every facet of the economy. There came into being so many laws that farmers could no longer farm, nor could workers work. Nearly everyone went on government-provided relief. This eroded the tax base, and the whole regime collapsed. Diocletian ignored an unavoidable truth: Government is, by definition, a parasite that feeds off the private economy.

During and after the Industrial Revolution there was a long adjustment period, as mentioned previously. Marx accurately saw abuses, but he wrote before the development of factory management skills became manifest. These skills eventually included humane treatment of workers and the efficient organization of cooperative efforts to produce more per person-hour of input, thereby increasing wages, profits, and living standards.

Thomas Paine wrote that there are only two sources of power in government. One is delegated, and one is assumed. "All delegated power is trust, and all assumed power is usurpation. Time does not alter the nature and quality of either."[14] Hayek wrote, "Such a power does not destroy, but it prevents existence; it does not tyrannize, but it compresses, enervates, extinguishes, and stupefies a people, till each nation is reduced to be nothing better than a flock of timid and industrial animals, of which government is the shepherd."[15]

Vladimir Lenin was a disciple of Marx. By 1921 Russia had struggled through World War I, the Bolshevik Revolution, and a civil war. The country was ready for a leader who could lead the way to prosperity for the first time in its history. A short time later, Lenin introduced socialism under the Communist Party. Central planning persisted for seventy years, and its apparent early success recruited other country governments as followers.

Lenin's government set about redistribution of wealth, but after three wars there was precious little to distribute. Only capitalism can create and accumulate wealth in the absence of violence, but Marx had predicted the demise of capitalism. In the end whatever wealth existed did indeed get redistributed—into the pockets of privileged cadres.

Government planners have introduced the notion of a social contract. This term was borrowed from the principle of sanctity of contract, to add legitimacy to the notion. It argues that citizens have entered into an agreement whereby they are subject to government controls and pay taxes as the price for living in a peaceful and orderly society. But David Bergland pointed out: "A contract requires knowing persons who voluntarily enter an agreement, accepting obligations in exchange for benefits they expect to receive. One essential characteristic of a contract is that one can choose to enter it or not."[16]

Because democracy includes free choice, the implication here is that "democratic socialism" is a contradiction in terms. In a free-choice democracy, thinking citizens will vote to reject socialism when they realize that this is the direction in which the government is moving. In this situation politicians don't want enlightened citizens, so they will be tempted to stretch the truth and divert people's thinking from this evolving reality.

As government pries ever deeper into the private lives of citizens, officials know full well that their actions are resented. This fact makes them paranoid, as they fear that someone will blow their cover. The elites then organize an internal security operation aimed at identifying dissidents and neutralizing them. Three of recent history's more egregious examples are Hitler's Gestapo, the KGB in the Soviet Union, and the Stasi in the former East Germany. As the vicious circle continues its downward progress, more dissidents see what is really going on. Eventually the regime must involve citizens spying on citizens; therefore, the cycle also breaks apart a society.

Citizens' resentment and feelings of alienation could easily flare up into open rebellion if they knew what was really going on in government. Therefore it becomes imperative for government planners to control information flows. Stalin issued an order that only the most vitally important cadres could have telephones, as his paranoia told him that phones were the logical resource to help dissidents organize a resistance. Today Russia is supposed to have a democracy, with free markets and an open economy wherein new businesses can start and prosper. Even today the legacy of Stalin's order undermines efficiency in business.

A paternalistic government impedes the natural maturation process of individuals, leaving them childlike and dependent on government. But the maturation process cannot be stopped, so people must struggle to work around, over, under, and through bureaucracies that have grown huge, irrelevant, and often corrupt. "No need to exert yourselves beyond work; the Party will care for all." The Communist Party bureaucracy promised care from womb to tomb.

Tocqueville commented:

> *[Government] likes to see the citizens enjoy themselves, provided that they think of nothing but enjoyment. It gladly works for their happiness but wants to be sole agent and judge of it. It provides for their security, foresees and supplies their necessities, facilitates their pleasures, manages their principal concerns, directs their industry, makes rules for their testaments, and divides their inheritances. Why should it not entirely relieve them from the trouble of thinking and all the cares of living?*

Note his appeal to the positive side of human nature. Citizens may pay high taxes, but the bounty never stops. Then comes the hidden agenda: "Thus it daily makes the exercise of free choice less useful and rarer, restricts the activity of free will within a narrower compass, and little by little robs each citizen of the proper use of his own faculties. Equality has prepared men for all this, predisposing them to endure it and often even regard it as beneficial."

Shades of Aldous Huxley's *Brave New World.*[17] People don't realize they are being deceived. Paine suggested that when the interest of the people in supporting such a government wanes, public officials may continue to harass them for a while, but eventually the system will facilitate its own fall.

In 1942 Lane predicted a situation that citizens of that time must have doubted could ever come about.[18]

> *Do you imagine that the planes can not be grounded, the factories close, the radio be silent and the telephone dead and the cars rust and the trains stop? Do you suppose that darkness and cold and hunger and disease, that have never before been so defeated and that now are defeated only on this small part of the earth, can never again break in upon all human beings? Do not be so short-sighted.*

Notes

1. Rose Wilder Lane, *The Discovery of Freedom.* Fox and Wilkes, 1993.
2. Edward O. Wilson, *On Human Nature.* Harvard University Press, 1978.
3. Alfred Toffler, *Powershift.* Bantam, 1990.

4. Lane, *Discovery of Freedom.*
5. Thomas Paine, *Rights of Man.* Knopf, 1915.
6. Paul Kennedy, *The Rise and Fall of the Great Powers.* Unwin Hyman, 1988.
7. Toffler, *Powershift.*
8. Joseph A. Schumpeter, *Capitalism, Socialism and Democracy.* Harper and Row, 1942.
9. Jim Powell, *The Triumph of Liberty.* Free Press, 2000, p. 343.
10. Alexis de Tocqueville, *Democracy in America.* Knopf, 1972.
11. *The Economist,* "Growth Is Good." May 27, 2000, p. 82.
12. Lewis H. Lapham, *The Wish for Kings: Democracy at Bay.* Grove Press, 1993.
13. Friedrich A. Hayek, *The Road to Serfdom.* University of Chicago Press, 1944.
14. Paine, *Rights of Man.*
15. Hayek, *Road to Serfdom.*
16. David Bergland, *Libertarianism in One Easy Lesson.* Orpheus, 1997.
17. Aldous Huxley, *Brave New World.* Harper Perennial Library, 1998.
18. Lane, *Discovery of Freedom.*

Chapter Three:
A History of the US Government

Those who are too smart to engage in politics are punished by being governed by those who are not.

—Plato

There were many prominent, intelligent, and dedicated men who were involved at the inception of the US government, including several who were truly outstanding. One man stood head-and-shoulders above all—Thomas Jefferson. This chapter conveys his thoughts, as he was arguably history's deepest thinker on the theory of democracy.

Jefferson possessed an insatiable curiosity about a great many subjects, including human nature, history, and science. The letters he wrote reveal a man of virtue, deference, and complete honesty. He was uniquely able to integrate his philosophy with daily experience as he traveled about with an open mind.

This carefully cultivated state of mind enabled him to listen intently to foreign philosophers, writers, politicians, and statesmen holding a great variety of beliefs. It also drove him to accumulate a library of some 10,000 books, which he offered to the Library of Congress after the British burned it during the War of 1812. His legacy may be considered the greatest single gift to the United States, which he loved fully as much as did George Washington.

The Early Days

In Central and South America the Spanish conquistadors left a trail of murder and devastation in their wake. In North America the situation was different, as early pioneers did not find developed civilizations clustered around masses of gold and silver. Many people were killed, certainly, but the motive was not naked conquest and plunder as families defended their homesteads and militias engaged hostile Indian tribes. The result was that newly independent citizens and their leaders in 1789 found themselves with a wealth of undisturbed natural resources and a blank political slate on which to write. This situation may have been unique in history; educated men and others who had fought for personal liberty hastened to take advantage of it.

For 6,000 years of recorded world history, the masses had lived in wretched poverty, scraping out a bare subsistence. Then in the space of only three generations a whole new world was created. There were two revolutions that contributed to this relatively sudden transformation: the Industrial Revolution and the American Revolution.

Benjamin Franklin was a major contributor to both. When he was posted to London in the 1770s he was shocked: "The extreme corruption prevalent among all orders of men in this old, rotten state, with its numberless and needless places, enormous salaries, pensions, perquisites, bribes, groundless quarrels, foolish expeditions, false accounts or no accounts, contracts and jobs that devour all revenue." This is what an unregulated monarchy can do to a government, and therefore a government to a people. When they began thinking in terms of rising up in revolution, the colonists may have been unsure of what they wanted, but on what they did **not** want there was little argument.

Franklin underlined this gap in an amusing incident when he engaged the old Duchess of Bourbon in a chess match. He threatened her king and then took it. "Ah," said she, "we do not take kings so." Franklin replied, "We do in America."

Jefferson saw law as servant of the people, not their master. Therefore the number of laws and lawyers should be kept to a minimum. He reworked the laws of the state of Virginia to include separation of church and state. Jefferson was a deep believer in education: Truth makes men free. "It is error alone which needs the support of government." With time, study, and reflection he came to appreciate the "unalienable rights" of man. This led to his prominent role in writing the Declaration of Independence.

This document contains three fundamental propositions. First, people have natural rights that precede and supersede rights created by any government. Second, the institution of government has but one main purpose: to protect those natural rights. This means citizens' rights do **not** come from government; rather, the people create government and delegate to officials carefully measured powers to help citizens protect those rights. The people and their government will work together toward a common objective. Third, whenever government fails to adequately protect those rights the people have the right to discipline, alter, or abolish that government as in their collective wisdom they may see fit. (The Declaration is in itself a powerful document in defense of this right.)

The year was 1776. In that year another honest man, Thomas Paine, saved his money in England so he could publish a forty-page pamphlet called "Common Sense." In it he urged confused colonists to fight for independence, set up a government, and do what they believe is right. "O! Ye that love mankind! Ye that dare oppose not only the tyranny but the tyrant, stand forth! There hath not been such an opportunity since the time of Adam. We have it in our power to make a new world." Later, General George Washington said, "Paine was worth more than the whole army." The pen was mightier than the sword. So began history's third great attempt to set free men's energies.

The Articles of Confederation were compiled in 1781 by those who deeply feared oppression by government. As an instrument of government the articles were all but useless, for several reasons. One of these was the requirement that for the central government to collect money from the states, all thirteen had to approve each specific request. Instances of unanimous approval were practically nonexistent. Washington expressed his deep concern: "Thirteen sovereignties pulling against each other and all tugging at the federal head will soon bring ruin on the whole." The general had seen hundreds of his soldiers shot, bleeding, and dying. They had sacrificed life and limb for **this**?

Yet all was not lost, as Rose Wilder Lane demonstrated:

> *Without unity, without money, without an army, without any social order or any ruling Authority, surrounded on all sides by the Great Powers and as helpless as Poland had been, how long would these rebels keep their shadowy independence? Based on all past European history, that was sound reasoning. It did not apply here, precisely because American government was weak. The opportunity to exercise human rights released a terrific human energy. No one expected what happened; no one could possibly have planned it. When individuals are not prevented from acting freely, they create the unprecedented.*[1]

After burying his beloved wife, Jefferson sailed to France in 1784 as minister (ambassador). There he took advantage of many opportunities to interact with knowledgeable people; his thinking matured during his five-year tour of duty. Like Franklin, he was appalled by the widespread human misery caused by oppressive governments in Europe. In a letter to his friend George Wythe on August 13, 1786, he wrote: "If all the sovereigns of Europe were to set themselves to work, to emancipate the minds of their subjects from their present ignorance and prejudices, and that, as zealously as they now endeavor the contrary, a thousand years would not place them on that high ground, on which our common people are now setting out."[2]

While serving in Paris, Jefferson was not available during the Constitutional Convention of 1787, and letters taking at least eight weeks for delivery were of little help. William Peters's account described often turbulent meetings during that hot summer in Philadelphia, where it seemed that only the towering presence of chairman Washington kept the convention from splitting apart with the job undone.[3]

As secretary, James Madison laboriously kept notes on everything said. He was adamant on keeping the power to declare war away from the president. Alexander Hamilton provided a rare insight into this issue:

The continual necessity for their services enhances the importance of the soldier, and proportionately degrades the condition of the citizen. The military state becomes elevated above the civil . . . [and commits] frequent infringes of their rights, which serve to weaken their sense of those rights; and by degrees the people are brought to consider the soldiery not only as their protectors but as their superiors. The transition from this disposition to that of considering them masters is neither remote nor difficult.

In this instance and in others, Hamilton appreciated the potential of the negative side of human nature: "Man is ambitious, vindictive and rapacious."

Madison also commented on legal systems: "What indeed are all the repealing, explaining, and amending laws, which fill and disgrace our voluminous codes, but so many monuments of deficient wisdom?" The founding fathers believed that citizens should make the laws under which they consent to be governed. Should the legal system deteriorate into the condition described by Madison, citizens would have only themselves to blame.

Lane wrote,

The Federal Constitution, for example, forbids men in office to increase their own salaries. It forbids the president to adjourn congress. It forbids him to make treaties, or even to appoint his own assistants, without . . . congressmen. . . . It forbids both the president and the congressmen to interfere with the courts. It forbids the president and the senators to appropriate money from the Federal treasury. It forbids them to impose, collect, or spend taxes; only the members of the house . . . are permitted to do that, and they are subject to recall every two years.[4]

She continued: "[The Constitution] also uses the Federal and State governments as checks upon each other. An American has two governments, or three, or more, including his county and his town. He should always aid the weaker to check the stronger, for this divided sovereignty is the protection of his freedom." This truth exemplifies the principle of federalism.

The finished document would not become the supreme law of the land until nine of thirteen state constitutional assemblies had ratified it. Thousands of citizens carried copies of it in their pockets, and there was widespread and spirited discussion and debate on its merits.

On June 21, 1788, New Hampshire became the decisive ninth state to ratify the US Constitution. Thus occurred history's first nonviolent transition from one system of government to another. Later, on March 4, 1797, George Washington became history's first head of state to voluntarily leave office.

In 1790 Jefferson reluctantly accepted Washington's urgent request for his services as secretary of state. On arrival in New York City (the nation's capital at that time) Jefferson was shocked to find a group of monarchists in charge of government. He took up the (nonviolent) fight immediately, and over the next few years he and Hamilton often found themselves toe to toe.

Some of Washington's former army officers came to him with the suggestion that he assume the crown; they would support him. Without a second thought he sent them packing, tails between their legs. Historians requested that Jefferson comment about Washington: "His mind was great and powerful, without being of the very first order; his penetration strong, though not so acute . . . and as far as he saw, no judgment was ever sounder. . . . He was incapable of fear. . . . His integrity was pure, his justice the most inflexible I have ever known."

The Bill of Rights, the first ten amendments, became a part of the US Constitution in December 1791. Lane wrote, "The name 'Bill of Rights' is English. . . . The English Bill of Rights is a statement of certain freedoms that the British government permits to its subjects. An American Bill of Rights is the exact reverse of the English one. . . . is a statement of the uses of force which American citizens do not permit to men in American government."

The first item of the Bill of Rights guaranteed freedom of speech, assembly, and religion. Jefferson remarked that this amendment built "a wall of separation between church and state." That remark has frequently been misconstrued. Later he wrote a letter that clarified his meaning, which was still later conveniently ignored: "Religion is a matter which lies solely between Man and his God." He argued that religious belief freely chosen in a tolerant environment nurtured morality, which supported a free society. Put another way, Jefferson meant to emphasize the individual nature of religious belief and not to permit or forbid group activities in government and schools.

In France, Jefferson had written letters arguing that this protection of citizens' freedom be part of the original constitution. Madison remained unconvinced, but Jefferson persisted until he changed his mind. Henceforth Madison was among the Bill of Rights' strongest advocates. This anecdote illustrates the value of keeping an open mind, even after having committed to a position on an issue. He had many opportunities to learn this important lesson when he listened to and engaged in furious debates during the Constitutional Convention. One important reason why deliberations were kept secret was that after courageously arguing his side of an issue a delegate felt secure in keeping a mind open to change. Were his original position a matter of public record, a switch would have been much more difficult.

In 1792 Paine published his *Rights of Man* in England. The British aristocracy promptly flew into a towering rage, stopped publication of the book, and put him on trial for sedition (a friend tipped him off beforehand, and he escaped to France). Jefferson wrote to him saying, "Go on then in doing with your pen what in other times was done with the sword: shew [*sic*] that reformation is more practicable by operating on the mind than on the body of man, and be assured that it has not a more sincere votary nor you a more ardent well-wisher than Yrs. &c."

The temptation of government officials to take improper advantage of their offices has existed since there were governments. The new government of the United States was no exception. Jefferson denounced the "shameless corruption" he found in the 1st and 2nd Congresses.

> *If ever this country is brought under a single government, it will be one of the most extensive corruption, indifferent and incapable of a wholesome care over so wide a spread of surface. This will not be borne, and you will have to choose between reformation and revolution. If I know the spirit of this country, the one or the other is inevitable. Before the canker is become inveterate, before its venom has reached so much of the body politic as to get beyond control, remedy should be applied.*

Paine addressed the same issue: "While they [political parties] appear to quarrel they agree to plunder."

In the 1796 presidential election, Jefferson ran against John Adams, was defeated, and by custom was seated as vice president. He promptly did battle against the monarchal tendencies of Adams's Cabinet, as "eating away at the basic guarantees of individual liberty, the re-introduction of despotism." He recruited allies: "Nothing rescued us from their liberticide effect, but the unyielding opposition of those firm spirits who sternly maintained their post in defiance of terror, until their fellow citizens could be aroused to their own danger, and rally and rescue the standard of the Constitution."

Gutless officials of today will not do battle on behalf of citizens. Rather, citizens must force politicians to help them protect their liberty. This means that power must lie in the people and in their ideas.

On March 4, 1801, Jefferson completed his inaugural address as president with this remark: "Relying, then on the patronage of your good will, I advance with obedience to the work, ready to retire from it whenever you become sensible how much better choice it is in your power to make." This quote from history's foremost democratic thinker is impressive; the president saw himself as a public servant.

Jefferson made another very important point: "No generation can contract debts greater than may be paid during the course of its own existence." This argument connects directly to natural law: A citizen's actions may not damage the rights of others. He gave a hypothetical example, wherein a French generation borrowed money from Dutch lenders at no interest for thirty-four years, after which interest would be paid forever at 15 percent annually. The borrowers then proceeded to eat, drink, and make merry until they died, leaving a huge burden of debt service for generations yet to come.

The number thirty-four was hardly arbitrary—it was the average life span at the time. "Every constitution, then, and every law, naturally expires at the end of

34 years. If it be enforced longer, it is an act of force, and not of right . . . that a law of limited duration is much more manageable than one which needs a repeal."

Perhaps Jefferson's most daunting challenge occurred when there came across his desk a plot of land for sale, and his window of opportunity was too narrow to ask the public what they thought. He had to act on his own, and this was against his principles. He agonized over the purchase of the Louisiana Territory before he authorized it, and with a stroke of the pen the size of the country was doubled.

The Inherent Difficulty in Representative Government

Strictly speaking, the United States did not begin its existence as a democracy. In a democracy citizens govern themselves without a middle institution, such as a Parliament or Congress. The founding fathers were visionaries, but they were also practical—they realized that a pure democracy could not work well in a large country where travel and communication was difficult (no cars, buses, or phones). Ratification of the Constitution was done indirectly, through state constitutional assemblies whose members visited among citizens before deliberating and voting. The nature of the government that arose from these deliberations and voting is properly called a republic.

In the early years of the republic the grim legacy of King George remained indelibly etched on citizens' memories. This attitude caused them to be extremely skeptical of members of Congress whom they had elected to office and whom they had to trust to act on their behalf. Before 1789 and the formation of the republic, this skepticism had been overdone, which is why the Articles of Confederation were so ineffectual. People realized that a compromise between monarchy and near-anarchy was needed.

Members of Congress were kept keenly aware of the feelings of their constituents as they faced the challenge of travel from home to the capital and back. Citizens were willing to trust them only as far as was absolutely necessary. In those days the job of a congressman was part-time because the vast bulk of the governing was democratic. It was done at home, where citizens could not only see and approve of the results but also get directly involved in producing those results. When the action was local, public officials could much more easily be held accountable for their actions.

These remarks point to the essence of the inherent difficulty in representative government—it lies in trust and accountability. This difficulty is minimized when reliance on trust is limited to a small number of issues. Unless this principle is strictly enforced, politicians will be subject to the tug of the negative side of human nature. Depending on the strength of the integrity within each one, sooner or later nearly all will feel this tug.

The farther away from citizens a government agency is located, the shorter the span of trust. Besides human nature there is another reason for deep concern about trust. The definition of government includes three main characteristics that combine to undermine trust. (1) Government is an unregulated monopoly; (2) government is a parasite on the private sector; and (3) government is force.

The implications are as obvious as they are terrible. This is why the major thrust of the US Constitution and Bill of Rights is restraint of government. This is why visions of King George wafted through Independence Hall in Philadelphia during the summer of 1787. For just one example, during those proceedings Madison said, "Executive powers . . . do not include the rights of war and peace." His colleague George Mason agreed, "Giving power of war to the executive because . . . [he is] not to be trusted with it."

Early Supreme Court Justice John Marshall wrote "that the power to tax involves the power to destroy; that the power to destroy may defeat and render useless the power to create." By 1913 the public's skepticism must have slipped a bit. After the Supreme Court rejected a law to tax citizens' incomes as unconstitutional, they stood by and allowed the proposal and ratification of a constitutional amendment that permitted Congress to tax personal incomes. Congress sold it to the people by reassuring them that the rate would never exceed a few percentage points.

So it was, for a couple of years. But Congressmen soon began to feel the tug. In 1917 the United States entered World War I and the top rate swiftly climbed to 77 percent. By 1927, well after the end of the war, government spending was more than double what it was in 1916.

Beginning in 1800 there occurred in government upheavals that could be described as revolutions, about every thirty years through 1932. Each of these upheavals provided a purge to the system. Jefferson believed that the constitution and the government should be scrapped and replaced with new models about every thirty years. This indicates that popular skepticism of politicians carried on through most of the history of this country, although it gradually faded in intensity as the nation grew in world prominence.

It is natural for people to assume that the blessings of liberty will always be there. Inherited wealth is an accurate analogy; if an individual does not need to work hard for it he or she will value it less. The founding fathers and many others of the time pledged "our lives, fortunes, and sacred honor" (from the Declaration of Independence). They knew that shortly after sending this parchment to King George they would have a fight on their hands.

Political freedom directly implies responsibility, including protecting that freedom from those in public office who feel the tug. The proper role of government is to limit some individual freedoms while protecting others. Decisions concerning which actions to allow government to restrict and which should be protected must rest with the citizens themselves.

Citizens tend to avoid the work that is necessary to make these decisions wisely. Public officials know this, and they find it easy to publicize benefits while keeping the costs hidden. Abraham Lincoln commented on the negative tug that produced this deception. "Politicians are a set of men who have interests aside from the interests of the people and who, to say the most of them, are, taken as a mass, at least one step removed from honest men." Mark Twain said there was "no such thing as a distinctly native American criminal class, except Congress."

THE GREAT DEPRESSION, WORLD WAR II, AND THE AFFLUENT SOCIETY

A story bearing an important lesson sets the stage. Its ramifications may be discovered throughout the nineteenth century and half way through the twentieth. In 1810 a steamboat was moving freight on the Hudson River, and entrepreneurs in New England were excited over the possibilities of this new type of craft. They applied for a monopoly for operation, justifying their position before government officials by saying that if others entered the business hundreds of jobs would be lost among sailors, ships' carpenters, rope makers, and so on.

Lane wrote:

> *Governments had always protected their subjects in precisely this way. This is the only way a government's use of force can protect any man's economic welfare . . . by preventing other men's economic activities; that is, by stopping economic progress. But such laws could not be enforced here. They were unconstitutional.*[5]
>
> *Three thousand years before, men had known the principle of the steam engine. 115 years before, a steamboat had run successfully on European waters. For 50 years, British government had been encouraging, protecting, subsidizing, and "controlling" the making of steam engines. In 12 years, Americans—not encouraged, not protected, not helped, and not "controlled"—covered the Western Waters with steamboats, and launched the first steamer that ever crossed an ocean; the first challenge from the dynamic New World to the static Old World.*

The lesson: Government should not restrain the creativity of mankind.

By the 1920s government at the local level was flourishing, largely because citizens were governing themselves. When a citizen got into difficulty the local ward heeler would come by, learn the nature of the problem, and find help through local government, churches, or civic organizations. In 1928 a county judge named Harry Truman learned that money had been borrowed for years from Kansas City banks at 6 percent interest. He shopped around, eventually finding money at 2.5 percent. Unhappy bankers claimed that Truman was cheating their shareholders out of profits, but he figured that taxpayers were the ones being cheated. Meanwhile, the national government was making inroads on citizens' freedoms.

In 1929 there began a series of economic events that most citizens of today understand only dimly and inaccurately. The following discussion will bring forth some little-known truths about the years 1929–39. Begin with an event in 1913: the passage of a law creating the Federal Reserve Board, who would control the supply of money in the economy.

In early 1928 the Fed, as it came to be known, was not quite fifteen years old and still learning about its complex job. Share prices in the stock market were increasing rapidly. People were borrowing money recklessly and dumping all of it into stocks; they were convinced that prices could go nowhere but up. Worried over loss of control over trading, the Fed raised interest rates to calm the market, but this act created a recession. Then came the famous stock market crash of October 1929, which drastically deepened the recession.

Ordinarily even a deep recession is over within about three years, but this time the government and the Fed combined in a comedy of errors to cause the Great Depression. At that time, most of the world was on the gold standard, which meant that a specified percentage of the money in circulation must be backed by gold reserves. As the US economy slowed, imports dropped more than did exports. This should have caused extra gold and money to flow into the country, expanding the supply and pulling the economy out of recession. But, still worried about inflation, the Fed pulled money out of the economy, which made a bad situation worse.

As prices decline, the natural tendency among consumers is to hold money and not spend it because its purchasing power is increasing. Therefore few people were spending, and consumer spending is what drives an economy forward. In an attempt to further reduce imports (which cause money to leave the country), the government passed the Smoot-Hawley Tariff Act. This act all but closed the US market to foreign goods. Other countries retaliated with their own tariffs (taxes on imports), and world trade ground to a standstill.

Farmers could not export their products, so they could not pay off bank loans. Around 10,000 rural banks failed. German companies lost their export markets, on which their government was depending heavily to pay off towering World War I debts that the Treaty of Versailles had slapped on it. This loss helped pave the way for Adolf Hitler's rise to prominence (he greatly revitalized the German economy after the recession). According to an old saying, "When goods don't cross frontiers, armies will."

The Hoover administration splashed out money in many directions for poor relief and subsidies for farmers, but then in 1932 it doubled the income tax to balance the budget and restore confidence. The government had one foot on the gas pedal and the other on the brake. Even today there are economists who claim that Hoover's capitalistic free-market policies caused the Great Depression. The truth is that the man intervened in the economy fully as much as did the next president, Franklin D. Roosevelt (and with similar tragic results).

Roosevelt entered the White House in March 1933, after campaigning on a free-market platform to differentiate his plans from the mess that Hoover had created. However, once in office he, too, took to meddling in a big way. Hans Sennholz wrote, "In his first 100 days, he swung hard at the profit order. Instead of clearing away the prosperity barriers erected by his predecessor, he built new ones of his own. He struck in every known way at the integrity of the US dollar through quantitative and qualitative deterioration. He seized the people's gold holdings and subsequently devalued the dollar by 40 percent."[6]

Between 1933 and 1936 government spending increased by 83 percent. The Agriculture Adjustment Act taxed processors of agricultural products and used the proceeds for massive destruction of crops and cattle. The National Recovery Act raised the cost of doing business by 40 percent, which was not exactly the best medicine for a depressed economy. Black markets expanded, only to be suppressed by violent police methods. For ten years Roosevelt raised income tax rates, eventually putting into force a top marginal rate of 91 percent. Raised amid wealth, the man had no concept of how business is conducted, so he consistently bit the hand that fed him.

In spite of all the abuse, by 1935 the economy was stirring a little from its slumber. But the National Labor Relations Act sent it spiraling downward again; Sennholz noted, "It took labor disputes out of the courts of law and brought them under a newly created federal agency, the National Labor Relations Board, which became prosecutor, judge, and jury, all in one. . . . The US thereby abandoned a great achievement of Western civilization, equality under the law."

As war clouds gathered in Europe, Roosevelt let loose a thunderous barrage of insults at the business community. By 1941 his infamous and ruinously expensive New Deal programs had done practically nothing to pry the economy loose from the Great Depression. One thing he did that helped was to authorize US companies to supply war matériel to the Allies who were fighting Hitler's armies.

History may eventually prove what is only speculation now. Desperate to see the economy humming again, Roosevelt may have purposefully ignored warnings that the Japanese fleet was heading toward Pearl Harbor. He knew that if nothing else worked, a war would boost the economy. But he also knew that the people were not in favor of getting involved, so he needed a tragedy to change their thinking and goad them into action.

The Japanese attack did the job. The president's emergency measures removed the fetters from the private sector, and its tremendous productive capacity came into full play. Most of the men were overseas, so for the first time in US history large numbers of women entered the paid labor force to make tanks, airplanes, jeeps, and so on. The war effort galvanized the entire nation; consumption was discouraged through rationing to maximize supplies for the military.

After the war, opportunistic politicians proudly seized credit for having pulled the economy out of the Great Depression. Very few citizens understood what had really happened, and public officials were firmly disinclined to enlighten them. Therefore the people did not question this assertion. Because they had suffered greatly during the long slump, they concluded that government was a capable social problem solver. Thus a healthy skepticism of government of some 160 years' duration quickly changed to one of abiding faith (read: blind faith) in government. Accountability evaporated overnight.

Politicians concluded that the people liked Roosevelt's social programs, so they left many of them on the books as the nation entered the era of the affluent society and these programs were no longer needed. In fact, these and other programs were used to buy citizens' votes, and the notion of the career politician became a reality. Due to the sudden increase in wealth and to their newly acquired blind faith, citizens did not mind when the government left high wartime taxes on the books. This lack of action caused huge amounts of money to come into Washington, DC. The pork barrel industry mushroomed, and so more votes were bought as members of Congress financed construction projects back home, such as roads, dams, bridges, parks, and so on. A responsible government cuts way back on spending once a war is over. Not this one.

Over the decades since World War II, Washington's public "servants" came to live very well. Today, part of Washington is the nation's wealthiest community. Career politicians had taken the affluent society seriously. So seriously, in fact, that by 1960 they thought there was still not enough money to spend, so they began borrowing.

Throughout US history there have been seven time periods when the government has consistently spent more than it took in. Six of these included major wars or deep recessions (including the Great Depression). But in every year since 1960 the government has operated in deficit; the national debt at the time of this writing is around $6 trillion. (Politicians claimed that 2001 finished in surplus, but applying the same accounting rules that government forces on the business community would have shown a deficit.)

In 1870 total public spending at all levels took less than 4 percent of the gross domestic product (the value of everything produced in a year). The total tax load of government at all levels amount to less than 5 percent of a family's annual income. Today governments forcibly take about 45 percent of a typical family's income. Since 1960 the cost of state and local government has increased by 350 percent in inflation-adjusted dollars. They take about $15,000 a year from a middle-income family of four, and the national government takes about $23,000.

Over the past forty years there has been a rapid increase in the number and percentage of two-income households. Apparently there is a reason for this trend.

Marc Fisher urged citizens to:

> *think back to the time before focus groups and the triumph of marketing over content. The "pop" in pop culture originally did not mean that something had sizzle; it meant that this was content that sprang from the people, from the bottom up. Pop was born in folk. . . . Then came the era of homogenization. Technology made mass culture possible: Radio, movies, TV, the car, the mall. And then marketing took over. Pop culture became something imposed from above, created by elites. The "pop"—the people—became the targets, rather than the creators.*[7]

This book will show that today the elite class controls the mass news media.

In April 1995 a Gallup poll showed that 39 percent of US citizens think the national government "poses an immediate threat to the rights and freedoms of ordinary Americans." These people are beginning to rethink their abiding faith in government as social problem solver. Jefferson noted, "It is the manners and spirit of a people which preserve a republic in vigor. A degeneracy in these is a canker which soon eats to the heart of its laws and Constitution."

Notes

1. Rose Wilder Lane, *The Discovery of Freedom*. Fox and Wilkes, 1993.
2. Thomas Jefferson, *The Life and Selected Writings of Thomas Jefferson,* edited by Koch and Peden. Random House, 1944.
3. William Peters, *A More Perfect Union: The Making of the United States Constitution*. Crown, 1987.
4. Lane, *The Discovery of Freedom.*
5. Ibid.
6. Hans Sennholz (ed.), *Taxation and Confiscation*. Foundation for Economic Education, 1993.
7. Marc Fisher, "Left and Right, a Nation Opts Out of Its Own Pop Culture." *News and Observer* (Raleigh, NC), May 2000.

Part II: How Government Gradually Became Bloated, Alienated, Gridlocked, and Corrupt

There is only one immortality, and that is government.
—Unknown

This part begins with the end of World War II and continues to the present. It provides details concerning how a political environment that triggers behavior based on the negative side of human nature brought on the state of government that is Washington, DC today. The people of the United States would never permit such a state to exist unless they were led to believe that all is reasonably well. Knowing this, career politicians have combined with other elites over the past fifty years to deceive the public. Part II exposes the Grand Deception.

Chapter 4 presents the reaction of society to a combination of three major new economic, social, and political forces: a sudden increase in wealth, the commercialization of television, and the advent of the career politician. This combination rocked the society to its foundations and set in train the forces that are described in subsequent chapters.

Chapter 5 demonstrates the career politician's need for unprecedented amounts of money to get reelected repeatedly, so in this way he or she can make a career out of elective office. Advertising and campaigning on TV was very expensive. Taxes made very demanding by the war provided a high platform on which to mount further increases in taxation. Still clinging to an abiding faith in government as social problem solver, citizens appeared not to mind, in part because politicians had learned how to hide tax increases and fake tax cuts.

Chapter 6 reveals where some of the mountains of money went: cradle-to-grave assistance to citizens. Over the past five decades the art of using its own money to buy and win votes from the public was perfected. As time passed very few people realized that a paternalistic government acts to keep them in a perpetual state of childhood. Therefore citizens could not assume the mantle of adulthood with its accompanying freedom of choice.

Chapter 7 discusses how constantly increasing taxes, laws, borrowing, and bureaucracies caused government to grow without limit. Lawyers in Congress passed laws to make more work for lawyers. The notion of group rights displaced the constitutional emphasis on individual rights. People did not realize that pitting each group demanding special benefits from government against many others fragments the society, even as the government's rhetoric emphasized integration.

Chapter 8 describes members of the elite class as they pursued personal power over ordinary citizens while using the people's money to do so. Huge concentrations of wealth in Washington turned otherwise honest heads and hearts. Citizens came to resent the privileges of the elite class, but they saw little that could be done about it.

Chapter 9 indicates how career politicians took advantage of the public's abiding faith in government to perpetrate many abuses. Elite worship of the status quo produced gridlock, even as society struggled to move forward. The news media cooperated in continuously lying to the public about what was really going on in Washington. As time passed some members of the elite class became more arrogant.

Chapter 10 summarizes the result of economic, social, and political trends described previously— the Grand Deception. Misleading communications have phased into corruption and outright thievery. The language of politics has been fogged to deceive the public. Laws and regulations have been rigged to favor the elites, while rhetoric continues to emphasize public service. The people's suspicions and disgust continue to grow with each passing year. They conclude that unless something serious is done the situation can only grow worse.

CHAPTER FOUR:
THE SIMULTANEOUS ARRIVAL OF WEALTH, TELEVISION, AND THE CAREER POLITICIAN

I am strongly in favor of common sense, common honesty, and common decency; this makes me forever ineligible for any public office.
—H. L. Mencken

The arrival of three economic and political forces (wealth, television, and the career politician) shortly after World War II caused shock waves. These occurred almost exclusively in the United States, because the horror and destruction of the war had left almost every other advanced economy in shambles. Even today, with the benefit of hindsight, it is difficult to fully realize and appreciate the manner in which these forces combined and their total impact on the economy. It is all too easy to assume that they have always been present and to ignore the negative incentives they brought with them. A few moments' reflection will reveal the potential for these incentives to influence public officials, and the resulting damage these officials' behavior has done to society over the past fifty years. This chapter will illustrate the reality.

THE POSTWAR SOCIETY ADJUSTS TO WEALTH

Seen through the lens of the whole of history, the 100 years' duration of the Industrial Revolution (1750–1850) set the stage for a sudden and dramatic increase in wealth. This increase was preceded by an equally dramatic liberation of human energy. Enterprising people, unencumbered by government restraints, invented new machines, multiplied efficiency in production, and rapidly increased living standards for themselves, their workers, and consumers. Never in history had so much wealth accumulated, not even in kings' vaults.

Never in history had there been a large middle class of people in any society. This development provided a huge tax base for postwar politicians, who did not fail to notice this potential for rapid expansion of government. They moved far more quickly than did the adjustment process in the culture as they took advantage of the newly acquired abiding faith in government as social problem solver.

People were used to high tax loads during World War II, and with extra wealth they complained only mildly when taxes were not reduced afterward. Tidal waves of money flowed into Washington, DC.

Today an individual who wins a lottery has difficulty adjusting to a very different lifestyle. An entrepreneur who starts a business that quickly becomes successful encounters difficulties, not just in terms of cash flow but also with respect to personal lifestyle. By its nature, capitalism provides opportunities for people to get rich quickly. As individuals completed the adjustment process, it became apparent that the onset of great wealth following the war was a mixed blessing; both sides of human nature were at work.

Robert Bork commented on the flip side of wealth: "Men were kept from rootless hedonism . . . by religion, morality, and law. These were commonly cited. To them I would add the necessity for hard work, usually physical work, and the fear of want. These constraints were progressively undermined by rising affluence."[1] Before World War II, these forces had kept people dependent on family, neighbors, and local government. The arrival of wealth changed everything. Many of the grandchildren of hard-working people became couch potatoes.

Writing in 1946, Wylie could see ahead clearly.

> *In a world that is engaged in the reckless rush for mass-produced material objects there is neither room nor time for honesty, consideration, integrity of thought, introspection, or the operation of conscience. In such a world—democratic, fascist, soviet, whatever the form of government—there will be no security because security comes from man's trust of man—man's confidence in man,—and the mills cannot manufacture it and the state cannot guarantee it. Only each man, working within himself to the best of his ability, can create temporal security.*[2]

Schumacher elaborated on this vital argument:

> *The exclusion of wisdom from economics, science, and technology was something which we could perhaps get away with for a little while, as long as we were relatively unsuccessful; but now that we have become very successful, the problem of spiritual and moral truth moves into the central position. . . . It is not wealth that stands in the way of liberation but the attachment to wealth; not the enjoyment of pleasurable things but the craving for them.*[3]

Wisdom is useless unless it is given an opportunity to adjust thinking and subsequent behavior, but a person constantly driven to acquire still more wealth (or, more often, spending) provides wisdom no window of opportunity.

Multitasking is a contemporary term used to describe someone who is doing two or more things simultaneously. Examples include people talking on cell phones as they drive, switching back and forth between multiple windows on their computers, and keeping people on hold while talking on the phone to others. Paul Gilster referred to this phenomenon as "this wall of noise, so similar to what you hear from too many vehicles on the roads, is indiscriminate: You can't escape it; it radiates out in all directions, a pollution as toxic as the dankest smoke-stack." [4]

By 1990 this country had more noncommercial vehicles than drivers. The average working adult spent seventy-two minutes a day behind the wheel of a car. This is more than twice as much time as the average parent spent with his or her children. Maureen Dowd wrote: "We want big. We want fast. We want far. We want now. We want 345 horsepower in a V-8 engine and 15 miles per gallon on the highway. If we don't wear our seat belts, it doesn't matter, because we have air bags. If the air bags don't deploy, it doesn't matter, because our cars are so beefy, we'll never get bruised."[5] A time for reflection surely seems to be appropriate.

Wealth is medium-quality power in that it provides both the "carrot" (positive side) and the "stick" (negative side). The US society has adjusted to the positive side by acquiring the means to live in a variety of ways and to do a variety of things. However, because freedom is not free, Bork's, Wylie's, and Schumacher's arguments demonstrate that wisdom, self-discipline, and reflection are necessary to truly enjoy the personal freedom that wealth delivers. Money is definitely nice to have, but it has no conscience or morality. Overemphasis on materialism can blind people to this truth.

As a middle-class family raises its young and increases its social status, it continues to accumulate material possessions. Walter Kerr's book *The Decline of Pleasure* attempted to identify a point where a family stops owning these myriad products, and they start to own the family.[6] The existence of this point may not be hypothetical; there is food for thought here.

Three generations ago spouses stayed married, due primarily to economic necessity. Today the failure rate of first marriages is commonly cited as about 50 percent. Nevertheless, the urge to mate persists, and so divorcees often remarry quickly. But some experts have estimated the failure rate of second marriages at 75 percent, and third marriages even higher. Studies have shown that families with women who work outside the home are more likely to divorce. Census data reveal that today 59 percent of mothers with a child under one year old work, with 36 percent of all such mothers are employed full-time. For the first time in the nation's history, a majority of couples with children at home are both employed.

With money worries attenuated, women tend to put more emphasis on the romantic aspects of marriage. But there is very little time for this, especially after children arrive. In a divorce the little ones often suffer even more than their parents, because they are not in a position to understand the forces involved and think only that a large part of their needed security will be gone. Here is another component of the flip side of wealth.

Poor adjustment to wealth and absence of the discipline to which Bork referred frequently causes overspending and deep debt. Before World War II fiscal discipline was externally imposed, but when wealth brought an end to this it became important to develop an internal self-discipline to supplant it. Poor money management combined with looser sexual taboos to make up additional components of the flip side of wealth.

The traditional extended family originated in the dawn of history. Only very recently has its importance diminished, and then only in advanced societies. After World War II the notion of the isolated nuclear family began to take hold, due not only to wealth but also to easier travel and increased occupational mobility. Workers could move to locations where they could earn better wages. Today the nuclear family is showing signs of strain, although the incidence of married couples in one dwelling remains a slim majority. Wealth brings increased choices, but not necessarily the ability to make the best choice.

The conclusion is that although people are basically good, some young people will grow up responding more often to negative incentives and some more often to positive. The key to the direction of these responses seems to lie in parental guidance. Parents who have learned to guide themselves effectively provide better for their offspring. But young adult children whose total assets nearly equal or exceed those of their parents may be disinclined to listen.

The social and familial impacts of increased wealth have been discussed, along with a hint of how the public sector adjusted. During the 1960s under presidents John F. Kennedy and Lyndon Johnson, politicians began to fully appreciate what wealth can do for their careers. Playing on people's natural concern for the poor, the Johnson administration created social programs called the War on Poverty, Model Cities, and Great Society. The economy grew so rapidly during this decade that officials thought they could also afford a war in Vietnam.

History has shown that the latter was a colossal mistake, although this conclusion takes nothing away from those who suffered and died. Some $4 trillion worth of poverty programs over the decades did little or nothing for poverty and the difficulties in inner cities. However, over the short term they bought millions of votes in elections. These actions set the tone for the future. Today's society is reaping what yesterday's politicians sowed.

President Johnson and his mandarins in the bureaucracy also produced another first in history. They perhaps inadvertently created the theory of accumulation of money, which states that whenever a mountain of money accumulates in one place and indications are that it will stay there for a while, otherwise honest public officials will feel the tug of temptation. The higher the mountain, the more will succumb.

The constant need to buy or otherwise win votes means that wealth in government is being misused. However, the misuse exists in the eyes of citizens who provide the money, not in the eyes of politicians. Therefore, huge amounts of money are spent for prisons, to make rich farmers richer, on the military, for election campaigns, and so on.

Regarding the latter issue, politicians spend more than taxpayer money to get reelected. The one-quarter of 1 percent of the population who are the super-rich plus various special interest groups make large donations. In return for this largess, they receive special tax breaks, credits, loopholes in laws, and subsidies totaling far more than the amount of their donations. These actions reduce the total tax revenue in Washington, so higher taxes on ordinary citizens are enacted to make up the deficit. The effect is a massive transfer of wealth from the middle class to the rich (as Chapter 5 will demonstrate).

To conclude this section, it is intriguing to reflect that sixty years ago there was far less per capita wealth and real incomes were much lower than they are today. Yet families got along reasonably well with just one breadwinner. Today, with far more inflation-adjusted money coming into a typical household, a family needs two or even three jobs to make ends meet. On top of this fact, today's typical family has fewer children. At the very least, this development is thought-provoking.

Television as a New Communication Medium

It hardly needs stating that TV has had a major impact on citizens' lifestyles. As with any major innovation, some time was needed for it to become institutionalized. Before and during the 1950s broadcasting companies were learning how to use the new medium. Journalists still went out into neighborhoods and communities to seek out and report local news. They were plain folks, just like those they interviewed; they lived with them. Their noses for news led them into companies, churches, bars, sports venues, civic organizations, and government agencies.

The media of that time saw their most important job as constant criticism of whatever government officials were saying and doing. Their task was to assist citizens in keeping government shaped up, because without this pressure officials would feel the tug of negative incentives. Reporters reinforced citizens' skepticism in their writing, often motivating them to act in their own behalf.

In New York during the 1940s journalists had a motto that stated, "We're against people who push other people around." James Fallows wrote: "By the 1990s, 'crusading' journalists on TV news-magazine shows might also say they were standing up for the little guy. But viewers would sense something phony in this pose. Reporters had moved into the class of Americans who can do the pushing."[7]

Print journalists still get comments such as "I liked your article," or "I think you're wrong on this one." With print media the reader is far more likely to examine and evaluate the content. TV news anchors are not reporters, and the feedback that they get relates to their personality or their charisma.

It is easy to fall into this trap. During the 1960s, so-called hippies and other concerned people massively demonstrated against the Vietnam War. The more active participants began to draw the very media coverage that they craved, but soon the trap was sprung. They became engulfed in the heady atmosphere of celebrity journalism, and so they lost touch with the masses whose interest they had formerly represented. Thus failed a valiant and (as this book will argue) desperately needed bloodless revolution against big government.

By the 1970s there was a TV in almost every home, and many had color sets. This meant that anyone who could get on the air enjoyed tremendous "reach." The same network broadcast would be received by millions of people. Campaigning politicians naturally saw the medium as heaven-sent. There was no longer any need to ride the rails for long periods, with whistle stops, hurried stump speeches, on to the next little burg, and continue to the point of exhaustion.

This also meant that national politicking became centralized in Washington, and candidates transformed their speeches to remove content and focus on charisma. The nature of TV is not conducive to serious thought regarding the content of programming. Most viewers of the first televised debate between presidential candidates were convinced that Kennedy prevailed over Richard Nixon due to a more telegenic image.

In the early days of TV candidates emphasized their clean, wholesome image. But as time passed a tradition of vicious negative advertising became established, which convinced the public that politicians were a bunch of barroom bums. Either way, the public remained unenlightened concerning candidates' actual positions on issues important to citizens.

Candidates for Congress no longer look forward to visiting with constituents and learning about their concerns. They seldom go home unless there is an upcoming election, and then they often stay just long enough to generate a few feet of videotape and a couple of photo-ops. If they do occasionally meet with ordinary citizens this is done in front of and for the cameras.

Prices of TV time have been increasing for decades. In 1976 the Supreme Court ruled that political **contributions** must be limited, because without limits there is potential for corruption. But **spending** by a candidate or party cannot be restricted, because that is free speech. This ruling provides strong incentives to work around restrictions on campaign contributions; one result is what is called soft money. The rhetoric states that the money is used to build party strength and get out the vote, but thinking citizens know the reality: It goes to candidates. In practice there are no limits on political money, so with every election it only grows worse. Members of Congress spend more than 40 percent of their time fund-raising.

No one gives money without expecting something in return; even donors to charities derive satisfaction or they would not donate. Members of Congress return the favor of money with favors given. These favors go to special interest groups in the form of laws, regulations, and tax breaks that give them unearned differential advantages over ordinary citizens, who continue to be taxed to pay congressmen's salaries and their many perks.

Mountains of money and TV's emphasis on personalities and personal power seeking have combined to concentrate great power in Washington. The news media cooperate, lest they lose access to the highest reaches of personal power. They know that in an environment of celebrity politics, these are the people about whom readers and viewers want to know.

The combination in TV of light, sound, action, and color fools viewers in several ways. One of these lies in the illusion that the attractive announcer has come to visit in the living room. The medium personalizes a distant human being, projecting his or her personality to the point where a viewer believes he or she knows the person. But what he sees is not what he gets, because the screen image is not the person. Rather, the person has been trained to act as someone likable. If successful, demand builds for appearances and speaking dates. With more fame, the price per appearance goes up. It's a business. But this business bears scant resemblance to accurate, balanced, responsible, and useful reporting of news.

A viewer tends to see a TV anchor's life as nothing but sweetness and light, and this generalizes into politics. Candidates soon discovered that their TV images were more important than their positions on issues relevant to their constituents. A new industry sprang up: spin doctors who could advise candidates on how to polish their persona. Hollywood and politics had intermixed before, but this was a new twist.

TV news and, to a lesser extent, print news are geared more to entertain than to inform. It is a competitive business, with careers rising and falling on TV show ratings and on subscriptions to newspapers. Therefore the news is dramatized, and it has nearly abandoned issues while it focuses on people. But the news as a product is different than any other: People learn about their government from it. They must be informed about their government, or they will not have a studied opinion. Without this there can be no democracy, because in a democracy accurately informed people govern themselves.

Politicians largely control the airwaves by issuing, withholding, and canceling licenses to broadcast, and by threats to cut off access to personal power centers if companies don't cooperate. This is done even though politicians are aware that they bore people with their empty rhetoric, but they need lots of face time on the tube to keep their names before the public at election times. The tradition of the news media acting as critics of public officials' positions on issues has all but vanished (with the positions).

In the early days news was crafted, and care was taken to be accurate. Today's news is mass-produced as the networks triple and quadruple weekly time devoted to news. An innovation of around twenty years ago is partly responsible—that of breaking news. Under this policy news is broadcast immediately as "breaking," without any analysis and often with practically no checking to determine if what little is broadcast is accurate.

Another innovation is the tendency to dart from one piece of news to another, as a hummingbird flits from one blossom to another. (A string of commercial messages sandwiched in between only accentuates the process.) The result is that people are drowned in entertainment and starved for information.

A third innovation, equally harmful, is the nine-second sound bite. Fallows explained that a sound bite is a clever play on words that refers to a piece of existing news. It often substitutes for going out into society and digging for real news.

News is like democracy in at least one respect. Trust, virtue, and decency are delicate blossoms, which frequently wilt in the absence of loving care and feeding.

In recent years even otherwise respectable news media have become bottom feeders as they broadcast one scandal after another. This practice keeps a lot of citizens entertained, but it does little to enlighten them concerning what is going on in government. Every editor knows that sex sells; this may be among the few topics left where people can still learn the results of investigative reporting. In his book *The Wish for Kings*, Lewis Lapham accurately compared today's Washington, DC to the scandal-soaked palace intrigue of the seventeenth-century French King Louis XIV.[8] This country's founding fathers had no use for a king, but it seems that today's citizens tolerate a monarch's lifestyle in the White House. (Thomas Jefferson would be appalled.)

The Pew Research Center for the People and the Press interviewed 552 journalists. Results showed that these journalists are as fully aware as the public that the credibility of the news media is rapidly decreasing. Causes mentioned included sensationalism, lack of objectivity, inaccurate reporting, and preoccupation with the bottom line. This is interesting in that if managers and editors are interested in profitability it would seem that something would be done about the other three causes stated. The grim reality is that customers apparently prefer to be entertained rather than informed. Either that or their abiding faith in government is unshakable.

Campaigning politicians desiring to entertain and not wanting to risk losing votes avoid taking positions on issues. However, they don't want to be seen as not having the courage to take positions, so they adopt an aggressive position with respect to their opponents. Viewers then get a combination of spin doctoring and vicious negative ads on TV. Neither conveys much useful information, so millions of voters conclude that they are not familiar with candidates' positions on the issues.

If they cannot cast an informed vote, why bother? Surveys by the Pew Research Center have shown that people think their votes don't count, so voting makes no difference in the outcome of an election.

Even debates are scripted to maximize their entertainment value. If an issue is admitted for discussion it is only because each candidate's campaign manager believes it can be manipulated so that post-debate straw polls will show his or her candidate a winner, or there will be more votes in it at election time.

Many citizens have argued for public financing of election campaigns, believing that money is not speech and elections should be won and not bought. They don't realize that a lot of the money spent on today's TV ads already comes out of taxpayers' wallets and purses. If certain criteria are met, campaigns qualify for millions of these dollars. Also, businesses spend millions of shareholder money buying special favors, and most of this money goes to finance campaign spending. (Including indirect holdings through insurance companies and pension funds, half of all citizens own stocks.) This applies as well to union dues and other organizations that lobby for favors.

In 1997 Britain ran a national election campaign that took six weeks from start to finish. Candidates spent an average of US$6,000, because radio and TV ads were not permitted. A logical question to ask is, How did British candidates get their messages across? They went into the towns and villages to talk to voters, and they held town meetings. This means each had a cohesive message to convey; otherwise citizens would have chewed him up and spit him out.

In contrast, the British newspaper *The Economist* reported that in 1996 the average campaigning incumbent US senator spent $4.5 million on his race.[9] This means he or she raised an average of $14,000 every week during six years in office. The cost is sky-high when TV ads are permitted, but the benefit to candidates is at least dual. First, they do not need to think through issues and develop credible positions on them; the second benefit is not having to mingle with the riffraff. The predictable result is alienation and mutual contempt between voters and candidates (see Chapter 8).

The conclusion is that, rather than being a medium of communication, TV is a barrier. Its entertainment value keeps erstwhile citizens in front of the box when they could be with family, friends, co-workers, and neighbors, discussing local issues and judging the performance of their elected public servants. This means politicians have the opportunity to develop new ways of hiding from problems, as ignorant and often complacent citizens have practically no access to their elected representatives.

Today TV audiences are fragmenting as hundreds of channels become available. This development could make it difficult for politicians to get their message across, and hence the need for still greater piles of money.

In his popular book *Bowling Alone*, Putnam reported results of many studies that looked into what he called "civic disengagement."[10] He found that "dependence on television for entertainment is not merely *a* significant predictor of civic disengagement. It is *the single most consistent* predictor that I have discovered." Putnam's conclusion: "Heavy television watching by young people is associated with civic ignorance, cynicism, and lessened political involvement in later years, along with reduced academic achievement and lower earnings later in life."

There was a story going about in the early 1950s in which a neighbor invited an old lady to come over and "watch television." She politely declined, saying "Oh, thank you, but no thanks. I've seen television."

THE NOTION OF THE CAREER POLITICIAN

The founding fathers did not anticipate that members of Congress would have full-time jobs. Having worked in the private sector for some years and been successful, some men might aspire to public service; these men would form the pool from which candidates would be selected to stand for office. Having spent long periods in the private sector, they would have acquired a respect for the free market's ability to contribute to economic development. Furthermore, each would want to serve for a limited time only.

During a visit, the Frenchman Alexis de Tocqueville noted the absence of "public careers" in America.[11] He was quoted in an 1836 issue of the *Democratic Review*: "We have no great faith in professional politicians." Throughout the nineteenth century congressmen served an average of one or two terms and then, having satisfied their aspirations, returned to their communities.

The founding fathers did not anticipate the advent of tremendous wealth and TV. It has been shown that these factors enabled politicians to think in terms of making a full career out of public service. This section will demonstrate how their mentalities evolved to respond to incentives derived from the negative side of human nature.

In the country's early years the average turnover of personnel was about 50 percent at each election. Today there is very little turnover of politicians from one election to the next one. *The Economist* reported on the outlook for election year 2002:

> *There will be fewer than 50 competitive races this time (meaning races in which the candidates are only a few points apart) compared with 121 ten years ago. Of those 50, only half will really be toss-ups. This is worsening existing trends. In 1998 and 2000, nine out of ten winning candidates in the House of Representatives won with 55% of the vote or more. That was the lowest percentage of close races of any election year since 1946, save one.*
>
> *Only six sitting congressmen were defeated in the general election in 2000, a re-election rate of 98%. Such a result, which would hardly shame North*

Korea, is becoming the norm: the re-election rate has averaged more than 90% since 1952. Not surprisingly, congressmen are reluctant to leave their warm nests.

The writer summarized: "The combination of larger numbers of safe seats and increasingly expensive campaigns is undermining the quality of American politics." [12]

Those who don't retire with fat, self-voted pensions often turn to lobbying or "consulting." Their contacts with active lawmakers are worth a lot of money to special interest groups seeking unearned favors. (Today in government "whom you know" takes precedence over "what you know.") Because these activities are unconstitutional, politicians often resort to deception to obtain the money to get reelected over and over again.

Recently there was a lot of press devoted to a deep tax cut spread over ten years. There is probably little truth in it, just as there was no truth to the Reagan income tax cut of 1981. That one was also scheduled to phase in over a period of several years. But beginning a couple of years later President Reagan raised payroll taxes in several steps. These steps not only wiped out any gain coming from the 1981 legislation, they actually increased the average citizen's total tax load. The news media cooperated in both instances, hyping the benefits of the tax "cut" while the payroll tax increases were kept under wraps.

Even politicians eventually age, retire, and are replaced by younger men and women. But nothing changes, because political parties are just as interested as members of Congress in perpetuating the current system. They often select candidates who sympathize with the status quo. (This includes primary elections.)

Once in a long while a young tiger comes to Washington determined to clean house. Very soon after arrival he finds himself seated in the office of a veteran, who explains, "You are right; government needs a sweeping change, but this will take time. You will need to become chair of one of the key committees, and when this happens you will have the power to effect real change. Meanwhile, I suggest that you become familiar with how we do things around here."

The Congress operates on a seniority system, so the tiger soon learns that he is fifteen to twenty years away from a chairperson's job. He must get reelected several times, and this means he must raise great quantities of money. For that period of time, therefore, his strategy must be, "To get along you must go along." He needs not only money; he also needs the cooperation of many veterans.

Time passes. Eventually he gets that vital chair position. But by now the tiger's fangs and claws have been dulled, and he owes favors to the many who helped him along the way. They don't want him to rock the boat, and he still needs money for the next election. In this way the system traps him, just as the veteran (probably still around) knew would happen.

Some of the needed campaign money comes from companies. In 1970 a few Fortune 500 big firms had offices in Washington, DC. By 1980 over 80 percent of them did. The name of the game of politics was gradually changing from governing to money, and executives accurately concluded that they had to be there to look out for their companies' interests.

One small example of the response by members of Congress to this presence was a vote to annually give $127 million of taxpayer money to several big companies to promote foreign demand for their products. The convenient reason given was a deficit in overall trade with other nations (greater value of total imports than exports, which sends dollars overseas).

If companies believed that money should be spent on promotion, one would think they would spend company money. But this means spending shareholder money, and recently these owners of companies have been more closely watching how their money is spent. Taxpayers are not as watchful, so taking a small amount of additional money from them will not cause ripples. Some of that money would not be spent on promotion; it would be kicked back into congressional reelection campaigns.

This example indicates how the system works to keep career politicians in office. Government officials sometimes pass laws to encourage recycling; this is how they recycle themselves.

A saying goes, those who cannot learn from history are doomed to repeat it. A career politician seeks to learn from history, but his purpose in seeking is not necessarily the public good. Rather, he has two purposes in mind. One is to learn what types of decoys and deceptions of the public have worked in the past, and how they can be adjusted to fit today's political reality. The other is to identify instances in the past that have the potential of embarrassing or harming the current regime. The record of these instances is then revised to more nearly accord with the desires of today's politicians and other members of the elite class.

Thinking citizens will recognize the last as "revisionist history," which was practiced extensively by the Soviet Russian and Chinese governments until recently. When embarrassing information is withheld from the public, the future job of revising is made easier.

There is evidence that some congressmen are living beyond their means, even though they recently voted themselves generous raises in pay. This means they are diverting reelection campaign money to their personal use. Dwight Morris maintains a page on the *Washington Post*'s Web site called "Money Talks," where concerned citizens can follow where money is raised and spent. In 1998, 109 **unopposed** House of Representatives incumbents raised an average of $392,225. (This book will elaborate on other abuses.)

Public officials know they are not accountable to citizens, but they apparently don't particularly care. Legalities are seldom a problem, because those in the

Congress are in a position to make almost anything they want to do legal. Future historians will select some year between 1955 and the present to mark the end of Rule of Law in this country (where no one, absolutely no one, is above the law).

Money is power, and without accountability power corrupts. If people in government think they can get away with it, acting on negative tugs will produce amazing if also predictable results. The theory of accumulation of money suggests that everyone has a price, even though few want to admit it.

From what has gone before it is easy to see how electioneering promises slowly become empty. If a candidate does not promise the moon or its equivalent, his or her opponent will. If the electorate has lost touch with the principles that guide good government, and no candidate runs on these or even on relevant issues, empty promises and perceptions of charisma will win contests. During the 1930s a prominent world politician believed that if he told citizens lies often enough they would eventually come to believe them as truth. In a society that has lost touch with truth, this stratagem can work. It surely did for Adolf Hitler.

Nobel Prize Laureate economist Milton Friedman, writing in 1967: "Time and again, extravagant promises have been made that this or that expensive program will solve this or that social problem. And time and again, the result is that both costs and problems multiply."[13] It is the promises that win headlines and votes. What happens later is precisely as Friedman stated, but the news media keep these failures hidden from the taxpayers. Because this devious behavior works, it is still in vogue more than thirty years later.

But sometimes promises can return later and boomerang on career politicians. An excellent example is entitlements, such as Social Security, Medicare, Medicaid, food stamps, farm subsidies, and others. Most were put into law with not just cost-of-living increases built in. As the population ages, some of these programs are growing at three times the rate of inflation.

They are called entitlements so that citizens are led to believe that they deserve these benefits, and they are someone else's money. Politicians have worked hard at conveying this impression. Today these programs are out of control by government; career politicians have painted themselves into a corner.

Programs to benefit the elderly, poor, and disabled make up half of all government spending. Older people vote far more often than do the young, so the programs are also politically untouchable. For thirty years they have been beyond the control of public officials, some of whom are the same ones who won millions of votes by passing the laws originally. Only very recently have politicians found the courage to dent these voracious programs, and then only a little.

This problem had its origin during the Great Depression and World War II, when government grew far more rapidly than at any time before. Public officials adopted the practice of taking large amounts of money through force from taxpayers, who saw the necessity for doing so.

But this practice did not stop with the end of the war. The US government kept growing, and today a vast bureaucracy skims 20 percent off the top of all revenues; another 20 percent goes to interest payments on a $6 trillion national debt; and ten years after the end of the cold war "defense" still claims around $380 billion annually.

Political promises will over time also generate a "what's-in-it-for-me?" mentality among citizens. Effective operation of a democracy requires a "what-can-I-contribute?" mentality. The former encourages people to form groups and lobby for what they want from government; this mentality has been called groupthink. The latter has individuals acting on behalf of good government, contributing their time and talents and deriving pleasure therefrom.

President Bill Clinton obviously subscribed to what's-in-it-for-me? as he set a new standard in promising. Citizens are beginning to realize that being inundated with blankets, cookies, and warm milk will not encourage them to become responsible, concerned, what-can-I-contribute? adults. Rather, by encouraging development of incentives based on the negative side of human nature, Clinton did his country a massive disservice.

Thinking citizens don't appreciate this treatment, as they know the realities of life: meeting challenges, competition, winning, losing, and plunging in for another go. When blankets and cookies get in their way, they don't like it, and they become alienated from government. An alienated electorate guarantees empty elections, which play directly into the hands of career politicians. Some journalists commented on 1996 presidential candidate Bob Dole's campaign as "uprooting himself from the senate and taking root in America." This pretty well says it: As a long-time senator he actually perceived himself as having lived in a different nation, known as Washington, DC.

Yet another way of making promises meaningless lies in finger-pointing. "We were all set to move on this one, but those damned Republicans/Democrats stopped it in its tracks." Of course, the tradition of shifting the blame did not originate in Washington. But the situation is different there, in that often politicians who don't want to pass a bill desired by citizens will rig the vote in advance to ensure failure. The so-called Republican revolution of 1994, with its media-hyped Contract with America, is arguably a case in point. Ditto for the Reagan revolution; both hardly dented the system's hide, which has grown thick with age. (Chapter 9 discusses how gridlock is designed into the system.)

In 1992 there came a fresh breeze from outside the system in the person of H. Ross Perot, a third-party candidate for president. He cared not a hoot about speechwriters or opinion polls; he tapped into his conscience and said what he felt like saying. He thoroughly embarrassed candidates George Bush and Bill Clinton in TV debates, forcing them to discuss the towering fiscal deficits and national debt that irresponsible government had built up over previous years. In this he rendered a great public service by speaking his mind, in stark contrast to what career politicians (including Bush and Clinton) do, saying only what the people want to hear.

In fact he aroused such fear among public officials that the two major political parties apparently resorted to a dirty trick to get him to back out of the race. (They interfered with his daughter's wedding.) He came back at them in 1996, but by then the major parties had figured how to screen him out of the debates.

"When the cat's away the mice will play," goes the old saying. But in this case politicians' toys are becoming horrendously expensive, nearly all of them courtesy of the taxpayer.

The term *contribute* has acquired a new meaning in Washington. Miller noted: "Members of Congress intimidate major contributors to support them, not their opponents, and use Federal Election Commission [FEC] reports to police their behavior."[14] Candidates tell "contributors" that even if they lose the election they will still be around long enough to hurt donors' causes. Therefore the real meaning of *contribute* is "extort."

The saga of election campaign finance reform need be discussed only briefly, because no career politician wants it and with an alienated and disinterested electorate there is no chance of passage. If perchance such a bill should become law, it will have no teeth in it. In 1974, in the wake of the Watergate scandal, an aroused public forced a law to be passed with some teeth, but two years later the Supreme Court gutted it with its *Buckley v. Valeo* decision. (For practical purposes, this decision said that money equals speech.) Miller continued: "More than two decades of research has concluded that the major effect of the 1974 reforms was to help incumbents ward off challengers."

Uncontrolled campaign finance violates the justice provision of the US Constitution: equal opportunity under a rule of law. This is because a candidate without megabucks has less than half a chance of success. Many good citizens who desire an opportunity for public service therefore decide not to run. When personal power seeking gets hold of politicians' souls even the Constitution gets steamrolled, just like everything else.

War hero, senator, and 2000 presidential candidate John McCain said:

> *Most Americans are convinced we are utterly incapable of acting. . . . That we have no greater priority than our own reelection. . . . That we will act openly or deceitfully to prevent the slightest repair of the system. . . . That we conspire to hold onto personal ambition, political advantage. . . . Some excuse six-figure donations, saying America spends more on yogurt and toothpaste. We're not selling toothpaste but integrity.*

This is accurate, except that by its definition integrity is not for sale, as are members of Congress.

Against this background, the argument that if the McCain-Feingold campaign reform bill were passed into law it would restrict political competition even further seems not surprising. In 1996 every House of Representatives incumbent who spent less than $500,000 won reelection, whereas only 3 percent of challengers won who spent as little as that.

Furthermore, McCain-Feingold would restrict self-financed challengers. Not only would members of Congress vote themselves discounted TV time, they would legally accept up to $6,000 from an individual contributor rather than the usual $1,000 maximum whenever incumbents ran against a wealthy self-financed challenger. Finally, because money is fungible and because these politicians are thoroughly familiar with every fiscal nook and cranny in Washington, a thinking citizen would surmise that the bill would never be passed without advance planning concerning how to negate its impact. Although no proof of this exists, only a bit of reflection on human nature leads to this conclusion.

The Economist apparently reflected on this situation in 2001: "When the US senate passes the boldest campaign-finance reform for 27 years, it would be churlish not to celebrate. . . . Well done to senators. . . . at least until their legal advisers have worked out how they can get around it."[15] *The Economist* concluded: "The painful fact is that nothing will keep money, galumptious amounts of it, from pouring through America's elections."

But in early 2002 the same newspaper must have reflected again: "By passing a bill to limit so-called 'soft money' . . . the House has paved the way for the biggest change in the financing of America's elections since 1974."[16] A thinking citizen would suspect that he or she is not the only one confused by the role of soft money in elections.

It is not just the money. In his book *Monopoly Politics*, Miller stated that a challenger must register with the FEC. To do this he is required to complete a 618-page questionnaire that weighs nearly two pounds. Indeed, career politicians truly leave no stone unturned.

Robert Mugabe is currently president of Zimbabwe. He is a tyrant by any reasonable definition, and in early 2002 he was preparing for yet another crooked election so that he could remain in power. Officials in the US government were leaning on him in an effort to obtain a free and fair election. The term *hypocrite* comes to mind. Maybe citizens should turn over a few stones here at home.

But the harassment does not stop there. Any challenger "is liable at any time to have a formal complaint to the FEC lodged against them. This device has become a routine way of orchestrating a 'hit' on an opponent—a charge that is leveled but whose veracity is never adjudged by the agency until long after the reelection returns are in."

The Electoral College is a mysterious institution that also helps preserve incumbent politicians in office. In January 2000 Raymond Steiber attacked it:

"With the dawn of another presidential election year, maybe it's time we finally admitted that the Electoral College system is broke, that it's been broke for over two centuries and that it's time we got rid of the thing."[17]

In theory citizens select their electors, but in practice they consist of all congressmen and senators. The winner of the popular vote in each state sends all its electors to Washington. "The loser, even if it's only by one vote, gets to send none. In other words, as far as the national election is concerned, his [or her] votes simply disappear."

About one month after the election an electoral head count is conducted in Washington. December 2000 marked the fourth time in US history that a candidate was elected who did not win the popular vote. Steiber continued: "If you're a republican living in Massachusetts or a democrat living in Texas, you might as well not even show up at the polls—your vote simply won't count in the national election." Furthermore, "it discriminates against independent candidates. Every time an independent . . . loses a state, he also loses all the votes. That means he can't build coalitions across state lines—which is the only way an independent can win. This is a fine state of affairs for the morally bankrupt republican and democratic parties, but it's hardly a benefit to the rest of us."

Without the electoral college, a person would vote as a citizen of the United States and not as a citizen of a particular state. When voting for someone to execute the public will over national and international issues, this seems only appropriate. The electoral college should be abolished as an outmoded and biased institution.

The Economist reported on the 2000 campaign.

> *But there is no doubt that the campaign-finance system is badly broken. A country that regards itself as an international torchbearer of democracy would be wise to make sure that its own political system is not rotting from within.*
>
> *This year's election has been the most expensive in American history. An estimated $3 billion has been spent on presidential and congressional races—including millions of dollars by unaccountable outside groups—and an additional $1 billion or more has been spent on state contests. Expenditure is up nearly 50% from the 1996 election, a contest that supposedly set an all-time low in money-grubbing and rule-bending.*[18]

On the subject of rule bending, law school dean Gene R. Nichol noted:

> *Gore and Bush are no strangers to putting principle aside to scramble for victory. Imagine how "principled" the governor of Texas felt running a campaign based on support for a Medicare prescription drug benefit, a Patients' Bill of Rights, an unyielding commitment to the protection of public education and a rock-solid guarantee of full Social Security benefits. If Bush believed in these things, you can't prove it by his record. But he did the polling and swallowed hard.*

Gore, on the other hand, ran as a populist. That's tough work for someone who has spent the last decade turning the Democratic Party into a marriage of Wall Street, Hollywood, and Silicon Valley.

When North Carolina's Frank Porter Graham ran for the senate in 1950 he said that if he had to forego his beliefs and set aside the common good to win, "then I don't want to be elected."[19]

At that time there was not much money around Washington compared with what's there today. The world *principle* had not yet been excised from the Washington lexicon. A thinking citizen might conclude there is a connection between money and principle.

In a November 2000 column, David Broder noted that the incoming freshman class of congressmen numbered forty-one. This is less than a 10 percent turnover of personnel. While observing that thirty-two of the forty-one have had substantial experience in government, he asked: "Who says American politics no longer attracts the talented?"[20]

It is easy to agree with Broder, until the question is raised: talented at what? Washington's greatest talents consist in emptying the pockets of taxpayers without an open rebellion, either taking it through force or threat of force or stealing it, and then wasting much of it (close to half, according to citizen survey results). The new crop of forty-one stalwarts will integrate smoothly into this system, as the aftermaths of previous elections have so amply demonstrated.

"Government of the people, by the people and for the people shall not perish from the earth." So said Abraham Lincoln at Gettysburg in 1863. It is hard to avoid the conclusion that it has perished; government of the people today is by the politicians, bureaucrats, lawyers, and special interest groups. All of these connect with money, which has become literally the coin of the realm in Washington, DC. Another conclusion is that in politics experience is a negative asset, because it connects closely with the negative tugs of human nature.

Madison argued for "a frequent change of men resulting from a frequent return of elections." Because human nature does not change, a wag was recently quoted: "Politicians are like diapers. They need changing frequently, and for much the same reason."

In his famous book *Memoirs of a Superfluous Man* (1943), Albert Jay Nock lamented: "The American people once had their liberties; they had them all; but apparently they could not rest o'nights until they had turned them over to a prehensile crew of professional politicians."

Notes

1. Robert H. Bork, *Slouching Towards Gomorrah*. Harper Collins, 1996.
2. Philip Wylie, *A Generation of Vipers*. Dalkey Archive Press, 1946.

3. E F Schumacher, *Small Is Beautiful: Economics as if People Mattered.* Harper and Row, 1989.
4. Paul Gilster, "A Pause in Technology's Headlong Rush." *News and Observer* (Raleigh, NC), October 9, 2000, p. 3D.
5. Maureen Dowd, "The Pursuit of Happiness, 2001." *News and Observer* (Washington, DC), May 22, 2001, p. 13A.
6. Walter Kerr, *The Decline of Pleasure.* Simon and Schuster, 1962.
7. James Fallows, *Breaking the News: How the Media Undermine American Democracy.* Pantheon Books, 1996, p. 76.
8. Lewis H. Lapham, *The Wish for Kings.* Grove Press, 1993.
9. *The Economist,* "How to Cost the Cost of Politics." February 8, 1997, p. 17.
10. Robert Putnam, *Bowling Alone: The Collapse and Revival of American Community.* Simon and Schuster, 2000, p. 231.
11. Alexis de Tocqueville, *Democracy in America.* Knopf, 1972.
12. *The Economist,* "How to Rig an Election." April 27, 2002, p. 29.
13. Milton Friedman, *An Economist's Protest.* Thomas Horton, 1972, p. 71.
14. James C. Miller, *Monopoly Politics.* Hoover Press, 1999, p. 79.
15. *The Economist,* "Goodbye, Soft Money." April 27, 2001, p. 22.
16. *The Economist,* "Soft Money, Tough Measures." February 16, 2002, p. 31.
17. Raymond Steiber, "Aren't We Ready for Democracy?" *News and Observer* (Washington, DC), January 9, 2000, p. 21A.
18. *The Economist,* "Selling America to the Highest Bidder." November 11, 2000, p. 43.
19. Gene R. Nichol, "What They'll Fight For." *News and Observer* (Raleigh, NC), November 29, 2000, p. 17A.
20. David Broder, "In the New House, Brains, Experience, and Big Red." *News and Observer* (Raleigh, NC) November 2000.

Chapter Five:
The Need for Mountains of Money and Predictable Changes in Tax Policy

A billion here and a billion there, and soon you're talking about real money.
—Senator Everett Dirksen

TV and the intrusion of excessive money into the political process have eroded the tradition of earning votes through effective representation of voters' interests. Buying and winning millions of votes now requires centralizing of billions of dollars in Washington, DC. The purchase of access and influence constitutes a massive bazaar with annual turnover of around $25 billion.

Career politicians do not advertise this fact; rather, they tell voters what they want to hear, and between elections they march to a different drum. Charles Adams's book *For Good and Evil: The Impact of Taxes on the Course of Civilization* is a useful resource for understanding the situation today.

A History of Taxation

Taxes have been an enemy within almost every civilization. In the rare exception taxes are only a potential enemy, soon to become a real enemy in the absence of constant vigilance. Politicians constantly warn the public against terrible military threats from abroad to divert attention from the enemy within. The daily news is rife with these warnings, and the media frequently stretch the truth. Officials encourage publication of these bulletins because taxes are the enemy only for those who live outside the centralized power centers. When one body of people can **legally exert force** nearly without limit on another body to collect money, the situation is ripe for abuse.

Although a tax system poses a threat, there is opportunity for good. This means a country can become a land of opportunity. This phrase once accurately described the United States, but hardly anyone even utters it today unless he or she is a recent immigrant.

The history of abuse stretches way back, and it is not limited to high tax rates and items taxed. Pharaohs of ancient Egypt taxed practically everything, but they occasionally gave back some tax money when they thought their scribes were taking too much. But then the scribes began keeping part of what they collected, so the pharaohs hired investigators to check up on them. Feeling the tug of the negative side of human nature, the scribes began buying silence among the investigators. In this way even an honest ruler found the system deteriorating from good to evil. In one form or another this trend has repeated itself throughout history.

In the second century bc Roman managers whose companies got into difficulty lobbied the Senate for tax breaks. Near the end of the 800-year Roman Empire, Emperor Diocletian actually had more tax collection agents than there were taxpayers. Charles Adams noted: "Civil liberties are adjusted to a tax system; the tax system is not adjusted to civil liberties."[1] He argued that the fall of Rome was due largely to the evil side of taxes.

Arabs guided by the Prophet Mohammed formed the Ottoman Empire to replace the failed eastern Roman Empire. At first they relieved the people of oppressive taxation, provided that they accepted Islam as their faith. But several centuries later the predictable happened, as sultans and caliphs piled on the taxes. In Egypt the local sultan triggered a major revolt. The Ottoman Empire survived until 1918, but by that time it was but a shadow of its former glory.

During the Hundred Years War in Europe (in the fifteenth century) there were tax revolts by peasants in France and England. The next 200 years saw one revolt after another throughout Europe. Peasants were given no voice in tax policy, yet they bore most of the burden. This may have been the original inspiration for disgruntled British subjects (American colonists) in 1774 when they called out that "taxation without representation is tyranny!" A study of the French tax system found seventeen ways to achieve tax immunity. Each loophole had its own political power base, and none involved the peasantry.

French cooking enjoys a worldwide reputation, which might suggest that their government originated the concept of "cooking the books." Martin Gross showed that no trade barriers slowed the process when this devious skill was imported into this country.[2]

In the 1993 bill, many of the new spending cuts have yet to be appropriated. In fact, it might be a case of congressional (and White House) creative accounting. The supposed $250 billion in 1994-98 "cuts" include $44 billion in reductions already provided in the 1990 bill. Twenty-five billion in increased taxes on social security beneficiaries are strangely thrown into the spending cuts column. Eighteen billion is actually new taxes in the form of user fees. Perhaps Congress should develop a new budget category called "Unreal."

Gross's observation suggests that members of the Congress are double-counting budget cuts. It also looks like they are double-dealing citizens. "To quote the legislative aide of a house budget committee member, 'It's a pure travesty.'"

Writing in *The Wealth of Nations* in 1775, English economist Adam Smith said: "There is no art which one government sooner learns from another than that of draining money from the pockets of the people."[3] In Germany, Frederick the Great wanted to know where all the tax money was going. His finance minister handed a piece of ice to the next minister, who passed it on to the next, and so on, until when it finally reached the king all he had was a wet hand. The lesson was clear: Many tax revenues are consumed by the bureaucracy.

English common law provides that a man's home is his castle, and not even the king or his agent may enter it to collect taxes. But although the taxman enforces law for others, he may not allow it to hamper his work. Thomas Paine wrote:

> *If, from the more wretched parts of the Old World, we look at those which are in an advanced stage of improvement, we still find the greedy hand of government thrusting itself into every corner and crevice of industry, and grasping the spoil of the multitude. Invention is continually exercised, to furnish new pretenses for revenue and taxation. It watches prosperity as its prey, and permits none to escape without tribute.*[4]

No delegate to the Constitutional Convention in Philadelphia in 1787 wanted to grant to future Congresses the ability to tax the public at will, yet the new government would need money to operate. Keenly aware of the grisly record of tax history (and that of human nature), delegates were concerned lest a group of public officials gain control of the tax system and exploit it for their own benefit. Delegates were convinced that controls were needed beyond the consent of the citizens, as this would be all too easy to imply from a variety of statements and actions. The result in effect was to establish uniformity by forbidding loopholes and tax breaks for anyone.

This uniformity provision tied in well with the concept of justice. Adams wrote, "It is just as immoral for governments to grant exemptions as it is for citizens to hide their income." It was not until the twentieth century that the graduated income tax undermined the uniformity principle. Passage of the Sixteenth Amendment in 1913 meant open season for future Congresses, and since then their penetration of society has grown ever wider and deeper.

Logically, to control tax increases, control over spending power is needed. For the founding fathers the meaning of the term *common defense* permitted no foreign wars. Alexander Hamilton commented that this was a new idea in history: ". . . tying up the hands of government from offensive war."[5]

Furthermore, the "general welfare" clause was meant to restrict government spending to those activities that benefit the whole nation. During the 1930s the Democratic Party reinterpreted this clause to justify forcing one class of citizens to give money to another class, calling it public welfare. This policy could mean a benefit to the whole country were it not forced by government; it robs some people of choice concerning how to help other people, and it robs recipients of their dignity.

Thomas Jefferson wrote in an 1816 letter:

> *If we run into such debts, as that we must be taxed in our meat and in our drink, in our necessaries and our comforts, in our labors and our amusements, for our callings and our creeds, as the people of England are, our people, like them, must come to labor sixteen hours in the 24, give the earnings of 15 of these to the government for their debts and daily expenses; and the 16th being insufficient to afford us bread, we must live, as they now do, on oatmeal and potatoes; have no time to think, no means of calling the mismanagers to account.*[6]

King George III was still in charge, and an overmature tax system had turned evil.

Adams commented on today's tax system: "Jefferson could not have imagined, nor could he ever have expected, an American to move to Europe to avoid American taxes. . . . Tens of thousands of Americans have moved to Europe to escape from a tax bureau known the world over as the world's worst in complexity, intrusions, and punishments."[7] In Jefferson's day, escape was in the other direction, and the reason could often be traced to taxes.

In 1894 a law in this country taxed incomes over $4,000 (equal to about $55,000 today) at 2 percent. Ninety-eight percent of the people were exempt, but the law was nonetheless attacked and defeated. Adams noted: "As one lawyer argued, if the rate was two percent today, it could be twenty percent tomorrow. No one suggested it might be ninety-one percent tomorrow; that would have been laughed out of court as an appeal to the absurd. But tax laws that are productive of revenue have a tendency to become absurd." Nevertheless, in 1913 the Sixteenth Amendment, which taxed personal income, was ratified.

In 1916 the US Treasury reported that there were 206 people with annual incomes over $1 million. The maximum marginal tax rate was 7 percent. In 1921, when it went to 77 percent, only 21 people reported incomes of $1 million or more. The rate increase had caused massive tax evasion.

The Fourth Amendment prohibited "unreasonable searches and seizures." Agents of the Internal Revenue Service (IRS) on the trail of suspected tax evasion could not enter a home or business without a court order. Today, this amendment has been gutted.

Before 1913 the tax system was unpopular with only a small minority, which means it generally catered to the positive side of human nature. The government was not fighting a foreign war, nor was it taxing and spending with reckless abandon. Supreme Court Justice Oliver Wendell Holmes thought he was getting a bargain for his tax dollar, so he enjoyed paying. Some citizens voluntarily contributed even if they did not owe tax.

Adams argued that later the Supreme Court developed a split personality. It outlawed racial segregation as "inherently unequal," but in 1976 it authorized collections of money by politicians and parties by claiming that these are free speech. The court saw fit to ignore restrictions on the free speech of candidates who lacked access to piles of money. Franklin Roosevelt's chief of staff Harry Hopkins had set the tone: "We're going to spend and spend, tax and tax, and elect and elect!"

In 1968 William Henry Chamberlain wrote:

> *Part of the blame for the steady chipping away and erosion of the taxpayers' income and standard of living rests with the undue meekness of the Forgotten Man. He is a law-abiding citizen and his impulse, on getting an increased bill from the tax collector, is to pay up without even marching to city hall and hanging the mayor and members of the council in effigy.*
>
> *Indeed, it is a problem for a psychologist why organized union groups will sometimes commit every crime in the book, assault and battery, willful destruction of property, mayhem, even murder, in order to extort a higher income while the taxpayer meekly accepts dose after dose of diminished income. The latter is surely a more serious grievance and one wonders what explosion would follow if an employer proposed the same work at reduced wages. That is what the state, thru one agency or another, is continually imposing on the Forgotten Man, the taxpayer whom the politician despises as a cow to be milked dry, a sheep to be shorn.*[8]

"How different was the reaction of early Americans to the imposition of what seems, in comparison with the present exactions, quite trivial taxes on tea and stamps!" At that time, citizens had to fight for their liberty. This has not been necessary for today's citizens; hence, they place less value on it. They must realize that liberty is excruciatingly hard to retrieve once lost.

Gross pointed out that today's family pays three times as much taxes, in constant dollars, as did its 1950 counterpart.[9] Since 1950 there has been a lot of inflation, but Congress did not adjust the exemption amount on IRS form 1040 until recently. Keeping the exemption constant adds to taxable income when it is subtracted from an increasing gross income. Also, inflation caused a worker's increasing taxable income to slip into higher tax brackets, even when what that greater income could buy did not increase. This meant that a person's purchasing power decreased, and the amount of that decrease equaled the increase for the government. (Money stolen through "bracket creep" was later eliminated.)

Some conclusions are in order. Ancient Greek historians believed that politicians who are given too much power become tyrants. Even wise taxation eventually turns bad, and tax history tends to repeat itself. Representative taxation seldom works as a system, because the line between a fair and an oppressive tax is fuzzy and people are seldom called on to make that distinction. Increases in taxes imposed during an emergency (such as a war) will often continue after it is over.

Adams wrote: "When a government taxes too much, there are . . . four things that can happen, and three of them are bad; rebellion, flight . . . and evasion. There are even more things that go bad with society: chronic inflation, low productivity and slow economic growth, strangulation of freedom by state regulatory bureaucracies, and gradual erosion of individual freedom and self-determination."

Jefferson: ". . . and shall not take from labor the bread it has earned."

Taxation Today

In spring 1986 the strong US dollar bought a lot of French francs and German marks. Europe braced for the summer's onslaught of tourists from this country. A German woman was quoted: "Why can't they just stay home and send the money?" The analogy is tragically accurate: The US taxpayer has for decades been staying home and sending the money to Washington, DC.

Milton Friedman stated that the income tax is like "a gun to the head."[10] The government can give nothing to anybody unless it first forcibly takes from another. "When a taxpayer is confronted by a civil 'servant' from the IRS, is there any doubt in either mind as to who is the master and who is the servant?" Tax experts outside of government argue that abuse of the income tax can endanger citizens' future liberties and even civilization itself. Career politicians love to spend someone else's money, and unless they are restrained there will be no end to it. Adams noted: "There is ample precedent in the opinions of the court in the nineteenth century to support a judgment that the Internal Revenue Code is so lacking in uniformity in so many ways as to be blatantly unconstitutional."[11]

The principle of fair value received guides the contracting, service, and payment of ordinary debts. But if taxation is law, this principle does not apply; the government has ordered it, and that is all. The income tax is a penetrating intrusion on privacy. It forces every worker to be a bookkeeper, and it forces every employer to collect the tax and forward it to the Treasury. The government pays no one for an estimated 400 million to 1 billion person-hours each year devoted to preparation and payment of taxes. It refuses to pay for the services of professional tax preparers. Finally, it ignores the real fear that taxpayers feel about an audit. The smallest error can be a cause for harassment.

Adams (quoted from *Those Dirty Rotten Taxes*):

Informers are not used in the modern world except in the US. Like the informers in the ancient world, US informers receive a percentage of the tax recovered. It is ironic that the US pursues a policy of promoting informers, when the American Revolution was sparked by a similar practice instituted by British revenue authorities . . . special training sessions to show agents how to enlist people to inform on their friends, neighbors, employers—even family members. It is all reminiscent of the Soviet Union, where children were taught by parents that "the walls have ears."

Adams also wrote: "In a free society the power of the government to spy on its citizens is strictly limited, restrained, and controlled." The IRS maintains records similar to those that used to be kept by the KGB in the Soviet Union, the Stasi in East Germany, and the Securitate in communist Romania. These agencies were concerned with internal security against rebellion. Tax agents in the United States are concerned with revenue security. "The ends differ, but the scope of the espionage does not."

There comes a point at which a government presumably committed to protecting its citizens' liberties begins to take them away. When and where does revenue security taper off and internal security take over?

Two immigrants from Russia who were making lots of money were interviewed on a talk show; the host asked how they liked life in the West. After saying they enjoyed it, they attacked the IRS, saying that not even in Russia was there an organization that could take half of a person's earnings. (The astonished host quickly changed the subject.) Congress recently passed the Bank Secrecy Act, but it does not protect the taxpayer against depredations of the IRS. Banks have been socked with huge penalties for not informing on customers who use a lot of cash or engage in other activities that the IRS wants to know about. Another recent law attempts to bind the IRS to the constitutional presumption of innocent until proven guilty. Hopefully this law will act to restrain overzealous agents.

Adams reported that "some years ago, the *Reader's Digest* published a series called 'The Tyranny of the I.R.S.' It shocked the country at the time, so much so that Congress held a hearing on the charges. The hearing turned out to be a total fraud. No one from *Reader's Digest* was invited to appear. The author was not invited." Even all-powerful congressmen quake in fear of the IRS. Their tax records are dicey at best, and agents know this. The conclusion is that the organization is totally out of control, accountable to no one.

The nonprofit Tax Foundation reported that on average the IRS in 1999 forcibly took $7,026 from each person (including children) in the country. Other levels of government took a total of $3,273, for a grand total of $10,299. This is more than most households spend in a year per person on food, clothing, and shelter **combined.**

The National Center for Policy Analysis reported that in 1999 central government tax revenue totaled 21.7 percent of the US gross domestic product (GDP), compared with an average of 18.6 percent from 1945 through 1992. This is a record high. Between 1998 and 1999, the take increased by 4.9 percent.

Summarizing, the total tax load on a typical family of four comes to $41,196, and this omits hidden taxes on companies that must be passed along to consumers. It also omits the cost of compliance with a multitude of government regulations (administrative law).

Corporations are also thoroughly gouged, according to Adams: "One example: Mobil Oil's tax counsel testified before the congressional Ways and Means Committee that 'It takes Mobil fifty-seven man-years at a cost of $10 million to prepare its income tax returns.' To prove his point, he brought along to the . . . hearings a stack of tax returns, four feet high, which weighed seventy-six pounds."

Public officials gradually designed and built the system of entitlements so citizens would think that their windfalls were someone else's money. Local politicians are told to actively sell this fakery to their constituents: "We'll take the heat on taxes, as we are far away and out of mind, and you can bask in the glow of entitlements. But this means you owe us one; when election time rolls around you will devote great efforts to helping our campaigns." This is in part why so much money takes the scenic route to Washington instead of staying near home, where it could do the most good for local taxpayers.

Most governments ask three things of a tax system: (1) pay for their operations, (2) redistribute money from those with more to those with less, and (3) give tax advantages to worthy causes. Most tax systems are severely stretched just to meet the first goal. The other two are open to abuse. Who should decide how much to take by force from those with more and how much to give to those with less, especially when both groups have incentives to hide income from whoever decides? Whenever a special interest buys a juicy tax break, the extra money that ordinary citizens must provide to make up the deficit is safely hidden away. Multiply this a thousand times every year and the system soon becomes a crooked, 10,000-page bucket of worms. (That is the size of the Tax Code.)

The withholding tax is surely clever. When a worker never sees a substantial part of the money he or she earns, he is inclined to believe it never belonged to him. Therefore a worker will probably not complain very loudly when the amount withheld is increased by a little, and later by a little more. In addition, many people rob themselves by asking extra to be withheld in anticipation of a "windfall" refund; the government uses their money without paying interest on it.

Social Security started out as a pension plan in 1935, but it quickly metamorphosed into a tax. This is also withheld, and normally never seen. Furthermore the worker often perceives it (when he looks for it at all) as saving for old age instead of a forced taking from a relatively poor worker to be given to an often-richer retiree. A young worker so taxed has less incentive to save for his or her own old age: Let the young of that time support him or her.

But life spans are increasing, and 30 percent of all public spending on the elderly occurs during the last six months of life. This means that numbers of seniors are increasing faster than are the young who will presumably support them. Combine all this with the fact that government has been spending all surpluses in the Social Security trust funds as fast as they accumulate instead of setting them aside to be used when needed much later, and the generation gap in the future is going to yawn much wider than it does now.

Even this does not do justice to the Social Security mess. By 1939 politicians realized that old folks voted more frequently than did young people, so they started increasing retirement benefits. In an ordinary pension plan, a worker's and the employer's contributions are saved with accumulated interest for retirement. But in the 1950s politicians put through several big increases in benefits, and each one took effect about a month before an election. This is how Social Security "pension funds" (old age, survivor, and disability) became a tax on young workers.

And here is how it evolved.

	1935	1955	1975	Today
Payroll tax rate	2%	4%	11.7%	15.3%
Portion of wages taxed, the first	$3,000	$4,200	$14,000	$65,400
The resulting tax	$60	$168	$1,638	$10,006
Share of total revenue from payroll tax	1%	12%	30%	36%

Some of the increase in wages taxed is due to inflation, but not the percentages. These increases were kept hidden from public scrutiny for obvious reasons. Furthermore, payroll taxes discourage entrepreneurs from starting businesses, because they must be paid whether or not the business is profitable.

This hits minimum-wage employees hardest because the law will not permit an employer to lower the wage enough to cover his or her half of the tax. (In effect, this is done for all other workers, which means they pay all of the payroll tax.) Of course this restraint increases unemployment among poor teenagers.

In 1996 an estimate put the unfunded liabilities of the Social Security trust funds at $8.5 trillion. Fifteen years in the future the baby boom generation will begin to retire in great numbers; at that time the retirement trust fund must pay out far more than it takes in. Workers being taxed then will pay in far too little money to meet obligations. The retirement trust fund will go broke.

Unless something is done a working family at that time will need to cough up an extra $37,000 a year in taxes, on top of its existing tax burden. Today a typical family is forced to pay government at all levels a total of 45 percent of its income. In the 2030 the tax bite would be 80 percent.

The government passed a law years ago that makes it illegal for private companies to carry unfunded pension liabilities on their books. But when the government does this and citizens not yet born will be taxed to help meet stupendous future obligations, is it then okay?

Public officials have become spendaholics. Since World War II, every time taxes are increased to balance the budget, they simply spend more. Today the budget is close to balanced, but this is not due to any restraint by government. During the 1990s the economy roared ahead. Therefore the private sector was able to create huge wealth in spite of government and not because of it, so tax money by the trainload came into Washington.

Politicians know the public is concerned about reckless spending, so many of them recently seized the opportunity to take credit for a balanced budget. They said this result proved that members of Congress can restrain their spending when they put their minds to it. There is no truth to these pronouncements. The news media even hyped a huge projected fiscal surplus, but knowledgeable analysts predicted today's stillborn status.

All this, and the talk about serious tax cuts is just that: talk. Logically any extra money should be devoted to debt reduction, but politicians hooked on the spending drug do not think logically. During 1997 revenues exceeded predictions by $45 billion, but instead of returning this overage to taxpayers or routing it to debt reduction members of Congress and the president spent it.

Adams wrote: "Looking back into history, whenever the power to tax and the power to spend reside in the same political body, . . . the power to spend will always overpower the power to tax. Governments will inevitably spend too much. . . . They will debase their coinage, if necessary; steal from helpless minorities; and create enormous debts that will be passed on to future generations."

Clinton is not the first president to trumpet legislation to soak the rich. Someone in 1929 projected population and incomes ahead to 1966, concluding that in that year there would be 6,500 people with incomes of over $1 million. The actual number was 626. This result could lead to a conclusion that the income gap between rich and poor had narrowed substantially. But a second look focuses on **taxable** income. In 1966 the top tax rate was 70 percent, compared to 25 percent in 1929. The high rate made it worthwhile for the rich to hire tax accountants and lawyers to exploit government-provided loopholes, subsidies, and tax breaks to reduce reported incomes and tax loads. Also, many of the wealthy shipped some of their income-producing assets overseas to what are known as tax havens (small island countries with practically no income taxes).

Adams previously mentioned three negative reactions by taxpayers to overly high taxes: evasion, flight, and rebellion. The first two have already been discussed. A thinking citizen might wonder when the time is ripe for the third.

In 1989 a "privileged persons tax law" enabled 1,081 people with incomes over $200,000 to pay no taxes. A 1999 Congressional Budget Office (CBO) report claimed that between 1993 and 1997 the take from taxpayers earning more than $200,000 a year went up by 83 percent. This number should be taken with a generous grain of salt, because the estimate came from the bowels of the US Congress. Furthermore, that level of income is considered upper middle class today; the super-rich behave as described previously.

A citizen who is unhappy about the thousands of government programs but please don't touch his or her favorite few is deluding himself. If he permits taxation to support these programs, he automatically permits taxation for those that everyone else wants. This book will argue that a person would be much better served if he were to work with fellow citizens at local levels to develop programs that benefit him- or herself and others, and the tax load would be slashed.

The phony Reagan tax cut of 1981 has been discussed. The famous tax reform legislation of 1986 involved the same sort of trickery.

The income tax code has been amended some 5,000 times since Reagan (presumably) simplified it. In 1994 it consisted of 5.6 million words. Notwithstanding this repeated subterfuge, when Reagan entered the White House the national debt was $994 billion. Twelve years later it had ballooned to $4.4 trillion.

In 2001 President George W. Bush compared his proposed tax cut package with the Reagan extravaganza some twenty years before. Republicans argued that the Reagan initiative released an era of unprecedented prosperity. Projected budget surpluses of $5.6 trillion over the next ten years fully vindicated Reagan's supply-side economic promises.

Molly Ivins saw the package differently: "The Bush tax cut, centerpiece of his presidential campaign and signature issues, is so bad [that] Jane Bryant Quinn, the business columnist who is not normally given to overexcitement, called it 'a contemptible piece of consumer fraud.' *Time* magazine's headline was 'Stupid Tax Tricks.'"[12]

A typical bit of government tax fakery is to backload a long-range cut. This means the real cuts don't kick in for several years hence. Ivins noted, "Bush was able to hide the true cost of the things, which is now estimated at $4 trillion for the second 10 years. That is, frankly, nuts." She added that the tax plan was "disingenuous and dishonest to begin with." Someone must have gotten nervous, because then committee members added a clause that would cancel the entire law at the beginning of 2011, thus resurrecting year 2000 tax rates.

Subsidies to farmers alone cost taxpayers around $30 billion a year, and this is just one of many farm programs. About 600,000 full-time farmers each receive an average of $3.5 million each year. A lot of this money is kicked back into congressional reelection campaign funds. In 1990 part-time farmers received about

18 percent of that $30 billion, and this was in addition to what they made farming and what they did when not farming.

The military is a still bigger business, consuming (as promised by President Bush) upward of $400 billion a year of taxpayer money. Members of Congress especially like to buy weapons, as defense contractors bid loosely for the business and kick back some of their excessive profits. Frequently the Pentagon does not want what Congress wants, but the latter is in the business not for war or peace but rather for bucks and votes.

They also like themselves. Over a twenty-year period Congress increased spending on themselves by 705 percent, which is more than twice the 280 percent rise due to inflation. Congressional staff in the 1950s numbered around 5,300; now the total is about 39,000. The total cost of the Congress in 1992 was $2.8 billion, compared with $343 million in 1970.

William Greider provided a deep insight into the inner workings of the Congress:

> *Therefore, in order to accomplish such distorted outcomes, the governing elites and monied interests are required to create a series of elaborate screens around the subject of taxes—a moving tableau of convincing illusions that distracts the public from the real content and gives politicians a place to hide. Meanwhile, behind the screens, the action proceeds toward the results they seek. In public, the two major parties struggle contentiously over tax issues. Yet the reality is the collaboration between them. Expert opinion is marshaled in behalf of broad economic goals that seem desirable to everyone—economic growth and jobs. Meanwhile, elites work out among themselves how these broad goals can be translated into reducing their own tax burdens.*[13]

Paine's eighteenth-century warning was prescient: "While they appear to quarrel they agree to plunder."

Gross noted,

> *Each year, our politicians use fresh pseudologic to convince us to part with more of our money for services we do not want, do not truly understand, and generally never receive. .... Politicians have always been somewhat deceptive, but the corruption of words is reaching new heights. Taxes become spending cuts. Spending becomes investment. Budget arithmetic is manipulated. Hidden agendas proliferate.*[14]

Survey results suggest that citizens believe 48 percent of what government takes in taxes is wasted. This amounts to about $19,774 for each taxpaying family of four. The mountain of money in Washington has grown so high that a staff of conscientious accountants could not manage it. Because it is not their money, government accountants have little incentive to even try.

As tax loads continue to increase, the predictable happens: Economic activity goes underground. New research suggests that the informal sector may make up one-seventh of total economic activity in the world's advanced countries. If government does not know a company exists, taxing it becomes a challenge. It appears that since the 1960s the shadow economy in the United States has grown three times as rapidly as the official one.

Taxes practically always increase by dribs and drabs to avoid ruffling taxpayer feathers. Therefore a look at the long term is revealing. In 1910 a typical family's **total** tax load was 5 percent of annual income. Today when the costs of taxes and regulation are added together they total about 57 percent of a family's income. Harry Browne wrote, "Of course, you get something in return for all the taxes and regulation. But what is it? Safe cities? Good schooling for your children? Safe and uncongested roads? A harmonious society? A nation secure from attack by terrorists?"[15] Today's concerned citizen is inclined to ponder this ninety-year trend in taxation.

Gross capably elaborated on the long-term trend in taxation with a story based on true statistics. In 1950, Mort Stevens had a wife and two children. Their total tax load, federal, state, and local, was $615, or 12 percent of their income. The scenario now shifts to the same little Long Island house in 1993, now worth $210,000. Sam Greene's thirty-year mortgage bears an interest rate of 8.5 percent, which is double that of Mort's mortgage. Sam works in the same factory as Mort did, and he earns $41,000 a year. But this is not enough to live on, so Mrs. Greene works at $17,500 a year for a combined $58,500.

This may look like enough, but by 1993 five different levels of government were in the tax collection business. There were excise taxes on gasoline, phone, liquor, tolls, and so on. The local school district took a whopping $5,700 a year from the small house, some twenty-five times the take in 1950. This alone grabbed 10 percent of their combined income. The state took $2,603, and Social Security took $4,500. The Greenes' federal tax was $10,025, so the **total tax load, even accounting for inflation, was three times as much** as it was for the Stevens family.

Politicians know that citizens are unhappy about taxes, so they frequently promise tax relief. In Washington jargon this means giving back to people their own money. But an accurate definition of *tax relief* is a reduction in the typical citizen's tax load, not taking his or her property through threat of force, skimming 20 percent of it off the top for the bureaucracy, and giving back some of the rest.

Studies indicate that 72 percent of citizens want a constitutional amendment that would require a referendum vote among them for every proposed tax increase. This may be sound in theory, but convincing evidence demonstrates that congressmen are masters at hiding tax increases, and they often ignore the US

Constitution when doing so. They have been getting away with this for decades, but a thinking citizen must wonder how much longer it can continue.

Another fact worth some thought is that the same group of officials is in charge of both taxing and spending: the House of Representatives. A private company would never permit this. Now, it is true that the president has the veto, but when he (or she) and the House combine forces to steal from the public, this check on power put in the Constitution by the founding fathers is not effective. Adams wrote: "If we are to preserve and pass on to our children the liberty and freedom we boast about, which our forefathers passed on to us, we must focus our attention on our tax system and the destructive forces we have put in motion, forces that are far more dangerous that any outside invaders." This quote needs amending, in that citizens did not put in motion these destructive forces; rather, those responsible are the representatives whom the people trusted and who betrayed that trust.

Adams concluded: "Liberty tends to carry the seeds of its own destruction. . . . Taxing powers will, if carried to excess, destroy the very liberty they sought to preserve."

Borrowing and Debt

Public officials have long known that voters don't like taxes but they do like benefits, so the convenient tactic for years has been to put costs on the cuff for later payment. Because they love to spend the people's money, politicians delight in this practice. It makes them look generous at election time, and the costs are well hidden. The same source of money must be used to give government employees increases in salary, but this shows up as an immediate expense, so the same interest in hiding increases in expenditure fattens their pensions.

To soothe taxpayers concerned about the national debt, politicians occasionally clamp a legislative lid on the amount. This is a simple operation, and it is equally simple to vote a higher ceiling whenever the existing one is threatened. This has been done time and again, to the point where the ceiling is meaningless. Today each citizen shells out $4 a day just to pay interest on the debt.

Sometimes when the ceiling is approached, the Treasury Department finds the financial markets not amenable to yet another issue of long-term debt. This is no problem for creative agencies, which issue BANS (bond anticipation notes), RANS (revenue anticipation notes), and TANS (tax anticipation notes). The main focus always is don't interfere with government officials' spending habits.

In 1994 Kevin Phillips remarked:

> *The Spanish, the Dutch, and the British, each in turn, proved unable to roll back their public debt once it gained momentum, because the vested interests involved were too strong. This is true again. The middle class of the 1990s*

> *looks askance at sacrifice, being too hard-pressed to give up the 5-10 percent of overall income that its largest membership, those in the 50th to 85th percentiles of the US population, receive from government transfer payments.*[16]

These three empires collapsed after repeated wars drained treasuries and left them hobbled by debt. The current threat from within is not without precedent.

Today the public debt is up to $6 trillion and counting, notwithstanding the rhetoric about a balanced budget. Annual interest payments swallow almost a fifth of revenues. During the 1992 election campaign the debt was rising much faster than it is now, and the government was spending nearly $400 billion each year more than it took in. In that campaign, Ross Perot debated seasoned political pros Clinton and Bush. He referred to the debt and the fiscal deficit that fed it as the "crazy aunt in the basement. Everybody knows she is there but nobody talks about her." By bringing this up he forced the other two candidates to debate the issue. This caused a lot of embarrassed harumphing and shuffling of feet; in his absence, neither major-party candidate would have said anything about this threat.

Interest on the debt takes nearly all of the nation's private savings, in part because people seem to emulate the government's emphasis on the short term and so they save very little of their income. Wealthy citizens and foreigners hold most of the Treasury bonds, so the money to pay interest is drained from the pockets and purses of ordinary citizens to fatten the investment portfolios of the rich. Like others, the public debt transfers wealth to the rich from the nonrich, and the latter get no return from their "investments."

In 1980 voters elected a president (Reagan) who promised to get big government off citizens' backs. "Government is not the solution; government is the problem." Harry Browne said, "When [Reagan] left office eight years later, government spending was 69% greater, tax collections were 65% larger, and $1.9 trillion had been added to the federal debt your children are supposed to pay."[17]

There is an organization called Lead or Leave, founded by a group of twentysomethings in 1992. Members spread the word about what they call generational politics. They are some of the children to whom Browne referred.

President Clinton loved to propose wonderful things for the nation's children. One analyst said whenever he mentioned "children, reach for your wallet." Politicians seldom kiss babies anymore, perhaps because they find it very difficult to do so while simultaneously hanging an $80,000 debt on the wee one. The law says adult children of a deceased parent are not required to take on the burden of any unpaid debts at time of death. However, when the government spends tomorrow's money to buy the votes of today's old folks, is this okay?

Reaganites knew the public wanted a balanced-budget amendment to the US Constitution, so they proposed one near the end of his term in office. They reaped the political benefits from the proposal, and if it should be ratified in the future,

Reagan and his reckless spending would be out of office and someone else would have to deal with the problem (unless it could be hidden from the public).

John Steel Gordon wrote a book called *Hamilton's Blessing: the Extraordinary Life and Times of Our National Debt.*[18] In 1916 the national debt could have been eliminated by the nation's richest man, John D. Rockefeller. Today the two richest US citizens, Bill Gates and Warren Buffett, would go bankrupt trying to pay just six months' **interest** on the national debt. Gordon identified seven periods when the debt steadily increased; six of these involved either a major war or economic depression. The seventh period began in 1960, and without major wars or depressions it has increased for more than forty years. (The economy in the 1960s was strong, so the damage due to the Vietnam War was not as serious.)

Browne noted, "Politicians don't plan to repay what they borrow in our names. They spend whatever they want, and the amount exceeding tax receipts is simply put on our tab. When they leave office . . . They just collect enormous pensions and praise themselves for a lifetime of 'public service.'"

There is one area in which politicians do plan for the long term—for their own families. Unless something is done, the debt will eventually get so high that lenders will balk. In that event, instead of defaulting on the debt public officials may "monetize" it. That is, they will print enough money to avoid either default or impossibly large interest payments. This will cause galloping inflation, and the purchasing power of the dollar will go into free fall. With money from those huge pensions invested, first here and later abroad when inflation gets hot, politicians' descendents will live comfortably through the catastrophe. Ordinary citizens of that time will be on their own.

The government not only spends the country into deep debt; it also lends money to students, small businesses, and other borrowers. A Government Accounting Office (GAO) report showed that agencies often make no attempt to collect these debts. Word of this policy has gotten to the borrowers, so they accurately perceive their loans as gifts from the taxpayers. The Small Business Administration (SBA) has a very high rate of default on their loans, largely because to qualify a borrower must not be creditworthy in application to any other lender. The bureaucrats are not concerned; it is someone else's money.

Citizens governing themselves will make mistakes; no single person or group is perfect. But they will be quickly aware of each one, and can and will equally quickly act to correct it. But government goes on making the same mistakes repeatedly. Rather than spend taxpayers' money to help citizens improve their lives, politicians spend it to buy votes. What is disturbing is that citizens quietly accept this tomfoolery and go on paying.

The conclusion is that private debt must be retired, because the alternative is bankruptcy. The unavoidable presence of this imperative restrains excessive borrowing. In the absence of accountability, public officials are not restrained.

Therefore, they are tugged by incentives connected to the negative side of human nature. When permitted for long enough, spending other people's money becomes an obsession.

THE CENTRAL GOVERNMENT BUDGET

In 1716 the king of England set up a sinking fund to pay off the national debt in a few years. But in 1733 Prime Minister Walpole raided it and used part of it to meet expenses. Parliament agreed, and after 1733 such raids became a habit. The same thing has been done in the United States to the Social Security trust funds. This is a misnomer twice over, as there are no funds each year after the raid, and surely there is no trust.

The total of fiscal deficits in the 1950s was $17.7 billion; for the 1960s it was $56.9 billion; and for just the first half of the 1970s the figure was $71.4 billion. This means that as time passed there were fewer factories built, products made, wages paid, and homes built than would have been accomplished without the deficits. Since 1955 the inflation-adjusted amount of the budget has tripled, while the population has increased only 65 percent. O'Rourke put it like this: "The budget grows because, like zygotes and suburban lawns, it was designed to do nothing else."[19] It is thus assumed that all government programs will grow. One Washington insider told a journalist that every activity done in government is being done by at least twenty agencies.

Section 7 of Public Law 95-435, approved on October 10, 1978, states that "beginning with fiscal year 1981, the total budget outlays of the federal government shall not exceed its receipts." Members at that time were fully aware of the pleasures of spending, so this law was and is merely window dressing. Maybe a citizen or group of them could go to court and get a judge to enforce this law. Maybe, but this book will show that most judges are also a part of the oligarchy.

The 1,500-page annual budget includes $2 trillion split among almost 200,000 separate accounts. If a citizen were to study each one of these for three minutes, this task would require five years to complete. Next year, here comes another one. It is naive to think that members of Congress read each budget before they vote on it; their leaders tell them how to vote.

It is also naive to think that any curious taxpayer could make any sense of this colossal mishmash. Jefferson wrote, "We might hope to see the finances of the Union as clear and intelligible as a merchant's books, so that every member of Congress, and every man of any mind in the Union, should be able to comprehend them to investigate abuses, and consequently to control them."

Control today is called accountability. To install this vital safeguard of the public trust, the government should be required by citizens to utilize open accrual accounting practices, privatize the Social Security trust funds (to remove the irresistible congressional temptation to raid them), and eliminate all off-budget activities and contingency funding. These safeguards would work under two conditions: minimal government and constant citizen vigilance.

Browne wrote,

> *In 1990 the republicans and democrats joined hands to enact a program to balance the budget by 1993; it included an enormous tax increase and stringent spending limits. The plan projected a $156 billion surplus in 1995—which turned out to be a $192 billion deficit. We still pay the oppressive taxes, but the spending cuts disappeared—and the politicians' projection was off by $348 billion. That's not close enough—not even for government work."* [20]

As a Texas congressman in 1968, elder George Bush castigated President Johnson after his State of the Union speech because he neglected to mention the "tremendous" budget deficit of $25 billion. Twenty-four years later in his own State of the Union address, President Bush played down a $269.5 billion deficit, which was nearly eight times larger (accounting for inflation).

In 1995 there occurred a Republican revolution, or so the news media reported. The 1994 midterm election placed an unusually large crop of neophytes in Congress. President Clinton vetoed the new Congress's first attempt to balance the budget. But over the next two years, public opinion underwent a shift in favor of balanced budgets. Clinton shifted, too, of course, and Republicans then accused him of stealing their thunder. The reality is that if a balanced budget is achieved it will be in spite of the spending drug, not because of anything government has achieved.

In 1997, after working hard on the budget for fiscal year 1998, politicians called it a great victory. President Clinton said it was a "historic agreement that will benefit generations of Americans." John Kasich, the chairman of the House Budget Committee said it was "a dream come true." *The Economist* editorialized: "This budget agreement is the epitome of political fudge and economic incoherence. Labeling it an historic achievement would be laughable, if it were not so sad."[21]

How did the news media handle this so-called historic agreement? The headlines trumpeted news of the first budget in thirty years without a deficit. Everyone in Washington must have thought there is no end to citizens' gullibility.

In his State of the Union message of January 1998, President Clinton called for using every dime of the budget surplus to save Social Security. A short while later he proposed a litany of big spending programs and higher taxes to pay for them.

Every agency submits a sub-budget before compilation of the big one, and each inserts an account for "other services" and includes a number. In 1993 someone totaled all these many items and got a mind-numbing $246 billion. This was nearly equal to the fiscal deficit for that year, and it was $17 billion more than the previous year. This practice creates open-ended slush funds that can be used to satisfy any whim among government operatives, and there is no practical way to trace the money.

Gross commented on the 1994 budget:

> *That pie chart in the 1994 budget is a masterpiece of obfuscation. It shows slices of defense, payments to individuals, interest on the debt, grants to states, then leaves only 6 percent for "other federal operations," which is supposed to be everything else. Really? Only 6 percent, or $90 billion, to pay for all the rest of the government? Apparently, the subliminal message is that there's nothing left to cut. Is that true? No, not at all. When the fake numbers are cut away, there's enough fat in that budget to fry a whale.*[22]

Expense items were cherry-picked to show those that officials thought taxpayers would accept.

In 1999 the CBO was at it again, making projections, even though the agency admits its five-year estimates miss the mark by an average of 13 percent. This means its projection of a fiscal surplus of $239 billion by 2004 could actually turn out to be wildly inaccurate. In 1997 Congress enacted deep cuts in spending beginning in 1999, but by then the political will to make them had evaporated.

Was this a willful violation of a solemn commitment to the people? Not exactly, as officials provided for relief from spending caps for "emergencies." But they neglected to define an emergency, so the result is open season (and déjà vu) on tax funds once again.

Historically there are instances of fiscal rectitude, however rare. Johnson wrote,

> *Indeed, Harding can be described as the only president in American history who actually brought about massive cuts in government spending, producing nearly a 40 percent saving over Wilsonian peacetime expenditure. Nor was this a wild assault. It was part of a considered plan which included the creation of the Bureau of the Budget, to bring authorizations under systematic central scrutiny and control. Its first director, Charles Dawes, said in 1922 that, before Harding, "everyone did as they damn pleased;" . . . Congress "a nest of cowards." Then Harding "waved the axe and said that anybody who didn't cooperate his head would come off;" the result was "velvet for the taxpayer."*[23]

Today the high and mighty in Washington are doing as they please and, as usual, on the taxpayers' dime.

Johnson directed his attention to a more recent president: "While he was in charge, federal spending as a percentage of GNP [gross national product], and with it inflation, was held to a manageable figure, despite all the pressures. It was a notable achievement and explains why the Eisenhower decade was the most prosperous of modern times." President Eisenhower was not a politician.

Finally, Johnson observed that in government nothing good seems to last, as he turned to the Lyndon Johnson administration.

> *By that stage, the government slice of the GNP had risen from 28.7 percent under Eisenhower to 33.4 percent. Treasury control disintegrated. Under Eisenhower, the*

very efficient Bureau of the Budget operated as Harding had conceived it: as an objective agency, . . . to supervise all spending. Under Kennedy, characteristically, the Office was politicized and under Johnson it became activist.

In May 2001 Krugman pointed out that today budget activism has phased into budget skullduggery:

> *Two missing pages happened to contain language crucial to the compromise that had persuaded moderates to agree to the budget.*
>
> *Whatever really happened, the fundamental cause of the mishap was that the republican leadership was trying to pull a fast one—to rush through a huge tax cut before anyone had a chance to look at the details. Now the case of the missing pages has delayed things. . . . You see, there seem to be a few other pages missing from the budget plan.*[24]

Krugman went on to describe the content of additional missing pages. They include the likely cost of a missile defense system, how a conventional defense buildup can be accomplished with no increases in spending beyond that proposed by Clinton, no extra money for prescription drug coverage, no provision for the approximate $300 billion loss of revenue caused by the Bush tax plan's treatment of the alternative minimum tax, and no allowance for the $1 trillion needed by the Social Security system when it is partially privatized.

Krugman finished: "Oh, and there's one more page missing. . . . [It] explains why . . . they should put their names to a budget resolution that is patently, shamelessly dishonest."

In February 2002 *The Economist* commented on President Bush's request for fiscal year 2003: "Budget is not for the faint-hearted. It is big. His $2.13 trillion spending plans for 2003 include a 14% increase in the defense budget, the biggest since Ronald Reagan."[25]

"Not only has he extended tax cuts, but he has tried to hide the cost of doing so with accounting techniques that would make Enron proud." Cooking the books is a pernicious practice of several decades' standing. Why should anyone wonder why Enron Corporation followed a similar recipe? Apparently it's okay for the government to do this, but if a private company does it then a great opportunity opens for public officials to distract the citizens from their own fiscal chicanery by launching several media-hyped investigations.

Confiscatory Taxes and Stupendous Borrowing Still not Enough

The French economist Frederic Bastiat defined government as "the great fiction, by which everyone hopes to live at the expense of everyone else." Over the years politicians have learned to live very well off public largess; a recent measurement showed that the part of Washington, DC, where many of them live is the nation's richest community. They must work hard to support this lifestyle, but the bulk of what they do while working benefits themselves.

In 1996 the Supreme Court opened a new way for political parties to work around campaign finance laws. Now parties can run radio and TV ads in congressional races so long as their actions are independent of the candidates themselves. But money is fungible, and it has no morals. Therefore no thinking citizen believes this fiction.

There are a few actively concerned citizens who complain about the abuse. The standard ploy is listening to their complaints, just giving the impression of truly listening. This is a skill that must be developed early in the career of a politician. If it is done right the complainer feels good about having gotten that one off his chest and goes about his or her business. Of course the politician promptly forgets about this issue as a hundred others crowd in on him, so nothing gets done about it. The money machine keeps cranking just as if there had been no complaint.

Besides taxation and borrowing, politicians have entered the kickback business in a big way. Because they operate a monopoly and can dispense favors through rigging laws and regulations with no competition, special pleaders have nowhere else to go. Members of Congress are not supposed to devote tax receipts to their reelection campaigns over and above what they have already provided for themselves, so they take advantage of their privileged position to demand kickbacks. This chapter only introduces the subject; there will be more on this topic later.

For example, a big defense contractor bids successfully for development of a new weapon. There are several big defense contractors, so there is at least the appearance of competition. This may help keep bids reasonable, or there may be a prior agreement between public officials and contractors to spread the wealth. However, once a contract is won future research and development is negotiated on a cost-plus basis. It is almost impossible to estimate the cost of acquiring new knowledge, so negotiations tend to be loose to be sure unanticipated costs are covered.

Politicians will get involved to be sure that extra costs are covered perhaps two or three times over, and the excess is routed back to them for their campaigns. This is how the kickback process works. The irony of this situation has voters reacting to attack ads on television with disgust, when their own money has paid for them.

Politicians grub for money from anywhere they can. President Clinton "rented" rooms in the White House, accommodating wealthy guests who contributed many thousands of dollars to the Democratic Party. The building is very large, it is owned by the public, and Clinton paid no rent to live there with his family. Apparently he saw nothing improper in running the building like a six-star hotel, and the idea that such "rental" income should by right go to the public probably never entered his mind. (There is no record of whether this income was taxed.)

Officials know citizens disapprove of their actions in trolling for more money, so they often create facades to hide behind. *The Economist* reported:

> *Foreign money provides a convenient distraction. While it is being comprehensively investigated, with CIA men parked behind screens and giant blow-up charts of the destinations of Mr. Huang's telephone calls, politicians can be left free to attend their dinners, go to their fund-raisers, and continue in all the ways they know best to let their consciences and their legislative proposals be shaped, like warm wax, by the promise of a check.*[26]

From the viewpoint of foreigners it is only natural that they want to tap into the system. Due to dramatically increased regulation during the 1960s, US companies by the dozen located offices in Washington. Later foreign companies who compete with these firms saw that they were being shut out, so it is no surprise to see them similarly involved. This is how the tawdry business grows.

The Economist continued: "While Mr. Thompson's hearings have been getting into gear, in other parts of Congress some fifty-seven separate bills to reform campaign finance have been dying for lack of interest. Should anyone really care how good clean American money flows through the machine of American democracy? Well, yes, gentlemen: someone should."

The airwaves are also public property, and the Federal Communications Commission (FCC) has responsibility for licensing bandwidth to broadcasting companies. Because politicians depend so heavily on getting their ads and persons on TV, licenses that could be sold through public auction to generate billions in receipts are often given away. But even this is not enough. Broadcast lobbyists in 1997 wanted to be sure their clients were getting an immense freebie, so they dumped $7.6 million into campaigns and party committees.

Another equally large gimmick through which politicians can hide expenditures is called off-budget enterprises (OBEs). Bennett and DiLorenzo wrote: "The Federal Financing Bank succeeds in making a lot of expenditures in such a way that the voters, in general, will not know they are made, whereas the beneficiaries will be very well aware of it."[27] The practice makes it easy to evade restrictions on taxation, spending, and debt. Bennett and DiLorenzo's book was written to demonstrate that a constitutional amendment to mandate a balanced budget would be an exercise in futility. Most of the operation takes place underground.

Fiscal legerdemain is perpetrated in three ways: (1) Simply place an agency off the books; (2) guarantee loans to privileged individuals, businesses, and governments; and (3) set up numerous privately owned (in name only) but federally operated and controlled enterprises. Examples of the latter include the Federal National Mortgage Association, Farm Credit Administration, Federal Home Loan

Bank Board, and Federal Home Loan Mortgage Corporation. "These agencies were at one time on-budget, but their large and rapidly expanding borrowings become an embarrassment to some members of Congress and were omitted from the budget in 1968." (Apparently congressmen in the 1960s were still capable of feeling embarrassed.) These companies with their national backing compete unfairly with truly private companies.

The procedure is quite simple. Quasi-public companies are created that issue bonds not subject to restrictions on public debt. They are called a variety of names, like district, board, authority, agency, trust, and so on. The taxpayer is presumably not liable should the company go under, so his or her approval is not perceived as necessary for its authorization. Of course the reality is different: From whence will the money come if a company folds while still owing money?

These companies are set up to cater to special interest groups, who are then interested in expanding the operation. The implicit backing of the taxpayer diminishes the incentive to operate efficiently. Bennett and DiLorenzo report that bankruptcies have been rare, due to politicians' concern lest their source of gravy dry up. Thousands of employees work in this public sector, but their numbers don't show up in official statistics concerning government employment. Lawyers, consultants, and contractors are interested in expansion of OBEs, as competitive bidding is not required and contracts are awarded to friends. No one checks up on these operations, so there is no accountability, and the now-familiar negative incentives come into full play.

The two authors wrap it up thus: "So anxious are federal politicians to distribute and local politicians to receive federal aid, that there are literally thousands of OBEs in existence which do nothing but collect federal grants. . . . There are at least 17,500 'toy governments' in the US which do not employ a single full-time employee, but nevertheless receive millions of dollars in federal aid." Taxpayers have gone to court on numerous occasions to protest these abuses, but they have gotten nowhere.

These activities have over several decades compiled a contingent liability for taxpayers of something like $18 trillion. This means that the total that must eventually be paid will most probably be considerably less than this, but the nature of contingency is that no one knows what the final amount will be. In combination with a $6 trillion on-budget national debt and $8.5 trillion in unfunded public pension liabilities, the prospect is deeply disturbing to say the least.

The need for reform is obvious. The Center for Responsive Politics has a Web page called Follow the Money (available online at www.crp.org). Anyone with a Web browser can see how much money is being contributed. The page includes proposals for reform.

Expecting an effective reform law to be passed by Congress is like asking a fox to guard the hen house. In late 1997 Senate Majority Leader Trent Lott had set ground rules for a vote on his amendment to a campaign finance bill. If it failed, the democrats would continue to push the McCain-Feingold bill in spite of a promised Republican filibuster. But if it passed, adding union restrictions to the legislation, the Democrats would filibuster. This is one of many examples of deliberately planned gridlock (discussed in Chapter 9).

The delegates to the 1787 Constitutional Convention were concerned lest a majority act to mistreat a minority. Today it seems as though the reverse has generated a greater concern. A relatively small group of elite rich people in Washington, DC are acting so deceptively and arrogantly as to be tantamount to tyranny of the majority.

If a government runs on money, the winners and losers are preselected.

Notes

1. Charles Adams, *For Good and Evil: The Impact of Taxes on the Course of Civilization.* Madison Books, 1993.
2. Martin L. Gross, *A Call for Revolution.* Ballantine Books, 1993.
3. Adam Smith, *An Inquiry into the Nature and Causes of the Wealth of Nations.* 1776.
4. Thomas Paine, *Rights of Man.* 1791.
5. Alexander Hamilton, in *The Federalist Papers.* Penguin, 1961.
6. Thomas Jefferson, *The Life and Selected Writings of Thomas Jefferson,* ed. Koch and Peden. Random House, 1944.
7. Charles Adams, *Those Dirty Rotten Taxes.* Free Press, 1998.
8. William Henry Chamberlain, chapter in Sennholz (ed.) *Taxation and Confiscation.* Foundation for Economic Education, 1993.
9. Gross, *A Call for Revolution.*
10. Milton Friedman, *An Economist's Protest.* Thomas Horton, 1972.
11. Adams, *For Good and Evil.*
12. Molly Ivins, "Back-Loaded, Top-Weighted and Phased-in-and-out Tax Cut." *News and Observer* (Austin, TX), June 11, 2001, p. 11A.
13. William Greider, *Who Will Tell the People: The Betrayal of American Democracy.* Simon and Schuster, 1992.
14. Gross, *A Call for Revolution.*
15. Harry Browne, *Why Government Doesn't Work.* St. Martin's Press, 1995.
16. Kevin Phillips, *Arrogant Capital.* Little, Brown, 1994.
17. Browne, *Why Government Doesn't Work.*
18. John Steele Gordon, *Hamilton's Blessing: The Extraordinary Life and Times of Our National Debt.* Walker, 1997.
19. O'Rourke, [See page 234, item 26]
20. Browne, *Why Government Doesn't Work.*
21. *The Economist,* "A Fiscal Failure." August 2, 1997, p. 14.

22. Gross, *A Call for Revolution.*
23. Paul Johnson, *Modern Times*. Harper Collins, 1991.
24. Paul Krugman, "Missing in the Budget: Realism." *News and Observer* (Princeton, NJ) May 8, 2001, p. 11A.
25. *The Economist*, "Unfurl the Fuzzy Maths." February 9, 2002.
26. *The Economist*, "The fear of Foreign Cash." July 26, 1997, p. 15.
27. James T. Bennett and Thomas J. DiLorenzo, *Underground Government: The Off-Budget Public Sector*. Cato Institute, 1983.

CHAPTER SIX:
PATERNALISM AND VOTES

When I was a boy I was told that anyone could become president;
I'm beginning to believe it.

—Clarence S. Darrow

Federal law prohibits the buying of votes: US Code, Title 18, Chapter 29, Sections 595-607. This chapter will expose today's reality in Washington, DC.

When the United States was created there were conflicting political philosophies among the founding fathers. The Constitution stressed individual rights, but the legacy of common law was inherited directly from England. (Lawyers among them probably recommended this.) For centuries England had had a top-down, aristocratic government.

On visiting this country in 1830 the Frenchman Alexis de Tocqueville predicted that citizens would lose sight of the basic principles of democracy 100 years before the process accelerated (under Franklin Roosevelt).[1] He also predicted an overregulated private sector that encouraged business managers to come to government for help, rather than rolling up their sleeves and meeting the competition head-on.

In nineteenth-century Germany, Otto von Bismarck regulated the entire economy and regimented the citizens, who felt that they were being treated well for a change. Rose Wilder Lane commented: "For the first time in German history, the Prince did not say, Eat straw. Very kindly he said, Give me your money and I will give you back some of it when I think you need it."[2] He gave his (presumably adult) subjects a monthly allowance in a manner similar to the way entitlement programs are run in this country today.

Take a child into a store where candy and toys are sold, and his desires know no bounds. As a child, he thinks in terms of cost-free benefits. Paternalistic government behaves in the same way, deferring the costs and keeping them hidden. President Bill Clinton proposed program after program for children. If he were honest he would also have pointed out that these same children would later be forced to pay for these benefits when they were adults.

Herbert Spencer wrote, "The ultimate result of shielding men from the effect of folly is to fill the world with fools." Tibor Machan noted: "In its protective care for people, the welfare state neither trusts its citizens to be intelligent guardians of their own good nor to be responsible guardians of the good of others. And in taking this line, the welfare state has produced a citizenry that is neither good nor responsible."[3]

It is human nature to improve oneself and to care about others. When citizens observe some people doing better than others, it is equally natural to ask why. Often unaware of the outcome described by Machan, people are tempted to turn to government to provide what they believe the private and volunteer sectors are not adequately providing. Who can object to the desire for everyone to have a good job, a certain level of wealth, adequate housing, health care, and so on?

But when government takes over these individual responsibilities the results are not equal, as might be anticipated. Government laws, regulations, programs, and policies restrain the individual person from deciding what job is a good job for him or her, how much wealth is enough, what is an adequate house, and how much health care he needs. These restrictions are based on the assumption that there is someone else who knows that person better than he himself does, and should therefore decide for him.

Who is this someone else? The US Constitution sought to guarantee equal opportunity for individuals. The distinction between equality of opportunity and equality of results is subtle but important, because it marks the boundary between democracy and an authoritarian government.

The Great White Father in Washington

In elaborating on his prediction, Tocqueville said:

> *Over this kind of men stands an immense, protective power which is alone responsible for securing their enjoyment and watching over their fate. That power is absolute, thoughtful of detail, orderly, provident, and gentle. It would resemble parental authority if, fatherlike, it tried to prepare its charges for a man's life, but on the contrary, it only tries to keep them in perpetual childhood. It likes to see the citizens enjoy themselves, provided that they think of nothing but enjoyment. It gladly works for their happiness but wants to be sole agent and judge of it. It provides for their security, foresees and supplies their necessities, facilitates their pleasures, manages their principal concerns, directs their industry, makes rules for their testaments, and divides their inheritances. Why should it not entirely relieve them from the trouble of thinking and all the cares of living?*[4]

Human nature makes people different from each other. In any society, therefore, some will be more successful than others. Those less successful will be tempted to turn to government for help. From the officials' viewpoint here are citizens needing help, and what is government for but to help citizens? Surely this is why they elected us.

On reflection it becomes obvious why the founding fathers sought to restrain government: to restrict it to keeping **only opportunities** available to citizens. Looked at over the long term, it is also obvious that Tocqueville's observation connects to the negative side of human nature.

During its first 100 years, the United States had a limited government. President Grover Cleveland vetoed a bill passed by Congress in 1887 that would have given $10,000 to distressed farmers. "A prevalent tendency to disregard the limited mission of (the government's) power and duty should be steadfastly resisted, to the end that the lesson should be constantly enforced that, though the people support the government, the government should not support the people."

Advocates of the so-called nanny state often point to market failures. Any institution that involves people will occasionally have failures. This chapter will show that government is all too quick to respond to these with new rules. Rules not only deny the market an opportunity to correct its mistakes, but the presence of new rules on top of old ones creates a situation that restrains citizens and provides more work for lawyers instead of solving the problem.

In the private sector the price mechanism operates to guide the amount of a product produced. If too many are produced compared with demand, the price drops to where some companies cannot make profits. The weaker ones turn to something else, and this restricts the supply until the price raises somewhat. Conversely, if too few items are produced, the price and profits will be high. This will attract additional companies to the market, which will increase supply and drive the price downward. Over a period of time the price tends to stabilize; this is known as the equilibrium price, where just enough products will be made to clear the market. (This is theory, but a free market works in practice approximately as described.)

Government is a monopoly. When it produces a product or service, there is no competition to discipline production, so officials don't know how many to make available and how much to charge. Therefore these decisions must be made by guessing. Competition spurs innovation as a weak company strives to grow stronger by creating a slightly different product that the market wants, thus enhancing sales and profits. In government this force is absent.

In an age of specialization the temptation is to leave such decisions to experts. But every citizen is different, and so the only way to promulgate a new program is to force-feed most of the people to meet the needs of the few. Mitchell and Simmons wrote,

> *In the market, prudent consumers must consider income and prices before deciding to buy, and this must be done at the margin and with an eye to one's future prospects and obligations. In the polity, in contrast, citizens are not con-*

> *strained by income or prices. The goods . . . of government are provided whether one wants them or not.*[5]

This action restricts consumer choice, not to mention forcing payment of the necessary tax. In this way money for national defense is determined by public officials, with citizens having to pay the approximately $380 billion price tag every year (the projected figure is $400 billion).

A taxpayer is interested in the total government budget and usually would like spending reduced. However, as a beneficiary one is interested in receiving payments, be they entitlements, subsidies, tax breaks, credits, and so on. Mitchell and Simmons ably pointed out the implications:

> *If a politician has a choice of dividing $1 million equally among 1 million citizens or equally among 1,000 people, he will rationally opt for the latter because he is more likely to win the gratitude of those who gained $1,000. . . . Conversely, if the same politician has to choose between taxing 1 million . . . $1 and taxing 1,000 taxpayers $1,000 each, he will . . . choose the former option. The logic is similarly clear; the electoral implications of concentrated gains and dispersed losses prevail.*

This example explains why public officials so often reward the few at the expense of the many while quietly ignoring the US Constitution. A thinking citizen can see from this hypothetical example how special interest politics works.

It eventually becomes political suicide to even reduce benefits; following any such attempt recipients will quickly organize and bring pressure on politicians and bureaucrats. This means programs almost never die, even though they may no longer be relevant. A vote is a vote at the ballot box, but a single dollar vote in a congressional office has a weight that differs from every other dollar vote.

Another parable has 100 people, 1 to a room, and each with 100 $1 bills. A politician makes the rounds, collecting $1 from each person, but at the end he gives $50 to one of them, who is pleased to receive it. After 99 more rounds, where a different person receives $50 each time, everyone is $100 poorer, $50 richer, and happy. The politician quietly leaves the building with his $5,000.

Politicians have arranged a lucrative life in Washington for bureaucrats, so naturally there is a surplus of applicants. Were this situation to exist in the private sector this surplus would quickly drive down the price of their services (salary and benefits). But in a monopoly where someone else is paying, this doesn't happen. An East Indian diplomat once said: "That society which routes its best and brightest young people into the public sector, which spends wealth, and not into the private sector, which creates wealth, shall not last indefinitely as a viable society."

Mitchell and Simmons argued that politicians become more important and command more resources from taxpayers if the economy is believed to be working poorly. The reality is that if left alone by government the private sector, with the occasional hiccup, will stimulate economic development and raise living standards far more effectively.

The human body is a complex mechanism. Therefore it seems logical that people need protection from medical charlatans and quacks, which could ruin that mechanism. Enter government. Licensing laws prohibit medical people without the proper license from performing certain procedures.

This surely seems reasonable, until on reflection the hidden agenda is revealed: Restrict the supply so that the price will rise. Licensing is thus appropriate as an aid to a patient's decision selecting who will treat an injury or ailment, but the generally less expensive option of allowing unlicensed practitioners to work will help keep the price reasonable for all. As the price offered by licensed physicians continues to rise it will cause more patients to opt for the alternative; thus, the restraint. (In the event of malpractice a patient has the same access to legal recourse no matter who treated him or her.)

The news media like to play up the fact that around 44 million people are without health insurance coverage. The lack of price restraint has made it difficult for a lot of people to buy insurance. However, this figure includes several million people who are wealthy and healthy enough to balk at the high cost of coverage, so they simply insure themselves. If government passes a law to require all businesses to provide medical insurance, thousands of small businesses that cannot afford to do this will go under. This will increase unemployment, more so when the same law inhibits new businesses from starting up.

In 1997 a law was passed that prohibited elderly patients from receiving medical care beyond that authorized by Medicare, even if they were willing to pay for it. The reason for this rejection of market demand based on common sense lies in the notion of socialized medicine: Everyone must have exactly the same benefits. If people were permitted to make choices there would be unequal results. But it also seems somehow unfair to force the elderly into the black market to get the care they want.

If one citizen claims a right to medical care, this means someone else is being forcibly taxed to provide it. The question then comes around again: How much medical care is this person entitled to? If the answer is as much as one needs, then there is little incentive to get healthy and remain so. Who decides, the taxpayer? If so, how does his voice get heard? Politicians are experts at faking listening.

The notion of a patients' bill of rights is a political ploy devoid of practical meaning. It is the government attempting to tell citizens who gets what; it is also a sleazy political take-off on the US Constitution's first ten amendments.

Medicare is a huge, $280 billion program that has nearly 40 million beneficiaries and processes some 800 million claims each year through 60 contractors. The theory of accumulation of money operates, so there is little control over disbursements.

In one example, a man set up about twenty-five phony medical clinics and applied for provider numbers for each (code used to submit bills to Medicare). No one bothered to check him out, so his assistant began billing the state Medicare office, and the checks began coming back. A bureaucrat lives to see his program expand, as this brings in more staff and promotions, and higher pay and benefits for him. There is no incentive to check on expenditures, and it is someone else's money anyway. In two years of part-time "work" the man cleared $500,000 of taxpayer money. It is bad enough that no one checks doctors and other medical personnel who have padded bills and engaged in other gimmickry to rake in unearned dollars. What is potentially worse is that there is evidence that organized crime has discovered this source of easy money.

As a second example, Malcolm Sparrow of Harvard's Kennedy School of Government devised an experiment in which a crook submits a bill for $1,500, which is paid.[6] He then submits 10,000 claims for the same procedure on 10,000 other patients, for a total of $15 million. "In every field site I went to, bar one, a $15 million check would have been issued without a hiccup." One executive told him, "We would probably never notice. It's not our money." Apparently the fake clinic man could have looted far more than a paltry $500,000 if he had realized the full potential.

In early 1998 Clinton proposed the largest expansion of Medicare in twenty-five years. The next day he proposed $22 billion for "the largest national commitment to child care in the history of the US." There was no limit to the great white father's generosity.

Two years and a thousand initiatives and executive orders later, *The Economist* noted:

> *[The] glass ceiling that prevents parents from rising to the top at work . . . You could almost hear that terrible ceiling crack as Mr. Clinton issued his executive order banning federal employers from denying people jobs or promotions because of their parental obligations. . . . "We wanted to send a clear signal to employers that there is nothing wrong with being a parent," said Bruce Reed, the president's chief domestic policy adviser, in one of the bravest speeches of his career.*[7]

One would hope so. *The Economist* then offered a stimulant for further discussion:

> *The White House was also worryingly silent on how to prevent women from bearing a disproportionate share of the burden of preparing all these family meals. Should the government offer tax credits so that more men can learn to cook? Or should it issue an executive order mandating that men must do all the table-laying and dishwashing?*

Is the writer indulging in a bit of tongue-in-cheek? Some folks argue that big government should regulate the family dinner ritual. Surveys indicate that over the past twenty years or so the number of families responding that they eat dinner together regularly has dropped significantly. Roper surveys of families with children aged eight to seventeen show a similar trend from 1976 to 1997. Taking vacations together dropped from 53 percent to 38 percent, watching TV together from 54 to 51 percent, going together to religious functions from 38 to 31 percent, and just talking together from 53 to 43 percent.

Today the regulatory apparatus has gotten so large as to be out of control. With the government awash in money and politicians so dependent on it, political expediency seldom gives the market a chance to correct imperfections in resource allocations. The health maintenance organization (HMO) issue is a case in point. The recent rapid expansion of this approach to health care was stimulated by spiraling costs of care, but the government's avalanche of regulations passed and being passed have already forced costs out of control again.

Under the old fee-for-service system there was practically no incentive to control costs; someone else was paying. (This applies to private insurance companies as well as Medicare.) Also there was very little concern for preventive care or good health.

In 1996 the estimated savings due to the presence of HMOs were between $23.8 and $37.4 billion. Employers thus saved money on benefit payments, workers received some of the savings in higher wages, and taxpayers paid less for Medicare beneficiaries who were in HMOs.

As with other innovations, the problem comes down to resistance by people who have a vested interest in the old way. Doctors and other medical personnel are seldom concerned with costs, as their training concentrates on healing the sick and injured and letting someone else worry about costs. Politicians reap rewards when their constituents read about seemingly miraculous medical breakthroughs, and they, too, have little concern about costs.

Against this background along comes an instance in which a mistake made by an HMO employee causes suffering or death. Naturally, shocked and grief-stricken family members strike at any target to vent their frustration. The news media learn of this instance and quickly realize the value in print sales and viewership potential coming from an emotional issue such as human health. They hype the story, politicians learn of it, the bashing begins, and more regulation is sure to follow. This predictably defeats the major objective of the institution as costs rise. Expansion of managed care several years ago (membership peaked at 70 percent of citizens) stopped the spiraling cost of medical care in its tracks, but now the outlook is for more increases as politicians and other activists continue to hammer HMOs.

Another paternalistic issue is connected to health—air and water pollution. Pollutants in the air and water vary widely with different locations in the country, so it is logical that local citizens work with sources of pollution and their public officials to minimize the harmful effects. The nature of pollution means that total elimination involves infinite costs, so the objective is to find levels that most people can accept and that are cost-effective. Here is an opportunity for the democratic process to work.

But people's health is an emotional issue. Therefore in the years up to 1970 environmentalists hyped it, the news media cooperated, and politicians responded with the Clean Air Act of 1970. Thousands of regulations followed.

But there are problems with this approach. One is that often government-mandated pollution abatement mechanisms don't fit the need in a particular power plant, so the result is not only to force the price of its output upward. The mandate also undermines the incentive to find a different, better, and cheaper way to reduce pollution at that plant. There is also an incentive to avoid cooperation with inspectors and to fight this intrusion by government into the plant.

Instead of allowing the democratic process full play, clean air and water politics are centralized in Washington, DC, where polluters can concentrate their power (read: money) in opposing restrictions. Politicians know their business, and whenever they see a source of money they do not pass up its vote-buying potential. The result is often watered-down regulations in certain areas where deep pockets contribute generously. Another result is the high probability that today the country's air and water would be cleaner with the democratic process and without three decades of regulation.

How might this be? Publicly owned air, lakes, and streams are apparently free garbage dumps, and it is obviously cheaper to dump than to scrub exhausts or transport and dispose of waste properly. In a socialist society under the Communist Party almost everything was owned by everyone and by no one. There was very little private property; hence no one had any concern about anything except the little that he owned. Workers regularly looted what they could from the job, and managers did not care, as they would send faked output figures upward anyway. Everywhere the landscape was desecrated.

The remedy to this situation emerges through the concept of private property, on which the founding fathers had to tread lightly to convince convention delegates from slave-holding states to support the proposed constitution. The phrase in the Declaration of Independence—"life, liberty and the pursuit of happiness"—is a modification of John Locke's "life, liberty and property." This weakness in protection of citizen rights by government should have been removed after the Civil War.

With laws on the books in support of the principle of private property, citizens who suffer from excessive air or water pollution can collect data, go to the source(s), and request that something be done. Without a positive response after a reasonable time, they would organize and recruit more people to the cause. This would probably generate a different response from the source, but if it did not then the logical sequence of events would be to public hearings, mediation, arbitration, and eventually litigation if the issue went that far. Polluters are concerned about costs, of course, but most are also public-spirited. Aware of local citizen concern and given the opportunity to devise their own solutions, there will be rare instances of noncooperation. But if a paternalistic government uses force the reactions will be quite different.

An Oregon law forced scrubbing of exhaust air only in new power plants, because retrofitting old plants was recognized as prohibitively expensive. The **predictable result** was that old plants were kept in operation longer and fewer new plants were built, and so the air only grew worse after passage of the law than it was previously. A logical conclusion: Bureaucrats do not think like business managers.

Paternalistic government can and does grow large as place-seekers try to avoid the rough world of employment outside government. Tocqueville observed that when public service is poorly compensated and working conditions are poor people will gravitate to the private sector, and the reverse.

Reformers in early seventeenth century Madrid estimated that in government the ratio of parasites to productive workers was about thirty to one. It is in the nature of parasites to feed and multiply until eventually they have destroyed their host and themselves. The great Spanish empire collapsed. Paul Kennedy's book described several other empires throughout history that had the same experience.[8] The Roman Empire lasted around 800 years, but it eventually succumbed.

An analogy can be found in the person who feels sick and goes to see a doctor. The problem is diagnosed as a bacterial infection, and a treatment is prescribed. The patient follows the recommended dosage and later feels better. This story is hardly unique, as it is played out millions of times every day. However, the medication does not kill the very last offending bacteria. Several million remain, but the important point is that now the patient's natural immune system can keep their number down to the point where they no longer bother him or her.

Bacteria are parasites. There is an analogy with government, which feeds on the private sector. If parasites in government are allowed to multiply without limit, the ultimate result is predictable; the proof lies in world history. Therefore whenever big government threatens to grow beyond control a "treatment" should be prescribed and administered (as Jefferson advocated).

But where is the doctor who will prescribe, and will the patient swallow the medicine as directed? Some bacteria in a person are beneficial; they facilitate certain body processes, such as digestion. They are like fire in that a little is necessary, but when out of control they are truly devastating. So it is with the growth of government.

When public officials try to control the energies of citizens, the people become frustrated at the resulting poor genetic fit and try to work around the new law. This causes more laws and regulations to go into force, and the predictable result is greater attempts by citizens to work around, over, and under them. From the politicians' viewpoint these problems cry out for **more** government, not less. This in turn brings on more laws, and eventually a vicious circle of ever-greater oppression of the people occurs as paternalistic government penetrates deeper into their private lives. Economic activity increasingly submerges into the underground market as laws are violated and respect for the law diminishes. The ultimate result is a police state and open rebellion.

Schudson wrote: "In 1961, in a classic study of urban politics, political scientist Robert Dahl wrote that for most people politics lies at 'the outer periphery of attention.' Not public affairs, but 'primary activities involving food, sex, love, family, work, play, shelter, comfort, friendship, social esteem, and the like' are at the center of people's interest."[9]

Forty years later, the distinction between primary activities and politics cannot be maintained.

Every one of Dahl's "primary activities" has been politicized. Dietary guidelines have become matters for congressional debate, the Center for Science in the Public Interest has attacked the popcorn sold in movie theaters, and a well-organized social movement has put laws against tobacco use on the books at local, state and federal levels. Today terms like "date rape," "marital rape," and "battered woman" are familiar. "Deadbeat dads" is a political rallying cry, and state policy about women's decisions on abortion has fueled the most extensive populist movement of our time. The notions of representation, justice, and political participation have extended far beyond the sphere of conventional politics into "private" life.

This lengthy observation barely scratches the surface. Paternalistic big government has injected itself into citizens' private lives in a way and to an extent that is without precedent in this country. This strategy enables the nanny state to exert constant control over the activities of its flock.

Harry Browne noted, "The Constitution gave the federal government no power to deal with common crimes, or to regulate individual conduct, or to take care of people in need. The founding fathers knew that politicians could use such power to reward their friends, punish their enemies, and gain control over your life."[10]

There is a story about a Polish economic advisor who sought direction from US policy makers about moving from a socialist to a market economy. They reminded him that markets are chaotic, difficult to control and predict, and produce inequitable distributional outcomes. They cautioned him to maintain direct government control and regulate economic activities. The Polish advisor listened politely and finally said, "Oh, we know all about regulation and control, we call it socialism. We want to try capitalism."

WELFARE: THE POLITICS OF POVERTY

President Theodore Roosevelt said, "Anything that encourages pauperism, anything that relaxes the manly fiber and lowers self-respect is an unmixed evil."[11]

For the millions with less, the problem is economic. For politicians, the problem is political. Due to radically different perceptions of the problem, it is understandable that programs intended to help the poor do more **to** them than **for** them. The public is naturally concerned about poor people, and it is logical to assume that their representatives in government are similarly concerned. This section will reveal a hidden agenda.

In 1992 then-Senator Bill Bradley said, "To say that you don't need a massive investment of perhaps $20 billion a year to reclaim the cities is ludicrous." The senator's argument was at least partly inaccurate in that spending any amount of money to support consumption is not investment. It does very little to create wealth.

Since the Lyndon Johnson administration the government has pumped $4 trillion of taxpayer money into poverty, mostly in the cities, where it is concentrated and politicians can grab media coverage and win votes. Studies indicate that the resulting benefits to the poor of all that spending are approximately zero; since Johnson's presidency the problem has only gotten worse. Adding $20 billion a year to this total could be described as counterproductive if not outright ludicrous.

In the 1930s the Franklin Roosevelt administration created programs intended to help the destitute. The founding fathers would have described these programs as poor relief, as they recalled the poor laws in England. In that country, churches provided for the poor, and taxpayers were required to help. The money was raised and spent locally. Because both groups of citizens were concerned about scarce money, great efforts were expended to get recipients back to work and paying taxes. However, the truly incapacitated were not ignored.

The Preamble to the US Constitution includes "to promote the general welfare." The intent was to enhance the well-being of the general population and not one or more groups among them. To do this would violate the uniformity principle in that document. But in 1933, when Roosevelt took office, society was hurting, and he felt that something radical must be done. His minions thought that a term borrowed from the constitution would help sell the programs to the public and the Supreme Court, even if their constitutionality was suspect.

These programs were originally intended to provide assistance to widows with young children, because during the Great Depression churches and other charities were overwhelmed. It was only later that the programs developed additional problems instead of solving the original one. These began when politicians discovered there were votes in this business. Browne wrote:

> *Still, as of 1962, the federal government was only a minor participant in the ugly business of demoralizing the poor, and the problems were minuscule compared to today's. . . . Shortly after the US government declared war on poverty, the downward trend in poverty came to a halt. It became obvious . . . that the more money the government gave to the poor, the less people would strive to avoid qualifying for help.*[12]

The historical stigma attached to the dole diminished.

The number of children age eighteen or younger increased by 42 percent from 1952 to 1970, but the number on welfare increased by 400 percent. New York City's population hardly changed between 1960 and 1971, but the number of welfare recipients went from 330,000 to 1.2 million. During most of the 1960s the economy grew at a healthy pace, which should have helped poor people get off welfare, get work, and get paid more while working.

There were two forces at work to create this anomaly. One was unlimited funds directed at the problem, and the other was assignment of the problem to a bureaucracy. These forces worked together over several decades, to a point where popular concern for the poor dissolved into bureaucrats' concern about empire-building and politicians' concern about winning votes.

One of many examples of perverse results is Medicare, a program created in 1965 to enable the elderly to get affordable medical care. Because a high percentage of older Americans vote, the hidden agenda here was manna for politicians. But the economic law of supply and demand interfered. This law increased demand for cheaper care and limited the supply as doctors either spent many hours filling out paperwork instead of treating patients or simply abandoned the profession. These developments predictably drove the price upward, so today the elderly pay twice as much **out of pocket**, even accounting for inflation, than they did before 1965.

Taxpayers object to giving their money away without some controls over expenditures. This lack enables a bureaucracy to get a foot in the door. As years pass and the problem seems to get worse, the logical response is more money. However, this response can remain logical in the eye of the taxpayer only if the real agenda remains hidden. Once open season has been established, there is no end to the expansion. After the recent welfare reform there remain about eighty government welfare programs, and many of these have overlapping responsibilities. The explanation can be completed with the observation that **bureaucracies thrive on problems and not solutions**; creation of more problems justifies more staff, new programs, more resources, higher pay and perks, job promotions, and so on.

After World War II there was a dramatic increase in charitable giving. However, starting in about 1961 the share of citizens' incomes devoted to philanthropy has diminished beyond the point where it obliterated postwar gains.

Roughly speaking, each additional dollar forced out of taxpayers by big government reduces charitable giving by thirty cents.

In 1950 Social Security and Medicare combined to take 0.3 percent of GDP (total value of all goods and services produced by the country in one year). In 1970 this take had increased to 3.7 percent, and in 1993 6.9 percent. Projections into 2010 have these programs taking 8.9 percent of the economy and in 2030 13.0 percent. Another projection has the economy producing $12 trillion of goods and services in that year, so these programs might take $1.5 trillion to subsidize consumption by millions of seniors, most of whom at that time will be well off or just plain wealthy. It is not difficult to identify who will be taxed to provide this mountain of money. In 1935 there were lots of older people in trouble. Some sixty-five years later the situation has surely changed, and yet the programs have only grown.

Gross noted: "The country didn't become great because the government gave anybody welfare. And surely no one ever became rich on the dole. If the millions who struggled their way through Ellis Island—Irish, Greek, Jew, Italian, Pole, Hungarian—had been given welfare, they'd probably now be victims of capitalism instead of its masters."[13]

In 1920 the illegitimate birth rate was 3 percent, and in 1960 it had increased to 5 percent. With the commencement of President Johnson's War on Poverty in 1965, the trend accelerated upward: to 10 percent in 1970, to 18 percent in 1980 and to 30 percent in 1991. This trend is easy to explain. The government paid poor young girls to have babies, and marriage was not part of the bargain. The rate of violent crime in 1960 was about 1,900 per 100,000 people, but by 1980 the rate was almost 6,000. The hidden agenda sees the light of day.

Poor girls did not want husbands, because the boys who impregnated them were often uneducated, unemployed, or on drugs, and hence unable to support them at the same level as did monthly welfare checks. If they married, the checks either stopped or the amount was reduced. Pieces of paper substituted for a father in the household, young men felt a lack of self-worth, and so they often turned to drugs and crime. It was said that in the inner cities Mother's Day was celebrated twelve times a year, on check day when absent fathers came by for a cut.

University of Washington researchers determined that when benefits increased by $200 a month the illegitimate birth rate soared by 150 percent. A Cornell University study showed that every 10 percent increase in benefits brought an 8 percent drop in marriage involving single mothers.

Negative feelings about themselves trigger incentives based on the negative side of human nature. Self-esteem is a matter of perception: If a person thinks she is worthless she is not motivated to seek work or otherwise improve her life prospects. However well-intended going in, the reality is the money is a barrier that keeps the poor "in their place." The bureaucracy does not attempt to regulate romantic love (at least, not yet), but apparently it does regulate self-love.

Most of the $4 trillion in tax money spent to date on poverty did not get to the poor; if it did, they would be poor no more. Rather, most of it was passed among social classes and not between. A building contractor, for example, must bid competitively for business in the private sector. Because others are likely to underbid the contractor, the competitors' presence in the market makes it difficult for him to make profits.

On the other hand, public money is easier to come by, as with unlimited funds bidding is far less competitive. The contractor goes to Washington, schmoozes with politicians, slips them some money, and comes away with a fat contract to build housing for the poor. Because he or she can make a very good profit he kicks back some of it to politicians in anticipation of the next juicy contract. The public goes on shelling out in the naive belief that their money is helping the poor. In England during the nineteenth century Thomas Macaulay said, "The country can have, there is no doubt of it, exactly as many paupers as it chooses to pay for."

After becoming mayor of New York City, Rudolph Giuliani checked on welfare recipients and found that half did not live at the address they gave on applications. Some were not who they said they were and had extra income not reported on their applications. Fingerprint tests revealed that close to 400 people were claiming benefits in both New York and New Jersey, and greater numbers were double-dipping in nearby counties in New York state.

Today a typical poor family's annual income averages about 25 percent more than that of a middle-class family in 1900, allowing for inflation. In 1963 a typical poor family's annual income was **twenty-nine times** greater than the **average** in the rest of the world. This is only what they report as income. Bureaucrats are not interested in getting at truth in this issue, because it could reduce the number of those eligible and undermine program expansion.

The poverty line is revised frequently by politicians to maximize its vote-winning potential. Economists repeatedly argue that the number is useless, in that it omits the value of free health care and education provided by government. But their arguments get little press. These statistics get in the way of politicians' plans, so they try to keep them hidden.

A comment about middle-class welfare is in order. The many entitlement programs are geared to convince the public that they are entitled to the money, which in total commandeers about half of the $2 trillion annual budget. Thirty years ago these programs took 10 percent, but since that time a lot of votes among older folks have been purchased. Because older people are living longer and **old** so often means **ill,** these programs are growing twice as fast as the economy. The core of the difficulty here is related to the politicians' hidden agenda, in that it is creating a society dependent on a paternalistic government. Tocqueville's 1830 prediction is being vindicated by today's grim reality.

Robert Samuelson noted: "Responsibility poses choices, recognizes limits, and clarifies accountability. Entitlement denies choices, ignores limits, and muddles accountability."[14] In today's society a young couple not yet fully mature often gets into marital difficulty. Instead of making the admittedly considerable effort to work through the problems, each spouse will often return to the parental nest for stroking and sympathy.

A major contributing cause of this new societal phenomenon lies in a paternalistic government that denies the young the opportunity to mature into responsible, fully functioning adults. Because this barrier has been in place for generations, parents raising children are similarly encumbered.

One unpleasant result of this deficiency has thousands of children on prescription drugs, such as Ritalin®. As they grow older, they become exposed to other drugs that are not dispensed by a pharmacist but by a street-corner salesperson. Still at a tender age, their difficulty in making a distinction between these two broad categories of drugs is understandable.

Schudson referred to Walter Lippmann's 1922 book:

> *What* Public Opinion *provides is a convincing exposition of the conclusions of the nascent sociology and social psychology of the day—that human beings have limited attention spans; that on the rare occasions when they do turn their attention beyond their immediate, personal worlds, they are guided more by emotion, transitory circumstance, and mood than by reason; and that a vast new machinery of institutionalized persuasion was all too willing and able to exploit the situation for selfish ends.*[15]

Recently there has been some movement toward common sense in welfare for the poor. The Personal Responsibility and Work Opportunity Reconciliation Act of 1996 may cause citizens to believe that public assistance is no longer a fundamental right. Each state receives a block grant each year, and its renewal is contingent on meeting several criteria aimed at reducing the number of recipients.

Early results are surprising, even dramatic: Many more people are abandoning welfare than even optimists predicted. This is due to three reasons, and no single reason can be easily isolated as a major cause. One is a resurrection of the positive natural feeling of standing with head held high, another lies in the strength of the 1990s economy, and a third relates back to the previous observation that families and individuals on the dole were actually taking in more money each year than they reported.

Recent surveys among states show that after getting off welfare between 61 and 71 percent of families included an adult who had a job at the time of the survey, usually full-time. Wages were low but apparently adequate, especially when supplemented from other (unreported) sources.

One point of curiosity is why the money for the block grants goes first to Washington and then, after the bureaucracy skims perhaps 20 percent off the top, it goes right back out whence it came. Surely it would be more efficient to keep the money at the start, somewhere close to where it will end. But politicians want that money to be run past them, and what they do with it before sending some of it on its way constitutes a mystery in the perception of the taxpayer.

Another point of curiosity: Politicians still see money in racial issues. Recent poll results suggest that relations between blacks and whites have never been better, and the majority of the blacks who respond say they are content and even optimistic. The difficulty here is that in an era of shock and drama contentment and optimism don't make very exciting copy for the news media, nor for politicians who love to give speeches behind a forest of microphones and in front of TV cameras (when they should be listening). They feel a strong need to be perceived by the many sheep as mighty, protective shepherds. Because it is human nature to want to mature into an adult form, they reinforce their power over citizens at every opportunity. Thus do positive and negative incentives do battle.

Putnam contributed an insight:

> *Child psychologists speak of a fairly primitive stage of social development called "parallel play" . . . two kids in a sandbox, each playing with a toy but not really interacting with each other. In healthy development children outgrow parallel play. But the public spectacles of television leave us at that arrested stage of development, rarely moving beyond parallel attentiveness to the same external stimulus.*[16]

Blacks almost equal whites in rates of high school and junior college graduation. Full-time workers have started to close the income gap. Any employer in a competitive marketplace who consistently discriminates against better-qualified minority workers will soon become less competitive. Company managers are generally sensitive to the need to hire, train, and keep the best. More and more blacks are working harder at becoming the best.

The problem here lies in the fear among civil rights groups that they may be put out of business. Racism has a tradition of generating government intervention. Today in spite of this tradition group rights are losing out to individual rights (as emphasized in the Constitution). In a June 1997 Gallup poll poor blacks said money, not racism, was their biggest problem. While 75 percent of them said their relations with whites were good, 53 percent were unhappy with their incomes.

There are three goals that poor parents should drum into their children before having a baby: finish high school, reach at least age twenty, and then get married. Accomplishing these objectives requires abstinence from illegal drugs. About 8 percent of children raised in this manner experience poverty, versus 80 percent of those who ignore these objectives.[17] It is important to note that attaining these goals also means looking within the individual and family for the needed inspiration to swim upstream in an often downstream environment.

The inescapable conclusion is that problems of the poor cannot be solved by simply throwing money at them.

Pork-Barrel Politics

"Bringing home the bacon," often used to refer to earning a steady paycheck, is also a long-standing tradition in many governments where politicians must be reelected to continue in office. Any kind of favor will do: bridge, dam, power plant, park, office building, military base construction, and so on. The enterprising politician is limited only by his imagination as he pursues one of his favorite occupations: buying taxpayer votes with taxpayer money. Former Chairman of the House Ways and Means Committee Dan Rostenkowski probably set a record that still stands; he brought millions of taxpayer dollars to his home district in and near Chicago. This section will identify and describe only a few of the more egregious abuses (there are whole books available on the subject).

Around thirty years ago Congress got the idea that compiling huge "omnibus" spending bills provided ample opportunities to insert pork where it would remain hidden from public view, but not just from the public. Leaders in both the House and Senate were in a position to sneak their favorite spending items into a bill immediately before a scheduled floor vote. They did this, knowing that other members would have no time to read through a document of perhaps 4,000 pages before voting on it. Not only this, they told their colleagues how to vote.

The result could be amusing, were it not so expensive. An example from a fiscal-year 1999 bill: "The conferees believe that the responsibilities of the Nurse Corps officers necessitate that they should be required to have baccalaureate degrees. This provision extends the 1998–1999 duck hunting season in the state of Mississippi." Any reference to parts of the Constitution that give Washington authority over either of these issues was omitted. This bill weighed twenty pounds, and each year there are about twelve others like it.

One representative recalled his first such vote in 1989. It took place on a Sunday, and no one expected to vote had actually read the bill. It came onto the floor in a corrugated box "tied together in twine, like newspapers scheduled for recycling." The omnibus crime bill had sandwiched in it $10 million for a criminal justice center at Lamar University in Texas, which is the alma mater of Congressman Jack Brooks. At the time he was the powerful chairman of the House Judiciary Committee. It is interesting to note that although members of both political parties were loudly denouncing this bit of pork, a committee was approving another appropriations bill that included money for the same project.

Pork violates the uniformity provision in the Constitution (Article IV), and it creates love-hate relationships. A recent poll by *Nations Business* magazine asked business executives, "Is Congress doing a good job?" Ninety-five percent said "no." To a related question 91 percent said members are mainly interested in protecting their jobs. But when asked about their own congressmen or -women, 58 percent said they should be reelected. At least in part, the explanation for this inconsistency lies in bringing home the bacon.

There was disagreement between parties on one program for fiscal year 1998: The House wanted to spend $40 million for a program called Economic Development Initiative, which would presumably create jobs for poor people. By definition any economic initiative comes from the private sector, but of course this issue generated zero debate time. The Senate plumped for $50 million. They compromised at $138 million. (There was no problem; it was not their money.)

Economist Steven Levitt studied pork and the results of its dispersal.[18] He predictably found that the more pork the more votes. Each additional $100 of pork per capita increased the vote in favor of the incumbent by 2 percent. The cost of each vote was approximately $14,000 of taxpayer money. This is a very inefficient way to buy votes, but as long as citizens don't think about the fact that it is their money, damage control will remain in place.

The set of space programs drips with pork fat, primarily due to cooperative news media hype of high-flying drama, painting astronauts as heroes, and organizing citizens as wannabes. This means that politicians not only buy votes through pork, but they also win votes as people watch shuttle flights on the tube.

It also means the government has hung onto these programs for far too long instead of hiving them off to the private sector for further development. Doing this would immediately inject fiscal discipline into the programs, but as long as there is no bottom to the money barrel, such discipline is lacking. Instead of cost efficiency, therefore, engineers have been encouraged to solve problems by throwing money at them.

A staffed space shuttle costs five to ten times more per kilogram than to launch a satellite. Scientists by the dozens have attempted to testify that nearly all experiments being done and planned by astronauts could be done on earth or by robots in space at less than a third the cost. Furthermore, they argue that very few of these experiments have or are likely to have any scientific value. But few hear about this testimony because these scientists are routinely denied access to the news media. Politically inspired glamour rules over scientific truth, especially when the money is right.

The international space station project went ahead even though the Russians remained way behind schedule in building their portion of it. In 1993 Publius II wrote to a prominent US news magazine, wondering what the Russians would charge to rent space on their *Mir* space station. This surely seemed a much less expensive way to do studies of questionable value, a potential saving of untold billions of taxpayer money. (Mir is history now, but its service life could have been extended for some years.)

The magazine did not reply. About then NASA administrator Daniel Goldin said, "I don't care what it looks like, smells like or feels like so long as the United States of America provides world leadership with a space station." Taxpayers have a different set of senses, or should have.

Pieces of the work on the space station were spread around to as many congressional districts as there are congressmen and -women who could insert pork into appropriations bills. This is a horribly inefficient way to build anything. It has been said that this project does not lend itself to cost-benefit analysis because the station is "a laboratory of the human soul." But the soul already has a laboratory up there.

Along with inefficiencies a comment about effectiveness is also in order. A recent assessment showed two explosions during launches and three satellites stuck in useless orbits. Another satellite burned in the atmosphere. There were six rocket failures in a nine-month period, and a Mars polar lander disappeared. Most of the total of $4 billion in losses involved taxpayer money.

The Economist observed, "It is not just the Mars program that is in trouble. NASA's four space shuttles are also causing concern. Last July, one of them almost had to make an emergency landing when two of its six computers failed and one of its engines went wrong. Since then, numerous problems with the shuttles have become known."[19] But not enough to avert the tragedy of February 1, 2003.

The Economist later observed that NASA clings to manned space flight for three reasons.[20] One is showmanship: high drama on TV. A second is keeping Russian scientists out of the pay of renegade regimes like Iraq. The third "and most disgracefully, it puts billions of dollars into the pockets of aerospace companies such as Boeing. It is, in other words, a disguised industrial subsidy."

Today the international space station has been saddled with a $5 billion cost overrun, two missions to Mars lost, and a $3 billion-a-year shuttle program of questionable value but essential to keep the space station aloft and doing at least something. *The Economist* concluded with a comment on the bureaucrats who run NASA: "On the one hand, he [Goldin] doggedly sought to cut costs and produce spacecraft under the motto 'faster, better, cheaper.' On the other, he maintained the agency's dedication to manned space flight, which is none of those things."

Surely there would be mistakes if the whole operation were privatized, because human beings would still run it. But there would be limited funds available, far fewer mistakes, and the taxpayer would not be repeatedly stuck with the bill. If government wanted to conduct experiments (only with taxpayer approval), officials could rent space on satellites or in rocket payloads.

Defense is a huge business, costing taxpayers around $380 billion each year whether or not there is an enemy available. The external threat theory has been utilized for centuries by political leaders to keep the population in a continuing state of near panic. This gimmick not only commands massive public resources, it is also very effective in distracting citizens from the real domestic problems.

Big defense contractors have plants spread throughout the United States, especially in California. Because contracts are bid very loosely, these firms can afford to pay workers very well and still show healthy profits. People with good jobs tend to vote for incumbent politicians. The big bucks are in weapons, so the 1996 budget gave the Pentagon billions more than it wanted, and this was not the only year it did so. Military installations also provide jobs and votes. There are well over 3,000 of these scattered over the US landscape, several hundred more overseas, and still more under construction as this volume is being written.

Following the cold war, attempts have been made to reduce this number, but congressmen and -women hang onto installations in their districts with the tenacity of pit bulls. In 1993 the Pentagon managed to close two large bases, in and near Indianapolis. One of these included 2,000 acres of pristine forest, which was converted into a state park. Unemployment did not increase, as there are also 4 million square feet of office space and nearly 1,000 homes. About 12,000 people work in the area and annual local tax receipts are $7 million; the military paid no taxes.

In 1995 the military targeted a second base for closure, which might have put 2,600 people out of work. But the entire operation was privatized, and Hughes Electronics was the winner among seven bidders. Ninety-eight percent of the workers went home on Friday as government employees and came to work on Monday as employees of Hughes.

The B-2 "Stealth" bomber runs $2 billion each. By 1997 there were twenty-one of these planes on hand or on order, and members of Congress were pressing for nine more. The Pentagon preferred that the money be spent on other projects, but politicians in Congress insisted. Seawolf nuclear attack submarines cost $3 billion each. Recently an additional two were ordered, and President Clinton added a third. No one is sure whom they will attack, besides taxpayers.

With the Pentagon less enthusiastic about weapons, Congress has been looking elsewhere. Today the United States has nearly 70 percent of world trade in weapons. This keeps a lot of defense plants busy. During the 1992 election campaign President Bush authorized the sale of 150 F-16 fighter aircraft to Taiwan, in violation of an understanding with China that this type of technology would not be sold to that country. He even paid a visit to one of the plants that would build them, bringing along the cameras, of course.

International trafficking in weapons is especially devastating for poor countries, which spend scarce money on weapons that should be devoted to building their economies instead of destroying them. Furthermore, they enable ruthless dictators to massacre their people whenever they rebel against oppressive rule.

When Reagan authorized development of the Strategic Defense Initiative (SDI), popularly known as Star Wars, thinking citizens concluded that the sky is not the limit when it comes to defense spending. A poll of the National Academy of Sciences revealed that 98 percent of members believed that the SDI would never "provide an effective defense of the entire US civilian population." Congressmen infected by the tug of spending saw to it that this poll result did not become public knowledge. By 1999 the bill was up to $55 billion, and still no part of SDI has worked. The program has almost everything prized by government and the military: special interests, contributions to election campaigns, cooperative news media, politically based decisions having little or nothing to do with national security, great slabs of pork, and an unenlightened public.

One contractor calls its product "theater high altitude area defense." It is designed to attack medium-range incoming missiles, and it has flunked five straight tests. At one point some frustrated army officers planted a remote-controlled explosive in a target missile so it would blow up whether hit or not. Now a new President Bush wants to dump additional billions of dollars into this black hole.

Defense projects are survivors. Many have stayed alive even when Congress stopped the flow of money. If the Pentagon wants a program to continue, it simply takes money from some other program. Some years ago the Air Force's request for $1.8 billion to build its first six F-22 fighter aircraft was denied, but the Appropriations Committee left $1.2 billion already in the program for research and development. Over the past ten years the Pentagon has dumped $20 billion into the program.

In June 1977 President Jimmy Carter decided against allowing the B-1 bomber to go into production because it was unnecessary and expensive. But the Pentagon found money to keep the program alive until 1981, when President Reagan authorized construction of 100 bombers.

In 1991 President Bush nixed production of the V-22 Osprey aircraft and authorized building just one Seawolf submarine. But Congress kept the programs alive until Clinton took office and authorized construction of 500 Ospreys and 2 more Seawolfs. Today the Osprey program is in deep trouble. The machines keep crashing and killing people in the absence of any enemy action.

An International Monetary Fund (IMF) study indicated that if the United States trimmed $250 billion from its military budget over five years, at the end of that period its $10 trillion economy would be $7 billion smaller but much richer thereafter. Part of the reason for this is that weapons don't create wealth. They just sit there; when used, they destroy wealth.

Defense contractors are opposed to converting their factories to making consumer products, quite logically because they would then be forced to compete for their money. They are demanding taxpayer money to help them convert. But after World War II thousands of companies converted without public assistance.

One company recently converted and was surprised to learn that rival firms used half the workers to do the same job. In 1991 Olin Corporation offered to sell its defense business, and a buyer was found in 1992. This was a logical move after the cold war when contracts would be fewer, and the Pentagon approved. But the Federal Trade Commission (FTC) blocked the sale on antitrust grounds.

In 1997 Congress passed a law giving the president line-item veto power, which means he could review a massive omnibus spending bill and excise any pork discovered. Presidents for most of this century have wanted this authority, the public was asking for it, and President Clinton finally had it.

The solution to the pork problem was in place, or so it seemed. Actually, Clinton made a great show of wielding the knife to remove two or three tiny items probably put in a bill just for this grand occasion. In 1999 the Supreme Court struck down the law.

The Economist could not resist commenting on the situation: "Budget politics is not known for its comic depth; but Bill Clinton's exercise of his new line-item veto powers on August 11th yielded some real thigh-slappers. . . . When he announced the vetoes, Mr. Clinton could not resist grandiloquence. 'From now on, presidents will be able to say no to wasteful spending.'"[21] What Clinton blue-penciled amounted to a grand total of 0.007 percent of the amount in the bill.

Nicholas and Koszczuk noted that public officials like to distract attention from their own porking.[22]

> *No one has been more critical of the White House's spending habits than Representative Tom DeLay, the third-ranking Republican in the House, who has said Clinton is "addicted to spending." But DeLay may need a little rehab himself: While condemning Clinton publicly, he has worked quietly to secure millions of federal dollars for projects for his suburban Houston district.*

The Washington writers continued:

> *President Clinton is wielding his veto pen to force the funding of some of his favorite projects, and the response from legislators of both parties is that if he's going to get his, we're damn sure going to get ours. As a result . . . spending for fiscal 2001 . . . is likely to be $100 billion more than allowed by the supposedly ironclad budget agreement of 1997.*

As the 2000 election campaign approached its climax, both candidates castigated each other's plans concerning what to do with a very large projected fiscal surplus. Unnoticed by most citizens were great slabs of pork being passed into law by Congress. Members apparently spent the surplus before it materialized.

The Economist weighed in:

The Congressional Budget Office's estimate of a $2.2 trillion surplus over ten years . . . assumes that discretionary spending will rise no faster than the projected rate of inflation over the next ten years: less than 3% a year. According to the Concord Coalition, a bipartisan group that vainly but nobly advocates fiscal probity, discretionary spending has actually risen by an average annual rate of 5.5% over the past three years.[23]

This did not include the latest explosion of such spending.

The Economist concluded: "Even without an economic downturn, the many rosy surplus forecasts that frame today's debate in Washington are little more than entertaining fictions." Citizens might recall the Reagan administration putting out similar fictional forecasts just before cranking up the spending machine. The logical conclusion is that spending taxpayer money is a strictly bipartisan effort.

Presidents and Congresses come and go, but pork goes on forever.

Winning Votes through Clever Rhetoric

In this section the term *clever* substitutes for misleading, evasive, and deceptive words. Indirect reference is continuously made to the old cliché, "Talk is cheap." Politicians can and do get away with this kind of talk, because citizens are kept in the dark and there is no accountability. Put another way, they know they will not be caught, so they can say practically anything they want to and avoid saying words they suspect they will have to eat in the future. The following are snippets from several books, the content of which are liberally sprinkled with clever rhetoric.

Wylie wrote, "Many people feel their way through life rather than think it through and they have, in the ability to direct their feelings, as useful a function of personality as they have in their ability to direct their thoughts—at least potentially. Besides, feelings have the advantage of operating swiftly."[24] Citizens who allow life in the fast lane to preempt serious thinking and reflection will pay the consequences, and not just in how they are governed. This reality is not lost on politicians, whose many speeches are aimed at people's emotions. This dodge enables them to hide truth and make themselves look good in front of the electorate.

In 1972 Milton Friedman referred to politicians seeking labor union votes by increasing the minimum wage: "These people confuse wage rates with wage income. It has always been a mystery to me to understand why a youngster is better off unemployed at $1.60 an hour than employed at $1.25."[25]

Alterman's book *Sound and Fury* described what he called the "punditocracy," a group of columnists who claim to know and report on the "real truth" in Washington.[26] They are very powerful, and in their writings, speeches, and public appearances they invariably seek to enhance their personal power. During the 1992 election campaign Bill Clinton's campaign managers wisely and successfully sought the assistance of this tower of power. Alterman quoted George Stephanopoulos, who was Clinton's deputy campaign manager: "They write the columns, the experts and the diplomats read the columns, the reporters interview the experts, the producers read the reporters and the next thing you know, Clinton's made the evening news, looking like a president." The public is given to believe that the pundits write truth, but the reality is that politicians, pundits, and other Washington insiders fear truth.

Greider noted:

> *Every few years, for example, usually just before presidential elections, a new 'crime bill' is enacted with bristling resolve in response to public fears. Over two decades these measures have had no measurable effect on crime or its causes, but they are popular in Washington as election-year gestures to the anxious voters. Likewise, various social programs are enacted in response to obvious areas of concern—hunger or homelessness or disadvantaged children—but none of them is equipped with the funds to accomplish what they promise."* [27]

The crime issue furnishes an excellent opportunity for male politicians to get in front of the cameras and polish their macho credentials. Their stomping, snorting, and turbo-charged windbaggery entertains viewers seeking high drama, along with taming of their fear of crime. Surely the great white father will protect their children from this terrible menace.

Violent crime today is down, which would lead naive citizens to believe that the new laws are working. The reality is that three factors account for nearly all of the reduction. They are: (1) the teen years are high-crime years, and right now this age group is much smaller in numbers than it was previously; (2) carryover from a strong and sustaining economy means more wealth widely distributed and hence less incentive toward crime; and (3) the 1973 *Roe v. Wade* court decision permitting abortion brought on a substantial increase in use of the procedure, especially among poor girls, so many thousands of poor were not born who would today be in their peak crime-producing years.

Lapham commented on the 1992 campaign: "The election was about what was in it for me—me the candidate, me the voter, me the purveyor of public opinion polls. Avoiding the difficult questions about either the nature or purpose of the American enterprise, the candidates were careful never to utter a word or a phrase that might be confused with a principled conviction."[28] Such a gaffe might lose votes, and the objective of the campaign from the perspectives of candidates and parties is not selection of the man or woman who is most capable of governing. Rather, it is to win the election.

Phillips wrote: "The *Washington Post* noted that the Clinton White House banned the press from the 1993 democratic senate majority dinner to keep them from describing the president 'consorting with all the fat cats he denounced during last year's presidential campaign.'"[29] During his 1992 campaign Clinton had said, "The last 12 years were nothing less than an extended hunting season for high-priced lobbyists and Washington influence peddlers." Electioneering is one thing; governing is quite another. The rhetoric stays in tune.

In his 1997 State of the Union address, Clinton called for using "every dime" of the budget surplus to save Social Security. But the next national budget said, "Spend it." Here came a litany of new spending initiatives and higher taxes to support them. The usual procedure was followed: At first the new spending was less than tax receipts, but later the former would swamp the latter. Of course Clinton would be out of office by then, and the next president would probably follow past practice and raid the Social Security trust funds while dreaming up a different line of rhetoric to divert the public's attention from what is really happening.

In a March 1998 column Thomas Friedman created a mock interview situation to spoof the clever rhetoric issue.

Student: "[Director of National Security Sandy] Berger, you now say NATO expansion will only cost $1.5 billion over ten years, when just last year the pentagon said it would be $27 billion . . . and CBO said it could be $125 billion over fifteen years. How come [the number] gets cheaper every day it gets closer to a Senate vote?" Berger: "Our NATO numbers were prepared by the same accountants who said the US budget was balanced. I rest my case."

Krugman wrote,

> *Could anything be worse than having children work in sweatshops? Alas, yes. In 1993, children in Bangladesh were found to be producing clothing for Wal-Mart, and Senator Tom Harkin proposed legislation banning imports from countries employing underage workers. The direct result was that Bangladeshi textile factories stopped employing children. But did the children go back to school? Did they return to happy homes? Not according to Oxfam, which found that the displaced child workers ended up in even worse jobs, or on the streets ... and that a significant number were forced into prostitution."*[30]

Senator Harkin probably received many votes after this proposal. Quite possibly he cared not what happened to poor children; his interest was probably limited to votes, whether won or bought. Furthermore, there is no evidence that he checked into the results, nor even that he asked Oxfam, a charity that operates in Bangladesh. Once votes are bagged there is seldom any further concern.

The Environmental Protection Agency (EPA) frequently makes policy decisions based more on emotions than on scientific evidence. In 1998 a federal judge caught them at it: "EPA publicly committed to a conclusion before research had begun; excluded industry by violating the [1986 Radon] act's procedural requirements; adjusted established procedure and scientific norms to validate the Agency's public conclusion." The agency is a bureaucracy. It is easier to procure increased funds and continue to grow if truth is bent by using rhetoric laced with emotional hype.

Pundit George Will in an October 2000 column, said, "This presentational dimension of the presidency is utterly unrelated to the skills, such as they are, which the 'debate' format used Tuesday rewards. The principal skill is the regurgitation of memorized phrases crafted as responses to anticipated questions." Will referred to the first campaign presidential debate as a parallel press conference. He also observed: "The point of October debates is to persuade those people who [are] still undecided. Who are such people, and how, besides intermittently, do their minds work?"

There's no business like show business.

Notes

1. Alexis de Tocqueville, *Democracy in America*. Knopf, 1972.
2. Rose Wilder Lane, *The Discovery of Freedom*. Fox and Wilkes, 1993.
3. Tibor Machan, *Private Rights and Public Illusions*. Independent Institute, 1995.
4. Tocqueville, *Democracy in America*.
5. William C. Mitchell and Randy T. Simmons, *Markets, Welfare, and the Failure of Bureaucracy*. Westview Press, 1994.
6. Malcolm Sparrow, *License to Steal*. Westview Press, 1996.
7. *The Economist*, "Parenting: Comedy, Cont'd." May 6, 2000, p. 31.
8. Paul Kennedy, *The Rise and Fall of the Great Powers*. Unwin Hyman, 1988.
9. Michael S. Schudson, *The Good Citizen: A History of American Civic Life*. Free Press, 1998.
10. Harry Browne, *Why Government Doesn't Work*. St. Martin's Press, 1995.
11. Theodore Roosevelt, "The Strenuous Life." *The Century*, October 1900.
12. Browne, *Why Government Doesn't Work*.
13. Martin L. Gross, *A Call for Revolution*. Ballantine Books, 1993.
14. Robert J. Samuelson, *The Good Life and its Discontents: The American Dream in the Age of Entitlement 1945–1995*. Random House, 1995.
15. Schudson, *The Good Citizen*.
16. Robert D. Putnam, *Bowling Alone: The Collapse and Revival of American Community*. Simon and Schuster, 2000.
17. William Raspberry, "A Three-Point Plan to End Black Poverty," *News and Observer*, August 25, 1998, p. 13A.
18. Steven Levitt, "The Cost of a Vote." *The Economist,* September 2, 1995, p. 26.
19. *The Economist*, "Annus Horribilis." April 1, 2000, p. 74.
20. *The Economist*, "Unmanned." October 27, 2001, p. 13.
21. *The Economist*, "Line-item Laughs." August 16, 1997, p. 22.
22. Peter Nicholas and Jackie Koszczuk, "Pork Rules as Congress' Sessions End." *News and Observer* (Raleigh, NC), October 2000 column.

23. *The Economist*, "If You've Got It, Spend It." October 28, 2000, p. 28.
24. Philip Wylie, *A Generation of Vipers*. Dalkey Archive Press, 1946.
25. Milton Friedman, *An Economist's Protest*. Thomas Horton, 1972.
26. Eric Alterman, *Sound and Fury: The Washington Punditocracy and the Collapse of American Politics*. Harper Collins, 1992.
27. William Greider, *Who Will Tell the People: The Betrayal of American Democracy*. Simon and Schuster, 1992.
28. Lewis H. Lapham, *The Wish for Kings*. Grove Press, 1993.
29. Kevin Phillips, *Arrogant Capital*. Little, Brown, 1994.
30. Paul Krugman, "Free Trade Isn't Pretty, But It's a Way Out." *News and Observer* (Princeton, NJ), April 25, 2001, p. 15A.

CHAPTER SEVEN:
TOP-DOWN BIG GOVERNMENT AND GROUPTHINK

We must create more jobs in industry and agriculture
to provide for the expanding needs of government.
—Unknown

Top-down big government is the direct result of public officials seeking personal power over others. It connects to the negative incentives of human nature, and it can occur only in the absence of accountability to the governed. People like to trust one another and tend to do so, but whenever this trust is coupled with complacency and extended to other people in government the result is predictable. This combination of circumstances is hardly rare; history is rife with examples, and even today it is widespread. But this fact does not mean it is best for citizens.

Anthony De Jasay's book's central theme is "how state and society interact to disappoint and render each other miserable."[1] At first blush it would seem that only the citizens are rendered miserable. However, this volume will show that a person who sacrifices honesty and morals to money is not and cannot be anything but miserable. "The state has a special kind of means: power over the conduct of its subjects that when exercised in particular ways is widely accepted as legitimate."

People who tend to trust others can be deceived. Therefore the negative side of human nature can tempt public officials to betray citizens' abiding faith in government as problem solver (which began with the Franklin Roosevelt administration). Placing trust in people is risky, but without risk there can be no progress.

Thomas Paine indicated how this power is exercised.[2]

> *Almost everything appertaining to the circumstances of a nation, has been absorbed and confounded under the general and mysterious word government. Though it avoids taking to its account the errors it commits, and the mischiefs it occasions, it fails not to arrogate to itself whatever has the appearance of prosperity. It robs industry of its honors, by pedantically making itself the cause of*

its effects; and purloins from the general character of man, the merits that appertain to him as a social being.

Mystery is perpetuated through secrecy, highly developed finger-pointing deflects criticism, and if something seems to go right politicians leap to claim credit. President Franklin Roosevelt the politician was quick to blame the business community when his massive New Deal programs did not lift the economy out of the Great Depression. But Friedrich Hayek, an economist, showed how intrusive big government restrains citizens' energies as well as efficiency in business activity.

Washington had nothing to do with helping victims of the great Michigan fire of 1881 because it lacked the resources. People left homes and jobs to hasten to the scene; railroads shipped tons of materials. Clara Barton and the newly formed American Red Cross met their first major challenge. A farmer and philosopher named Horatio Bunce told his congressman: "If . . . you were at liberty to give to any and everything which you may believe, or profess to believe, is a charity, and to any amount you may think proper, you will very easily perceive what a wide door this would open for fraud and corruption and favoritism, on the one hand, and for robbing the people on the other."

Today the tentacles of disaster relief reach into hundreds of small, local episodes, and those who know the territory could address relief much more effectively if government were to keep out of them. But for big government the issue is not disaster; it is votes. (It is interesting to note that many such relief efforts backfire because, due in part to lack of understanding of local conditions, inflated expectations of desperate citizens are either not met or not met in good time.)

An aristocracy or oligarchy is better at making laws than is democracy. Evidence that the job can be done much more efficiently comes forth in blazing color in Washington, DC each year, as 7,500 pages of new legislation and 75,000 pages of administrative law are cranked out. However, human nature has people supporting what they help to create, but the reverse is also true. This means the more laws, the more crime.

In 1933 members of the House of Representatives were each permitted a two-person staff. By 1970 the total congressional staff was up to 10,739. In 1930 there were 73,000 total federal government employees; by 1970 the number was 327,000. In 1930 the population of the United States was 123 million ; today it is about 280 million, which is nearly 2.3 times as many people. If citizens since that time had been vigilant and kept government from growing, there would be about 2.3 times 73,000 or 168,000 national government employees today, instead of about 3 million—almost nineteen times as many. Harry Browne said: "Today the Bill of Rights is just a quaint piece of parchment that few in Washington take seriously . . . lest it interfere with government's power do to what's right for you."[3]

An occasional drink obviously does little harm to a person; millions indulge their pleasure. However, everyone knows that drinking more than occasionally can lead to alcoholism, an addiction from which recovery is a major challenge. The analogy with government is accurate: For more than five decades citizens indulged their government. It grew ever larger, until today rectification is a daunting task.

In the twelve years 1981–92 big government swallowed huge gulps of otherwise productive capital. Budgetary deficits added up to $2 trillion, tripling the national debt and taking a large part of the people's savings. The Reagan administration did most of the damage by annually projecting an impracticably rosy economic outlook designed to convince people that future growth would amply cover current huge expenditures. Reagan's campaign rhetoric against big government proved to be hollow, once he settled into office.

In state governments during 1982–89, spending increased at an annual rate of 8.5 percent, more than double the rate of inflation. From 1980–89 state taxes almost doubled. State employment rose by 19 percent, but the population grew by only 9 percent. Public employee unions increased their membership by 30 percent, and between 1980–87 salaries increased by 59 percent, whereas salaries in the private sector went up by 35 percent. Benefits also increased rapidly.

Is the Era of Big Government Over?

The institutions of any government should be oriented to serve the needs of constituents. If these institutions are organized and maintained by government, the negative side of human nature will guide the efforts of public officials. Officials in big government have over the years worked through hundreds of turf battles over allocation of tax receipts, to the point where there is very little room for maneuvering. Pecking orders have been set in stone. This means the institutions of government do not change with changing needs of citizens. But improvement in life is inherent in the human condition.

A candidate promises voters that he or she will oppose new government spending if elected. But on arrival in Washington the candidate is surprised by an unforeseen condition. If he or she votes against, say, a highway bill, the constituents back home may be deprived of money and roads. This is because there is no connection between taxes levied and the amount spent in any particular congressional district. If the candidate votes no, other members have that much more money to spend in their districts.

Today the rhetoric concentrates on balanced budgets and fiscal surpluses, which would have some merit if action followed rhetoric. This is unlikely. However, the media hype serves another purpose that is not made public: It distracts public attention from the absolute total tax loads big government is hanging on its constituents.

Miller reported on a lengthy study of income tax rates in this country.[4]

Using data for the period 1949 to 1989, Gerald Scully found that the "optimal" (that is, growth maximizing) tax rate for the US government would have been twenty-two percent instead of the observed thirty-five percent. If this tax rate had prevailed over the period, the rate of economic growth would have been 5.6 percent instead of 3.5 percent; total wealth created would have been $76.4 trillion instead of $29.9 trillion; and tax revenue would have been $17.5 trillion instead of $13.8 trillion. Scully's conclusions are in accord with similar research based on US data by Peter Grossman, Edgar Peden, and Richard Vedder and Lowell Gallaway.

Another group of researchers analyzed data from several advanced countries and came up with an optimal tax rate of only 10 percent. However, career politicians from any such country don't want results like these publicized.

Top-down laws are not made by those who must live under them, so one-size-fits-all programs are ill suited to almost everyone where they are implemented. This country embraces great variety geographically, culturally, and ethnically. President Bill Clinton discovered this in 1993 when he traveled about the land pushing a top-down plan for comprehensive health care. Even among those who approved (of course, these were the only ones interviewed in front of the cameras) each complained about different parts of the bill.

In 1995 the economy passed a milestone of sorts. In that year government employment at all levels surpassed employment in manufacturing. Over several decades automation has acted to reduce employment in making products. Nevertheless, the trend deserves some discussion.

Lapham described the elite group in charge of government and other institutions, which he estimated at about 4 million people.[5] "By and large they are the people who manage the government, own the media and the banks, operate the universities, print the money, and write the laws. I don't know why so many people fail to take the point." On reflection, Lapham would see that people kept in the dark about these institutions and how government manipulates them cannot appreciate what is happening and hence appreciate its impact on their daily lives. Later he seemed to answer his own question: "A democracy supposedly derives its strength and character from the diversity of its many voices, but the politicians in Washington speak with only one voice, which is the voice of the oligarchy."

During his State of the Union speech in January 1998, President Clinton grandly proclaimed: "We have the smallest government in thirty-five years." Immediately after this blockbuster statement, he offered a laundry list of initiatives for additional spending, practically none of them authorized by the US Constitution. What is truly amazing is the way the news media hyped this statement. In January 1998 the Cato Institute calculated that the government will spend more money during the current fiscal year than **the inflation-adjusted total of all expenditures of US national governments from 1787 to 1930**. (That is not a misprint.)

Government has become so large that presidents control their operations only with difficulty. President John F. Kennedy had most of his staff in place three months after taking office—118 senior appointments. President George W. Bush probably took a full year to complete today's 300 senior appointments. Each new scandal generates a multiplicity of bureaucratic tests. Today prospective appointees must answer over 230 questions, including those pertaining to illegal nannies. Then they must be dragged through the wringer by Senate confirmation committees. A lot of very good people decide not to accept nomination.

In his book *Modern Times*, Paul Johnson commented:

> *Lincoln had to pay a secretary out of his own pocket. Hoover had to struggle hard to get three. Roosevelt appointed the first six "administrative assistants" in 1939. Kennedy had twenty-three. The total White House staff had risen to 1,664 in Kennedy's last year. Under Johnson it was forty times the size of Hoover's. Under Nixon it rose to 5,395 in 1971, the cost jumping from $31 million to $71 million.*

Browne wrote:

> *So government never has to say it's sorry—never has to take responsibility for the misery it causes. Instead, it can blame everything on personal greed, profit-hungry corporations, and the "private sector." . . . And, even though government controls over fifty percent of the money spent on medical care, politicians freely refer to the high cost of a hospital stay as a "failure of the free market."*

Officials have honed finger-pointing to a high art. "Each government program carries within it the seeds of future programs that will be 'needed' to clean up the mess the first program creates." Because this process has been going on intensively since 1960, it has become impossible to identify that first program, which is probably still on the books. The sequels provide employment for hordes of expensive lawyers.

Travel in the early days was by stagecoach over rough and often muddy roads; some trips to Washington required ten days one-way. Nevertheless, members of Congress returned home frequently to sample the opinions of their constituents. Today's elite politicians hate to go home for at least three reasons. One is because they know that citizens are beginning to smell something rotten. Related to this suspicion is another reason: Due mainly to big money slipped to them by the National Rifle Association (NRA), there are more guns per capita in this country than almost anywhere else. A third reason lies in their reluctance to meet and interact with people whom they perceive as riffraff. Birds of a feather flock together, so they much prefer life in Washington, schmoozing with their own kind.

A good example of top-down local government comes to mind: the Rebuild Los Angeles project, which followed destructive riots in the wake of the Rodney King verdict in 1992. Talented executive Peter Ueberroth took charge and recruited help from government, community groups, and businessmen. About $500 million was raised, most of it from corporations. Enthusiasm was infectious, but the approach was top-down without local citizen involvement in planning, so the whole project was a failure. It is possible even now that Ueberroth does not fully understand why it went wrong.

The elites' grand plan has citizens split into contentious factions. Someone called this strategy groupthink, and it runs counter to the notion of tolerance. This country could never have developed in the way it did in the absence of tolerance, but the elites encourage "diversity," which they interpret as groupthink, even as it sounds like tolerance of different personal appearances, mannerisms, and beliefs.

Yet another special interest group descends on Washington looking for unearned special favors. Two negative incentives combine in these instances, that of personal power seeking and what's-in-it-for-me dependency on paternalistic government. Once this process has acquired momentum there is no end to the groups coming to Washington.

Mentioned in Chapter 6, the race issue mainly acts to divide citizens, whereas recent studies have shown that relations between members of different races have never been better. Tolerance is spreading through the culture in spite of the efforts of big government and their media lackeys. The census form for 2000 included six discrete Asian races: Asian Indian, Chinese, Filipino, Japanese, Korean, and Vietnamese. There is another box, labeled "other Pacific Islander." This list more or less proves that the very notion of race is a myth. Wilson noted: "Most scientists have long recognized that it is a futile exercise to try to define discrete human races. Such entities do not in fact exist." [6] If the government were not preoccupied with groupthink the census form would not include a question on race (and multiethnic champion golfer Tiger Woods could fill out his copy without becoming confused).

The Economist ably summarized this section:

> *The simplest measure of the economic role of the state is the share of national income spent by government. This averaged 30% in the rich industrial countries in 1960. By 1980, after the acknowledged excesses of the previous decade, the share had increased to 42.5%. The next ten years saw a great change: accelerating deregulation, technological advance and global economic integration. As a result the state . . . er, . . . increased its share again, to 45% of the economy. Since then, [it] increased its share a bit more, to 46%. Decade by decade over the course of this century and before, in war and in peace, in sickness and in health, government . . . has done nothing but grow.*[7]

When Big Government Regulates Activity in the Marketplace

Two hundred years ago, James Madison warned of the danger of an overcentralized, expensive government. He said our democracy could turn into an oligarchy, or top-down rule by an elite few. The first instance of government regulation of economic activity was enacted in 1789, which was the year George Washington took office as our nation's first president.

It has been truly said that the invisible hand of politics works counter to the invisible hand of the marketplace. Public officials know that citizens do not approve of personal power seeking, and so they strive to make their actions invisible. Adam Smith wrote about the invisible hand of the marketplace in 1775, describing it as an unseen guide that helped untold millions of sellers and buyers to **voluntarily** agree on trades, wherein each instance both seller and buyer came away from the exchange with perceived gains. This section will show that because the political hand is **force**, the result is distortion of markets, loss of efficiency, and outright corruption.

Miller wrote: "During the second half of the nineteenth century the railroads expanded dramatically, but were unable to realize monopoly power because each time they established minimum rates the cartel fell apart. In despair they turned to the federal government, which obliged by establishing the Interstate Commerce Commission in 1887."[8] In effect the government helped the railroad barons to form an unconstitutional cartel.

The ICC forced railroads to charge at least minimum rates, presumably to prevent "ruinous competition" among rail carriers. But then in the 1930s along came trucking companies, which threatened the railroad cartel. Rather than close down the ICC, Congress authorized regulation of these firms also. Later airline companies, smarting from competition and seeing how comfortable were the railroads and truckers, sought a place at the table. Congress obligingly created the Civil Aeronautics Board.

Enter the lobbyists. Protected from the rigors of competition, the transportation companies made enough extra profits that they could hire people to give money to politicians and twist bureaucrats' arms for more protection. Customers had little choice but to pay predetermined rates, so free markets in interstate transportation vanished. Later on many special interest groups saw the obvious advantages in seeking their places at table, and the movement mushroomed without limit. Miller concluded: "To the extent these costs are hidden, voters will demand too much government."

Government could increase taxes or borrow to accomplish its aims, but these actions are visible. More cunning is required for government to have its way. Regulation wins votes now, and the costs are hidden in the future. Furthermore, government does not need to find the money to meet the vast bulk of these costs;

officials need only administer the programs while costs of compliance are borne out in the field, ultimately by consumers.

Regulated businesses must pass their costs on to customers in the form of higher prices. What does compliance cost citizens? Samuelson said, "By one careful study, all government regulations imposed about $500 billion in annual costs by the early 1990s; that roughly equals a third of on-budget public spending."[9] Thomas Hopkins of the Rochester Institute of Technology estimated that this cost in 1995 was $668 billion, or $7,000 per household. This was about $1,000 more than it paid in income taxes that year. Clearly this lack of accountability allows rampant personal power seeking as Congress passes laws vaguely worded, so that bureaucrats are free to impose horrendous costs on the public while presumably correcting market "failures."

Other hidden costs are not amenable to computation. These take the form of new products that do not reach the market, new businesses not started, and job opportunities not offered. Businesspeople who envision these good things do not move forward because projected costs of regulation obliterate anticipated profits.

The market is not perfect, although when given time for an innovation to integrate into the marketplace it comes closer than any other alternative. The problem for politicians lies in the imperative of taking some action whenever the media publish an apparent imperfection. This action must be taken immediately, before the next election, so the candidate will be perceived as doing something about the problem. This means that the market is all too often given too little time to adjust to eliminate the imperfection. The resulting distortion is often more harmful to society than was the original flaw, especially as more regulations follow that are presumably aimed at correcting the distortion.

By the 1980s, the public suspected that regulation of business was not quite the boon to living standards that the hype suggested. Therefore some deregulation was put in place by the Reagan administration (the transportation sector definitely benefited). However, again political expediency intervened as flaws made their appearance, and so reregulation was instituted. This caused more distortion, as some people in the right place at the right time exploited temporary advantages during the adjustment process.

Well-intentioned consumerists frequently do more harm than good when they describe the market as a zero-sum environment: Any gain by a seller must accompany a loss suffered by a buyer. Competition is cut-throat, most prices are too high, labor is weak and exploited, monopolies are everywhere, profits are way too high, advertising is wasteful and manipulates consumers without their knowledge, and the consumer is helpless. To the extent that people hold these opinions there will be demands for government to do something.

With acknowledged rare exceptions, the reality is that competition spurs companies toward excellence. It keeps prices from increasing more than necessary for some profit, without which a company cannot continue in business. As for labor, employees are sellers of effort, skills, and dedication. Any good worker will be sought by several companies, so he or she has a broad choice of employment. There are very few monopolies, and none that are not regulated (save government). Finally, a smart consumer will seldom be manipulated by advertising. (Note the reference to responsibility on the part of both workers and consumers. The market is not one-way.)

Those who believe that big companies call all the shots might reflect on the fact that only a tiny portion of today's Fortune 500 companies existed during the 1920s. Most of that era's large firms have disappeared. Government was around during that decade, although in much smaller form than it is now. But it was and is an unregulated monopoly, so there is no limit to its growth. Because government is force public officials can call many more shots than can private companies.

Mitchell and Simmons summarized ably:

> *Regulators gain more positions with more authority, higher salaries, and more status; the politicians gain votes, campaign monies, possible positions in the regulated industry once they retire or resign, income from the industry lecture circuit, and, perhaps, bribes. Obviously, the consuming public loses from all these cozy arrangements: They suffer reduced supplies, increased prices, and higher taxes.*[10]

Rarely will a reporter or columnist follow up on a regulatory program. In 1997 Jacoby noted that at least eighty-seven people have been killed by automobile air bags that worked as designed.[11] The chief bureaucrat who forced auto companies to install air bags rejects any responsibility for the deaths, most of whom were women and children. These people never apologize. They just issue orders, and citizens such as family members of those killed must live with the consequences.

Although it is true that air bags have saved many lives, the key concept here lies in consumer choice. That is, car buyers had no choice but to fork over an extra $1,300 to $2,200 for a product so equipped. Later the bureaucracy did in fact have second thoughts, so they permitted consumers to have an on-off switch installed in a car's air bag system. This cost another $150 to $200. These extra costs have the perverse result of causing young, inexperienced, financially poorer, and more accident-prone drivers to buy older and less safe cars, thus increasing the frequency of accidents causing personal injuries instead of decreasing it. Maybe it is time for another regulation.

Perverse results can affect people with illnesses. Kreuger reported that Glaxo Wellcome (now GlaxoSmithKline), a drug company, recently pulled Lotronex®, a medication to relieve irritable bowel syndrome, from the market after receiving reports of severe health problems with some people who were taking the drug.

Chief medical officer Dr. Richard Kent: "I guess we are voluntarily doing it after our conversation with the FDA, which left us essentially with no viable alternative."[12]

Irritable bowel syndrome afflicts close to 52 million people in this country. This drug had enabled many thousands of them to lead normal lives for the first time in many years. Kreuger interviewed a medical sales representative with the syndrome: "It's going to tremendously impact my life. It's going to be miserable again. I don't have an option. I have nothing else I can use to keep me feeling well. I can't tell you how bad that news is for me." (The drug has been reinstated.)

Because every body is different, a competent doctor in a free market will prescribe a drug for a patient at first on an experimental basis, perhaps using a limited dose regimen. Further experimentation will determine whether and how much of the drug is best for the patient. But when the FDA regulates the availability of a medication the market is distorted, and doctors and their patients no longer have a free choice. The result can be and often is extensive and unnecessary suffering.

Browne wrote, "Government has been involved in medicine since before any of us was born. . . . Its policies are the cause of medical care's high cost and the difficulty of obtaining health insurance—the two problems the politicians now propose to cure with more government."[13] Browne also pointed out state laws that force insurance companies to cover certain conditions; these predictably increase the cost of buying coverage. The price often goes up so high that many citizens choose to do without. This perverse outcome pads the figure hyped about so many millions of citizens without health insurance, so surely the government should "do something."

Prominent author James Michener wrote,

> *My wife and I had five cancers to deal with, and I had a massive heart attack, a quintuple bypass, . . . new hip, . . . [and] kidney failure . . . [and we] had superb medical care. But when it came to paying . . . we found ourselves in a jungle so insane that we could not even guess who might have been sufficiently addled to have devised it . . . inkling of the tremendous waste in our medical system. . . . [The] government system was as confusing as that of the private company. Both seemed to be vying for a prize to see which could have the stupidest bookkeeping system and the most lost records. It was a draw. The snafu that most angered my wife came when a kindly Medicare secretary told her they were sorry to hear that I had died.*[14]

During the past several decades the inflation-adjusted prices of manufactured goods have declined by 40 percent, whereas prices of education and health care have risen about three times as fast as inflation. To a thinking citizen the explanation is obvious: Making things is a mundane process, but the two services are subject to emotional responses. Therefore politicians have stuck their long noses into practically every detail of these processes, thus denying the market a chance to work toward correcting any flaws.

Regulations are sometimes written by lawyers who work both sides of the street. They are hired by organizations being regulated to write regulations that either contain loopholes or are impractical to enforce. Because bureaucrats work with firms being regulated, they welcome the reduction in their workload. Then lawyers work the other side by showing companies how to evade the impact of the same regulations they themselves wrote. There are lots of dollars being made promulgating regulations, second-guessing them, putting out more to correct the "oversights," minimizing the impact of these, and so on (no prize for guessing whose dollars).

Each year about 75,000 pages of regulations are written. Some pages are removed, as the Code of Federal Regulations is now "only" around 150,000 pages thick. Sixty agencies issue 1,800 rules each year.

Bureaucrats generally hang onto their jobs even in the face of new technological developments that would do a far superior job. For example, before 1920 thousands of babies died annually in New York from drinking contaminated milk. The use of pasteurization eventually prevailed over the strenuous objections of dairy inspectors.

Also, over the past forty years hundreds of thousands of people have gotten ill with food poisoning and thousands have died. Irradiation treatment has been available for all that time. It does not make food radioactive, nor does it change taste, texture, or appearance. What it does do is kill all bacteria without exception, which enables food to be preserved safely for long periods. The World Health Organization and the American Medical Association approve of the process. If used it would have prevented the widespread illness in 1997 caused by contaminated hamburger from Hudson Foods, and it could kill the salmonella that infects up to 60 percent of poultry and eggs. Yet a new Department of Agriculture meat inspection system commencing in that year did not even mention irradiation, even though the process was invented forty years ago.

In California, Proposition 113 placed a ceiling on what auto insurance companies could charge customers. The industry got a court to invalidate the law. The activists planned an initiative in 1992 that would set up a nonprofit public organization to provide low-cost insurance to drivers in competition with the private companies. But this would not work, as drivers with high accident rates would flock to this organization and their frequent accidents would quickly drive the firm into deep debt. Then taxpayer-provided subsidies would be required to bail it out.

With high-claim customers dwindling, owners and managers of private insurance companies would see their profits rise. Over a period of time competition would drive rates downward, but when combined with an increase in taxes to cover the subsidies all eventually would come out in the wash. **Someone** has to pay; the market cannot be denied, although big government has been known to give it a whale of a try.

The Occupational Safety and Health Administration (OSHA) was established to ensure safe and healthy working conditions for every worker. How could anyone object to this agency? Its establishment must have won politicians millions of votes. Inspectors visit factories and give orders regarding use of safety devices. The workers might resent taking orders from someone other than their bosses, who generally make requests for voluntary actions instead of barking orders. So perhaps they use bureaucrat-ordered safety equipment only when a scout among them flashes news of inspectors' imminent arrival.

Thus the scene becomes a contest of wills. Furthermore many supervisors believe that trying to make everything idiot-proof is itself dangerous. Workers do not have to think, and bosses are too tied down with paperwork to supervise them effectively.

Factory managers and their workers share an interest in job safety and health. This is nothing more or less than good business. But apparently government is convinced that it can manage these aspects of the job better than can those who perform it. A recent study compared accident rates in the construction industry between Ohio and Michigan, the former highly regulated and the latter not. There was no significant difference; however, it revealed a more positive attitude toward safety in plants where managers and workers assumed responsibility for themselves.

The EPA has a rulebook that consists of seventeen volumes of fine print. Ever since the original legislation (1970) environmentalists have hyped this issue, playing to the emotions of the masses. Four main subissues stand out in their concerns: (1) natural resources are running out; (2) population growth will eventually cause a shortage of food; (3) species are becoming extinct, forests are disappearing, and fish stocks are diminishing; and (4) the Earth's air and water are becoming more polluted. The news media have cooperated fully in the hype, of course.

In its zeal the EPA has frequently seen fit to stretch truth and interpret science to suit its aims. A new book by Bjorn Lomborg is titled *The Skeptical Environmentalist: Measuring the Real State of the World.* In it the statistician author utilizes different data and different interpretations to prove that nearly all the environmental hype is false. The reaction to the book by environmentalists has been ferocious. (They know from experience that emotions generate far more press than science.)

Discrimination on the job has been and is an emotional issue, so government by one count has 168 programs that give some kind of preference in hiring and on the job. This could be another instance of layering more regulations on top of previous ones.

Basic economics guides decisions in the private marketplace, but it is unfortunate that so few people understand it. Aside from the law of supply and demand there is not much necessary to know. Recently several hurricanes harassed East Coast residents and destroyed billions in property, mostly through floods. There is an established tradition that has government spending public money to reimburse flood victims. Tragedy and high-drama rescues ensure plenty of vote-grabbing media coverage. The perverse result here has such people rebuilding again and again, right where the next flood is sure to hit. Due to this forced taxpayer generosity, few homeowners in the area buy flood insurance.

As if this were not enough, government also forbids local merchants to charge market prices for food, bottled water, flashlights, plywood for windows, and so on. This means that some people who get to the supermarket first buy large quantities and hoard them, thus denying others who come later.

The law of supply and demand says that when demand rises and supply is limited the price will rise; the reverse is also true. But if government clamps a ceiling on a price, merchants have little incentive to really hustle to provide more at greater expense to them (rush orders are always costly). Now, a politician will argue that price gouging will deny the poor access to emergency goods. But if there aren't any available at all, the price is irrelevant.

Social activists pushed for better housing for migrant workers from Central and South America. Farmers performed economic analyses and discovered that although they would be spending more to further mechanize their operations, they would be better off if they could avoid spending even more on housing. Of course this put many migrant laborers out of work.

No one asked the workers if they thought their accommodations were adequate; the activists just kept pushing. If asked the workers might have said their housing was okay, even better than what they left back home. Surely they would have said they preferred having jobs to unemployment, as this was the reason they left home and family in the first place.

The Family Leave Act was President Clinton's first legislative achievement. It requires businesses to give pregnant women twelve weeks of unpaid leave from the job. Women's rights advocates hailed this law as a major triumph for women. Who can object to a law to help women and babies? Politicians harvested millions of votes.

Now small businesses, which create most of the new jobs, avoid hiring young women without children. But this is discrimination, say the women's rights people. Big government had previously provided business managers with a convenient response while hiring older women: They are only conforming to another government regulation, which forbids discrimination based on age.

At one point recently the government raised the minimum wage and simultaneously acted to get welfare recipients back into work. But the first action made it more difficult and expensive for employers to conform to the second goal.

Who can object to keeping city apartment rents reasonable? But rent ceilings make it uneconomic for landlords subject to rising costs of maintenance to make profits. Therefore they try to sell and invest their money elsewhere for a better return, but prospective buyers are not stupid, so landlords simply abandon their properties. As they gradually become uninhabitable and people move out, they may be turned into crack houses. This response increases demand for apartments not subject to rent control.

After the terrible Exxon *Valdez* oil spill in Prince William Sound, Alaska, emotions were understandably aroused among the public. Politicians responded with a law that hit the industry hard: strict and unlimited liability regardless of whether the tanker or the company was at fault. Votes poured into their hoppers.

Today financially strong oil transport companies avoid hauling to the United States. When they do they use old, unsafe tankers so that the loss is minimal if the government seizes one as compensation for a spill. They charge higher prices, claiming a need for much greater insurance coverage due to the new law.

Decades ago milk prices dropped and farmers were having it rough, so Congress arranged for regulations to guarantee minimum prices. If the price dropped below a specified level the taxpayer made up the difference. This took practically all the risk out of dairy farming, so thousands of people entered the business. Had Congress refused to "help," weaker producers would have left the market, thus reducing supply and enabling the price to increase to where remaining dairies could make profits.

The original price drop was due to a **surplus** of milk products, not a shortage, so the new regulations must have seemed confusing to economists and ordinary people, but not to politicians, who saw votes in helping poor farmers. For consumers the result is higher taxes to prop up prices for farmers and higher prices in the supermarket. They get gouged both going and coming.

In the 1980s Japanese automakers were beating the pants off US firms, who hired lobbyists to ask President Reagan for assistance. He clamped restrictions on imports of Japanese cars and small trucks. This predictably increased their prices; consumers were paying 20 percent over sticker price for new imported cars. Detroit responded by increasing prices of their products, even though there was no increase in quality to match them. During one four-year period the estimated extra cost to consumers, over and above their expenses without import restraints, was $26 billion. This figure was not published, nor was an estimate of how many products might have been purchased with that $26 billion and how many people would have been hired and trained to produce them.

The computer industry was not regulated during 1981–95, when prices dropped by 95 percent even as the machines became many times faster and more powerful. The next major regulatory challenge for government lies in the Internet, as it poses a real danger to public officials who need to keep hidden a multitude of sins. The Net penetrates into every facet of society, just as does big government, but government does not (yet) have control over it. It can also flash information around the world in an instant; this could mean importing dirty political laundry while politicians remain unaware of what is going on. This alarming situation violates the oligarchic imperative: Public officials know what is really going on, but citizens do not (see Chapter 9).

Regulation has traditionally made a distinction between private and public communication, but the Internet makes no such distinction. This book will demonstrate that top government officials must maintain control over information flows if they want to perpetuate their privileged positions. Put another way, secrecy is absolutely essential.

Due to lack of government interference, "wired" citizens are able to take more responsibility over their own lives, making decisions otherwise made for them by big government. Unless the nanny state can get an effective handle on regulation of this communication medium, it may eventually help millions of citizens to become truly mature.

The Economist published a study that ranked eleven European Union countries by how heavily their economies were regulated and by growth in economic output.[15] It found that Great Britain and Ireland, with markets mostly free, had the highest growth rates. Most heavily regulated Greece had the lowest growth rate.

A logical conclusion is that regulation is counterproductive for several reasons. One is that any form of government intervention has been proven to be misguided over and over again. A second lies in the potential for abuse with Washington insiders working both sides of the street. A third is that in most of the regulated industries conditions are changing so rapidly that regulators haven't a prayer of keeping up. Fourth, most industries are going global, and if they cannot be effectively regulated when domestic it will be impossible when they are multinational. Fifth, perverse results occur often, thus prompting bureaucrats to overlay still more regulations. A sixth has Congress passing vaguely worded laws to give bureaucrats a wide range of options. (This last also provides opportunities for lobbyists to grease congressional palms.)

There is a story about a friend finding famous comedian W. C. Fields reading the Bible. Asked why, Fields replied, "I am looking for loopholes."

Many people believe that if enough laws and regulations are put into effect they will eliminate any and all loopholes that might enable a privileged person or group to evade the impact of the law. The truth is that no amount of law can cover all situations in the field. In fact, the more laws the more loopholes, whether planned or not. A plethora of rules undermines initiative. Most accidents, mistakes, and trial and error result in useful learning and therefore progress. About fifty years ago, Hayek stated that Soviet Russian central planning with its tons of rules "kills the human faculty that makes things work."

In his book *The Death of Common Sense*, Philip Howard drove the point home with another reference to the great economist: "Law is not coercive, Hayek noted, if it permits you to adapt. But if it tells you exactly what to do, it has all the characteristics of coercion. Coercion by government, the main fear of our founding fathers, is now its common attribute. . . . We now have a government of laws against men."

Micromanagement of the entire economy is precisely what the Kremlin of the old Soviet Union tried to do for seventy years. The Clinton administration seemed bent on emulating this example, instead of taking great pains to avoid that tragic result. High public officials think only of regulating others. The principle, enshrined in the US Constitution, of citizens regulating government no longer enters their thinking.

Regulated companies keep the rigors of competition at a distance, so they grow fat, lazy, and less efficient. This means they must periodically return to the well for more government handouts, and this becomes a vicious circle. Eventually they get trapped, just like individuals on public welfare.

Thomas Jefferson wrote, "Were we directed from Washington when to sow and when to reap, we should soon want for bread."

The Anatomy of a Bureaucracy

Laws are passed that are designed to look like they benefit the public, but because these actions are public by law members of the elite class have difficulty in keeping their true intent secret. But secrecy is no problem among bureaucrats. Therefore laws are deliberately written vaguely, to give maximum flexibility to mandarins as they work to favor the elite class and guarantee that Congress and the bureaucracy remain in power indefinitely. This is how the symbiotic relationship between the two groups plays out.

Public service in a bureaucracy attracts a certain type of person who is oriented toward job security and is therefore risk-averse. Such a person comes aboard with great enthusiasm, but soon the system gets to him or her, and he realizes that survival requires entrenchment. A bureaucracy does occasionally suffer a politics-caused reduction in force (RIF), which always blows over. The bureaucrat soon learns how to weather these events by keeping a low profile and writing justification memos to the file. Once entrenched, even a political earthquake will not dislodge him. (RIFs in the Soviet Union were called purges.)

This need for security becomes more acute with more big government intervention in people's private lives, as this causes feelings of insecurity. Such people search for a hole where no one will bother them and the money is steady. Perhaps not intentionally, in this way the supply of future bureaucrats is assured. Soon after beginning work they turn into time servers, oriented to problems and not solutions. If a program were to succeed there is the real danger of job loss, and one purpose in joining public service was to avoid this unstable situation.

Salaries are standardized and move upward in lockstep in accordance with seniority. This means there is little incentive toward excellence in job performance, which suits a seasoned bureaucrat. Years ago, salaries were equalized with those typically paid in the private sector, but this omits consideration for the less stable job environment that typifies any private company as it faces often tough competition. This oversight further sweetens the opportunities in public service.

The standard modus operandi is to go with the flow and don't try to find and solve problems. One bureaucrat said: "It makes too many headaches for too many people. You get political flak, you get press. A lot of people in the federal bureaucracy are quite happy with that system. They are the ones, largely, who survive and get promoted. The higher they get, the more cautious they become." Don't rock the boat; but a thinking citizen may wonder how the operation gets anything done.

Bureaucracy can predominate, but it cannot lead. No one is interested in leading the organization, as this means a relatively high (and risky) profile.

But this takes nothing away from its hypersensitive nose for money. The resurrected National Missile Defense System is a case in point. No one even knows if a system can be built at any price that will protect us from incoming missiles. But the external threat of such missiles (see Chapter 20) is a very emotional issue, so Congress will probably get authority for, say, $60 billion of taxpayer money. Spending this wad will move research along, even if there remains no solution. However, would it not be foolish to allow $60 billion of utter waste? This would not look good, so Congress will probably authorize another $60 billion, and so on. In this way gigantic slabs of pork are spread over much of the US landscape.

Projects like this employ many scientists. Passmore said, "Pretending to absolute objectivity, they in fact seek to secure their own position in society; they will serve any government, acquiesce in any form of social arrangement, whether it be capitalism, communism or the Third Reich, provided only that it will provide them with the funds they need for their experiments."[16] Some of them are not above a bit of fudging of either the results or the interpretation, as they know whence comes the money. In the case of the nebulous project under discussion here, the opportunity and hence the temptation is considerable.

The iron triangle consists of politicians, bureaucrats, and voters, who benefit from and hence approve of government's behavior. Bureaucrats work hard at increasing the demand for their services; then they go to the politicians who serve on appropriations committees with extensive justification statements to support requests for more money for the coming fiscal year. Politicians wish to impress the third leg of the triangle and thereby win votes, and bureaucrats want to expand their operations. This mutual dependency encourages the spending of more public money.

Mitchell and Simmons noted:

> *The conspiracy may be benevolent but the outcomes are not. . . . Bureau budgets [are] twice the size of the average budgets for analogous private firms operating under competition and three times the size of those for private monopolies. . . . Finances padded costs; in short, the added funds go to overstaffed agencies employing costly procedures, to provide higher incomes and unnecessary perks to employees, and to underwrite a more pleasant life style than their counterparts in private enterprise. . . . Still, we get too many services from too many bureaus.*[17]

A desired "free" good will generate many customers. Bureaucrats appreciate this increase in demand, because it plays to their natural tendency to expand their turf. But nearly all public services cater to consumption and not investment, which in the private sector creates new wealth and economic growth. This means not only that money must be diverted from private investment, but any growth must be paid for by asking for more taxpayer money.

It is well said that the job is not finished until the paperwork is done. Howard put it this way: "After years of bureaucratic paper-pushing, courts are presented with gargantuan records, whose size, Judge Friendly observed, 'varies inversely with usefulness.' What the courts generally do is ignore the massive records and, after reviewing whatever the parties bring to their attention, make their own decisions."[18]

Occasionally a new issue will be hyped by the news media. Bureaucracies by the dozen instantly grab for it—here is another opportunity for growth. Turf battles are fought, although they are often resolved in terms of friendship with a key politician. Often a whole new bureaucracy takes root and begins growing. But pieces are distributed to others; this is why nearly every activity in government is being done by about twenty different agencies.

Another example lies in illegal immigrants. Although most plug into the economy with jobs, however lowly, some answer the siren call of the bureaucrat and go on welfare. These people are not reported to the Immigration and Naturalization Service (INS), because bureaucrats could lose clients if they were. When discovered, private companies who hire illegals are prosecuted.

A bureaucracy grows for years and eventually it ages, just like people. There is an important difference, however. A person has the option of learning and self-renewal in old age, but a bureaucracy gradually loses sight of the original purpose for its formation, assumes the trappings of eternal life, and does not change with the changing needs of its clients. As time passes people find themselves working harder to get around, through, or over what they see as a barrier to progress.

As a bureaucracy ages, the rulebook expands. It is said that a fading organization's last big gesture is to promulgate a bigger book of rules. The more that people in any organization (and in society) depend on rules, the less members trust one another. Today whenever a citizen makes a mistake, his first impulse is to reach for his lawyer instead of his conscience.

Against all this evidence, it is intriguing to note that poll results over the past ten years indicate that people want more controls, not fewer. Either the polls are administered by bureaucrats who rig the results, or citizens are truly unaware of the damage that they are visiting on themselves (hidden costs make awareness rare).

Another unfortunate and largely unnoticed development lies in the gradual displacement of traditional family habits and remedies by rules laid down by experts unknown to the ordinary family. Recent discoveries regarding an individual's genetic code suggest that each person is truly unique. However, he has no choice but to follow uniform rules made for the masses. The family is one of several traditional institutions that have been undermined by experts in bureaucracies. Another is the public education system.

Putnam reported on many studies of what he called "civic disengagement."[19] "Professional staff could often do a more effective, and more efficient job in the task at hand than 'well-meaning' volunteers. However, disempowering ordinary members of voluntary associations could easily **diminish grassroots civic engagement and foster oligarchy**" (emphasis added).

A typical active citizen in a town may get concerned enough about a toxic waste dump to go to the local bureaucracy for assistance in rectifying the problem. He would probably get only a run-around, and so would naturally begin thinking about getting government to pass another regulation. But any rule passed is intended to be one-size-fits-all, whereas in fact it does not. The US government did establish a tax-supported clean-up fund under President Jimmy Carter. But several years later someone looked into the results of implementing this program, and found that 88 percent of the money spent at that point had gone to lawyer fees.

Bureaucratic regulations are also known as administrative law. Because bureaucracies are always expanding, there are far more laws made by them than by Congress, and bureaucrats need not stand for election. They are essentially accountable to no one, and this is dangerous.

Robert Bork compared the bureaucracy to a democracy:

> *If equality is the ultimate and most profound political good, there is really very little to vote about. Only a society with a profusion of competing values, all regarded as legitimate, needs to vote. In such a society, there being no way of say-*

ing that one outcome is a priori better than another, it is the legitimacy of the (democratic) process that validates the result; not, as in a thoroughly egalitarian society, the morality of the result that validates the process." [20]

The first process is bottom-up, and the second is top-down.

Another institution that has suffered damage is the church (including the mosque and the synagogue). Local churchpeople often personally know others who have come onto hard times. They understand the precise nature of their needs, and they can identify freeloaders in order to show them the door until they shape up. The bureaucrat wants as many freeloaders as he or she can recruit. In this way the force of big government interferes with any church's ability to effectively serve the community's spiritual and emotional needs.

Milton Friedman showed that in New York City during the early 1970s bloated welfare programs eroded the tax base as people and businesses left the city in the face of ever-higher taxes.[21] This exodus reduced the amount of money available to (presumably) help the poor. What did get to the poor was "largely wasted because it encourages them to substitute a handout for a wage." Especially in the South Bronx area, the more money spent, the worse the disease became.

The Economist commented following the terrible terrorist attacks of September 11, 2001: "Opinion polls show a greater appreciation not just of big government but also of the work of once-demonized institutions such as the FBI and CIA."[22] A thinking citizen might wonder why he or she saw or heard nothing in the news that referred to the abominable incompetence in these two agencies that enabled a large group of men to hijack four airplanes, each destined to destroy a major target. Around 3,000 innocent people killed and billions in property damage could have been averted, not to mention the widespread paranoia that keeps President Bush's popularity rating propped up. (In another article *The Economist* called it "one of the biggest intelligence failures the world has ever seen." But this magazine is a British publication, and only a very few US citizens read it.)

Sennholz thought back to a different time:

> *How surprised and shocked would have been the men who fought against a foreign tyranny at Lexington and Bunker Hill and Saratoga and Yorktown if they could have foreseen today's bureaucratic monster, in the shape of federal, state, and local governments, costing almost $9,000 a second to operate, and doubling its exactions from the labor of its citizens every ten years.*
>
> *When more people see the state as a robber baron that takes from them, not as a Santa Claus that gives to them, the prospects will have improved for the dismantling of the bureaucratic monster.*[23]

If nothing is done about the kudzu vine along the East Coast of the United States, there will eventually be no trees left. This analogy needs no further explanation.

Howard wrote,

Making judgments is hard, and some failures are inevitable. It's far easier to lounge around the basement TV room, hooting at any mistake or apparent unfairness. . . . The media will do their best to egg us on; headlines are more exciting when the needle oscillates wildly. All we have to do is fall for it, and demand instant legal fixes whenever a problem arises, and we'll be right back under law's shadow.[24]

Special Interest Politics

James Madison said: "By a faction I understand a number of citizens, whether amounting to a majority or minority of the whole, who are united and actuated by some common impulse of passion, or of interest, adverse to the rights of other citizens, or to the permanent and aggregate interests of the community."[25] This observation suggests that either a majority or a minority may install tyranny. The Bill of Rights was designed to protect the minority against the majority, but only citizens' vigilance can protect their freedom from the formation and depredations of elite minorities. "Among the numerous advantages promised by a well constructed Union, none deserves to be more accurately developed than its tendency to break and control the violence of faction."

Today lobbyists pound the corridors of congressional office buildings, bearing wads of money to purchase unearned special favors for the interest groups who hire them. This activity provides security for sponsoring enterprises, which sometimes takes the form of protection from the rigors of competition in the marketplace. Difficulties enter when members of groups without enough money are denied equal opportunity to succeed, and also when striving for security gets to the point where liberty is undermined. This happens when increased security awarded to one group increases the insecurity of others.

Naturally, other groups see what is going on and come looking for their seat at the table. Gradually the society becomes infected by a "what's-in-it-for-me?" mentality. The negative side of human nature is thus activated, and it prevails over the positive side: "What can I contribute?" The process turns vicious when each group perceives purchasing activity engaged in by some other group as unfair; the playing field is never perceived by all as level.

Kevin Phillips said,

The notable expansion in the Washington parasite structure during the 1970s and 1980s came from outside the federal government . . . from an explosion in the ranks of lawyers and interest-group representatives out to influence Uncle Sam, interpret his actions, or pick his pockets for themselves or their clients. The gunslingers, card sharks, and faro dealers were checking into Gucci Gulch [corridors of Congress].[26]

In 1950 just under 1,000 lawyers were members of the local bar; by 1975 there were 21,000 and by 1993 61,000. Phillips noted: "No other major US city matched the capital's per capita concentration of lawyers." Lawyers write regulations to favor their sponsors. "When policy decisions were made, attendance would be taken, checks would be totaled, lobbyists would be judged, mail would be tabulated—and if a group wasn't on hand to drive its vehicle through the Capitol Hill weighing station, that organization was out of luck."

The game continued to grow ever more expensive as more groups kept jumping in and upping the ante. The 1960s saw rapid growth of the consumer movement, paced by Ralph Nader's famous book *Unsafe at Any Speed.* (That volume tweaked the nose of the nation's mightiest corporation.) Company executives saw this trend and accurately concluded that they also needed to come to Washington, DC.

During the 1970s and into the 1980s the response movement developed to where executives hiring lobbyists could obtain a larger money return on "invested" capital by playing the game than by private investment in better products, services, and processes (which go to improve quality, productivity, wages, and living standards). A very big industry, such as oil, could, through buying just a small tax break or subsidy, realize an increase in profits of member companies that exceeded their total "contribution" by perhaps four to six times.

But now the picture has predictably changed. Most of the companies and other interest groups came to Washington because they felt they had to come, but as more arrived and more favors were dispensed, the carrot was slowly replaced by the stick. That is, executives eventually realized that with so much competition for favors the extra return on investment was no longer so lucrative, and so they began to want out. The president of a group of top company executives was interviewed recently; he complained that the game has evolved into a shakedown as politicians constantly badger them for even more money. He said that key congressional committee chairs were in position to do serious damage to a firm that did not come across as "requested." Enter the stick; today some congressmen's behavior closely resembles that of the Mafia.

Interest group activity does not contribute to economic growth. New wealth is not created; rather it is only transferred, usually from the pockets of one fat cat to those of another. No pay, no play. Note that whenever a special interest buys a tax break the deficit must be made up somewhere. Because taxpayers are an unorganized interest group they are forced to pick up the tab.

Friedman commented on the oil industry: "Few US industries sing the praises of free enterprise more loudly than the oil industry. Yet few industries rely so heavily on special governmental favors. . . .These special favors cost US consumers of oil products something over $3.5 billion a year. . . . This staggering cost cannot be justified by its contribution to national security."[27] (This observation saw print in 1967.)

Shortly after the Bush administration took over the reins of government, Vice President Dick Cheney trumpeted a report that "indicate[s] that over the next 20 years US oil consumption will increase by 33 percent." Krugman noted that the increase over the twenty years to 1999 was less than 5 percent.[28] "What's behind Cheney's greasy math? . . . The Cheney plan provides an array of subsidies, explicit and implicit, for energy producers. Indeed, the libertarian Cato Institute calls the plan a 'smorgasbord of handouts and subsidies for virtually every energy lobby in Washington.'" There is no earthly reason why taxpayers should subsidize or otherwise support big oil. Big government is already transferring too much wealth from the middle class to the rich.

The dairy lobby occasionally publishes position papers: "Dairymen enthusiastically support a strong and flexible federal milk marketing order program. Such a program is essential for the maintenance of orderly marketing of milk in fluid and manufactured dairy markets." "Orderly marketing" translates into elimination of risk of loss to dairy farmers through taxpayer-financed milk price supports. In a free market any business must accept risk of losses as it pursues profits.

Price supports drew thousands of new producers into the market, thus making it awash in milk. Instead of removing the supports, government bought and slaughtered 1.6 million cows (again with taxpayer money). The explanation for this crazy action and loss of resources to the market lies in the annual $2 million of tainted money the dairy industry contributes to congressional reelection campaigns.

Some truth about entitlements needs to see the light of day. Social Security and Medicare are financed separately through FICA taxes on payrolls. Some fourteen other entitlements are promoted through a cooperative press as benefits for the average citizen. Martin Gross wrote: "But they seem to have almost nothing to do with the average citizen . . . as Washington would like us to believe. What they really are is a bag full of give-aways for special interests."[29] He pulled few punches:

> *Did you know that the taxpayer-paid health insurance for government retirees, some of whom are getting pensions of $75,000 a year, is a $4 billion entitlement? . . . In fact all $15 billion in farmer's subsides in 1993 were entitlements. Doesn't that thrill you nonfarm people who make up ninety-eight percent of the population? Did you know that those supposed entitlements for the middle class include $35 billion each year for federal civilian employee pensions?*

Gross described an entitlement that enables federal employees to buy stocks and bonds. Now, if the game described herein persists to its logical conclusion, those stocks and bonds will be worthless. The poor get many billions in entitlements such as Medicaid, food stamps, SSI, earned income tax credits, Aid to Families with Dependent Children (AFDC), child nutrition, and social services from state governments, as well as from Washington. "So on net, how much of these entitlements do non-special-interest, ordinary, sweating, working, middle class Americans get from Washington? The answer is Nada, Nothing, Rien, Zippo, Zero. The sucking sound you hear is the money being vacuumed out of your pockets to pay for the entitlements of others." (Welfare reform has since somewhat lowered these takings from the middle class.)

Most citizens have found government inscrutable, so they don't scrutinize it. This of course means open season for the elites. A **true** public servant considers constituents as a special interest group, which means he or she has over several decades become an endangered species.

In a climate where optimism about people's ability predominates and where public service involves some sacrifice, talented elites will direct their energies toward the private sector. Maybe later in life a successful citizen will feel an urge to devote a short time to public service.

THE PROBLEM WITH GROUP RIGHTS

Samuelson said:

> *Is the "right" of someone to a disability hearing really as important as the "right" of free speech? Is the "right" to a welfare check as important as the "right" to freedom of religion? The first set of "rights" here involved details of government—who gets what benefits and under what conditions—while the second set involved fundamental principles of social and political conduct that have guided Americans since the eighteenth century.*[30]

The distinction between political or natural rights and economic rights is subtle but nonetheless vital, as it separates equality of opportunity from equality of results, and therefore democracy from authoritarian governments.

Thomas Paine wrote:

> *If we look back to the riots and tumults, which at various times have happened in England, we shall find, that they did not proceed from the want of a government, but the government was itself the generating cause; instead of consolidating society, it divided it; it deprived it of its natural cohesion, and engendered discontents and disorders, which otherwise would not have existed.*[31]

Paine referred in this observation to the natural human tendency to seek affiliation with others: cohesion. This section will show that the notion of group rights divides society, thus robbing it of its natural cohesion.

Because society cannot function well without a government, the appropriate question for discussion is what kind of government is best for the mass of citizens. If the rights of the individual are truly held to be unalienable as argued in the

Declaration of Independence, no group of people can assume authority over any other group. A government that adheres to the principles of individualism and bottom-up self-government cannot organize as the kind of authoritarian government known as oligarchy.

The United States began a new life in 1789 under a constitution that was designed to protect individual rights against an admittedly necessary central government. In the country's early days, an individual was free to carve out a destiny as his or her heart may direct. But he easily recognized the need for others in a particular endeavor, and so he sought and received their voluntary cooperation. The person would return the favor at first opportunity, and because people trusted one another back then each knew he could count on a person's assistance with the next joint project or emergency.

The key word here is **voluntary**; cooperation at that time extended across ethnic and religious boundaries, because for practical purposes such frontiers didn't exist. Paine's "natural cohesion" had prevented them from forming.

However, when equality of opportunity is permitted, diversities within human nature will induce one individual to fare better than someone else, and the latter will often feel left behind through no perceived fault of his or her own. To preserve self-esteem, one will naturally look around for a scapegoat and for recourse (or "equality") through some means outside of himself. Dissatisfied with government's protection of individual rights, a person is likely to join with others who see themselves similarly deprived and approach government for help in redressing a serious and jointly perceived wrong.

This natural tendency has recently spawned development of the victimology movement, which is group-oriented. Because the issue is emotional, lawyers are attracted to it. Bureaucrats also like it, because they can spread their wings to embrace group after group. Isn't this what government institutions are for?

Howard noted:

> *There are rights for children and elderly; the disabled, the mentally disabled; workers under twenty-five and over forty, alcoholics, and the addicted. . . .*
>
> *Whenever there is a perceived injustice, new rights are created to help the victims. These rights are different: While the rights-bearers may see them as "protection," they don't protect so much as provide . . . new, and often invisible, form of subsidy. They are provided at everyone else's expense, but the amount of the check is left blank.*[32]

But under the US Constitution, "rights were not the language of government action. Rights were protections that **prevented government** (emphasis added) from telling us what we could say, where we could travel, or who our friends could be."

These new laws have brought paranoia to the workplace. Minorities are hurt most as employers hesitate to hire people who can possibly sue them later for the smallest perceived slight. People talk less at work, which undermines employee morale and efficiency. The logical conclusion is that government is fragmenting the populace. The reality is a conspiracy, and the lawyers love it.

Under capitalism and free markets everyone is free to make money. Individual talent and effort are rewarded. But the notion of group rights undermines this basic belief, because an organized group seeks **unearned** economic betterment from government. If a country reaches the point where this type of work carries more weight than hard work on the factory floor, a vital value will have perished.

Bork pointed out that the "intellectual class" has traditionally disapproved of individual rights.[33] Indeed, some members consistently see themselves as part of an oligarchy. This group of people influences the courts, so whenever personal liberty and equality of results come into conflict the decision will often come down on the side of equality.

In 1821 lawyer and former President Thomas Jefferson worried that "the judiciary of the US is the subtle corps of sappers and miners constantly working underground to undermine the foundations of our confederated republic. They are construing our constitution from a coordination of a general and special government to a general and supreme one alone. This will lay all things at their feet." A negative incentive connected to human nature known as personal power seeking was at work early in the country's life.

Jefferson referred here to the principle of federalism: His "general and special government" were the national and state governments, respectively. The principle states that power is divided between these two levels of governments, so that one may not prevail over the other. Should the general government prevail, the result is oligarchy and eventually despotism. Should the state governments prevail, the general government would be hollowed out and the result would be the same situation as when citizens suffered under the Articles of Confederation (guarded boundaries between states, trade tariffs, different currencies, noncooperation in capturing fugitives).

Lawyers have formed a special interest group to demand extra unearned privileges from government. They clearly enjoy an inside track, because nearly half of congressmen are lawyers. The American Trial Lawyers Association (ATLA) has one of the most powerful lobbying forces in Washington. In 1991 Vice President Dan Quayle spoke before the American Bar Association: "Is it healthy for our economy to have 18 million new lawsuits coursing through the system annually?"

Members of Congress and lawyers frequently combine to pass laws intended to make more work for lawyers. Texas professor Stephen Magee contended: "When lawyers artificially stimulate the demand for legal services through politics, we cannot rely on the usual market forces of supply and demand to control their numbers." Today Japan has about half the population of the United States, and the country has 18,000 lawyers. Were this proportion applied to this country there would be around 36,000, but the reality is 891,000 or nearly twenty-five times as many.

Because special interest groups seeking favors from government are organized and have money, lawyers leap at the opportunity to represent them. Because other members of the fraternity pervade the membership of Congress, getting requested laws and regulations enacted is not difficult. The matching dramatic rise in federal lawsuits is not difficult to explain.

One excellent example of lawyer dominance may be found in the area of school discipline. Richard E. Morgan quoted Edward A. Wynne: "Some of my older friends, . . . have sometimes asked me, 'What has happened to the tough teachers of my youth? The legendary tiny old maids who could tongue-lash adolescent giants into humble submission?' . . . 'The legends were real. I saw them in operation when I was a child, and they won fear and respect.'"[34]

Lawyers were not involved at that time, and an unruly giant knew that a strong and coordinated power structure consisting of school system and concerned parents backed up a tiny teacher's admonitions. A student knew that if he or she did not shape up, expulsion would be imminent. Students of that time really wanted to finish school.

But today's lawyers have perverted the Fourteenth Amendment to the Constitution, which provides for "due process of law." Morgan: "Once the schools get into the business of writing codes, holding hearings, and legalizing discipline, a logical momentum drives them to ever more elaborate innovation in order to stay ahead of what will now . . . be constant nit-picking and claims for 'true fairness' by people whose real grievance is that they are being disciplined at all." The problem was most serious in large cities, which suffered from the greatest middle-class flight and also the highest concentration of rights industry lawyers.

The latest incarnation of the school code movement is called zero tolerance. Perverse results include the following bizarre instances: a twelve-year-old Virginia boy expelled for waving a stapler around on a school bus, a Florida girl suspended for bringing a nail clipper to school, and an Ohio boy who wrote 'You will die with honor' when asked to write a fortune cookie message. Also harassed were a girl for possessing a bottle of ibuprofen, a boy for using a mouthwash after lunch, and a kindergartner who brought a beeper on a school trip.

Codes are a one-size-fits-all group-oriented approach to situations that were formerly handled on the spot by utilizing an individual approach to each. What is truly amazing is that zero tolerance goes head-to-head against the US Constitution's defense of tolerance of people who look and behave differently than the majority. However, lawyers created this situation, and so they like it. But students have difficulty in respecting authority when they see adults suing one another, evading lawsuits, and enforcing discipline in trivial matters.

Lack of individual discipline at school and home leads directly to crime. Children need discipline just as they need love, and when it is not forthcoming it is amazing the lengths to which some will go to obtain it. Famous poet Rudyard Kipling wrote: "If you can keep your head when others about you are losing theirs . . ." Blake Pirtle, a death row inmate, said, "This was at the age of nine or ten, during the fourth grade. . . . They thought it was funny to see me stoned out of my mind and falling down drunk, and I was more than pleased to do it, for it provided me the attention I so desperately needed."[35]

The subject of rules deserves further comment, especially in view of what the national government has been creating over the past twenty years. Morgan pointed to a law enforcement officers' manual of 1,000 pages. "The manual is a third-year law student's delight; as public policy it is a disaster." Experts, lawyers, and judges seldom venture out into the streets where police officers work, so they don't realize the impracticability of writing code to cover every situation in its infinite variety. An old German proverb goes: "The more laws, the less justice." There is a clear need for intuition and trust, experts' pronouncements notwithstanding.

New rules are being written, primarily for the edification and benefit of the lawyers, judges, and bureaucrats who have taken over the institutions of government, and they have spread their influence beyond these groups to interfere with private institutions. The elites favor themselves over the rabble, who continue to pay the bills. The privileged feel the tug of negative incentives, and without accountability to those who support them they will continue the abuse. Nay, they will expand it.

The democratic process is often inefficient and even chaotic, as ideas and recommendations are criticized and debated by concerned citizens to strengthen them and mold the best of these into law. It is human nature to want stability, even as it is also human nature to want progress.

The key lies in a mix of stability and life on the edge, its nature delineated by citizens. But such a balance is not easy to attain; hence the chaotic nature of the democratic process. Therefore a citizen often finds it easier to join a group whose desires and feelings of inadequacy closely match his or her own, thereby circumventing the process.

Government officials are motivated to cooperate because they are always on the prowl for votes. They justify this cooperation by stating that it is their job to listen to legitimate concerns from all quarters and act on them. At first glance this surely sounds like the democratic process, but when money enters into the negotiations the original goal of equality of opportunity among citizens becomes transformed into special and unearned privilege for the few.

As group goes up against group and more groups join the fray, the media play up the conflict, because executives know conflict sells almost as well as sex. Occasionally an analyst will get carried away and an editor will print hyperbolic nonsense. For example, one recent article playing up the "familiar 2050 problem" produced the following (column by John Leo which criticizes an article): "Hispanics, will be about 25 percent of the national total and, when added to the black and Asian-American totals, will produce enough political power to neutralize or overthrow the existing order."[36]

This projection assumes that such people will always vote as a monolithic bloc and never based on their own individual interests or beliefs. It also assumes that all of these groups will unite in their voting behavior against whites and other ethnic groups. But surveys indicate that Hispanic attitudes generally closely match those of whites. The conclusion is that such articles not only mislead the public but also exacerbate divisions between ethnic groups and thereby spread the popular belief in group rights. Uninformed readers will tend to believe this tripe when the news media make little effort to publish truth as a basis for comparison.

Before 1960 school systems in the United States emphasized indoctrinating young immigrants to be Americans. Children who could not speak English were placed in schools where only English was used, and they eventually became proficient in the language. This institution was a unifying force, which taught tolerance of people whose appearance and beliefs were different. Today's school systems are administered in a top-down manner by experts and bureaucrats, where parents have very little to say about how their children's schools are managed.

One authority actually advocates government intervention to preserve and promote different cultures. He believes public officials should "celebrate its holidays, teach its history, foster its language and expound its values." This well-meaning gentleman has not thought through the consequences of his recommendation. There are an infinite number of cultures in this country, and if every holiday were celebrated in any particular area there would be few working days. Also, teaching the language and history of all cultures would crowd out everything else from a school curriculum. Finally, it would fragment the community, pitting neighbor against neighbor. This conclusion is not to discourage the perpetuation of cultures, as there is much to recommend preservation of the flavors of their heritages among the young. But societal cohesion will benefit if this is done through the family and clubs.

The concepts of nationalism and race look inward and backward. The concept of democracy looks outward and forward. The first foments envy and disharmony, whereas the second encourages tolerance and a unity of purpose. With competent leadership these will suffice to overcome diversity of viewpoints and stimulate natural cohesion.

Berliner and Hull wrote:

> *The diversity movement claims that its goal is to extinguish racism and build tolerance of differences. This is a complete sham. One cannot teach stu-*

dents that their identity is determined by skin color and expect them to be colorblind. One cannot espouse multiculturalism and expect students to see each other as individual human beings. One cannot preach the need for self-esteem while destroying the faculty that makes it possible: reason. One cannot teach collective identity and expect students to have self-esteem.[37]

When a special interest forms a group its money-soaked vote carries more weight than does those of an equal number of individuals. When this condition prevails the constitutional notion of "one person, one vote" has been displaced by the unconstitutional notion of "one association, one vote." Voters know this, and the recent historical record of declining voter participation reflects this knowledge.

Putnam expressed alarm at "explosion of interest groups represented in Washington since the 1960s that these studies reveal is ever more groups speaking (or claiming to speak) on behalf of ever more categories of citizens."[38] He went on to indicate that "the most visible newcomers . . . are headquartered within ten blocks of the intersection of 14th and K streets in Washington."

These interest groups are gathering together to share a common interest: taxpayer money. Now, what can be wrong with people sharing a common interest in the national government? Is this not democracy? But the problem lies in what is done with the money that their lobbyists give to public officials. The result is a populace that is fragmented into thousands of splinter groups, each one striving to live at the expense of the others.

Perhaps another law is in order? But the justice clause in the US Constitution, if observed, would eliminate lobbying. Now, the First Amendment mentions freedom of assembly and petition to government "for a redress of grievances." However, there is nothing in the language of the amendment about bringing money along with the petition or that any official is authorized to accept it even if brought.

The notion of group rights plays directly into the hands of the elite class. Members know that a fragmented citizenry cannot practically unite in an organized rebellion against the oligarchy. With more money coming into Washington with each passing year, the system only becomes more deeply entrenched.

Morgan argued:

We must face the fact that beginning after World War II, and especially over the past twenty years, the American law of civil rights and liberties has been increasingly manipulated, redefined, and expanded at the urging of people with little understanding or sympathy for the traditions and ideas on which this body of law is properly based. A consequence of this, largely unintended by the rights-and-liberties militants, has been to marginally disable major American institutions, both governmental and private. It has also rendered more difficult the already daunting task of maintaining minimum standards of public manners and morals.[39]

All this is done in the name of enhancing civil rights, a movement that began with the best of intentions but swept forward on a foundation of emotion and in the absence of reasoned discourse. The zealots did not stop with desegregation of schools as supported by the US Constitution; they went beyond this to force integration on a disapproving public through busing and quotas. Morgan commented, "Not for them to weigh and balance; it was for them to achieve 'social change.' . . . concentrating on their moral mission, became more and more remote from public opinion, and indeed from common sense."

There was a time when nongovernmental institutions, such as families, schools, churches, civic organizations, and neighborhood groups, operated based on an accepted moral cohesion to discourage deviance and crime. These combined to create a stronger influence on rates of crime than did numbers of police, their level of professionalism, and tough judges. Today top-down big government has undermined the effectiveness of these traditional institutions, because top-down actions predictably cause an increase in crime. (Recent news media hype about a decline in violent crime is misleading. In major cities since 1969 violent crime has risen by 40 percent.)

Plea bargaining and shorter sentences for some crimes puts criminals quickly back onto the streets, and the public is reassured by stiffer sentences for murderers and jammed-packed prisons. This tactic swells the statistics, which in the perception of the elites demands more police, SWAT teams, bigger weapons, and deeper penetration of government into private life. The privileged class in its luxurious gated communities does not care if these actions only make the situation worse; the public image is that of caring and doing something. The hidden agenda is the eventual attainment of a police state, when individual rights will all but vanish (see Chapter 10).

Putting patrol officers in cars and rushing them to trouble spots means they ignore the ordinary chores of a police officer, such as checking doors, helping citizens in difficulty, breaking up gangs of loitering youths when the noise bothers merchants, and so on. Small wonder that cops are not perceived as friends by the middle class (who don't get to know them) and as the enemy by the lower classes (who are harassed by powerful strangers).

Admittedly, high-speed chases and shoot-outs make more exciting viewing on the evening news, but innocents who must suffer the consequences prefer a more mundane existence. Furthermore, there is the fear of being bothered by disorderly people like panhandlers, drunks, addicts, loud teenagers, prostitutes, and so on. Cops in cars have little to do with these problems as they are preoccupied with more serious offenses, which could be sharply reduced if police and citizens were to cooperate with one another.

This problem seems to admit a relatively easy solution: put more patrol officers on the beat. This has been tried with some success. The difficulty lies in lawyers and other rights activists who object to police officers stopping people to ask for identification and an explanation of their presence in a time and place that arouses suspicion. The courts favor the activists over policemen and -women.

Experts (read: lawyers) among the rights industry people have fogged the English language, which increases demand for their services. This is nothing new: Doctors and lawyers have been doing this for centuries. But the effect also tends to draw to its practitioners responsibility for interpreting rights law and making new rights into law, a group Morgan described as "an increasingly closed guild." Because government is force, this concentration of power by lawyers tends to reduce ordinary citizens to the role of serfs, as described in Hayek's famous book *The Road to Serfdom*.[40] As with democracy, individual freedom is a delicate flower that must be constantly nurtured.

Politicians on the campaign trail appeal to groups in several ways. One is to provide favoritism in law making (if the price is right), and another consists in offering benefits to groups. In 1996 there was a typically Clintonesque instance in which the latter tactic assumed its zenith. First there was a mandatory forty-eight-hour minimum stay in the hospital for childbirth, which appealed to women aged eighteen to forty. Then the Senate recommended a law to require mammograms for women aged forty to fifty. Finally, a mastectomy bill would require a long hospital stay for women over age fifty. The combination comprehensively covered all voting-age women, and the ever cooperative media spread the word shortly before the fall election.

"Talking heads" earn livings from manipulating words and symbols instead of rolling up their sleeves and sweating a little. They fit comfortably into the elite class, and so they get disproportionate media coverage. This coverage helps elevate charisma and drama over the mundane task of producing and distributing products and services that people want and buy.

Talking heads attempt to equate intellectual ability with intelligence, but thinking citizens can see through their pontificating. Unfortunately, the rush and whoosh of today's lifestyles mean there are few thinking citizens who can separate wheat from chaff. When presumably thinking judges and lawyers cooperate in the scheme, the implications are frightening.

Throughout US history it has been true that local institutions, such as well-run churches, schools, civic organizations, and charities, have been necessary for a successful society. When these are undermined by whatever force, the importance of the family as a foundation for individual morality increases. But without the support of these institutions, socially desired family cohesion is often poor or lacking.

Lawyers concentrate on rights, because if people accepted responsibility for what they say and do there would be little need for lawyers. If everyone concentrates on getting more rights and neglects responsibility for their actions, there can be no civilized society; no matter how many laws on the books, it would be law of the jungle.

By Definition, Government Is Force

George Washington said, "Government is not reason, it is not eloquence—it is force! Like fire it is a dangerous servant and fearful master; never for a moment should it be left to irresponsible action."

Thomas Jefferson said, "The God who gave us life, gave us liberty at the same time: the hand of force may destroy, but cannot disjoin them." Jefferson said citizens have their God-given liberty regardless of what government does, but government can make citizens' lives miserable nonetheless. (He saw this misery in France during his service as ambassador.)

Adolf Hitler said, "I am restoring to force its original dignity, that of the source of all greatness and the creatrix of order."

Rose Wilder Lane commented,

> *What holds the public official to his oath? Nothing but his conscience, and the vigilance of multitudes of citizens. His honor and patriotism in theory carry him in office even though he has sworn to obey a constitution that limits his personal power. But incentives tied to the negative side of human nature tempt him to seek personal power and prestige. If he wants to do good (as he sees good) to the citizens, he needs more power. If he wants to be re-elected, he needs more power .... If he wants money, he needs more power; .... And what prevents him from using more power? Constitutional law, words on paper. Its only force is moral.*[41]

Friedman showed that government frequently forces people to act against their own interests in the name of a general interest that is never spelled out in detail.[42] These forces "are therefore countered by one of the strongest and most creative forces known to man—the attempt by millions of individuals to promote their own interests, to live their lives by their own values. . . . It is also one of the major strengths of a free society and explains why governmental regulation does not strangle it."

Most citizens today devote little time and thought to government except during election campaigns, and even this effort is undermined by campaigns strung out until they are nearly continuous. Therefore the threat of a negative vote has no impact, especially when pressure groups and money enter into the picture.

A hundred years ago a judge would listen to a case and determine what an offender must do to make restitution to the victim and the family. Everyone in town cooperated to see that the miscreant did exactly as required.

Civil law settles disputes between citizens, whereas in criminal law the issue is between one or more citizens and the government. There has been a long-term trend in this country—moving away from civil law and toward criminal law. This trend draws power away from citizens and toward the elites, as it both increases demand for lawyers and ultimately forces ordinary citizens to live in fear of the law. The second of these outcomes is insidious in that on the surface a citizen may not feel threatened, but after reading about and looking at thousands of newscasts that report on terrible crimes, a natural tendency to keep a low profile and not speak out against government creeps into his or her psyche.

A recent example had President Bush promising to go after identity thieves and "make it a criminal offense to sell a person's social security number." This is correctly a civil matter between victim and thief. Government may help identify and catch the latter, but then the matter should be resolved through tort law. Mr. Bush probably won thousands of votes with his campaign promise, but following through means yet another bureaucracy and big government growing bigger.

Lane noted,

> *Stupid men believe that force can improve other men's morals. . . . They dream that because a law can make any action a crime, it can stop that action. . . . To these ardent reformers who want to do good (as they see good) by using force upon the greatest number of their inferiors, add the groups of those who want to rob others by force without risking going to jail.*

Lane argued that it is illogical to have people who produce nothing barking commands at people who produce and contribute to economic development.

Harry Browne, in his book *Why Government Doesn't Work*, wrote: "But there are far more prisons today than there were forty years ago, far more police, far tougher laws . . . far tougher sentencing, far more money spent. [But this] has done nothing to make you safer. . . . [The] crime rate has risen sharply since the 1950s. Obviously, more government hasn't worked."[43]

Public officials in Washington and in state governments know that most of this avalanche of laws will not be obeyed. They use the convenient reasoning that people want to feel safe and secure to justify piling on still more laws and regulations, many of which interfere with the exercise of citizens' natural rights. So long as citizens refrain from thinking and talking among themselves about this situation, it will only grow worse.

James Bovard in his powerful book *Lost Rights*, said: "(Then) Attorney general Janet Reno recently told a group of federal law enforcement officers: 'You are part of a government that has given its people more freedom … than any other government in the history of the world.' If freedom is a gift from the government to the people, then government can rightfully take freedom away."[44] Not only is Reno's pronouncement misleading, it is false. Bovard made a vitally important point when he argued that in a free society freedom is not given to the people.

Rather, government helps citizens to protect their God-given freedom from the depredations of big government. (It is amazing that Reno apparently did not understand this basic tenet of democracy.)

Today there are thirty times as many laws on the books as there were 100 years ago. Agencies publish about 200 pages of new rules and regulations in the *Federal Register* every day.

Law enforcement officials seize apartment buildings to punish landlords for not eliminating drug dealing (but they leave drug-infested public housing projects alone for some reason). The Justice Department gives money to informants, and so thousands cooperate in seizures of private assets and arrests of dealers, often without due process of law. Because the Fourth Amendment to the US Constitution (preventing unreasonable searches and seizures) is ignored, the victims have no recourse.

This means any bum with a personal vendetta against someone else can legally harass him or her at will. The situation in large cities is reminiscent of the old Soviet Union's KGB: Ordinary Russians lived in constant fear of a 2 AM knock on their doors. Furthermore, no compensation is given for private property seized through force.

Bovard noted: "If Congress proposed to forcibly alter all private deeds and titles in the US by adding a clause stating that the government acquires ownership rights if any law enforcement official hears a rumor about a property's possible illicit use, the public backlash would raze capitol hill. But, increasingly, that is the law of the land." The rules of evidence are ignored, a person is guilty until proven innocent, and there is no access to a lawyer. In practice the policy is a convenient way for local police forces to augment their salaries.

Browne analyzed the contents of the infamous 1993 health care proposal.

> *In the . . . debate of 1992–94, words like compassion, right, need, and fairness showed up frequently. But a number of relevant words were ignored. For example, I never heard the words force or coercion in public discussion. . . . There are some revealing terms in the proposal—such as prison (which shows up seven times), penalty (111 times), fine (6), enforce (83), prohibit (47), mandatory (24), limit (231), obligation (51), require (901), and so on.*

It appears that government was dead set on seeing that all citizens had health coverage, even if it had to force-feed it to them.

If government forces insurance companies to cover people regardless of previous health conditions, most people would not buy insurance until they develop a chronic illness. This was tried in the state of Washington, where the government forced companies to accept patients with chronic illnesses. The result was thousands of such people moving to Washington, and the flight from the state of nineteen companies.

Public officials who believe everyone should be equally well off economically never say how much inequality they are willing to tolerate simply because they cannot. Even if complete equality were possible it could never stay put, because the talented and energetic would no longer have any incentive to work hard to keep the indolent in clover. But the political appeal of the notion persists, due to people's natural concern for the underprivileged. Therefore government continues to experiment with use of force against society's more productive people.

Urban renewal is another case in point. This program began in 1949 with the goal of placing every family in a decent home and suitable living environment. But between that time and 1971 the government razed five times as many homes as it built, and forcibly evicted about 1 million people from their dwellings and businesses.

Bovard mentioned one homeowner named Kam Chin,

> *who, with her husband, lost her art supply store, which she had spent 15 years building up. Chin had fled China in 1969 after the communist government seized her father's art supply store. The New York Times reported that the couple saw the problem as much the same as in Communist China. "They're doing the same thing," Mrs. Chin said of the city. "They condemn my property. They take it away like in a communist country. Not only that, but they give it to the rich. The whole thing is really sick."*

Big government's force is not restricted to large cities. In 1992 the Department of Agriculture made it a federal crime for California farmers to sell nectarines less than 2 and 5/16 inches in diameter and peaches less than 2 and 3/8 inches. In a court case in Texas, federal prosecutors argued that if a company "put the contents of one eyedropper of hazardous waste into the ocean, the entire ocean then becomes hazardous waste under the law."

Some years ago Friedman observed: "The private economy has become an agent of the federal government. . . . At least fifty percent of the total productive resources of our nation are now being organized through the political market. In that very important sense, we are more than half socialist." The average citizen today works more than half of each year to pay the cost of government taxes and regulations.

Those who argue that the big multinational corporations rule over most people are reminded that no company can force young people into military service, imprison them for behavior it disapproves of, or tell them where they cannot go. Unrestrained government does all these things and worse. Paine stated that being forced to pay for abuse of personal freedom is "the excess of slavery."

Some of the wealthier members of the not-quite-elite class are acting on their own. *The Economist* reported "abandoning the state: living on private roads, sending its children to private schools, paying for its own private police force, playing golf at private clubs. Why bother supporting public service when you get all yours delivered privately?"[45]

Two forces drive this trend: increasing wealth and declining faith in government and public services. Quite possibly further progress will see such communities setting up and operating their own governments, with minimal political influence and undermining of personal freedoms permitted from outside the gates.

This chapter concludes with a quote from Ayn Rand's compelling novel *Atlas Shrugged*. In view of what has been discussed, there is a lesson in it. Protagonist Francisco d'Anconia holds forth:

> *Such looters believe it safe to rob defenseless men, once they've passed a law to disarm them. But their loot becomes the magnet for other looters. . . . Then the race goes, not to the ablest at production, but to those most ruthless at brutality. When force is the standard, the murderer wins over the pickpocket. And then that society vanishes, in a spread of ruins and slaughter.*
>
> *Do you wish to know whether that day is coming? Watch money. Money is the barometer of a society's virtue. When you see that trading is done, not by consent, but by compulsion—when you see that in order to produce, you need to obtain permission from men who produce nothing—when you see that money is flowing to those who deal, not in goods, but in favors—when you see that men get richer by graft and by pull than by work, and your laws don't protect you against them, but protect them against you—when you see corruption being rewarded and honesty becoming a self-sacrifice—you may know that your society is doomed.*

Notes

1. Anthony de Jasay, *The State*. Liberty Fund, 1998.
2. Thomas Paine, *Rights of Man*. 1791.
3. Harry Browne, *Why Government Doesn't Work*. St. Martin's Press, 1995.
4. James C. Miller, *Monopoly Politics*. Hoover Press, 1999.
5. Lewis Lapham, *The Wish for Kings*. Grove Press, 1993.
6. Edward O. Wilson, *On Human Nature*. Harvard University Press, 1978.
7. *The Economist*, "The Invisible Hand." September 20, 1997, p. 17.
8. Miller, *Monopoly Politics*.
9. Robert J. Samuelson, *The Good Life and its Discontents: The American Dream in the Age of Entitlement 1945–1995*. Times Books, 1995.
10. William C. Mitchell and Randy T. Simmons, *Markets, Welfare and the Failure of Bureaucracy*. Westview Press, 1994.
11. Jeff Jacoby, "Ensnared in Government's Safety Nets." *News and Observer* (Raleigh, NC), November 1997.
12. Bill Kreuger, "Glaxo Agrees to Pull Lotronex." *News and Observer* (Raleigh, NC), November 29, 2000, p. 1A.
13. Browne, *Why Government Doesn't Work*.

14. James Michener, *This Noble Land: My Vision for America*. Random House, 1996.
15. *The Economist*, "Two Rules Good, Four Rules Bad." October 12, 1996, p. 85.
16. John Passmore, *The Perfectibility of Man*, 3rd ed. Liberty Fund, 2000.
17. Mitchell and Simmons, *Markets, Welfare and the Failure of Bureaucracy.*
18. Philip K. Howard, *The Death of Common Sense: How Law Is Suffocating America*. Warner Books, 1994.
19. Robert D. Putnam, *Bowling Alone: The Collapse and Revival of American Community*. Simon and Schuster, 2000.
20. Robert H. Bork, *Slouching Towards Gomorrah*. Harper Collins, 1996.
21. Milton Friedman, *Capitalism and Freedom*. University of Chicago Press, 1982.
22. *The Economist*, "The Imperial Presidency." November 3, 2001, p. 39.
23. Hans Sennholz (ed.), *Taxation and Confiscation*. Foundation for Economic Education, 1993.
24. Howard, *The Death of Common Sense.*
25. James Madison, Federalist Paper no. 10, in *The Federalist Papers*. Mentor, 1961.
26. Kevin Phillips, *Arrogant Capital*. Little, Brown, 1994.
27. Friedman, *Capitalism and Freedom.*
28. Paul Krugman, "A Crisis for Energy Producers." *News and Observer* (Princeton, NJ), May 23, 2001, p. 19A.
29. Martin L. Gross, *A Call for Revolution*. Ballantine Books, 1993.
30. Samuelson, *The Good Life and its Discontents.*
31. Paine, *Rights of Man.*
32. Howard, *The Death of Common Sense.*
33. Bork, *Slouching Towards Gomorrah.*
34. Richard E. Morgan, *Disabling America: The "Rights Industry" in Our Time.* Basic Books, 1984.
35. Blake Pirtle, "As the Walls Close In," in Claudia Whitman and Julie Zimmerman, (eds.) *Frontiers of Justice Volume 3: The Crime Zone*. Biddle, 2000.
36. John Leo, "A Dubious 'Diversity' Report." *US News*, June 23, 1997, p. 15.
37. Michael Berliner and Gary Hull, quoted in Donald N. Wood, *Post-Intellectualism and the Decline of Democracy: The Failure of Reason in the 20th Century*. Praeger, 1996.
38. Putnam, *Bowling Alone.*
39. Morgan, *Disabling America.*
40. Friedrich A. Hayek, *The Road to Serfdom*. University of Chicago Press, 1944.

41. Rose Wilder Lane, *The Discovery of Freedom*. Fox and Wilkes, 1993.
42. Friedman, *Capitalism and Freedom*.
43. Browne, *Why Government Doesn't Work*.
44. James Bovard, *Lost Rights: The Destruction of American Liberty*. St. Martin's Press, 1995.
45. *The Economist*, "America's New Utopias." September 1, 2001, p. 25.

CHAPTER EIGHT:
ASSUMPTIONS OF THE ELITE CLASS AND PERSONAL POWER SEEKING

When men are pure, laws are useless;
When men are corrupt, laws are broken.
—Benjamin Disraeli

Jeffrey Bell introduced his book *Populism and Elitism* with these assumptions:

Populism is optimism about people's ability to make decisions about their lives. Elitism is optimism about the decision-making ability of one or more elites, acting on behalf of other people. Populism implies pessimism about an elite's ability to make decisions for the people affected. Elitism implies pessimism about the people's ability to make decisions affecting themselves.[1]

There is an implication here of a lack of trust in someone else to do a good job of exerting control over a person's life. The recorded history of government indicates that this skepticism is well placed, due in large part to human nature.

Elites adhere to the PANG principle: People Are No Good. They are weak, stupid, incompetent, dishonest, and so on. Therefore they need direction from others to enjoy good lives through good government. The problem with this assumption is that if the premise is true, then why should anyone trust another human being or group to rule over him or her at all? The elites get around this truth by designating themselves as the "chosen few" who are good, who are willing to sacrifice a better life elsewhere to bring good government to the masses. Someone should ask: Who, or maybe what, chooses these people?

Acting on the elitist assumption, politicians in Washington, DC say to citizens "Our experts have studied your problems, we know what they are, and aren't you lucky? We're here to solve them for you." To reinforce the PANG principle, public officials create more problems for citizens by complicating the issues so that the average citizen cannot understand them (lawyers are accomplished at this skill). Thus confronted with frustration after frustration, citizens are tempted to throw up their hands and agree to allow the elites to "solve" the problems.

This abdication sets elite power in stone, even as it connects to the negative side of human nature.

Benjamin Franklin said:

> *Sir, there are two passions which have a powerful influence on the affairs of men . . . the love of power and the love of money. . . . When united in view of the same object, they have in many minds the most violent effects. Place before the eyes of such men a post of honor that shall at the same time be a place of profit, and they will move Heaven and earth to obtain it.*

The urge to personal power acts on some people exactly like a drug. They try a little of it, like it, reach for more, and eventually get hooked. The record throughout world history weighs in to support this conclusion.

Today's Washington elite class is a subset of the entire elite class; it consists of just half of one percent of the US population, but its money buys access and influence among the high and mighty way beyond its numbers. Ellen Miller is executive director of Public Campaign:

> *The public believes campaigns cost more and more with each election cycle; that those who give the money get something ordinary people don't get—access and influence over the system; that there is a nonstop fund-raising chase, so the candidates spend more time raising money than they spend doing other business; and that good people can't run for office without becoming enslaved to the system, which is both the money chase and the special-interest influence that ensues.*

She paused for a moment, then added, "They're right."

The collective wisdom of the mass of citizens nearly always stays close to the truth. In this instance the news media give out very little detail, but the public has gotten the message anyway. Getting together for political discussions and criticisms of ideas not only is a vital part of the democratic process but also enables citizens to bring out truth far more reliably. In the issue of money politics, the truth has become so obvious that suspicion has apparently spread broadly over the landscape even without extensive discussions among citizens. This development could be interpreted as a measure of the arrogance of the elite class, as they make little effort today to conceal the nature and extent of their underhanded dealings.

Concentration of Wealth in Washington

Alexander Hamilton noted that "man is ambitious, vindictive and rapacious." By nature, humans crave power and wealth and also revenge. Hamilton understood these negative incentives within people. He wrote most of the eighty-five *Federalist Papers* in 1788, in which he, James Madison, and John Jay urged ratification of the new constitution then under public discussion. The major thrust of that document lies in restraining these incentives that lurk within public officials, so that the positive side of human nature guides officials' behavior.

Thomas Paine said, "A constitution is the property of a nation, and not of those who exercise the government."[2] However, if citizens allow the concentration of great wealth in one place, such as Washington, the elites will be tempted to possess the constitution as their own. From this point forward the reality is "we" and "they." Government will no longer work with citizens to help them protect their rights, as the Constitution specifies. "What is called the splendor of a throne, is no other than the corruption of the state. It is made up of a band of parasites, living in luxurious indolence, out of the public taxes."

During World War II centralization of power was necessary if the United States was to help the Allies by supplying massive quantities of war matériel and by fighting a major war. It was only after the conflict that the economy took off and vast wealth began to flow into Washington. After previous wars, US governments had allowed the economy to settle back to its prewar mode with a small government.

But this time was different. Even though economists attributed to the war the force necessary to drag the economy out of the Great Depression, the political imperative among congressmen was to give President Franklin Roosevelt's New Deal programs credit for the recovery. Therefore the programs were allowed to continue operating even though the need for them had evaporated (churches and charities were again sufficient to help vastly reduced numbers of poor), and taxes were kept high to support them. The government has expanded rapidly ever since.

The free market disperses wealth because there are myriad opportunities to earn it, and there are few restrictions on the location of a typical business. On the other hand, Washington's huge masses of programs, laws, regulations, and money are concentrated in one place, where they can do serious damage to those who must live outside the system.

The original idea for expansion of regulation sprang from the apparent failure of the free market during the Great Depression. Officials in government claimed to have lost faith in the market as an efficient method of allocating such resources as land, labor, capital, and management expertise. The reality is that through a series of extremely poor policy decisions the government caused the Great Depression (politicians don't like to admit this truth).

The rise of elitism in a democracy leads to concentration of power in the central government, and by extension less active citizen participation in local government. The setting of community standards as a basis of civic pride has been preempted by a remote group of elites and their experts, who do not understand local concerns.

For the average citizen, participation in government has been reduced to elections, paying taxes, and viewing political races on TV. But the damage is done between elections. Richard Moe, a lawyer-lobbyist, said, "Because of regulation and so forth, everybody feels the need to be here—and they brought a lot of money with them."

Lapham described the result in detail:

> *The presumption of entitlement seeps downward through the whole of the government bureaucracy, and it is not surprising that the Congress in 1992 allocated $2.8 billion to the cost of its own privileges and comforts. The comparable sum in 1970 amounted to $343 million. . . . Over the last twenty years the Congress has increased the spending on itself by 705 percent—more than twice the 280 percent rise in inflation or the 311 percent rise in the defense budget. As the costs have increased, so also has the number of congressional household servants. . . . In the 1950s, [Congress] made do with a staff of 5,373; the two houses of Congress now employ a staff of 38,696.*
>
> *Each member of Congress . . . receives an annual salary of $129,500 [it's $141,000 now], but the pay is augmented by perquisites—worth an additional $38,722 a year. The pensions . . . as much as $155,000 a year . . . Together with the routine luxuries of free parking, subsidized meals, gymnasiums, attending physicians, valets, florists, and hair stylists, . . . services of 89 video producers—who arrange their publicity, and at least 4 upholsterers—who tend their office furniture."* [3]

All this is at taxpayer expense. Some years ago members of Congress became concerned about complaining citizens, so they slowed the frequency of their self-voted increases in salary. This did not affect pensions, however, which shot upward and are unique in that they compensate most retired members in amounts greater than their salaries while working.

The most recent bit of chicanery on congressional salary has members establishing a deadline beyond which a salary increase takes effect in the absence of a vote against it. Then a vote against is taken, just **after** the deadline. In this way each congressperson can tell his or her constituents that he voted against a raise but was outvoted.

Nobel Prize laureate Milton Friedman said,

> *Our minds tell us, and history confirms, that the great threat to freedom is the concentration of power. Government is necessary to preserve our freedom; yet by concentrating power in political hands, it is also a threat to freedom. Even though the men who wield this power initially be of good will and even though they be not corrupted by the power they exercise, the power will both attract and form men of a different stamp.* [4]

Friedman referred to the duality of human nature: originally the positive incentive—good will—but later the negative—(and also the attraction of office for the initially negatively inclined).

Taxpayers are spread around the countryside, they have diverse interests, they are not organized, and each has little time, money, or motivation to confront what Friedman referred to as the "Frankenstein monster." By contrast, elites are a small minority concentrated around Washington, they have single interests, they are organized around those interests, and they have lots of time and money. Put these attributes together, and it is obviously futile for a citizen to confront the monster.

Each taxpayer takes only a small additional hit with each new tax or regulation, and so it is not worth the effort to either complain loudly or organize a sufficient number of others similarly gouged. The elites have thus created a largely closed system.

One example will illustrate how misguided assumptions favor the elites over citizens. Bergland wrote:

> *First, people typically assume that polluters can only be stopped by regulatory officials working for the EPA or similar state agencies. Second, many assume that private owners of property have some perverse motivation to destroy its value in the pursuit of short-range profits alone. Third, many people think that only public spirited bureaucrats can manage forest, grazing lands or wilderness in a manner that does not destroy their long term value. Each of these assumptions is false.*[5]

These issues can be addressed locally through the notion of sanctity of property. That is, if some person or group dumps waste on someone else's property or person without consent, the victim has recourse through individual negotiation, publicity, mediation, arbitration, or, if all else fails, litigation. If many people are victimized they can organize at the local level, point out the nature of the damage and its cause, and request either a cease-and-desist order or compensation. Once they are organized, they can bring great pressure to bear on the offender.

However, if clean-air or clean-water politics is concentrated in Washington, polluting industries can concentrate their money and lobbying in the interest of gutting any laws or regulations that may be put into force. Furthermore, they can utilize their superior technical knowledge in support of their position. Recently one expert gave an opinion suggesting that today's air and water would be cleaner if the issues had remained local.

The second of Bergland's assumptions can be addressed by thinking like a landowner. The tax on land is based on its logical and efficient use and the potential for income from this use. If the owner destroys it for that use, he or she remains liable for tax. He might sell the land and thus avoid the tax, but in its present condition the owner will not find a buyer. Therefore most land managers will be oriented to long-term value, and they have a private incentive to learn how to manage their own land better than would a bureaucrat (which supports Bergland's third assumption).

As the heads of public officials get turned in a money-soaked Washington the traditional notion of public servant gradually metamorphoses into master in a classic role reversal. The citizens who pay for government end up as servants (anyone who has been audited by the IRS knows the feeling). Taxpayers have virtually no influence on lawmaking in the national government; the one who pays the piper no longer calls the tune.

In 1998 the Government Accounting Office (GAO) issued a report suggesting that the presence of mountains of money in Washington reduces concern about each dollar. This applies especially when it is someone else's money. The report demonstrated a failure to account for billions of dollars of property, equipment, materials, and supplies. The government could not accurately estimate the cost of most federal credit programs; it did not know the amounts of its various obligations; nor did responsible officials know the net costs of government operations.

The question comes down to how much real power a public official has if he or she lives from one pot of special interest money to the next one. He can sell influence in a monopoly government but this produces little value for the dollar that is of practical use to the average citizen, except to return a small portion of his own tax money to him in the form of pork and entitlements.

Today's Washington is literally awash in money. Place seekers, lobbyists, lawyers, "consultants," hacks, con artists, and thieves are streaming into the city. Most will become hooked on the money drug, if they have not already been victimized. There is little honor or friendship among these types of people, so when the population grows larger than some indefinite number they may turn against one another. Should this grisly scenario actually happen, the outcome would be unpredictable. (This will happen shortly after the enormous amount of tax money coming into Washington stops growing.)

THE BIG PLAYERS ON THE WASHINGTON STAGE

The title of this section appears to be flawed in that it reinforces Rose Wilder Lane's argument that based on millenniums of history, people tend to look up to an authority figure without questioning it.[6] This section expands on the reality that evolved, primarily since World War II, as the emphasis in governing and campaigning completed its shift from issues to personalities.

Alexander Hamilton thought:

> *It will always be far more easy for the State governments to encroach upon the national authorities than for the national government to encroach upon the State authorities. The proof of this proposition turns upon the greater degree of influence which the State governments, if they administer their affairs with uprightness and prudence, will generally possess over the people.*[7]

Hamilton never believed in democracy; yet he had the good practical sense to advocate ratification of the constitution as the best alternative at the time. To this end he wrote eloquently in the *Federalist Papers*.

The quotation has truth in it, but only when two very important "ifs" are resolved in a positive direction. The first of these is clearly mentioned: "If they administer their affairs with uprightness and prudence." Today's state government officials exhibit very little of this behavior, and with good reason. That reason connects with the second "if," which came into being much later and of which only a tiny minority of today's citizens are aware. It has been kept hidden for a reason, which will quickly become obvious.

Article I, section 3 of the Constitution states that senators shall be elected by state legislatures, but the Seventeenth Amendment removed this provision and required election by the people of each state. The surface rationale was obvious: It is clearly superior to have all elected public officials voted on directly by the citizens. What has been kept carefully hidden is the original intent of the founding fathers, who anticipated the eventual concentration of political power in the nation's capital and purposefully inserted section 3 in accordance with the principle of federalism. This principle requires an equal division of power between national and state governments. Put another way, the principle serves as a vitally important restraint on the personal power seeking of officials in the central government.

Therefore section 3 sent senators to Washington who would jealously guard the power of their state governments against growing central government power. But the effect of the Seventeenth Amendment, ratified on April 8, 1913, is to bypass state legislatures, thus removing this restraint. As implied, on this issue it was easy to fool the public and also officials in at least three quarters of the state legislatures (required to pass the amendment), who apparently thought they were responding to the public will. Thus the second "if" refers to the principle of federalism.

The elites often recruit the services of experts on issues to reinforce their arguments for rule over the masses. Recruitment is not difficult, so long as the elites hold the power of the purse. This power may suggest a lack of integrity among scientists and analysts, but thousands of these people depend on national government grants for funds to conduct research. This means a constant temptation to skirt the bounds of integrity while analyzing data and presenting results: The stream of grant money may dry up. In this way many experts' behavior is molded to suit the interests of the elite class.

In 1912 presidential candidate Woodrow Wilson said:

> *What I fear . . . is a government of experts. . . . God forbid that in a democratic country we should resign the task [of governing] and give the government over to experts. What are we if we are to be scientifically taken care of by a small*

number of gentlemen who are the only men who understand the job? Because if we don't understand the job, then we are not a free people.[8]

Bringing in experts with their sophisticated terminology and research methods will surely cause a "complexification" of the issues, to the point where the average citizen cannot understand them and is tempted to hand power over to public officials and their expert lackeys. Wilson's fear was real. This is one of several forces that separate governors from governed and generate alienation and mutual contempt.

Concentration of immense power in Washington has caused top public officials to see themselves as powerful players. Power in the absence of integrity will inflate egos. The following discussion provides examples.

Harry Truman may have been the last politician to perform well as president (he was originally a farmer, soldier, haberdasher, and county judge). Dwight Eisenhower was a good leader, but he was not a politician. Those who followed were poor or worse in the job, largely because government grew too big to manage and the negative side of human nature asserted its influence on their behavior.

Members of Congress assert their authority by passing volumes of laws and pump their egos by getting in front of TV cameras as often as possible. Many citizens do not realize that officials responded to public pressure to televise legislative sessions by prohibiting the cameras from panning the Senate or House of Representative chambers. This is because most speakers direct their remarks at a chamber that is nearly empty, so this restriction deceives viewers.

Little serious thought is required to conclude accurately that the absentees are most often busy raising money for their reelection campaigns. Members of Congress know that to become big players they must be reelected several times, and this requires big money.

In 1993, one analyst thought that members of the House of Representatives behaved like they were in business for themselves instead of their president or their party. He did not mention citizens, whose interests said members are sworn to represent. Lapham described the antics of one pedigreed and presumptuous bureaucrat on his arrival in Washington:

What had been a public or common entrance on Fifteenth Street [Robert] Mosbacher appropriated to his private use, decorating it with a red awning . . . and furnishing the adjacent lobby with an extravagant show of flowers. When the work was completed, Mosbacher announced that the new entrance was reserved for the comings and goings of only six people.[9]

In 1420 the Forbidden City was built in Beijing, China, for Ming Dynasty emperors. The huge central gate on the edge of Tian 'Anmen Square could be used only by the emperor.

Today there are around 80,000 professional lobbyists in Washington, about half of whom are active at any one time. These people are generally lawyers, and their business is helping those who pay them very well to influence legislation and regulation in favor of their sponsors. When calling on members of Congress they frequently bring great quantities of money, and because members need similar quantities for reelection there have evolved mutually beneficial relationships. It is thus easy to see why the analyst mentioned above omitted ordinary citizens in his remark.

Concentrating great political power in Washington makes buying influence more efficient than when power is dispersed. It concentrates minds as well as money, but it also alienates the citizen from the political process.

Most of the lawyers were hired by the government and special interest groups. Japan has 1,000 engineers for every 100 lawyers; in the United States these figures are reversed. Engineers are far more often employed in the private sector, where they contribute toward wealth creation and economic growth. Lawyers in Washington contribute practically nothing toward economic growth; the money they take in is transferred, not invested. Some are paid in excess of $600 per hour. Ronald Cass, dean of the Boston University School of Law, said: "The question . . . will be whether lawyers are serving any real purpose in life or whether lawyers are simply engaging in semantic arguments that don't make sense to ordinary people."

Williams commented on the tornado in Washington after lawyer Jack Quinn won a Clinton pardon for fugitive financier Marc Rich.[10]

> *The backbiting offers a rare glimpse at the unwritten tenets of the Washington access culture. . . . The first sin was to get caught at a game that is played every day of the week in Washington. In seeking a pardon for a notorious fugitive who had never been tried, Quinn may have played a gaudier hand than most do. But it was still just a daring version of the trade that is plied by every lawyer in Washington who claims a practice in "government relations."*

Williams assured her readers that after some time for the smoke and dust to settle, Quinn will be back plying his sleazy trade. Her prediction is reliable, because the money is just too good.

Eric Alterman wrote: "The punditocracy is a tiny group of highly visible political pontificators who make their living offering 'inside political opinions and forecasts' in the elite national media. And it is their debate, rather than any semblance of a democratic one, that determines the parameters of political discourse in the nation today."[11]

These people exert great personal power, and they are accountable to no one. Their writings and speeches have gone far to reduce Washington to an outsized Peyton Place. Citizens are not informed by the news media and the punditocracy; rather, they are either entertained or mesmerized.

So long as this situation persists pundits can work their magic through manipulating attitudes and empty perceptions. They care nothing for democratic debate, as this would undermine their power base. Indeed, they strive to convince the public that their debates can replace democratic ones. Are they not as close to the issues as anyone can be? What citizens don't realize is that substantive issues long ago departed the scene in Washington, having been displaced by money, big players' personalities, sound bites, and empty perceptions.

Thousands of laws are written in vague terms and passed by Congress. They are written in this way to enhance the power of the bureaucrats who write and implement regulations based on them. Furthermore, due to the Seventeenth Amendment, state legislatures have few resources with which to fight back whenever the national government decides to force them to comply with even more regulations. In this way state taxes are driven upward and blame is deflected away from public officials in Washington.

As already mentioned, bureaucrats thrive on problems and not solutions. Therefore bureaucracies continue to grow ever larger even when the original purpose for their existence may have vanished. Roosevelt's New Deal laws and regulations are a case in point; some of these are still on the books over sixty-five years later.

A vital traditional role of journalism in a free country is to provide constant criticism of government. Today accurate reporting is limited to who died, the weather forecast, who won the ball game and the score, who killed whom, and any big fires, earthquakes, wars, hurricanes, or floods. Professional journalists with masters' degrees think it is beneath them to go into local bars and attend civic meetings to collect news of real use to readers; this is one reason why people don't read newspapers as much.

As mentioned, TV news no longer informs. Today's journalists would have people believe they are reporting truth about the high and mighty in Washington, but were they to do this they would quickly lose their vital access to the big players. Therefore they and cooperating TV news anchors put their spin on existing news, which was collected by someone else and not analyzed for significant meaning before going on the air.

Writer Ken Auletta stated: "When you're treated like a celebrity, and people know your face, you become full of yourself. It robs you of the humility you need to do your job as a journalist, which is fundamentally based on asking other people questions."[12] In 1993 TV celebrity Sam Donaldson said, "I'm trying to get a little ranching business started in New Mexico. . . . making out those government forms." In supposedly relating to the struggles of the average small businessperson, he continued to draw his base salary of $2 million a year. Later he did a piece that attacked farm subsidies, without mentioning that "those government forms" enabled him to collect almost $97,000 in sheep and mohair subsidies over two years.

High drama, sex, and violence have displaced substantive news, and therefore an uninformed public cannot vote intelligently, much less actively participate in government. The news keeps them entertained and lulled. Like sheep grazing, they collect their monthly subsidies in the form of entitlements.

The use of the term *big player* is not based on random selection. The action in Washington today is in fact a theater in which, judging by the price of admission, each taxpayer is occupying one of the best seats in the house. But all he or she can do is watch, and so much is going on behind the drawn curtain between scenes that he begins to wonder if it is worth the time to watch.

Phillips identified several political upheavals in the past, which he called revolutions.[13] They occurred about once each generation, beginning in 1832. It is interesting to note that his argument related to Jefferson's recommendation that a new constitution and government be established every thirty years or so. "No longer. Yesteryear's transformability started to vanish as Washington expanded in the 1930s; then the larger system's political fluidity and openness to a purge began to dissipate as Washington mushroomed into the power center of the world during the 1940s, 1950s and 1960s—and the Permanent Washington took shape."

Phillips pointed to the causes of permanent Washington as power and money, and also the fact that the political party out of power no longer functions as a loyal opposition. This means that the parties are colluding with one another, just as Thomas Paine warned in 1792: "While they appear to quarrel they agree to plunder." Paine was not alone in this suspicion; in 1887 E. L. Godkin charged that party politicians "are all banded together for plunder."

Someone suggested that people could be divided into two groups: those who want to **be someone**, and those who want to **do something**. Lapham compared the palace court of King Louis XIV with today's Washington to beautifully illustrate how a member of the first group tries to be someone.[14]

At the court of Louis XIV in 17th-century France, people occupied themselves with the great work of making small distinctions: those greeted at the door; those offered arm chairs; those deemed worthy of being seen off in their coaches. In official Washington in late 20th-century America the court occupies itself with similar distinctions: those assigned government cars; those awarded parking spaces at National Airport; those invited to sit in Jack Kent Cooke's box at RFK stadium. Against the sum of such tremendous trifles, the questions of yesterday's riot or tomorrow's debt beat as heavily as the wings of moths.

Gross provided another example:

When Harry Truman was vice president, he was frugal (actually cheap). He had a staff of four and lived in a two-bedroom apartment on Connecticut Avenue, for which he paid the $140 a month rent out of his own pocket. Today . . . the VP [Al Gore at the time] lives royally in a mansion on Navy grounds and enjoys a motorcade of cars, a jet plane, a $90,000 entertainment allowance, sixty employees, and four government offices including one in Tennessee, which has nothing to do with his being vice-president.[15]

The mansion was recently refurbished at a cost of $3.5 million in taxpayer money. "It is proving to be an expensive ritual, which is peculiar because Mr. Gore is supposedly a waste cutter."

Gross went on to report the congressional vote on a $151 billion highway bill. Leaders forced the vote, even though there were no copies of the bill available for reading prior to the vote. Apparently it is not just ordinary citizens who think their votes do not count for much.

Then Gross pointed out another hidden taxpayer subsidy:

> *In addition to his regular staff of nineteen, the democratic whip . . . has seventeen party workers. But, most amazingly, they are not paid by the party. They are all on the federal payroll. That's only the beginning. The majority leader, who incidentally is elected by nobody except his party pals, has twenty-six party workers on the taxpayer tab, including three foreign affairs advisers. . . . The bill for his party work, picked up by all of us, runs an extra $1 million a year.*

The House of Representatives has a total of 160 party employees, all on the taxpayer dime. The senate has 201. Gross: "Like the congressional leadership, political parties are mentioned nowhere in the Constitution. . . . In his farewell address in New York, Washington warned 'of the baneful effects of party.'" Party chairmen have tremendous personal power, yet they are accountable to no one.

Perhaps the most serious recent contender for a prize for the biggest ego is Henry Kissinger. Isaacson said: "This 'reluctance to be reduced to the dimensions of a mere mortal,' he readily admitted, was also driven by his own ego, the size of which amused even him. When he arrived in Rome to do a television special for NBC, he was told the Pope was busy planning a beatification ceremony for two new saints. 'Who is the other one?' he asked."[16]

Summarizing, the big players in Washington are in the business of micromanaging the entire economy, putting into force myriad laws and regulations. There is a benefit somewhere in all this for every special interest whenever the price is right. But the grim reality is that the government cannot manage itself, and in mismanaging the economy public officials injure it and make life more difficult and expensive for everyone in it. Well, not for *everyone*. The big players live in their own separate economy. A thinking citizen would wonder how this dichotomy connects to democracy.

Rule of Law Sacrificed to Personal Power

> *Power tends to corrupt and absolute power corrupts absolutely.*
>
> —Lord Acton

The democratic principle of Rule of Law was built into the Constitution by the founding fathers. Its intent was to allow no one in government to violate any law, no matter the time, position, or circumstances, with absolutely no exceptions. However, the principle got off to a questionable start because lawyers in government at the time naturally clung to their previous training in British common law when compiling the Constitution.

British common law relied heavily on precedent as a guide to lawyers' arguments and judges' decisions. A particular case may therefore turn on a similar one that was decided centuries in the past. Because many law cases connect with human nature, the core of the problem is not the distance into the past but human nature acting on laws made at any time. That is, if a regime of government is not democratic it is top-down, and therefore laws are much more often made to favor officials in government rather than citizens. The result is a massive volume of law that ill-serves the people who must live under it. This evaluation holds more or less for practically every government in Europe over the past 500 years.

Paine wrote in 1792:

> *Government by precedent, without any regard to the principle of the precedent, is one of the vilest systems that can be set up. In numerous instances, the precedent ought to operate as a warning, and not as an example, and requires to be shunned instead of imitated; but instead of this, precedents are taken in the lump, and put at once for constitution and for law.*[17]

Paine's admonition should have been a guide, especially in this infant country where precedent in law was all but nonexistent. His argument acquires more weight when it is considered that in a democracy citizens make the laws under which they consent to be governed.

Paine wrote during the middle of the Industrial Revolution. This great technological upheaval created the capacity for society to advance far more rapidly than it could have previously. Therefore decisions in law that reach backward over centuries for support are rendered even more irrelevant. Few people of Paine's time or in the present have thought through this important issue.

In view of these facts, it is not surprising that the national government would eventually become something less than what was envisioned by the founding fathers. Their vision, although far-reaching, was less than perfect.

In a despotic regime without Rule of Law, political winds change direction frequently, but laws tend to remain on the books forever. Lawyers are too busy drafting new laws to be bothered with removing old ones, and their overbearing impact generates a demand for more lawyers to try to make some sense of them. Furthermore, if these lawyers are separated from the citizenry, their work tends to most greatly benefit themselves and those who are close to them.

Hayek commented on a

> *general distinction between Rule of Law and arbitrary government. Under the first, the government confines itself to fixing rules determining the conditions under which the available resources may be used, leaving to the individuals the decision for what ends they are to be used. Under the second, the government directs the use of the means of production to particular ends.*[18]

The second is top-down government, so it is not difficult to surmise which "particular ends" will be selected.

To accomplish equality of results among citizens, a government must forcibly discriminate against some of them and in favor of others. This is incompatible with Rule of Law, because under this principle all must receive equal treatment. Indeed, this is the basis of justice under Rule of Law; it is incompatible with arbitrarily determined distributive justice, even if administered by the chosen few. Similarly, any private individual who discriminates against another individual is undermining Rule of Law and should therefore be restrained from continuing that behavior. Equal political freedom for individuals is a fundamental principle, which restrains government as well as other individuals.

Carried to its logical conclusion, Rule of Man (in essence, government by whim) can be described as found in Rand's book: "Questions of truth do not enter into social issues. Principles have no influence on public affairs. Reason has no power over human beings. Logic is impotent. Morality is superfluous."[19] Rule of Law connects to principle; Rule of Man abandons principle. This conclusion may seem extreme until Wylie's comment on human nature puts it into perspective: "Man's ego—the importance he puts upon his limited awareness of who and what he is—has become all of man to man, so far as man himself is concerned. This unholy, starveling error is responsible for the trouble he has with himself. And there are national egos just as there are individual and mob egos."[20] If a man does not know himself, he cannot discipline himself, and this means open season for the negative tugs of human nature (see Chapter 19).

Confucius lived in China in the sixth century bc, and he believed in Rule of Man. The emperor was considered to be Son of Heaven; his personal power was truly arbitrary. Thus began a long history of rulers who subscribed to Rule of Man. Its attraction was not only in that it fed the ego, but personal power was unlimited because the ruler was accountable to no one.

Greider brought the concept forward to the present:

> *Once again, the terms of the law were subverted . . . by strenuous industry lobbying. Once again. . . protracted litigation. The message . . . is that restoring reliable authority to law is not something that even the lawmakers are likely to accomplish on their own. The political system itself is stacked against the law . . . even laws made with reinforced steel.*[21]

The Economist noted: "If right-wingers stand for one thing, you would have thought if you had been listening carefully during the past 20 years, it is individual freedom against the collectivist, oppressive, intrusive forces of the state."[22] If a thinking citizen had listened carefully enough and reflected on what was heard, he or she would have concluded that all of it was rhetoric aimed at harvesting votes. Once in office it has been, is, and quite possibly will be business as usual in big government.

The elder President George Bush believed in nonpartisan government, which in his view translated into administrative decree. However, in a democracy every issue is partisan; that is, there is active and argumentative dialog preceding enactment of every issue into law. At one time on his watch, Bush requested $30 billion for covert activities, mostly for use in the Central Intelligence Agency (CIA), which is one of some twelve cloak-and-dagger agencies in government. (Prior to becoming president, Bush had served as director of the CIA.)

Due to a convenient rationale often called national security, no citizen or organization outside a severely limited group of people in government could know what Bush would do with that huge lump of taxpayer money. Even today the CIA is authorized to take unlimited money from any or all of a variety of other agencies. This rationale is ancient, having kept Rule of Man alive and thriving for centuries.

Like father, like son according to *The Economist*:

> *The collapse of the twin towers [in the terrorist attack of September 11, 2001] jolted both Mr. Bush and his office back into life. Washington immediately reorganized itself around the executive branch. And Mr. Bush equally immediately reorganized his presidency around the struggle against terrorism. The distracted dilettante became a purposeful monarch. Almost at once, the administration persuaded Congress to approve a $40 billion recovery package that also strengthened intelligence and security. An anti-terrorism bill that hugely increases the executive's power was also passed quickly.*[23]

In a democracy even the president is a public servant. How on earth can any current president retain an appropriate mentality with hundreds of "assistants" constantly fawning at his feet? He would seem to have little choice but to assume the mantle and scepter of a king (which is the point that Lapham made in *The Wish for Kings*[24]). Greider: "The presidency cannot be counted upon to uphold the law because the White House has become the capstone of lawless government . . . an institution that rewrites law behind closed doors for the benefit of the few who have political access." Note that the Constitution authorizes Congress, and only this body, to write law. The president heads the executive branch of government and is charged by the Constitution to enforce Congress-made law. But today he has a huge staff of bureaucrats who are doing precisely as Greider described.

Such rewriting is a clear violation of the Rule of Law. An enlightened citizen who watches the presidential inauguration would be appalled to think of the millions of people who believe that a president is sincere when he places his left hand on the Bible and, with great pomp and ceremony, raises his right hand to recite the oath of office, guided by the chief justice of the US Supreme Court. He solemnly swears to protect and defend the Constitution, all the while knowing that he does not mean it.

In his 1993 inaugural speech President Bill Clinton said: "And so I say to all of you here, let us resolve to reform our politics so that power and privilege no longer shut down the voice of the people. Let us give this capital back to the people to whom it belongs." A few days later the Democratic National Committee deposited $3.5 million that it had just raised. The occasion was a dinner in New York's Lincoln Center, in which the guest of honor was Bill Clinton.

Dowd remarked,

> *With [the] Monica Lewinsky [scandal], Bill Clinton subverted the legal system and sullied the presidency. With Marc Rich, he perverted the legal system and may have traded a constitutional power for personal benefit. . . . He can't argue that our interest in this transgression is a violation of his privacy. The Clintons ran a cash-and-carry White House. They were either hawking stuff or carting it off.*[25]

Selling coffee to supporters in that public building at $50,000 a cup comes to mind.

Krauthammer noted,

> *Perhaps even more outrageous than the Rich pardon was the commutation he issued to the four N.Y. Hasidim who set up a totally fraudulent religious institution to bilk the government out of millions of dollars. . . . Now, we can't prove that Bill Clinton traded this pardon for this isolated sect's political support of Hillary . . . but we do know that this village voted 1,359 to 10 for Mrs. Clinton.*[26]

Krauthammer continued: "Perhaps the measure of a president's corruption—a Presidential Corruption Index—is how many laws are changed in order to prevent future presidents from acting as scandalously as this one. . . . There is not a flurry of proposed changes in the law." He concluded: "We're also in the midst of a movement to reform the campaign finance laws, which were totally shredded by the 1996 Clinton campaign."

All this was committed with impunity. These acts will enter history as a shocking and embarrassing smear on the United States of America.

Clinton established a new dimension for sleaze, paving the way for Gary Condit's towering arrogance and scandal. *The Economist*:

> *But [Condit's] is the perfect Washington story in a more profound way: because of what it reveals about the way the city works. It demonstrates the casual hubris of the powerful, and also shows what extraordinary methods ordinary people have to adopt if they are to combat the dissimulation of an insider.*
>
> *For what else besides hubris can explain the congressman's behavior? He conducted an affair with an impressionable young woman entirely on his own terms. . . . And when she disappeared, he put his own reputation above every-*

thing else. He not only failed to come clean with the police about the nature of their relationship; he even bamboozled his own staff into lying on his behalf.[27]

Condit probably thought he could get away with this, as did the president. "Bill Clinton not only lied about his relationship with Monica Lewinsky; he used the White House spin machine to discredit people who tried to tell the truth."

Washington insiders have challenged the epitome of arrogance. They don't care what people think, simply because they believe citizens cannot touch them. For the elitists there is no law, provided they can keep the scandals coming regularly. This fulfills two aims. One is creation of a jaded public: Ah, well, here comes another one. Yawn. The other is to keep scandals coming rapidly enough so that each fades from the public radar screen before the results of any investigative reporting can be aired.

In early December 1997 *The Economist* "dramatically" illustrated Rule of Man:

The drama is running according to its script, so Bill Clinton went to an evening basketball game in Washington; Al Gore ate a restaurant pizza after visiting a school in Connecticut; and republican politicians stood in front of television cameras to exude indignation. As predicted, Janet Reno . . . had decided on December 2nd not to ask for an independent counsel to investigate alleged fund-raising abuses by the president, his vice-president and his former energy secretary, Hazel O'Leary. In the theater of Washington politics, it pays for the administration to affect nonchalance as the opposition affects outrage.[28]

President Clinton exemplified the rule of love, which has supplanted Rule of Law. Instead of providing leadership, he who would be king recruits fans. No president should have either a fan club or a hate club. Citizens should love or hate ideas, recommendations and policies, not people. If the president, **as a public servant**, did not have such a towering, media-hyped public profile, there would be less temptation for citizens to either perceive him as a king or hate him.

The notions of a big person, wheeler-dealer, or insider all refer to people who have managed to manipulate others into believing they are important. Each of them may not have a single idea worth its salt; this is unimportant. What is important to the power-seeking insider is the perceptions of others, who have not managed as well to manipulate still others into believing that they are all-powerful. When ideas and debate become irrelevant, perceptions, however empty, rule.

Lapham noted, "An anxious public yearns for the shows of omnipotence, not only on the part of its rulers but also from its scientists, its ballplayers, its divorce and bankruptcy lawyers. Omnipotence doesn't exist in a state of nature. It must be manufactured, and the supply increases with the demand. Authority vested in institutions gives way to authority vested in persons."

But Lapham did not stop there:

> *Just as the cost of a friend at court prices most Americans out of the market for political expression, so also the rule of grace and favor exempts the government from the nuisance of obeying its own laws. If the well-placed bribe can so easily rescind the will of Congress, then George III or the Emir of Kuwait might as well rule us. From the point of view of most of the government functionaries whom I've known in Washington, the shift to monarchy would require nothing more difficult than a change of costume.*

Who would want to work at a company with a little over 500 employees, 29 of whom have been accused of spousal abuse, 7 of whom have been arrested for fraud, 19 of whom have been accused of writing bad checks, 71 of whom cannot get a credit card, 8 of whom have been arrested for shoplifting, and in 1998, 84 of whom were stopped for drunk driving? Small wonder that no upright citizen would want to be associated with this "company"—the 535 members of the US Congress.

Since the passage of the Clean Air Act of 1990 there has been lots of activity and press on this issue. Probably none of these machinations mentioned the fact that the US government is by far the nation's worst polluter. Greider noted, "The federal government . . . enjoys a crucial advantage in its ability to evade laws. It owns the prosecutor."

In 1991 many of the barons of Congress owed the House restaurant over $300,000. Someone leaked this information, so they voted to shut it down in 1993, after having written 8,331 bad checks. Journalists sought the names of the offenders under the Freedom of Information Act, but when casting that one into law members of Congress had exempted themselves from its provisions. Due to public pressure the matter was referred to the House Ethics Committee to determine what should be done, but the chair of the committee was one of the bad check writers. The TV networks largely ignored this scandal, so the leaker contacted muckraker Rush Limbaugh. The broadcasting company tried unsuccessfully to muzzle him.

The news media cooperate with Rule of Man for several reasons, including vital access to the high and mighty. During the Reagan and first Bush administrations, James Baker and Richard Darman exercised great skill in selectively leaking information to friends in the press. This policy generated lots of friends, but it also put the press at these men's knees and kept it there.

Eric Alterman, in his book *Sound and Fury*, showed how pundits provided another dimension to the shroud fogging the relationship between citizens and their government.[29]

> *In this selfless pursuit, political punditry would do "what every sovereign citizen is supposed to do but has not the time or the interest to do for himself." The theory's fault lies with its vulnerability to human idiosyncrasies. To work effectively, the theory required two enormous assumptions: First, that the pun-*

dit could accumulate the requisite "insider" information from those who control it via disinterested inquiry . . . rather than through some implicit quid pro quo of sympathy and support. Second, the notion assumes that the pundit will continue to identify with the interests of the outsider class vs. those of the insider elite. It does so despite the fact that virtually their entire professional and social lives were likely to be dominated by interaction with that same ruling class. Should either of these two assumptions be undermined, the pundit becomes not an agent of democracy but an accomplice to its subversion.

These idiosyncrasies connect to the negative side of human nature: personal power seeking. Alterman argued that rubbing shoulders with the elite class constitutes an elixir fully as powerful as money. Pundits are oriented to personal power, so their writing and public appearances emphasize the cold war (even though it is past history) and the external threat to the country. This bias combines with the withholding of truth to increase citizens' fear of the unknown, and hence their willingness to continue to allow governing by the elite class.

Judge Robert Bork demonstrated the involvement of the Supreme Court in undermining Rule of Law:

We are no longer free to make our own fundamental moral and cultural decisions because the court oversees all such matters, when and as it chooses. . . . The Founders had no idea that a court armed with a written Constitution and the power of judicial review could become not only the supreme legislature of the land but a legislature ***beyond the reach of the ballot box.***[30] (emphasis added).

This statement completes coverage of the three branches of government as established by the Constitution. Proof now exists that not only does Congress make law, but so do the other two branches and without any constitutional authority.

The Economist provided some details:

Supreme Court justices . . . set the shape of cyberspace, addressed America's view of individual liberty, and challenged the existing balance of power between federal government and the states. They redefined insider trading; they determined manufacturers' responsibility to people exposed to asbestos; they ruled on whether private prison operators could be sued. In few other countries would judges decide on so many questions of social and economic policy, let alone on so many issues that touch life's deepest moral quandaries. And yet Americans, so intensely democratic, delight in the power of these aristocrat-philosophers . . . even though their decisions are as consequential and controversial as any politician's act.[31]

The Constitution states only that judges of the Supreme Court and other federal courts shall hold their offices "during good behavior." In theory a judge can be recalled, but practically speaking this is impossible. Therefore they are accountable to no one. As discussed, they frequently respond to requests from members of Congress to put into force laws that, if enacted by Congress, would generate such political heat as to endanger their campaigns for reelection (although they can only do so in the context of court cases). Lapham wrote: "Rehnquist spoke for a majority, not only of the court but also of the American governing and possessing classes, when he ruled that the democratic experiment had gone far enough and that the republic no longer could tolerate the risk implicit in the freedom of speech and the freedom of thought." William Rehnquist is chief justice of the US Supreme Court.

Men and women who are honest in their private dealings may well lie in their roles as public officials for "reasons of state." Service to the state presumably excuses actions that would be considered immoral if not illegal if committed by private citizens. It is logical to conclude that this is the effect of the system on individuals; they feel the tug of the negative tendencies of human nature. It is interesting to speculate whether subsequent presidents would have so willingly and so often violated the law had Richard Nixon been punished for his crimes instead of pardoned by his successor.

In the game of personality politics, political parties select candidates with charisma who can win. There is no longer any concern with ability to lead or govern in the public interest. Top party cadres continue to increase their personal power even as public support wanes. A recent study showed that 37 percent of citizens call themselves independent, 35 percent said they were Democrat and 28 percent Republican. Public officials in Washington have enacted a great variety of laws and policies intended to discourage any attempt by a third party or independent candidate to win high office. These actions demonstrate that they know they are not doing a good job for citizens; if they were competent, they would welcome competition as a means of improving their public services.

Arianna Huffington called the Republican Party the "most famous third party in American history."[32] Founded on July 6, 1854, it "went on to win a plurality of seats in the US House that fall. If current states' laws had been in effect then, the GOP would have failed to get on the ballot in over half the states."

Violations of law and disrespect for the Constitution on the part of political "leaders" cause the same within the citizenry. Without a voice in the formulation and enforcement of laws and with unnecessary thousands of laws on the books the average person loses interest in good citizenship, becomes fearful of the law, or both. Crime should be a community concern, but it is an emotional issue, so there are votes in it for the national politician who can convincingly harangue the public on television (and burnish his macho credentials).

Alexis de Tocqueville said:

But I think that administrative centralization only serves to enervate the peoples that submit to it, because it constantly tends to diminish their civic spir-

> *it. Administrative centralization succeeds, it is true, in assembling, at a given time and place, all the available resources. It brings triumph on the day of battle, but in the long run diminishes a nation's power. So it can contribute wonderfully to the ephemeral greatness of one man but not the permanent prosperity of a people.*[33]

Tocqueville illustrated the tendency for a large, strong central government to favor Rule of Man.

In 1992 the chair of the House Banking Committee was a maverick named Henry Gonzalez. Greider quoted Gonzalez's sincere lament:

> *When the president can bomb a foreign leader who's unpopular, we no longer have a constitutional democracy. If a president can do what Reagan did in Lebanon and Grenada and Nicaragua and Libya and what Bush did in Panama, we don't have a constitutional democracy. I'm still in kind of a daze. We have learned nothing. It demoralizes me. Makes me, not sad, but sick of heart. It's too great a country to go by default. We have so traduced democracy, cut off the participatory side, that the people don't see any point. . . . I find that the people can see through things. The people are there. But what can they do? When they have no choice between the two parties, no real choice between the overwhelming preponderance of candidates?*

Leaders like Gonzalez have become an endangered species in Washington.

The Economist noted "American and British government, faced with a new terrorist threat, now seem to hanker after . . . the power to get things done unfettered by the pesky rules of law. Though tempting, the idea that casting aside most legal constraints is necessary to fight terrorism, or will make Americans and Britons much safer, is a delusion."[34] The writer referred to one of several points: "John Ashcroft . . . recently imposed a new change in prison rules allowing conversations and letters between terrorist suspects and their lawyers to be monitored without a judicial warrant, suspending the Constitution's sixth-amendment right to effective counsel."

From this stance it is a simple matter to declare anyone whom the elitists dislike a terrorist suspect. It could be argued that terrorism can be effectively fought only through individual initiative, providing people are willing to seize it. In turn, this persuasion occurs only when democracy prevails in government. This concept in place, there would be no impetus for terrorists to ply their grisly trade.

In Ayn Rand's novel *Atlas Shrugged* Francisco d'Anconia takes over his father's business and begins to deal with government:

> *It was then that I began to see the nature of the evil I had suspected, but thought too monstrous to believe. I saw the tax-collecting vermin that had grown for centuries like mildew on d'Anconia Copper, draining us by no right that anyone could name—I saw the labor unions who won every claim against*

me, by reason of my ability to make their livelihood possible—I saw that any man's desire for money he could not earn was regarded as a righteous wish, but if he earned it, it was damned as greed—I saw the politicians who winked at me, telling me not to worry, because I could just work a little harder and outsmart them all. I looked past the profits of the moment, and I saw that the harder I worked, the more I tightened the noose around my throat—I saw that my energy was being poured down a sewer, that the parasites who fed on me were being fed upon in their turn, that they were caught in their own trap,—and there was no reason for it. [35]

There **is** a reason, amigo. It lies in human nature and lack of accountability to the people. However, when carried to a point near that which elicited d'Anconia's outburst everything of real and lasting value is being sacrificed on the altar of stolen wealth and privilege.

Alienation and Mutual Contempt

Stephen Carter wrote:

In the world as the framers of the Constitution imagined it, Tip O'Neill was precisely right: all politics was local. The federal government had little to do. The aspects of governance that affected people most were carried on at levels they could influence: the state house, the parish, and the town meeting. The cumbersome machinery for electing a national legislature every two years was designed to slow the national legislative process to a crawl: unable to anticipate modern transportation and communications, the framers assumed that the rascals could do relatively little damage in two short years.[36]

Tip O'Neill was Speaker of the House of Representatives; this position carries with it enormous personal power. He knew his statement was false when he uttered it. Carter's book *Integrity* suggested that a person has integrity when he (1) studies an issue until he can take a position on it that he knows is morally right; (2) acts on this conclusion; and (3) has the courage to state his position in the face of expression of opposing views.

Paine castigated the aristocracy of the late eighteenth century:

The more aristocracy appeared, the more it was despised; there was a visible imbecility and want of intellects in the majority . . . that while it affected to be more than citizen, was less than man. It lost ground more from contempt than hatred; and was rather jeered at as an ass, than dreaded as a lion. This is the general character of aristocracy, or what are called nobles or nobility, or rather no-ability, in all countries.[37]

Because the notion of aristocracy ties into human nature, its modern counterpart appears to be little different. "Government with insolence is despotism;

but when contempt is added, it becomes worse; and to pay for contempt is the excess of slavery."

The notion of big government has been around for centuries. Its officials attempt to broadcast dependency in a manner similar to that used by the ancient priesthood to subjugate the citizenry. When citizens are forced to pay for this kind of treatment, Paine's criticism is accurate.

Barber reported that in the nineteenth century an Irishman named Feargus O'Connor was elected to the British House of Commons and started the Chartist movement.[38] Members were attacked by police, who beat men, women, and children. Among the movement's beliefs were "foxes ought not to represent geese—that wolves ought not to represent sheep—and that hawks ought not to represent pigeons." O'Connor was later declared insane and placed in an asylum. In the Soviet Union, dissidents who attempted to start a movement that criticized the regime were removed (or "purged") in the same manner.

Today the world is getting smaller due to rapid improvements in transportation and communication. Cell phones, fax, email, and Web sites facilitate instant communication throughout most of the advanced world, and airline ticket prices have fallen since deregulation. A citizen's intuition suggests that these developments should enable citizens to become closer to their governments at all levels. Yet the opposite is happening; feelings of alienation and contempt keep growing. The elites continue to believe that big government policies and programs can substitute for weakened values in communities.

Phillips said: "Over the last half century, . . . a capital city so enlarged, so incestuous in its dealings, so caught up in its own privilege that it no longer seems controllable or even swayable by the general public."[39] This bloated entity annually demands and receives $2 trillion in tax dollars. Because citizens are beginning to see truth in this issue, a deep contempt regarding Washington is developing.

What they may not realize is that this contempt is mutual: The elites see the population as an alienated and stupid bunch of peasants. What is truly galling is that this tiny minority has the chutzpah to continue to refer to this country as a democracy, even as they rule their subjects rather than govern their citizens. (Even more galling: the press cooperates.)

David Brinkley was interviewed in 1992: "This country is really turned off on politics and politicians . . . and I know why. Because (the American people) have been lied to so much, and deceived so much. Cheated. Abused. Taken advantage of by pols. It would be surprising if they weren't turned off. They deserve to be turned off. I'm turned off."

In August 2000 Westphal said: "The Vanishing Voter Project weekly tests America's sentiment toward the campaign. One finding: Distrust of the political system is profound. 'We asked how many found politics disgusting and about seventy-five percent said yes.' . . . 'If you had asked that in the early 1960s, you might have had ten percent saying yes. This is really a sea change.'"[40]

Empty elections make it much easier for incumbent career politicians to get reelected. Citizens who are turned off don't think about the election and vote only through a feeling of obligation. Therefore they tend to opt for the devil they know.

During the fall 2000 campaign CBS allocated more hours to a soap opera called *Big Brother* than to coverage of the Democratic National Convention. The Fox network showed the action movie *Most Wanted* in lieu of Al Gore's speech accepting his party's nomination for president.

The elites don't know their constituents back home; furthermore they don't **want** to know them. There is no common ground between the elite culture and the vast majority of citizens. This is why, in practical terms, "home" is Washington, DC.

Therefore after completing their "public service" most of them stick around. Robert Dole gave up his Senate seat to campaign for president in 1996. After some thirty-five years in Washington, going back to Kansas apparently didn't seem so attractive. But there was another attraction: Due to his long service he had many important contacts in government, many friends, some of whom owed him favors. In a culture in which whom you know and can influence is more important than what you know, Dole's services were in demand, and he knew it.

A prestigious law firm called Verner, Liipfert, Bernhard, McPherson, and Hand quickly added Dole to their stable of big names. Their jobs were to "make rain," which means using their rich contacts to bring the firm millions of billable hours each year. Dole does not lobby directly, but he provides guidance to those who do. So instead of "Joe sent me" as it was during the days of Prohibition and speakeasies, today it's "Bob Dole sent me." Whom you know guides formulation of government policies in many countries today: China, Russia, India, Iran, and Iraq, to name just a few.

The pundits of Washington continue to claim that they speak for the public. But Alterman questioned this statement, referring first to the public:

> *They believe, by wide margins, that to build the world's "strongest education system" is more important to the nation's well-being than to accumulate its "strongest military force." In an extensive fall 1990 survey of the foreign policy beliefs of the American public compared with those of its appointed "opinion leaders," the Gallup organization found that fully twenty-eight percent of the American people considered "crime" and "poverty" to be among the nation's "two or three biggest problems." The two categories did not even place among opinion leaders. . . . One in five leaders responded that "Iraq" belonged in the "biggest problem" category, while the respondents questioned in the large public survey did not even mention it.*[41]

Alterman concluded that the pundits are a barrier to enactment of legislation that could revitalize decaying institutions. In addition their writings reinforce feelings of alienation among citizens, who are beginning to see through the facade.

The elites often claim they are doing what the people want, as indicated in poll results. Clearly this is not always true, and it is easy to rig (or simply misread) poll results. Therefore it is easy to use implied citizen consent to do pretty much what the elites want, and so the reality is that the people indirectly choose to be ruled rather than led.

The public's side of most issues is described as emotional, whereas the elite side is rational and is backed up by science (or pseudo-science when straight science cannot support a position). The former is considered a weakness, and the latter is promoted as strength. Of course the reality is that what is or is not rational is determined by the elites; the public has no voice.

Protest leaders find it easy to stir a naive public to action, because protest is based on emotion. Those who are less educated and do not take time to think through an issue are most susceptible. The result is often a misguided protest, which is easy for the elite class to put down as empty and baseless passion.

The average citizen interested in contributing to local government finds his or her way at least partially blocked by national government programs presumably designed to help. Here are a few examples from Bovard's book *Lost Rights*:

> *Skamania County, WA residents voted ten to one against the proposed scenic river restrictions but were still dragooned under federal controls. Government officials dictate what colors families can paint their homes and even decreed that local homes cannot function as bed-and-breakfasts except for those listed on a historic register—and even those houses cannot serve breakfast to hunters or fishermen before 5:00 A.M.*[42]

Recently frustrated citizens thought of a way around the bureaucracy—by calling for constitutional amendments. Such callings included amendments for a balanced budget, victim's rights, campaign finance, English as the national official language, political term limits, school prayer, unfunded mandates, abortion, flag burning, and supermajorities required in Congress to increase taxes. Poll results as reported by John Leo indicated that some of these were very popular:[43] 69 percent approved the supermajority measure, school prayer was supported by 73 percent, the balanced budget by 83 percent, and term limits by 73 percent. None of these initiatives will go anywhere, only in part because the founding fathers purposely made it difficult to amend the Constitution. They are nonstarters because the elites don't want them.

Article III of the Constitution set up a branch of the national government called the judiciary. The intent was to make and keep it independent of the other two branches (legislative and executive), and thus to act as a check on their activities. The founders knew that an independent judiciary was essential to the preservation of liberty. The Supreme Court has no constitutional power to make laws, nor can it redo any part of the Constitution itself. It is intended to uphold the Constitution by striking down and changing laws that are unconstitutional.

However, since the 1930s the Supreme Court has seen fit to make laws (in the context of court cases) and intrude into the private lives of citizens. The nine justices have done this, primarily because they believe they know what is best for the people. They are in a position to force the issues, because they don't need to stand for election and it is all but impossible to remove them in any other way.

Daniel Pilla wrote: "[Then] chief justice Warren Burger went on to explain that the courts must strike a 'balance' between the rights of the citizen and an 'overriding' governmental interest. He reasoned that when the government could show such . . . it could infringe the plain and clear constitutional rights of the citizen."[44] The potential for abuse is without limit, because the elites determine the definition of *overriding.*

These disturbing trends have gradually created a breakdown of trust in society. This means more police, more people in prison, and far more highly paid lawyers than there were only a few years ago. Fukuyama wrote in *Trust*: "By contrast, people who do not trust one another will end up cooperating only under a system of formal rules and regulations, which have to be negotiated, agreed to, litigated, and enforced, sometimes by coercive means."[45] It is obvious that many lawyers are needed in such a society.

Many career politicians follow poll results in governing. In 1990 President George Bush (Sr.)'s popularity rating was down when Saddam Hussein moved his army into Kuwait after a brutal eight-year war against Iran that cost him nearly a million men. Saddam did have several legitimate grievances against his neighbor, but this caused Bush no pause whatever. There is nothing like a war to boost a leader's popularity rating, and this one promised to be over quickly and with few body bags coming home. The timing was nearly perfect, so he bypassed the United Nations and charged ahead.

In the event he was right—his rating soared. But the idea that it would stay up all the way through the 1992 election was naive. His minions probably thought this could be done, but due to alienation they didn't know the public. After about six weeks the rating plummeted downward to where it had been before (and there went the election).

The inescapable conclusion is that US government institutions have declined to the point where they are not only irrelevant but also barriers to good government. On inquiry, however, insider elites will reassure concerned citizens that said institutions are as healthy as ever. Such a response is not new. Similar reassurances came from insiders in the governments of Rome, fifteenth-century Spain, seventeenth-century Holland, and eighteenth-century Britain, each shortly before getting into deep trouble and even extinction.

Italy has seen almost as many governments since World War II as the number of years since 1945. In 1997 officials finally resolved to do something about this situation, so they drafted a new constitution. *The Economist* reported on the result: "The proposed new constitution is a triumph for the old politics. . . . The idea of turning the current senate into a punchier chamber with a stronger remit for speaking for the regions was stymied by the current crop of senators, who proved unwilling to risk losing their own seats or perks."[46]

There are two lessons in this. Jefferson provided one, when he recommended that "before the canker is inveterate . . . remedy should be applied." The second applies when remedy has been delayed; it states that those who profit from the status quo are not about to install the necessary major changes. Only an organized outside force can do this, and up until recently it was accomplished only through terrible bloodshed and misery. Today, with the advent of the Age of Reason, there exists a nonviolent alternative. (See Chapter 22).

Why Central Government Promotion of Good Education Is Only Rhetoric

Restless natives are likely to disturb the current system of government. Educated natives are more likely to be restless, generating and promoting new and different ideas that could eventually threaten the system. The negative incentive of personal power seeking and holding therefore causes behavior intended to keep the rabble dumbed down. The rhetoric, of course, is simply saying what the public wants to hear on an issue that everyone knows is vital to the nation's future.

The elites' vision of that future naturally differs from that held by ordinary citizens, who have always been and remain deeply committed to their children. Therefore the rich send their children to exclusive private schools, while attempting to keep the rest of the population's children in inferior systems.

For about 900 years the University of Cairo (Egypt) operated on the principle of free inquiry. Near the end of the nineteenth century, Egypt became a British colony. After that event, educational policy changed from free inquiry to what the British thought young students should know.

In 1787 Jefferson wrote to Madison, wondering "whether peace is best preserved by giving energy to the government, or information to the people. This last is the most certain and the most legitimate engine of government. Educate and inform the whole mass of people. Enable them to see that it is their interest to preserve peace and order, and they will preserve them."

When visiting this country in 1830 Tocqueville saw a time in the future "in which freedom, public peace, and social stability will not be able to last without education."[47] Hayek, writing in 1943, said:

> *Only since industrial freedom opened the path to the free use of new knowledge, only since everything could be tried—if somebody could be found to back*

it at his own risk—and, it should be added, as often as not from outside the authorities officially intrusted [sic] with the cultivation of learning, has science made great strides which in the last hundred and fifty years have changed the face of the world.[48]

Any national government role in education is dangerous. Powell provided a nineteenth-century example: a freed slave named Frederick Douglass. He and his students violated laws against educating blacks at great risk. Why was this so bad? Government officials feared educated slaves, believing they would probably revolt. It takes but little thought to generalize this fear beyond blacks and slaves; educated natives of all colors can get restless.

In 1989, Schumacher demonstrated the extent of a disturbing change in orientation:

Strange to say, under the influence of laboratory science many people today seem to use their freedom only for the purpose of denying its existence. Men and women of great gifts find their purest delight in magnifying every "mechanism," every "inevitability," everything where human freedom does not enter or does not appear to enter. A great shout of triumph goes up whenever anybody has found some further indication that people cannot help being what they are and doing what they are doing, no matter how inhuman their actions might be.[49]

A thinking citizen would argue that this development is not so strange for two reasons. First, the very notion of personal freedom has been gradually and insidiously squeezed out of people's thinking; without this trend, the grand deception could not flourish as it does (Chapter 10). The second explanation lies in government-financed research. The "men and women of great gifts" are in fact gifted. They are also gifted enough to know who is paying them, so the results are frequently adjusted accordingly, and interpretations are also adjusted so it looks like the scientists have not compromised their integrity. The negative side of human nature pervades the entire process of paternalistic subjugation.

Lane, writing around the same time as Hayek, referred to the predominance of private schools in the United States in 1900.[50] Creative ways were found to pay the costs of elementary school education, and students habitually worked their way through high school and college. But "this American method of education never fully developed; it was stopped about forty years ago, by the eager German-minded reformers, who believed that the State can spend an American's money for his, or his children's, education, much more wisely than he can."

Bergland elaborated:

Nineteenth century advocates of state schooling made no attempt to hide their agenda. They openly argued that children were not self-owners, but rather the property of the state. They contended that the school's function was to indoctrinate the children so that they would be patriotic, unquestioning, obedient cit-

izens whose first loyalty was to the government; and that the primary obstacle to achieving these purposes was interference from the students' parents and families.[51]

It was a different era when the predominant belief among people involved in education was free and open inquiry, intended to build critical minds whose thinking would range far and wide. This kind of thinking combined with dedication and tolerance in implementation to build a great nation. There seems to be a connection between tolerance of ideas and tolerance of people with different beliefs. Good ideas can reach across gaps in ethnic background, but only when allowed full play.

If a society puts greater value on whom you know than on what you know, it has no need for a good education system. If there is no need for a good education system, there is no need for a good society. "That society which routes its best and brightest young people into the public sector, which spends wealth, instead of into the private sector, which creates wealth, shall not long endure as a viable society."

In 1984 a blue ribbon commission published a voluminous report on the state of the US education system. The title was "A Nation at Risk." It contained a dire warning: Unless recommendations for drastic reform are carried through and quickly, the nation would be in serious trouble. Today it is difficult to identify any of the commission's recommendations as having been completed in practice. George Bush (Sr.) called himself the "education president," and Clinton passed up few opportunities to trumpet the virtues of education, but practically no concrete action followed. It is true that a Department of Education was formed, but the real intent was to provide a forum for dissemination of misleading rhetoric.

George Will commented on President Bush's hoopla over the inappropriately named No Child Left Behind Act.[52]

> *Federal education legislation is rarely edifying. In 1994 the senate, enacting the "Goals 2000" education bill, . . . imperious commands to the future. Only two goals were quantifiable: By 2000, America's high-school graduation rate would be "at least 90 percent" and students "will be first in the world in mathematics and science achievement." Sen. Pat Moynihan, comparing these goals to Soviet grain production quotas, said: "That will not happen."*
>
> *And of course it did not. In 2000 the graduation rate was about 75 percent, a figure inflated by "social promotions." American students ranked 19th among 38 surveyed nations in mathematics (right below Latvia) and 18th in science (right below Bulgaria).*

Wood noted "that *a free people—unless they have sufficient intellectual strength—will willingly choose slavery over freedom*; we will readily embrace security in place of independence."[53] This is inaccurate in that most citizens are not aware that they are making this choice willingly (nevertheless, a point). Artful politicians appreciate the value to them in keeping this decision beyond public awareness.

Wood quoted prominent newsman Walter Cronkite:

> *[We] recently observed that education "lies at the very bottom of every problem we have. If the people were truly self-informed, were truly philosophical, were truly aware of our associations with one another, (then) presumably our dialogue and our reporting would be considerably better than it is." He continued: "The tragedy is, we aren't educated to any degree. Education levels are so low that the public does not have a capability of making an informed judgment . . . so we're handicapped from the beginning."*

Here is a rare instance of someone in the news media criticizing the institution, pointing out how, in the absence of demand for truth, news reporting misleads the public. Wood continued: "In 1993, the Department of Education released the results of 'the most comprehensive study of its kind,' which indicated that literacy rates for people ages twenty-one to twenty-five have dropped significantly since 1985. . . . twenty-three percent of the adult population (44 million people) are illiterate or 'can perform only the barest of tasks.'"

This report came nine years after "A Nation at Risk," and it showed continued deterioration. Apparently the report of a blue ribbon commission holds little weight in Washington. Fixing an institution like education admittedly takes time, but it surely seems that further decline could have been arrested.

Charles L. Glenn was commissioned by the Department of Education in 1989 to conduct a study and write a book called *Educational Freedom in Eastern Europe*. He found a deep concern among postcommunist reformers in education, and also instances in which parents enjoyed a wider school choice for their children than in this country. But the book was not published during the remaining two years of President Bush's administration, and Clinton canceled it immediately after taking office (January 1993). Finally, in 1994 a mere 200 copies were released.

Apparently these two presidents liked to emphasize rhetoric above action. Nothing much moved toward Bush's much-hyped Goals 2000 program, and Clinton recently argued that everyone should have at least two years of college.

But improving colleges without doing something about the sorry condition of grade-school systems is like fixing the roof when the foundation is crumbling. Today very few grade schools teach civics as it connects to democracy. Public school systems respond to pressures from public officials in government, who don't want the riffraff thinking about what government is really doing.

Diane Ravitch was Assistant Secretary of Education under George Bush. In 1997 she urged Clinton to place the national testing program with an independent agency, outside the Department of Education. Her experience in the department had acquainted her with its hidden agenda. National testing would bring the education issue under widespread public scrutiny, and thus force serious reform. Poor and mediocre teachers would lose their jobs. Ravitch said: "Unfortunately, this did not happen, and now the Clinton administration is well on its way to destroying the credibility of its good idea."

It did not stop there. The plan was for national tests to emphasize "whole language" theories of reading instead of phonics, and promote so-called fuzzy math, where the process of problem solving took precedence over finding the right answer. The administration pushed ahead without public hearings or explicit congressional authority.

Still continuing, in 1999 the Department of Education published guidelines warning of potential discrimination through use of "high-stakes testing." If approved, this would have made it very difficult to use tests under any circumstances. In the winter of 1997–98 Public Agenda, a nonpartisan polltaker, found that 78 percent of African American parents agreed that testing "calls attention to a problem that needs to be solved." (The published "guidelines" included a threat of litigation for noncompliance.)

In terms of the objective of the elites, TV is a windfall resource. What little useful learning is offered attracts a tiny minority of viewers, and even this does not often address political issues. (C-SPAN is not orchestrated to appeal to viewers.) Therefore this communication medium is perceived as a device for entertainment and not information.

Will castigated recent TV programming: "So NBC sank to the challenge of thinking lower. . . . Its competitors in the race to the bottom will not rest, and the bottom is not yet in sight."[54] He referred to long-standing research results:

> *For more than 20 years, research has shown that children [are] less likely to get good grades. . . . Too much TV:*
>
> - *Slows the development of thinking skills and imagination*
> - *Shortens attention spans*
> - *Slows the growth of reading and speaking skills*
> - *Conditions a child to the dual distractions of sound and images, a constant level of stimulation not found in most classrooms.*

Some school authorities are now proposing banishing homework, because its existence tends to widen inequalities between students with attentive parents and those without. Astonishing as this is, it seems to tie in with the overall deterioration in this country's education system.

The Economist reported a large research project on educational standards that included forty-one countries.[55] In math the US score ranked it twenty-eighth of the forty-one. The Czech Republic achieved Europe's highest score and was ranked sixth, below several East Asian countries. The Czech Republic spent one third as much per student as the United States did.

Listening to strident calls from public educators for more money, the average citizen may be forgiven for some confusion. The Kansas City experience will help clarify. In 1986 its school system was about the worst in the entire country with drugs, crime, guns, vandalism, and attacks on teachers. A judge ordered that a whole new system be designed and put in place. About $1.3 billion bought many new and refurbished buildings, art studios, science labs, computers—practically everything that money could buy.

The results after seven years? Although near the bottom in 1986, math scores **dropped** still further. The dropout rate was bad going in, but it **increased** to a mind-numbing 60 percent. Thousands of parents and taxpayers were shaking their heads and wringing their hands, but there was no need for this anguish, as about 200 published studies done previously had shown the same result: The more money, the worse the performance. (Throwing money at a problem will not make it go away.)

Reflection can provide an explanation based on human nature. Some of those on the inside of the system had devoted much of their careers to moving upward to privileged positions, and these people exerted great personal power in stale bureaucracies. For them, deep reform was a threat, so they fought it. Therefore when more money came their way, it was put to work doing more of the same counterproductive things that they had been doing to get the system into such difficulty in the first place. (The Kansas City judge ordered a new system, not new buildings, but he did not get it.)

In the 1970s a new issue loomed on the political horizon: bilingual education. Bureaucrats jumped on it, but once the program got started practically all instruction was in Spanish. In 1996 a survey revealed that 81 percent of Latino parents wanted their children to learn English as soon as possible; they felt that bilingual education was a poverty trap, from which they had come to the United States to escape. (The program was phased out, but apparently not a single bureaucrat saw fit to say, "I'm sorry.")

The National Association of Scholars (NAS) studied the catalogs of fifty top-quality universities for academic years 1914, 1939, 1964, and 1993. Bork reported:

> *The findings were devastating. They bear out in full columnist Robert J. Samuelson's conclusion: "You should treat skeptically the loud cries now coming from colleges—that the last bastion of excellence in American education is being gutted by state budget cuts and mounting costs. Whatever else it is, higher education is not a bastion of excellence. It is shot through with waste, lax academic standards, and mediocre teaching and scholarship." . . .*
>
> *From 1914 to 1939, the percentage of institutions with literature requirements fell from 57 percent to 38 percent. By 1993, only 14 percent . . . The same pattern held true in philosophy, religion, social science, natural science, and mathematics. . . . Average number of days classes were in session during*

the academic year dropped precipitously. . . . The average was 204 days in 1914, . . . to 156 days in 1993.[56]

The Economist expressed alarm when informed of a new policy in the vast University of California (170,000 students and 20 Nobel Prize laureates). The policy eliminates the Scholastic Aptitude Test (SAT) in evaluating candidates for admission to the university. "It cannot be entirely coincidental that America's SAT-backed universities are the envy of much of the world, whereas many of its high-schools, without any objective national testing, are dreadful." [57]

"The politics is simple. The abolition of affirmative-action programs in 1997 led to a dramatic reduction in the number of blacks and Latinos in the university, in part because . . . worse than whites and Asians in SATs."

The writer finished with a devastating critique: "Getting rid of SATs not because they are uninformative but because they are all too informative. . . . It is foolish to deal with unpalatable information by shooting the messenger. The right way to deal with it is to work like fury to change California's schools. And that surely means more testing, not less."

Geyer pointed out that "America is losing its national memory. This would be serious enough in any country, but it is deadly for a unique historical entity such as the US, whose very existence and coherence depend on the perpetuation of an idea."[58] That idea is democracy. She referred to a survey

> *by the Roper Organization, conducted among top seniors at fifty-five leading colleges. [It] found that while nearly 100 percent could identify the cartoon characters Beavis and Butthead . . . only one-third were able to identify the Constitution as establishing the division of powers in the US government. . . . Indeed, only twenty-five states now require any civics education in public schools at all.*

Citizens have lost touch with the principles and ideas that made their nation great. There are two causes. The first lies in overbearing big government discouraging education, and the second may be found in the lack of discussion of civic issues. The automobile, long commutes to work, TV, and bedroom communities have combined with massive increases in wealth to discourage co-workers, family, friends, and neighbors from getting together to discuss politics and government. Geyer concluded: "More and more, too, America [is] obsessed with form while the substance fades away. That should surprise no one. That is what happens when a nation forgets its history . . . and it is worst of all when the citizens do this to themselves."

It can be argued that reducing academic requirements encouraged the same kind of free inquiry that prevailed in the University of Cairo for so long. However, there is no evidence that this was encouraged; indeed, there is evidence that these requirements were replaced by less demanding courses.

The finding that less than half of the year's 365 days devoted to classes might seem acceptable today (with so many courses offered via correspondence and on the Web), but not in 1993. Perhaps criticism of universities is unfair: Over the years the quality of their raw material inputs has deteriorated at a rate that roughly matches that of the nation's K–12 systems.

Bork wrote:

> *What caught my eye about the Michigan report is how the new stupidity shows up in college writing classes. . . . Embedded in the theory is the notion that standards, grammar, grades, and judgment are bad. Self-expression, self-esteem and personal rules are good. . . . Rules, good writing, and simple coherence are sometimes depicted as habits of the powerful and privileged, sometimes as coercion of the poor and powerless.*

Even this was not enough. "A better example . . . [was an] article in the *English Leadership Quarterly* urging teachers to make intentional errors in English as 'the only way to end its oppression of linguistic minorities.'" What is appalling to any thinking citizen is that this article, written in good English by two professors, won an award from the magazine. It is a publication of the National Council of Teachers of English.

Harvey C. Mansfield is a professor at Harvard University who has kicked up a lot of dust with his castigation of grade inflation. *The Economist* capably summarized his case:

> *Perhaps the simplest argument for Mr. Mansfield's cause is that anybody who has ever been well taught knows that he is right. People who work under demanding taskmasters usually learn to respect them. People who are coddled—despise the system they are exploiting. Living on a diet of junk grades is like living on a diet of junk food. You swell up out of all decent proportions without ever getting any real nourishment. And you end up in later life regretting your disgusting habits.*[59]

A good education enables a citizen to understand him- or herself. With this understanding comes a feeling of comfort and security within the self and a lack of apprehension when becoming acquainted with others of different appearance, speech, background, and outlook. The result is tolerance, and a successful melting-pot society; this is a vital component of the history of the United States. When tolerance is lacking people tend to avoid others, and this causes a lack of acquaintance, increased apprehension, and ultimately a fragmentation of the culture.

Today's wired world clutters the mind during every waking moment in the day. William Safire noted: "What with cell phones and palm pilots and satellite-controlled pagers and messengers, the world is too much with us. In our lust to be in constant hand-held communication, we fritter away our long-held value of personal freedom."[60]

This condition suits the elite class perfectly: with no time for private self-learning, reflection, and discussion peasants cannot know what top-down, big government is doing to them. Safire continued: "Too many of us are gripped by the fear of being alone. If we are not in demand round the clock, goes this worry, we don't count." But the truth of the matter is that wired citizens don't count when they don't think about what society is and what it could be.

With school authority undermined, children will learn less. The combination of poor learning and an overabundance of lawyers fits in well with the elites' grand plan for the society, as this book will demonstrate in Chapter 10. A possible harbinger occurred in Nebraska, where seven fathers were thrown in jail for educating their own children in a church school. These children scored higher on standard tests than did their public school counterparts and were willing to be tested repeatedly.

Friedman wrote in 1982:

> *If one were to seek deliberately to devise a system of recruiting and paying teachers calculated to repel the imaginative and daring and self-confident and to attract the dull and mediocre and uninspiring, he could hardly do better than imitate the system of requiring teaching certificates and enforcing standard salary structures . . . in the large city and state-wide systems.*[61]

A small minority of excellent teachers works long and hard anyway, because they are prisoners in the system. That is, their love of learning and children confines them.

Economists Ballou and Podgursky reported on five years of research.[62] They found that "the quality of America's teachers has more to do with how they are paid rather than how much." The National Education Association (a teachers' union) opposes merit-based pay. Salaries based on experience and education are called "massively unimportant" in determining how well students do, according to Podgursky. "The uniform pay scale invites what economists call adverse selection. Since the most talented teachers are also likely to be good at other professions, they have a strong incentive to leave education for jobs in which pay is more closely linked to productivity. For dullards, the incentives are just the opposite." When test scores were used to verify this finding, the brightest teachers were the ones who left. The results of the study supported Friedman's conclusion.

In 1998 Friedman was interviewed. He argued that government controls the education market. Government control of the economy in Russia and Eastern Europe has ended. "Why should socialism work better for education than for anything else?"

Friedman made no claim to something new in this matter. Herbert Spencer wrote *Social Statics* in 1851, which explained how governments in Greece, Rome, China, Russia, Austria, France, and Britain controlled education to maintain their power over the people. Spencer commented on government schools, writing,

"They are among the last places to which anyone looks for improvement in the art of teaching."

Mark Twain said, "In the first place, God made idiots. This was for practice. Then He made school boards." Although this remark may overstate the issue, here is a tradition that apparently should be discussed.

The Economist illustrated how government will distract the public from truth while serving its own purpose.[63]

> *Take education. The government's race-based solution to poor black performance has been to allow admissions standards at colleges . . . to be lowered to admit more black students. Yet the basic problem has nothing to do with race: it lies in the appalling state of too many primary and elementary schools, and in the refusal of the teachers' unions to countenance reform or experiment.*

There are two reasons for using this dodge. One is that even though race relations have dramatically improved over the past forty years there are still votes to be gleaned in racism. The other lies in the dollar-based need to appease the teachers' unions, as they regularly donate millions to congressional reelection campaigns.

Whenever truth is skirted the results can be bizarre. In 1990 Cathy Nelson was selected the state of Minnesota's Teacher of the Year. But when she received the award she didn't even have a teaching job, because under a union-set last-hired-first-fired policy she had previously been laid off.

In his 1997 State of the Union speech a freshly reelected Clinton thundered, "The enemy of our time is inaction!" And then, "My number one priority for the next four years is to ensure that all Americans have the best education in the world." Thinking citizens reached an accurate conclusion: One of US history's most accomplished purveyors of rhetoric was on the podium, plying his trade.

The ramifications of this national malaise reach far and wide. Officials in the state of Massachusetts administered a statewide test for candidates hoping for public school teaching positions. Almost 60 percent failed. Thirty percent failed a basic test of reading and writing, and 63 percent failed the math portion. Schools of education in the nation's universities have entrance standards so low that they repel the more highly qualified students.

In 1999 a federal judge stopped Cleveland's school voucher program. Possession of a voucher, usually tax-supported, gave parents a choice concerning where to send their child. When administered without restrictions, this major change in the present system has the tremendous potential of stimulating competition among schools, as they struggle to improve their operations to attract students.

Predictably, union officials welcomed the judge's decision while parents of disadvantaged students were distraught. Cleveland has one of the worst school systems in the entire nation. Rees reported that in 1999 only 38 percent of students graduated from high school, and only 22 percent of its fourth-grade students and 12 percent of sixth-graders passed math proficiency tests.[64]

Without vouchers, poor parents have no choice but to plug their offspring into an educational abomination. An annual poll by Phi Delta Kappa, an association of professional educators, showed that support for school vouchers among public-school parents rose from 51 percent in 1994 to 60 percent in 1999. A poll by the Joint Center for Political and Economic Studies found that 60 percent of blacks and 70 percent of blacks under age thirty-five favored use of vouchers.

The Economist wrote : "Pro-voucher blacks have established a lobbying group to plead their cause. The Black Alliance for Educational Options [BAEO] is only a few months old."[65] The writer continued:

> *In Florida . . . the threat that children would receive vouchers to attend private schools spurred the seventy-six worst-performing schools to make big academic strides. And, even if you get stuck in the many squabbles about such studies, there is the most powerful evidence of all: word of mouth. Blacks are telling each other that vouchers work.*

There is nothing like competition to concentrate minds.

In Cleveland and elsewhere, the superior work of Catholic schools gets very little press. For at least thirty years educators have been watching these schools outperform public schools, to the point where the mystery is how this situation has been so successfully kept under wraps. *The Economist* provided an insight:

> *Put in a call to Hales Franciscan school in Chicago, and the answerphone message tells you that "100 percent of our 1996 students were admitted to college." Arrive at the school at 8:45 in the morning, and 300 black teenagers in crisp white shirts and ties are getting down, in total quiet, to a school day heavy with English and mathematics. . . . It sits in a part of the city where most of the children have no financial assistance and where, as one local man put it, "You would not want your car to break down."*[66]

These schools have no bureaucracy, no tenure for their teachers, and no unions. Furthermore, they missed out on the "progressive education" movement that began over forty years ago, so teachers can and do discipline disruptive students. Finally, there is no bilingual education, no dumbing down of standards, and no obsession with self-esteem.

Charter schools allow parents and teachers control over school policies, although the money still comes from taxpayers. A North Carolina group named FREE applied for a charter to open a school, not realizing the full nature and extent of the bureaucratic obstacle course they would be obliged to navigate. First, the dean of the UNC School of Education said that UNC would not grant any charters. The local school board was prejudiced against charter schools, so the group approached the State Board of Education. After several meetings they finally obtained a charter.

The next hurdle involved finding a building for the school. After the town of Chapel Hill approved an application, the group met with the owner to sign a lease, only to find he had leased it to someone else. After this disappointment they met with the state Department of Public Instruction, who told them exactly how things would be done in the school, no discussion allowed.

The group found that teachers who transfer to a charter school cannot continue their membership in state pension plans, unless the group allows local school boards to appoint 80 percent of its board of directors. There would be no start-up money available, and lenders would not provide financing, because if the venture failed all assets would revert to the school district. This carefully contrived series of barriers is reminiscent of what incumbent career politicians have erected to discourage competition. A thinking citizen might well conclude there is a connection.

There are no known solid statistics in home schooling, but it appears that the movement is growing at around 15 percent a year. Twenty years ago home schooling was illegal in many states, but the climate has changed because advocates have become a potent political force. When a Gallup poll first asked about home schooling in 1985, 73 percent of respondents disapproved and 16 percent approved. The same question asked in 1997 revealed only 56 percent disapprovals and 36 percent approvals. Apparently parents are actively searching for viable alternatives to public school systems.

James Barber noted:

> *The Nazis relieved people of the trouble of thinking and decision making and responsibility. They removed all doubt, and in return for "blind obedience" provided thrilling spectacle and song, romantic adventure, the prospect of conquest, and the assurance of belonging to the "master race." . . . The Nazi idea of education is eerily echoed in the recent fashion for deconstruction in American universities. This theory of criticism displays the same contempt for reason and reality the Nazis did. One of the most prominent deconstructionists of the 1970s and 1980s, Professor Paul de Man, wrote much Nazi propaganda in the Europe of the 1940s.*[67]

Sayers wrote:

> *The combined folly of a civilization that has forgotten its own roots is forcing them to shore up the tottering weight of an educational structure that is built upon sand. They are doing for their pupils the work which the pupils themselves ought to do. For the sole true end of education is simply this: to teach men how to learn for themselves; and whatever instruction fails to do this is effort spent in vain.*[68]

Educated natives do get restless.

Notes

1. Jeffrey Bell, *Populism and Elitism*. Regnery Gateway, 1992.
2. Thomas Paine, *Rights of Man*. 1791.
3. Lewis Lapham, *The Wish for Kings: Democracy at Bay*. Grove Press, 1993.
4. Milton Friedman, *Capitalism and Freedom*. University of Chicago Press, 1982.
5. David Bergland, *Libertarianism in One Easy Lesson*. Orpheus, 1997.
6. Rose Wilder Lane, *The Discovery of Freedom*. Fox and Wilkes, 1993.
7. Alexander Hamilton, Federalist Paper No. 17, *The Federalist Papers*. Mentor, 1961.
8. Woodrow Wilson, in Robert J. Samuelson, *The Good Life and its Discontents: The American Dream in the Age of Entitlement 1945–1995*. Random House, 1995.
9. Lapham, *The Wish for Kings*.
10. Marjorie Williams, "Misplaying the Game of DC Politics." *News and Observer* (Raleigh, NC), February 15, 2001, p. 15A.
11. Eric Alterman, *Sound and Fury: The Washington Punditocracy and the Collapse of American Politics*. Harper Collins, 1992.
12. Kenneth Auletta, in James Fallows, *Breaking the News: How the Media Undermine American Democracy*. Pantheon Books, 1996, p. 76.
13. Kevin Phillips, *Arrogant Capital*. Little, Brown, 1994.
14. Lapham, *The Wish for Kings*.
15. Martin L. Gross, *A Call for Revolution*. Ballantine Books, 1993.
16. Walter Isaacson, *Kissinger: A Biography*. Simon and Schuster, 1992.
17. Paine, *Rights of Man*.
18. Friedrich A. Hayek, *The Road to Serfdom*. University of Chicago Press, 1944.
19. Ayn Rand, *Atlas Shrugged*. Penguin Books, 1992.
20. Philip Wylie, *A Generation of Vipers*. Dalkey Archive Press, 1946.
21. William Greider, *Who Will Tell the People: The Betrayal of American Democracy*. Simon and Schuster, 1992.
22. *The Economist*, "Conservatives and Liberty." October 14, 2000, p. 23.
23. *The Economist*, "The Imperial Presidency." November 3, 2001, p. 39.
24. Lapham, *The Wish for Kings*.
25. Maureen Dowd, "Time for the Clintons to Pay." *News and Observer* (Washington, DC), February 13, 2001, p. 13A.
26. Charles Krauthammer, "Up Next: Ex Post Clinton Laws." *News and Observer* (Washington, DC), February 4, 2001, p. 31A.
27. *The Economist*, "Secrets, Lies and Hubris." July 14, 2001, p. 29.
28. *The Economist*, "The Lady's Not for Turning." December 6, 1997, p. 25.
29. Alterman, *Sound and Fury*.

30. Robert H. Bork, *Slouching Towards Gomorrah.* HarperCollins, 1996.
31. *The Economist,* "Judges, Suicide and the Resurgence of the States." July 5, 1997, p. 25.
32. Arianna Huffington, *How to Overthrow the Government.* Harper Collins, 2000.
33. Alexis de Tocqueville, *Democracy in America.* Knopf, 1972.
34. *The Economist,* "Terrorism and Freedom." November 17, 2001, page 11.
35. Rand, *Atlas Shrugged.*
36. Stephen Carter, *Integrity.* Basic Books, 1996.
37. Paine, *Rights of Man.*
38. James D. Barber, *The Book of Democracy.* Prentice Hall, 1995.
39. Phillips, *Arrogant Capital.*
40. David Westphal, "Parties Scramble for Fewer Votes." *News and Observer,* August 2000 column.
41. Alterman, *Sound and Fury.*
42. James Bovard, *Lost Rights: The Destruction of American Liberty.* St. Martin's Press, 1995.
43. John Leo, "I'd Like to Amend That." *US News,* November 25, 1996, p. 30.
44. Daniel Pilla, *The Freeman,* September 1997, p. 543.
45. Francis Fukuyama, *Trust.* Free Press, 1995.
46. *The Economist,* "As You Were in Italy." July 5, 1997, p. 18.
47. Tocqueville, *Democracy in America.*
48. Hayek, *The Road to Serfdom.*
49. E. F. Schumacher, *Small Is Beautiful: Economics as if People Mattered.* Harper and Row, 1989.
50. Lane, *Discovery of Freedom.*
51. Bergland, *Libertarianism.*
52. George F. Will, "Lessons Unlearned in School Bill." *News and Observer* (Washington, DC), January 6, 2002, p. 23A.
53. Donald N. Wood, *Post-Intellectualism and the Decline of Democracy: The Failure of Reason in the 20th Century.* Praeger, 1996.
54. George F. Will, "Programming Pitched at the Maggot Level," and Stephen Jurovics and Kathleen Clarke-Pearson, "For Children, Worse than a Waste of Time." *News and Observer* (Washington, DC), June 21, 2001, p. 17A.
55. *The Economist,* "Education and the Wealth of Nations." March 29, 1997, p. 15.
56. Bork, *Slouching Towards Gomorrah.*
57. *The Economist,* "Disabling the National Education Defense System." February 24, 2001, p. 36.
58. Georgie Anne Geyer, "Do We Know What Day It Is?" *News and Observer,* column in May 2000.

59. *The Economist*, "All Shall Have Prizes." April 14, 2001, p. 32.
60. William Safire, "Breaking Out of the Work Cell." *News and Observer*, column June 2000.
61. Friedman, *Capitalism and Freedom*.
62. Dale Ballou and Michael Podgursky, reported in *The Economist*, "Paying Teachers More." August 26, 2000, p. 18.
63. *The Economist*, "Black, White and Wrongheaded." August 30, 1997, p. 14.
64. Nina S. Rees, "Cleveland's Vouchers Are Rescuing Students." *News and Observer*, September 1999 column.
65. *The Economist*, "Blacks v Teachers." March 10, 2001, p. 27.
66. *The Economist*, "Answered Prayer." April 5, 1997, p. 27.
67. Barber, *The Book of Democracy*.
68. Dorothy L. Sayers, "The Lost Tools of Learning." In *Education in a Free Society*, ed. Anne H. Burleigh. Liberty Fund, 1973.

Chapter Nine:
The Public's Abiding Faith in Government and History's Most Elaborately Contrived Lie

People never lie so much as after a hunt, during a war or before an election.
—Otto von Bismarck

Thomas Jefferson wrote, "The art of government is the art of being honest." Artful politicians might agree with Jefferson, but they would be lying.

In 1830 Alexis de Tocqueville admired the healthy skepticism of government that was built into the typical US citizen of the time.[1] This skepticism persisted right up through the 1930s, when the Great Depression laid low the entire economy. President Roosevelt and many other politicians put the blame for widespread misery on the business community, when the real culprits were shortsighted and wrongheaded policies enacted by government itself.

When World War II finally lifted the economy out of the hard times, politicians leaped to claim credit: The New Deal policies had worked to alleviate the misery. From that point on long-suffering citizens kept an abiding faith in government's ability to solve social problems, and passed that faith along to their children. Today this faith distracts public concern from what government is really doing.

Walter Lippmann was a prominent journalist and analyst of the political scene more than fifty years ago. "A community that lacks the means to detect lies also lacks the means to preserve its own liberty." Especially in today's age of information technology, it is extremely important for a citizen to develop and retain an ability to distinguish wheat from chaff. Unfortunately, government and the media see fit to avoid helping the concerned citizen with this vital task.

Robert Bearce noted:

> *We ought to see that many reporters, commentators, editors, publishers, and news anchors are not the fair, objective, accurate, and honest people they would like us to believe. Instead, they are prejudiced against freedom. They show a*

clear bias in favor of more government . . . a support for more government intervention that daily translates into a corruption of the truth.[2]

The nation's prominent news media are under the thumb of big government, whose officials enhance their personal power by micromanaging nearly every aspect of the nation's economy. This chapter will demonstrate that the oligarchy fears truth, and this fact impels officials to falsify communications with the public in order to suppress it.

A prominent world figure during the 1930s believed that if he told the public a lie often enough and cleverly enough they would eventually come to believe it, even if it was not good for most of them. That person was Adolf Hitler. He and others such as Göring and Goebbels conspired to install a dictatorship in a Germany decimated by its experience in World War I and by the huge reparations demanded in the Treaty of Versailles. Hitler was a student of human nature: "What luck for rulers, that men do not think."

As in the United States, German citizens were suffering. Grasping at straws, they placed their trust in Hitler. US citizens did the same thing, depending on President Franklin Roosevelt to relieve their misery.

These observations suggest that there is a conspiracy alive today in the United States. A recent survey found that only one in five people today said they trust the government to do what is right most of the time; this is down from nearly two-thirds in 1964. More than just a suggestion is the feeling of alienation and frustration with government that pervades today's society.

Greider said: "Instead of a politics that leads the society sooner or later to confront its problems, American politics has developed new ways to hide from them."[3] President Reagan's "feel-good" politics comes to mind. The man's acting ability was far more effective in the White House than it ever was in Hollywood.

The Imperative of Controlling Information Flows

On May 23, 1792, Thomas Jefferson wrote to President George Washington:

Of all the mischiefs objected to the system of measures before mentioned, none is so afflicting and fatal to every honest hope, as the corruption of the legislature. As it was the earliest of these measures, it became the instrument for producing the risk, and will be the instrument for producing a future king, lords and commons. . . . Withdrawn such a distance from the eye of their constituents, and these so dispersed as to be inaccessible to public information, and particularly to that of the conduct of their own representatives, they will form the most corrupt government on earth.

Today's citizen might read this quote and conclude that the culture has changed over the past 200 years to make people much more accessible to public information: Print and broadcast media are full of information about representatives' speeches and actions. A second thought points to Lippmann's admonition. A conspiracy is by its nature carried out in secrecy, because it cannot work unless the victims do not realize that their thinking is being manipulated.

Russian citizens suffered for centuries, right up to World War I. This tragedy was followed immediately by the Bolshevik Revolution and then civil war. Furthermore the Soviet Union lost 20 million young men during World War II, and the economy was left in a shambles. Stalin fully appreciated this grim history, and he also knew that communism sat very poorly with his war allies in the West. Therefore he sought to clamp a tight lid on information flows to the West. He also worried about another revolution from within, so he directed that only key party cadres have telephones. Today's Russia is still paying the price in restricted ability to communicate.

Playwright Friedrich Schiller wrote *Wilhelm Tell* in 1804. Powell noted:

> *When Adolf Hitler heard that Schiller's Wilhelm Tell justified the toppling of tyrants, he banned the work. From . . . Don Carlos, Nazi censors cut the famous line, 'Give freedom of thought!' which always inspired a burst of applause from the audience. But on subsequent performances, as the action got to that point in the play, audiences applauded the missing line, and further performances were banned.*[4]

People everywhere crave personal freedom, so it is difficult for a tyrant to keep them silent.

Governments in the so-called third world restrict information flows, even though it is well known that a good communications system enhances economic development. The usual reason used for clamping down on the media is that they interfere with the government getting on with the job. The reality is that an effective media institution bridges the gap between concerned citizens and public officials, bringing to both groups constructive criticism without which government cannot do its job well. This illustrates the contrast between the negative tug of human nature—personal power seeking and holding—and the positive side—good government working with citizens to preserve their freedom.

Hayek went beyond this: "It is not difficult to deprive the great majority of independent thought. But the minority who will retain an inclination to criticize must also be silenced."[5] Creative officials have developed a great variety of methods of accomplishing this objective.

In his biography of Henry Kissinger, Isaacson wrote:

> *Laird [defense secretary] even kept up with the most secret Kissinger secret of all: the private peace talks with the North Vietnamese in Paris. "Hanoi's negotiators sent very good reports, full of Henry's sniveling, back from Paris every time Henry went over there," Laird said. These cables quickly appeared on Laird's desk, even though Kissinger was going to great lengths to make sure that*

the Pentagon and the State Department did not even know that these negotiations were under way.[6]

Isaacson continued:

The underlying assumption here is that decisions made without public scrutiny are better than those made after an open discussion. But even if one accepts this premise, one can still be taken aback by the disdain for democracy implied by his [Kissinger's] assertion that there is something "brutal" about allowing a congressional committee or newspaper readers to know about the debate. . . . In addition, reliance on secret channels wasted the time and creativity of Kissinger's staff. Winston Lord had to organize three versions of many briefing papers, for example. Kissinger and Nixon relied on the channels more because it suited their personalities than because it suited the security interests of the nation.

Kissinger's preoccupation with secrecy became an obsession when Nixon suggested that his own staff may be responsible for a series of embarrassing leaks. Kissinger eventually bugged the phones of his staff, but that bit of information was also leaked. The biggest leak came with the publishing of the Pentagon Papers. Isaacson observed: "Those who witnessed Kissinger's fury at the . . . meeting would long marvel at the scene, speaking of it like old salts recalling a historic hurricane. 'This will totally destroy American credibility forever,' he ranted as he paced around waving his arms and stamping his feet. 'It will destroy our ability to conduct foreign policy in confidence.'" There was a lesson in this, but it apparently was lost on Kissinger and the government.

In 1982 President Ronald Reagan signed an executive order authorizing classification of documents (which makes them secret). In 1984 the government classified 19,607,736 documents, a 60 percent increase over 1973 when there was a war still going on in Vietnam. In April 1986 Reagan put into force thirteen measures to increase secrecy, including prosecution of public officials for leaks and reducing their access to classified files. These actions reversed a trend begun by President Dwight Eisenhower that limited classification of documents. Today's presence of a demand for leaks suggests that citizens' suspicions are growing.

Sussman commented on the invasion of Grenada: "The US distributed government films that provided favorable coverage on the landing, detained several US reporters already on the island, and threatened to shoot others who tried to reach Grenada on their own."[7] Generals had previously sworn that the media caused their defeat in Vietnam, so they "adjusted" coverage in Grenada, and later in Panama, Iraq, Kosovo, and Afghanistan.

Bad government regulation of banking before 1988 put into place a policy in which if a major bank failed taxpayers would finance a government bailout. When savings-and-loan managers fully understood the implications of this policy, they realized that their risk of failure had been eliminated, and so they began to play fast and loose with depositors' money. They sunk it into extremely high-risk ventures and proceeded to lose billions.

The situation came to a head during the 1988 presidential election campaign. Desperate concern on the part of cadres in both political parties led them to muzzle the news media until after the campaign. Had the issue been aired in a timely manner the damage would have been easily controllable; most of the errant managers could have been forced to make good their losses.

Robert Dugger, a lobbyist, remarked:

> *Everyone knew the game was: democrats don't bring this up, republicans don't bring this up. Because a firefight on this issue will have more bodies on both sides than anyone wants to lose. The financial community knew that and we knew where the play was: Wage the presidential campaign on all issues, but don't use the thrift crisis. We all know it has to be dealt with. We'll do it right after the election.*[8]

Thus was launched a campaign of tight secrecy reminiscent of the Mafia's code of Omerta. When the scandal erupted after the election the damage was far worse than it would have been. After the smoke and dust had settled, taxpayers got stuck with a $100 billion bill. Officials "sold" this huge lump to the public as a "patriotic obligation." Controlling information flows assumes even greater importance just prior to an election, and this is but one such instance.

The CIA is one of thirteen government agencies that handle cloak-and-dagger work. This type of work opens up nearly unlimited possibilities for withholding information and deceiving the public. Lapham stated:

> *At the behest of various presidents a succession of compliant CIA directors . . . rearranged the intelligence estimates (about Vietcong troop strength or the geography of the Bay of Pigs, about the military and economic capacities of the Soviet Union, about the Arab oil reserves and the democratic aspirations of the shah of Iran) in order to align the facts with whatever preferred image of the world happened to be in fashion at the White House. Judged by the standards of intellectual honesty, the record is a disgrace; weighed in the balance of Washington politics, the record can be judged a success as great as the savings and loan swindle because the events that followed from the deconstruction of the texts advanced the careers of the court officials who revised or deleted the offending paragraphs.*[9]

In fall 1994 Budget Director Alice Rivlin and her staff compiled a memo for the president that showed what real choices the government had ahead of it. They were grim. Someone leaked it, and immediately another hurricane blew up as Rivlin was cussed up and down by officials in both political parties. Truth lurks in the shadows as a towering threat to any regime that seeks to withhold it from the public.

Today the White House press corps is very large, and yet citizens feel ill-informed because concentration of personal power requires withholding information from the public. Therefore the corps is fed disinformation to feed in turn to the public. Citizens thus get an avalanche of "information," but because they cannot separate the wheat from the chaff they remain poorly informed.

Johnson observed that President Calvin Coolidge handled the press quite differently. "Not only did he keep no press secretary and refuse to hold on-the-record press conferences; he resented it if a journalist addressed any remarks to him, even 'Good morning.' But if written questions were submitted in advance . . . would write the answers himself: short, very dry, but informative and truthful."[10] He could retain a copy of his answer, and the press knew it. This threat boxed it in very effectively.

But today's White House does not stop at simple obfuscation. Helm noted: "The US Department of HHS [Health and Human Services] initially refused to disclose which antibiotics were being used to treat the Florida anthrax outbreak or where the drugs came from 'for security reasons.' Private . . . companies said they could not discuss vaccines or antidotes because the administration told them not to."[11] Helm continued: "The administration has also waded into the editorial content of US news outlets and talk shows."

One of the most widely distributed newspapers in the Soviet Union was *Pravda*, which in the Russian language means *truth*. Well before the collapse of the Soviet Union, practically every citizen knew the real truth about this publication. The reason why so many US citizens have been deceived over the past fifty years lies in the abiding faith thesis mentioned at the beginning of the chapter. Due to centuries of abuse of citizens by governments in Russia, this faith had no opportunity to develop. Therefore top cadres knew that conspiracy was not an option. Centralization of power and oppression of the masses was the only alternative.

Citizens' abiding faith in this country's government has been jarred over the past thirty or so years, toward distrust and suspicion. Putnam showed that young people believe they no longer get useful information in the daily news:

> *Daily newspaper readership among people under thirty-five dropped from 2/3 in 1965 to 1/3 in 1990, at the same time that TV news viewership in this same age group fell from fifty-two percent to forty-one percent. Today's under-thirties pay less attention to the news and know less about current events than their elders do today or than people their age did two or three decades ago.*[12]

These findings suggest that the elites' attempt to withhold information from the public is working.

Colleges and universities have traditionally taken great pride in being places where open minds could pursue free inquiry aimed toward revealing truth. To abandon this noble search would be a great tragedy, but the politically correct movement and its more recent reincarnations are doing exactly this. The consequent denial of truth to young people has two obvious implications: It fits well into government's concern with withholding information, and it guarantees that nearly all citizens of the future will be docile.

In 1989 the Bush administration classified as secret another 5,506,720 documents. Sussman offered a hypothetical example of the counterproductive effects of overclassification: "Imagine if the Germans in 1875 had classified the internal combustion engine. The French then in retaliation would have classified the gearbox, and Goodyear would have classified the vulcanization of rubber. The automobile industry would have had a very hard time."[13] This example goes far to explain the litany of failures by the CIA: It is protected by a shroud of secrecy in the name of national security.

For forty-five years the phrase *covert action* has been used to conceal activities that interfered in the internal affairs of other countries. Codevilla was a senior staff member of the Senate Select Committee on Intelligence from 1977 to 1985.[14]

> *The US has been surprised by every major world event since 1960. . . . The Tet offensive that proved to be the turning point in the Vietnam war; the Soviet invasion of Czechoslovakia; the Yom Kippur war in 1973 and the ensuing Arab oil embargo; the Soviet invasion of Afghanistan; and the rise of the Polish Solidarity trade union in 1980, and the manner in which it was crushed in 1981, to name just a few. The revolution that swept Eastern Europe in 1989, an event that ranks in importance with World War I, was wholly unheralded by technical intelligence.*
>
> *Just about all of the CIA's actions in Vietnam were well known to the enemy. What purpose, then, was served by keeping them secret within the US government and from the American people?*

In the absence of reliable information the rumor mill will often fill the need. In this instance rumors were extensively **discussed and molded into truth** by the collective wisdom of a large mass of concerned young people, some of whom were being drafted into military service through a system that they described as "body bingo" (random selection by birth date). The end result was a government that remained uncertain as to why the United States was fighting a brutal war in a far-off land, and a public that knew the truth.

Codevilla wrote,

> *In 1978 five Cubans had testified . . . that they had offered their services to the CIA, had been accepted, and for ten years had served as double agents, fooling the CIA on behalf of Cuban intelligence. . . . According to a CIA report that found its way to the press, "Most East Germans recruited by the CIA as spies since at least the early 1950s were double agents secretly loyal to the Stasi."*

The CIA wrote in its 1987 *World Fact Book* that the per capita GNP (value of all goods and services produced in a year) of East Germany exceeded that of West Germany, just two years before the Berlin Wall came down and revealed the truth.

In 1982 a captured Nicaraguan soldier told the CIA that he had been trained by the Soviets to help overthrow the government of El Salvador. The US government had been trying to prove this very point, so agents put the young man before a press conference. He denied the whole story and accused the United States of kidnapping, drugging, and torture. Codevilla noted: "They had not questioned the teenager's motives, much less had they taken the elementary precaution of staging a 'dry run' before a fake audience. A 19-year-old armed with the fundamentals will outdo a whole government that forgets them, every time."

Another agency, the Bureau of Intelligence and Research, probably did not know enough to judge the accuracy of Soviet missiles based on purloined data. But it did know enough to fudge them on the side of improved accuracy, because this conclusion would reinforce calls for more taxpayer money for defense. This was nothing new; the national security ruse had covered a multitude of sins for centuries. Codevilla ventured a comment on human nature: ". . . that other people are moved by love, hate, devotion to God, lust for vengeance, the cruel joy of conquest, or political ideology." These tendencies affect agency operatives, of course, but they often pull in a different direction when protected by the shroud of secrecy.

Eventually these and other "intelligence" agencies took on the trappings of stale bureaucracies. For years they had refused to admit that communism was devastating economies throughout the world. "Finally, while the collapse of communism in Eastern Europe prompted most bureaucracies in Washington to draft plans to reshape themselves for a new world, the US intelligence community seemed to want very much to stand still." These agencies had had several decades to adjust to the cold war. Bureaucrats felt comfortable and secure in their niches. Therefore the reaction to a major change in the intelligence environment was deer-staring-into-headlights panic.

Barber commented on the Iran-contra scandal: "On Poindexter's authority . . . Oliver North lied to Congress to obscure his secret actions, thus corrupting democracy. He took pride as a soldier in fighting with the weapon of deceit against the people's representatives, whom he perceived as the enemy."[15] What is incredible about this episode is the number of citizens who perceived North as a hero. This apparent criminal even had the temerity to run for governor of the state of Virginia (he was defeated). Barber: "Secrecy is the greatest advantage of those who would abuse human rights."

The 1991 war against Iraq was sold as the outcome of a UN resolution, but its real cause was a need for President Bush to boost his sagging popularity rating. Saddam Hussein was unlucky enough to enter the world stage at almost precisely the right moment, with a presidential election coming up soon afterward and the time to begin campaigning just about then.

There was also an image problem, in that the US public perceived Saddam as the tin-pot dictator of a tiny country exhausted from a grisly and greatly damaging eight-year war against its neighbor, Iran. This image had to be changed, or the citizens would not accept the idea of giving the man and his country another pounding. Therefore a reputable public relations company was hired to enlarge Saddam's image to that of an 800-pound gorilla (Kuwait paid the $10.8 million tab). The Bush administration ignored the fact that surveys showed American citizens reluctant to trade blood for oil.

The generals carefully orchestrated media coverage during the war, so that it resembled a TV miniseries. It included only bombs and missiles that hit their targets, for two reasons. The first was to make a hero out of their commander-in-chief, Bush, and the second was to convince a gullible public to spring for additional billions of dollars to replace parts of an already huge arsenal of weapons and to add still more (well-paid jobs in defense factories readily translate into votes for incumbents).

Before he became president of France, Jacques Chirac said privately, "The best press law contains just one sentence: The press shall be free. You should say that publicly while you are out of power, to commit yourself. Otherwise, the temptation to act differently is too great, once you come to power." The man was right: Once in office, he ignored his own sound advice.

Alterman showed that the pundits "had access to the highest reaches of the government, and in turn were expected to exercise good judgment about just how much truth was healthy for Americans to hear."[16] Not only does this control over flows of information contravene the US Constitution; what is released to the public is biased and thereby skirts the edges of truth. Pundits live, work, and party among the elites, so it is not difficult to surmise the direction of their biases.

Bureaucrats get entrenched into public employment with the intent of staying until retirement regardless of whether the agency is doing good for anyone besides bureaucrats. A part of this strategy lies in invention of a language that fogs the issues for outsiders, thus making it difficult to understand what they are doing. Jefferson mused:

> *I thought it would be useful . . . [to] reform the style of the later British statutes, and of our own . . . which, from their verbosity, their endless tautologies, their involutions of case within case, and parenthesis within parenthesis, and their multiplied efforts at certainty, by saids and aforesaids, by ors and by ands, to make them more plain, are really rendered more perplexed and incomprehensible, not only to common readers, but to the lawyers themselves.*

In 1774 Jefferson was hard at work on this task: organizing and rewriting for clarity the laws of the colony of Virginia. In today's central government it looks like someone should be hard at work.

At this point it would be encouraging to relate an instance in which concerned citizens forced their government to be more open about their operations. In fact an attempt was made in 1966 with passage of the Freedom of Information Act. But in casting it into law Congress saw fit to exempt itself from enforcement. Later it exempted several agencies, including the CIA. Lawsuits have been brought under the act, but with very limited success because Rule of Law is all but nonexistent in today's Washington.

Reeves observed that a citizen might see archived records of a former president, but he or she would need permission from both former and present incumbent.[17] "There are rules upon rules about which presidential papers become available and when . . . and some of them defy all reason." Citizens are paying government officials to act in their behalf. How can they determine sincerity if denied information they paid for? Reeves concluded, "It's hard to see how double presidential oversight will speed things up, unless the idea is to just say no. And I think that is the idea."

George Will elaborated on this theme in an assertive manner: "The basis of political-speech regulation is the 1971 Federal Election Campaign Act. . . . Because of it, for the first time Americans were required to register with the government before spending money to disseminate criticism of its officeholders."[18] For example, "The first FECA enforcement action came in 1972, when some citizens organized as the National Committee for Impeachment paid $17,850 to run a *New York Times* ad criticizing President Nixon. His Justice Department got a court to enjoin the committee from further spending to disseminate its beliefs.

Will wrote about a man who designed a Web site for the same purpose. The Federal Election Commission shut it down, interpreting his purchase of a computer as spending money to criticize the government. Finally, Will noted that "litigation has become a campaign weapon: Candidates file charges to embarrass opponents and force them to expend resources fending off the speech police."

A potentially more encouraging development lies in the Internet, which has thus far proven difficult (if not impossible) for the central government to control. Although to date it has been crammed with fluff, it is possible to send truth over it, and this incipient threat has high public officials feeling paranoid.

They are trying to control the Net. In January 2001 *The Economist* noted:

> *It seems likely that 2000 will be remembered as the year when governments started to regulate cyberspace in earnest; and forgot, in the process, that the reason the worldwide network became such an innovative force at all was a healthy mix of self-regulation and no regulation. [Britain] now gives the police broad access to e-mail and other online communications.*[19]

Hopper quoted a muckraking congressman named Jay Inslee: "Americans should not have to worry about federal agencies monitoring their Internet activity, yet this audit found seven examples of invisible Web bugs on Navy, Air Force and Marine Corps Web sites."[20]

But, wait. Columnist Friedman reported from the Middle East: "The Egyptian government censors *The Cairo Times* when it comes into Egypt. And what do the editors . . . do? They now print in bright red letters on their Web site (cairotimes.com) everything the government takes out."[21] However, if Walter Lippmann were around today he would predict that this news outlet would not realize its potential for dissemination of truth until the public learns how to distinguish truth from lies.

Growing Comfortable with Lying

There is little doubt that Bill Clinton could write this section better than anyone else. But he was no pioneer in this devious skill. Woodward, in his book about Federal Reserve Chairman Alan Greenspan, communicates the predominant flavor in Washington as people's behavior reflect the negative tugs of human nature:

> *"This is a town that is full of evil people," Greenspan had said. "If you can't deal with every day having people trying to destroy you, you shouldn't even think of coming down here." Normal human beings could look you straight in the face and lie about things they had done, Greenspan warned. It had happened to him. . . . Greenspan maintained that it was morally evil to lie outright.*[22]

Patrick Henry said:

> *It is natural to man to indulge in the illusions of hope. We are apt to shut our eyes against a painful truth, and listen to the song of that siren, till she transforms us into beasts. Is this the part of wise men, engaged in a great and arduous struggle for liberty? Are we disposed to be of the number of those who, having eyes, see not, and having ears, hear not, the things that so nearly concern their temporal salvation? For my part, whatever anguish of spirit it may cost, I am willing to know the truth; to know the worst and provide for it.*

Henry used his excellent speaking and dialectical skills while promoting revolution against King George III.

The affluent era for the United States commenced right after World War II, when an economy stimulated yet undamaged by war raced ahead. With acquisition of wealth it was natural to relax scrutiny of government. This opened the door for lying and deceit.

Lapham illustrated the consequences of telling too many lies:

> *Failing to hold themselves responsible—to the summons calling them to become more than they thought they could become, they destroy the chance of their own freedom. The same thing can be said of governments, most especially*

of democracies. More than anything else we have need of a believable story because without a believable story we have no means of connecting the past to the present, the dead to the living, the citizen to the state, the now to the then.[23]

Lapham argued that citizens need the courage to seek truth. With this vital possession they can force into place a credible government and keep it there.

Carter noted: "We, the people of the United States, who a little over two hundred years ago ordained and established the Constitution, have a serious problem: too many of us nowadays neither mean what we say nor say what we mean. Moreover, we hardly expect anybody else to mean what they say either."[24] This is another way of presenting the result when a society loses its grip on honesty. In an August 1998 column, Carter wrote: "If the polls are correct, we do not really care very much whether the president lies to us as long as we are otherwise happy with his performance. This alarming display of cynicism teaches our children that what matters most is not right or wrong but getting what we want."

The implications for society are dangerous. How could citizens be happy with Clinton's performance if they didn't know the truth about it? The sad truth is that during his entire administration Clinton consistently exhibited a thoroughgoing disdain for truth.

Mike Royko in a January 1996 column stated that

all politicians tell lies at one time or another. If they didn't lie, most would never be elected because they'd have to declare their candidacies by saying: "I seek this office because I have an enormous ego. I love power and wheeling and dealing; crave admiration, recognition and approval; am infinitely more intelligent than the rest of you; have an insatiable need to impose my will on others." . . . So they tell us lies about what they will do for us, rather than what they will do to us. . . . This is as it must be. We would have chaos if politicians told us only the truth.[25]

If this statement is accurate, a thinking citizen would be hard put to refer to the government as a democracy.

A political buzz term called *current services baseline* drew a comment from P. J. O'Rourke:

This is how a president can—using last year's actual budget figures—claim that he plans to increase spending on some piece of federal tomfoolery while congressmen in the opposing party can—using the current services baseline budget figures—claim that the president plans to drastically cut the same identical folly. And they can both be telling the truth—or, to put it in layman's terms—lying.[26]

O'Rourke here suggested that Washington has adopted a new and vastly different definition of *truth* (as did the Soviet Union and other countries).

Lapham argued that Reagan taught the country that there was no need for expertise on any important issue. "Government was a salesman's smile and a gift for phrase. But it turned out that lies did make a difference: the lies and the Reagan administration's relentless grasping of illegal and autocratic privilege."

Alterman commented on Reagan's budget director:

> *The substance of Stockman's story could hardly have been more devastating to the Reagan administration. He was saying that at base, the entire edifice was phony. . . . Literally "no one" knew "what was going on with the numbers." The costs of the willful self-deception involved in conferring competence on the Reagan administration would be demonstrated over and over again during the course of the next eight years.*[27]

"Yes sir/ma'am, I definitely identify with your concern on this issue, and I pledge to exert my every effort to resolve it as you so adroitly suggest. Thank you for bringing it to my attention." This canned response always follows a carefully rehearsed and faked listening routine. The rehearsals are necessary to convince the complaining citizen or organization that the career politician is really listening, whereas the hidden agenda is get rid of the serf and get back to the real business of government. Faked listening is a vital skill that is learned early on in the career of a politician.

Elder president George Bush encouraged citizen polls, because he believed that these would convince the people that he was listening to them and would act on their suggestions. In 1988 one firm asked what should concern the new president. Back came the usual: environmental regulation, toxic wastes, the poor, the homeless, trade laws, health insurance, and so on. The list had absolutely no impact on his campaign or later when he was in office. He governed at variance to and sometimes opposed to what the people wanted; his reasoning was that the people must want the same things the president wants or they would not have elected him. The ultimate result of this line of reasoning is that the **people come to depend on politicians** for their political positions, rather than the other way around.

There are two basic methods of accounting—cash and accrual. The first covers cash in and out only, so the opportunities to make spending commitments where the costs can be hidden in the future are unlimited. The second must include every fiscal decision, even including what are called contingent liabilities (which may or may not ever require payment). The government naturally prefers the first method, even though the law requires publicly owned companies (corporations) to use accrual accounting when they publish their annual reports.

With this in view it is not difficult to imagine that data that compare the government's operations under both methods are hard to come by. In one year, 1974, the government reported a fiscal deficit of $6.1 billion. Were that figure to be calculated by the accrual method the deficit would have been $95.1 billion. By 1984 the total national government debt (accumulated deficits) was $1.3 trillion when figured by the cash method, and $3.8 trillion by the accrual method. Forty years ago Congress passed a law that requires use of the accrual method in government, but officials have ignored this law ever since, and apparently no one has called them on it.

Lying to the electorate about the government's use of their money is also not difficult. In October 1990 the Bush administration said that a tax increase would reduce the fiscal deficit for the next year to $63.1 billion. Bush got the "Read my lips: no new taxes!" tax increase, but by the end of 1991 the deficit was $384.6 billion. Lapham wrote, "The numbers speak to the contempt with which the court at Washington regards the American public."

Due to the political atmosphere in Washington, it is very difficult to winnow truth from the mass of fluff in the media. Therefore it is frequently necessary to go abroad in search of this elusive commodity. *The Economist* provided some truth in an area where emotion often prevails.[28] In 1972 the Club of Rome said total global oil reserves were 550 billion barrels. President Jimmy Carter said, "We could use up all . . . by the end of the next decade." Between 1970 and 1990 the world used 600 billion barrels of oil, so there should have been a deficit of 50 billion barrels. The club did not see fit to apologize for its error in prediction.

The news media often trade on emotion, not facts.

Lester Brown of the Worldwatch Institute began predicting in 1973 that population would soon outstrip food production, and he still does so every time there is a temporary increase in wheat prices. In 1994, after twenty-one years of being wrong, he said: "After 40 years of record food production gains, output per person has reversed with unanticipated abruptness." Two bumper harvests followed and prices fell to record lows. Yet Mr. Brown's pessimism remains as impregnable to facts as his views are popular with newspapers.

There were people who in 1970 predicted abundant food, who in 1975 predicted cheap oil, who in 1980 predicted cheaper and more abundant minerals. Today these people . . . are ignored by the press and vilified by the environmental movement. For being right, they are called "right wing."

The Economist discussed the acid rain scare of the early 1980s as the "doom du jour" of that decade. In the end the trees recovered, and the total stock in Europe actually increased during that ten-year period.

Now it is time for global warming. *Newsweek* magazine wrote in 1975: "Meteorologists . . . [predict a] cooling trend. . . . But they are almost unanimous in the view that the trend will reduce agricultural productivity for the rest of the century." Al Gore in 1992: "Scientists concluded—almost unanimously—that global warming is real and the time to act is now."

The truth is that insufficient data are available today to make an accurate projection so far into the future. Reliable weather records go back slightly more than 100 years, which means that both of the opposite predictions mentioned relied on nearly the same batch of weather records. (A recent study, reported in *Nature*, of long-wave infrared radiation looks convincing. However, data representing just two years [1970 and 1997] only twenty-seven years apart had to be manipulated to get the results.) Furthermore, there are benefits to global warming, such as longer growing seasons for crops. But in today's political climate these remain underreported. President Bush was vilified by environmentalists for his criticism of the Kyoto protocols, but more recent study and reflection indicate that his position may have merit.

The Economist commented further: "In two years, elephants went from imminent danger of extinction to badly in need of contraception (the facts did not change, the reporting did)." Scientists otherwise renowned for their integrity but dependent on federal grants for their work are occasionally tempted to adjust interpretations of results to match the current direction of political winds.

An entrepreneur has organized a business in Washington that reveals intentional bias in statistical reporting. The global warming controversy illustrates what is widely known: Statistics can be interpreted to suit most arguments. David W. Murray says that half the information "everybody knows" is not supported by facts. (He hastens to add that he has no political ax to grind.) Considering the amount of statistics that Washington turns out and the prevalence of bias in that town, the outlook for the business has to be good.

The logical conclusion is that if citizens want truth in their news media they will not get it until they demand it. They will not demand it until they fully realize that their thinking is being manipulated.

> An *Economist* article entitled "The Price of Perjury" was published, not coincidentally, in November 1998.[29]
>
> *Two centuries of lawmaking, compounded by the cumulative ingenuity of lawyers, have created statutes and precedents that touch on every part of life, multiplying the chances that citizens will find themselves obliged to give evidence in legal proceedings. Meanwhile, the use of oaths in such proceedings has multiplied as well. For the first century of the republic's life, this sacred device was invoked sparingly.*

The litigation explosion has combined with great numbers of trials on television to render the taking of an oath by ordinary citizens close to meaningless.

Unfortunately, in high public office, where perjury can do much more damage to the social fabric, the same situation prevails. "As a result, respect for the law has been diminished. It would be better if the excesses of legalism were rolled back, so that Americans feel readier to impeach the next perjurious president." The apparent lesson here is that future presidents need not worry about perjuring themselves. Therefore a generation yet to come may have to suffer through one who surpasses Hitler's grisly record.

In a January 2001 column, Will commented on Bill Clinton:

As president he was fined $90,000 for contempt of court, and there is no reasonable doubt that he committed and suborned perjury, tampered with witnesses and otherwise obstructed justice. In the words of Richard A. Posner, chief judge of the seventh circuit, Clinton's illegalities "were felonious, numerous and nontechnical," and "constituted a kind of guerrilla warfare against the third branch of the federal government, the federal court system." [30]

Will concluded that "Clinton is not the worst president the republic has had, but he is the worst person ever to have been president."

Krauthammer said,

But it was more than just the power of Juanita Broaddrick's charges . . . that altered the post-impeachment mood. It was the shame visited upon democratic leaders who were required, by party loyalty and by the stock they had already invested in Bill Clinton's innocence, to dismiss her charge with "it's just a he-said, she-said" rape story so "let's move on." One can only imagine the embarrassment, the self-loathing, of those who for years decried the marginalization and victimization of women with stories exactly like Juanita Broaddrick's, now publicly dismissing her with a shrug.[31]

Here is a prime example of Lapham's courtier spirit (page 222). Therefore there was far less self-loathing than Krauthammer implied in this column.

This grisly event further demonstrates the tremendous strength of the negative tug that impels people to seek personal power over others and then cling to it through hell and high water. Just a shred of honesty and integrity would have been needed to remove Clinton from office and thus restore some political credibility for the nation's generations to come. (At the time *The Economist* argued repeatedly that he should be removed.) Lacking this, the only logical conclusion is that the impeachment process was staged after the protagonists had agreed on a script.

Russia-born Ayn Rand thought deeply about truth and honesty in government.[32] "There is no conflict, and no call for sacrifice, and no man is a threat to the aims of another . . . if men understand that reality is an absolute not to be faked, that lies do not work, that the unearned cannot be had, that the undeserved cannot be given, that the destruction of a value which is, will not bring value to that which isn't."

Jefferson commented, "He who permits himself to tell a lie once, finds it much easier to do it a second and third time, till at length it becomes habitual; he tells lies without attending to it, and truths without the world's believing him. This falsehood of the tongue leads to that of the heart."

Massive Waste Covered Up

O'Rourke noted: "It is a popular delusion that the government wastes vast amounts of money through inefficiency and sloth. Enormous effort and elaborate planning are required to waste this much money."[33] It is impractical for anyone or any government to control two trillion dollars and adequately account for all receipts and expenditures. This reality combines with the fact that no one spends somebody else's money as carefully as they spend their own, opening the way to massive waste of resources (along with outright thievery). Nowhere else in the world is the money mountain nearly so massive as it is in Washington, DC.

When Transportation Secretary Federico Peña was told his department owned 304 airplanes with 2 assigned to the secretary, he replied, "I don't use them. I fly commercial coach." He said nothing about the other 302. The Inspector General checked Federal Aviation Administration (FAA) records and found a total of 1,384 airplanes owned by the government, including 237 that were apparently missing. Thirty-one planes were registered to agencies that were not supposed to have any. Another 152 were somehow transferred to state and local governments. The inspector general estimated that this operation wastes a half billion dollars a year.

Gross dug for facts about government expenditures for furniture and decorating, finding that between $1.3 and $2 billion a year were spent.[34] His informant lost his job for supplying this information to a published author.

Gross continued digging. "Between January 1993 and April 1994, FAA officials took 247,840 free flights . . . [including] a Washington-area evaluator who flew to West Palm Beach . . . for a week of leave; an Atlanta employee who made twelve trips to visit family; a Washington evaluator who made a trip to London for a two-week vacation; and a Washington evaluator who used twenty-two tickets to visit his family in Philadelphia, as well as six tickets to Atlantic City . . . and Las Vegas." Department of Transportation (DOT) Inspector General A. Mary Schiavo referred to air traffic controllers' trips: "The numbers were so high that we stopped counting. . . . At least 83 percent . . . were for personal gain."

Energy Secretary Hazel O'Leary chartered a luxury jet and took along 119 others plus photographers to South Africa. This cost $560,000, even though the United States has no nuclear power plants or waste in South Africa. She also chartered a luxury jet with a bar and a kitchen for a trip to China and Pakistan.

The National Park Service thought a new shopping center under construction next to Manassas Historic Battlefield in Virginia was an eyesore, so the Congress bought it and paid more than $200,000 an acre. Gross said: "I asked what will happen when a shrewd entrepreneur who knows the government's mind puts up another eyesore shopping center outside the new boundaries. Will the government buy that one too for another $130 million? They just tittered." According to estimates, a different particular tract of public land containing deposits of platinum and palladium was worth $32 billion. The government sold it for $5.40 an acre.

Then there was $315,000 to make a historic site of the South Carolina home of Charles Pinckney, a signer of the US Constitution. But Mr. Pinckney had died before the house was even built.

When business makes an offer, the consumer immediately knows (or can easily learn) what it will cost. He or she can therefore make a far more informed decision than when he hears or sees a politician's blandishments. He votes, maybe, and the bill arrives much later, in spurts and dribbles and from myriad directions, such that the citizen never knows how much he is paying for any particular bit of fluff. These prices are not advertised, so only with the most painstaking of inquiry can a citizen learn about those numbers.

Shortly before the Gulf War the army ordered 12,000 hand-held global positioning satellite (GPS) navigation aids to enable soldiers to accurately pin down their locations on the battlefield. A defense contractor estimated the cost at $34,000 per unit. Each would weigh seventeen pounds and would be available in eighteen months. Then two private companies got the business, filling the order in three months with three-pound devices at $1,300 each.

A 1996 estimate put central government waste at $350 billion. The budget deficit for that year was $120 billion. Gross estimated in 1995 that the total bill for government at all levels was $2.55 trillion, and of that $600 billion was wasted. Since 1960 the cost of state and local government has increased about 350 percent in inflation-adjusted dollars, and it is now over $1 trillion. That is, $15,000 a year for a typical family of four, in addition to the $23,000 a year taken by Washington.

There are some ninety early childhood programs spread across eleven agencies. There are eleven rural development programs in six agencies, and each has its own set of regulations for local officials. The Department of Education administers more than 200 programs, and thirty other agencies manage another 308. Eighty-six programs spread across nine agencies deal with teacher training. Gross noted ". . . there are 150 different training and employment programs operating out of fourteen agencies. According to the inspector general of labor, the cost is $17 billion a year. Yet seventy percent of the jobs obtained are for $5 an hour or less . . . positions that need no training." (A 1996 estimate has 163 programs spread among fifteen agencies.)

In his 1996 State of the Union speech Clinton said there were more than seventy redundant job training programs in the Department of Labor that should be consolidated, but the budget proposal sought a spending increase for the existing maze of unworkable programs and added two more. This instance exemplifies the result of decades of turf battles among career bureaucrats.

Gross soundly castigated the growth of the executive branch of government, focusing especially on the Department of Agriculture.

> *The department is no longer famous for what it does but is known for the irrationality of its size . . . and how much money and manpower it wastes on its ever-decreasing mission. It's a massive organization with 124,000 employees and an extravagant $62 billion annual budget. . . . Without fear of exaggera-*

tion, we can say that the D of A is so mired in bureaucratic morass and skewed goals that nothing will improve the reputation of the federal government until most of this department is eliminated.

The extraordinary story is that the department kept growing larger as its mission got smaller. At the turn of the century, there were five million farms. Some 20 million people were directly involved, plus millions of others dependent on farmers. We're talking about a third of the nation. How large was the D of A then? All of 3,000 people, one lonely bureaucrat for every 1,800 farms.

Today? You won't believe it. There is one bureaucrat for every 16 full-time farmers. There are 12,000 field offices . . . 40 percent of all 30,000 government outposts in the nation. . . . . (In 1994) farmers of corn, barley, rice and cotton received $379 million to limit their production while they received $66 million in irrigation subsidies to produce more crops.

A top staffer in the House Agriculture Committee provided an insight: "There's a swap. The farm congressmen back all that money that goes to the cities and welfare, and city people back our farm subsidies. That's how the country is run."

Taxpayers were beginning to catch a whiff of this publicly financed quid pro quo, and they were predictably less than enamored with the arrangement. Running scared, politicians in 1996 generated what is called the Freedom to Farm Act. *The Economist* said, "[The act] ended half a century of farm policy in which the government told farmers how to use their land in exchange for subsidizing the crops they grew. . . . They will get $30 billion in 'transition payments' between 1997 and 2002, but these are no longer linked to what goes on in the fields."[35]

This conclusion sounds strange, as the passage of that half-century has seen hundreds of new government farm programs, and these have gradually separated many full-time farmers from their land. Such a farmer spends more time "farming" the corridors of congressional office buildings seeking greater subsidies, set-asides, payments for not growing crops, irrigation payments, and payments in kind than farming the land. There are 600 full-time farmers who annually get $1 million or more of such payments.

Stephen Budiansky was also skeptical:

Reports that farm subsidies are dead are premature, however. Payments under the Freedom to Farm bill will decline only modestly over seven years. . . . [It] also retains the $2 billion-a-year Conservation Reserve Program, which pays farmers to keep 36 million acres of highly erodible farmland in wildlife habitat. Though touted as saving $13 billion over seven years, the bill may save less than $1 billion, says the CBO.[36]

Amendments to decrease taxpayer support for wealthy peanut and sugar producers were defeated, thus enabling forced payments from the nonrich to the rich to live on unmolested.

In 1997 Clinton issued an executive order to declassify all secret documents more than twenty-five years old. The CIA had 166 million such pages, and the Department of Defense had 998 million. But the thirteen intelligence services balked. In 1984 Congress shielded CIA files from public access through the Freedom of Information Act, on condition that a special review panel be set up. Historian George Herring sat on that panel from 1990 to 1996. "It was like nailing jelly to a wall. Now I'm from Kentucky, and I'm not supposed to be swift, but it didn't take too long even for me to realize that I was being used to cover the agency's ass while having no influence." If these files had seen the light of day, the exposure of massive waste and fraud probably would have buried the agency.

The Economist elaborated:

> *As well as the CIA and the FBI, America maintains eleven other intelligence agencies, which duplicate each other's work. There are rival groups of intelligence analysts working for the army, the navy, the air force and the marines; on top of this the defense establishment has the Defense Intelligence Agency, the National Security Agency, and two other bodies. Then there are intelligence operators at the Department of Energy, the State Department, and even at the Treasury. The head of the CIA is supposed to lead all thirteen agencies, though he controls only one of them. . . . This blundering costs America good will among its allies. It costs taxpayers dearly, too: the thirteen . . . consume around $30 billion a year (the precise figure is secret). By contrast, the State Department budget comes to a paltry $2.5 billion.*[37]

The government apparently believes that spying on governments of other countries is nearly twelve times as important as making and keeping friends among them. It also partially explains why many foreigners perceive the United States as a big bully (see Chapter 21).

London columnist Gwynne Dyer was solicited by a Russian spymaster.[38] He was not serious, explaining to her that he simply needed to maintain a certain number of informants and one of his existing had just been killed in a traffic accident. Her conclusion after additional research:

> *It IS just a game. Huge amounts of money get spent, hundreds of thousands of people are employed, and some of them go to jail or even get killed, but it is all quite pointless.*
>
> *In wartime, good operational intelligence can make a big difference, but in peacetime (including the whole Cold War) the whole gigantic machinery of espionage is pure waste. Most of those engaged in it are cynical drones like Khmyz, or romantic fools, or greedy fools. In America, at the moment it seems to be the latter who predominate.*

The Department of Defense reinforces this dubious world image, but sometimes the president also helps. The B-2 Stealth bomber is a case in point, because the president continued to order the airplanes even though the Pentagon didn't want them. *The Economist* commented:

> *The B-2 Spirit bomber is a case study in how politics drives the shaping of America's arsenal. Spurned by George Bush and the chiefs of staff, and at first discontinued by Mr. Clinton, this hugely expensive aeroplane has now been resurrected from the grave. The reason for doing so, in large part, is presidential politics. "I don't think the defense bill is a jobs program," says a congressman from California, "but some people see it in that perspective." . . .*
>
> *Bush . . . would cancel cold war plans to build seventy-five B-2s . . . get by with twenty. That, most people reckoned, was the beginning of the end for the B-2. [By] early February . . . Clinton . . . halt[ed] the order at twenty. He knew the decision could hurt him in California . . . until the presidential campaign came along. . . . On March 20th Mr. Clinton reversed himself. He ordered one more B-2. . . . One aeroplane may not sound like much, but it will keep the assembly lines warm and set a precedent for ordering more. . . . Mr. Clinton is so afraid of looking anti-military that he will flout the wishes of the brass and buy it an aircraft it does not want.*[39]

One B-2 airplane costs $2.2 billion. *The Economist* had previously opined that "ounce for ounce, America's B-2 stealth bomber is more valuable than gold." The writer meant it costs more; the difference in meanings is meaningful to a taxpayer.

The Economist also could not refrain from commenting on the international space station: "It has been touted as a stepping stone on the way to Mars, an exemplar of international cooperation in space, and an orbiting research laboratory. Sadly, the International Space Station is none of these things. . . . But the truth . . . [is that] at a cost of over $100 billion, is a monumental waster of time and money."[40]

Thomas Schatz addressed the concerns of the young and unborn:

> *What about future generations? In . . . fiscal 1995 budget, an entire chapter was devoted to "intergenerational accounting," which calculates the tax burden on future generations due to Washington's wasteful ways. But last year and again this year, the president hasn't addressed this vital issue. There's a good reason . . . he doesn't want anyone to know that the next generation faces an eighty-four percent tax rate to pay for all government spending. Even under the "drastic" republican budget, that rate is seventy-one percent.*[41]

These words were published in 1996. Since then the strength of the economy has apparently softened the projected impact on future taxpayers of politicians' reckless spending, but no one can be sure because with the continuing economic good news has come a new avalanche of proposals for additional spending. Now a recession has brought the above discussion back into accurate perspective.

Jefferson: Actually, there is no quote available, because during his time in government it was so small that officials could not afford to waste anything.

The Illusion of Motion in Government

Michael Kramer wrote,

Sometimes art gets it just right. In a particularly delicious scene in The Distinguished Gentleman, the latest Hollywood film about political corruption, a lobbyist asks the movie's protagonist his position on sugar price supports. The con artist turned congressman . . . has gone to Washington to commit legalized larceny, but he doesn't have a clue about sugar. Which position would prove most profitable? he wonders. It doesn't matter, [Eddie] Murphy is told. If he favors the program, the sugar producers will fill his campaign coffers; if he opposes it, the candy manufacturers will kick in. Similarly, Murphy is assured, he can make a bundle on either side of the medical malpractice issue: doctors' groups and insurance companies will fund him if he supports limiting claims; the trial lawyers will be in his debt is he opposes caps. Well, asks Murphy, "if that's true, how does anything get done?" "It doesn't," the lobbyist retorts. "That's the beauty of the system." [42]

"Beauty is in the eye of the beholder," goes the old saw. But the same pair of eyes apparently differ from one time to another. In 1787 Rufus King was a delegate to the Constitutional Convention in Philadelphia. He objected to setting a date for Congress to meet each year because he "could not think there would be a necessity for a meeting every year. A great vice in our system was that of legislating too much." At present each year Congress and president pass into law approximately 7,500 pages of text, and the executive branch creates administrative law (regulations) to the tune of around 75,000 pages. O'Rourke asked: "When can we say, stick a fork in it, it's done?"[43]

The Economist reported:

One of the great confusions of our age is to mistake active government for purposeful government, or . . . good government. Most conservatives, supposing . . . advocates of small government, are roughly as keen as . . . expansionists for politicos to keep busy, busy, busy.

America's constitution allows even greater scope for activity as an end in itself. Changes in domestic policy have to be approved by both Senate and House . . . which facilitates the conceit that the House has done this or the Senate that . . . when next to nothing has actually happened. The same is true of the White House, only more so. The president's independent powers in domestic policy are extremely weak: he can do virtually nothing by himself. This requires, and allows, an even more impressive display of activity leading nowhere: presidential commissions, taskforces and panels of every kind, not to mention the full-

time eager beavers on the White House staff, help Bill Clinton, as they would say, to leverage his prodigious work rate . . . to no effect whatever.[44]

When in doubt, order another round of due process. If anyone is unhappy, order another hearing. Still unhappy? How about a new study or task force? The slightest excuse—a phone call or disparaging remark—can unhinge proceedings of several years' duration. Big government knows its position on every issue, and it knows if the public holds a different position. Ergo, bury it in studies, blue-ribbon commissions, and so on, until the issue eventually fades from the public radar screen. Then all is well once again in Big Washington.

During nearly his entire tenure in office Clinton poured forth a continuing blizzard of initiatives, apparently intended to win votes. Even while in office he never stopped campaigning. Encumbered as he was with weak powers to actually put these into law, very few of these initiatives went that far, but this reality slowed him down not at all.

It seems simple to prepare a bill that contains a position on at least one issue supported by Republicans and opposed by Democrats, and at least one position where the reverse applies. When it fails to pass, professional finger-pointers in both parties then whine: "See what happened? I tried so hard, but those damned Democrats/Republicans . . . "

Does this actually happen in Washington? *The Economist* reported on an attempt at tax reform: "But instead of presenting Americans with one well-thought-out proposal, Mr. Armey will argue passionately for a flat tax while Mr. Tauzin, with equal passion, will promote a national retail sales tax."[45] The only challenge in this charade lies in equating passions and votes to be sure neither bill passes. For if one or the other wins the day there would be a serious risk of real change in the 10,000-page income tax code.

In early 1999 the Clinton impeachment proceedings came in handy as an excuse for inaction on Medicare and Social Security, even though Clinton had promised forward motion on desperately needed reforms. This inertia was strung out until Labor Day, which was designated the official start of the presidential election campaign. Each party wanted these two issues as ammunition during the campaign. Citizens were apparently not too upset at the lack of action; they were also willing to pay candidates in public office their salaries and perks while they waged a campaign over fourteen months.

But reflection brings out another hidden agenda. By November 2000 citizens were so sick and tired of the campaign that few bothered to vote. Career politicians love empty elections, because this reduces the risk of upsetting their beloved status quo.

Massive wealth is a mixed blessing. Among individuals it has the potential to do good, both in the business sector through investment and in the nonprofit sector through altruism. But in Washington it creates loose and poorly controlled mountains of money, bloated salaries and perks, flexible ethics, and a stupendous gravy train that might be derailed if any serious debate were permitted. Spirited citizen debate is the only way to create and preserve democracy, but it has no place in an oligarchy.

Phillips wrote:

> *The naive perceive nothing more than gridlock, an ineffectiveness that is merely superficial, in which the mechanisms and processes of Washington can be unlocked with the right lubrication and the right leadership. But . . . it is difficult for politicians—not just late-20th-century US politicians—to develop the needed debate over what no longer works for a nation and then to look down revealing historical pathways for clues to appropriate remedies.*[46]

Doing this requires courage, a commodity in perennially short supply among career politicians who constantly face reelection.

In the Soviet Union the Communist Party ruled with an iron fist. Once in power, cadres naturally sought to hold onto it, and this meant planned gridlock. Low-level *apparatchiks* lived in constant fear of the next purge, which was intended to cleanse and reinvent government. But these actions always originated from within the oligarchy because there was no opposition party to initiate them. Therefore they invariably went nowhere and the system continued to deteriorate. Al Gore wrote a book about reinventing government. Had he consulted with the Soviets, he might have saved some wasted time and effort.

When big government intrudes deeply into private economic activity talented individuals who are willing to work hard and assume risks are frustrated: they can keep less and less of what they earn through their efforts. They no longer see productive effort being rewarded. The result over time comes down to a negative incentive: It is easier to take someone else's wealth through buying special favors than it is to create one's own new wealth. As this situation gains momentum, the sea anchor dragging down the economy commensurately increases in size and weight.

Lee said:

> *When all ships are productively employed shipping the goods, a large amount of wealth can be generated. But if sanctions against piracy are eased a few shippers may find it to their personal advantage to stop shipping and start pirating the merchandise being shipped by others, even though this reduces the total wealth available. This piracy by the few will reduce the return the others receive . . . there will be an increase in . . . piracy. Eventually the point may be reached where everyone is sailing the seas looking for the booty that used to be shipped but is no longer. No one is doing well under these circumstances, and indeed, all would be much better off if everyone would return to shipping the goods. Yet who will be willing to return to productive shipping when everyone else is a pirate?*[47]

This analogy would be amusing if it were not so accurate and potentially tragic.

Lapham noted:

> *So volatile a state of affairs is intolerable to the societies at court. The courtier spirit is about the wish to make time stand still, about being, not becoming. . . . The time at court is always noon. Favors come and favors go, and so do wars and presidents, but the court lives forever in the land of the perpetual present, preserved—in Hollywood and the universities as well as in Washington—in the precious amber of incumbency.*[48]

He went on to describe the courtier mentality.

> *People reduced to playing the role of the courtier cannot afford to admit acquaintance with their own thought or their own feeling. Admiring everything and nothing, they conceal a servant's envious rage behind the mask of an ingratiating smile and so abandon not only their courage of mind but also the chance of making a future that doesn't already belong to somebody else.*

It takes a certain kind of person who is willing to abandon his moral self in the interest of taking others' money without earning it. The negative impact on heart, mind, body, and spirit must keep a lot of marriage counselors, psychiatrists, gastroenterologists, and ministers busy in and around Washington. A thinking citizen might find it curious that the activities of these people generate no ink.

Having learned from the Reagan revolution of 1981, Republicans trumpeted their Contract with America in 1995, with about the same zero results. In March there was a little action that seemed to hold promise. The corridors of Congress immediately filled up with lobbyists. One side represented trial lawyers and consumer groups who swore that Republicans were trying to deny due process to victims. The other side consisted of lobbyists for corporations, who argued that a litigation explosion was imposing huge costs on them. This was a business expense that they had to pass on in higher prices, often to the same consumers who were screeching on the other side of the fence. Predictably, nothing came of the issue.

The strategy was to hype the contract shortly before the 1994 election and, sure enough, a (recent) record number of Democratic incumbents were removed from office. But as for meaningful progress on the ingredients in the contract, **there was no intent to act**. The objective was votes; once these were banked it was back to business as usual while the rhetoric faded slowly enough to convince naive voters that the contract was still in force.

Politicians hasten to reassure citizens that everyone wants stable government, because this situation means families can plan their futures free of uncertainty at the hand of government. But long-range planning must take economic and social change into consideration; without these there can be no progress.

Conceived outside the central government several years ago, the information technology revolution still generates enormous press. But if this revolution continues forward, and it will because it must, it will soon slam into an immobile government. Conjured and set in stone by Washington, the political environment retards rapid technological changes and hence social progress.

Phillips said:

The entrenchment tools of the status quo range from state laws that give the republican and democratic parties automatic ballot position (while curbing access by potential rivals) to a whole range of federal campaign subsidies, assistance to party-affiliated institutions, and preferred postal rates. Stacked alongside the financial support that the republican and democratic parties enjoy from their particular interest groups, these favoritisms add up to what economists call a "duopoly"—the two-party version of a monopoly. Independent political movements can surge and become powerful, but they cannot institutionalize; they cannot win the White House or take more than a few seats in Congress.[49]

If public officials and their parties believed they were doing a good job they would welcome competition, because there is nothing more effective in keeping any institution shaped up. But the elites are thoroughly familiar with what is really going on behind the shroud; thus the barriers thrown up against any outside force that might threaten the system. Phillips showed that the reality of today in Washington is single-party government. The loyal opposition party has vanished, and with it any semblance of serious criticism of government laws and policies.

But not just in Washington. *The Economist*'s report on the current situation in Japan contains an insight into what the elite class in Washington fears most.[50]

Japan is changing rapidly, ... Its politics remains eternally the same. How long can it last? . . .. But almost half of Japan's 100m eligible voters do not support any particular party these days. Their frustration is with the whole system, and with the LDP [Liberal Democratic Party] as the system's entrenched representative. There is a widespread feeling that the country is in dire need of a whole range of social as well as economic reforms, but that the government—bound by its powerful ties to special interests—is incapable of doing the job.

The writer went on to discuss a sharp rise in crime and noted that Japanese TV has become even bloodier than in the United States. Then the article presented the following insight:

The . . . people sense that the time has come for a "third opening" . . . the introduction of a wholly new way of doing things comparable to the Meiji Restoration or General MacArthur's post-war reforms. What goes unmentioned, however, is that the Meiji Restoration destroyed the livelihoods of a ruling class of 1.5m samurai; and that the post-war reforms drove 200,000 wartime leaders from office. . . . That is why Japan's political leaders want nothing to do with reform.

Note especially the absolute imperative generated by the negative tug of human nature: Hold onto great personal power **at any cost**. The alternative is considered unthinkable. The reality is that Japan's government is even more severely constipated than is Washington, and the outlook is for more of the same. Pity the long-suffering Japanese people. (And, unless something is done, pity the future US citizen.)

The Japanese and East Asian concept of *wa*, or an emphasis on harmony, suggests that a citizen or government official is culturally restrained from rising above others and assuming the risks that accompany assertive leadership. But the heritage in this country is quite the opposite. When mixed together, these facts constitute food for thought.

Serving in Paris during the Constitutional Convention of 1787, Thomas Jefferson wanted to include a date when the document would cease to exist (about twenty to thirty-five years after its ratification). His thinking was that each succeeding generation should have the right to begin again with a statement of principles that would guide lawmaking in accordance with their desires.

This did not happen. Although the constitution got off to a great start and wore remarkably well over the past two centuries, today the document is arguably overdue for a major overhaul or possible replacement (see Appendix). At the very least, citizens should force their public servants to adhere to its principles.

John Gardner, in his book *Self-Renewal*, noted: "Failure to face the realities of change brings heavy penalties. Individuals become imprisoned in their own rigidities. Great institutions deteriorate. Civilizations fall. Yet decay is not inevitable. There is also renewal."[51] Governmental institutions have been renewed throughout history, but nearly always by means of armed rebellion or conquest by a foreign army.

Today the advanced world stands on the threshold of the Age of Reason, when armed conflict will fade into history (see Part V). Apparently realizing this potential, Gardner issued a warning: "If people are apathetic, defeated in spirit, or unable to imagine a future worth striving for, the game is lost."

Why the News Media Cooperate in the Lie

Based on the Constitution's First Amendment, establishing freedom of the press, a tradition of investigative journalism was established early in the nation's history. But the institution had a rough time in getting established; in 1807 Jefferson wrote: "It is a melancholy truth, that a suppression of the press could not more completely deprive the nation of its benefits, than is done by its abandoned prostitution to falsehood. Nothing can now be believed which is seen in a newspaper. Truth itself becomes suspicious by being put into that polluted vehicle."

Once the institution was firmly established, reporters frequently worked hard to dig up a story, verify it through independent sources, and write it with the intent of communicating truth to readers. Because travel and communications were expensive, readers got more depth on local issues than a broad cross-section of national news. Better informed on fewer issues, they could analyze and discuss them and develop clear conclusions. This tradition persisted up until about 1950; applied to government, it reinforced a healthy skepticism concerning what public officials were actually doing in office.

But devious elements were at work. Schudson referred to E. Pendleton Herring's writing in 1928; he "found Washington . . . 'the happy home of propaganda and the paradise of the press agent.' Not only lobbying organizations but the government itself churned out. . . 'tons of press material and manufactured news by the gross.' It is hard . . . to distinguish the work of the press agents from the work of the journalists."[52]

Due to the gradual accumulation of tremendous political power in Washington, people today have come to expect news about the high and mighty. Journalists now almost always have college degrees. They congregate around the elites to get stories about them, and the feeling of elitism rubs off on the journalists. This has a strong influence on what they write and how they write it, and the ultimate result is an institution consisting of pussycats who climb up on the laps of the high and mighty, lap warm milk, and purr. The public gets the "information" the elites choose to release. This reduces the role of the journalist to that of government press agent. The new tradition that started a long time ago is still in place, and it has gotten worse.

Kovach and Rosenstiel argued that reporters "have lost touch with voters, with regional politics and with campaigns as national conversations. . . . Campaign journalism increasingly tends to see voters as abstractions, through polls, or as targets of campaign manipulations, to be interviewed in artificial focus groups or panels assembled to observe debates."[53] These are scripted to appear as spontaneous encounters, but if people have not made the effort to understand the issues through discussions and debates **among themselves**, they can be manipulated without realizing it.

Kovach and Rosenstiel continued: "Politics is considered deadly for ratings, and that has translated into less political coverage on the nightly news." The matter comes down to a vicious circle: If the media don't offer some meat people will not watch, and hence less meat, fewer viewers, and lower ratings. Members of the elite class don't want to stimulate citizen discussions among themselves, as this democratic process might reveal something embarrassing about the most gigantic scam in history. (See Chapter 10).

Recently WBBM tried to break the cycle.[54] The station "ditched the burgers and fries of local news: no more overblown crime coverage, no Hollywood promos dressed up as news stories, no live shots from outside dark buildings where news had happened hours earlier, no choreographed chit-chat between anchors and no obligatory pet stories." Instead came stories as long as five minutes and live interviews with important political leaders from around the world, conducted by an award-winning journalist.

The results? "Critics like the new format, but, so far at least, viewers have voted with their remote controls. . . . [WBBM has] continued to lose viewers. . . . But, even if WBBM has stumbled it does not prove that trash is king. The other stations have all been shedding viewers." These grim results suggest that people are no longer capable of separating wheat from chaff. Lies come cheaper than truth, so attention to the bottom line means that so long as lies continue to sell they will remain the coin of the realm.

The journalistic tradition of "get it first, but first get it right" has been replaced by smaller penalties for being first, even if it is wrong. Now, if citizens don't know or care who is right and who is wrong, there will be no penalty. Today spin is considered news, and lies turned out in great quantities by the White House are not refuted. Ethics in the greater society has deteriorated over the past fifty years, and journalists have always reflexively stated that their writing accurately reflects society.

Putnam put it like this: "In 1948, when the median American adult had nine years of formal schooling, daily newspaper circulation was 1.3 papers per household. . . . Fifty years later schooling had risen by 50 percent, but newspaper readership had fallen by 57 percent, despite the fact that newspaper reading is highly correlated with education."[55] Educated people especially know when they are wasting their time.

Many journalists complete a temporary side trip into government service before plying their trade. This helps the elites to indoctrinate them. This orientation is important, because without cooperation from the media in a country with a free press an oligarchy cannot be established and maintained.

Advancing technology has enabled the news media to bring viewers "breaking news." A news anchor on TV rapidly skips from one snippet to the next, having no familiarity with the content of each as it is quickly thrust onto his or her desk. Because there is no elaboration, much less analysis, a typical viewer becomes confused (not to mention the anchor).

Subsequent massaging of breaking news by further breaking it into sound bites will not clear up any confusion. The nation's three major all-news networks are wired into at least 40 million homes, and yet on a typical day only 0.1 percent of the occupants actually watch them. Apparently people don't appreciate being kept confused.

Schudson attacked TV as a news medium: "Nearly everyone believes television is a failed political medium. It is not a new mode for expressing citizenship but a new barrier to expression, not the speakers' corner for a new virtual community but a trivialization of the politically serious and perhaps even the leading cause of declining civic participation."[56] A thinking citizen might question the use of the word *perhaps*, believing that TV is in fact a strong contributing cause.

Schudson continued:

> *Theodore White wrote the epitaph for democracy's experiment with television even as he announced its birth. . . . [It] "should have provided" a forum for issues, but the demand . . . for quick answers and its incapacity to allow any dead airtime for the candidates to think invalidated it as a medium of reason. "Neither man could pause to indulge in the slow reflection and rumination, the slow questioning of alternatives before decision, that is the inner quality of leadership."*

Jefferson would agree.

G D Gearino also agreed; he asked

> *"With So Many Opinions at Hand, Why Form Your Own? The contemporary world is not a place that encourages pondering. Events happen too quickly and are reported too efficiently for people to dwell on them. If a dark horse candidate scores an upset primary victory, or if the economy of an Asian country takes a sudden dive, you need not spend time thinking about what it means. That will be done for you. . . . There are experts on every topic available at a moment's notice, and they will tell you what all this means.*[57]

Often the experts have little time to ponder, and their opinions may mislead the public. Later one of them may realize his or her mistake, but new events crowd in and there is little or no opportunity to publicly rectify the error.

"The more media available to you, the less time you invest in simple pondering and mulling. It shouldn't be that way. If anything, this runs contrary to the way common sense suggests it ought to be. Thinking and information do not exist in separate, mutually exclusive spheres. Information should reinforce and encourage thinking, not dampen it." Citizens don't realize that without taking time for reflection and discussion with others to determine whether or not there is truth in a news bulletin, there is no way to know whether today's blizzard of information contains any benefits for them. They spend hours each week watching, listening, or reading news, thinking that this time spent keeps them current with events that impact their daily lives, and therefore it is valuable. But if the news media are Washington's puppets, the value accrues to the elites and not to the peasants.

Referring back to Chapter 8, an insight emerges. Big government can utilize mesmerizing TV to keep the natives from getting restless, but only if officials act to keep them dumbed down.

Lapham wrote: "The news media's devotion to the status quo accounted for their active and unanimous endorsement of governor Bill Clinton during the final months of last year's [1992] election campaign. No other candidate seemed likely to preserve both the fictions of democracy and the interests of oligarchy." The man was typecast. "Clinton was one of the media's own, a politician fluent in the ritual language of the issues and careful to observe the pieties embodied in the editorial pages of the *Washington Post*, and the journalists at court expressed their gratitude by favoring him with easy questions and prominent photo placements."[58]

Time magazine selected Clinton as Man of the Year only seven months after publishing an article titled "Why Voters Don't Trust Clinton." An intervening election caused courtiers on the editorial staff to instantly turn their coats inside out. The media also misled their customers when a blizzard of news accompanied the death of Lady Diana, whereas coverage of the nearly simultaneous death of Mother Teresa was buried in page six of one prominent newspaper. Celebrity journalism does not inform.

Promulgating the external threat theory (terrible foreign power threatening) suits the elites, and therefore the media are attracted to wars. Lapham noted: "The promise of blood brings with it the gift of headlines, audiences, single-copy sales, Nielsen ratings, Pulitzer prizes, and a swelling of the media's self-esteem. A television network on assignment to a war imagines itself outfitted with the trappings of immortality." Reporting on the Gulf War from Baghdad in early 1991, Peter Arnett was perceived as larger than life.

Samuelson described the "extent to which modern political groups must exploit conflict to survive. Villains not only exist, they are required. Groups' grievances not only exist, they must be nurtured. These campaigns, full of pessimism and condemnation, feed on one another and are reflected in the press."[59] There are two important reasons for this near obsession. First, mass conflict sells (so long as it is "over there"). Second, conflict tends to keep citizens in a state of fear or at least uncertainty. The ploy works as long as citizens are kept separated from truth.

Today the time-worn fear of Russia still gets play in the media, primarily because the people don't know the whole truth about the economic and social chaos that plagues that country. This sad condition makes it impossible for the Kremlin to mount a large-scale sustained conflict; nevertheless recent consumers of the news got graphic pictures and stories about almost every shot fired in Chechnya.

This hype got so bad that Shnurenko proved that news of a presumed massacre of Chechen civilians by Russian troops was faked.[60] The report generated wide dissemination, but there were no apologies when the truth was published. Even North Korea, with its dysfunctional economy, is played up as a dire threat. All this media hype distracts the public's attention from the enemy within.

In this day of huge databases and computers supplying information everywhere, citizens apparently know less about their government today than they did 200 years ago, when letters sealed by wax took months to cross the Atlantic Ocean. Fallows remarked: "The more prominent today's star journalists become, the more they are forced to give up the essence of real journalism. . . . Issues that affect the collective interests of Americans—crime, health care—are presented mainly as arenas in which politicians can fight."[61] But these "fights" are unreal; they are scripted.

In 1996 there was speculation in the news media about a possible run at the presidency by then-Senator Bill Bradley.

> *Two days after his announcement, Bradley was interviewed by Judy Woodruff [a] widely respected and knowledgeable reporter, but her interaction with Bradley was like the meeting of two beings from different universes. Every answer Bradley gave concerned the substance of national problems that concerned him. Every question she asked was about short-term political tactics. . . . Bradley gave a long answer about how everyone involved in politics had to get out of the rut of converting every subject or comment into a political "issue," used for partisan advantage. . . . As soon as he finished, Judy . . . asked her next question: "Do you want to be president?" It was as if she had not heard a word.*

The viewer probably felt like he or she was watching two TV sets, facing one another but tuned to different channels.

The media believe that people are bored with good news. Carter wrote:

> *A reporter will ask: "What do you think of X?" I will say, "Well, the good outweighs the bad." I will go on to list the many good points and the few bad ones, and the enterprising journalist, for whom controversy trumps accuracy, will then write . . . a story that mentions only the bad things I mentioned. . . . Integrity is being harmed by the need to make the facts fit the story rather than making the story fit the facts. All too often, having made up their minds that the story has a certain ending, reporters and editors are disdainful of evidence that the ending is wrong.*[62]

In his research, Karl Marx either distorted or rejected results that disagreed with his grand vision.

For example, bashing Muslims is in vogue, so when a disgruntled army private and a friend blew up the Alfred Murrah building in Oklahoma City and killed some 170 people, the media unhesitatingly cast blame on Muslim terrorists. The media had not a shred of evidence, but a long history of biased reporting had led people to expect that fanatic Muslims extremists were responsible. So the media gave their audiences what they wanted. Not just the news media are to blame; in the last ten years Hollywood has produced around twenty-five movies in which US soldiers kill Arabs.

No matter that much terrorist activity is state-sponsored, the media put the blame on religious and ethnic groups. For the fifty-plus years since the establishment of the state of Israel, the US government has systematically harassed Muslims in the Middle East. Quite naturally, groups have formed who engage in terrorism as a last resort; they cannot directly challenge Israel and the United

States combined. The reality is that these young men constitute a tiny fraction of 1 percent of the whole population of Middle Eastern Arabs and Muslims, but they garner practically all the press.

Other facts bear on the terrorist issue. The name *Islam* translates into "peace," and the Koran teaches tolerance of Christianity and other religions. Mohammed was the prophet of Allah, but Jesus Christ is also considered a prophet. Many Arabs and Muslims perceive Israeli soldiers as terrorists.

When suitably hyped by the media, here is another example of the external threat. In 1998 Congress increased the FBI's antiterrorism budget from $118 million in 1995 to $286 million, a 142 percent boost. And now there comes another huge increase after the tragedy of September 11, 2001.

Lapham illustrated the pussycat nature of the news media by referring to the "Rubbergate" check-cashing scandal of 1994: "By the third week in March the political grandees in Washington were renouncing their privileges—limousines, prescription drugs, stationery, meals, flowers, barbers, aerobic instructors, paintings on loan from the National Gallery, etc.—as hastily as escaping burglars emptying their pockets of evidence."

Most of these elite perks had been put on the taxpayers' tab. A few concerned citizens made bold to complain. "The American people were doing nothing more unusual than expressing their opinion of their elected government, but the news media, faithfully reflecting the interests of the government in question, heard their modest complaint as both an insult and an outrage."

To convince the public that they are getting straight truth, the president and members of Congress hold frequent press conferences. The viewing public is led to believe that the official giving it is being grilled mercilessly from several different directions by journalists bent on revealing for citizens the darkest of secrets. The reality is that many if not most of these meetings are at least partially scripted, and politicians have developed a keen talent for dodging the few genuine questions while appearing to provide answers.

Rev. Martin Luther King Jr. began his civil rights crusade by rallying citizens at the grass roots in one town after another. As he and his followers worked harder over time, media coverage was not what they had hoped for. Eventually they felt they had to change their tactics. J. Hunter O'Dell was one of King's early lieutenants: "In the end, it means a new kind of addiction to media rather than being in charge of our own agenda and relying on mass support as our guarantee that ultimately the news covering apparatus must give recognition to our authority." Dr. King's murder spurred extra efforts, and the movement went forward in spite of the lack of cooperation within an institution that had become wired in to the high and mighty.

That was in the 1960s, when the news media refrained from full cooperation with a bottom-up, democratic movement aimed at providing constitutional rights for African Americans. It is interesting to observe a sweeping change since that time. Now that so much has been accomplished in terms of individual initiatives by these people, the media continue to drag their feet.

Martinez elaborated: "The *Washington Post* ran a front-page story last week that proclaimed minorities in the US still face incidents of discrimination. Whoa—stop the presses! I find it amusing when predominantly white-owned and operated media find racial discrimination big news."[63]

Martinez quoted from results of a study of a state's highway patrol traffic stops. "Yet when the survey asked 'Have you ever been unfairly stopped by police because of your racial and ethnic background?' the overwhelming response was no, African-American 61 percent, Hispanic 79 percent, and Asian 85 percent." Another question: "'During the last 10 years, have you experienced discrimination because of your racial or ethnic background, or not?' Majorities of African-Americans (53 percent), Hispanics (60 percent) and Asians (58 percent) said no." Martinez may not realize that the oligarchy continues to see votes in racial issues, even though these issues may have largely disappeared. Officials seldom allow truth to get in their way, and their media lackeys cooperate.

An entrepreneur might catch a whiff of suspicion among consumers of news and organize a news company aimed at providing truth in coverage of government. The way would be very rough, because the center of news today is at the center of political power, and the high and mighty don't want the truth published. Therefore access for this courageous entrepreneur would be cut off. One reporter might make the effort to dig up some truth about a politician's activities and get it published. But there is no reward in this, as citizens would not know whether to applaud the effort or ignore the piece as just another cheap shot at a politician.

Large syndicates today control most news media. Managers (not journalists) run these, and they move more or less in unison in their pursuit of the highest reaches of political power. There is little room for dissent, even though it is widely known that any society that does not tolerate dissent has a limited life. Lapham noted, "Like every other important newspaper in the country, the *Tribune* didn't concern itself with the routine injustices committed by the people who owned the wealth of the country—for the logical and very good reason that the same people owned the press."

Elite journalists frequently take issue with criticism of their attitudes and work. Fallows remarked: "In response to suggestions that the press has failed to meet its public responsibilities, the first instinct of many journalists is to cry 'First Amendment!,' which is like the military's reflexive use of 'national security' to rebut outside criticism of how it does its work." In the media view, reference to the First Amendment is irrelevant. What is relevant is the bottom line, which is largely why so much reporting comes across as conflict (fabricated if deemed appropriate).

"Criticize reporters or editors for their negativity, and you will be told that they are merely reflecting the world as it is. Objecting to news coverage, they say, is merely 'blaming the messenger;' the press claims no responsibility for the world that it displays." This apparently means it is okay to bash Muslims and any others without evidence.

Fallows pointed out that there is evidence that cynicism and emphasis on violence on the part of the press tends to make society's problems harder to solve than they would be otherwise. A *Times-Mirror* study in 1997 found that 71 percent of the people believe the news media actually interfere with a nation that is trying to solve its problems.

In 1999 the Pew Research Center for the People and the Press interviewed 552 journalists about how they perceive themselves and their profession. Major problems cited included sensationalism, a lack of objectivity, and inaccurate reporting. Also included was too much emphasis on profits, competition, and declining audiences. Finally, respondents were concerned about loss of credibility. There was apparently no inquiry regarding elitism. Adhering to the example provided by high public officials, today's news media institution exempts itself from the same standards of integrity that it tries to enforce on ordinary citizens.

Haynes reported on an intriguing instance of integrity originated by citizens, and in which justice was obstructed by the US Department of Justice (not a misprint).[64]

> *In the summer of 1989, the US attorney impaneled a grand jury to investigate whether officials at the Rocky Flats Nuclear Weapons Plant willfully committed hundreds of environmental violations, including dumping radioactive waste into drinking water. After questioning 100 witnesses and reviewing 860 boxes of documents for nearly three years, jurors returned indictments against eight plant and government officials. But the US attorney refused to sign the orders before disbanding the jury.*
>
> *Federal law forbids grand jurors disclosing anything that has gone on during investigation and deliberations. Breaking silence could mean jail time. But now, in an unprecedented move, 19 of the 23 jurors are attempting to go public with charges that federal prosecutors obstructed justice. . . . Since launching their battle, they have been the subject of relentless media attacks by prosecutors, and an FBI probe.*

The loyalty of the media to their masters does not waver even when ordinary citizens, presumably customers of the same media, are harassed and mistreated. Indeed, they go so far as to actively participate in the obstruction of justice. The issue of nuclear waste is hot, and so the wagons had to circle quickly.

Lapham commented: "If the media succeed with their spectacles and grand simplifications, it is because their audiences define happiness as the state of being well and artfully deceived." It is human nature to seek truth, so citizens on the whole can be fooled for a limited time only. How much time is "limited" remains to be seen.

Sussman, writing in 1989, said,

> *We concluded—twenty years ago—that the unease with American journalism was a threat to the democratic system. We thought representative audiences should be invited regularly to see television newscasts to determine how audiences react, what they understand, and what they feel they have missed. Funding could not then be secured for such 'consumer' research. It was never undertaken. The idea is still on the table.*[65]

Notes

1. Alexis de Tocqueville, *Democracy in America*. Knopf, 1972.
2. Robert Bearce, "The Spirit of Freedom." In *The Foundations of American Constitutional Government*, ed. Robert Gorgoglione. Foundation for Economic Education, 1996.
3. William Greider, *Who Will Tell the People: The Betrayal of American Democracy*. Simon and Schuster, 1992.
4. Jim Powell, *The Triumph of Liberty*. Free Press, 2000, p. 343.
5. Friedrich A. Hayek, *The Road to Serfdom*. University of Chicago Press, 1944.
6. Walter Isaacson, *Kissinger: A Biography*. Simon and Schuster, 1992.
7. Leonard R. Sussman, *Power, the Press and the Technology of Freedom*. Freedom House, 1989.
8. William Greider, *Who Will Tell the People: The Betrayal of American Democracy*.
9. Lewis H. Lapham, *The Wish for Kings: Democracy at Bay*. Grove Press, 1993.
10. Paul Johnson, *Modern Times*. Harper Collins, 1991, p. 221.
11. Mark Helm, "Is It Your Right to Know?" *News and Observer* (Raleigh, NC), October 28, 2001, p. 23A.
12. Robert Putnam, *Bowling Alone: The Collapse and Revival of American Community*. Simon and Schuster 2000, p. 231.
13. Sussman, *Power, the Press and the Technology of Freedom*.
14. Angelo Codevilla, *Informing Statecraft: Intelligence for a New Century*. Free Press, 1992.
15. James D. Barber, *The Book of Democracy*. Prentice Hall, 1995.
16. Eric Alterman, *Sound and Fury: The Washington Punditocracy and the Collapse of American Politics*. Harper Collins, 1992.
17. Richard Reeves, "Making History Harder." *News and Observer* (Washington, DC), November 18, 2001, p. 33A.
18. George F. Will, "Speech Suffers under Campaign 'Reform.'" *News and Observer* (Washington, DC), March 11, 2001, p. 31A.

19. *The Economist*, "Stop Signs on the Web." January 13, 2001, p. 21.
20. D. Ian Hopper, "Defense Web Sites Secretly Track Visitors, Audit Shows." *News and Observer* [AP], June 6, 2001, p. 7A.
21. Thomas L. Friedman, "In Cyberspace, Arab Democracy Gains a Foothold." *News and Observer*, July 2000.
22. Bob Woodward, *Maestro: Greenspan's Fed and the American Boom.* Simon and Schuster, 2000.
23. Lapham, *The Wish for Kings.*
24. Stephen Carter, *Integrity*. Basic Books, 1996.
25. Mike Royko, "Little Lies and Whoppers Keep the World Spinning," *News and Observer*, January 1996.
26. P J O'Rourke, *A Parliament of Whores*. Atlantic Monthly Press, 1991.
27. Alterman, *Sound and Fury.*
28. *The Economist*, "Plenty of Gloom." December 20, 1997, p. 19.
29. *The Economist*, "The Price of Perjury." November 28, 1998, p. 32.
30. George F. Will, "Judging a Dismal President." January 2001 column.
31. Charles Krauthammer, "Destroyed by Scandal, Clinton Fades into Insignificance." March 1999 column.
32. Ayn Rand, *Atlas Shrugged.* Penguin Books, 1992.
33. P J O'Rourke, *Parliament of Whores.*
34. Martin L. Gross, *A Call for Revolution*. Ballantine Books, 1993.
35. *The Economist*, "The Farmbelt Breaks Free." July 12, 1997, p. 21.
36. Stephen Budiansky, "Subsidies Are Dead, Long Live Subsidies." *US News*, February 19, 1996, p. 36.
37. *The Economist*, "The World's Most Thankless Job." March 22, 1997, p. 29.
38. Gwynne Dyer, "My [Brief] Career in Espionage." *News and Observer* (London), February 28, 2001, p. 19A.
39. *The Economist*, "The Morning after High Noon." August 10, 1996, pp. 20–21.
40. *The Economist*, "A Waste of Space." October 28, 2000, p. 76.
41. Thomas Schatz, article in *Waste Watch*, spring 1996, p. 2.
42. Michael Kramer, "The Best Pols Money Can Buy." *Time*, December 14, 1992, p. 4).
43. O'Rourke, *Parliament of Whores.*
44. *The Economist*, "Don't Just Do Something, Sit There." December 23, 1995, p. 11.
45. *The Economist*, "Binning the IRS." October 4, 1997, p. 20.
46. Kevin Phillips, *Arrogant Capital.* Little, Brown, 1994.
47. Dwight R. Lee, "The Political Economics of the US Constitution." In *The Foundations of American Constitutional Government*, ed. Robert Gorgoglione. Foundation for Economic Education, 1996.

48. Lapham, *The Wish for Kings.*
49. Phillips, *Arrogant Capital.*
50. *The Economist*, "Sunset for the Men in Suits." July 1, 2000, p. 26.
51. John W. Gardner, *Self Renewal.* Norton, 1981.
52. Michael Schudson, *The Good Citizen: A History of American Civic Life.* Free Press, 1998.
53. Bill Kovach and Tom Rosenstiel, "Media Can Still Learn from Election Humiliation." *News and Observer*, November 2000.
54. *The Economist*, "Come Back, Ed Murrow." October 7, 2000, p. 42.
55. Putnam, *Bowling Alone.*
56. Schudson, *The Good Citizen.*
57. G D Gearino, "With So Many Opinions at Hand, Why Form Your Own?" *News and Observer* (Raleigh, NC), February 13, 2000, p. 23A.
58. Lapham, *The Wish for Kings.*
59. Robert J. Samuelson, *The Good Life and its Discontents: The American Dream in the Age of Entitlement 1945–1995.* Random House, 1995.
60. Igor Shnurenko, "War Crimes—or Faked News?" *News and Observer* (Raleigh, NC), March 10, 2000, p. 18A.
61. James Fallows, *Breaking the News: How the Media Undermine American Democracy.* Pantheon Books, 1996, p. 76.
62. Carter, *Integrity.*
63. Rick Martinez, "Lingering Bias Isn't the Story." *News and Observer*, June 26, 2001, p. 19A.
64. V. Dion Haynes, "Denver Grand Jury Charges Prosecutors Scuttled '89 Nuclear Probe." *Chicago Tribune*, February 1997.
65. Sussman, *Power, the Press and the Technology of Freedom.*

CHAPTER TEN:
THE GRAND DECEPTION AND THE MASS OF FLIMFLAMMED CITIZENS

The masses have little time to think.
And how incredible is the willingness of modern man to believe.
—Benito Mussolini

In almost any type of government besides democracy, oppression of the people is obvious to all. When citizens who are unhappy with government have no recourse, there is no need for deception. Because the negative tug of human nature operates continuously, even democracy has a limited life without equally continuous vigilance. Jackson Pemberton, writing in 1976, referred back to the days of the British colonies:

> *In our day the tyrant came to us in open defiance of our rights, with hostility and violence, with sword and cannon. Through tears, prayer, and blood we threw him off and drove him out.*
>
> *Now he is among you again, but not in open war upon your houses and lands, but in subtle disguise, bearing gifts of free money, free food, free houses, and free security; trading them to you in the name of equality, rights, and liberty; offering the goods he took from you by heavy taxes and a deliberate inflation. With flattering words he coddles your vanity, legalizes your selfishness, and leads you through a political mirage into his fool's paradise where he has appointed himself the Grand Regulator. Yet, your greatest danger lies in none of these things, but in your failure to recognize the pattern he follows, for it is ancient; what he cannot accomplish by force and violence he will attempt by lure and deceit.*[1]

The key lies in keeping the gullible in the dark concerning what is really going on. This chapter can only remove the shroud of deception. It would require several books to reveal all, but there is enough information here to convince a concerned citizen of the United States that there is a serious problem with contemporary government.

A Brief Lesson in Washingtonspeak

About sixty years ago, Rose Wilder Lane accurately predicted the future of education:

> *Today the confusion of the meaning of words in these United States is a danger to the whole world. Few American schools any longer require a pupil to dissect his words to their roots, and to know what he means when he speaks. And for 20 years the disciplined members of the Communist Party in these states have been deliberately following Lenin's instruction, "First confuse the vocabulary."* [2]

Pursued to its logical conclusion, such activity will fuzz the distinction between truth and falsehood. Once this has been accomplished, citizens have no way of knowing when they are being flimflammed.

Hayek showed how this is accomplished:

> *The coming of socialism was to be the leap from the realm of necessity to the realm of freedom. The subtle change in meaning to which the word 'freedom' was subjected in order that this argument should sound plausible is important. To the great apostles of political freedom the word had meant freedom from coercion, freedom from the arbitrary power of other men, release from the ties which left the individual no choice but obedience to the orders of a superior to whom he was attached. The new freedom promised, however, was to be freedom from necessity, release from the compulsion of the circumstances which inevitably limit the range of choice of all of us.* [3]

Though this argument is attractive on the surface, the fallacy lies in the reality that **each individual** wants the freedom to satisfy his or her basic necessities as he sees fit. One-size-fits-all programs sponsored by government tend to limit this freedom. Also, reduction of freedom of choice impinges on a citizen's pride in person; it retards maturation and weakens the sense of self. Put another way, man seeks security just as he does freedom, but these goals constitute a trade-off. Too much freedom tends toward anarchy, whereas too much security tends toward dictatorship. Even today there are Russians who feel so insecure in their new freedom that they long for the "secure" days of communism.

Hayek continued:

> *The worst sufferer in this respect is, of course, the word "liberty." It is a word used as freely in totalitarian states as elsewhere. Indeed, it could almost be said—and it should serve as a warning to us to be on our guard against all the tempters who promise us New Liberties for Old—that wherever liberty as we understand it has been destroyed, this has almost always been done in the name of some new freedom promised to the people.*

The word "truth" ceases to have its old meaning. It describes no longer something to be found, with the individual conscience as the sole arbiter of whether in any particular instance the evidence . . . warrants a belief; it becomes something to be laid down by authority, something which has to be believed in the interest of the unity of the organizational effort and which may have to be altered as the exigencies of this organizational effort require it.

Truth is often bent to suit the elites in charge of government. Soviet authorities controlled the content of the newspaper *Pravda*, which means "truth" in Russian. The individual citizen had practically no freedom to seek truth, and does not now enjoy this privilege in either Russia or in this country.

In a similar manner "facts," "research," and "ideas" are distorted, usually by "experts" paid to craft the particulars of Washingtonspeak. Lawyers and lobbyists help the process along. Gross noted: "Politicians have always been somewhat deceptive, but the corruption of words is reaching new heights. Taxes become spending cuts. Spending becomes investment. Budget arithmetic is manipulated. Hidden agendas proliferate. It's even possible that we're no longer witnessing traditional political hype."[4]

Some contrasts in word definitions and usage are presented here:

Liberal: What government says: A welfare state caring for the poor, entitlements, rights for everyone without obligations.

Liberal: The reality: This word was originally used to apply to individual freedom of choice in a free market, which included political freedoms as well as economic. The Democratic Party distorted its meaning during the 1930s to win support for its unconstitutional social programs.

Tax Cut: What government says: Taxpayers deserve a break, so we are reducing amounts collected.

Tax Cut: The reality: Either a reduction in the rate of increase in taxes or a myth clothed in smoke and mirrors. The same twisted reasoning applies to program "cuts."

Farm Programs: What government says: Assistance to small farmers, to help them ensure a steady food supply for all citizens.

Farm Programs: The reality: Routes citizens' tax money mostly to full-time farmers, who are already richer than nearly all citizens. (Race horses are tax-deductible as part of a farm program.) Part of this wealth is regularly kicked back into congressional reelection campaigns, which means these are financed in part by taxpayers.

Social Security: What government says: Programs in which workers and employers "contribute" to trust funds, from which citizens withdraw their money in the event of old age, loss of a spouse, or disability.

Social Security: The reality: Scarcely four years after the retirement trust fund was established Congress began increasing benefits for retirees, inserting each increase shortly before an election. Therefore the system changed to a tax on the young to support retirees. Furthermore, for about twenty years the government has stolen every dollar of surplus funds as the balance grows in anticipation of later retirement needs of today's baby boom generation. This has been done so the budget deficit will not look so bad before the public. This means there is little Social Security here, and certainly no trust.

Truth: What government says: When a high public official speaks, this is truth; when a reporter or columnist writes, this is truth.

Truth: The reality: The government has, over the past four decades, blurred the distinction between truth and lies so much that citizens have lost touch with truth. They don't know. Many don't like not knowing.

Campaign "contributions" were originally volunteered by lobbyists for special interests. Later they were considered investments, and the return in unearned profits gradually became greater than when the same money was invested in the private sector to create new wealth instead of transfer existing wealth. But today the definition has changed again, to extortion.

Many "donors" either disliked the Clintons or disliked being shaken down by the Clintons (or both). They saw it as protection money, and the calls and letters came almost every day. The Committee for Economic Development is a sixty-year-old public policy institute backed by corporations like General Motors, Xerox, and Merck. Twenty of its members support a ban on unlimited contributions. Charles Kolb is president of the organization: "These people are saying: We're tired of being hit up and shaken down. Politics ought to be about something besides hitting up companies for more and more money." Other executives have complained that members of Congress are in position to hurt their companies if they don't pay up.

At this point, so much money is demanded that most companies would be better off investing it in productive enterprise, but if managers do this public officials may make good their threat. A precedent was set during the 1930s, when the Franklin Roosevelt administration repeatedly and brutally bit the hand that fed it.

The trial of principal figures in the Iran-contra scandal was conveniently scheduled to take place after the 1992 presidential election. President George Bush (Sr.) pardoned all of them just a few days before the trial. (Doing so before the election would have torpedoed his candidacy.) When he explained to the press that this was the *honorable* thing to do, thinking citizens added this word to their Washingtonspeak dictionary.

In May 1999 the Supreme Court faced a major challenge: finding a definition of *disabled* that would include those who truly need assistance and omit those who do not. When he pushed the Americans with Disabilities Act, President Bill Clinton probably evaluated it in terms of its voting-getting potential without thinking how it would work in practice.

Victimology had a fling during the 1960s, and later it faded. Clinton brought it back, and it became customary to blame anything and everything for a person's misfortune: government, parents, schools, movies, television, sugar, tobacco, TV, sexism, racism, and so on. This trend brought with it a culture of irresponsibility, but when everyone concentrates on rights and neglects responsibilities society cannot exist. President Harry Truman had placed a prominent sign on his desk: THE BUCK STOPS HERE.

Alterman provided a thought-provoking analysis:

> *Consider the terms "freedom," "leadership," "democracy," "strength," "credibility," "security." All can be said to represent fundamental virtues to which Americans profess allegiance and which American politicians promise to uphold. Yet in the context of the contemporary American politics, all have become buzzwords for nothing more than the willingness to go to war, to threaten war, and to fund, subsidize, and prepare for war. We defend tyranny in the name of freedom. We behave obsequiously in the name of leadership. We subvert elections in the name of democracy. We allow ourselves to be crudely manipulated in the name of strength. We lie in the name of credibility. And we poison our beautiful country in the name of national security.*[5]

Alterman's words go far to illustrate and underscore the malaise that affects the United States. But the implications are still worse when a citizen begins thinking of what can be done: "How could any American presidential candidate—Perot included—ever rise above these linguistic perversions and 'talk sense' to the American people when the words needed to express the values to which he would appeal imply their definitional opposites? How could Americans hear him?"

Vladimir Lenin knew precisely what he was doing. However, Alterman's observation needs amending: **We** have **not** wreaked this terrible and unpardonable damage to our country. Rather, the culprits are public officials, whom we entrusted with the responsibilities of high public office. Today circumstances have risen to the point where they have willfully betrayed our trust. Furthermore, they have refused to accept responsibility for their deeds, as did President Truman in the 1940s.

Arblaster noted that the

> *definition of democracy has been revised, adapted, narrowed, and diluted to render it compatible with the persisting belief in the necessity of the virtue of rule by elites, with an equally persistent mistrust of "the masses," and, perhaps most important of all, to render it compatible with the existing political systems of the western world which call themselves "democracies." Given this revised definition, it becomes* ***natural to talk about preserving and defending democracy rather than achieving it*** (emphasis added).[6]

Posturing and Hype

Today television dictates the practice of politics. Because people watch TV primarily to be entertained rather than informed, a politician whose natural bent is toward bluster and shades of meaning utilizes the medium just like other entertainers: to enhance his or her public image. Therefore over the past fifty years, the age of TV, citizens have come to select their public officials based on perceptions of image, rather than on their leadership and ability to evaluate public opinion and act on issues that concern citizens.

Public officials in Washington, DC, generate larger TV audiences than at state and local levels. They have elevated windbaggery to an exalted status. The trick is to look and sound like profound eloquence while saying nothing for whatever length of time a TV company will allow. This is the age of personal power seeking, and TV ably facilitates the quest. Alterman commented: "So long as American politics remains in thrall to show business, after all, the best we can hope for from our national discourse is that it keeps us entertained."[7]

Among the more recent heroes who were typecast for the modern era was Ronald Reagan with his feel-good politics. "Fellow citizens, it's morning in America!" His telegenic personality was honed in Hollywood. He tried to make everyone feel just fine while the entire society ignored reality. He knew he could sell fantasy far more effectively than truth. However, the ground had been prepared for him decades beforehand.

Those who are not typecast have a more difficult time. Vaclav Havel was a playwright in what was then Czechoslovakia when he became prominent in the underground movement against communism. After the 1989 Velvet Revolution nonviolently overthrew the regime, he was elected president of the country (now the Czech Republic). He was not a career politician when he was thrust into high public office. His lament:

> *I never fail to be astonished at how much I am at the mercy of television directors and editors, at how my public image depends far more on them than it does on myself. . . . I know politicians who have learned to see themselves only as the television camera does. Television had thus expropriated their personalities, and made them into something like television shadows of their former selves. I sometimes wonder whether they even sleep in a way that will look good on television.*

Men like Havel are rare in public life. Another is the United States' own: chairman of the Federal Reserve Board Alan Greenspan. Woodward reported:

> *In this culture, politicians, actors and nearly all public figures are produced and handled. Greenspan emerges as one of the few who seems to maintain a steady and sober detachment. Most other powerful figures have a television persona, often defined by glibness and efforts at cleverness. The public gets a flash of*

B-roll stock footage of the chairman walking across the street—arriving at an FOMC [Federal Open Market Committee] meeting, he always looks the same—grim, even gloomy, briefcase under his arm, an unrevealing look on his face.[8]

The man is honest and straight, so he sees no need for a false public image. He earned his spurs in the field of economics and finance, not politics. It must be frustrating for the elites, as they can't manipulate him as they do practically everyone else.

Today in the United States the external threat theory is having a difficult time justifying abuse of citizens' wallets, now that the Soviet Union no longer exists. Nevertheless, the hype goes forward as Washington's politicians and pundits furiously scratch around for an enemy. Slobodan Milosevic has fizzled and there are no asteroids in the heavens bearing down on the world, so either Saddam Hussein or North Korea is apparently the ogre du jour. The reality is no different than it was during the cold war: The hype is a decoy, intended to divert public attention from the true enemy within. (See Chapter 20.)

The pundits fed on the cold war and grew powerful, so today they fear loss of personal power. Attempting to regain lost influence, their writings and speeches supported Congress when it created a Committee on the Clear and Present Danger, to cast about for a credible threat from offshore. Both Congress and the president like to create committees, blue-ribbon commissions, and so on. These actions are intended to convince citizens that they are actively working on problems.

Clinton loved to soak the rich, and so he frequently hyped initiatives to increase the top marginal income tax rate or harass them in some other way. The reality is that the super-rich have many tax lawyers and accountants, who will help them avoid high taxes regardless of what the government does. But this alone is not enough; they have also bought a lot of congressmen to be sure that any tax legislation includes loopholes, subsidies, and tax breaks to favor the rich. The income tax code is a 10,000-page mishmash, so hiding these favors within it is not difficult.

Today President George W. Bush is hyping a huge tax cut, but as usual the big cuts are delayed until several years down the road, when economic conditions will have changed and politicians can figure ways to avoid its impact. But in the short term the news media are playing up the "fact" that prime beneficiaries of the tax cut will be the rich. This is rhetoric only; these folks can and do look out for themselves regardless of any tax cuts, real or unreal.

Politicians love crime for its macho potential. Every year they collect TV cameras and wave fists, pound lecterns, and carry on like crusaders. "Lock 'em up and throw away the key!" "Three strikes and you're out!" and so on. The reality is there is very little vote-buying money in crime laws, so congressmen's theatrics are aimed at winning votes. They concentrate their spending where it will buy votes, so they pass laws that force state governments to build prisons at their own expense.

Occasionally the White House tussles with the Congress to see who is tougher on crime. In 1996 a law was passed in which states would be required to test millions of convicts for drug usage to qualify for funds for prison construction. This would be expensive, but Washington provided only a little money. This meant that most states would not seek construction funds, a result that would neutralize the impact of the law and which the elites anticipated. But in the short term politicians won votes with the legislation.

The news media continue to push conflict anyhow, because it sells. Therefore the nightly news is stuffed with car-jackings, sexual predators, workplace gunmen, home robbers, murderers, and road rage violence. Police use statistics garnered from these news shows to pad their budgets, politicians use them to win votes, purveyors of security systems use them in advertising to increase sales, the networks use them to improve ratings, and citizens feed their fear. The reality is thus lost on nearly everyone.

Russell Day remarked on prison routine: "The staff didn't show compassion or a true desire to understand. Corrections Officers were there to condemn us for every petty rule broken, rules they created to establish order and discipline, not morality and virtue. Over time, you learn how to manipulate the system. You learn to think like a criminal, the very thing they're supposed to be stopping."[9] As rules proliferate on the outside, order and discipline also prevails over morality and virtue. Day's example indicated that citizen's reactions to this oppression could have been predicted.

The 1995 Contract with America was a case study in hype. A survey showed that 62 percent of citizens predicted that the "revolution" would be a success. Two years later, a citizen would be challenged to find more than one or possibly two half-baked results. Therefore the hype was a success, but the outcomes predictably fizzled. The status quo is simply too rewarding for the elites.

The values debate has surface credibility, because debate is an important part of the democratic process (as this book will show in Part IV). But the debaters are Washington insiders and not the public, which means their debates are hype. The reality has a thinking citizen wondering how a government so renowned as a moral wasteland can preach values to a society whom it does not know or understand, nor even cares to understand.

The rights revolution generates lots of hype. This one also has surface credibility; it was intentionally created to get the public to think in terms of the Bill of Rights (ditto for patient rights). The reality has Washington's lawyers pushing group rights and not individual rights, as set forth in the Bill of Rights. The hidden agenda pits special interest against special interest, ethnic group against ethnic group, white against black, and rich against poor. Thus the administration's grand strategy comes down to divide and conquer. That is, keep the society fragmented so that members cannot organize to replace the current oligarchy with democracy. The strategy works.

In 1992 Clinton and Gore hyped themselves as futurists: global competition, high-tech, more jobs, and so on. Once in office, they quickly melted into the regime's status quo imperative: Don't rock the boat.

The 1992 horse race may have been a small cut better than the 1988 campaign, when voters were asked to choose which candidate (George Bush or Michael Dukakis) was tougher on flag burning, would kick Willie Horton harder, or who looked meaner which sticking his helmeted head out of a tank. When candidates stake out positions on such complex issues, intelligent voting becomes a major challenge.

Fallows wrote:

> *Now TV pundits are the best-paid and best-known representatives of the journalist's craft. Their work makes it harder, rather than easier, to cope with the nation's problems, because of their relentless emphasis on discord, prediction, and political spin. And it undermines the entire process of journalism, by suggesting that it should be viewed as a sideshow, most successful when it draws gawkers into the tent.*[10]

Gawkers seek entertainment, not enlightenment.

> *Through the C-Span camera, which was fixed steadily on the podium, Gingrich looked as if he were addressing a packed chamber, with eye contact, pauses, and gestures appropriate to a speaker before a vast crowd. In reality the house was usually empty as he spoke.*

Practicing a speech in front of a bathroom mirror would have had the same impact. "During tapings of 'Crossfire!' producers are shouting constantly in the earphones of the hosts, 'Cut him off!' 'Interrupt!' This makes for lively talk TV. But the culture of artificial polarization and overstatement spills over into the rest of journalism. Ambitious reporters know that these traits are rewarded." There is no longer any concern for the traditional tasks of journalism: digging for facts and constructive criticism of all institutions, especially government.

Anti-tobacco crusaders in the Environmental Protection Agency (EPA) were caught twisting truth in their emotional hype. They stated that secondhand smoke causes 3,000 lung cancer deaths annually. A federal judge said: "EPA publicly committed to a conclusion before research had begun; excluded industry by violating the [1986 Radon] act's procedural requirements; adjusted established procedure and scientific norms to validate the Agency's public conclusion."

The tendency for bureaucrats to distort and exaggerate is always there, as moderate conclusions on the dangers of hazards do not generate big budget increases. Adherence to established law is apparently a secondary consideration.

During the 1988 presidential campaign, Dick Gephardt said: "The Wall Street rentiers can make money and are making money out of the decline in the American economy. So long as they are making big profits they'd just as soon see it go on. They don't care. Takeover attempts, putting together financings, trashing companies . . . the transition can go on for years . . . it's killing us."

As a career politician Gephardt probably had limited understanding of how business is done. Profits are not only the reward for taking risks; they are also invested in creation of new wealth, jobs, and improvements in living standards. Competition keeps profits from becoming excessive. Takeovers occur in theory to strengthen weak companies (not all are successful), and when a company is beyond saving it is either absorbed into another company or liquidated (trashed), so that its resources can be put to work more productively elsewhere. These actions are what drive an economy forward; they are not killers. What does have the potential for killing (in the sense that Gephardt used the term) is an overblown, overbearing big government, because it is a gigantic parasite on the business sector. But a career politician feels a need to divert people's attention from this reality.

Logically, therefore, in his speech Gephardt bit the hand that fed him. In saying what he did, he relied on previous "education" of the public by Hollywood and academia to help him convince the public that he spoke truth.

Politicians in the two major parties routinely fight like cats and dogs, but this is hype. The reality is collaboration in the interest of maximizing the take in special interest money. When citizens in sufficient numbers discover this reality, they will wish a plague on both parties' houses.

The Economist noted:

> *Once upon a time, governments were made to conform to the popular will by the mechanism of elections. This is now passé; politicians are striving to replace elective democracy with a new, pre-emptive version. In pre-emptive democracy, politicians employ the wizards of opinion polls and focus groups to tell them what the people want, and then deliver promptly. It is a system fitting for the modern age. Food is fast, credit is immediate, manufacturing is just-in-time. So why not instamocracy?*[11]

Several reasons come to mind. One is that democracy is not an instant process; open debate and deliberation are required. A second is because people cannot distinguish truth from falsehood, they can be flimflammed as they respond to opinion polls and participate in focus group interviews. A third is lack of control over selection of those who participate, because polls commissioned by elites' lackeys (the press) have a built-in bias. (Even presumably independent pollsters are attracted to the money.) Finally, the process of delivery can be manipulated to appear as though the public will is being respected.

INFORMATION AS SMOKE SCREEN

The age of information and technology has arrived, but thinking citizens are confused because in spite of a blizzard of information they feel like they are less informed than they were ten years ago. Part of the Kremlin's operations in the old Soviet Union provides an insight. The government developed the art of disseminating **disinformation** to its logical epitome; the idea was to convince the public that they were well informed about political issues, while the real business of governing went on behind closed doors. This ploy can work only when citizens cannot separate truth from lies (or when an oppressive government denies them any other choice, in which case it is not a ploy).

The Economist described the tactics of Charles Taylor, president of Liberia:

> *Some ministers are not corrupt, and Mr. Taylor himself can talk to visitors well enough about his worthy aims for the country. The visitors are often impressed. But are they right to be? What is happening on the surface may be no clue to the way the country is run behind the scenes. Mr. Taylor recently passed a law that gives him the right to dispose of all "strategic commodities." These are defined as all mineral resources, all natural forest products, all art . . . and anything else the president chooses to call "strategic." Liberia is, in fact, Charles Taylor, Inc.*[12]

Clinton and his mandarins in Congress did much the same thing. Having set up budget limits, they routinely transcend them to spend taxpayer money on anything that tickles their fancy by simply calling them emergencies. This enabled them to circumvent the limits; it also meant a hollowing out of government. What people saw was no clue to how their government operates behind the smoke screen. The United States was not Bill Clinton, Inc., because many other elites were on the inside with him. But the impact on the ordinary citizen differed from that in Liberia only in degree (and not many degrees at that).

With 5,000 journalists making up the White House press corps, surely nothing that happens in the vast bureaucracy constituting the executive branch of government escapes their scrutiny. This statement is probably accurate, but what they see and what they report are not the same. Instead of reporting on controversial political issues that might generate productive discussion, and instead of offering constructive criticism of national legislation and policies, they report on personalities, personal power, and scandals. Sex scandals are preferred, because these cause the media to ignore everything else. A citizen could be forgiven for concluding that this is tabloid journalism.

Alterman said:

> *Almost everyone seems to agree that objective reporting is something to which journalists should aspire. Yet the rules of objective reporting often prevent the media from providing exactly the kinds of contextual information that*

would allow a reader to understand what is truly going on. This not only impedes our ability to judge a story's significance but it also gives politicians enormous latitude with the truth.[13]

If the rules of **objective** reporting impede **objectivity**, something is out of sync.

As any bureaucracy grows, its people enhance their sense of self-importance by inventing new terminology, often called neologisms. They tend to write memos in a dialect that is understood only by fellow bureaucrats. One memo analyzed using the Fog Index Readability Guide received a rating of twenty-six, which means a reader would need twenty-six years of school to read it comfortably and understand it.

Complicating the issues thus becomes a part of the smoke screen. If no one else can understand what is happening or being proposed, the bureaucrat has succeeded in convincing others that he or she is indispensable to the success of the operation. Inquiring citizens will often throw up their hands and agree that such business must be left to government, because it has the "experts" who can understand the issues. In this way the bureaucracy works toward achieving citizens' abdication of responsibility.

Carter said: "I worry deeply about the number of us who seem happy to drift through life, activists in behalf of none of our beliefs."[14] Big government creates such citizens—success in this endeavor keeps the rabble quiet. But then, it is hard to get active and involved when the issues are fogged to the point where they are difficult to understand.

Greider wrote:

Typically, political reporters separate 'politics' from substantive 'issues' as though they were two different subjects. Yet, in government, even the dimmest member of Congress understands that the ***substance is the politics.*** *No one can hope to understand what is driving political behavior without grasping the internal facts of governing issues and asking the kinds of gut-level questions that politicians ask themselves in private. Who are the winners in this matter and who are the losers? Who gets money and who has to pay? Who must be heard on this question and who can be safely ignored?*[15] (emphasis added)

It is becoming more obvious that the citizens fit into the second category in each of the last three questions. But in writing them Greider was not thinking of citizens; rather, he was describing the inner workings of the vipers' nest that is Washington. This is behind-closed-doors politics; it is not the politics of representative democracy.

Peggy Noonan is a former White House speech writer: "Make all your scandals complex and you can beat the rap every time." She referred to the Whitewater caper, which the media could not easily reduce to a short story line.

The trend in creation of smoke screens has led to a demand among viewers of the news for sound bites, clever and otherwise. Young people today spend more time on computers than on watching newscasts, partly because they perceive the mainstream news media as lacking in content and controlled by the elites.

The Center for Media and Public Affairs said the three network newscasts carried 868 show-business stories from 1990–1993, almost as many as the 1,025 stories on education and the environment combined. Leo noted in October 1997:

> *The Pew polls list only 31 news stories since 1986, that more than half of Americans say they followed very closely. The [Space Shuttle] Challenger explosion was first. [Princess] Diana's death came in 18th. Most . . . were crashes, explosions, and disasters of various kinds. Only two, near the bottom, were clearly Washington stories . . . Clinton's election in 1996 and the Supreme Court's decision on flag burning. Editors understand this shift away from sheer information, toward drama and emotional story telling. This is particularly true on TV, which specializes in emotional moments.*[16]

In a later article Leo demonstrated the contempt that contemporary news media have for truth.

> *One newsmagazine made the mistake of paying big money for newly discovered diaries of Adolf Hitler, but the [journals were] . . . fake. The magazine ran long excerpts anyway, telling readers, "Genuine or not, it almost doesn't matter in the end."*
>
> *This is believed to be the first time that any news organization announced that fake news is just about as good as real news. The other [major news error was] Tawana Brawley's claim that she was kidnapped and raped by white law-enforcement officers. Unwilling to give up on the story, the Nation ran an article claiming that "this faked crime" was useful in calling attention to the suffering of blacks, so "in cultural perspective, if not in fact, it doesn't matter whether the crime occurred or not."*[17]

The competitive imperative to be first with a story interferes with the reporter's natural tendency to check it out before writing it. In these two instances, the media did not see fit to apologize to their readers for misleading them. In this age of rights and victimization, few people accept responsibility for their errors, and the society suffers accordingly.

Leo continued. "A California therapist helped a patient convince herself that her parents had abused her. The patient sued her parents, and the therapist told *Frontline*: 'I don't care if it's true . . . . What actually happened is irrelevant to me.'" If the jury concluded similarly, there is in this an excellent business opportunity for the therapist. All that would be needed is to engage a lawyer and look around for adult children estranged from their parents. There would be no problem finding a lawyer who will cooperate.

Leo also wrote,

The recent case involving racial slurs by Texaco executives displays the "almost" mentality in action. The uproar and the damage to Texaco was so great . . . [that they] settled [at a cost of]. . . $176 million. But the Times was wrong. The nasty "N" word in the transcript turned out to be a holiday reference to "St. Nicholas." The "black jelly bean" comment was innocent, too: It referred to word and images supplied by a diversity trainer who was working with Texaco executives."

Nevertheless several news organizations continued reporting these "slurs" as real news. "The story line—racist company brought to heel—was so strong that the actual facts never penetrated the consciousness of the media or the public." This has long been a problem for any high-profile company, because the news media love to pan big business. Combine this tendency with one for disregarding truth, and the result is as shown. Leo concluded: "As a rule, use of the 'almost' phrase indicates that someone is in the process of selling you snake oil, so it is best to turn off your hearing aid quickly and check to see if your wallet is still there."

Some of the costliest false hype originates in the Pentagon, the CIA, and other cloak-and-dagger agencies. This is understandable: Hidden within the external threat theory lies their bread and butter. For decades the Pentagon and the CIA fed the media false stories about the ferocity of the Soviet military. If the truth had been forthcoming, hordes of bureaucrats would have had to seek productive work, probably in the private sector.

This prospect caused deep fear and bigger lies as the Soviet economy and its military grew weaker. Lying is also easier than going out among the enemy and digging up real data. Therefore the end of the cold war came as a complete surprise to these and other agencies.

Alterman noted: "While polling 250 people selected at random from the Denver phone book during the gulf war, [it was] discovered that the more television news and commentary the respondent claimed to have watched about the conflict, the less he or she was likely to understand about its causes and consequences."[18] President Bush did not want anyone to know that the war was staged to boost his popularity rating. Also, the generals orchestrated all the media coverage, and they knew less about directing performances than, say, Stephen Spielberg.

A few months after the war, in June 1991 President Bush outlined his plan for arms control in the Middle East. Two days later his defense secretary, Dick Cheney, announced during a visit to Israel that the United States was planning to stockpile military equipment there for use in regional conflicts. Chapter 20 argues that weapons drive conflict and not the reverse. As this is being written, some of former secretary (now vice president) Cheney's weapons are probably being used to kill Palestinians.

The elites perceive the masses as the enemy within. Yet their rhetoric tells citizens how important it is to preserve and protect democracy. To the extent this message is believed, the masses are convinced that they have the requisite strong voice in their government. Therefore they will remain passive and submissive while the elites push forward with preserving and protecting **their democracy**.

Because government has stolen the citizens' democracy the next logical step in the sequence of events becomes feasible. David Shipler served in Moscow for a number of years. "Political control [was] . . . convenient for the authorities to have most Soviet citizens in a constant state of illegality, always arrestable on apolitical grounds. . . . [An] individual feels frail against the massive righteousness of the state . . . . And the concept of crime becomes blurred, disorienting, until synthetic and regular crime fade in and out of one another." In the United States the mechanisms can be seen: More prisons and longer sentences in the name of preserving citizens' safety, more activities criminalized, ever higher mountains of laws, concentration of political power in Washington and in state governments, and media answerable to the elites and not to the masses.

President Clinton's trial for perjury and obstruction of justice was staged, although the media saw fit to avoid mention of this. Every senator knew in advance that the president would not be convicted. Krauthammer commented:

> *From the beginning, it was clear that this trial was not about truth. Truth was not going to alter anyone's ultimate vote, certainly no democrat's. (Sen. Richard Byrd . . . declared publicly that Clinton was guilty of high crimes and misdemeanors, then voted to acquit.) This was about feeling, and in particular, about feeling comfortable and good. . . . Good grief. The trial of a president—the closest thing a republic gets to regicide—as group therapy.*[19]

This fiasco suggests incredible arrogance on the part of the senators; they apparently didn't care if the public believed that members of the two major political parties were in bed together. This example combines with others to suggest that this country has a single-party government.

Bowman reinforced this conclusion when he referred to Gore and Bush in fall 2000.

> *They differ on abortion, gay rights, prayer in schools, and vouchers for private schools . . . all issues where the ruling establishment has no financial stake, and where the federal government has no constitutional role. These non-issues have been deliberately used by the elite to divide the American people and to fool them in thinking that they have a real choice between two different parties.*[20]

Margasak's report leads a citizen to wonder who is fooling whom.[21] "The Pentagon agency charged with exposing fraud destroyed documents and replaced them with fakes to avoid embarrassment when its own operations were audited, an internal inquiry found. The unsuspecting IRS reviewers found 'no problems' with the Pentagon's audit work after poring over the phony documents."

THIEVERY MADE LEGAL

Recently someone said, "America is the finest country anyone ever stole." This is an impressive compliment, as public officials have stolen some fine countries throughout history. In 1900 the total tax take from all levels of government amounted to an average of 5 percent of a family's annual income. Including the estimated costs to a family of government regulation, today's take exceeds 50 percent. This development suggests that government today is ten times better than it was in 1900. Or, more likely, it suggests that today's citizens are not getting their money's worth; politicians are stealing some of the mountains of taxpayer money going to Washington and other levels.

Today the inflation monster has apparently been tamed, although constant vigilance will be required to keep it in that condition. But public officials like inflation for selfish reasons.

The "money illusion" is a notion that depends on citizens inability to recognize when they are being taken; it works as follows. As inflation erodes the purchasing power of the dollar, workers believe that increases in take-home pay are making them and their families better off, when the reality is often the opposite. For example, if a worker receives an average annual three percent increase in pay but inflation is five percent, what his or her income will buy is reduced by two percent each year.

During the 1960s the government intentionally inflated the currency, because officials wanted to launch several gigantic social programs and pay for the war in Vietnam at the same time. They needed more purchasing power, so they stole it from citizens through two processes. One of these was discussed in Chapter 5: responding to inflation, employers provided increases in the dollar amount of families' annual incomes. These increases made the totals fall into higher tax brackets, and therefore more taxes were owed and the family retained less purchasing power. The oligarchy quietly pocketed the excess tax revenue.

The other process stole purchasing power by not adjusting for inflation the amount of an exemption on IRS Form 1040. This failure meant that less purchasing power (but the same number of dollars) was subtracted from a family's gross annual income, thus leaving more income taxable. At least one critic called both processes "intentionally dishonest."

Historian W. H. Chamberlain thought about this situation in 1958 as the government was putting these processes into motion:

> *One of the most insidious consequences of the present burden of personal income tax is that it strips many middle-class families of financial reserves and seems to lend support to campaigns for socialized medicine, socialized housing .*

. . socialized everything. The . . . income tax has made the individual vastly more dependent on the State and more avid for State handouts. It has shifted the balance in America from an individual-centered to a State-centered economic and social system.[22]

Chamberlain wrote this during the height of the cold war, when public officials and the media were exceptionally busy stoking fear in the populace (helped in great measure by a misguided zealot, Senator Joseph McCarthy). Today a different interpretation is in order, as the external threat posed by the Soviet Union no longer exists. Now the primary emotional hook has vanished, and citizens are becoming more rational and more inquisitive concerning what the government is doing to them.

When a burglar enters a home or business the loss is obvious; no burglar will take just a little money. Insurance will cover most or all of the loss, and the thief will not return again and again. When government enters homes and businesses, it takes only a little each time (examples are withholding, payroll, and sales taxes). This conceals the loss, so that it can return time and again, frequently unnoticed and frequently increasing the amount. These intrusions have been made legal, and there is no insurance available to cover these losses.

Bovard noted: "Before the income tax, the government existed to serve the people, at least in some vague nominal sense; now, the people exist to provide financial grist for the State's mill. . . . IRS seizures of private property have increased by 400 percent since 1980 and now hit over two million Americans each year." In his book *For Good and Evil* Charles Adams demonstrated that this increase in the use of violence by tax collectors has ample historical precedent, especially in the case of taxes on incomes.

Bovard continued: "From 1985 to 1991, the number of federal seizures of property under asset forfeiture laws increased by 1,500 percent . . . reaching a total of $644 million. . . . 80 percent of the people whose property is seized by the federal government under drug laws are never formally charged with any crime." Local police departments have found these laws convenient for enhancing their operating budgets, because usually the former owner cannot retrieve the property without a court decision. Without charges there is no court appearance, and it is often too expensive to pursue recourse through civil action.

The Fifth Amendment to the Constitution reads in part: "No person shall . . . be deprived of life, liberty, or property, without due process of law; nor shall private property be taken for public use without just compensation." It is thus hard to avoid the conclusion that citizens are being robbed and the Constitution is being ignored.

Bovard also wrote,

If a group of neighbors voted to seize someone's front yard to make a picnic ground for themselves, that would be seen as rank thievery. But if the same neighbors incorporate into a local government, do the same thing, and offer the yard owner only 10 cents compensation on the dollar for his losses, this is supposedly fair play. It is important to have a sounder distinction between democracy and thievery than simply counting votes.

This is reminiscent of two wolves and a sheep voting on what to have for dinner. The needed protection resides in the Constitution, but when public officials ignore key parts of the document in their lawmaking there is little point in keeping it, other than as a curiosity for tourists.

The current designation "historic" has proven excellent for undermining fundamental rights of property ownership. If concerned citizens really want a particular property to be preserved as historic, all they need do is organize, raise enough money, and buy it. (Rarely will an owner refuse to sell at any price. Should this happen, the property will still be around when the owner is no longer.)

The Cato Institute commented:

Today, there is no worthy end—from the uniformity of zoning to the preservation of flora, fauna, wetlands, views, historic sites, and more—that property owners are not expected to pay for by forgoing their rights and bearing the loss that follows. It is time to end such theft, which is precisely what to call it when government takes what it wants from individuals without paying for it. . . . If the public had to pay for what it took, it would think twice about whether the goods were worth the price. Absent that discipline, the public appetite would in principle be infinite . . . which is precisely what has happened under the reign of "free" regulatory takings.[23]

Hidden safely within the income tax code are thousands of tax breaks, subsidies, tax credits, and other favors to rich election campaign contributors. Often their donations are made tax-deductible, simply because Congress is in a position to make a great variety of activities legal. (Human nature often impels them to make laws that favor themselves and their rich friends.) Representative Les Aspin was not the only one to found his own think tank, through which he received tax-deductible contributions from defense contractors. Some lawmakers have even organized their own personal foundations (tax-exempt of course).

The problem with all this lies in the need for the ordinary taxpayer to make up the slack through increased taxation. People don't like tax increases, so it must be done in an indirect way so that the impact is kept hidden.

Farm subsidies are great for full-time farmers, who kick some of the loot back to members of Congress who vote for the subsidies. What is less known is that consumers get it from two directions: They were taxed $30 billion in 1993 to pay for the subsidies, and they paid another $12 billion in higher food prices. Those who think food prices are too high have a point.

Bovard said,

> *Discretionary power has been granted to bureaucrats by many laws, because congressmen don't have the courage to say openly what they want the bureaucracy to do, leading to government by stealth. In September 1990, for the first time and under federal court order, USDA [Department of Agriculture] officially solicited comments from orange farmers on its plan to restrict their sales. By a 10-to-1 margin, farmers vehemently opposed USDA's plan to prohibit them from selling much of their harvest. . . . Despite the farmers' opposition, the agency prohibited California and Arizona farmers from selling 32 percent of their fresh navel oranges to other Americans in the 1990-91 season.*

The bad side of human nature has been on grisly display in Washington for decades. The good side recognizes the propensity to give, to contribute. It holds "What can I contribute?" above "What's in it for me?" People who like to help people resent constantly contributing toward the care and feeding of thieves, especially when the "contributions" are collected through force. Stealing is stealing, legalized or not. Someone said, "We put the petty criminal in jail, but the really big thieves we elevate to high public office."

Lapham commented: "Other oligarchies at other moments in the nation's history have conducted similar raids on the public treasury, but mostly they had the wit not to give press interviews and the good luck not to wreck the economy that provided them with their new fortunes."[24] One reason why this time is different lies in the immense accumulation of wealth in the US economy since World War II; therefore the economy is not yet wrecked. The difference between thievery and robbery is that the former is sneaky and the latter is open and sometimes brutal. Lapham seemed to suggest that from the perspective of the people the conversion of public officials from thieves to robbers is ongoing. In a police state there is no need for thievery.

Arrogance on the part of Washington insiders has grown with their wealth. They are aware of an incipient suspicion among citizens, so they have raised the profile of the GAO as an internal auditor, or watchdog. This agency monitors government actions, presumably on behalf of citizens. Once in a while this office will publish some damning evidence, but nothing referring to thievery will be exposed, simply because bureaucrats in that office know from whence their salaries and perks are coming. The occasional bit of criticism is intended to convince concerned citizens that the GAO is doing its job.

However, once under the influence of legal thievery and the spending drug, politicians either believe that they can fool all of the people all of the time or in their arrogance they simply don't care. With all of Washington plunged so deeply into fantasy and moral depravity, insiders are losing touch with reality.

Humanity has the ability to renew itself periodically. Therefore the perpetrators of history's greatest scam cannot stop; they are propelling themselves, lemming-like, to their own destruction by the hand of the citizen.

In 1870 Spooner emphasized a stark contrast. "The highwayman takes solely upon himself the responsibility, danger, and crime of his own act. He does not pretend that he has any rightful claim to your money, or that he intends to use it for your own benefit. He does not pretend to be anything but a robber." The question begs a discussion: When does the government's legitimate right to a citizen's money stop, and robbery begin? The answer is very difficult to determine. Therefore over a period of years and without direct accountability to taxpayers the negative tug of human nature will gradually turn public officials into a pack of thieves.

Politicians like to say to citizens, "In a democracy, **you** are the government." They choose to interpret this truism to mean that anything they do is by citizen consent. The national debt is now over $6 trillion, presumably due to citizen consent.

That unimaginably stupendous number prompts discussion of the most pernicious aspect of government thievery: stealing from generations to come. The politician's view of the national debt is simple: "We owe it to ourselves." The reality is not so simple: who are the "we" and who are the "ourselves"? Reflection on this question leads to realistic answers. Members of Congress over the past several decades have run up a towering public debt, in large part through buying the votes of older people, who vote a lot compared to the young. Today many of these former voters are dead, so they will not be contributing toward the interest and principal on that debt.

Social Security had its beginning in 1935 under President Franklin Roosevelt. The Great Depression had left millions of citizens impoverished and destitute, so three programs were established: one to accept employee and employer contributions and keep them with accumulated interest until they are paid out monthly after retirement; a second to compensate destitute widows with young children; and a third to support those who are incapacitated. The second two programs were essentially taxes, as no money was paid into the programs aside from that collected from taxpayers and borrowing. How did the state pension plan work out over the long term?

In theory, contributions on behalf of each employee and accumulated interest were monitored. After retirement, monthly payments were calculated based on a worker's life expectancy and disbursed. At first the fund accepted contributions according to the plan, but soon it began to accumulate large surpluses because few contributors retired in the early going. After World War II members of Congress got the idea that they could remain in office as long as they wanted through buying votes among the retired, and so they increased benefits and expanded eligibility. They did this in each election year throughout the 1950s; almost every one of these raises took effect one month before an election. In just the first five years, retirees' benefits more than doubled.

By the time the program was in effect fifteen years the government had transformed it from a "defined contribution" pension plan into a "defined benefit" plan. Put another way, it had become a tax on the young to support the old.

Economic growth was strong during the 1960s, so payroll taxes flowed into Washington by the ton. But instead of holding the surplus Congress again expanded benefits, this time by 83 percent. A 20 percent increase took effect just five weeks before the 1972 election. By this time the retirement community in the United States had become the richest in the world, but the bite on the struggling young continued to get deeper. Now it becomes obvious that "we owe it to ourselves" is meaningless.

Jefferson wrote: "I sincerely believe . . . that the principle of spending money to be paid by posterity . . . is but swindling futurity on a large scale." Not only are today's young being forced to support the old at a high level of living, the national debt will be their responsibility and that of generations as yet unborn.

Disgusting as it is, the end of this issue is not yet near. For years the pension fund has been running huge surpluses in anticipation of the retirement of the huge baby boomer age group, beginning around the year 2015, when the fund will operate in deep deficit. Hooked on the spending drug, members of Congress have for years taken every dollar and spent it, while leaving unsecured IOUs in their places. The pension plan's unfunded liability is now more than $8.5 trillion. At this point there is no need to ask who will be responsible for at least a major part of that colossal obligation.

Future citizens cannot complain about this situation because they have not yet been born. But they are the unwitting victims of thievery nonetheless. Young women might be thinking twice about giving birth, when each newborn carries an $85,000 debt right from the start. But if thousands of women acted on this thought the situation would be far worse. Small wonder members of Congress keep raising their salaries and pensions; they are providing for their progeny as well as for themselves in old age.

People in the future who are not Washington insiders will be on their own. As citizens begin to understand this grim prospect, more of them will apply to become insiders.

Word about the annual congressional raids on the Social Security trust funds has got out only recently: There are no **funds**, and surely there is no **trust**. So in his 1998 State of the Union address President Clinton said he would reserve "every penny of any budget surplus" for Social Security. What he actually did was to increase government spending by $20 billion, getting around budget restraints by calling the expenditures "emergencies."

The ruse worked, and he never presented any plan to save the system. Hence all the media hype about the first government fiscal surplus in thirty years amounted to just that: hype. Now, the media did report surpluses for a couple of years. But this is rhetoric at best, and in any event honest, accrual accounting was surely not utilized. If any real surplus should develop, the rhetoric will focus on the national debt while the reality will be increased activity by the spendaholics in Congress.

The steal-and-spend syndrome has apparently spread beyond Congress. Congressman Dick Armey said in July 2001: "Let me just be very clear about this. The House of Representatives is not going to go back to raiding Social Security and Medicare trust funds." As he spoke, the administration was raiding Medicare.

Lane wrote: "Government must take the wealth they consume, from the wealth that productive men create. The important question is, What amount can they take *safely*? Because they use force, they have no means of knowing the answer to that question."[25]

Hospers said, "Special interest pays tribute to predatory politicos who suck the marrow from the bones of society, individuals are reduced to ever more meaningless atoms in the social cosmos. All of life becomes politicized, which means corrupted by power. And as individual liberty and individual rights die, all that is decent in human society dies with them."[26]

Laws and Regulations

When placed in an unearned position to coerce others, anyone can become power-drunk. The illusion comes in as people find ways around the implementation of this power. This of course causes even more rules to be put into effect, followed by more evasion, and the vicious circle continues until citizens see no alternative other than open rebellion.

Madison wrote,

> *The internal effects of a mutable policy are still more calamitous. It poisons the blessing of liberty itself. It will be of little avail to the people that the laws are made by men of their own choice if the laws be so voluminous that they cannot be read, or so incoherent that they cannot be understood; if they be repealed or revised before they are promulgated, or undergo such incessant changes that no man, who knows what the law is today, can guess what it will be tomorrow. Law is defined to be a rule of action; but how can that be a rule, which is little known, and less fixed?*

At the time Madison wrote the above passage in the *Federalist Papers*, Jefferson was serving as ambassador in Paris. In a letter to Col. Edward Carrington, he referred to European governments: "Under pretense of governing, they have divided their nations into two classes, wolves and sheep. I do not exaggerate. This is a true picture of Europe. Cherish, therefore, the spirit of our people, and keep alive their attention."

Charles Dickens called British common law an ass. Depending on precedent stretching possibly back several centuries, the system had lawyers and judges researching legal history for principles established in common law for use as guides to arguments and decisions. But it is difficult to see how good principles can be found in bad laws, and many thousands of these were created over the centuries. The primary and often exclusive reason why these laws were bad is that they were put into force by kings and judges (possibly at personal whim) instead of by the people through the democratic process.

The result is frequent reference to legal precedents put forth in the Europe that Jefferson described when making arguments and rendering decisions in the United States, even today. This section will certify that the hundreds of thousands of laws and regulations on the books today were not made by the people of the United States. Rather, they were made in a top-down manner by paternalistic governments.

Thomas Paine said,

> *We now see all over Europe, and particularly in England, the curious phenomenon of a nation looking one way, and the government the other . . . the one forward and the other backward. If governments are to go on by precedent, while nations go on by improvement, they must at last come to a final separation; and the sooner, and the more civilly they determine this point, the better it will be for them.*[27]

Paine wrote during the late eighteenth century, when the Industrial Revolution had just acquired significant momentum. Common law worked fairly well before this time, when there were few technical and social changes in society from one century to the next. But afterward society moved forward much more rapidly, and old laws were rendered even more irrelevant.

This grim legacy then must combine with the natural human tendency by public officials to meddle in the private sector. The news media, apparently just as naturally, cooperate, pointing to numerous market "failures" that must be rectified through government intervention. The welfare economist concentrates on the economy and does not recognize the impact of the political system on the shape of the economy. This recognition is easily avoided if the expert has no corresponding theory of government operation, and easier yet if a typical intellectual has no interest in learning about such a theory. Such is life under government by experts.

In a democracy public officials have faith in citizens. Because markets are made up of citizens, it logically follows that officials have faith in markets. Because no human institution is perfect, markets will occasionally develop imperfections. However, a government with faith in citizens knows that, given a little time, the market will correct a temporary imbalance. Whenever that faith weakens, the political urge to meddle will assert itself. The negative side of human nature is always on red alert.

Conventional wisdom among political scientists and welfare economists suggests that someone with a strong record of accomplishment in the private sector changes his or her psychological stripes on entering public service. He identifies with a cause greater than himself. But this runs counter to human nature, as when accountability weakens and there is lots of money around he will be tempted to act on his own behalf.

Mitchell and Simmons noted:

> *As a taxpayer, the citizen is interested in the aggregate size of the budget and supports reduced spending. . . . As a beneficiary of government spending, the same citizen supports an increase in subsidies or favors for his company or employer and governmental regulation of his profession; he has little interest in the total size of the budget. Predictably, these latter interests are generally apt to be more intensely felt than taxpayer commitments.*[28]

This explains in large part many citizens' lack of concern with the total national budget and their demand for more government.

The potential of this feeling has not been lost on career politicians; hence the presence of thousands of laws that provide something for nearly everybody in the populace. The result, also predictable, is continuing growth of government.

This tendency also explains why favors and special programs never stop. Once momentum has been established, it is relatively easy for concentrated interests to maintain a program and increase the money.

Early Supreme Court Chief Justice John Marshall declared in 1820 that the US Constitution dictated that contracts are inviolable. Private property is acquired through a contract between a willing buyer and a willing seller, in which price and other conditions of sale are agreed. But today politicians and bureaucrats regularly interfere with private contracts, sometimes completely nullifying them.

Bovard wrote,

> *Americans today must obey thirty times as many laws as their great-grandfathers had to obey at the turn of the century. Federal agencies publish an average of over 200 pages of new rulings, regulations, and proposals in the Federal Register each business day. The growth of the federal statute book is one of the clearest measures of the increase of the government control of the citizenry. But the effort to improve society by the endless multiplication of penalties, prohibitions, and prison sentences is a dismal failure.*[29]

This, too, can be explained through human nature: People support what they help create. Every one of the regulations in this daily blizzard was created in a top-down manner by bureaucrats, many of whom are obsessed with their personal power over others. Thus the bureaucrats support what they create, for themselves.

In 1977 Nobel Laureate Milton Friedman performed in a ten-part TV series called *Free to Choose.*[30]

> *In one of the most memorable scenes, Friedman talks while walking behind stacks of the Federal Register . . . arranged in chronological order. There are only one or two volumes per year from the 1930s, so viewers can see his full figure. Then during the 1940s came increasing numbers of regulations, and each year's stack of volumes blocks view of his legs. The 1960s brought an explosion of regulations, and the stacks of volumes are so high that Friedman can no longer be seen.*

This passage graphically described the administrative law of the land to the 1960s. Thinking about the implications of this subterfuge beyond the 1960s, a citizen might feel like asking Friedman to produce *Free to Choose 2.* However, he might turn down the offer as an exercise in futility—the gentleman stands only five feet three inches tall.

Bovard elaborated on the power theme,

> *We have far more federal agencies, and the agencies are under less restraint than they used to be. The federal judiciary has created an overwhelming presumption in the legality of the actions of federal agencies, thus approving more and more acts by government officials that once would have been considered outrageous, illegal, or unconstitutional. The sheer volume of federal action . . . makes effective judicial oversight of federal agencies a near impossibility.*

The founding fathers agonized for weeks in 1787 over the concept of separation of powers in the new national government, which they were proposing in the US Constitution. The finished product, though not perfect, worked remarkably well for some 160 years.

"The more often the law is revised, the more the law becomes simply a series of arbitrary political commands that must be obeyed, a grant of unlimited power to government officials." What would Madison say to this?

Bovard presented a laundry list of abuses. For example, "dumping" in international trade refers to a company pricing a product for export at below cost or less than a fair price; the potential for abuse is great when a country wants to restrict imports to protect jobs in its own factories. Recently Japanese flat-panel displays for laptop computers were slapped with a 63 percent dumping penalty even though there were no viable US makers. This increased prices on laptops to the point where they could not compete with foreign-made computers. Therefore Apple shifted its manufacturing from Colorado to Ireland, Compaq shifted from Houston to Scotland, Toshiba from California to Japan, and Dolch Computer from California to Germany. These moves eliminated nearly 3,000 jobs, when the original purpose of the dumping penalty was presumably to preserve jobs.

Bovard wrote that "it is a federal crime for a woman to sew buttons on a dress for pay in her own home." The long arm of the law knows no limit when it comes to limiting people's freedom.

The FDA has for years tested drugs for safety before permitting release to the market. This huge bureaucracy has recently and on its own decided that it will rule also on efficacy. Doctors will admit that every **body** is uniquely different, even between identical twins. This unavoidable fact makes it difficult to justify certifying a drug as safe, much less whether it will work as advertised by its maker. For example, Procter and Gamble tested its Rely tampon on thousands of women of all types, colors, weight, hair and skin color, and most ages with no negative effects whatever. Then it was marketed, and it killed or maimed several users. But the challenge of testing for efficacy means no limit to future expansion of the bureaucracy.

In 1989 in Costa Mesa, anyone standing within 300 feet of certain areas who looked guilty of an intent to solicit work was subject to arrest. Ninety-six men were arrested for the crime of asking for work. The *Orange County Register* editorialized: "If declaring that certain phrases, like 'Need some work?' or 'How about a job?' are grounds for imprisonment isn't an unconstitutional infringement on free speech, it's difficult to imagine what is."

The 1968 National Housing Act created heavily subsidized mortgage loans for low-income families to own homes. Bovard wrote, "The most serious problem . . . was housing abandonment . . . emptied and left to rot in previously stable neighborhoods. . . . since most families had almost no equity in their homes, it was often cheaper for them to abandon . . . than to repair them. . . . It took only four years of the . . . program to reduce a neat, middle-class neighborhood into a shattered, decaying slum."

In 1985 a typical decision was made by Congress: Farmers were paid not to plant corn, wheat, and other subsidized crops on their land and were paid up to $200 an acre to grow any other crop they chose. But this boosted supplies of unsubsidized crops and therefore dropped their market prices, and ruined farmers who were not being paid to grow the same crops. Due to taxpayer-financed subsidies, there is often tremendous overproduction, and the surpluses are stored at taxpayer expense.

The government's drug war has created a variety of bizarre results. A pain specialist has had his office searched eighteen times by Drug Enforcement Administration (DEA) agents and local police. Frank Adams commented: "Drug agents have been turned loose and are totally out of control and they do not know how to discriminate between the legitimate and illegitimate use of these drugs. This is police-state medicine."

In 1990 the number of people sentenced to prison for drug crimes exceeded those sentenced for violent crimes. This was happening at a time when far more people died each year from legal drugs than from illegal ones. In one year about 400,000 deaths were associated with tobacco, and there were 6,756 deaths from illegal drugs.

Bovard once more:

> *While the police were awaiting bandits, they witnessed store clerk Elaine Ott sell a copy of Playboy to two 16-year-old boys. The police quickly arrested, strip-searched, and jailed the 52-year-old woman, who faced five years in prison and a $5,000 fine for the felony. . . . Ott complained that she could not understand why she could sell condoms to minors, but not magazines. The following night, after the police were no longer there, Mrs. Ott's husband was robbed at gunpoint.*

As long as the government can meddle in the broadcasting business, free speech will remain in jeopardy. Issuance and revocation of licenses and promulgating regulations give politicians opportunities to flatter and protect themselves, and also to threaten any station that criticizes government policies and programs. In effect the threat of license revocation is censorship.

Around 800 different trades and professions are licensed; anyone lacking a license who performs services that are restricted to licensed practitioners is subject to fines and imprisonment. The logical and convenient rationale is protecting the public from charlatans, but the hidden agenda is restriction of supply of services so that the law of supply and demand will operate to raise their prices and keep them high.

The logical solution is twofold: publicize the work records of all, including complaints, and allow those without licenses to practice while probably charging a lower price. This policy would make services available to poorer customers. In this way customers have a broader choice of services available along with information about them, and there would be very few brain surgeons practicing without a license. Furthermore there would be far fewer poor people lining up for treatment under taxpayer-financed state Medicaid programs.

Mitchell and Simmons noted, "Government can coerce payment from taxpayers whether they consume the good or not, but there is still no guidance as to the optimal amount to produce or the appropriate price to charge. Given the other limitations faced by government, the arguments for public provision of public goods are not as compelling as they may seem at face value."

In the former Soviet Union there were no prices to guide production of one factory's goods to be routed to another factory as inputs to its production. The ultimate result was chaos. Some factories actually subtracted value during the process of manufacture: Outputs were worth less than inputs.

A market-clearing price helps equalize supply to demand; without it efficiency will decrease. Also, without competition spurring development of new ideas far less new wealth is created.

Politicians and bureaucrats deliberately create instability, as this increases demand for their services when citizens complain about lack of ability to plan ahead. Officials become more important and can demand more money. "Appearing to fight inflation and deficits is . . . politically astute. Actually fighting them may be political suicide." If things can be kept stirred up, citizens will continue to believe their public servants are laboring on their behalf.

Since the end of the Soviet Union, Russian presidents Yeltsin and Putin and the Duma (parliament) in the Kremlin have passed thousands of laws, probably as many new laws and regulations as has the US government during the past decade. On reflection a citizen might conclude that the results have not been very different. Steven E. Landsburg is professor of economics at the University of Rochester. He believes the public probably suffers less when ostensibly competing businessmen agree to break laws than when ostensibly competing political parties conspire to make laws. He is probably right; in the private sector competition lurks around each corner, even when executives conspire to restrict this economic force.

People support what they help create, and people don't support what they don't help create. This explains much of the violence that plagues society today, especially among the young. Not only are they ground down by top-down lawmaking; they are also getting mixed signals from government.

O'Neill explained:

> *Following his extended coverage Tuesday night about Columbine High, Koppel told viewers to hang on just a few minutes longer. There had been a spectacular series of explosions in downtown Belgrade. A building suffered a direct hit by US missiles, and "Nightline" was ready with up-to-the-minute details about military mayhem in Yugoslavia. Quickly viewers had to make the transition from violence as wasteful and tragic to violence as good and necessary.*[31]

For members of the sound-bite generation, this transition is not difficult: bad violence is here at home, and good violence is over there. All it takes is a decline in morality in the culture and feeling for those poor, innocent, suffering souls in Yugoslavia vaporizes.

O'Neill continued,

> *Violence is unacceptable in school, they are told, but military recruiters are free to set up shop in schools, to recruit our children into the perfectly acceptable vocation of warrior. Parents and religious leaders embrace war as a necessary evil. . . . On the one hand we want our children to think, to follow their consciences in moral matters. At the same time we give our moral stamp of*

approval to war, where obedience to authority is the bottom line and conscience is irrelevant.

In December 2000 a pundit posed this question: "What should be the principal source of government . . . the judiciary or the political branches?" This question penetrates to the core of the issue under discussion in this section. Specifically, it **omits mention of the citizens as the source of government**. This is oversight is as astounding as it is predictable. In its essence it omits, and even refutes, democracy.

Selling Influence Is Corruption

In 1790 Thomas Paine was in England. He discovered that every politician had his price, apparently "at the expense of a deluded people." Mitchell and Simmons commented: "Successful politicians become the mirror image of what they do, shifting, smoothing, evading, concealing, lying, and diffusing hostility. Insincerity and flattery are common forms of political behavior; so, too, are paranoia, hatred, envy, and cynicism."[32]

These words omit few of the emotions that connect with the negative side of human nature. This is the life of the career politician; the only real compensation is money, lots of it. Everything of real and lasting value is sacrificed on the altar of mammon.

When corruption infects the government of a poor country there is limited wealth available, and so a tiny minority becomes very wealthy at the expense of the dirt-poor masses. When a country is wealthy many people flock to feed at the public trough, and the more money the more looters. They acquire strong vested interests, and they have the wherewithal to defend them. Eventually they come to believe their exalted position and perks are part of their birthright. This is how aristocracies were formed centuries ago. It describes how oligarchies are formed today.

In 1991 P. J. O'Rourke wrote: "When buying and selling are controlled by legislators, the first things bought and sold are legislators."[33] An experienced lobbyist who was the self-described "money guy" for several senators indicated that not all senators could be bought through flattery, dinners, gifts, money, and so on: only around 95 percent.

Phillips said,

> *In a city where influence mongering is so often the pot of gold at the end of the public service rainbow, we should not be surprised that work-for-anybody gunslinger lobbyists are as lionized—and as little inhibited by law enforcement—as their six-gun predecessors were in the fast-draw years of Abilene and Dodge City. Federal lobbying statutes, meanwhile, have had the stopping power of blank cartridges. They are designed not to matter.*[34]

Citizens suspect that their wishes are being preempted by dirty money; hence an occasional legal straw man is used to divert their attention away from the action. Schudson reported that perhaps the first record of this deceit occurred with the passage of the Federal Corrupt Practices Act in 1910.[35] It was amended the following year to set spending limits for campaigns for Congress, but there were no enforcement mechanisms. Another presumed attempt became law in 1925, but this one also had few teeth. After 1927, no one was prosecuted under the law.

Gross wrote,

> *So much of the nation's treasure is funneled into Washington every day from a large trough running from all corners of America down into the low-lying beltway, that the smallest change in a tax code, a regulation, or a subsidy law can mean hundreds of millions, even billions, of dollars for the organization paying the lobbyist's bill. No wonder the lobbying industry is sometimes called "The Fifth Branch of Government," the fourth being the press.*[36]

Pundits are wired into power politics, but they occasionally criticize government to induce the public to believe they are writing truth. At other times they will defend government or mislead the public. Broder argued that the bulk of the so-called dirty money is actually spent on television ads rather than stolen or used to create special favors.[37] "A report earlier this month from the Alliance for Better Campaigns, a bipartisan public interest group critical of the broadcasters, said that 'stations in the top 75 media markets took in at least $771 million . . . last year. . . . Total take probably reached $1 billion." What Broder did not say is that this money is little more than pocket change when compared with the $25 billion annually spent in the grand influence bazaar.

Will made bold to defend corruption: "However, those crying 'corruption!' must show that legislative outcomes were changed by contributions . . . voted differently than they otherwise would have done."[38] Well, if the special interests who hire lobbyists to dump money into congressional pockets were not getting something for their millions they surely would not be contributing them.

Will continued: "To prove corruption one must prove that legislators are acting against their principles, or against their best judgment, or against their constituents' wishes." This is admittedly difficult, because career politicians have no principles except to maximize the money (which means that in accepting contributions they are acting in their best judgment). However, there is ample evidence that they are acting against constituents' wishes: term limits, referendum vote for any tax increase, less military, smaller government, and so on.

On the same op-ed page Molly Ivins challenged Will: "Hard to see how the influence of campaign contributions on politics could get clearer than the credit-card industry's purchase of a harsher bankruptcy law, industry's purchase of the repeal of rules to prevent repetitive stress injuries and High George Dubya's 180 on CO_2."[39]

In 1993 Clinton issued Executive Order #112834, which contained presumably stern rules against lobbying. But the fine print all but negated the impact. Ditto for the Lobbying Disclosure Act of 1993.

Gross continued:

> *The appearance of integrity has become the key in newly frightened Washington, as long as there is no bite to it. Too much is at stake among the $250,000-plus-a-year crowd to jeopardize their industry because of any new morality, pretended or otherwise. . . . Says Charles Lewis of the Center for Public Integrity . . .. "Lobbying in Washington is out of control. Not only is legal corruption rampant, but it has become a way of life . . . one in which the mercenary culture has overtaken the public interest. And it's worse than it's ever been."*

The outlook? More of same. Attracted by mountains of easy money, new gangs of looters come into Washington almost daily.

Many citizens believe that members of Congress are the prime recipients of dirty money, as they need tons of it for their reelection campaigns. But over recent decades there has been so much money coming in that many laws are worded only vaguely, so that bureaucrats in the executive branch can enhance their personal power and perks through issuing thousands of regulations. Regulations are a politician's dream, because as they are put into force they cost no direct and immediate money and they are dressed up to look like many benefits for citizens.

Greider elaborated:

> *The transactions where this occurs are mostly submerged in the executive branch, scattered across hundreds of bureaus and agencies and focused mainly on the esoteric language of federal regulations and enforcement. The regulatory government is a many-chambered labyrinth, staggeringly complex and compartmentalized into thousands of parts. But one does not have to study a dizzying organization chart . . . to understand how it works. One need only visualize what happens to a law after it is enacted to grasp the antidemocratic dynamic.*[40]

A September 15, 2000, *New York Times* editorial indicated that justices of the Supreme Court apparently don't like to be left out of the sleaze.

> *At a moment when the federal judiciary needs to tighten its ethical prohibitions on accepting money or gifts from private interests . . . Chief Justice William Rehnquist . . . move in the opposite direction. With Rehnquist's approval, senator Mitch McConnell . . . tucked a provision into a spending bill in July that would lift the 11-year-old ban on judges' collecting honorariums for appearances. The ban was imposed in 1989 to protect the integrity and impartiality of the judicial system against outside influence.*

The piece continued: "Fairness and impartiality of the federal judiciary is already being seriously undermined by allowing federal judges to accept free vacations at posh resorts from private interests bent on influencing." The negative virus seems to spare no one in Washington.

A November 1998 issue of *Time* magazine published something rare: a piece of investigative political reporting. Although members of both parties staged varied debates, Don Barlett and Jim Steele discovered that the great variety of subsidies, tax breaks, low-cost loans, and so on produce nothing for taxpayers. Politicians handed out $125 billion to companies during a time of strong economic growth in a way very similar to that used by traditional welfare programs.

"It is unfair, destroys incentive, perpetuates dependence and distorts the economy." Furthermore, it rewards the wealthy rather than the poor. Big Fortune 500 firms have reduced their total employment over the past decade, yet they are the largest recipients of these handouts. The hidden agenda, of course, it that corporate lobbyists purchased that $125 billion with perhaps a few million in "contributions."

The 1996 Freedom to Farm Act allowed farmers to plant whatever they wanted and still receive subsidies. However, eventually government would stop supporting farmers. *The Economist* noted: "But commodity prices plummeted, and five years later federal farm aid soared to $32 billion (bringing the total disbursement over the past 40 years to around $350 billion)."[41] This huge lump of taxpayer money has gone in mostly two directions: one to make already fat farmers still fatter, and the other to make already fat politicians still fatter. This is one more massive transfer of wealth from the middle class to the rich.

The Economist went on to explain that rich farmers use some of their windfall to bid up the price of farmland, which makes it more difficult for young people to buy land. Therefore, although the rhetoric from Washington emphasizes helping small farmers, the reality is government hastening the decline of small farming towns.

In early August 1999 another $7.4 billion of taxpayer money went to farmers, presumably in response to falling prices and droughts. An economist might figure that with drought yields will be lower and that will drive prices upward. Or, an economist might figure that showering money on farmers would help them produce more, and thus cause prices to fall further.

But a politician uses a different calculus. The government ladled out $6 billion to farmers during the previous fall, which the news media assured readers was a one-time fix. Then came another $7.4 billion; a substantial part of both chunks of money will find its way back into reelection campaign coffers. Even this is not the end of the story. In June 2000 President Clinton shoveled out another $15 billion of taxpayer money to farmers.

In October 2001 Congress did it yet again, and *The Economist* was on the job.

One of the glories of American farm policy is that, whenever you think it cannot get any loonier, it promptly finds a way of doing so. After pumping some $70 billion of public money into farms over the past four years, and thereby stimulating even more over-production of food, the House of Representatives has now passed a farm bill approving the payment of $173 billion over the next ten years (roughly $70 billion more than had been budgeted for).[42]

Farmers and congressmen could and did predict what happened. These people are not naive; it is a conspiracy against the taxpayer. It is difficult to see the situation in any other light.

Less than 2 percent of Americans are on farms today, and only a small fraction of those are the wealthy ones under discussion here. Their lobbyists are obviously very accomplished at maintaining the rich farmers' direct pipeline into taxpayer pockets. Thinking citizens might wonder if they have missed their calling; they should be farmers.

Greider described the influence monger industry:

You want facts to support the industry's lobbying claims? It pumps out facts. You want expert opinions from scholars? It has those in abundance from the think tanks corporate contributors underwrite. You want opinion polls? It hires polling firms to produce them. You want people . . . live voters who support the industry position? Jack Bonner delivers them.

Bonner will supply influence in any desired direction, if the price is right.

"In actuality, earnest citizens are being skillfully manipulated by powerful interests—using 'facts' that are debatable at best—in a context designed to serve narrow corporate lobbying strategies, not free debate." An influence monger will ask a lobbyist how much pressure he wants to put on Senator Phoghorn: maybe ten groups of poll respondents, maybe a few hundred letters, or maybe a thousand phone calls. In this way the good senator can say he heard from the folks back home on this issue, so this is the way he will vote. Once again, these scams can work only so long as citizens cannot distinguish truth from lies and hence don't know when their thinking is being manipulated.

Capital budgeting is a financial term that describes a process within a business of evaluating investment alternatives with respect to projected profit and risk. Then one or more projects are selected, depending on the amount of money available for long-term commitment. This is where new jobs are created. If lawmakers were for sale this would add another alternative to the mix of proposed projects. Frequently a lobbyist will show that the "profit" on an "investment" in government is higher and the risk lower than any other alternative being considered by the firm.

Executives are indirectly hired by shareholders to work hard to maximize shareholder value (the stock price). This assigned task suggests that managers can be forgiven if they maximize value by "investing" (read: "stuffing dirty money into campaign war chests") in government.

The difficulty here lies in the reality that no new wealth and jobs are being created, as they would be if the money were invested in a new plant, addition, specialized equipment, research, training, and so on. Rather, existing wealth is just being transferred from one deep pocket to another. Furthermore, because competition is reduced through these activities, companies become weaker. They can afford to pay their employees less, and prices to consumers and business customers are higher. These two factors combine to slow the rise in living standards for families in the greater society.

But these are side effects for corrupt politicians, and they themselves don't suffer from them (only consumers do). Huffington said,

> *[Senate Majority Leader] Lott scored nearly a million dollars in contributions for his party from casino interests following a trip to Las Vegas with [Senator] McConnell aboard casino magnate Steve Wynn's corporate jet. Afterward, Lott tucked a 10-year, $316 million tax break for the casino industry into an I.R.S. reform bill. "No other industry benefits from it," said Frank Clemente, director of Congress Watch.*[43]

Dwayne Andreas, head of Archer Daniels Midland, is an old hand at this business. He even managed to one-up Steve Wynn, as Huffington continued:

> *Over the last four election cycles . . . have heaped over $3 million in soft money on both parties . . . in an effort to protect federal subsidies for ethanol. . . . .This generous spreading of financial manure has proven to be the best investment in town. Of the $600 million taxpayers will be forking over to ethanol-producing companies every year until 2007, half will go to ADM . . . which no doubt will turn around and reinvest a portion of it in enormous campaign contributions.*

Just one instance of thousands, this example graphically illustrates how the game is played. A citizen might ask, is Andreas in the ethanol business or printing money? Huffington asked another interesting question: "Some people look at laws and ask, Why not? I look at them and ask, Who paid for them?"

In 1977 the government passed the Foreign Corrupt Practices Act, which prohibited US firms from paying bribes to do business overseas. Today foreign companies come to Washington, and—er, pay bribes.

The newspapers mentioned a fund-raising dinner in 1994, but they neglected to say anything about Team 100. Players on this team have contributed at least $100,000 in soft money, presumably to political parties. Common Cause, a public interest organization, totaled contributions that evening, and they came to $25 million. But the favors in the marketplace purchased with that money amounted to over $100 billion. If a wealthy individual could obtain a return like this

(400,000 percent) on an investment in the business sector, within a few years he would be worth more than Bill Gates.

Ivins commented on a magazine article:

> *Speaking of campaign contributions, Time magazine reports Cheney's aides consulted with the West Virginia coal baron Buck Harless, a Bush "Pioneer" (contributing at least $100,000); Stephen Addington of AEI Resources, whose executives gave more than $600,000 to republicans last election; and of course, our old favorite Peabody Energy—the biggest coal miner in the country—whose chairman gave over $250,000. Could this pay-off possibly be more obvious?* [44]

The news media repeatedly claimed that inflation had been tamed. This left a thinking citizen confused when, only five years later, he read about a Team $1 million. Fred Wertheimer is a veteran of several campaign-finance wars: "When you solicit and institutionalize million-dollar campaign contributions, you are putting the government up for sale in a manner that is unprecedented in modern times. The ultimate price will be paid by the taxpayer in the form of billions of dollars of government favors and tax breaks given to Team $1 million donors." The citizen must ask, where is the end to this abuse?

During the 2000 election campaign, Richard Reeves raised the following issue: "There are things that should be unsaid and unseen. For instance, democrats raising $26 million by explaining how outraged they are at raising $26 million. If you're going to be a sleazebag, be a sleazebag. But don't put it on television where children and other ordinary citizens can watch."[45]

A concerned citizen would disagree: Put it right there, on prime time. Let the public know the truth about political parties and their corrupt behavior.

Reeves concluded his column with two observations:

> *As television and direct mail have become the media of time-efficient, depersonalized campaigning, the only way politicians can meet people is by taking their money. . . . The endless shakedown is also what allows politicians to live far beyond their means. Most everything they do—from golf to the flights to where the rich and famous people congregate, for example—is paid for by campaign funds.*

Most writers and political analysts have concluded that the public will go on accepting the grim fact of politicians selling their souls to the highest bidder.

Because whom you know in Washington swings so much more weight than what you know, congressmen, top executive branch bureaucrats, and party chairs stay around after they retire. Their connections are worth so much that their incomes often far exceed the mere $141,000 plus $40,000 in perks that a member of Congress earns. The name of the game is access—lobbying their former colleagues and getting to the big people to offer money for special unearned favors. Returning home is not an attractive option, especially when citizens are beginning to smell something unpleasant and there are so many guns everywhere. For these people, home is Washington, and home is where the money—er, heart—is.

It has long been well known that sex in the media sells very well. What is less well known is its ability to furnish cover for monetary shenanigans, distracting public attention from the ongoing bazaar in Washington. Thomas Jefferson may have fathered several children by one of his slaves. However, citizens at the time were free of one worry: They knew Jefferson was not in bed with campaign contributors, either before, during, or after his overseas tour of duty.

No one was capable of convincing Attorney General Janet Reno to appoint a special prosecutor to investigate alleged irregularities in financing during the 1996 Clinton-Gore campaign. However, a committee was convened to look at the same in foreign lobbying. At one point it had spent $5 million to investigate $3 million in questionable funds. As usual, the media cooperated, so almost no one noticed how much dirty money was being passed around among buyers and sellers in the domestic bazaar.

Dwight Morris writes a column on the *Washington Post*'s Web site, called *Money Talks*. In the run-up to the 1998 election he reported that 109 **unopposed** House incumbent politicians had raised an average of $392,647 each. A group of 111 who were opposed raised an average of $421,647 each. Not one of their challengers had raised more than $10,000. Newt Gingrich raised $4,878,472, and his opponent raised less than $5,000. There seems little need to explain why unopposed candidates were unopposed.

The Supreme Court, in its 1976 *Buckley v. Valeo* decision, stated in effect that the First Amendment means no restriction on political money. This decision goes far to explain the numbers just cited. If money is speech, citizens in this country do not enjoy equal opportunity to participate in their government. Because equal opportunity (political freedom) is enshrined in the Constitution, this ruling is hard to understand.

A plausible explanation is that the act of equalizing money to speech cleverly utilizes the Constitution as a foil. Citizens are led to believe everyone's right to free speech is protected, but the reality is protection of wealth's claim to a larger voice. In a democracy speech is more important than voting, because citizens must be fully informed on issues of concern to them before they can vote intelligently and make a meaningful contribution to their government.

In 1992 the Federal Election Commission (FEC) gave each of the two major parties $11 million of taxpayer money to stage nominating conventions, although the nominees had been selected previously through primary elections. Then it sent George Bush (Sr.) and Bill Clinton each a check for $55 million to spend as they saw fit. Furthermore, a policy of matching small donations means that the 1992 campaign cost taxpayers a total of $42,742,815. Gross: "Unfortunately, the largest piece of our money went for inane television advertising . . . as Americans paid for their own political stupefaction." The IRS Form 1040 has a box where tax return filers can **voluntarily** donate $3 to presidential election campaigns. It surely seems like enough is not enough; it is too much.

Law permits individuals to give only up to $1,000 to a presidential candidate and $20,000 to a political party. But the letter of the law leaves openings for fat cats to give as much as they want to political parties, and what happens to it afterward remains hidden. The money that slips through the cracks is called soft money; it buys access to the highest reaches of political power. Furthermore the McCain-Feingold proposal relaxes limits on individual donations if the incumbent is up against a wealthy, self-financed challenger. The elite class leaves no stone unturned in its zeal to remain in power.

Donating really big money can buy an ambassadorship in, say, Paris. The *New York Times* suggested changing the label from soft money to sewer money, but the rest of the media chose to stick with the first term. Members of Congress have become full-time fund-raisers and part-time legislators, which makes a citizen wonder how they can crank out 7,500 pages of new laws each year.

Someone invented a statistic called Gross Influence Selling Product (GIPP), which can be used as a rough measure of transfer activity. Today the grand bazaar in Washington does in excess of $25 billion in "business" each year. With turf wars largely over, the average parasite concentrates efforts on collecting more dollars from existing sources. The last thing he or she wants is interference from the public; he or she craves freedom to play one special interest off against another to raise the ante.

The Economist noted: "The moment a congressman has five minutes free—sitting in his car, waiting at an airport—out comes the cell phone and the list of donors' numbers."[46] A citizen with imagination might envision a House or Senate floor vote coming up on an issue crucial to special interests and their lobbyists. Cell phones get punched during the debate, big money is pledged on one side, and then bigger money on the other. Then perhaps a call back to the first lobbyist, to inform him that the opposition has just one-upped him, and does he want to sweeten the pot?

Even though Congress has the ability to make almost anything it wants to do legal, some members have created legal defense foundations in case they get caught in some act that is illegal. Lobbyists' contributions are tax-deductible. These help contributors to get around what little restrictions on tax deductibility may exist. Ellen Miller is director of the Center for Responsive Politics: "These foundations become another pocket of a politician's coat into which companies can stuff money."

Gross went on to cause a citizen to wonder why congresspeople keep raising their salaries and pensions. "Hundreds of politicians regularly dip into their campaign funds for their personal use, something the voters, and the contributors, find hard to take. . . . Up through the end of 1992, all unspent campaign money became the personal fortune of representatives once they left Congress!" And on top of this the price of a congressman keeps rising.

In August 1999 the Senate passed the Deceptive Mail Prevention and Enforcement Act, which was apparently intended to clean up the direct mail industry. A short while later citizens received a "Priority Express-Priority Service" envelope from President Clinton, which was dressed up to look like a personal message. A note inside asked for a citizen's views on several issues, promising that responses would be shared directly with the president.

The recipient was led to believe he or she would have some influence on policy and also that the president needed an "urgent contribution." A thinking citizen might conclude that the president was violating a law just passed by the Senate through a unanimous vote.

"Face time" with the president went for around $100,000 per hour donated to the Democratic Party. Not long ago the oligarchy decided that Clinton's appearance at trial with Paula Jones should be delayed until he left office, because the president's time was too valuable and he was too busy for that sort of thing. The oligarchy was right; here is the evidence.

Greider: "The way to understand political money is to think of it as building 'relationships.' . . . Nobody is buying anybody—these are old friends. When money passes among friends, they need not ask what it is for. It is for friendship—the bonds of loyalty and trust." If preservation of friendship requires passing of money, the government in Washington is made up of fair-weather friends.

Huge defense contractors are notorious for their generous donations to politicians. Douglas Waller reported on an especially tawdry deal, in which President Clinton in 1997 canceled a restriction on arms sales to countries in Central and South America.[47] Since President Carter established this restraint in 1978, many Latino countries have replaced dictators and military juntas in favor of serious attempts at democracy. Now this impressive progress may have been reversed.

"Classic Washington tale of bureaucratic intrigue, skillful press manipulation, high-powered industry lobbying and fat campaign contributions had foreordained the outcome." Sophisticated fighter aircraft were on the block at $24 million a copy. Bernard Aronson was the State Department's assistant secretary for Latin America during the senior Bush administration: "We should be promoting arms control in the region first, not arms sales." It would seem better policy to use the money spent on weapons to help build economies. Fighter planes can only destroy them.

A problem came up when no one wanted to buy the planes; this forced the Pentagon to get involved in extra promotion to arouse interest among Latino generals. It hired Puerto Rican pilots to fly them around in the F-16 fighters, and it sent a fleet of them to a big air show in Chile.

A survey done in 1993 showed that one-third of those queried thought the offices of the Congress might as well be auctioned to the highest bidder. But this is the reality today; such auctions occur every day in the grand bazaar that is Washington.

In a democracy the collective wisdom of the mass of citizens seldom errs, but this depends on a plentiful supply of relevant and accurate information and extensive discussion of issues. Today these vital resources are denied the citizens, but they have come up with the right answer anyway: The rich own politics. Because government today is all politics, they own the government.

In a March 1997 statement, James Glassman introduced the reader to Chapter 11 of this book. "Cut the scope of government, and you'll cut the flow of dollars. . . . Nothing else will work. Nothing."[48]

The *New York Times*: "Congress is unable to deal objectively with any issue, from a patients' bill of rights to taxes to energy policy, if its members are receiving vast open-ended donations from the industries and people affected."

CONCLUSIONS

The US Constitution was created to protect the ordinary citizen from his government. This means that the **vast majority of those millions of laws and regulations on the books are unconstitutional**.

Arblaster wrote:

> *It is only in the 20th century that theorists have attempted to produce a version of democracy in which popular participation is treated with suspicion, if not regarded as positively undesirable. . . . It was understood on all sides that democracy meant . . . popular power, popular sovereignty, popular participation. There is no good reason why that traditional understanding should now be abandoned, however inconvenient it may be to some of those who would otherwise like to shelter under the umbrella of the term "democracy."*[49]

The enabling factors in the grand deception lie in distance, apathy among the multitudes, several decades of time, and purposeful complication of the issues. Henry Ward Beecher said, "There is no liberty to men who know not how to govern themselves."

When big government reaches its long arm into community affairs, the people lose their previously valued sense of attachment, and with this loss the urge to reach out directly to one another. As they search for other ways to reach out, it seems that bureaucracies are everywhere. Citizens tend to become dependent on them, rather than neighbors, friends, and family. The Cato Institute remarked: "The decline of values in America is due, not to greater freedom, but to greater dependence on government and to the overlegalization of society. When government and law replace individual manners and morals as the basis for social order, government and the law will fail, and so will society."[50]

This warning is reminiscent of Paul Kennedy's book *The Rise and Fall of the Great Powers*. In it he described the repetitive nature of the pattern illustrated in the book's title, and he tied it to human nature. This is the way in which society renews itself. It is important to observe that Kennedy's book is shot through with accounts of bloodshed and misery. Parts 4 and 5 of this book will demonstrate that societal renewal at present need not involve such tragedy.

The intrusive government trend shows up in the fact that neighbors no longer know one another, and people today are not as considerate of others as previously. (The latest manifestation of decline is called road rage.) People no longer trust one another, and lawyers are feeding on and exacerbating these negative feelings. Greider said, "A successful family that is bound together by trust and loyalty and mutual purpose can be thought of as an intense microcosm of a larger society that has developed the same capacities. If families are wounded and struggling in modern America, so too is the political order."[51] As the social fabric frays, so also do nerves (see Chapter 19).

This development is not lost on the powers in Washington. They have therefore set up several advisory councils, blue-ribbon commissions, projects, and programs, all aimed at reviving civic morality through such institutions as families, schools, and religious organizations. These efforts are not having and will not have any impact, and public officials know this. They know they are not in a position to preach morality to anyone, and furthermore they are not interested in a moral society because then citizens would be more curious about immorality in government. To be effective a movement must originate among those citizens who consent to be guided by these institutions in their daily lives; they must themselves do the reviving.

Free speech today is reserved for public officials; private citizens are frequently denied this right through operation of a new type of lawsuit called Strategic Lawsuit Against Public Participation (SLAPP) by sociologists. When a citizen dares criticize a high public official, the official directs his or her lawyer to SLAPP down the infidel. Consumer advocate Ralph Nader has formed a coalition of lawyers to defend public-spirited citizens against SLAPPs.

Bovard wrote: "The federal ban on steroid use or possession created hundreds of thousands of criminals overnight. The New Jersey and California bans on assault rifles created hundreds of thousands of lawbreakers. . . . The more new crimes politicians have invented, the less government has protected citizens against the old crimes."[52]

This example capably illustrates Washington's hidden agenda: Citizens complain about of lack of protection against violent crime, and this gives politicians carte blanche to create still more laws and force states to build still more prisons. This vicious circle not only relates to the negative tug of human nature, it also gradually fulfills the elites' objective of turning the country into a police state. Once this has been accomplished, there will be no need for a hidden agenda.

The September 11, 2001, terrorist attacks have caused millions of citizens to hunker down, afraid of another terrorist attack. But big government was working toward this end before the attacks, with its laws on laws and regulations overlaid on others. Therefore in a supreme irony the terrorists have aided the very government they had hoped to convince to change its foreign policy, but only because the Bush administration saw fit to answer violence with more violence (see Chapter 21).

The term *soviet* refers to a council, which in the Soviet Union was originally a group of workers, but which later evolved into the Supreme Soviet. This governing body was composed of 1,500 people, and it functioned as a puppet of the Communist Party of the Soviet Union. USSR stands for Union of Soviet Socialist Republics. Economist Milton Friedman noted that today various levels of government combine to take more than half a typical family's income, and therefore this country is half socialist. A thinking citizen might project the upward trend of single-party government taking of power as pointing toward a Union of Soviet Socialist States. As elections become emptier politicians will come to realize that citizens can no longer touch them.

The Clinton administration's antidrug budget allocated only one-third to education, prevention, and treatment. The rest went to interdiction, supply reduction, and law enforcement. Something around half of people in jails and prisons today have been convicted due to drug-related offenses.

A Justice Department report showed that in 1999 1.86 million people were imprisoned. This is an increase of more than a million over 1985, and it is a new record. The rate of imprisonment today is approximately equal to that in Russia. The current zero tolerance discipline policy in public schools may have been designed to prepare children for adult life in the police state.

Robert Bork is a jurist, nominee to the Supreme Court, and a capable writer. However, one instance of his thinking as written in his book *Slouching Towards Gomorrah* is misguided. "A distinctive feature of modern liberalism is its unwillingness to deal with crime with the rigor it deserves and that the general public wants." Politicians have responded to this desire with inflammatory rhetoric and an avalanche of laws and regulations, but there are so few citizens who see into the line of reasoning behind the facade, that apparently even Bork has yet to fully appreciate the grim reality.

Over the past ten to fifteen years among thinking citizens there has been developing a feeling of distrust of government, phasing into contempt. What most of these people have not fully realized until the present is that Washington insiders feel the same way toward citizens. They perceive ordinary citizens as riffraff, and taxpayers perceive officials as a pack of arrogant thieves.

With nothing done to assuage these feelings, the next logical step is a seething undercurrent of outrage lying beneath a relatively calm surface. The people are beginning to smell something rotten. But because of big government's efforts over the past forty years or so aimed at fragmenting the culture, this outrage lacks focus and a medium of expression. The standard media will not cooperate, but there may be a way to organize citizens' ideas in cyberspace. However, this book will demonstrate that the best way to get at truth and install democracy is through citizens in a neighborhood and community who are directly involved in face-to-face interaction.

Citizens who remain skeptical of the elites' ulterior motive may be interested to know about a new way the Pentagon has found to spend taxpayer money: this program develops nonlethal antipersonnel weapons. These weapons incapacitate people without inflicting death or permanent injury. Examples include sonic weapons that vibrate the insides of a person, either stunning them, putting them to sleep, or causing intense nausea. Another weapon sends beams that make an intruder more uncomfortable the closer he gets to an objective. An electromagnetic gun can induce seizures like those of an epileptic. Still another heats the body to a very uncomfortable 105 degrees.

It is widely known that the government sends weapons and military personnel over much of the world, presumably to defend the country's interests. News reports about laser-guided smart missiles hitting only their military targets and surgical strikes notwithstanding, the reality is broadcast damage, mass killing of civilians, and untold (read: "muzzled news media") misery. Clearly the Pentagon and its commander-in-chief (the president) care little about any repercussions coming from the use of lethal weapons overseas; it is equally clear that they believe that might makes right (Chapter 21).

Therefore it is logical to ask for what purpose these new weapons are being developed. Unaware of the government's hidden agenda, local police chiefs are already ordering them for use by SWAT teams. Put these developments together with the knowledge that the nation's soldiers and national guardsmen are unlikely to be willing to fire lethal weapons at their fellow citizens, and the logical analysis has been concluded. (Douglas Pasternak's article in *US News* on July 7, 1997, from which this information was gleaned, wrote "But these programs—particularly those involving anti-personnel research—are so well guarded that details are scarce.")

Some of today's police trainees may be planning ahead for themselves and their families. When they look ahead and see police departments gradually phasing into jack-booted gestapos, they want to be on the "might makes right" side. Friedrich Hayek argued that the problem is not barbarians at the gate. They are already inside.

But there is hope, because truth constantly lurks in the shadows. This means it is only a matter of time before the lid blows off Washington's cover, so it also means that elite insiders live in constant fear of truth. Truth can bury the insincere, the thieves, and the immorals. But truth lies as much in the perceptions of people as it does in the objective realm. Furthermore, knowledge of truth is not enough; **people** in sufficient numbers must **appreciate it and also have the courage to act on it.**

There is one more vital ingredient: faith. In this instance faith means security in the knowledge that if given the opportunity, ordinary citizens can and will develop a collective wisdom that brings them much closer to truth than does any conventional wisdom coming at them top-down from Washington.

Theory suggests that in the Land of Opportunity citizens have this ability, but the reality is the government has gradually convinced them that they lack it. Why have the people permitted this monstrous taking of their freedom? The answer lies in the apathy that developed with acquisition of wealth over many years, and the consequent loss of accountability. During the 1992 election campaign, nonpolitician Ross Perot said, "You want to know where the ultimate problem is? Look in the mirror." Citizens didn't want to hear these words, but there is truth in them and therefore implicit in his remark was a call for the courage to confront this truth. (A politician never says something that citizens don't want to hear.)

Less than four years later *The Economist* laid bare the core of the problem and also the cause: big government doling out benefits in all directions in order to fragment the populace.[53]

> *What Americans need in 1996 is a referendum on government, rather than a referendum on rhetoric about government. They can have the former if they reject the latter. But if they again vote for candidates who bash government while promising to save Medicare, support students, defend farmers, bolster defense, protection pensions and generally preserve all the nice bits . . . then let them stop raging against the government they get. It is no more messy and muddled than they are.*

Jefferson wrote, "It is the manners and spirit of a people which preserve a republic in vigor. A degeneracy in these is a canker which soon eats to the heart of its laws and constitution."

Passmore commented, "But only if it be presumed that man is 'naturally good' and yet has nevertheless gone hopelessly astray in a manner he will not, given a fresh start, repeat, is there any ground for expecting that the new society which is to arise out of the ashes of the old will be any better than its predecessors. In a reborn society many may well reforge the chains that bind him."[54] Manners and spirit indeed.

Jackson Pemberton is a Jefferson fan, and he possesses a compelling turn of phrase.[55]

Is there a cause more just, a goal more worthy, a need more clear, or a pastime more sweet than this; to bind up the wounds of the national character, to reassert the natural rights of man, and to secure the blessings of liberty to yourselves and your posterity? You . . . my Sons of Liberty; ponder it in your hearts, speak of it in your gatherings, and pray for it in your secret chambers! Let the cry go forth throughout the land and echo across a world groaning and starving under the crush of tyrants: restore the rights of man!

Notes

1. Jackson Pemberton, "On the Destiny of Liberty." In *The Foundations of American Constitutional Government,* ed. Robert Gorgoglione. Foundation for Economic Education, 1996.
2. Rose Wilder Lane, *The Discovery of Freedom*. Fox and Wilkes, 1993.
3. Friedrich A. Hayek, *The Road to Serfdom*. University of Chicago Press, 1944.
4. Martin L. Gross, *A Call for Revolution*. Ballantine Books, 1993.
5. Eric Alterman, *Sound and Fury: The Washington Punditocracy and the Collapse of American Politic*. Harper Collins, 1992.
6. Anthony Arblaster, *Democracy*. University of Minnesota Press, 1987.
7. Alterman, *Sound and Fury*.
8. Bob Woodward, *Maestro: Greenspan's Fed and the American Boom*. Simon and Schuster, 2000.
9. Russell Scott Day, "The Search for Home." In *Frontiers of Justice Volume 3: The Crime Zon*e, ed. Claudia Whitman and Julie Zimmerman. Biddle Publishing, 2000.
10. James Fallows, *Breaking the News: How the Media Undermine American Democracy*. Pantheon Books, 1996, p. 76.
11. *The Economist*, "The Kennedy Mystique." August 24, 1996, p. 23.
12. *The Economist*, "The Heart of the Matter." May 13, 2000, p. 22.
13. Alterman, *Sound and Fury*.
14. Stephen Carter, *Integrity*. Basic Books, 1996.
15. William Greider, *Who Will Tell the People: The Betrayal of American Democracy*. Simon and Schuster, 1992.
16. John Leo, "No More News, Please." *US News*, October 20, 1997, p. 20.
17. John Leo, "I Almost Didn't Write This." *US News*, November 10, 1997, p. 20.
18. Alterman, *Sound and Fury*.
19. Charles Krauthammer, "The Senators Nuzzled Warmly . . . And Voted with Feeling." *News and Observer* (Raleigh, NC), February 1999 column.
20. Robert M. Bowman, "Where Do We Go From Here?" *Space and Security News*, November 2000, p. 2.

21. Larry Margasak, "Report: Pentagon Fakes Documents." *News and Observer*, June 6, 2001, p. 8A.
22. James Bovard, *Lost Rights: The Destruction of American Liberty*. St. Martin's Press, 1995.
23. Cato Institute, *Cato Handbook for Congress*, 1995.
24. Lewis H. Lapham, *The Wish for Kings: Democracy at Bay*. Grove Press, 1993.
25. Lane, *The Discovery of Freedom.*
26. John Hospers, "Freedom and Democracy." In *The Foundations of American Constitutional Government,* ed. Robert Gorgoglione. Foundation for Economic Education, 1996.
27. Thomas Paine, *Rights of Man*. Knopf, 1915.
28. William C. Mitchell and Randy T. Simmons, *Markets, Welfare, and the Failure of Bureaucracy*. Westview Press, 1994.
29. Bovard, *Lost Rights.*
30. Milton, Friedman, (Reported in Jim Powell, *The Triumph of Liberty*, Free Press, 2000 chapter 8).
31. P M O'Neill, "If We Want Peaceful, Schools, Why War?" *News and Observer*, April 1999 column.
32. Mitchell and Simmons, *Markets, Welfare.*
33. P J O'Rourke, *A Parliament of Whores*. Atlantic Monthly Press, 1991.
34. Kevin Phillips, *Arrogant Capital.* Little, Brown, 1994.
35. Michael Schudson, *The Good Citizen: A History of American Civic Life*. Free Press, 1998.
36. Gross, *A Call for Revolution.*
37. David Broder, "What's the Money Chasing?" *News and Observer* (Washington, DC), March 22, 2001, p. 19A.
38. George F. Will, "'Corruption:' Only Innuendos." *News and Observer* (Washington, DC), March 21, 2001, p. 15A.
39. Molly Ivins, "Money's Clout: On the Record." *News and Observer* (Austin, TX), March 21, 2001, p. 15A.
40. Greider, *Who Will Tell the People.*
41. *The Economist*, "In the Great American Desert." December 15, 2001, p. 26.
42. *The Economist*, "Just Plant Dollars." October 13, 2001, p. 31.
43. Arianna Huffington, *How to Overthrow the Government*. Harper Collins, 2000.
44. Molly Ivins, "Bush Digs Deep for Contributors." *News and Observer* (Austin, TX), May 6, 2001, p. 33A.
45. Richard Reeves, "Obscene Show in the Capital." *News and Observer*, May 2000 column.
46. *The Economist*, "If in Doubt, Spend." June 13, 1998, p. 25.
47. Douglas Waller, "Arms Deals." *Time*, April 14, 1997, p. 48.

48. James Glassman, chapter in James C. Miller, *Monopoly Politics.* Hoover Press, 1999, p. 109.
49. Arblaster, *Democracy.*
50. Cato Institute, *Cato Handbook for Congress.*
51. Greider, *Who Will Tell the People.*
52. Bovard, *Lost Rights.*
53. *The Economist,* "Hollow Politics, Deluded Voters." January 27, 1996, p. 15.
54. John Passmore, *The Perfectibility of Man,* 3rd ed. Liberty Fund, 2000.
55. Jackson Pemberton, "A New Message on the Constitution." In *The Foundations of American Constitutional Government,* ed. Robert Gorgoglione. Foundation for Economic Education, 1996.

Part III: A Distant Beacon

Never be afraid to try something new. Remember that a lone amateur built the ark. A large group of professionals built the Titanic.

The citizens of the United States have concluded that the Republican-Democratic party has worn out its welcome. Something clearly and very different is in order. Part III presents a vision of what a modernized version of the founding fathers' concept of democracy might look like. The approach is not prescriptive; rather, the intent is to stimulate discussion among citizens. A passage from *Rights of Man* by Thomas Paine gets discussion off to a stimulating beginning:

> *Government on the old system is an assumption of power, for the aggrandizement of itself; in the new, a delegation of power, for the common benefit of society. The former supports itself by keeping up a system of war; the latter promotes a system of peace, as the true means of enriching a nation. The one encourages national prejudices; the other promotes universal society, as the means of universal commerce. The one measures its prosperity, by the quantity of revenue it extorts; the other proves its excellence, by the small quantity of taxes it requires.*

Chapter 11 brings forth the principles that are necessary in a free society to guide discussion among citizens, and from which citizen-made law might emanate. It tracks the thinking of and discussion among the founding fathers as they strove to compile a document that would preserve individual freedom. Freedom always pits itself against two major threats of harm to the individual: one from the depredations of another citizen, group, or nation; and the other from encroachment by government into the private life of that individual.

Chapter 12 presents the theory of democracy and some insights into the roles a citizen might fill in contributing to the operation of such a government. The chapter emphasizes the importance of the individual citizen becoming informed on relevant issues and taking the initiative in acting on this information.

Chapter 13 argues for the absolute necessity of a strong educational system if democracy is to have any chance of success in a society. If citizens are to govern themselves they must be capable of forming intelligent positions on important issues, so they can accurately communicate their will to elected public officials. Democracy works in both directions: Officials must be receptive to citizens' conclusions, act on them in their capacity as leaders, and actively solicit criticism of public service performed.

Chapter 14 forecasts an open society in the future, which will be the case no matter what type of government any advanced nation may select (or have foisted on it). This means a strong presence in human behavior of the old saw that claims that honesty is the best policy. First and foremost, citizens will be able to demand and get honesty in government. Just as in the past, if citizens don't enjoy the virtue of open government they cannot have the information that they need to govern effectively. An important side benefit is mutual trust and confidence among the people.

Chapter 15 provides a framework for discussion about taxes in a democracy. The historical record on this issue is truly grim due to at least two factors. One lies in egomaniacs as top leaders constantly demanding money for unending warfare, and the other factor is lack of accountability directly to those who are paying for government. Human nature causes accountability to decrease directly with increases in amounts of money accumulated in one location.

Chapter 16 outlines the traits of a good leader in a democracy and offers a contrast with leadership in a top-down society. The separation of the idea from the personality of its originator is very important, because in this way an idea proved weak through open discussion and criticism does not reflect on that person. Therefore a citizen whose idea was rejected will retain an active interest and motivation toward further contributions to good government. An effective leader will argue that a poor idea rejected contributes nearly as much as a good one accepted.

Chapter Eleven:
The Constitution and Limited Government

The important thing is not to stop questioning.
—Albert Einstein

Peters wrote: "By his very nature, man was a mixture of good and bad qualities. By encouraging the good in man—his sociability, reasonableness, generosity, and lover of liberty—education, religion, and government might help to repress the bad—his selfishness, passion, greed, and corruptibility. And of all potentially corrupting forces, the most dangerous was political power."[1] This thought provided the founding fathers with a framework for discussion and debate on May 25, 1787, when they finally attained a quorum in Philadelphia's Independence Hall and were thus able to open the Constitutional Convention.

Lapham provided a further insight into their thinking:

> *The founders of the American republic entertained few illusions about the perfection of human nature, but as an advance over the pagan belief in a pantheon of gods and heroes, they proposed the countervailing ideal of a civil government conducted by mere mortals. They put their faith in the resourcefulness and self-discipline of the free citizen. No man was deemed indispensable. Given the instruments of the law, and the institutions directing the use of those laws, otherwise ordinary men were presumed capable of conducting the business of the state. The authors of the Constitution recognized in themselves and their fellow men the familiar vices of vanity and greed, but they preferred the risks of freedom to the assurances of monarchy.*[2]

The notions of faith, self-discipline, and freedom interact in an intriguing manner. Maintenance of the faith that the positive side of human nature can guide human behavior is founded on self-discipline. A citizen who lacks the ability to control his or her own impulses will abuse his individual freedom. Possession of self-discipline is in turn founded on self-knowledge, which is the product of a good education and the exercise of freedom of choice in life. Finally, a citizen who disciplines himself will discipline the government. Without these dynamics, true democracy cannot exist.

It should be understood that the protracted struggle that went on in Independence Hall produced not a cure-all that the delegates threw down on the citizens, but a document on offer for approval or rejection. Having recently concluded a long and bloody fight for freedom, monarchical dictatorship was not an option. But would their strong faith in ordinary people to govern themselves be ultimately vindicated? No one knew, for there existed in history no precedent (ancient Greek city-states' democracies had faith only in property-owning males as voices in government). Therefore they knew they were launching the newly minted United States on an experiment that was as risky as it was noble.

The political concept of fundamental human freedoms had its origin in the Magna Carta, signed by King John in 1215. This document proclaimed that certain basic rights of people were immune to trespass, even by kings. The principles of lawful judgment of peers and due process traversed the intervening centuries and found their way into the US Constitution. A later outgrowth of the Magna Carta was also included: No taxation without representation.

Originating also about that time were what are known today as Anglo-Saxon virtues. These included independence, self-reliance, individual initiative, local responsibility, reliance on voluntary actions, noninterference with a citizen's neighbor, tolerance of those who are different, respect for custom and tradition, and a healthy suspicion of authority. These virtues contribute to mutual trust and confidence, which in turn help members of society work together toward better lives.

The ideal situation is where neither politics nor law can touch basic human rights, as they are enshrined in the hearts of citizens and in those of **public-spirited** officials in their government. Political rights are protected, as is the opportunity to work toward economic betterment. Some people will do better, at least by their judgment, than will others. Government is there to guarantee equal opportunity.

1787–88: How the US Constitution Came into Being

Pemberton noted:

The Constitution is based on three timeless truths. First, it is founded on the fact that government is necessary in a society, that the citizen must either control himself by his own moral self-discipline, or he must be restrained so that he cannot abuse his liberty. Second, it is the nature of man to seek recognition, then influence, and then power in his relationships to his fellows. Third, it is the nature of man to work untiringly for himself when he is confident in the usefulness of his effort.[3]

The first truth refers to both positive and negative tendencies in human nature. The next one reveals the risk of behavioral tendencies slipping from positive to negative. The third truth emphasizes the positive side—the innate tendency in every person to improve his or her lot in life.

During the American Revolution, colonists assembled in their various states to compile constitutions. Citizens had engraved in their recent memories the horror of rule by England's King George III, so they feared central government power. Therefore they created state constitutions that denied essential powers to the national government. The Articles of Confederation, which guided the central government, were so weak as to be nearly ineffective as an instrument of government. For example, the Continental Congress found it impossible to raise money to operate.

The results of these deliberations were a serious error on the side of anarchy and a lesson was learned: Some sort of compromise had to be found between too much government and too little. Noah Webster wrote: "So long as any individual state has power to defeat the measures of the other twelve, our pretended union is but a name, and our confederation, a cobweb."[4] Something had to be done, so there was much discussion among citizens.

Peters quoted George Washington (1786):

> *What astonishing changes a few years are capable of producing! I am told that even respectable characters speak of a monarchical form of government without horror. From thinking, proceeds speaking, and thence to acting is often but a single step. But how irrevocable and tremendous! What a triumph for our enemies to verify their predictions! What a triumph for the advocates of despotism to find that we are incapable of governing ourselves, and that systems founded on the basis of equal liberty are merely ideal and fallacious!* [5]

Washington had seen the great sacrifices of life and limb by hundreds of his soldiers. They had bled and died for **this**?

Paine said a constitution is not an act of government but an act of the people making up a government. He thought this subtle distinction was important, and he was clearly not alone in this.

James Madison noted: "There never was an assembly of men, charged with a great and arduous trust, who were more pure in their motives, or more exclusively or anxiously devoted to the object committed to them than were the members of the Federal Convention of 1787."[6]

Everyone knew that George Washington would be selected as presiding officer, but even the great man had qualms. "It is too probable that no plan we propose will be adopted. . . . Perhaps another dreadful conflict is to be sustained. If to please the people, we offer what we ourselves disapprove, how can we afterwards defend our work? Let us raise a standard to which the wise and honest can repair. The event is in the hand of God." He went on to lament "my want of better qualifications, and claim the indulgence of the house towards the involuntary errors which my inexperience might occasion."

There was no single time when all of the fifty-five delegates were in the same room at the same time. Their experience was, however, considerable. Eight of them had signed the Declaration of Independence, forty-two had served in the Continental Congress, and seven had been governors of their states. As secretary, Madison did not miss a single session during the long, hot summer of 1787. He made copious notes with his quill pen and ink well.

The need for secrecy was established early on. This does not sound democratic, but there were two important reasons for this policy. First, there was such keen citizen interest in the proceedings that if word were to get to the public before the conclusion there would ensue such a ruckus that the work could probably not be completed at all. Second, with secrecy a delegate could take a firm position on an issue, listen to opposing arguments for a month or more, and then feel no constraint about changing his position. Were his original position to be made public, a switch would have been far more difficult. The delegates decided to present the finished product for acceptance or rejection as an indivisible whole.

The summer was exceptionally hot, but all doors and windows had to remain tightly shut in the interest of secrecy. The heat was terrible, but in spite of spirited arguments there was no record whatever of a single instance where passion displaced reason. This is amazing.

The issue of faith in the average citizen to govern him- or herself generated discussion. Peters quoted Virginia's George Mason: "Every family attachment, ought to recommend such a system of policy as will provide no less carefully for the rights and happiness of the lowest than of the highest orders of citizens." The delegates' heritage tied in with humankind's natural tendency to form pecking orders, but Mason argued for justice for all.

Pennsylvania's Gouverneur Morris: "The ignorant and the dependent can be as little trusted with the public interest." But Benjamin Franklin took issue with his colleague's remark: "It is of great consequence . . . that we should not depress the virtue and public spirit of our common people, of which they displayed a great deal during the war and which contributed principally to the favorable issue of it." He also did not think "the elected have any right to narrow the privileges of the electors."

In 1784 Jefferson had accepted a five-year assignment in Paris as ambassador, probably not anticipating that a constitutional convention would be assembled in his absence. In those days a letter took weeks to travel across the Atlantic Ocean; he must have felt frustrated. "Let me add, that a bill of rights is what the people are entitled to against every government on earth . . . and what no just government should refuse, or rest on inference." The current Bill of Rights was not a part of the finished document, but within three and a half years the Bill was enacted through ratification by three-quarters of the states. It consisted of the first ten amendments to the Constitution.

Lawyer Jefferson also complained about the organization of the Supreme Court. "The composition of the Plenary court is, indeed, vicious in the extreme; but the basis of that court may be retained, and its composition changed. Make of it a representative of the people, by composing it of members sent from the Provincial Assemblies, and it becomes a valuable member of the Constitution." Unfortunately, this recommendation was not adopted.

In 1816, Jefferson, finally retired to his beloved home at Monticello, indicated that he had accurately predicted what eventually happened. "The judiciary independent of the nation, their coercion by impeachment being found nugatory." Justices were nominated by the president and confirmed by the Senate by a process that quickly became politicized; therefore there was (and is today) no practical way to obtain the requisite two-thirds vote in Congress to remove a justice.

The revered elder statesman of the convention, Franklin, helped control passions when the sensitive small-versus-large state issue was discussed (found in Peters).

> *It has given me great pleasure . . . to observe that till this point . . . our debates were carried on with great coolness and temper. If anything of a contrary kind has on this occasion appeared, I hope it will not be repeated; for we are sent here to consult, not to contend, with each other; and declarations of a fixed opinion, and of determined resolution never to change it, neither enlighten nor convince us.*

The lesson here should be generalized well beyond the convention, for Franklin implicitly referred to any public official when he emphasized listening to others and being open to the possibility that a position taken is subject to change. Chapter 16 will present and discuss the relationship between power, ideas, and self-discipline in a democracy.

Animated debate continued with many different attempts to resolve the small-large controversy. Eventually the convention was deadlocked. Delegates wondered whether their efforts were in vain. Mason rose to speak: "It cannot be more inconvenient to any gentleman to remain absent from his private affairs than it is for me, but I will bury my bones in this city rather than expose my country to the consequences of a dissolution of the Convention without anything being done."

Washington wrote to Alexander Hamilton, who was back in New York: "In a word, I almost despair of seeing a favorable issue to the proceedings of the Convention and do therefore repent having had any agency in the business. . . . I wish you were back." Three days later, he was.

Hamilton commented on the qualifications of the holder of the nation's highest office. "This process of election affords a moral certainty that the office of president will seldom fall to the lot of any man who is not in an eminent degree endowed with the requisite qualifications. . . . It will not be too strong to say that there will be a constant probability of seeing the station filled by characters pre-eminent for ability and virtue."

During the deliberations Pennsylvania's Edmund Randolph wrote: "In the draft . . . two things deserve attention: 1) To insert essential principles only, lest the operations of government should be clogged by rendering those provisions permanent and unalterable which ought to be accommodated to times and events; and 2) To use simple and precise language and general proportions according to the examples of the constitutions of the several states." These remarks guided the final writing.

Madison provided a warning: "Mere demarcation on parchment of the constitutional limits of the several departments is not a sufficient guard against those encroachments which lead to a tyrannical concentration of all the power of government in the same hands." This document cast into law a foundation for a legal system that was aimed at discouraging and counteracting the natural human tendencies as described by Hamilton when he said, "Man is ambitious, vindictive, and rapacious."

The use of language here needs emphasis: **aimed** at discouraging; **aimed** at counteracting. The clear inference is that a piece of parchment by itself, however well compiled and with the noblest of intentions, is insufficient to preserve citizens' liberty. "Aimed at" is as far as the Constitution can take this preservation. From there, the burden passes to the citizens.

Suffering from gout, Franklin struggled to his feet.

> *Mr. President: I confess that there are several parts of this Constitution which I do not at present approve, . . . but I am not sure I shall ever approve them. For having lived long, I have experienced many instances of being obliged by better information or fuller consideration to change opinions, even on important subjects. . . . Thus I consent, Sir, to this Constitution, because I expect no better and because I am not sure that it is not the best. . . . On the whole, Sir, I cannot help expressing a wish that every member of the Convention who may still have objections to it would with me, on this occasion, doubt a little of his own infallibility and, to make manifest our unanimity, put his name to this instrument.*

Peters continued: "Washington is said to have told another delegate he didn't expect the Constitution, if approved, to last more than twenty years. But what was more remarkable than their doubts was their unspoken belief that a nation founded on words . . . might work."

Franklin expressed the one feeling of unanimity: The delegates had done their utmost. Nevertheless, he left the convention with a dire warning: "And there is no form of government but what may be a blessing to the people if well administered, and believe further that this is likely to be well administered for a course of years and can only end in despotism, as other forms have done before it, when the people shall become so corrupted as to need despotic government, being incapable of any other."

THE FOUNDERS' INTENT

To begin, a caveat is in order. English language usage in 1787 vastly differed from what is customary today; language evolves with passage of time. Books have been written, each dedicated to diving the true intent of the founders back then. There is controversy. This section will interpret the founders' intent in light of the theory of democracy, although even this is subject to debate. If there is a lesson here, Jefferson expressed it when he recommended that the Constitution be completely voided and replaced every thirty years or so.

The founding fathers called the document the "supreme Law of the Land," but this is slightly misleading in that it is not a body of law but directions for organizing the national government and a statement of principles that should guide formulation of law. The organization and principles were intended to attain two major objectives. One is to protect citizens' fundamental freedoms from an overbearing government, and the other is to prevent one branch of government from dominating the other two. Both constitute a restraint of government, one against citizens and the other against itself.

Paine wrote:

> *When it is in a constitution, it has the nation for its support, and the natural and controlling powers are together. The laws which are enacted by governments, control men only as individuals, but the nation, through its constitution, controls the whole government, and has a natural ability to do so. The final controlling power therefore, and the original constituting power, are one and the same power.*[7]

Paine stated that the Constitution belongs to the people, not the government. If it belonged to the government there would be no restraint on government's power over the people. It is **vitally important that citizens understand and assimilate this point.**

The Bill of Rights doesn't cover the natural rights of citizens that inhere in their existence—moral freedoms—rather, they spell out what government **may not do** in making laws binding individual behavior. For example, no law may interfere with the practice of religion unless such practice infringes on the natural rights of others; a citizen cannot be prevented from speaking freely, especially in criticism of government laws and policies; government may not prevent peaceful assembly to present a grievance; there can be no search and seizure of private property without a warrant; fair treatment and due process of law is required for those accused of crimes; and no citizen may be deprived of life, liberty, or property without due process of law. These are some of the principles that guard people's freedoms from encroachment by government.

If a government were to persuade or force the people to accept one big idea or grand vision, blind faith would enable public officials to organize a hidden agenda to win power over the people. Examples of such officials include Mao Zedong, Ho Chi Min, and Fidel Castro. According to Isaiah Berlin, these men triumphed in revolution and then offered their people the glory of victory, causing them to feel uplifted.[8] But freedom is very different from this; a free citizen has an inviolable political space that no authority may invade.

The Declaration of Independence states: "We hold these Truths to be self-evident, that all Men are created equal, and are endowed by their Creator with certain unalienable Rights, and that among these are Life, Liberty, and the Pursuit of Happiness." This statement underscores another principle, that of individual choice. This principle was developed during a seventeenth- and eighteenth-century philosophical movement called the Enlightenment. Principles contained in the Declaration of Independence found their way into the Constitution.

Alexander Hamilton, James Madison, and John Jay wrote the *Federalist Papers.* They appeared in New York newspapers during early 1788 as articles over the signature Publius, and they were intended to convince citizens of that crucial state to persuade their delegates to the state constitutional convention to vote to ratify the Constitution. Governor George Clinton was against ratification. (Later, the crucial ninth state convention ratified it. Then New York followed with a close vote in favor.)

In Federalist Paper #57, Madison argued cogently for the principle of Rule of Law (later roughly incorporated in the Fourteenth Amendment): "House of Representatives . . . that they can make no law which will not have its full operation on themselves and their friends, as well as on the great mass of the society. This has always been deemed one of the strongest bonds by which human policy can connect the rulers and the people together . . . but without which every government degenerates into tyranny."

In a January 2001 column, pundit Krauthammer argued that President Clinton should receive a pardon.[9] This would "establish a post-Nixon tradition that presidents are not to be hounded with prosecution after leaving office." Were he around today, Madison would be hopping mad, as according to the US Constitution this is dead wrong.

Krauthammer attempted to cover his tracks with "Clinton had his trial in the senate. That's enough." But, is it? Although admittedly lacking airtight proof, a reader having covered Part II of this book would logically conclude that the trial was staged for public consumption. Thinking about the Nixon pardon and legal infringements by subsequent presidents, one might further conclude that for the high and mighty in Washington today there is no law. Were the reader to get seriously interested in this issue, he or she might conclude that without the deterrent of certain punishment for violations of law presidents and other high public officials in the future would do precisely as they please. Accountability is absolutely essential.

What kind of democracy is this? Madison knew. Nixon and Clinton should have been punished (and not just those two). A Congress that believed in the US Constitution would have done this in both instances, and with alacrity. A Congress that has joined with other branches of government in a conspiracy to defraud the citizens would not.

During the Constitutional Convention Madison shared a deep concern felt by nearly all delegates: Vigilance should be stated as a principle, even though entering it into the document will not guarantee vigilance in perpetuity. "The people who are the authors of this blessing must also be its guardians. Their eyes must be ever ready to mark, their voices to pronounce, and their arms to repel or repair, aggressions on the authority of their constitutions." The Ninth Amendment reads: "The enumeration in the Constitution of certain rights shall not be construed to deny or disparage others retained by the people." In today's parlance, the language is not explicit, which places additional responsibility on the citizens.

The Preamble to the Constitution includes "promote the general welfare." In 1791 Jefferson foresaw the danger in this phrase: "that of instituting a congress with power to do whatever would be for the good of the United States; and, as they would be the sole judges of the good or evil, it would be also a power to do whatever evil they please." Were Congress to adopt such a stance, the protections in the Constitution against tyrannical power might as well be scrapped and along with them the document itself.

Madison in Federalist Paper #14 noted:

> *In the first place it is to be remembered that the general government is not to be charged with the whole power of making and administering laws. Its jurisdiction is limited to certain enumerated objects, which concern all the members of the republic, but which are not to be attained by the separate provisions of any. The subordinate governments, which can extend their care to all those other objects which can be separately provided for, will retain their due authority and activity. (#51): Ambition must be made to counteract ambition.*

Madison referred directly to the principle of federalism: Powers granted by the people to state and local government officials should counterbalance those granted by them to national government officials.

The Tenth Amendment further bolsters the principle: "The powers not delegated to the United States by the Constitution, nor prohibited by it to the states, are reserved to the states respectively, or to the people." Or, they would if today's Washington respected it.

The founders planned a government of three branches: legislative, executive, and judicial. The first would make law, the second would enforce it, and the third would interpret it in terms of the Constitution. Fully aware of the negative tendency to grab personal power, the founders placed in the document checks on the power of each branch. Examples include an opportunity for the president (chief executive) to veto a bill before it became law and a required two-thirds vote in each house to override a veto; power in the House of Representatives to impeach the president; confirmation in the Senate of a president's nominee to the Supreme Court; and justices in the court have power to strike down a law passed which they judge does not accord with the principles in the Constitution.

What was only implicit in the Constitution was that alert and concerned citizens would monitor the activities of all three branches to prevent possible collusion among them. In Federalist Paper #25, Hamilton foresaw this eventuality: "The supposed utility of a provision of this kind must be founded upon a supposed probability, or at least possibility, of a combination between the executive and legislative in some scheme of usurpation. Should this at any time happen, how easy would it be to fabricate pretenses of approaching danger?"

Today all three branches and the news media (frequently called the fourth branch of government) are cooperating in a scheme of usurpation. Hamilton understood human nature and the external threat theory (see Chapter 20).

Another principle lay in faith in the ordinary citizen to govern him- or herself. From Paris in January 1787, Jefferson wrote:

> *I am persuaded my self that the good sense of the people will always be found to be the best army. They may be led astray for a moment, but will soon correct themselves. The people are the only censors of their governors; and even their errors will tend to keep these to the true principles of their institution. To punish these errors too severely would be to suppress the only safeguard of the public liberty.*

To err is human. Jefferson referred to the collective wisdom of the people, which will be discussed in Chapter 12.

Educated citizens know themselves, and hence can discipline themselves. They are aware of the likely impact on others and their rights of a particular contemplated action. Because they have the ability to make this judgment, they can utilize reason to make a decision pro or con. This ability translates to a need for few laws; honest and moral people trust one another.

Lacking this individual self-discipline, society in the form of overbearing government and a plethora of laws will infringe on the rights of all just to control a few. Citizens will demand these laws without thinking through the implications for their liberty, and power-seeking public officials will be only too happy to oblige.

Nobel laureate Milton Friedman frequently referred to the Bill of Rights in his writing: "We have heard much these past few years about using government to protect the consumer. A far more urgent problem is to protect the consumer from the government."[10] This is what the Constitution is designed to do, but its success or failure lies in the conscience and actions of the citizen.

The original intent of the First Amendment's reference to religion was to avoid giving government's blessing to one religion over any other. The current interpretation of total separation of church and state may have entered the founders' minds, as history to that time was rampant with conflict and bloodshed in the name of religion. (Tragically, this triumph of passion over reason is still prevalent in much of the world.) But theirs was a government of reason, and they didn't anticipate anything like a modernized version of the Crusades. Rather, the intent related to the principle of free choice.

Developed during the Enlightenment, the principle of private property had a weak beginning in this country due to the need for unity with convention delegates from slave states. Carson noted that Jefferson said, "the exercise of a free trade with all parts of the world was possessed by the American as of natural right."[11] Carson elaborated as follows: "Actually, the freedom to trade is a corollary of private property. The right to dispose of property on whatever terms he will to whomever he will is necessarily a part of the full ownership of property."

Communist countries, such as the People's Republic of China and the former Soviet Union did not permit private property rights. Although ideologically opposed, government officials in both nations have recently begun to see the light. But even today the fundamental rights of private property get scant respect from the US government. The Constitution's weakness in this area should have been corrected in 1865, immediately after the Civil War.

There was a judicial action. After 1868 the Supreme Court struck down congressional attempts to violate the sanctity of labor contracts by regulating working hours, conditions, and pay. In handing down this decision, it referred to the due process clause in the Fourteenth Amendment. The argument turned on restriction of freedom of workers and employers to enter into contracts mutually agreed on, but it did not clarify private property rights per se.

The final principle in this section is that of public servant. The following is excerpted from President Jefferson's inaugural address of March 4, 1801:

> *With all these blessings, what more is necessary to make us a happy and prosperous people? Still one thing more, fellow citizens—a wise and frugal government, which shall restrain men from injuring one another, which shall leave them otherwise free to regulate their own pursuits of industry and improvement, and shall not take from labor the bread it has earned. This is the sum of good government, and this is necessary to close the circle of our felicities.*

Jefferson demonstrated that a commitment to public service means answering to a public that demands limits on government size and spending. At the end of his remarks he referred to a trait that seems foreign to today's popular view of public officials, humility. "Relying, then, on the patronage of your good will, I advance with obedience to the work, ready to retire from it whenever you become sensible how much better choice it is in your power to make."

THE NOTION OF INDIVIDUALISM

Frederic Bastiat in *The Law*, noted: "We hold from God the gift which includes all others. This gift is life—physical, intellectual and moral life. . . . Life, faculties, production—in other words, individuality, liberty, property—this is man. And in spite of the cunning of artful political leaders, those three gifts from God precede all human legislation, and are superior to it." Bastiat wrote of human nature, the individual person, and of natural law. Other philosophers of human nature have contributed their thinking to the notion of individualism; their ideas have been combined into a Western tradition of human freedom.

Gardner captured the essence of this tradition:

> *The premonitions of modern individualism in the Renaissance were amply confirmed in the course of the next three centuries. The Reformation, the rise of science, the Enlightenment, the Industrial Revolution—each in its own way contributed powerfully to the dissolution of embeddedness as a social norm. Only as this process gained ground did it become possible to think of the free society as we conceive it today—a society in which every person is encouraged and expected to become a free and responsible individual.*[12]

God helps those who help themselves. This old saying suggests that a person should seize the initiative as he or she acts on the innate urge to improve his lot in life. This done, God will enter that life with love, grace, and assistance.

Absent that initiative, God will still love the person, but He is less likely to help him or her improve. (Perhaps God wants the individual to feel a sense of accomplishment.) These observations suggest that unless the person can muster the courage and creativity to seize the initiative at each opportunity, he is resigned to muddle through life.

Thus was the way prepared for revolution in this country. Pioneers and colonists not only rebelled against King George and his redcoats; they also bore in their minds and hearts an ideal based on a tradition of individual sovereignty and initiative. That ideal suggested that people could govern themselves. The American Revolution won; the grand experiment commenced.

When the Frenchman Alexis de Tocqueville visited the United States in 1830, he was captivated.[13]

He obeys society not because he is inferior to those who direct it, nor because he is incapable of ruling himself, but because union with his fellow seems useful to him and he knows that that union is impossible without regulating authority. Therefore in all matters concerning the duties of citizens toward each other he is subordinate. In all matters that concern himself alone he remains the master; he is free and owes an account of his actions to God alone.

Tocqueville argued that a citizen is governed by natural law, up to the point where he joins with others in a cooperative project, such as work, family, or government. In discussing plans about a project he is equal to others; once a decision is cast, he subordinates his opinion to that of the majority. If his voice was heard during the discussions he will continue to feel free, because it is natural that people support what they help create.

Ralph Waldo Emerson spoke of self-reliance: "Take away from me the feeling that I must depend upon myself, give me the least hint that I have good friends and backers there in reserve who will gladly help me, and instantly I relax my diligence and obey the first impulse of generosity that is to cost me nothing and a certain slackness will creep over my conduct of affairs." This observation referred to the individual person standing tall and proud, whatever the forces in his life that could furnish convenient excuses for something less than his or her best effort.

The tradition of freedom guided the founding fathers, as Lapham demonstrated:

The Constitution was made for the uses of the individual. . ., and the institutions of American government were meant to support the liberties of the people, not the ambitions of the state. It was the law that had to give way to the citizen's freedom of thought and action, not the citizen's freedom of thought and action that had to give way to the law. The Bill of Rights stresses the distinction in the two final amendments, the ninth (the enumeration in the Constitution, of certain rights, shall not be construed to deny or disparage others retained by the people) and the tenth (the powers not delegated to the United States by the Constitution, nor prohibited by it to the states, are reserved to the states respectively, or to the people)." [14]

Although worded perhaps differently than they might be today, the phrases above hold meaning that remains clear: The government shall exert neither force nor fraud that undermines the natural rights of citizens. The fact that the people are mentioned in both amendments demonstrates that the restraint applies as well to all levels of government. Furthermore, due to the emphasis on individualism it demands that any majority decision must respect the fundamental rights of the minority.

The Englishman Macaulay remarked on the original manifestation of the Industrial Revolution.[15]

> *We see in almost every part of the annals of mankind now the industry of individuals, struggling up against wars, taxes, famines, conflagrations, mischievous prohibitions, and more mischievous protections, creates faster than any governments can squander, and repairs whatever invaders can destroy. We see the wealth of nations increasing, and all the arts of life approaching nearer and nearer to perfection, in spite of the grossest corruption and the wildest profusion on the part of rulers.*

The Industrial Revolution was primarily economic and technological, but there were also political implications as advanced economies raced ahead of the dead hands of their governments.

In the 1920s Albert Jay Nock wrote *On Doing the Right Thing.*[16] "The practical reason for freedom, then, is that freedom seems to be the only condition under which any kind of substantial moral fibre can be developed. . . . We have tried law, compulsion and authoritarianism of various kinds, and the result is nothing to be proud of." Nock went on to argue that an individual possesses an indefinite potential for improvement, and the freer one is the more he will improve.

It was previously demonstrated that Washington, DC cannot preach family values. Gray illustrated what government can do: "The formation of individual character cannot itself be a direct concern of government—it is rather the task of intermediary institutions, families, churches and voluntary associations. Nevertheless, government has an indefeasible obligation to tend and nurture those intermediary institutions."[17]

Such are the subtleties of government that even this observation needs an amendment. If citizens allow these institutions to be created **by government**, the tending and nurturing will go astray. Gray should have made this point and then stated that government will help tend and nurture them under citizens' direction following their creation **by the people**.

Institutions provide support systems wherein the individual can find the resources to help develop a vital inner self-confidence, which is so necessary to move forward in adult life. "I can handle it" is a mentality, a manifestation of self-confidence. Citizens who have been generally successful find it difficult to relate to those who think they have had no success. The wealthy are often challenged to appreciate the full depth of the meaning of self-confidence in others not so fortunate.

In this instance, nurturing means providing an enabling environment; this is the proper role for government. Democracy is a delicate blossom, which can easily wilt in the absence of adequate sunlight, soil, water, and tender loving care. Frequent removal of weeds (negative incentives) is also important.

Secure in institutional support systems, a citizen may look inside himself for an additional resource in deciding on an action; when this happens, morality comes forth as a guide. When the outcome of an action is judged as good, the experience builds self-esteem. When it is not good, one finds therein an opportunity to learn. Put another way, everyone does dumb things in their lives; the key to success lies in what can be learned from these experiences.

Gardner offered some homespun wisdom that accurately describes many of today's citizens.

> *Human beings have always employed an enormous variety of clever devices for running away from themselves, and the modern world is particularly rich in such strategies. We can keep ourselves so busy, fill our lives with so many diversions, stuff our heads with so much knowledge, involve ourselves with so many people and cover so much ground that we never have time to probe the fearful and wonderful world within. More often than not we don't want to know ourselves, don't want to depend on ourselves, don't want to live with ourselves. By middle life most of us are accomplished fugitives from ourselves.*

Jefferson knew that managing time is little more than setting priorities. Though admittedly living in a slower-paced era, he had a habit of frequent reflection on his surroundings, and what he had learned was well advised. This habit combined with a fertile and receptive mind to enable him to become history's most proficient thinker on the theory of democracy. There is much to be said for a person adjusting his or her priorities, but the process requires self-discipline. However, few citizens today even bother to set down New Year resolutions, let alone live by them.

A prominent motivational speaker said that people can be divided into three groups: those who make things happen, those who watch things happen, and those who wonder what happened. Naturally, the emphasis of his presentation focused on the first group. However, in the absence of some time taken for watching and wondering, an ambitious person will often make the wrong thing happen. And, if denied the learning opportunity available through reflection, he may make the same mistake again.

The meaning of the word *empowerment* is often misconstrued. In an individualist society, it means looking within the self to find a feeling of self-confidence and control over one's destiny. In a collective society, it means developing the ability to exert personal power over others.

The reality in any society is that life exists on the edge. Change is the edge that is perceived as a threat by some people, the losers, and as an opportunity by others, the winners. No form of government can cancel this truth. However, in a free society a loser need not remain so because he or she is free to learn. Seizing this opportunity makes a loser smarter when he is ready to have another go.

In this country, examples abound. By 1954 Ray Kroc had tried a couple of times to start a business and had failed. In that year he was pounding the road at age fifty-two, selling milkshake mixers. When he died in 1984 he was worth around $100 million, having developed and successfully promoted the concept of fast food under the name McDonalds. Sam Walton was the founder of Wal*Mart stores (and Sam's Club); his story and wealth are similar.

Equality of opportunity is political equality. When government rules narrow the wage and income gap between top and bottom earners this is socioeconomic equality; it was attempted in socialist countries under communist governments. Socioeconomic equality can be measured, but political equality cannot. Public officials trade on people's natural concern for the less fortunate in society by ostensibly transferring wealth from rich to poor. But they don't listen to the poor, most of whom don't want handouts. They want only an opportunity for self-improvement. Part of the intent of the Constitution is to protect this opportunity.

Responsibility is an individualist concept, whereas entitlement focuses on the rights of groups of people. Gardner was concerned about the long-term trend toward group orientation: "One of the deep tidal currents—perhaps the most fateful—is the movement over recent centuries toward the creation of ever larger, more complex and more highly organized social groupings. . . . The capacity of society for continuous renewal depends ultimately upon the individual." Referring to the group(ing) called government, the bigger and more complex it becomes, the more difficult becomes renewal. At present, renewal is possible only through a force outside government.

Bergland wrote: "Each person has the right to make all the decisions about his or her own life, body, and honestly acquired property. Further, each person must bear responsibility for those decisions. I have no right to force others to pay for my mistakes."[18]

The Economist summarized:

> *A jury in New Jersey upheld the death penalty for a child abuser who had himself been abused in childhood, rejecting the argument that a man's boyhood trauma diminishes his responsibility for his behavior as an adult. That same day the news was dominated by a deal to transform the regulation of tobacco, parts of which imply that adults are not fully responsible for the decision to smoke. These two incidents—one affirming responsibility, the other doubting it—together offer a lesson about the faith in individualism that is the basis for all liberal societies. And the lesson is this: even when individualism seems to triumph, its enemies are regrouping, plotting, attacking on a new front.*[19]

Eternal vigilance is the price of liberty.

Virtues of Limited Government

Kevin Phillips in his 1994 book *Arrogant Capital* argued that Jefferson was

. . . all too prophetic. His passage in the Declaration of Independence proclaiming the right of a citizenry to change its form of government after "a long train of abuses" is the first of many citations in this book that will quote our third president on the dan-

gers of an overgrown Washington, a grasping judiciary, or a too-powerful financial establishment. Awareness of the reemerging relevance of Jefferson's warnings and of America's need to reawaken the radical spirit of the Declaration of Independence has grown in the last few years.[20] Jefferson's thinking has recently won a lot of fans among concerned citizens.

Writing in 1791, Paine's *Rights of Man* took a different approach to discussion of limited government.

> *It is but few general laws that civilized life requires, and those of such common usefulness, that whether they are enforced by the forms of government or not, the effect will be nearly the same. If we consider what the principles are that first condense men into society, what the motives that regulated their mutual intercourse afterwards, we shall find, by the time we arrive at what is called government, that nearly the whole of the business is performed by the natural operation of the parts upon each other.*[21]

Paine argued that honest, upright, moral citizens can work through "nearly the whole" of their difficulties without the aid of government. Furthermore, they will engage in "civilized life" if given the opportunity. Along with Jefferson, Paine held a deep faith in people's ability to live together in harmony. In fact, in 1788–89 citizens of the United States demonstrated this faith in themselves when they agreed to adopt the new Constitution, but only if the federal government was given limited and specified powers.

Browne wrote: "The Constitution didn't limit what citizens could do. Its only purpose was to spell out . . . enumerate . . . what was permissible for the federal government to do. . . . The Constitution was the most successful attempt ever made to keep the dangerous servant from becoming the fearful master. And it made possible the freest, most prosperous country in all history."[22]

Having witnessed both the ruthless oppression caused by a central government that was too strong and the chaos caused by one that was too weak, the founding fathers incorporated the principle of federalism into the Constitution. They interpreted this to mean absolute authority granted to the central government by citizens, but only in narrow, carefully defined areas. Acting in their own interest, the citizens would ensure that these areas were not violated. A second objective was a balance of political power between the federal government and state and local governments.

Pilon discussed the crucial difference between powers and rights:

> *Federal power, flowing from the people to the government, . . .Indeed, it was the enumeration of powers, not the enumeration of rights in the Bill of Rights, that was meant by the Framers to be the principal limitation on government power. For the Framers could hardly have enumerated all our rights, whereas*

> *they could enumerate federal powers. By implication, where there is no power, there is a right belonging to the states or the people.*[23]

(The last statement paraphrases the Tenth Amendment.)

Natural law, and therefore natural rights, lie deep in the human psyche and are impractical to enumerate. Rights can be protected only indirectly through implication, and this fact creates a crack in the door that can be exploited by artful politicians. Vast wealth in contemporary society opens the door wide, and as people become wealthier they tend to let down their guard. John Gardner wrote that "dispersing power is an endless task; it never stays dispersed for long."

Limited government is more likely to attract public-spirited public servants. These people have no interest in making a career in public service, so they will help curious citizens learn about the otherwise mysterious inner workings of government. Tocqueville noted: "When official appointments are few, ill-paid, and insecure, while at the same time industry offers numerous lucrative careers, all those in whom equality is daily breeding new and impatient desires naturally turn their attention to industry, not to administrative work."[24]

Limited government has places for few officials; ill-paid means they will not be tempted to serve for a long period of time; and insecure suggests that they may be removed from office after the next election (or possibly before). All three of these restraints combine to minimize temptations toward abuse of power.

The Constitution puts limits on the democratic notion of majority rule. If the vote of a majority of citizens or their representatives in government were not restrained in some way, they could vote to take all the gold in Ft. Knox, or slowly plunder all taxpayers except themselves. (Without citizen vigilance, apparently a minority can do much the same thing.)

Professor Yale Brozen commented:

> *The state has typically been a device for producing affluence for a few at the expense of many. The market has produced affluence for many with little cost even to a few. The state has not changed its ways since Roman days. . . . Welfare which would be more abundant if politicians would not expropriate the means they used to provide the illusion that they care about their constituents.*[25]

Brozen referred directly to the grand deception, but he also indicated that human nature has not changed in 2,000 years.

Hayek connected the principle of limited government to that of Rule of Law: "The Rule of Law thus implies limits to the scope of legislation: it restricts it to the kind of general rules known as formal law and excludes legislation either directly aimed at particular people or at enabling anybody to use the coercive power of the state for the purpose of such discrimination."[26]

Hamilton said: "It is one thing to be subordinate to the laws, and another to be dependent on the legislative body. The first comports with, the last violates, the fundamental principles of good government."[27]

With a majority approval by citizens, a national budget would pass into law. State officials would closely monitor the money during the period of operation covered by the budget and demand rigorous explanations of deviations on behalf of their constituents. Citizens would carefully watch their state officials for any sign of collusion between them and their counterparts in Washington, DC. In the event of detection of any sign the news media would combine with the voting booth to rectify the situation.

Federalism directs that citizens at local levels carry out the vast bulk of governing; under this restraint Washington would be subjected to the judgment of citizens for its operating funds. The vast bulk of the money would be raised where it will be spent, so citizens can watch their money as it goes to work. It is well known that accountability and honesty make a tight bond.

A free society is not a law-governed society; it is a moral society. Free men and women realize that without morality a society with minimum laws cannot function. Therefore peer pressure and moral suasion combine to steer a citizen along the path of virtue. This is how a healthy society works.

In 1816 Jefferson wrote to Joseph Cabell:

> *No, my friend, the way to have good and safe government, is not to trust it all to one, but to divide it among the many, distributing to every one exactly the functions he is competent to. Let the national government be entrusted with the defense of the nation, and its foreign and federal relations, the State governments with the civil rights, laws, police, and administration of what concerns the State generally; the counties with the local concerns of the counties, and each ward direct the interest within itself. . . . By placing under every one what his own eye may superintend, that all will be done for the best. What has destroyed liberty and the rights of man in every government which has ever existed under the sun? The generalizing and concentrating all cares and powers into one body, no matter whether of the autocrats of Russia or France.*[28]

Notes

1. William Peters, *A More Perfect Union.* Crown, 1987.
2. Lewis H. Lapham, *The Wish for Kings: Democracy at Bay.* Grove Press, 1993.
3. Jackson Pemberton, "A New Message on the Constitution." In *The Foundations of American Constitutional Government,* ed. Robert Gorgoglione. Foundation for Economic Education, 1996.
4. Noah Webster, in Peters, *A More Perfect Union.*
5. Peters, *A More Perfect Union.*
6. James Madison, Federalist Paper No. 48, *The Federalist Papers.* Mentor, 1961.
7. Thomas Paine, *Rights of Man.* Knopf, 1915.
8. Isaiah Berlin, *Four Essays on Liberty.* Oxford University Press, 1969.

9. Charles Krauthammer, "A Triple Play for Bush." *News and Observer* (Raleigh, NC), January 2001 column.
10. Milton Friedman, quoted in Eric Alterman, *Sound and Fury: The Washington Punditocracy and the Collapse of American Politics.* Harper Collins, 1992.
11. Clarence B. Carson, "The Fruits of Independence." In *The Foundations of American Constitutional Government.*
12. John W. Gardner, *Self Renewal.* Norton, 1981.
13. Alexis de Tocqueville, *Democracy in America.* Knopf, 1972.
14. Lapham, *The Wish for Kings.*
15. Thomas B. Macauley, in Jim Powell, *The Triumph of Liberty.* Free Press, 2000.
16. Albert Jay Nock, in Powell, *The Triumph of Liberty.*
17. John Gray, *Beyond the New Right: Markets, Government, and the Common Environment.* Routledge, 1993.
18. David Bergland, *Libertarianism in One Easy Lesson.* Orpheus, 1997.
19. *The Economist,* "White Smoke, and Black." June 28, 1997, p. 16.
20. Kevin Phillips, *Arrogant Capital.* Little, Brown, 1994.
21. Paine, *Rights of Man.*
22. Harry Browne, *Why Government Doesn't Work.* St. Martin's Press, 1995.
23. Roger Pilon, "A Government of Limited Powers," in *The Foundations of American Constitutional Government.*
24. Tocqueville, *Democracy in America.*
25. Yale Brozen, in Murray Rothbard, *For a New Liberty.* Fox and Wilkes, 1973.
26. Friedrich A. Hayek, *The Road to Serfdom.* University of Chicago Press, 1944.
27. Alexander Hamilton, Federalist Paper No. 70, *The Federalist Papers.*
28. Thomas Jefferson, in *The Life and Selected Writings of Thomas Jefferson,* ed. Koch and Peden. Random House, 1944.

Chapter Twelve: **Democracy and the Bottom-Up Approach to Governing**

Of all the things I've lost, what I miss most is my mind.
—Finley Peter Dunne

Upset citizens by the millions and politicians haranguing on the need to preserve and defend democracy combine to create an inconsistency that is felt throughout the land. This book has explained the first half of this dilemma; now it is appropriate to investigate the second.

The elites' need to distort the language of government was discussed in Chapter 10. To clarify the issues to be presented in the following chapters, a few definitions are in order.

Freedom: Citizens create an institutional environment in which each individual can do as he or she may please, as long as he exerts neither force nor fraud on others. A citizen conforms to laws created by fellow citizens and agreed to in the community, state, and nation where he lives.

Rule of Law: In a democracy, when laws are made by those who agree to live under them, absolutely no one is above the law. This includes the president of the country, governors, and mayors, whom citizens hire as agents to help them enforce the law.

Equality: Everyone has equal opportunity to enjoy success in accordance with an individual's talents, effort, and persistence. Government bestows no special privilege due to membership in any group, however constituted.

Justice: Every individual receives equal treatment before civil or criminal law, which in turn means that swift and sure restitution or punishment fits the offense, no one may be punished twice for the same offense, and no one suffers harsher remedy than another for the same offense.

Truth: This is an elusive goal eternally pursued in a democracy. It is a guide to governmental activity and the objective of all serious inquiry.

Honesty: An individual is open in his or her relations with others and expects the same in return. It is a total and consistent lack of deceit. The first priority is honesty with oneself.

Integrity: An individual office holder will occasionally be visited by temptation. Rejection is consistent, no matter the offer. After the period of service is completed, he or she does not exert undue influence in contacts with current office holders under any circumstances. For a similar reason, he frowns on nepotism and patronage (soft jobs for friends). Publication of all gifts received includes the name of the donor, the amount, and the circumstances.

Liberty: This is a feeling that an individual has as he or she enjoys a maximum of freedoms while being restrained by a minimum of laws. It is the fundamental goal of every good government to protect the liberty of its citizens.

Participation: A participating citizen is active in the government at all levels and offers initiatives and opinions before group meetings. He or she also provides constructive criticism to add strength and relevance to ideas put forth by others. Ideas and initiatives are kept separate from personalities, and reason guides free and open debate.

Accountability: Citizens place trust in their public servants, but, knowing human nature, they also keep a close and continuing watch over officials' activities and quickly expose deviations from the line of duty. It is their money, so they are demanding bosses. They patronize only news media that cooperate with them. Citizens are quick to remove any offending official and punish him or her if appropriate.

Democracy: Has anyone recently seen or heard anything that objectively defines democracy? It seems hard to come by. The following section fills this void.

A Citizen's Curiosity about Democracy

Because a simple definition of democracy is hard to come by, some effort is required to assimilate the concept. Lapham provided a useful beginning:

> *It means the freedom of mind and the perpetual expansion of the discovery that the world is not oneself. A democracy is about individuals who trust their own judgments, rely on the strength of their own thought, and speak in their own voices. . . . People who live for others and not for the opinion of others, who believe that they can forge their energy and their intelligence into the shape of their own destiny. . . . People who recognize in other people the worth of their variant theories, tastes, customs, and opinions.*
>
> *Democracy is better understood as a habit of mind than as a system of government, and . . . candor is probably the one most necessary to the success of the proposition. The energy . . . flows from the capacity of its citizens to speak without cant, from their willingness to defend their interest, argue their case, say what they mean.*[1]

Individual citizens in a democracy think and believe differently; therefore intellectual combat is very much a part of the democratic process. However, if people "live for others," reason will prevail over passions during criticism and debate. If they are to "say what they mean" and be understood, they will need active and empathetic listeners, as well as working definitions of terms. Minds may differ. But if the difference is clearly stated and understood to be in principle, hearts will remain united.

Therefore, democracy is a mentality. If this mentality in citizens is oriented to security and not to risk, they shall not fail. Nor shall they succeed. Their destiny is not of their free choice, and so they are reduced to muddling along through life with no opportunity to proudly wear the rich rewards of success.

Citizens who are not averse to risk may fail, because that is the nature of risk. But with the proper orientation they will pick themselves up, brush off the dust, reflect on their experiences, and learn something that will enhance their prospects for success when the next opportunity presents itself. (It is vitally important that they know there will be a next opportunity.)

Lincoln said: "As I would not be a slave, so I would not be a master. This expresses my idea of democracy. Whatever differs from this, to the extent of the difference, is no democracy."

Greider presented some characteristics of democracy:

> *Accountability of the governors to the governed. Equal protection of the law, that is, laws that are free of political manipulation. A presumption of political equality among all citizens (though not equality of wealth or status). The guarantee of timely access to the public debate. A rough sense of honesty in the communication between the government and the people. These are not radical ideas, but basic tenets of the civic faith.*[2]

Because democracy is a mentality, each individual will generate and adjust over time his or her own interpretation of the concept. However, the general flavor is becoming clear, and it includes mutual trust and confidence among moral citizens. Other characteristics include majority rule with minority rights; power resting in ideas and recommendations; limited government; universal suffrage; freedom of speech, religion, and peaceful assembly; natural law and individual rights; and acceptance of responsibility for words said and actions taken. Honesty in the conduct of affairs means no secrets in government, and hence fully informed citizens. Finally, in the words of Lincoln, "that government of the people, by the people and for the people."

Barber discussed what he called the four major requirements for democracy.[3] The first states that democracy must control violence, especially the military and the police. The second says that democracy must provide freedom and equality. Government must refrain from intruding into citizens' private lives. The third has democracy providing what Barber called "real law. Law is meant to provide justice: rules that are constant, steady, well known, impartial, and objective." (Today real law is all too often bent to favor money.) The fourth requirement refers to reason. "Knowledge is a necessary ingredient for a good life, but it is crucial for democracy. Because we have to know what's wrong and what works, and democracy requires a knowledgeable citizenry participating in frequent public political discourse."

This concludes a static analysis of democracy. Now the discussion proceeds to dynamic analysis: what democracy does, or rather, what citizens in a democracy do in theory (Part IV will turn theory into actual practice).

Due to its nature, democracy is difficult to build and maintain. The beacon will shine brightly sometimes and dimly at other times. Good government is not high drama, violence, or tragedy, which today's media are so prone to emphasize. Without continuing concern on the part of citizens, it will slide along largely unnoticed. It is just this situation that attracts the attention of the ambitious and unscrupulous politician.

On the other hand, democracy has within it the potential to bond diverse citizens in a neighborhood or community into a shared interest in a better civic life. Through use of the institution of government as a resource, each citizen carves out his or her own destiny while making sure that others doing the same will minimally interfere with this ambition.

Democracy is questioning, argument, constructive criticism, listening, bonding, debating, leading, following, reflecting, committing, and maintaining minds that are open to change. (Minds are like parachutes; they function only when open.) Democracy is holding no fear of change, because actively participating citizens have influence over its direction and timing. Democracy is anticipation of a better life for a citizen and his or her family and actively thinking and working toward that end.

Democracy is also inefficient, even sloppy; it is the confused cries of a thousand citizens. Frederick Douglass said: "Those who profess to favor freedom, and yet deprecate agitation, are men who want crops without plowing up the ground, they want rain without thunder and lightning. They want the ocean without the awful roar of its many waters."[4]

Not everyone can speak and argue like Abraham Lincoln or Martin Luther King, Jr. But the democratic process creates government that people want, because people support what they help create. As John Gardner said, neither uncritical lovers nor unloving critics make for good government. The first allows unlimited power grabs by politicians and the second is simple complaining, which in the absence of sound recommendations for improvement accomplishes little.

Holmes commented: "Parties will always feel frustrated by the procedural delays in any liberal court of law, Montesquieu wrote. But time-consuming procedures is the price citizens pay for liberty. Such exasperating delays provide an indispensable chance for reconsidering legal principles, double-checking facts, correcting first impressions, and cooling turbulent emotions."[5] Holmes applied this remark to interpreting the law, but it readily generalizes to political meetings among citizens.

There is a vital component of democracy, which compensates for its inefficiency. Over a period of operation in a neighborhood or community, a collective wisdom develops among citizens. It seldom errs, and whenever it does the mistake is quickly and simply corrected. Furthermore, the discussions and debates that bring collective wisdom to bear on an issue enable the quest for truth to come closer to its full realization.

That society whose government does not tolerate dissent cannot continue indefinitely as a viable society. If a government has been built with respect for truth, neither citizens nor officials need fear dissent. In fact, dissent is encouraged because every potentially good idea originates in a tiny minority: one concerned and thinking citizen.

Lapham wrote: "If democracy can be understood as a field of temporary coalitions between people of different interests, skills, and generations, then everybody has need of everybody else. The democratic proposition fails (or evolves into something else) unless enough people perceive their government as subject rather than object, as animate organism rather than automatic vending machine." A mechanic is skilled at maintaining and adjusting the existing, whereas a gardener is skilled at making things grow and planting different things. Both skills are needed in a good government. Depending on the issue and stage of discussion, each predominates in turn.

The troubles in Northern Ireland bring out discussion of the role and fate of minorities in a democracy. About eighty years ago, an act of the British Parliament separated the country from the rest of Ireland, and since 1974 London has ruled Northern Ireland. The Protestant majority abused the Catholic minority for decades, and result has been almost continuous strife and misery.

In a democracy diversity is welcomed, so there are political minorities only with respect to various issues. For most of these, a minority will not be strongly opposed. Members' opposition will be softened when they realize that their political freedoms are unaffected by a decision that goes against their position. Also, they know they will live to fight another day; that is, there will be other opportunities to bring the majority around to their viewpoint. Finally, **having been heard** during discussions and criticisms, they feel like they helped bring the meeting to the conclusion chosen. Furthermore their arguments during discussions may provide insights into difficulties ahead during implementation of the final decision.

An excellent example comes to mind. When the Massachusetts constitutional convention met in 1788 to debate ratification of the new US constitution, a minority of delegates argued strenuously against ratification. They lost the vote.

Immediately afterward a member of the minority rose to speak. He stated that in spite of having lost the argument he and his colleagues would support the constitution "as if they had voted for it." A finer example of citizenship may not exist.

Hayek said:

> *It cannot be said of democracy, as Lord Acton truly said of liberty, that it "is not a means to a higher political end. It is itself the highest political end. It is not for the sake of a good public administration that it is required, but for the security in the pursuit of the highest objects of civil society, and of private life." Democracy is essentially a means, a utilitarian device for safeguarding internal peace and individual freedom.*[6]

What people by their very nature desire is freedom of choice, but every other type of government denies this freedom to some extent. Freedom is not "free"; some sacrifice is necessary. However, once democracy is in place and functioning most citizens will discover that their sacrifice has turned into a stimulating hobby. Furthermore, through its active practice they will earn the respect of their descendents, who will perceive future benefits to them and their offspring as having emanated from their parents' talents and efforts. The generation gap can be closed.

John Gardner in his book *Self-Renewal* pointed out that through democracy a society can accomplish needed change without revolution.[7] Just a glance at world history would convince anyone of the importance of this point. "But for an ever-renewing society the appropriate image is a total garden, a balanced aquarium or other ecological system. Some things are being born, other things are flourishing, still other things are dying. . . . But the system lives on."

Just as it is with ideas, some people are beginning life, others are flourishing, and some are dying, but the system lives. There is truth in this, but only when the society is self-renewing and ever-renewing. The only way to have and enjoy such a society is with a carefully and continuously nurtured democracy.

Individual Initiative, Rights, and Responsibilities

Berlin wrote, "Forcing men to do what they have not willed or consented to? Only in the name of some value higher than themselves. But if, as Kant held, all values are made so by the free acts of men, and called values only so far as they are this, there is no value higher than the individual."[8]

The Enlightenment questioned religious dogma, and thus encouraged people's thoughts to range far and wide. Through this freedom Einstein developed his theories, and they in essence displaced Newtonian physics. Furthermore, Freud's investigations into the human psyche similarly stimulated new thinking. These theorists combined to demonstrate the potential of free inquiry and personal freedom. Prominent writers such as Locke and Hume also made significant contributions.

However, folks were not sophisticated at that time, due in large part to the legacy of religious dogma. Therefore they were open, but what the typical person perceived was an intellectual vacuum.

This caused one's mind to be receptive to a philosophy that had its beginning in the thinking of Karl Marx. He wrote during the end of the Industrial Revolution, when inexperienced factory managers were exploiting workers. Thus was the vacuum filled, but time proved that the new philosophy was misguided.

That said, with the end of the cold war people's minds may again be open to new thinking. Quite possibly another vacuum has evolved. But if so, it is currently being filled with fluff that comes at people through TV and an overemphasis on a materialistic imperative.

The current social malaise has been exacerbated by big government's deemphasis on education over the past fifty years. The elites know that educated citizens are thinking citizens, so that any vacuum may be filled with thoughts of a better existence guided by a better government (perhaps self-made). They also know that the only better government is a small government, and there would go the elite class and its oligarchy. There is admittedly some speculation here. Nevertheless, there is the possibility that this book could make a significant contribution.

Some of the assumptions of hierarchy survived the making of the Constitution; Hamilton was himself an elitist. But when Jefferson became president in 1801, he turned the tide in favor of the individual citizen. Later he referred to this turning as "the revolution of 1800."

John Stuart Mill's *Essay on Liberty* extolled the virtue of man as a free individual. Berlin was a disciple:

> *What made the protection of individual liberty so sacred to Mill? In his famous essay he declares that, unless men are left to live as they wish "in the path which merely concerns themselves," civilization cannot advance; the truth will not, for lack of a free market in ideas, come to light; there will be no scope for spontaneity, originality, genius, for mental energy, for moral courage. Society will be crushed by the weight of "collective mediocrity."*

There is open season for individual initiative in a democracy. This book will show that public officials governing under this system must be receptive to citizen initiative, or they are not doing their jobs. Mill supported his own argument: "All the errors which a man is likely to commit against advice and warning are far outweighed by the evil of allowing others to constrain him to what they deem is good."

Mill worried that truth, once approximated, had little staying power unless questioned. Berlin summarized: "He says that unless it is contested, truth is liable to degenerate into dogma or prejudice; men would no longer feel it as a living truth; opposition is needed to keep it alive. 'Both teachers and learners go to sleep at their post, as soon as there is no enemy in the field,' overcome as they are by 'the deep slumber of a decided opinion.'"

Once it becomes conventional, conventional wisdom is no longer wisdom. Furthermore, whenever citizens grow inattentive, ever vigilant public officials will quickly become aware of fading accountability, and then the negative side of human nature enters in. The force of wisdom which counteracts **conventional** wisdom is the **collective** wisdom generated by concerned and participating citizens discussing, criticizing, and debating issues. Thus is truth renewed continuously, kept alive, dynamic, and vibrant.

Paine wrote: "Natural rights are those which appertain to man in right of his existence. Of this kind are all the intellectual rights, or rights of the mind, and also all those rights of acting as an individual for his own comfort and happiness, which are not injurious to the natural rights of others. Civil rights are those which appertain to man in right of his being a member of society."[9] Nothing is unthinkable, but acts are preferably first thought through with an eye to the natural rights of other citizens.

Schudson pointed out that the young nation's institutions took a while to adapt to their proper roles in the grand experiment.[10]

> *By the 1820s, newspapers began to compete with each other to gather news, not just to express outrageous opinions. . . . The newspapers were by no means the sole form, nor even the sole printed form, of communication between the government and the citizens. Of particular importance were the circular letters many congressmen sent. . . . An additional infrastructure grew to support reading . . .established libraries. New associations of people sprang up centered on reading and discussion.*
>
> *Beginning with the* New York Sun *in 1833, a new breed of newspaper . . . divorced from party preferences . . . selling for a penny instead of the six cents at which they were commonly priced. The new papers were hawked on the streets by newsboys instead of . . . subscription.*

This innovation caused a previous direct connection between a newspaper's sponsors and its readers to be severed, because no one knew precisely who the buyers were. Thus the argument that these penny sheets represented the only truly free press. However, the emergence of a generally free press was not to be for some years yet.

Schudson continued: "Tocqueville later expressed satisfaction in noting that the greater the number of newspapers and the more they are dispersed around the country rather than concentrated in a capital city, the less influence journalism has. For Tocqueville, a great virtue of the American press was its weakness." Political information is emotionally loaded. Therefore a good newspaper should work hard at objective reporting, because this is as elusive as truth. Slanted journalism is nothing more or less than caving in to power and influence, which is surely tempting whenever the bottom line grows thin. (The notion that an institution can be simultaneously virtuous and weak is intriguing.)

Greider referred to a modern organization.[11] "The mountain training center endures, a staff member explained to the circle, as 'a school for people to learn how to act to exercise their rights, which is what we think democracy is all about.'" There could be merit in what this school is teaching, but if the emphasis is on group rights, this is wrong on one count; the lack of emphasis on responsibility is wrong on a second count. A society with only rights and no responsibility cannot survive.

Donnelly clarified a vital contrast: "Underlying such arguments is the distinction between 'negative' rights that require only forbearance on the part of others, and 'positive' rights that require others to provide goods or services if they are to be implemented."[12] Worker A is paid well, and he saves and accumulates wealth. If he knows his wages and wealth will be taxed to support Worker B, who gambles away her wages as soon as they are hers (or is unemployed), will Worker A have an incentive to work hard and save?

Donnelly classified rights under several groups: personal, legal, civil, and political rights. Personal includes bodily and moral integrity, such as protection against discrimination, threats, slavery, and torture. Legal rights include habeas corpus (the right to appear before a judge or court), protection against arbitrary arrest, and presumption of innocence until proven guilty. Civil includes rights to speech, press, association, and assembly. Political rights include the right of participation in speech, press, and government.

He went on to list several groups of economic and social rights: subsistence or the right to food and health care; economic, such as social security, work, rest, leisure, and trade unions; social, such as education and family maintenance; and cultural, such as the right to participate in the cultural life of a community.

The first category (personal, legal, civil, and political) consists of negative rights, and the second includes positive rights. That is, the former restrains government from invasion of an individual's private space, and the latter takes from Worker A to support Worker B. Worker A may put up with the latter arrangement for a while, because he is not told where his tax money is going. But the system that enforces this situation is inherently unstable, and it becomes more so with each increase in forced transfer payments from one pocket to another. As his incentive to work decreases, Worker A's suspicion and resentment increases. Worker B's resentment also grows due to diminished self-esteem.

Schudson interviewed law professor Mary Ann Glendon to bring forth the flip side of the positive rights movement and recorded her conclusions.

> *It has created a language not truly about human dignity but about "insistent, unending desires." It legitimates individual and group egoism and emphasizes at every turn the individual, self-gratification over self-discipline, the*

economic over the moral, the short term over the long term, the personal over the social. . . . Rights-based politics is anti-democratic in removing political controversy from the legislatures to the courts. . . . [It] makes our politics far too dependent on lawyers.

Schudson continued:

A frequent result of a rights-oriented politics is to call forth additional governmental regulation or judicial intrusion in areas of life the state once left alone. A quest for liberty has often produced a growing governmental presence, and invariably a growing disaffection with government. . . . Glendon . . . would have Americans . . . speak of individual rights in a way that also gives credit to social responsibilities.

The gimmick referred to here is tried and true, having been tested by countless previous governments: Intrude ever deeper into society in the name of protecting citizens' rights.

Big government backed off a little on August 22, 1996, when a welfare reform bill was passed through Congress. *The Economist* commented: "Poor mothers—women and their children make up 90% of those on welfare—would have to look for work, and, even if they did so, they would no longer just get federal money on demand. . . . States received bonuses for moving people into work."[13]

The writer continued: "Welfare rolls have fallen more than even supporters predicted: from 5.1m families at the peak in 1994 to just over 2m now." For years unemployment among single mothers had been stuck at 40 percent. It quickly dropped to 28 percent by 1999. Annual wages for the bottom rungs of single motherhood increased by 80 to 100 percent. A 20-year upward trend in out-of-wedlock births was stopped in its tracks. Only a student of human nature would remain unsurprised at these figures.

The idea of acceptance of individual responsibility for things said and actions taken seems to have faded. The trend was exacerbated by career politicians, who are renowned for their finger-pointing ability. When a large firm in South Korea recently went bankrupt, its vice chairman took full responsibility. At age sixty-two he became a busboy at a restaurant in Seoul. In Japan, Prime Minister Ryutaro Hashimoto suffered defeat in parliamentary elections, so he resigned saying, "Everything is my responsibility," and "The results are attributable to my lack of ability." (Can anyone imagine Bill Clinton, or indeed any recent president, saying something like this?)

In 1982 Argentina invaded the Falkland Islands. British foreign secretary Lord Carrington immediately resigned, not necessarily to admit culpability, but because this embarrassment happened during his tenure. In this country, were citizens to have heard Presidents Roosevelt, Nixon, or Reagan even indirectly hint at some shred of responsibility, they would have been astounded. Instead of this they got "Mistakes were made" (Reagan) and "No controlling legal authority" (Gore).

Harry Truman had a sign on his desk indicating that he was ultimately responsible for his actions.

A logical conclusion points to the necessity for a morality that connects rights to responsibilities. This should be done locally: Citizens would clarify and focus through lawmaking the generalities of civil rights in accordance with their thorough knowledge of local conditions. Along with this they would provide for responsibilities through collective wisdom, reached in turn through free and open discussion.

Readiness to accept responsibility is a sign of maturity. In his treatise on human nature Wilson referred to Lawrence Kohlberg's sequence.[14] Stage one has the child acting in simple obedience to avoid punishment; stage two is conformity, to obtain rewards; stage three is conformity to avoid censure and rejection; stage four is an orientation to duty to avoid censure by distant authority; stage five is a legalistic orientation, recognition of the value of formal agreements and maintenance of the common good; and stage six is an awareness and appreciation of the importance of principles.

Wilson wrote that the "great majority of people reach stages four or five, and are thus prepared to exist harmoniously." In stage six, "the individual selects principles against which the group and the law are judged." This stage can be reached only through extensive self-knowledge and development of self-discipline. However, a carefully developed collective wisdom in a neighborhood or community will be a resource that can help citizens recognize and discuss principles. (Even this does little to reduce the need for a good education system, as Chapter 13 will demonstrate.)

Arblaster made a point about seizing the initiative, "But even when consent is given a more positive content, and a definite 'yes' is required rather than the mere absence of 'no,' it remains an indelibly passive concept. Consent is essentially a response to initiatives taken by someone else."[15] Then he turned to a question of faith: "Is it realistic to expect initiatives to come from the people themselves? For that to be possible there are certain conditions, . . . which must be fulfilled. First, there must be a climate of freedom within which opinions can be freely expressed and discussion conducted without fear or restraint. Democracy requires freedom." To this it is necessary to add active encouragement by public officials of initiatives from citizens and careful listening to them when they speak.

Bork castigated leaders who preach group initiatives for black people.[16] "Race-holding allows a black to retreat into his racial identity as an excuse for not using his talents to the full out of fear that he really cannot compete. Paranoia is fed by . . . professors of black studies, who teach resentment and fear. These are persons whose careers would be diminished or ended by progress in racial reconciliation; it is in their interest to preserve and exacerbate racial antagonisms."

Thomas Sowell is an enlightened black writer, who promotes individual effort by blacks rather than group efforts, such as demonstrations, voting drives, and affirmative action. Recently researchers have changed their approach, concluding that the difficulties under which many African Americans suffer are more a problem of class than race. Racism has been perceived as a crutch; this ties in closely with Sowell's campaign. Blacks today are looking about them and seeing more successful people with dark skin. They are forming their own conclusions as individuals.

What is particularly galling is the media, ever sensitive to violence, giving far more space and time to blacks who are in trouble with the law than to a prominent social trend with potential. In the future more black people will provide the answer to Arblaster's question. They will be concerned and contributing citizens, and they will erase racism once and for all. Moreover, they will force the media to report truth.

Meanwhile, in today's political environment people are afraid to speak out, lest others perceive them as weird or crazy. (Soviet Russian leaders locked up thousands of dissidents, conveniently calling them insane.) Lacking discussion with others, they don't realize that their feelings of resentment and alienation are not unique to them. Berlin wrote, "For in the past there were conflicts of ideas; whereas what characterizes our time is less the struggle of one set of ideas against another than the mountain wave of hostility to all ideas as such." Today there are conflicts only among personalities, and even these fights are often faked.

Schudson commented: "A public sphere may come to life in verbal give-and-take at a tavern, in a public square, on the courthouse steps . . . or in the pages of a newspaper or pamphlet. It is the playing field for citizenship; democratic citizenship may bear fruit in the formal acts of voting or legislating, but it germinates in the soil of a free public life." Without public discussion, criticism, and debate, voting and legislating are only empty gestures.

Rose Wilder Lane noted: "Responsibility-evading citizens in this Republic, if they become numerous enough, can wreck the Republic."[17]

The Potential of Bottom-Up

Paine demonstrated his familiarity with human nature with this insight:

> *There is existing in man, a mass of sense lying in a dormant state, and which, unless something excites it to action, will descend with him . . . to the grave. As it is to the advantage of society that the whole of its faculties should be employed, the construction of government ought to be such as to bring forward . . . all that extent of capacity which never fails to appear in revolutions.*[18]

Paine also showed that no one can predict when and from whom wisdom will assert itself, and he did not connect it in any way to wealth or intelligence. This means that if bottom-up government is to work as the founding fathers envisioned, everyone should be invited—nay, exhorted—to participate, to contribute to the collective wisdom as people strive to govern themselves.

President Jackson's postmasters were instructed to exclude antislavery literature from the mail, but pitted against this order were hundreds of petitions flowing into Washington and bearing thousands of signatures asking for abolition of slavery. With Jackson's support, Congress passed a resolution prohibiting discussion of the issue. Schudson wrote:

> *Meanwhile, petitions kept coming: 130,000 in 1837–38 asking for abolition of slavery in the District of Columbia, 32,000 asking for repeal of the gag rule, 21,000 to ban slavery from Western territories, and 23,000 to end the interstate slave trade. . . . In 1840, the gag order was replaced with a standing house rule that disallowed congress from even receiving, let alone responding to, anti-slavery petitions.*[19]

President Jackson was not called Old Hickory for nothing. His predecessor, John Quincy Adams, also had a nickname: Old Man Eloquent. As one of US history's very few former presidents who served in Congress, he spoke against the gag rule, and it was dropped. During years of protest Adams staunchly defended the right of citizens to a voice in their government, insisting on the sacred right of petition. He did not stop with slavery, arguing: "Why, sir, what does the gentleman understand by 'political subjects?' . . . Are women to have no opinions or actions on subjects related to the general welfare?"

Former congressman Thomas "Lud" Ashley remembered the old days. "But we had precinct captains and twenty-two ward chairmen and there were monthly ward meetings that you went home and talked to. They were robust, well-attended meetings . . . half business, half social. The business took 45 minutes or an hour and then it was 'let's get into the beer.'" During that era congressmen had to face voters and take whatever guff they dished out, and an important issue could generate an aroused citizenry.

Fallows reported on current times.[20]

> *The study came up with a list of traits that distinguished groups and communities with healthy, active political life from those where people felt estranged and cynical. . . . All the traits . . . were at direct odds with the norms of mainstream journalism. For instance . . . [some] emphasized the importance of "connection." Citizens understand that issues run together . . . that the problems of schools are connected to family structure, which is connected to the changing job market, which is connected to taxes and . . . But by journalistic convention these are treated as separate "items" on a political or legislative agenda.*

Conventional wisdom, a thinking journalist might say.

There is no continuity to a typical TV newscast, as the anchor flips back and forth among events from all over the world. Were a citizen to make bold to attempt a connection, his or her effort would be splintered by a string of commercial messages.

President Woodrow Wilson was an elitist. Schudson reported that "when he spoke . . . some of the best questions came from 'the least well-dressed in the audience—the plain fellows—whose muscle was daily up against the whole struggle of life.'"

In 1935 radio was spreading throughout society. "Town Hall helped establish listening groups around the country." The program generated around 2,400 letters each week. "Stressing always the nonpartisan virtues of public debate, town meeting advocates praised listeners not stuck in party loyalties but willing to courteously and tolerantly look at all sides of a question."

President Roosevelt could hardly be faulted for empathizing with the poor during the Great Depression; those were difficult times. However, with benefit of hindsight showering taxpayer money on these people (top-down) rather than encouraging formation of additional volunteer organizations (bottom-up) was wrong. These organizations would have supplemented what overwhelmed churches, the Salvation Army, and other charities were doing. Such emergency-oriented nongovernmental organizations would have helped the armies of poor through the depression, and then they would have disbanded when the job was completed.

Instead, Roosevelt built a vast bureaucracy. Bureaucrats don't disband. Later, businesses and other interest groups got wind of benefits being handed out to whoever sought a seat at table, so they pulled up chairs. As they say, the rest is history.

Decades later a naive citizen, Lois Marie Gibbs, executive director of Citizen's Clearinghouse for Hazardous Wastes, did battle over the famous pollution at Love Canal. "When I started, I believed democracy worked. I believed everything I had learned in civics class. What I saw was decisions are made on the basis of politics and costs. Money. So much for civics class."

In the early days of the nation the bottom-up approach was not used exclusively; negative human nature occasionally won, and there was personal power seeking. During most of the nineteenth and early twentieth centuries, bottom-up made great strides. But since World War II the trend toward top-down has accelerated dramatically. Public officials in Washington are involved in a huge variety of activities not authorized by the Constitution.

One issue continuously generates a lot of press: the drug war. Washington knows this fight cannot be won with a top-down approach, but it also knows that this emotional issue causes concern, and officials want to be seen as reacting to a serious problem. However, any neighborhood or community with civic pride would, if they truly desired to, organize to banish drugs and drug dealers by utilizing a bottom-up approach. This has been done, but only rarely. These instances of success are rare, because Washington's policies do not leave communities free to solve their own drug problems. This explains why successful efforts are newsworthy; working around a bloated and irrelevant bureaucracy is a major challenge.

Bottom-up works for at least two reasons. One is that local people know the territory, and so they know its problems far better than does Washington. Their decisions tend toward maximizing genetic fit (genes and culture). The other reason lies in the great truth in human nature that people support what they help create. If a community wants to paint a new political landscape, citizens should put a paintbrush in every hand.

If a community wants a government that will provide a lot of services and tax accordingly, citizens can argue for this and win the necessary votes. If at a later time they become aware of the waste and corruption that has probably occurred, they can pare their government down as they desire and do more things directly for themselves. The key points lie in citizen choice and the democratic process. It is natural for citizens in a neighborhood to reach out and talk with others. When people are informed, there is much less frustration when a project is delayed for whatever reason.

John Perry Barlow is an Internet activist. Several years ago he published a manifesto called "Declaration of the Independence of Cyberspace."[21] "Governments of the industrial world, on behalf of the future, I ask you of the past to leave us alone. You are not welcome among us. You have no sovereignty where we gather. You have no moral right to rule us nor do you possess any methods of enforcement we have true reason to fear. Cyberspace does not lie within your borders."

The Internet community is today mostly controlled from the bottom up, which means it has excellent potential as a resource for democracy (at least until big government finds a way to regulate it). Organizations like the World Wide Web Consortium, the Internet Engineering Task Force, and the Internet Corporation for Assigned Names and Numbers develop and set standards and coordinate protocols. Communication is more direct and open than in the real world. False and deceptive information proliferates, but educated users quickly identify these ruses. Citizens may be able to more efficiently become properly informed and vote. Even discussion may be possible, but there remain strong arguments for face-to-face interaction when criticizing and debating.

Lawyers make law for lawyers; citizens make law for citizens. There is no mystery to this, as the incentive for self-improvement lies in human nature. If citizens create their own laws they will write them in plain English. There will be little need for judges to interpret the laws, and because moral citizens are the authors they will obey them.

They will build and operate jails for the occasional miscreant, who will be the subject of swift, sure, and mild punishment that fits the nature of the offense. Because civil law will prevail over criminal law, there will be little need for prisons. Those that exist will be built and operated by private contractors, each of whom might receive a bonus for every year an ex-con stays out of prison. In this way contractors will have an incentive to help convicts rehabilitate themselves and properly prepare for the world outside. Contractors may hire successful ex-cons, who would return to prison as resources to help inmates with their preparation.

In bottom-up government there is a place for specialists. At a local level they can be very useful; at meetings they can bring their expertise to bear on technical problems. But such meetings should be run by generalists who will help citizens see how various issues interconnect. Later, after a project is approved, an expert may also assist in implementation.

Saul Alinsky organized the Industrial Areas Foundation (IAF) about twenty-five years ago. Greider interviewed Edward T. Chambers about Alinsky, and he said, "You believe that men and women are the most precious treasure this country has, and the most important thing we can do is to develop them, let them grow, let them flower, let those talents flourish."[22] Greider continued:

> *One Alinsky principle, known to all IAF members as the "the Iron Rule," is frequently invoked during their meetings: "Never do anything for someone that they can do for themselves. Never." The organizations, for instance, are launched with financial aid from the sponsoring parishes and churches, but the members must immediately develop their own capability to be self-sustaining and financially independent.*

People support what they help create; no one should deny them this pleasure. It is also interesting to observe Alinsky's expression of faith in people. This faith is essential for democracy.

"Statewide candidates from both parties would be invited to attend the celebration and experience an 'accountability night.' This is an IAF ritual in which the politicians are required to sit and listen, while citizens stand at the rostrum and do most of the talking." This requirement poses a stark contrast to the politician who waxes profoundly from behind a forest of microphones and in front of several TV cameras. Greider described many meetings for the purpose of building political relationships. "The San Antonio meetings pose a tantalizing question: Is this what the dialogue of a genuine democracy would sound like?" These days, who knows?

In 1990 in Nairobi, Kenya, Rubi Hassan pushed a handcart with candy and sodas chilled on a block of ice. She had started from scratch, but then a representative from Coca-Cola furnished a trolley, and later a kiosk, electric refrigerator, tables, umbrellas, and a picket fence. The business is now a corner store, serving 300 customers a day (including twenty crates of cola products). Rubi and her husband now earn enough to put all their children through high school. They purchased a used car and have invested in another business. They clearly support what they created. God may have sent the representative to help her, but only after Hassan had seized the initiative.

In Birmingham, England, 500 residents took to the streets and told the prostitutes, pimps, and drug dealers to leave. With some outside help, St. Paul's Development Trust was organized thirty years ago as a preschool in an abandoned church. Now it is a private company with charitable status. It has playgrounds, schools, provision for elderly clients, a farm, and a newspaper. Furthermore, it provides workplace skills and language training. Any resident can become a shareholder and vote for directors at the annual meeting. Civic pride has been regained.

Chicago's Cochran Gardens neighborhood had gotten so bad that even police avoided it. Then a teenager named Bertha Gilkey started working to improve the area. Ten years later, Cochran Gardens had been completely redone and was being operated by tenants. Tenants provided day care, a senior citizen residence, a medical clinic, and meals on wheels. All this happened because a teenage girl refused to back down in the face of dozens of hardened, gun-toting criminals twice her size.

The local newspaper in an Iowa town printed cut-out coupons that said, "I've had enough of drugs in my neighborhood! I have reason to believe that ________________ is using/dealing drugs." The police reported an excellent response.

There was also Montgomery, Alabama, and Rosa Parks during the civil rights movement in the 1960s. "The real victory was in the mass meeting, where thousands of black people stood revealed with a new sense of dignity and destiny," said Dr. Martin Luther King, Jr. One among many, Dr. King saw that top-down could drag down. This was especially applicable to people of color.

Formerly white and middle-class, Five Oaks had become half black and 60 percent renters. Conditions had deteriorated to the point where residents felt like they were living in a war zone. Three years later the prostitutes and dealers were gone, and children were playing in the streets. Residents and police had got together and decided to do something. Along with an ambitious cleanup, a consultant was hired, who recommended installation of gates to limit through traffic. In the first year crime dropped by 25 percent, violent crime by almost 50 percent. Through traffic was reduced by 67 percent, and accidents were down 40 percent. Prices of housing increased by 15 percent. One leader was quoted: "The beauty of it is that we don't have one wonderful white man giving us a million dollars a year. We've got 100,000 black people giving us $10, and 100,000 black people giving us $1, and that becomes a spigot that you can't shut off." People support what they help create: This is the mantra of the bottom-up approach to neighborhood and community problems.

The Rev. Floyd Flake was also a congressman who resigned before the end of his sixth term. The school that he founded in 1982 is still in existence. Then came the $23 million Allen African Methodist Episcopal Church, a credit union, a clinic, Head Start classrooms, a 300-unit apartment complex for the elderly, and 50 two-family bungalows. Rev. Flake spoke of black leaders for whom "the highlight of their lives was the civil rights movement, have not done the hard analysis that is indicated" by the achievements of the era.

Black columnist William Raspberry referred to a study of the inner city, in which the recommendation was to encourage entrepreneurship: "Thar's gold in them ghettos, waiting only the arrival of smart prospectors to dig it out. And the question inner city residents and their advocates ought to be asking is: Why aren't we digging?"[23]

Years of top-down poverty programs from Washington have generated a defeatist mentality within many inner cities. "We don't have the start-up capital, and white-owned banks won't lend us the money. Government assistance programs will give us just enough to fail. Black shoppers won't support black businesses." Big government has made losers of these people, so they dig, but not for gold. Rather, they dig for excuses. Victimology blinds its victims to opportunity.

In 1993 Vice President Al Gore published a report intended to reinvent government. This was the eleventh such attempt since 1905, and the results have been identical each time—nothing. No major change will occur within any organization that is a monopoly, because there is no competitive pressure. Furthermore, there are deeply entrenched vested interests to protect. Sweeping change can come only from outside the organization, from a bottom-up initiative. (It is worth noting that a dynamic democracy obviates the need for sweeping change.)

Gross stated that there are twenty-three states with "initiatives" in their constitutions.[24] "All voters have to do is sign a petition that they want a specific law . . . and it's automatically placed on the next ballot. If the voters win, no one, neither the legislature nor the governor, can tamper with it." California's experience suggests that such proposals must be worded very carefully to avoid misleading voters (if people discussed politics more often, this would not be necessary). This bottom-up approach to legislating may have great potential.

Gross went on to mention that amendments to the Constitution could also be proposed in this manner (through Article V): In response to applications from two-thirds of the state legislatures, Congress must call a convention to consider an amendment. If three-quarters of the state legislatures ratify a proposed amendment it becomes part of the Constitution. The procedure essentially bypasses the president and Congress. (This has never been done, a fact that is thought-provoking in itself.)

Because each neighborhood is uniquely different from every other one of the thousands in the nation, issues like gun control must be addressed through local initiative if they are to be effective. If after extensive discussion and debate a neighborhood or community should decide to eliminate guns in homes, say, everyone will cooperate with police in the task of enforcement. A nearby community might decide to accept ownership of specific kinds of firearms under specific conditions. People would then be free to choose where to live in accordance with their attitude toward guns.

But Washington cannot leave this emotional issue alone, so a few gun control laws have been passed in spite of fierce lobbying by the National Rifle Association (NRA). Not only have those passed been watered down due to this money—er, influence, there is evidence that the NRA is interfering with enforcement. In fact, this issue is so hot that many studies promote biased results. Therefore, truth is hard to come by, and discussion by citizens is in order.

The Economist reported a study by Mark Duggan that addressed the difficult issue of causation.[25] "From an empirical perspective, gun ownership could promote crime by facilitating violence; or it could deter it by implicitly threatening retribution." The researcher was meticulous and apparently unbiased as he worked. The Economist: "Still, the central tenet of Mr. Duggan's findings stands: on balance, the evidence suggests that guns foster crime, not the other way around."

Human nature suggests that almost everyone has it in for someone at one time or another. If guns were difficult to obtain, as they used to be in cities, at least, such a person would probably seek to injure his target in some way. But with a gun murder would be far more likely. Moreover, if the gun is immediately handy he is more likely to act before the passage of time that is required to calm down and regain reason. These difficult-to-measure factors contribute to the rate of homicide. They would be given due consideration in a neighborhood political meeting in which the issue came up for discussion and formulation of law or policy.

Public officials in Washington have furnished ample proof that everyone needs to be accountable to someone. When the bottom-up approach to governing is used, citizens are accountable to themselves. This is the essence of self-government, which the founding fathers enshrined in the Constitution. However, citizens must also hold their public officials accountable for faithful performance of the task assigned to them. If most of governing were bottom-up these officials would seldom be far away. They would know they must face their constituents in public debate on demand, so it would be hard to get away with any chicanery.

This applies not only to officials' behavior in their interactions with the people, but also with respect to their management of the taxpayers' money. That, too, is never far away: Money should be raised where it will be spent.

In a democracy public officials must be selected with great care, because in their jobs they must walk a tight wire. To err on the minus side excites little progress among the turbulence that is the democratic process. To err on the plus side will cause the people to chafe under what they perceive as oppression. In the former situation little would get done, whereas in the latter citizens are likely to remove their servant.

The dismal record of the Environmental Protection Agency (EPA) has been discussed. This is a good example of the failure of top-down, one-size-fits-all governing. The solution lies in the democratic process: Several citizens in a hypothetical community who live near power plant A have respiratory problems that can be attributed to their proximity to the plant. They organize additional concerned citizens, who send a petition to the plant manager. If there is no response, a stronger initiative is in order, then other actions as necessary, possibly then a local law requiring the plant to reduce its emissions until they meet some defined specification. Punishment would be specified for noncompliance after a reasonable time.

Because there was no EPA to require the wrong technology, cases of recalcitrant managers would be rare. Democracy may be inefficient, but when citizens organize around a cause and get results, community pride waxes eloquent.

Rose Wilder Lane wrote: "Abraham and the prophets after him knew that every human being is self-controlling and responsible. Christ knew it. Mohammad knew it. This fact is the hope of the world. For only unknown individuals can create and maintain conditions in which men can act freely . . . to improve the human world."[26] Her observation connects with the positive side of human nature, as perceived by three men whose importance in history is widely acknowledged.

"Only an individual who recognizes that his self-controlling responsibility is a condition of human life, and fully accepts the responsibility of a creator of the human world, can protect human rights in the infinite complexity of men's relationships with each other. Only this individual protection of all men's rights can keep their natural freedom operating on this earth."

The Citizen as a Member of a Winning Team

As envisioned by the founding fathers, the Constitution has one paramount obligation. This is to provide an environment in which each individual is free to attain the highest potential in accordance with his or her unique interpretation of this goal. Four principles in place and undisturbed can create that environment: a low tax burden, free markets, protection of property rights, and stable money. Within such an environment citizens will find it not just necessary but also convenient to come together in institutions that act as facilitators. Government is but one of a group of facilitators, such as family, school, work, and so on.

When this has been accomplished, citizens will perceive institutions as helping hands instead of barriers. Genetsky wrote:

> *A nation where a significant portion of the population behaves as dependents can never be a great nation. It can only be a nation of individuals who*

> *have failed to attain maturity and independence; a nation of individuals who will insist on blaming others for their problems; a nation of individuals who constantly look to government, as a child looks to a parent to solve its problems.*[27]

But a paternalistic government is not equipped to help; its policies can only make the situation worse and thus create citizens who are more dependent.

Friedman commented:

> *The use of political channels, while inevitable, tends to strain the social cohesion essential for a stable society. The strain is least if agreement for joint action need be reached only on a limited range of issues. . . . Every extension of the range of issues . . . strains further the delicate threads that hold society together. If it goes so far as to touch an issue on which men feel deeply yet differently, it may well disrupt the society. . . . The widespread use of the market reduces the strain on the social fabric by rendering conformity unnecessary with respect to any activities it encompasses.*[28]

In his comment on the range of issues straining the delicate threads, Friedman referred to the notion of genetic fit. Diversity within an individual can flourish, and he or she is thus free to seek his own unique destiny. Furthermore, he may combine with others of like mind, whenever and wherever he may see fit to do so. Any such combination is voluntary for all concerned.

Diversity is important in an individualist society, because with blind conformity no potentially good ideas will ever see the light of day. It is said that for any couple married for a long time and who has never had a disagreement, at least one of them has not voiced a thought during that time. The same applies as well in other institutions. (Chapter 16 will show how to keep reason in charge of discussion of a controversial issue.)

Blind conformity puts every individual in the same boat with every other with no land in sight. It is hard to combine people into a team when there is no shared goal. This is stability carried to its logical extreme. Friedman's interpretation of a stable society states that there is some turbulence in government, but it is created by citizens working together in their mutual interest. They do not perceive it as turbulence, as in the case of an outside force, such as a hurricane. They are themselves the force; to paraphrase a line from the movie *Star Wars,* they see the force as being with them.

There exists a paradox in the capacity of diversity and political conflict as a method of bringing people together in the joint effort of creating and operating good government. Its resolution lies in human nature: People support what they help create. If citizens carefully select their leaders and these people do the job right, civic pride will be the gratifying result. "Those people in the next neighborhood (or community) are very good, but we are a little better." An appropriate analogy is that of a league in which athletic teams compete.

The feeling of communal solidarity is more important than economic development. The latter creates wealth, which is of course good, but the negative side of wealth accumulation often brings irresponsibility and even corruption. Civic pride can contain this tendency, but the presence of wealth by itself cannot guarantee pride in community.

Civic pride causes many people to be active in the community; activities include a watchful care over those who have difficulty in adjusting to community life. Citizens will work with police, who will be free to assume different roles from those that prevail today. The term *community policing* will take on a different meaning, the precise nature of which is hard to predict.

A British town recently provided an example of how not to do community policing. A law was passed that required neighbors to be notified whenever a pedophile or other sex offender is released from jail and comes to live in a neighborhood. The difficulty lay in lawsuits by parents not notified in the event of an additional offense, and irate offenders who with advance notification were subjected to harassment. It seemed that the police were damned if they did and damned if they didn't. But then, the law was passed and administered in a top-down manner.

A community with civic pride would learn of the new arrival and immediately organize a corps of volunteers, who would maintain a respectfully distant watch over the offender for as many hours a day as appropriate. If they succeeded in getting the person involved in improving government, he might find something better to do with his spare time. (He might ask citizens to help him toward a healthy adjustment.)

In today's environment, should some crazy person threaten to kill or harm someone, police are likely to say their hands are tied until a crime occurs. In a fit of passion anyone can issue an empty threat. But how to be sure? With civic pride there is no need to wait until a person acts on this negative impulse. Either family members or a group of citizens would go talk with the person. If he or she could not be dissuaded, volunteers would organize accordingly with cell phones: home, car, workplace, and so on. Any potential victim would keep the team current with his or her location; whenever victim and assailant got close to one another, police would be called.

In Ayn Rand's novel *Atlas Shrugged,* intelligent hero John Galt observed the tragic deterioration of a formerly healthy society under an ever more ruthless top-down government (vicious circle).[29] Unable to stop this juggernaut by any other means, he organized a "brain strike," which removed the few remaining producers to a far-off and secret location. With the trains about to stop, all production about to cease, and city lights about to be turned off, he spoke to the public on a clandestine radio. The following is an excerpt.

His own happiness is man's only moral purpose, but only his own virtue can achieve it. Virtue is not an end in itself. Virtue is not its own reward or sacrificial fodder for the reward of evil. Life is the reward of virtue . . . and happiness is the goal and reward of life. Just as I support my life, neither by robbery nor alms, but by my own effort, so I do not seek to derive my happiness from the injury or the favor of others, but earn it by my own achievement. Just as I do not consider the pleasure of others as the goal of my life, so I do not consider my pleasure as the goal of the lives of others. Just as there are no contradictions in my values and no conflicts among my desires . . . so there are no victims and no conflicts of interest among rational men.

Galt argued for the Age of Reason, wherein each individual stands tall in his or her own evaluation. However, the lack of conflicts of interest among people is an ideal that can be approached if, according to Friedman, there are a minimum of issues delegated by citizens to government that contain within them the seeds of conflict. Combine these, and the result is both pride of person and civic pride. Put another way, the team is ready to get the job done.

A citizen grows old. He or she may often think backward, of what was not accomplished, opportunities forgone. The result is that he becomes grouchy. However, if a citizen lives in a community with civic pride and continuing learning, new opportunities for making contributions toward improving government constantly appear. In this environment the older citizen feels useful, looks forward, and enjoys the stimulating hobby of participation. He is too busy to be grouchy.

Notes

1. Lewis H. Lapham, *The Wish for Kings: Democracy at Bay.* Grove Press, 1993.
2. William Greider, *Who Will Tell the People: The Betrayal of American Democracy.* Simon and Schuster, 1992.
3. James D. Barber, *The Book of Democracy.* Prentice Hall, 1995.
4. Donald N. Wood, *Post-Intellectualism and the Decline of Democracy: The Failure of Reason in the 20th Century.* Praeger, 1996. Douglass quoted in Chapter 14.
5. Stephen Holmes, *The Anatomy of Antiliberalism.* Harvard College, 1993.
6. Friedrich A. Hayek, *The Road to Serfdom.* University of Chicago Press, 1944.
7. John W. Gardner, *Self Renewal.* Norton, 1981.
8. Isaiah Berlin, *Four Essays on Liberty.* Oxford University Press, 1969.
9. Thomas Paine, *Rights of Man.* Knopf, 1915.
10. Michael Schudson, *The Good Citizen: A History of American Civic Life.* Free Press, 1998.
11. Greider, *Who Will Tell the People.*

12. Jack Donnelly, *Universal Human Rights in Theory and Practice.* Cornell University Press, 1989.
13. *The Economist,* "A Lesson for the World." August 25, 2001, p. 14; and "America's Great Achievement." p. 25.
14. Edward O. Wilson, *On Human Nature.* Harvard University Press, 1978.
15. Anthony Arblaster, *Democracy.* University of Minnesota Press, 1987.
16. Robert H. Bork, *Slouching Towards Gomorrah.* Harper Collins, 1996.
17. Rose Wilder Lane, *The Discovery of Freedom.* Fox and Wilkes, 1993.
18. Paine, *Rights of Man.*
19. Schudson, *The Good Citizen.*
20. James Fallows, *Breaking the News: How the Media Undermine American Democracy.* Pantheon Books, 1996, p. 76.
21. *The Economist,* "The Internet's New Borders." August 11, 2001, p. 9.
22. Greider, *Who Will Tell the People.*
23. William Raspberry, "Business for the Taking." *News and Observer,* November 1997 column.
24. Martin L. Gross, *A Call for Revolution.* Ballantine Books, 1993.
25. *The Economist,* "Do Guns Mean Crime?" January 13, 2001, p. 76.
26. Lane, *The Discovery of Freedom.*
27. Robert J. Genetsky, *A Nation of Millionaires: Unleashing America's Economic Potential.* Heartland Institute, 1997.
28. Milton Friedman, *Capitalism and Freedom.* University of Chicago Press, 1982.
29. Ayn Rand, *Atlas Shrugged.* Penguin Books, 1992.

CHAPTER THIRTEEN:
EDUCATION AND THE PUBLIC-SPIRITED CITIZEN

Education is a better safeguard of liberty than a standing army.
—Edward Everett

An Eastern sage once said: "The pleasures of the senses are ephemeral. The pleasures of the heart may turn to sorrow. But the pleasures of the mind are with you till the end of your journey."

Thomas Jefferson said, "Educate and inform the whole mass of the people. Enable them to see that it is their interest to preserve peace and order, and they will preserve them. And it requires no very high degree of education to convince them of this. They are the only sure reliance for the preservation of our liberty."

Benjamin Franklin wrote: "An investment in knowledge always pays the best interest. If a man empties his purse into his head, no one can take it away from him."

A person must know himself before he can really get to know another. He must know himself before he can love himself (self-esteem), and he must love himself before he can truly love another. A good education is very helpful in acquiring these vital attributes. Furthermore, a good education reveals to a student that learning can be enjoyable; given this, the student will be motivated to go on learning throughout life. He can remain acquainted with himself and continue to love himself as he changes from year to year and from decade to decade.

Reference to the flip side shows a not-whole person dependent on others for his or her daily needs. Often, resources immediately available to him he finds inadequate, so he looks to government fill some of those needs. Government responds in the only way officials know: top-down. This approach very often misses the target, and so the unfortunate citizen asks for more. A dependent relationship makes for an unstable life.

Biographer Gilbert quoted Winston Churchill at age eighty-one: "I am being taken through a course of Monet, Manet, Cezanne and Co. by my hosts who are both versed in modern painting and practice in the studio. . . . Also they have a wonderful form of gramophone which plays continuously Mozart and other composers of merit. . . . I am in fact having an artistic education with very agreeable tutors."[1] Although hard proof is understandably elusive, Gilbert in his eponymous book attempted to explain how Churchill acquired the joy of learning at an early age.

An Educational System with Potential

Bennis described **maintenance** learning as "the acquisition of fixed outlooks, methods and rules for dealing with known and recurring situations. . . . It is the type of learning designed to maintain an existing system or established way of life."[2] **Shock** learning occurs when events overwhelm people. It is also known as crisis management. If institutions do not change over time maintenance learning will assume a predominant role, and people will endure frequent shocks. Company managers will become more like fire fighters than managers. Bureaucrats will become deeply entrenched in their jobs, so they can weather the shocks without changing policies.

Bennis described **innovative** learning as "anticipation, learning by listening to others, and participation." Anticipation is "being active and imaginative rather than passive and habitual. Participation is shaping events, rather than being shaped by them." Bennis would agree that these are the traits acquired by someone who enjoys learning. He also recommended time spent in reflection after and between learning experiences. These pauses enable a person to critically analyze what has been learned and to make appropriate adjustments (separating wheat from chaff, for example) before assimilation.

Jefferson believed in the value of reflection, as did Thomas Paine:

> *Two distinct classes of . . . thoughts . . . those that we produce in ourselves by reflection and the act of thinking, and those that bolt into the mind of their own accord. I have always made it a rule to treat those voluntary visitors with civility, taking care to examine . . . if they are worth entertaining, and it is from them I have acquired almost all the knowledge that I have. . . . Every person of learning is finally his own teacher.*[3]

Paine was a great writer and revolutionary, even though he had practically no formal education. Today reflection is a lost art; memory leads to quotation, but thought explores. The lives of Jefferson and Paine made real the potential of reflection.

The framers of the Constitution wanted everyone to have an equal opportunity for success in life, and they acknowledged the reality that not all will have equal success. However, since the time of Jefferson and Paine, society has radically changed from agrarian to industrial and now to what some call postindustrial. These changes put extra weight on education as a major factor in constitutionally guaranteeing everyone equal opportunity. This chapter recommends a system that can provide this equality.

Early in the life of the United States, school reformers began to look to public education as an advantageous replacement for attempts at private enterprise. The movement seemed to make sense, because the Industrial Revolution brought with it new educational requirements. Citizens agreed to be taxed to support this effort, as at that time people generally did not move away from the locality of their birth, so well-educated adults would make better contributions to the community.

In about 1900, educational philosopher John Dewey's theories advocated free inquiry by students. But advocates of public education chose to interpret his theories to favor the rigid curriculum and administration that would be necessary for public education to become entrenched.

Burleigh commented on a paper by Goodrich and Rogge:

> *Because it is assumed that the purpose of education in an unfree society will be to serve the whim of the dictator, proletariat, priest-king . . . The state will have no purpose of education at all. Rather . . . totally a matter of individual concern. . . .*
>
> *Other arguments against the current method of financing education through public subsidy. First . . . inefficiencies in management that in a competitive, private system would be weeded out. Second . . . fails to sort out those students who do not care to be in school and have no intention of trying to learn. If schools were private, only those students with high motivation would care enough to pay the full price. . . . Finally, when teachers are not awarded salaries commensurate with their talents, when they are given fixed salaries regardless of how hard they work, when they report not to the parents of their students but to the state government, then they, too, lack motivation.*
>
> *"In summary, then," say the authors, "tax-supported education tends to make of our schools and colleges a collection of nonstudents under the tutelage of non-teachers and the administration of the incompetent."* [4]

These remarks summarize a prevalent feeling of many years' standing among concerned educators. A recent study has impressed such people:

> *[Caroline] Hoxby's work inspires a kind of awe among many economists: for its clarity, its empirical thoroughness, and its wonderful ingenuity in finding ways to answer hard questions.*
>
> *Four results stand out. First, choice reduces spending on education . . . the improvement in performance is achieved at lower cost. Second, it has the biggest effects on school productivity in states where districts have greater financial independence. Third, it reduces demand for private education: "policies that reduce choice among districts—or the benefits of choice—are likely to increase the share of students in private schools and reduce the share of voters who are interested in the general well-being of public education." Fourth, the effects barely differ as between prosperous families and poor families. . . . The view that*

greater choice favors the rich at the expense of the poor gets no backing. Everybody gains. . . . Except bad teachers.[5]

And politicians, as will be seen. A useful proxy measure to separate good teachers from bad might develop from school choice: The good would welcome and encourage it, whereas the bad would fight it tooth and nail.

During the early part of the twentieth century, Maria Montessori was experimenting with teaching "defective" children. Powell noted: "Incredibly, the children she taught learned how to read and write as well as ordinary children."[6] She promptly revised her approach to apply it to the latter. She was given a class in a poor section of Rome, Italy.

The children were an unpromising lot: sullen, withdrawn, and rebellious. Yet Montessori made a series of startling observations as she worked with them: that children have a powerful, inborn desire to learn and achieve independence, that they learn spontaneously where they have enough freedom, that they develop remarkable concentration on tasks that they choose, that they prefer exploring real things—the world of grownups—rather than conventional toys, and that they blossom in an atmosphere of dignity, respect, and freedom.

Montessori was a sensation. Aspiring teachers came from thousands of miles away to be trained by her. In December 1913, she visited the US. . . . She encountered ferocious opposition from academics, especially in the United States.

Even today public education continues its long-standing attempt to bury Montessori's legacy.

In one of the last of the many popular books he wrote, James Michener reflected on his years as a young teacher:

Arrived at a list . . . 1. Living in a family that has an orderly dinner every night at which there is lively discussion of important subjects. 2. Instruction in fundamental moral values. 3. It helps if a growing child has other children to play with, and if there are no siblings, preschool is a strong substitute. 4. Although the first six years of schooling are very important, they do not carry the intellectual weight or significance that the later years do. 5. When young students enter high school . . . [it is] essential . . . really get down to work.[7]

Michener's prescription sounds a bit archaic today, but nevertheless there is some food for thought when organizing the home for learning and parental participation in schools.

However, much later Rothbard pointed out, "If the mass of the populace is to be educated in government schools, how could these schools not become a mighty instrument for the inculcation of obedience to the State authorities?"[8] Years ago communities were small and scattered, and the central government did not interfere in school administration. Today Rothbard has a point; the national government recently established a Department of Education. Chapter 8 portrayed its impact on educational policy.

A state government might grant to each child a "scholarship" to grades K–12, paid for by the taxpayer and equalized throughout the state. Ideally, money should be raised where it is to be spent. However, different parts of a state have lower tax bases than do others. Due to the problem of obedience already described, a better arrangement is a government that grants tax breaks to private foundations that are formed to underwrite the costs of educational vouchers to be issued to parents of each child.

During the agrarian era a child could learn how to operate a farm while growing up. He needed little formal education, because his future was more or less predetermined. Today the cost of formal education is beyond the reach of nearly all young parents. Would private foundations be capable of accepting this towering challenge? The answer is not available now, but it is worth noting that there exist today around 5,000 private foundations that finance a great variety of worthwhile activities.

Citizens who have no children or grandchildren of school age would also benefit from a good education system. Educated adults commit fewer crimes, so society would be rendered more stable. Citizens would feel safer, less likely to be robbed, injured, or killed. There would be fewer poor people, and these would be helped by charities supported voluntarily by citizens. Taxes to support police and prisons would be lower. On the receiving side, educated citizens would obtain better jobs and broaden the tax base almost regardless of what kind of taxation system is in place (Chapter 15 discusses this issue). Combining these reasons suggests that nearly all citizens and most businesses would donate to private educational foundations.

The subject of educational vouchers has generated a lot of interest. The strongest argument in favor of vouchers lies in the exercise of free school choice by parents; its founders inserted the concept of free choice in the Constitution. Choice in turn means competition for customer favor. Because competition has acquired a dubious reputation in some minds, the following may be instructive (the quote was obtained from a businessman in East Asia and it bears repeating).

A TRIBUTE TO MY COMPETITORS

My competitors do more for me than my friends. My friends are too polite to point out my weaknesses, but my competitors go to great expense to advertise them. My competitors are efficient, diligent, attentive and would take my business away from me if they could. They keep me alert and make me search for ways to improve my products and services. If I had no competitors I would be lazy, incompetent, inattentive. I need the discipline they enforce upon me. I salute my competitors. They have been good to me. God bless them all!

Competition is indeed a blessing, in that its presence compels every organization to strive to improve. This is a major reason why government does not improve with age; it is a monopoly. The same applies to an educational system; in the absence of competition, its components will be "lazy, incompetent, inattentive."

The Economist, in a November 1997 article, wrote:

> *Vouchers inspire a flood of objections, none convincing. Schemes being pioneered in several American cities face legal challenges on the ground that, since many of those given vouchers choose Catholic or other religious schools, this violates the constitutional separation between church and state. But voucher schemes give public money to individuals, not institutions. Furthermore, precedents for these have been set by both the GI Bill in the 1940s . . . and more recently the Pell Grants (offering disadvantaged students a state-funded college place). In both cases the beneficiaries could . . . study theology at church-affiliated colleges."*
>
> *In fact it is the poorest families, who have no chance of paying private school fees, and whose schools are already sink schools, who would gain most. . . . That is why a group of several thousand black parents in Denver is suing the local school board for the right to be given them. Cleveland's voucher scheme has led to the founding of new schools, free from the dead hand of school board bureaucracy, offering poor families . . . choice.*[9]

Probably not all poor black and other poor parents are familiar with the Constitution's support of free choice, but they are obviously intelligent enough to know a bad deal when they see one.

Safire reported on a more recent study.[10] School vouchers make a big difference for black students. That is the conclusion of a two-year study in three cities—New York, Washington, DC, and Dayton, Ohio—conducted by a team from Harvard, the University of Wisconsin, and the Brookings Institution.

"If the trend line continues, the report says, 'the black-white test gap could be eliminated in subsequent years of education for black students who use a voucher to switch from public to private school.'" This study was commissioned by a group of foundations, not the government. Denver's concerned black parents are apparently onto something significant. As the educational gap closes, so also fade the last pale vestiges of racism.

President Clinton also knew a good deal when he saw one (*The Economist* continued): "Mindful of how important a constituency teachers are to their parties, both Bill Clinton and Tony Blair [prime minister of Britain] will not allow vouchers a chance to prove themselves." Chapter 10 discussed corruption. This is the issue here, because for decades teachers' union officials have contributed generously to political parties and candidates. The influence accompanying that money says do not change anything; just give teachers more taxpayer money.

Politicians at almost every opportunity loudly proclaim their concern for poor children, but this is rhetoric. The reality lies in the money. Therefore Clinton's "good deal" was a good deal for politicians, not for children and their parents.

It is interesting that Clinton **appeared** to be rock-solid in support of children. Almost weekly he seized the initiative on an issue related to children, emphasizing what his latest proposal would do for them. The matter had gotten to the point where a commentator observed, "Whenever Clinton refers to kids, reach for your wallet." (It is also interesting to note that *The Economist* is a British newspaper, and that articles like this one seldom if ever appear in a US news publication.)

The Economist continued:

> *Two-thirds of the voucher parents reported that they were "very satisfied" . . . compared with fewer than a third of public school parents [with no] voucher . . . also twice as likely to be "very satisfied" with the safety, discipline, moral values and individual attention offered by their schools. And the children are doing better. . . . [They] gained . . . five percentage points in reading and 15 points in maths.*

About 75 percent of voucher students are poor, and two-thirds are black. Given a good opportunity, there is no reason whatever to believe that a child of any color cannot perform equally with any other child (as Montessori so conclusively proved). Furthermore, private schools on average get a superior job done at a significantly lower cost to the donor or taxpayer per student.

"Critics of vouchers complain that schools would be ruined by having to compete with each other for pupils. This is nonsense. . . . Far from ruining the education system, more competition is exactly what is needed to improve it."

President Bush is far from enthusiastic about vouchers, but Ontario, Canada's premier Mike Harris is not so bashful. His voucher program offers a tax credit to parents who enroll their children in private schools. The most important aspect of the program is that the money goes directly to parents.

In 1998 Amity Schlaes interviewed Milton and Rose Friedman.[11]

> *Merely giving parents and charter schools the independence to set school policy or jawboning about "small school empowerment" won't do the trick. Parents need to control the money as well. Otherwise the state or federal government can intrude when it pleases. "The fundamental problem is that these schools remain government entities," says Friedman. "You may have competition in demand. But you don't have free market competition in supply. It's still socialism."*

The Friedmans apparently advocate support of education by private foundations. This idea is not new; many companies and corporations are sponsoring schools today. Executives recognize the value of educated employees, primarily because they are more trainable and, perhaps more important, will actively contribute their thinking along with their muscle to the success of the operation.

Joan and Jeff Fortune retired in their fifties from lucrative jobs, having attained considerable wealth. They cast about for opportunities to do good with some of it. They visited Nativity Prep in Boston and learned about starting a non-denominational school that would emphasize morality as well as academics and discipline.

Michael Ryan reported:

> *Since it opened two years ago, Academy Prep has made an offer to boys in the fifth, sixth, seventh, and eighth grades that you might think they would be glad to refuse: the chance to spend 9.5 hours a day in school, 11 months a year. And for nine of those months, they attend a two-hour study hall each evening . . . and go on field trips on Saturday. At present 60 boys, mainly African-Americans, are enrolled. . . . They say "Yes, sir" or "Yes, ma'am" to their elders and line up in neat rows for three assemblies a day. In everything they do—including basketball and baseball practices—they are taught discipline and civility.*[12]

Donations totaling $1.2 million came from Mr. Fortune's former company, a local bank, and other businesses. Volunteers planted trees and landscaped. Many of the twenty-seven teachers are retired and work for free, and others are new teachers who work for room and board and a small stipend. Each family also pays a $10 monthly fee to gain a feeling of sacrifice on behalf of their child's education. A logical conclusion is that if one public-spirited couple can accomplish this much, a foundation could do more.

Technology has acquired a role in K–12 education, involving students in activities that stretch their imaginations and creative skills. Computers enable individualized instruction and achievement-based learning instead of the current time-based method, where a student completes a grade and may be moved onward in spite of not having acquired the requisite skills of the former grade. The computer is infinitely patient with a student who is having difficulty with a problem. Also, teachers can function as resource people instead of standing in front of a class and trying to move all students ahead at the same pace when each naturally learns at his or her own speed.

"Social promotion" has massively contributed to the abominable educational system that dogs the nation today. The real world is achievement-based: A worker either performs in the job or is dismissed. Employers would value far more a diploma that reflects this type of learning; they would know precisely what mix of skills they are buying when they hire someone. Testing goes on every day in every business, and it is the business sector that finances government and practically all charities and other nonprofit organizations. The conclusion is that if education is to prepare young people for the real world, it, too, must be achievement-based. If a person with a high school diploma can't read, something is seriously wrong.

The Carbo Reading Styles program owes its existence to Dr. Marie Carbo. It has one overriding attribute: It recognizes that every single student learns in his or her own unique way. The implicit criticism of teachers who stand in front of a classroom and expect every student to perform in one uniform way is obvious.

About fifteen years ago Chris Whittle started the Edison Project, which utilizes computer-assisted instruction, achievement-based learning, and vouchers worth the same as those given to parents by taxpayers for use in public schools. There were critics, of course, who questioned the idea that a vital part of a democratic society should be entrusted to someone who is in it for the money. The response to such complaints was simple: If Mr. Whittle did not deliver the goods, he could be fired, and that was that. (Bureaucrats in this situation would sound the strident call for more money, and they have, time and again.) To date he has delivered.

Other critics argued that Whittle's efforts divert attention from attempts to reform the system from within. But entrenched bureaucrats will surely kill any serious inside attempt, because that is where their power base lies. These folks are Bennis's maintenance learners, who were educated in the same system through which parents and children are suffering today. One or two generations later, the system is predictably in even worse shape.

Whittle claimed he could help a child acquire the equivalent of today's high school education by age twelve, through using another tool called discovery learning. In this method a child manipulates a computer, and up comes something entirely new. (In the traditional classroom method of instruction, the teacher speaks, and the child often perceives what comes forth as predigested "baby food.") Teachers in the Edison Project frequently experience young squeals of delight with these discoveries. The new system has the potential to infuse joy of learning at an early age, with unlimited implications for the child's future. This is the anticipation, listening, and participation of Bennis's innovative learning.

Experience with the Edison Project in Wichita, Kansas, was reported by Ross and Robiglio:

> *At Dodge Edison Partnership Elementary, kids and teachers put in extra hours and learn in innovative ways, aided by top-flight research and an abundance of technology. "Edison has delivered on every guarantee they've made," said Larry Vaughn, superintendent. . . . "I'm a satisfied customer." Edison promised to bring up student test scores, foster a greater sense of community between parents, teachers and students, but without an increase in cost. . . .*
>
> *Now three years into the partnership in Wichita, the program has overcome the skepticism of parents, teachers and administrators and has renewed optimism that public education can work. . . . Walk through Dodge Edison and you'll see a school where instruction has spilled out into the halls. Tutoring is almost constant in the Edison method, and outside of most classrooms are small*

tables where educators and parent volunteers work with pairs of students to overcome an identified challenge.[13]

For stimulating thinking about course content, Whittle might look into Dorothy Sayers's Trivium.[14] This intriguing approach to learning was developed in 1948; it emphasizes development within the child of effective tools of learning. The approach is firmly grounded in developmental psychology.

Still other critics have complained that pulling students out of poor schools to send them to better ones will cause such a school to lose students and good teachers. These losses will further weaken the school, and a vicious circle will eventually bury it.

They are right; this could happen. However, managers of good schools would be constantly looking for opportunities to expand their operations, so they would compete strongly to acquire any school that is in trouble and add it to their successful company. Therefore parents who live in this area would have available a far better school to choose from among others already improved. When the system is well established, this could happen to any school that shows even small signs of weakness. Furthermore the influence of religion will probably diminish as more companies establish secular schools.

Recently in England, a regime of nationwide testing of students completing several different grades was established as an aid to parental choice. When results were first published there was more excitement among parents and students than might be found at a soccer game. When a test system is in place in this country, parents would look at aggregate scores when selecting a school. School managers would look at individual scores in recruiting students, because top scores would improve aggregate scores and hence their school's ability to attract the very best teachers.

Testing would be contracted out, with several testing companies competing for the contract. Care would be taken to avoid teachers teaching strictly for test scores. Actually, with computer-assisted discovery learning this would not be a major problem. Contract renewal would come up, say, every five years.

How does the slow or handicapped student fit in? With achievement-based learning, all have the same skills at any particular grade level. Furthermore, a student from a poor neighborhood who is sharp would be sought after by several schools, including those in wealthy neighborhoods. There is no reason why an outstanding school would not be located in a poor neighborhood (Academy Prep). This fact reveals the extent of equal opportunity that is possible with the system, especially when parents become actively concerned (the Edison Project strongly encourages such participation).

It is human nature to want to be a part of and contribute to a dynamic and relevant bottom-up institution. Small schools dispersed throughout neighborhoods would make it easier for parents to participate. This dynamism would apply especially to any parent who loves his or her child.

One day President Theodore Roosevelt went to the residence of famous retired Supreme Court Justice Oliver Wendell Holmes. The butler showed him into the study, where the president found Holmes reading Plato, and Roosevelt asked why. "To improve my mind, Mr. President," replied the ninety-four-year-old judge.

Tolerance Writ Small and Large

Jesus said, "Love thy neighbor as thyself." This is a major challenge in many parts of the world today, especially when neighbors are shooting at each other. This section will reveal the potential for harmony that tolerance—admittedly a couple of steps short of love—can accomplish from within neighborhoods and among nations.

Paine wrote eloquently on the subject: "But with respect to religion itself, without regard to names, and as directing itself from the universal family of mankind to the divine object of all adoration, it is man bringing to his Maker the fruits of his heart; and though these fruits may differ from each other like the fruits of the earth, the grateful tribute of every one is accepted."[15] He went on to argue that religion loses its benign nature when it becomes entangled with government. "The Inquisition in Spain does not proceed from the religion originally professed, but from the mule-animal . . . [It] drove the people called Quakers and Dissenters to America."

Paine was impressed with how the people in this country came together.

If there is a country in the world, where concord, according to common calculation, would be least expected, it is America. Made up, as it is, of people from different nations, accustomed to different forms and habits of government, speaking different languages . . . it would appear that the union of such a people was impracticable; but by the simple operation of constructing government on the principles of society and the rights of man, every difficulty retires, and all the parts are brought into cordial unison. There the poor are not oppressed, the rich are not privileged. Industry is not mortified by the splendid extravagance of a court rioting at its expense. Their taxes are few, because their government is just.

In 1799 George Washington wrote his last will. During this task he thought long and hard about the fate of his slaves. The finished document specified that on his death his slaves would be freed. It provided for support for those too old and too young to work, and there was a plan for educating and training the young. He knew that after being freed, former slaves would be hard put to adjust to freedom. He also knew that these provisions would not only end slavery at

Mount Vernon, it would end Mount Vernon as he knew it. Nevertheless, he completed the task. (Later in that year he died.)

Stephen Carter, in his book *Integrity,* noted: "Tolerance is the reason that the most liberal Americans must accept hateful speech and the most conservative Americans must accept homosexuality. It is not that nobody could hold the view that one or the other is morally wrong; it is rather that history has taught us to be careful about enforcing our moral views as law."[16]

Tolerance should never be inflicted, because attitudes cannot be legislated. However, it can be sold through persuasion, and education is an effective selling tool. Educated people understand themselves and their capabilities. Therefore they do not fear the unknown, such as someone else who appears, thinks, speaks, and acts differently. Rather, they perceive a meeting with such a person as another learning opportunity, and so they embrace it. Naive, timid people can be taught how to handle freedom and opportunity, and then they will acquire tolerance.

The Frenchman Tocqueville elaborated on what he called enlightened self-interest: "I do not think, by and large, that there is more egoism among us than in America; the only difference is that there it is enlightened, while here it is not. Every American has the sense to sacrifice some of his private interests to save the rest. We want to keep, and often lose, the lot."[17] Citizens in this country were not afraid or reluctant to reach out to others, even at some sacrifice.

Commenting on George W. Bush's January 2001 inauguration, Alan Dershowitz faulted Franklin Graham's inaugural prayer. "The plain message . . . non-Christians are welcome into the tent so long as they agree to accept their status as a tolerated minority rather than as fully equal citizens."[18] This well-intentioned man may not realize that his comment reflected a groupthink orientation: Non-Christians as a group are apparently the victims of discrimination because a Christian minister said a prayer in public.

But tolerance means reaching out in friendship to those whose beliefs are different, cooperating with them in a shared interest in good government as well as in other endeavors. A person's religious belief is his or her own, individually. When a person is comfortable in this (as in others aspects of the self) he or she will reach out to others, and one beneficial result will be pride in community.

Parent choice of schools would mix children of different ethnic backgrounds when they are young. At that age they have not yet acquired prejudice, and with the new system involved parents would be far less likely to teach their offspring this vice. Were a thinking citizen to reflect on this arrangement the long-term implications for the future of this country would become obvious. It has been mentioned that minds are like parachutes in that they function only when open. A similar reasoning applies to hearts.

For example, if an employer dislikes African Americans or Asian Americans, but certain individuals of this background bring to the job skills that are equal to or better than those possessed by other workers, he or she would be left at a significant disadvantage versus more tolerant competitors. Workers of minority background are often more motivated to succeed, especially immigrants. Profits would suffer as the employer paid dearly for discrimination.

In democracy a political meeting will attract a variety of citizens to free and open debate of relevant issues on the agenda for the evening. Rich, nonrich, and poor will mix, and the same goes for their ideas. A competent leader will see that each idea with merit gets adequate discussion, regardless of who proposed it. A poor citizen may contribute an idea with excellent potential, in which case his or her wallet may remain thin but his self-esteem will be enriched.

The recent movement called bicultural and multicultural education was misguided, in that it taught children about just one culture: their own. Minds and hearts expand through integrating various subjects, and culture is surely a part of this enlightening process. Members of different ethnic groups are protected from discrimination by the Constitution's equal opportunity. However, it does not authorize provision of taxpayer subsidies for educating such members.

Today's media are, if anything, damaging to the pursuit of tolerance. Over the past ten years two dozen movies have been made that show US soldiers killing Arabs. One studio even asked for comment from the Council for American Islamic Relations and the Arab-American Anti-Discrimination Committee, but it ignored the responses when producing *The Siege*. Both movies and the media also tend to ignore state-sponsored terrorism; they tend to portray all as ethnic or religion-based.

This emphasis has had an impact. Today the public thinks nearly all Arabs and Muslims are terrorists. As blindly attached as they are to violence and drama, the media will probably never publish any information relating to the tolerance that is built into the Koran, or the fact that a huge majority of Muslims practice peace and tolerance in their daily lives.

The Economist noted in 1998: "Latinos . . . are a heady mix of different races united mainly by a language. Yet it is precisely this variety that makes them so vital to America. Simply because they cannot cohere, they have never united around bitterness or some notion of group rights; instead, they have concentrated on those quintessential American tasks, getting up and getting on."[19] Many Latinos are so grateful for work that their thinking just doesn't dwell on foraging for additional rights. They believe in the land of opportunity, even if their skills are minimal. (They know this is temporary.)

Last year, President Clinton set up a commission to talk about race in America. It was heavily staffed by blacks who have been unable to see beyond the Great Divide. Perhaps it should have been staffed by Latinos, who cannot see a Great Divide at all: only bridges to be crossed, chances to be seized, another day's march along the road to completing the world's greatest multicultural experiment. Chapter 7 outlined Clinton's position on this issue when it discussed groupthink.

Tolerance writ large suggests that "a government who does not tolerate dissent has a limited life." Eduard Shevardnadze was foreign minister of the Soviet Union under Gorbachev; today he is president of the country of Georgia. An observation in his book, *The Future Belongs to Freedom,* is appropriate.[20]

> *It is more convenient to crack an opponent's head than to crack the ideas he comes up with. Under the rules of the system's power monopoly over the individual, you must bear without a murmur all attacks upon yourself and must accept as our due the diktat of the political patriarchate, which arrogates to itself the right to decide your fate. While it decides what to do with you, sit tight, do your work, and take advantage of the privileges and benefits offered to you. Don't try to yank the fish hook out of your mouth, or it will be certain death.*

Thus the limited life of an intolerant society. The absence of a colossal blood bath in 1991, when the Soviet Union collapsed, was a miracle. Shevardnadze himself was raised in a different family. "And if I inclined toward one opinion, I did not reject the opposing view out of hand. . . . If you eat such bread in childhood, you will always have a taste for it."

Throughout history dictators of every stripe have trampled on the rights of their own and other subjects. Grisly records like these made good fodder for Paul Kennedy's book *The Rise and Fall of the Great Powers.* The cycle repeats itself over and over again, proving the need for tolerance in governing and in international relations. The recent creation of a World Court in the Netherlands and the detention of former Chilean dictator Augusto Pinochet in England—both in the interest of punishment for crimes against humanity—are good signs. They will send an important message to other dictators. More recently the court reinforced this message: Serbia's Slobodan Milosevic is in The Hague standing trial on war crimes.

With adequate support, the United Nations could become the world's most effective salesperson for tolerance. The importance of this task is amply underscored by a fact of human nature. Whenever passions overrule reason, utter folly frequently governs behavior. People lose the connection with their humanity, and so the resulting conflict is extremely difficult to stop. The successful sale of tolerance will finally prevent conflict and thereby usher into the world the Age of Reason (Chapter 22).

There were about 50,000 Serbs among the 380,000 people who were trapped in Sarajevo, in the former Yugoslavia, when Serbian troops' artillery rained daily hell on the city. Many survived, together with Muslims and some Croats, helping one another when in trouble. Ordinary Serbs thought there was no victor in the battle. One said, "If there is a victory it is simply that we are still alive." This has become the way of war in the twenty-first century, as Chapter 20 will illustrate.

The recent fiasco in Kosovo illustrates a point. On the surface this was a NATO operation, but without US military presence and money it would not have happened at all. This war was an invasion of a province in a sovereign nation by an army from far away, representing a country not threatened by either that province or the country of which it is a part. It is true that Slobodan Milosevic had a grisly reputation as an "ethnic cleanser," but that unfortunate part of the world has been suffering through recurrent ethnic cleansing for nearly 700 years.

Some analysts wondered about the US failure to anticipate the tragedy in Kosovo. They didn't realize that lack of anticipation was actually a part of military planning. Government officials and generals want passions to govern behavior and conflict to break out, so they can keep their army in top fighting form and use up tons of weapons. Replacement of these will keep hundreds of thousands of workers employed back home and provide generous kickbacks for congressional reelection campaigns.

The man in charge of the fight, Gen. Wesley Clark, strongly claimed that the NATO goal is a multiethnic Kosovo. But tolerance cannot be brought about by force of arms, and surely 78 days of bombs and missiles will not erase 700 years of interethnic hatred. The poor people of Kosovo and elsewhere in Balkan countries need to realize that revenge is God's privilege and not theirs, but bombs cannot convey this vital message.

The Public-Spirited Official's Need for Educated Citizens

Peters described the making of the Constitution:

> *Since man's natural state is one of freedom and equality, legitimate government represents a mutually agreed compact among equals who sought protection of their natural rights in return for their pledge of obedience to its rules. The very basis of government, therefore, was the consent of the governed.* ***Those chosen to govern were the servants, not the masters,*** *of the people. But government, like man, was corruptible, and the task of those devising a system of government was therefore to prevent corruption and the oppression that would inevitably follow.*[21] (emphasis added)

One hundred fifty years later Friedrich Hayek claimed that "only scoundrels seek public office." Education can erode democracy if historical truth is distorted; if courses in civics are politicized; if personalities are emphasized in public service over logic, ideas, and debate; and if the top-down approach to governing is emphasized over the bottom-up version. Journalism can erode democracy if the institution neglects its primary and irreplaceable raison d'être: a constant thorn in the side of government, a constant and constructive critic. Entertainment can erode democracy if celebrities are lionized by citizens instead of ideas, political debate, and criticism.

The behavior of a career politician is governed by the negative incentives referred to by Peters. In politics experience soon becomes a negative asset.

The founding fathers inserted into the Constitution a number of principles. A public-spirited citizen official would take a stand on principles and rise or fall with them, because he or she would be a person of principle. A career politician necessarily lacks principles on which to stand or fall, as the major and often only objective is reelection. Therefore a career politician does not stand for any principle; rather, he crawls, maintaining a low profile and speaking in weasel words concerning an issue that relates to principle. This prepares the politician for the time when the issue is resolved, at which time he comes out roaring, stoutly maintaining that this was his position all along.

Wealth has little to do with public-spirited public service, because there are nearly as many definitions of success as there are successful people. However, its presence may contribute to a successful citizen's hankering for an opportunity to serve the public.

A campaigning public-spirited citizen will make few promises, especially those on which he knows he probably cannot deliver. He will state his position on as many issues as the people may desire. These positions develop from talking and listening to people over a period of years, participating in government, and integrating his own morality, study, and careful reflection into what he has learned. From this process, he has determined that he has the ability and the desire to make a contribution; otherwise he would not choose to stand for election.

There will be questions and complaints. He or she will respond to the questions, and ask complainers for their ideas on what can be done. This action separates the chronic complainers from the constructive critics. He will take time to listen to the people; as difficult as this is to believe today, in a democracy a public official will spend more time listening than talking. (He may reflect on the fact that God gave him two ears but only one mouth.) He will debate with an open mind, which means it is subject to change so long as in his judgment his principles are not violated.

An idea is easier to understand than a person, although both require effort. The presumption in personality-based campaigning (image merchandising) is that the real persona of the candidate is on display, so viewers are able to make intelligence judgments concerning whom to support. This presumption is just as false as the image being sold, and a campaign manager will often change a candidate's image partway through a campaign as the direction of the political winds changes.

The effort needed to understand an idea and forge it into something useful involves the process of discussing, debating, and criticizing. In this way the collective wisdom of the mass of citizens reveals truth.

A public-spirited citizen does not strike a high profile, because he or she knows there is no need for this. Aspiring heroes become stars in sports and other forms of entertainment. Seekers of wealth enter the business sector, where they can help create wealth and jobs, broaden the tax base, increase productivity, and raise living standards.

There is no need for a public servant to be an intellectual giant. The more important traits are dedication and a strong desire to serve, to make a contribution to the neighborhood or community. The action that makes these traits manifest emphasizes listening to ascertain the public will on an issue, act on it, and seek feedback later to be sure the job was done right. The success of this process depends on educated citizens working together to develop and nurture a collective wisdom. No public official can do his job well without this vital resource.

The educated public servant has acquired self-knowledge and hence self-discipline. This vital possession doesn't just insulate him or her from the temptations of office. He also has the ability to identify with citizens who desire to discipline their government. As a leader he would be likely to see the possibility of promulgating this desirable trait as far as his remit would permit.

Furthermore, there is no need for tons of money. In a democracy citizens do for themselves and delegate to their public servants only those tasks that they cannot conveniently accomplish by themselves. The more that is done by individuals, the less the opportunity for controversy that cannot easily be resolved through the democratic process. Finally, when citizens keep their freedom away from a grasping government, they will be motivated toward significant accomplishment as individuals; it is human nature to act to improve one's lot in life.

A public-spirited official would feel no tug toward reelection, as there would be no mountain of money and consequent urge toward personal power seeking to goad him or her into campaigning. With rare exceptions two terms of whatever length would be sufficient. For any re-election, he or she may respond to a call from citizens but may not seize the initiative himself.

The top leader of a democratic country is also a servant. Because of a tendency to feel personal power in such a position, the incumbent must constantly remind himself, every day, that he serves at the pleasure of millions of bosses: the electorate. Of course, guardianship runs both ways; if the bosses neglect assertion of their authority, accountability will fade and in its place will enter human nature's negative incentives. At age seventy-five Churchill sat through a long and impressive introduction preceding a speech in Copenhagen. He began his remarks with "I was only the servant of my country."

Today's senior citizens in this country often feel neglected, not only by their adult children but also by a society that appears to have put them out to pasture. They vote often, so politicians pay attention to them. They don't seem to enjoy being old, even as it becomes well-known that old does not have to mean sick.

The Economist commented:

> *Yet the Americans are surely unique in their determination not to grow old gracefully. Last year, for example, they paid almost $2.8 million in cosmetic procedures, from 'tummy tucks' to hair transplants, which were designed either to adjust reality or to stave off the inevitable.*[22]

In a democracy, these people would have no one to blame but themselves for feelings of neglect. Opportunities to contribute would knock again and again.

A public-spirited official should be a generalist. In today's culture specialization is rewarded, so generalists are in short supply, but this would change. The ability to connect seemingly disparate issues requires such a person, because if collective wisdom resolves one issue while neglecting others that bear on it, the result is likely to cause more harm than good.

Citizens will ensure there are no opportunities for patronage available to their public officials. The old spoils system or "jobs for the boys" cannot function in the absence of extra money to compensate friends and family placed on the public payroll. An official may have a small staff of dedicated assistants. He and his staff will be paid little, and there will be practically no perks. If these people cared much about their salaries, they would not be serving. (Until 1855, members of Congress were not paid salaries, just travel costs and per diem.)

Just as everyone is an amateur philosopher, every citizen is an amateur politician. An important point for an official to bear in mind is that he or she does not "know the territory" nearly as well as do the constituents, even if he has lived in the neighborhood for a long time. This means that officials need inputs from those who know. Once this imperative has been assimilated, an official will actively seek those inputs, and contributors will feel good when providing them. In this way a symbiotic relationship will be established and maintained. All the political education the average citizen needs is what he already has: knowledge of the thoughts and feelings of himself and of those in the neighborhood or community. However, good intellects will be important during discussions.

People eventually die, and occasionally nations do also, as they lose their vitality and are then subject to outside control and possible oppression. Nations and their citizens can build vitality into their social fabric. The most effective way to do this is for people to preserve the freedom to improve themselves. Put another way, the people's vitality can maintain that of their government and vice versa. Jefferson said, "It is the manners and spirit of a people which preserve a republic in vigor."

Gray stated: "Tacit knowledge is that vast fund of practical, local, and traditional knowledge that is embodied in dispositions and forms of life and expressed in flair and intuition, which can never be formulated in rules of scientific method, say, and of which our theoretical or articulated knowledge is only the visible tip."[23] Gray's inference is that educated citizens can reach further into this latent storehouse, especially when stimulated through dialog with others. There have been many such instances in the past, when later on reflection a person concludes that "I didn't know I had it in me." Confucius said, "Learning without thought is labor lost; thought without learning is perilous."

Some of this is wisdom, as Paine indicated: "Whatever wisdom constituently is, it is like a seedless plant; it may be reared when it appears, but it cannot be voluntarily produced. There is always a sufficiency somewhere in the parts of society, it is continually changing its place. It rises in one today, in another tomorrow, and has most probably visited in rotation every family of the earth, and again withdrawn."[24]

Both of these observations testify to the importance of active inquiry on the part of a public servant. He must be sensitive to comments and arguments by citizens, he must listen intently, and he must remain open to a change in position on his own part (and admit it). Servants everywhere need guidance concerning their duties, that they be discharged in the most accurate and efficient manner.

Debates should take place within a defined ideology, because this will enlist support for getting things done. However, political leaders should become and remain sensitive to the gathering momentum for change and give it free play at a time deemed appropriate by all concerned.

In summary, a public-spirited public servant might bear this saying in mind: "Better to remain silent and be thought a fool, than to open one's mouth and remove all doubt."

Notes

1. Martin Gilbert, *Churchill: A Life.* Henry Holt, 1991.
2. Warren Bennis, *On Becoming a Leader.* Addison-Wesley, 1989.
3. Thomas Paine, *The Age of Reason.* Gramercy Books, 1993.
4. In Anne H. Burleigh, introduction in *Education in a Free Society.* Liberty Fund, 1973.
5. *The Economist,* "The Difference That Choice Makes." January 27, 2001, p. 78.
6. Jim Powell, *The Triumph of Liberty.* Free Press. 2000, p. 182.
7. James A. Michener, *This Noble Land: My Vision for America,* Random House 1996.
8. Murray Rothard, *For a New Liberty.* Fox and Wilkes, 1973.
9. *The Economist,* "Don't Mention the 'V' Word." November 29, 1997, p. 18.
10. William Safire, "Get on Board the Voucher Train." *News and Observer* (Raleigh, NC), August 2000 column.
11. Amity Schlaes, "School Vouchers; the Next Great Leap Forward." Introduction to the *Hoover Digest;* booklet.
12. Michael Ryan, "This School Demands Excellence . . . And Offers Hope." *Parade,* August 15, 1999, p. 10.

13. Kirk Ross and Debra Robiglio, "Kansas School's Success Coveted." *News and Observer,* November 1997 column.
14. Dorothy Sayers, essay in Burleigh, *Education in a Free Society.*
15. Thomas Paine, *Rights of Man.* Knopf, 1915.
16. Stephen Carter, *Integrity.* Basic Books, 1996.
17. Alexis de Tocqueville, *Democracy in America.* Knopf, 1972.
18. Alan M. Dershowitz, "An Unwelcoming Opening Prayer." *News and Observer* (Cambridge, MA), February 2, 2001, p. 15A.
19. *The Economist,* "A Minority Worth Cultivating." April 25, 1998, p. 21.
20. Eduard Shevardnadze, *The Future Belongs to Freedom.* Free Press, 1991.
21. William Peters, *A More Perfect Union: The Making of the United States Constitution.* Crown, 1987.
22. *The Economist,* "Venerable Elders." July 24, 1999, p. 51.
23. John Gray, *Beyond the New Right: Markets, Government and the Common Environment,* Routledge, 1993.
24. Paine, *Rights of Man.*

CHAPTER FOURTEEN: THE OPEN SOCIETY AND HONESTY IN GOVERNMENT

When you put your head in a hole to hide from the truth,
like an ostrich you don't always show your better parts.

—Author unknown

Alfred Schopenauer said, "All truth goes through three stages. In the first it is ridiculed. In the second it is violently opposed. In the third it is accepted as self-evident." One important truth is that no matter how much smoke and mirrors citizens get from the government, truth always lurks in the shadows.

This means that personal power seekers lead paranoid lives; they fear truth. They know that people assembled to discuss political issues are seeking truth. Mesmerized viewers of television don't talk much, and when they do they are not likely to discuss politics and government.

Thomas Paine wrote of honesty: "Of more worth is one honest man to society, and in the sight of God, than all the crowned ruffians that ever lived." In another context, he explained the importance of open government: "There is no place for mystery; nowhere for it to begin. Those who are not in the representation, know as much of the nature of business as those who are. An affectation of mysterious importance would therefore be scouted. Nations can have no secrets; and the secrets of the courts, like those of individuals, are always their defects." In the open society the occasional attempt at secrecy would immediately arouse curiosity and suspicion, just as in a healthy marriage.

This chapter will show that today the old saying "Honesty is the best policy" needs to be amended. It should read, "Honesty is the only policy."

A PARTY-LINE CULTURE

In view of the recent explosion in telecommunications technology, older people are challenged to recall the old rural party telephone line. A call for one household would ring in each of the other households on the same line; thus alerted, several other people might pick up their receivers and listen in. The result was few secrets in a typical small town. Today society is approaching a modernized version of the party line: an era where the only secrets will be some aspects of personal finance, the voting booth, and the bedroom.

There still are telephones and phone lines, but their functions are multiplying and the cost of their use is dropping at rates that strain credibility. Having made copper lines obsolete, fiber-optic cable can handle hundreds of thousands of transmissions simultaneously. A portable satellite terminal converts any place in the world into an instant phone booth. Dial up, and the message is relayed by satellites flying 20,000 miles up in the sky. They can relay calls, transmit faxes, and tap into databases almost anywhere.

Government officials around the world are used to being spied on by satellites owned by superpowers. Soon more sophisticated satellites will be available to private interests as well; anyone will be able to obtain a remarkably clear and detailed image of anything going on in any part of the world. As the definition of these images increases their cost decreases. Public officials have no practical choice other than to live with this condition. Put another way, they will have to come clean, for a change, and be honest.

There are cell phones, faxes, portable notebook, laptop and handheld computers, data, graphics, video transmissions, and two-way beepers. Moore's Law says that computing capacity doubles every eighteen months, and the cost of a computer has dropped to the point where they are occasionally even provided free to users. The forecast is that the cost of a phone call to anywhere in the world will approach zero. The conclusion is that no one needs to be wealthy to have access to this amazing litany of communication capacity.

It is rapidly becoming impractical to name a topic about which information is not available on the Internet. But this phenomenon cuts both ways. The millions of people who use the Internet do not realize how much personal data about them are being stored in massive databases, and these data are regularly sold and thus join other databases.

This process has been going on for decades; in the business sector it is called market research. But today there are differences—in the amount of information being acquired, in the depth of penetration into people's private lives, and in the speed of its diffusion among many users.

Private eyes have also been around for decades, but the tools of their trade have changed dramatically. They have cameras so small they can fit on a pair of glasses or inside a watch. Clear pictures can be made from up to a quarter-mile away. A device can be attached to a car that will record where it went, at what time, and how long it stayed there. What used to require hours or days can now be acquired in minutes on the Internet, including product preferences, insurance and criminal information, and even some medical data. This means that someone who lacks online sophistication can hire a private eye to collect information on another person or group, and it is not expensive.

The Economist recently published an article entitled "No Hiding Place for Anyone."[1] "The Hitachi chip is the world's smallest wireless identification device. It measures 0.4 millimeters square and is thin enough to be embedded in paper." The writer concluded with a warning: "By the same token, chips in clothing—linked to their owner's identity at the time of purchase—could mark the wearer's location anywhere on earth." One of these mini-tattlers costs less than twenty cents. Right now its broadcast range is only twelve inches, but future capacity and ability is another matter.

The debate about free flows of information—what is private, and what is public—is currently being settled by engineers, not politicians. This is the reality; the sooner people accept this fact and adjust to it, the less unhappy they will be. The clear implication is that in the future honesty will be the only policy.

Some authorities believe that a new field called biometrics will regain privacy for individuals. A person's face, fingerprint, voiceprint, hand geometry, and eye pupil are unique, and these things can be reliably measured. However, these characteristics can be used to penetrate existing privacy. Today these traits are hard to forge, but the future is problematic.

Konrad and Ames provided an implication.[2]

> *Major e-mail providers, such as Yahoo!, Microsoft's Hotmail, and America Online, would not provide specific information on the security of their products. But Yahoo! runs banner ads that boast, "Only you can see your Yahoo mail." In fact, products like Yahoo! mail are susceptible to "sniffer" programs, which are becoming increasingly popular. Carnivore, the FBI's online surveillance technology, is one of the best-known sniffers.*

For privacy advocates, this is surely cause for concern. Konrad and Ames continued: "Yahoo! announced in August that it would team with ZixIt, a Dallas-based encryption company, to let its e-mail account holders use data scrambling to protect the privacy of their messages." But big government had previously announced that it needs the ability to penetrate private emails to protect a vulnerable public against terrorists and other bad guys. Concerned citizens label this as a convenient rationale for deeper penetration into their private lives—yet another government restraint "sold" to them in the name of protecting their safety and freedom.

If the Yahoo! strategy works, how long will it do so? People seem to be obliged to continue their email and other communications business while betting on whether the government or the private sector will win this one. Unless citizens unite to take back their lost government, the odds will favor George Orwell's Big Brother.

The law of supply and demand works for a great variety of things, where a surplus of supply relative to demand forces the price downward (as already illustrated) and the reverse. The law also works with information: When demand exists for some kind of information that is not available, someone will find a way to fill the need. Government, however organized, will not be able to control the resulting flow.

For example, during the 1980s in Poland, samizdat (underground) publications numbered about 400, and circulation of some of them approached 30,000. The group of trade unions called Solidarity broke into government radio and TV programs with messages such as "Solidarity!" and "Resist!" In 1989 Poland's communist government crumbled; the presence of Solidarity was a contributing factor.

In this country the beating of Rodney King by police in Los Angeles would have been just another beating, but someone videotaped it, and dissemination of this information ignited a firestorm of protest. *The Economist* commented:

> *Nothing out of the ordinary; many of the poorer areas of Brazil's big cities are violent places. But two things combined to turn these incidents into a national scandal. First, the thugs were uniformed policemen. Second, residents had become so fed up that they arranged for the incidents to be filmed by concealed video cameramen. On April 7th, TV Globo showed policemen beating, punching and kicking a group of men lined up against a wall in Rio. . . . Almost a year ago, President Fernando Cardoso launched a national human rights plan meant to deal with such abuses. But progress has been slow . . . until the latest incidents.*[3]

Police and their superiors are having second thoughts.

A large quantity of documents was recently smuggled out of China. They were filched from Communist Party archives, and they describe in detail the events and thinking of top cadres that led to the events in Tian 'Anmen Square on June 4, 1989. Experts have examined the documents and determined them to be authentic. The mole who stole them said that the only place where a publisher would cooperate with him was in the United States.

News media in the United States cooperate with the elites in Washington to perpetuate the grand deception. This is why a recent report published in the *Washington Post* and the *Boston Globe* caused raised eyebrows. These newspapers displayed evidence that CIA operatives in 1991 who had joined the arms inspection team in Iraq had been given an assignment in addition to looking for weapons production and stockpiling: They were collecting information that could be used in toppling Saddam Hussein from power. This embarrassment to the administration may be a small indication that the open society is penetrating government secrecy. There was a demand for information, and someone filled it.

If a demand exists it could soon have an impact on election campaign money. Candidates and their campaign managers may indicate a willingness to divulge sources and amounts, but more trustworthy sources of information would be sought elsewhere. Demand for truth would force the news media to cooperate.

If the Johnson and (especially) the Nixon administrations had believed in the open society, they might have undermined the efforts of critics of the war in Vietnam. Whenever people feel that they are being denied information that affects them—not just in the pocketbook but also in terms of young lives—they will become angry. An unhappy populace played directly into the hands of the critics; their outrage eventually tipped the balance, forcing an end to the war. What is sad today is that instances of citizens forcing government to do anything are so few and far between.

Published in 1971, the Pentagon Papers gave details of government deception of the public regarding officials' waging of the Vietnam War. This revelation strongly reinforced public suspicions and thus hastened the withdrawal of US troops. It also underlined the importance of cooperation of the news media if the government was to continue the grand deception (the papers were published by the *New York Times*). Unfortunately, instances of news media criticism of government policies have since become even more rare.

China's famous leader Mao Zedong once said, "Let a hundred flowers bloom. Let a hundred schools of thought contend." The Chinese quickly learned that he did not mean it; tight control of information continued as before. Wei Jingsheng is just one man, but once a dissident grows prominent, an authoritarian regime finds it internationally embarrassing to execute him. Beginning in 1978, when he was imprisoned for writing messages promoting democracy, Wei has fought the regime, and until his departure from China had spent more time in prison than out. Today he is in the United States with his health restored, but he has not given up. He leads a dissident group that smuggles messages by the hundreds into China.

Congress organized a Radio Free Asia station, patterned after Radio Free Europe, which operated successfully during the cold war. It broadcasts criticisms of China's government to citizens in that vast nation. Needless to say, top officials in that country's government are unhappy because their control of information about what they are doing is being undermined.

A little reflection leads to the conclusion that this is a part of the democratic process: different ideas brought into a community or nation for consideration by citizens as an alternative to the present regime. If members of Congress believe in freedom of information and democracy, as they often say they do, then they could hardly object if China were to set up a radio or TV station and broadcast into this country criticisms of its government. This station would fill a demand that domestic news media steadfast;y refrain from filling.

Washington might jam the signal, just as the Soviets did years ago, but sooner or later citizens would wonder about this denial of information. Their concern would cause demand to intensify. Someone would see an opportunity and cast about among many alternative communications media to find a way to fill it (fortunately, entrepreneurship still exists in this country). Both governments and all others need to rethink their policies of withholding information from concerned citizens.

Some of these citizens might ask, What about Big Brother? They are probably referring to George Orwell's famous book *1984*, which was published in 1949. In this novel, Big Brother is an overpowering and impersonal government whom no one knows anything about. There is a "telescreen" in every room that monitors all movement and sound. "Thought police" screen every thought, and there is complete and utter regimentation of everyone by an unseen power. "War is peace; Ignorance is strength; Freedom is slavery." These slogans are promulgated over and over again as truths.

Adams noted,

> *What is most likely to occur, and most frightening, is that our Social Security cards will become like our VISA cards and MasterCards. With every commercial transaction we undertake, the card will be zipped through the little computers they now use in almost every store. . . . Instantly everything we do could be recorded on our record at the tax bureau, a record that will be no longer private as it once was. A paranoid president or FBI chief could instantly know just about everything about you . . . your beliefs, actions, probably what you are thinking, and where you are at the moment.*[4]

Openness is a strength in an economic world, where the merchant has replaced the warrior. Strength will be derived indirectly from a weakness caused by futile attempts by some governments, companies, and individuals to maintain secrets. Secrecy was important in the era of conquest and plunder, as the element of surprise made for a significant advantage over an enemy. But trade is not a zero-sum game, where any gain on the part of one participant must come at the expense of others. Rather, whenever parties agree to a **voluntary** transaction, both must feel they will gain from it or there will be no transaction.

Artists and performers complain loudly about bootleg videos, fake reproductions of works of art, plagiarism of the written word, and unauthorized reprints. Napster was an online company that made music available free to anyone with a computer and modem. The artists have a point in that royalties are an important part of their reward for effort expended. Patents protect inventors, they rightfully argue.

There are so many methods of piracy in the market that talented people have diminished incentives to create because of insufficient compensation. For example, there are practically no famous native folk singers today in Vietnam because tapes and records of their songs are instantly pirated, thus denying them royalties.

In the open society, if someone sets up a copying facility in a basement, someone will soon find out about it. If such a facility should happen to be located in Vietnam, say, that someone has only to take out a cell phone, punch in some numbers, and word would go immediately to a local law-enforcement agency.

But this might not protect artists from companies like Napster (which is now defunct). Another alternative open to artists is to invite competitive bids from companies who are organized to assume the risk of success or failure of the creation and also to fight the pirates. The artist would sell all rights to a creation for a lump sum or a series of payments. Just as in any transaction, with this arrangement there is a risk for both parties. The creation might not sell as projected, in which case the company would lose. On the other hand it might sell mightily, in which case the artist would miss out.

For example, inexperienced author Margaret Mitchell probably settled for a pittance for her classic novel *Gone With the Wind.* (Spin-offs are still churning out money sixty-five years later.) This sounds unfair, until the buying company's viewpoint is brought forth: Here is an unproven author, so there is a high risk in accepting this deal. However, once an artist has acquired a reputation, the shoe is on the other foot.

A computer hacker might become frustrated, penetrate the medical files of many patients, and sprinkle them with bad data or even erase them. But if this happens there would be a need established for information. Recently there was a story about just such a person, but another hacker penetrated his operation and caught him.

In Europe the TV industry is highly regulated, and there has been a backlash against incursions by programs made by US studios. But if viewers demand these programs, even governments cannot ban them. There are ways to bring them to customers that governments cannot control. European producers have three options: accept the reality, get more creative and make program content that can meet the competition, or find some other line of business.

If citizens permit the establishment of a police state in this country, citizens could learn what is going on, but they could not act without bloodshed. Every type of government except a democratic one has a keen interest in prying into citizens' personal lives. Public officials know their subjects are unhappy, and they know that insurrections are most efficiently nipped in the bud. They spread their tentacles accordingly. But this phenomenon cuts both ways: Citizens can utilize free flows of information to control their government rather than the reverse. However, they must organize and act before it is too late.

PROJECTED METAMORPHOSIS

Benjamin Franklin said, "I must express my dislike of everything that tends to debase the spirit of the common people. If honesty is often the companion of wealth and if poverty is exposed to peculiar temptation, it is not less true that the possession of property increases the desire of more property. Some of the greatest rogues I was ever acquainted with were the richest rogues." Those who are not caught share a dishonest destiny. The richer the rogue, the easier it is for him to cover his tracks. He might even buy silence today. But the future will not be so easy.

James Madison spoke of a press that was free but not yet mature.

> *It is better to leave a few of [the press's] noxious branches to their luxuriant growth than, by pruning them away, to injure the vigor of those yielding the proper fruits. . . . And can the wisdom of this policy be doubted by any who reflect that to the press alone, checquered as it is with abuses, the world is indebted for all the triumphs which have been gained by reason and humanity over error and oppression?*

Madison left open the question of who will assist the press toward maturity and keep it there once attained. In a democracy the answer to this question is the market. If the people demand honesty and truth, a news medium that does not supply them is soon out of business.

During the post–September 11, 2001 months there was a plethora of ink concerning new legislation increasing the ability of big government to spy on citizens. Any authoritarian regime collects private information on its citizens, either clandestinely or openly whenever officials know citizens can do nothing about it. For example, in any war or warlike situation privacy advocates are obviously put at a disadvantage. Knowing this, government quickly puts more laws into force aimed at deeper penetration into citizens' private lives. They are practically never repealed; thus oppression by government continues to grow over the decades. (Fully aware of this negative tug, President Bush reinforced it when he declared "war" right after the attacks.)

Then officials withhold information about government operations from the public. In this way they maintain personal power over the downtrodden masses, and making it very difficult to dislodge the regime. The mass media help by generally publishing only what government permits. In any situation suggesting conflict, however remote, the national security ruse is trotted out to provide a convenient shroud behind which the elites operate as they see fit.

In a democracy spying is still practiced, but the direction is reversed. That is, citizens are constantly spying on their government at various levels in order to hold public officials' feet to the fire. In this political environment the media also cooperate, but with citizens and not big government. Utilizing the art of investigative reporting, they publish what government is doing, criticize it, and help communicate to public servants what citizens want government to do on their behalves. Officials help citizens govern by broadcasting their thinking and actions. In this way information flows both ways in a truly open society.

To demand truth seems easy, and yet it has rarely been successfully done. Lings noted: "If it can be said that man collectively shrinks back more and more from the Truth, it can also be said that on all sides the Truth is closing in more and more upon man. It might almost be said that, in order to receive a touch of It, which in the past required a lifetime of effort, all that is asked of him now is not to shrink back. And yet how difficult that is!"[5] This explains why the demand has not stuck, and the media continue with business as usual. The answer lies in courage, in free and open debate, and in good leaders to help citizens focus on the objective and the process.

Stephen Carter's book advanced eight principles to guide the return of government and society to a politics of integrity.[6]

1. "The nation exists for its people." Carter argued that the "elite mentality" should be discarded. This mentality suggests that Washington has all the answers to social problems if only the riffraff would go along. The elites think that the people should not be heard but rather be manipulated: ". . . As the clay rather than the potters." In 1992 Ross Perot said Capitol Hill was the only place he knows of where the employees can park and the owners cannot. Today the reality is that the phrase "politics of integrity" is a contradiction in terms.
2. "Some things are more important than others. Ever since the 1970s, voters have been electing presidents who promise a government that is smaller and . . . more controllable. That is, the American people quite sensibly see government size as related to government accountability."
3. "Consistency matters. . . . a politics of integrity requires that the principles for which our parties and institutions stand truly be treated as principles. A principle is not a principle if we will bend it to help our friends."
4. "Everybody gets to play." Carter pointed out that a law requiring a private restaurant business to admit certain types of people as customers infringes on the right of property. This observation is interesting from another viewpoint: Carter is African American. However, the owner of any business who discriminates based on skin color is also discriminating against his or her own body: cutting off one's nose to spite one's face. There are almost no private businesses that can thrive through consistent and arbitrary discrimination, but the principle of property rights stands just the same.
5. "We must be willing to talk about right and wrong without mentioning the Constitution. I say this as a longtime teacher of constitutional law and as one who truly loves our foundational document. . . . Individual rights are a good thing, but to make a cult of individualism can lead to social disaster."

Carter pointed directly to the cause: "Our well-known national inability to engage in moral conversation means that once a right exists, nobody seems to feel comfortable urging that it not be exercised." The reality here is that lawyers have smothered moral conversation, because they insist that every moral issue is instead legal. Put another way, urging is preferable to force. The Bill of Rights provides freedoms, but it says nothing about the morality of their exercise. It can and does intend to protect citizens' basic freedoms, but not from their foolish and immoral utilization of them to break apart the society into mutually alienated fragments. If the people but knew what they are doing to themselves, and if they could clearly see a better way, they would change their thinking and behavior.

6. "Our politics must call us to our higher selves. . . . We must respond to politicians who talk of the national interest and our shared obligations, not merely those who promise to enrich us." This argument refers to leadership in public officials, which is addressed in Chapter 16.
7. "We must listen to one another. A politics of integrity is a politics in which all of us are willing to do the hard work of discernment, to test our views to be sure that we are right. . . . This in turn implies a dialog, for in the course of our reflections, especially in a democracy, it is vital to listen to the views of our fellow citizens."
8. "Sometimes the other side wins. This is, perhaps, the most important principle of an integral democratic politics, and yet little need be said about it." Carter referred to a top-flight tennis match that took place years ago between amateur Ted Schroeder and Pancho Gonzalez. Gonzalez served a ball that landed inside the service area, and that Schroeder was unable to return, thus giving his opponent the point. Both players and the crowd saw it that way. But the line umpire called the serve outside, and the referee would not overrule him. Schroeder deliberately did not attempt to return the next serve, thus giving Gonzalez the point that he had earned previously. In the end, Schroeder lost a close match, but he preserved his integrity. It is worth reflecting whether such a scenario is likely to occur in high-level competition today.

Bennis elaborated on the return to individualist honesty: "Knowing Yourself . . . means separating who you are and who you want to be from what the world thinks you are and wants you to be."[7] Most citizens find it more convenient to just muddle through life.

"No one can teach you how to become yourself, to take charge, to express yourself, except you. But there are some things that others have done that are useful to think about in the process. I've organized them as the four lessons of self-knowledge. They are:

One: You are your own best teacher.

Two: Accept responsibility. Blame no one.
Three: You can learn anything you want to learn.
Four: True understanding comes from reflecting on your experience.

Nothing is truly yours until you understand it . . . not even yourself. Our feelings are raw, unadulterated truth, but until we understand why we are happy or angry or anxious, the truth is useless to us."

The educational system in this country is aimed at measuring up to someone else's standards, such as those of parents, teachers, coaches, and clergy. These people are useful as learning resources, but they cannot be expected to understand an adult person's inner self, especially when that person does not understand (and, it could be argued, a person is not an adult until he or she does understand).

The citizen in a democracy needs an honest and open government. The reality is that government by the people cannot function in the absence of reliable information, which citizens use to guide discussions among themselves and also the behavior of their public servants. In the Age of Reason the timeworn ruse of national security, used for centuries as an excuse for withholding information from the public, is no longer credible. This book will show that the Age of Reason and the open society would work together if citizens truly desire a better future (Part V).

Disseminating information about government to the citizenry serves two purposes of major importance. One purpose is making available new ideas, arguments, and recommendations to many people for discussion, criticism, and debate; the other is airing dirty laundry or revealing skullduggery. If people talk among themselves the first purpose will be served simply because conscientious and responsible media will not be able to remain aloof from the democratic process. Reporters will want to know what political issues people are concerned about, and so they will be active in seeking relevant information. Furthermore, there will be no problem with dirty laundry because concerned citizens will be hypersensitive to this issue and the media will know it and act accordingly. The market will govern the actions of the news media, forcing companies to fill customers' needs for information.

The question arises: Will democracy create politicians who are uniformly honest? Today's citizen may see this possibility as difficult to imagine. However, if the people do the governing they would talk with one another about politics and governing, and the news media would cooperate. A dishonest politician would soon stick out like a sore thumb. He or she and others of like mind would be accountable to their bosses, or be summarily thrown out of office by them at the next opportunity.

Continuous video on the Internet might reduce a challenger's need for big money while campaigning, because this medium would be far cheaper than TV for getting the message out. However, a voter would still need to be able to distinguish truth from lies, and this means active participation in government.

To date, career politicians in national and state governments have been getting away with rampant chicanery. A recent development in the country of Ethiopia can be used to illustrate a relevant point. In past decades, public officials in that country have behaved like terrorists in treatment of their own citizens. Predictably, there was a revolution. Now a new government is paying lawyers to defend those previously in charge as they go to trial for genocide and other crimes against humanity. Ordinary citizens who have seen relatives and friends tortured and killed especially appreciate the trials.

The point being made relates directly to human nature. That is, if anyone, politician or otherwise, thinks there is a real risk of being caught and brought to account, he or she would think long and hard before acting on negative tugs. The incentive applies as much to financial wrongdoing as it does to the physical variety.

In contrast, today's congressional Ethics Committees "investigate" abuses by their own members as a foil before the public; then they administer slaps on wrists with great fanfare. But this hardly comes as a surprise, as fraternity brothers typically stick together.

Tocqueville noted in 1830:

> *The federal government does confer power and renown on those who direct it, but only a few can exercise influence there. . . . It is in the township, the center of the ordinary business of life, that the desire for esteem, the pursuit of substantial interests, and the taste for power and self-advertisement are concentrated; these passions, so often troublesome ailments in society, take on a different character when exercised close to home and, in a sense, within the family circle.*[8]

Maximize the number of local public offices compared with state and federal, raise money where it is to be spent, and the question of accountability is more easily manageable. Accountability encourages—nay—forces, official behavior based on the positive side of human nature.

A logical conclusion is that the country would function more efficiently if each individual no longer needed to wonder about the nature of the hidden agenda that lurked behind every piece of published information (who paid for it). Also, with honesty prevailing in society it would be far more difficult to get away with a lie; people would have acquired the ability to distinguish truth from lies.

In his book *Trust,* Fukuyama argued that the information revolution "will spell the end of hierarchy of all sorts . . . political, economic, and social."[9] The result "will be a devolution of power downward to the people and a liberation of everyone from the constraints of the centralized, tyrannical organizations in which they once worked."

This encouraging prognosis can be realized only if there is an ample supply of citizens who are properly educated and committed (Chapter 13). With such people involved in both private- and public-sector activities, Fukuyama concluded: "With technologically powered communications, good information will drive out bad information, the honest and industrious will shun the fraudulent and parasitic, and people will come together voluntarily for beneficial common purposes."

The Economist projected a role for the Internet in this scenario, arguing that government should not attempt to regulate it.[10]

> *This entirely new sort of communication poses several new sorts of problems for would-be regulators. Two matter particularly. Intrinsic to the Internet is its ability to leap borders. . . . Second, regulation has traditionally distinguished between public and private communication: you can say things in a bar that you could never say on television. But the Internet is both a private conduit for messages between individuals, and a public one.*

This fact causes confusion, which *The Economist* attempted to resolve. "And where the Internet provides access to more pornography and hate speech than governments can stomach, it also provides the tools to let their citizens protect themselves. Thus can a little technology, backed by a global network, replace a lot of government." Self-disciplined people can and will protect themselves from the undesirable aspects of cyberspace, just as they do when they refrain from, say, attending a violent film in a theater.

Moral discipline constitutes a vital component of individualism, which is in turn a vital component of democracy. It is individual people restraining themselves through their own morality, not big government restraining individuals with one-size-fits-all, top-down laws.

Lord Acton said,

> *I exhort you never to debase the moral currency or to lower the standard of rectitude, but to try others by the final maxim that governs your own lives, and to suffer no man and no cause to escape the undying penalty which history has the power to inflict on wrong. . . . History does teach that right and wrong are real distinctions. Opinions alter, manners change, creeds rise and fall, but the moral law is written on the tablets of eternity.*[11]

Naturally, the tablets of eternity are still around, but they have gathered so much dust that they are hard to read.

The Economist continued: "Ultimately the Internet could breed a new approach to regulation, less paternalistic and more trusting in market forces." But the oligarchy is hard at work figuring out how to regulate the Internet. They know very well the implications if they fail. No oligarchy can survive as such unless members of the elite class can control the information made available to the public (Chapter 9).

The Economist concluded: "Citizens who have the power to take such actions on their own may be harder for governments to protect, but they will also need less government protection. That freedom can make adults of us all." This conclusion elicits the memory of a part of Emma Lazarus's poem, which is inscribed in bronze at the base of the Statue of Liberty: "Give me your tired, your poor, your huddled masses, yearning to breathe free." To this profound exhortation might be added "and adult."

One of history's foremost scientists and thinkers, Isaac Newton, concealed from publication some of his writing because it ventured outside the bounds of the conventional wisdom of the time. He was afraid he would lose his tenured position at Cambridge University. Therefore scientists continued in their research to build on existing theory while remaining ignorant of some of Newton's monumental work.

MUTUAL TRUST, BUT ALSO ETERNAL VIGILANCE

Early immigrants to the New World had to face the heartache of parting with members of their extended families, along with the very real possibility that they would never again be united. This meant that once settled in their adopted country, they had to reach out to neighbors who were not family members and often came from different ethnic backgrounds. Each pioneer delivered on his promise, as he had no way of knowing when he would need help from the very neighbor he was helping in the first place. In this way a tradition of tolerance and mutual trust was built.

Putnam wrote: "A society that relies on generalized reciprocity is more efficient than a distrustful society. . . . Honesty and trust lubricate the inevitable frictions of social life."[12] In contrast, a society whose members don't trust each other gradually becomes infested with laws and lawyers. Putnam concluded: "In short, people who trust others are all-round good citizens, and those more engaged in community life are both more trusting and trustworthy." Reaching out gets to know, and mutual trust logically follows. But the favorite evening activity for today's typical family is watching TV.

Fukuyama commented:

> *Traditional sociability can be said to be loyalty to older, long-established social groups. Medieval producers following the economic doctrines of the Catholic Church fall into this category. Spontaneous sociability, by contrast, is the ability to come together and cohere in new groups, and to thrive in innovative organizational settings. Spontaneous sociability is likely to be helpful from an economic standpoint, only if it is used to build wealth-creating economic organizations. Traditional sociability, on the other hand, can frequently be an obstacle to growth.*[13]

For early citizens, necessity was the mother of invention. They were reared in a traditional European environment, but on arrival in the New World it was either change or perish. The long legacy in Europe of kings and queens imbued in them a belief in the PANG principle (People are No Good). It was in large part the rejection of this legacy that drove pioneers to risk a perilous ocean crossing and an uncertain life afterward.

Harris's observation brought out the individualism in a person, and also a need for and ability to work through others.[14] "I am a person. You are a person. Without you I am not a person, for only through you is language made possible and only through language is thought made possible, and only through thought is humanness made possible. You have made me important. Therefore, I am important and you are important. If I devalue you, I devalue myself."

The implication of mutual trust pervades this remark. Fukuyama added: "One of the most important lessons we can learn from an examination of economic life is that a nation's well-being, as well as its ability to compete, is conditioned by a single, pervasive cultural characteristic: the level of trust inherent in the society."

Arab businessmen frequently wear dark glasses when negotiating contracts, because they believe that a negotiator's eyes involuntarily dilate when he hears something in which he is keenly interested. Often a sound negotiating strategy involves not laying all the cards on the table at once. The objective, of course, is mutual trust, because before an agreement is struck all cards possessed by both parties will come forth. Trust involves sharing of information, but it is more than this.

With a communal feeling widespread and trust an important currency of choice, few laws will be needed. Tocqueville wrote that US citizens were enthusiastic joiners of organizations, which created links across ethnic groups.[15] He considered it most important that their interactions were guided by a shared moral vision. More recently, researchers are finding that people do less and less together. This trend is disturbing in that it tends to cause a loss of trust in government, and in one another.

Henry Stimson was born in New York City, educated at Harvard and Yale Universities, and served as secretary of state under President Hoover. Henry Kissinger is a Jewish man who was born in Germany whose family suffered through part of the Holocaust before coming to this country. He too served as secretary of state, under Presidents Nixon and Ford. Isaacson wrote:

> *Henry Stimson, lived by the maxim he learned at Yale's Skull and Bones [a secret society] that the only way to earn a man's trust is to trust him. Kissinger, on the other hand, was more like Nixon: he harbored an instinctive distrust of colleagues and outsiders alike. Stimson rejected the notion of a spy service by say-*

> *ing that "gentlemen do not read other people's mail;" Nixon and Kissinger established a series of secret wiretaps on the phones of even their closest aides.*[16]

The contrast is stark; it is difficult to imagine that a government or any other organization can be administered under the outlook shared by the latter two men.

It has been shown that during the eighteenth and nineteenth centuries citizens made law in this country (indirectly, through their representatives). Phillips commented on the present situation: "America's curse-of-the-one-million-lawyers will be a hard one to shake. Too much of the nation's current overabundance of lawyers, legalism, and litigation is the product of a two-century evolution. Moreover, reversing the situation faces a slight technical hitch: the lawyers in the White House, Congress, the courts, and the state legislatures are the people who make the laws."[17] This reality flies in the face of the Constitution, which specifies that law evolves through citizen consent. The implication in that document has consent emanating from active participation by citizens in the law-making process.

Today's lawyers in government and their immediate predecessors have had several decades of experience in passing laws that create more work for lawyers. They have betrayed that vital ingredient of any healthy society—mutual trust and confidence. Without trust disputes can be settled by negotiations between honest citizens far less often. Recourse is thus made to litigation, which has seen explosive growth over the past thirty years.

P. J. O'Rourke offered a cryptic comment on the situation today: "A little government and a little luck are necessary in life, but only a fool trusts either of them."[18] This observation provides a fitting introduction to the notion of vigilance.

Someone said, "Eternal vigilance is the price of liberty." It is human nature to seek personal power over other people; this means that someone somewhere will always be nibbling at the edges of citizens' liberty. Relax vigilance, and the nibbling changes to gobbling.

Accountability is another name for vigilance. The farther away an organization is located from those who must hold it accountable the larger it becomes, the more money it attracts, the greater the challenge placed before those who are responsible, and hence the greater the effort required to control it. Because Washington is the one level of government most remote from citizens, it should be trusted the least.

The explanation lies in human nature, but honest citizens find it nonetheless amazing. A rough rule of thumb might be 75 percent of the thinking, debate, and actions of government should take place locally, 20 percent at county and state levels, and trust just 5 percent to Washington. Even the latter powers should be selected with great care and spelled out in detail and in plain English, such that the average citizen could ascertain for him- or herself that those powers are not being abused (as Jefferson recommended).

Browne provided a useful guideline for action:

> *And each reduction in government has to be complete. Reducing an agency to a small fraction of its current size leaves intact the mechanism by which it can grow again. Like a weed it has to be pulled out by the roots . . . not cut back. In each case, there are only two choices: 1. Get rid of the program and get rid of it quickly; or 2. Resign ourselves to living with it forever. There is no middle ground.*[19]

Perhaps the most effective way to remove a program is to cut off the money supply and then watch closely to be sure other public money does not find its way to the bureaucrats.

Another aspect about accountability needs discussion. If a nation has seen abuse in government in the past it should be rectified, but some provision should also be made to guard against future abuse of trust in public officials. This suggests discussion of what should be done to discipline or punish public malfeasance. Citizens should take up this subject in their deliberations and make decisions. However, they should not be lulled into believing that, once punishment has been meted out, future vigilance is no longer necessary. Public officials, however well intentioned at the beginning, always need to clearly understand that if they deceive the public they will be caught **and** punished. Rule of Law means exactly that.

History (and popular opinion) has shown that perhaps President Ford should not have pardoned Nixon. Due in large part to this pardon, succeeding presidents may have felt free to skirt the bounds of law. To date none have been punished, and so the democratic principle of Rule of Law has been rendered almost entirely impotent.

A citizen can prepare for the open society and for mutual trust by resolving to be an honest person. Such resolutions traditionally occur in profusion with every New Year's celebration, but in the future there will be good government setting the example, so the impact on individuals will be different. Mutual trust will replace mutual alienation and contempt. Without secrets there will be trust: People will rely on information received, and they will feel obligated to reciprocate in a similar manner. Lives will be improved through better decisions based on more reliable information.

Effort and persistence will be needed. However, honest efforts by honest people treating one another with mutual trust and respect will go a long way toward reducing insincerity and deception. As hearts unite, heads will be held higher.

Jefferson said "that truth is great and will prevail if left to herself, that she is the proper and sufficient antagonist to error, and has nothing to fear from the conflict, unless by human interposition disarmed of her natural weapons, free argument and debate, errors ceasing to be dangerous when it is permitted freely to contradict them."

Notes

1. *The Economist* Technology Quarterly, "No Hiding Place for Anyone." September 22, 2001, p. 10.
2. Rachel Konrad and Sam Ames, "So, You Think You're Protected." *News and Observer* (Raleigh, NC), October 22, 2000, p. 4E.
3. *The Economist,* "Policing the Police." April 12, 1997, p. 42.
4. Charles Adams, *For Good and Evil: The Impact of Taxes on the Course of Civilization.* Madison Books, 1993.
5. Martin Lings, *Ancient Beliefs and Modern Superstitions.* Perennial Books, 1964.
6. Stephen Carter, *Integrity.* Basic Books, 1996.
7. Warren Bennis, *On Becoming a Leader.* Addison-Wesley, 1989.
8. Alexis de Tocqueville, *Democracy in America.* Knopf, 1972.
9. Francis Fukuyama, *Trust.* Free Press, 1995.
10. *The Economist,* "Hands Off the Internet." July 5, 1997, p. 15.
11. John Emerich Acton, in Jim Powell, *The Triumph of Liberty.* Free Press 2000, p. 350.
12. Robert Putnam, *Bowling Alone: The Collapse and Revival of American Community.* Simon and Schuster, 2000.
13. Fukuyama, *Trust.*
14. Thomas A. Harris, *I'm Okay; You're Okay.* Avon Books, 1973.
15. Tocqueville, *Democracy in America.*
16. Walter Isaacson, *Kissinger: A Biography.* Simon and Schuster, 1992.
17. Kevin Phillips, *Arrogant Capital.* Little, Brown, 1994.
18. P. J. O'Rourke, *A Parliament of Whores.* Atlantic Monthly Press, 1991.
19. Harry Browne, *Why Government Doesn't Work.* St. Martin's Press, 1995.

Chapter Fifteen:
A Good Tax System and the Future Taxpayer

The power to tax is the power to destroy.
— John Marshall

The need for some government has been established, so the old adage that says the only certain things in this life are death and taxes has some truth in it. This chapter will inquire into what could be the parts of a citizen-friendly tax system, and suggest guidelines for citizens as they make their own tax decisions in such a system.

The original tax system in ancient Greek city-states demanded little from the taxpayer. A tradition of liturgy was established, whereby the rich voluntarily contributed to public projects. Sometimes rich donors competed for the honor of sponsoring an endeavor, and they frequently managed execution of the project. Progressive taxation was not necessary.

In his book on taxation, Adams showed that what happened a few centuries later was to be repeated many times over in the future.[1] As tax loads gradually grew more onerous, revolts and civil wars took place as other city-states were bled dry to support the upper class in Athens. Eventually the Peloponnesian War drained Athens's treasury, because the other cities would not pay more. As a result, ancient Greek civilization faded into history. The lesson to be learned from the repetition of this experience over centuries is that at first tax systems emphasize voluntary activity, only to phase into coercive actions later, and eventually to revolts as the negative tugs of human nature come into full play.

During the Middle Ages there was in England a Great Council to whom the king had to apply for money to wage war. But the council would not grant money unless the proposal was for a defensive war. Adams wrote, "The rights of Englishmen would be secure as long as the king was denied the power to tax permanently. Each year the process of debate and bargain for taxes would repeat itself." In the English government after the signing of the Magna Carta in 1215 the king could spend money but he could not tax the people to collect it; Parliament could levy taxes, but it could not spend money.

King Henry VIII got around this restraint on spending by appropriating the English assets of the Roman Catholic Church. He had Parliament proclaim him supreme ruler of the Church in England; in this way, new taxes were not needed. But even this was not enough, and Henry ran up a colossal national debt that took his eventual successor, Queen Elizabeth I, fifteen years to retire.

Queen Elizabeth I was a unique ruler. 'Never before nor since has a monarch behaved toward taxation the way she did. . . . She decided to be loved by her subjects and accept what revenue they were willing to give her. It was Elizabeth who said, To tax and be loved is not given to man.' Elizabeth did not ask Parliament for money. If revenues were small—and they were—then her government would adjust to what Parliament provided."

Low taxes permit economic growth because scarce resources are not drained off into the public sector where much is squandered, a lot is spent inefficiently, and none is productively invested in the private sector. The record is convincing: Queen Elizabeth's reign (1558–1603) launched the dawn of the British empire.

For most of US history, government was small and demanded little. Budget surpluses were the norm up until the end of the 1950s. It was only the Civil War that caused a tax on personal income to be enacted; afterward it was repealed, not to reappear until 1913. Adams reported that the Sixteenth Amendment to the Constitution passed only because politicians promised that the tax rate would never exceed a few percentage points.

Up until the Franklin Roosevelt administration (1933–45) economists favored taxes that matched benefits received by taxpayers as closely as practical. Sennholz wrote: "Government activity consisted primarily of defense and police protection of the basic human rights: life, liberty, and property. These benefits of activity were believed to be proportionate to income, which justified proportionate taxation. Classical economists from Adam Smith to John Stuart Mill favored proportionate taxation as the most equitable distribution of tax burdens."[2] (Proportionate means everyone was taxed at the same percentage, together with an implied lighter burden on the poor).

Early in the twentieth century, the influence of the writing of Karl Marx and others began to infiltrate the thinking of economists. From subsequent writing and discussions came the doctrine of ability to pay. Marx wrote: "From each according to his ability, to each according to his need." This doctrine introduced the notion of the progressive income tax, where those with higher incomes were taxed at a higher rate. The rationale was that they had more property to be protected by the taxpayer even if they had no additional life and liberty. The argument that they could afford to hire any additional protection that they freely chose to be necessary was apparently ignored.

This transposition got the government into a new business—that of redistributing income from wealthy to poor in accordance with decisions made by public officials who presumably knew best how and where to spend someone else's money. It also provided an opportunity to dramatically expand national government revenues. The 1913 promise to keep tax rates down to a few percentage points was forgotten.

Although the original impetus was based on the positive side of human nature, the growing presence of massive amounts of money over the decades since 1913 predictably excited the negative side into action. Personal power concentrated among politicians on Capitol Hill, as special interests seeking tax breaks and other favors poured their money into congressional reelection campaign coffers. Interest groups' power was also concentrated, but that of the taxpayer remained dispersed. Even if a citizen could see what was going on, organizing to resist this new tax system was perceived as not worth the effort. This conclusion meant that the process could continue indefinitely (and Chapter 5 demonstrated that it has).

It is interesting to observe that the media publish practically nothing concerning thoughts and recommendations regarding a good tax system. Thinking citizens therefore have no food for thought available to them. Big government does not want citizens thinking about tax systems.

Citizens Taxing Themselves in a Democracy

In a republic citizens consent to measures proposed by their representatives in government. In a democracy the citizens govern themselves, and public officials respond to their initiatives for taxation and other actions of government. Although not widely known and appreciated, this distinction is important. Although not purely coercive, the former is a top-down approach to tax making.

In a republic it is very easy to assume citizen consent. President Bush (Sr.) once said that the people must approve of what he was doing, or they would not have elected him. In general, he governed opposite to what he said he would do while campaigning.

In a democracy people support what they help create. Taxes are generally paid voluntarily, even though they are backed by force of law to bring in money from the occasional recalcitrant citizen.

When taxes are high, the recalcitrant citizen is no longer an occasional occurrence. In Chapter 10 W. H. Chamberlain described how high income tax rates drain away a family's reserves and thus indirectly force it to seek "socialized everything. The personal income tax has made the individual vastly more dependent on the state and more avid for state handouts."

The Economist commented:

Consider the three things that most governments now demand of their tax systems. First, they expect to raise enough revenue to pay for their own activities. . . . They want to redistribute income from those with more to those with less. Lastly, they want to give tax advantages to causes deemed worthy, or at least popular. . . . After a half century of experimenting, it is clear that these goals are simply too much for any one tax system to deliver. Indeed, the first objective is taxing enough. . . . Unfortunately, it is also a necessary cost of government. . . .

The other two, however, are not. And they wreak havoc with the goal of raising revenue efficiently. . . . The ease with which these favors can be dished out makes them irresistible to politicians and voters alike . . . dole out a juicy tax break . . . the extra taxes that everyone else must pay are safely hidden away.[3]

Every year lobbyists come again into town, laden with dirty money aimed at keeping existing breaks and loopholes and prying open new ones.

Milton Friedman said that government cannot give anything to anyone unless it first takes it away from another by force of law. Government has no business in giving back to taxpayers some of their own money, after the bureaucracy in Washington has skimmed 25 percent off the top and met roughly $750 billion of other taxpayer-financed expenses. Rather, public officials at national level should provide requested services only, and citizens should ensure that those services are limited to those which they themselves and local and state government cannot conveniently provide.

There are two possible reasons why Adams's vicious circle has not yet caused a taxpayer revolt. One is there is such wealth everywhere that even though people realize that they are being taken in, they don't feel it in the pocketbook as keenly as did those in bygone eras. Another reason points to a new deception: People believe politicians when they say that every dollar of projected fiscal surpluses will go toward saving Social Security and/or paying down the national debt.

Surpluses in the Social Security pension fund have been accumulating for about thirty years, but instead of saving them for future needs the government has spent every dime and left IOUs in the account. When 2020 arrives and members of the massive postwar baby boom generation begin to retire in great numbers, trillions of dollars that should have been saved will not be there when the pension fund plunges into deep deficit.

Browne suggested a radical solution to this huge problem: Sell national government lands to nonprofit trusts and private individuals, who will continue to operate them for the benefit of the public.[4] This idea has merit in many instances because management by bureaucrats is often poor, and the land is suitable mainly and sometimes only for public recreation.

He said if this were done, "Everyone who has become dependent on social security can receive a private annuity. We can balance the budget. . . . We can pay off the entire accumulated federal debt by the year 2003." (Browne's book *Why Government Doesn't Work* was written in 1995, when he ran for president.)

Sennholz observed that during the period from the end of the Civil War in 1865 until the beginning of World War I unbelievable change and advancement took place. "The degree of individual freedom that prevailed during this period led to an expansion of economic activity and an accumulation of capital unmatched in human history. Neither before nor since has a more rapid rate of growth been experienced by a group of people than during the twenty years from 1870 to 1890 when the real incomes of the people more than doubled." For the first time large numbers of people attained middle-class status.

The Industrial Revolution was over about 1850, so it took only a few years in a free market and limited government for human energies to dramatically raise living standards. But shortly afterward the natural government urge to meddle in the private sector started eating into the new wealth, as some politicians saw in this an opportunity to raise **their** living standards. Today big government feeds like a school of piranhas.

Adams commented on the tax system in Switzerland. Citizens there see a direct connection between democracy, liberty, and taxes. That is,

> *liberty is centered in one's pocketbook. We have drifted far from that early consent, but the Swiss have tenaciously held fast to the belief that liberty, to be real, requires privacy, especially financial privacy. . . . In Switzerland the final decision on revenue is made by the voters. . . . Legislators cannot vote themselves a salary increase. . . . If increases are to be made in tax rates, voters have to approve.*
>
> *In 1975 the Swiss government submitted a referendum to the voters for an increase in the income tax rates. The voters turned it down cold. When one prominent Swiss citizen was asked what this meant, he said, "The government will have to live on what it has—like the rest of us.*

This tax regime comes about as close to that put into law (about 1560) by Queen Elizabeth I as any system; the only differences are that she didn't ask the citizen-subjects and her tax policy started the ascendancy of the great British empire.

Philosopher John Locke's 1690 treatise on government was so radical at the time that he dared not even sign his name to it.[5] He argued that people are sovereign, not government. Government "can never have a Power to take to themselves the whole or any part of the Subject's Property, without their own consent. For this would be in effect to leave them no Property at all." Locke continued his argument, saying that rulers "must not raise Taxes on the Property of the People, without the Consent of the People, given by themselves or their Deputies."

He went beyond this position, making explicit the people's right to revolution. "Whenever the Legislators endeavor to take away, and destroy the Property of the

People, or to reduce them to slavery under Arbitrary Power, they put themselves into a state of War with the People, who are thereupon absolved from any farther Obedience." It is worth nothing that Jefferson drew on Locke's arguments when he drafted the Declaration of Independence:

Prudence, indeed, will dictate that Governments long established should not be changed for light and transient Causes; and accordingly all experience hath shewn, that Mankind are more disposed to suffer, while Evils are sufferable, than to right themselves by abolishing the Forms to which they are accustomed. But when a long Train of Abuses and Usurpations, pursuing invariably the same Object, evinces a Design to reduce them under absolute Despotism, it is their Right, it is their Duty, to throw off such Government, and to provide new Guards for their future Security.

After Queen Elizabeth I died, the urge to tax reasserted its presence. But in the 1860s English Prime Minister William Gladstone engaged the special interests in a classic political battle. Powell reported:

The policies were a stupendous triumph. Every effort to cut income taxes, tariffs and other taxes involved a fight with affected interest groups, yet Gladstone persisted, and ***the more he cut the cost of government, the more people prospered****. "The improved living standards of manual workers," reported economic historian Charles Moore, "were paralleled by improved living standards both for the middle class and for the very rich."*[6] (emphasis added)

Hong Kong was a British colony for 150 years, but immediately after World War II it was mired in poverty. However, its English governor had faith in entrepreneurs, believing that the risk-takers in the private sector could make better investment decisions than can bureaucrats in the public sector. On July 1, 1997, the colony was handed back to the Chinese government as a wealthy society. Taxes had been kept low throughout.

After Japan's defeat in World War II the occupying government forced high taxes on the Japanese. There was a highly progressive income tax in this country at that time. Adams noted:

As soon as they could, the Japanese started to lower and eliminate all heavy taxes. . . . They permitted all kinds of go-go depreciation, reserves against remotely possible losses, interest income tax free, capital gains tax free, tax rebates. . . .

One of the strangest checks on excessive taxation—a built-in safety valve for evasion—is the postal savings system. These secret accounts are a kind of check on the government's taxing policies. If the rates get too high, flights to these accounts will increase. . . . The high savings rate can be explained by the tax-free and low-tax nature of interest income rather than any cultural inclination to save.[7]

A Japanese citizen can shelter up to $62,000 of savings from taxes. The average citizen saves 26 percent of his income, whereas savings in this country vary from 4 percent to negative amounts.

Adams did not mention government policies in effect that discouraged consumption. Japan's current economic difficulties are due to factors other than the saving rate. Nevertheless he made an important point in that if Japanese citizens were unhappy with their government's tax policy they could do something about it.

In Article I section 8 of the US Constitution, Congress is authorized to levy taxes to raise money and to spend money to provide for defense and "general welfare." Although the Constitution is a truly magnificent document, no one has ever said it is perfect. In section 8 lies a major error: placing authority in the same body of government for both raising money and spending it. Having experienced since 1781 several years of a central government unable to collect taxes from citizens under the Articles of Confederation, delegates to the Constitutional Convention felt they needed to put teeth in tax making and collecting. (It is true that the president has authority to veto both taxing and spending bills, but if he elects to cooperate with Congress in fleecing the public there is no protection whatsoever.)

In 1788 there were no career politicians subject to the temptation provided by mountains of money. (Put another way, there were no mountains of money, and thus no career politicians to be tempted.) The founding fathers and other citizens therefore believed that Congress could be trusted to spend scarce taxpayer money frugally, provided that citizens kept a close watch on members' activities. Adams noted, "To be blunt, without strict and clear constitutional standards for tax making, ratification wouldn't have had a prayer."

Adams argued that the discrepancy in section 8 should be corrected as soon as possible, because it opens the door for massive abuse. One example has today's congresspeople interpreting the "general welfare" clause to mean they can tax for any purpose they please.

Today the situation is demonstrably different. Adams pointed out that parts of the Constitution are being ignored and even violated by government. He referred especially to the uniformity clause, which requires that everyone be treated the same under the law (justice). "We would be shocked if any citizen were granted immunity from the criminal law, yet we tolerate immunity from the tax law on a grand scale."

A thinking citizen may wish that this observation was totally true, but recently Congress apparently granted President Clinton immunity from criminal law. The news media indicated that few people were shocked, but then the same citizen might question the veracity of this news.

In the end a vicious circle takes over: ever higher taxes cause flight across international borders and evasion, but these reactions combine to reduce government revenues. Therefore taxes are increased still more, and then more flight and evasion, and so on, until eventually society dissolves in rebellion. According to Adams, world history has inscribed this process in stone.

Adams concluded: "If we are to preserve and pass on to our children the liberty and freedom we boast about, which our forefathers passed on to us, we must focus our attention on our tax system and the destructive forces we have put in motion, forces that are far more dangerous than any outside invaders." (Correction: "Destructive forces that **career politicians** have put in motion.")

ATTRIBUTES OF A GOOD TAX SYSTEM

This section presents the results of some sound thinking concerning tax systems. It makes no effort to prescribe an optimal system, as this issue is properly left to discussion and debate by citizens.

In a democracy any tax system should fulfill two objectives—fairness and control by citizens. There are three unavoidable characteristics of government, any one or a combination of which can derail a good tax system. These characteristics are (1) government is an unregulated monopoly, (2) government is a parasite on the society whom it governs, and (3) government is force. Were citizens to realize the full potential of these causes of abuse of their fundamental rights, they would eagerly participate in discussion and control of their tax system.

In 1787 the thinking of the delegates to the Constitutional Convention was heavily influenced by a movement known as the Enlightenment, which had its main impetus in the seventeenth-century philosophical writings of men like Descartes, Hobbes, and Locke. These men believed that knowledge could be acquired more usefully when guided by reason instead of church dogma, against which they argued. Equally important were the contributions of scientists like Newton. By the eighteenth century, ideas previously discussed had been expanded to include politics and social concerns. Then they were put into practice, most notably by the American and French Revolutions.

Adams wrote about the legacy of the Enlightenment, which he cast into the form of principles.

1. "Government is at best a necessary evil." He quoted Thomas Paine: "There are two distinct classes of men in the Nation . . . those who pay taxes and those who receive and live upon taxes. . . . When taxation is carried to excess it cannot fail to disunite those two." Adams again: "When governments tax too much, they steal from their citizens by taking the fruits of their industry and property. Instead of providing protection for the people's liberty and prosperity—which is the state's sole justification for existence—the state turns out to be a real enemy of the people, just as villainous as a foreign invader."

2. "The imaginary wants of the state." Montesquieu's book *The Spirit of Laws* exerted great influence on the founding fathers. Adams quoted the baron: "The real wants of the people ought never to give way to the imaginary wants of the state." He gave the example of the Vietnam War, during which Lyndon Johnson campaigned as a peace candidate, the real want of the people. But in office he pushed war, the imaginary want of the state.
3. "Governments should stay out of business." The business of government is not the government of business.
4. "Liberty carried the seeds of its own destruction." Montesquieu noted that people living in a state of liberty tend to relax their guard and allow large increases in taxes. Later they realize their error, but by then it is often too late to force a rollback because the state has used the extra money to consolidate control over their lives.
5. "Direct taxes are the badge of slavery, and indirect taxes the badge of liberty." Taxing the individual bears down heavily on his or her life, whereas taxing merchandise permits liberty through the exercise of relatively free choice.
6. "Tax evasion is not a criminal act. . . . Governments had no right to make 'criminal' what did not conform to the laws of Nature." This principle criticizes part of the trend through the past several centuries of creating more and more criminal law, as opposed to civil law. The former frequently involves incarceration, whereas the latter generally involves disputes between individuals and organizations other than government.
7. "Liberty's most dangerous foe: arbitrary taxation." Discussions during the Enlightenment produced three principles that, when followed, would protect a society from arbitrary taxation: (a) taxation by consent of the people; (b) apportion of taxes among the citizens by a definite standard understood by all; and (c) equality, which removes the temptation for one individual to shift part of his tax burden onto someone else.
8. "Common sense economics: the supply-siders." Low tax rates promote more earnings, savings, and investment. All these expand economic activity and therefore the tax base, taxable income, and wealth. Ronald Reagan took office in early 1981 with great fanfare about supply-side economics, but his administration never did practice it. Queen Elizabeth I practiced the concept, whether or not she understood it.
9. "The marks of a bad tax system: Adam Smith's four points: (1) A tax was bad that required a large bureaucracy for administration; (2) A tax was bad that 'may obstruct the industry of people . . .'; (3) . . . encouraged evasion; and (4) . . . puts the people through 'odious examinations of the tax-gatherers.'"

10. "What a good tax should be: Lord Kames' six rules. They are: (1) When the opportunity for evasion exists, taxes must be moderate; (2) Taxes that are expensive to levy should be avoided; (3) Arbitrary taxes are 'disgustful to all;' (4) . . . the poor should be relieved of any significant tax burden; (5) . . . [Taxes that] sap the strength of a nation should be avoided. Such taxes 'contradict the very nature of government, which is to protect not oppress;' and (6) Taxes that require an oath are to be avoided." Adams completed his presentation with the following pithy observation: "In the twentieth century westerners were seduced by the philosophy of socialism . . . [and] the thinking of the Enlightenment passed away."

In his classic 1776 book *Wealth of Nations,* Smith provided four characteristics of a good tax: fair, easy to collect, difficult to evade, and minimum distortion of the economy. That the founding fathers were also influenced by this famous philosopher and economist came forth in President Jefferson's first annual message, dated December 8, 1801:

> *There is reasonable ground of confidence that we may now safely dispense with all the internal taxes, comprehending excises, stamps, auctions, licenses, carriages, and refined sugars . . . remaining sources of revenue will be sufficient to provide for the support of government, to pay the interest on the public debts, and to discharge the principals in shorter periods than . . . contemplated.*

To the extent feasible, those who benefit from government services supported by a tax should pay it. Today's citizens don't know exactly which organizations are being favored; they know only that the system is not fair to them. Furthermore, the income tax code is changed almost monthly, which makes it very difficult for families and businesses to plan for the long term. Therefore little such planning takes place, and the orientation of both government and citizens is to the short term. This restraint tends to destabilize society.

History has shown that Smith's four characteristics will not guide top-down tax making. The people must be involved, or the negative incentives in human nature will eventually turn a good system into a bad one. Paine in his *Rights of Man* quoted from the French Declaration of Rights, compiled shortly before the French Revolution.[8] "Every citizen has a right, either by himself or his representative, to a free voice in determining the necessity of public contributions, the appropriation of them, and their amount, mode of assessment, and duration." History has shown the grim result when citizens do not exercise their voices in taxation.

Foley used a different approach in his proposal.[9]

> *Under the proportional gross receipts tax system, every person, corporation, foundation, or other entity (save for governmental units) would pay a flat percentage (e.g., one percent) of its annual gross receipt of funds from every source.*

> *There should be no exceptions, limitations, exclusions, deductions, credits, or exemptions, thereby greatly simplifying the whole tax preparation process. This system would produce sufficient revenue to support necessary governmental functions and would result in a great saving of creative energy now utilized in the regulatory and compliance process.*

Foley argued that there is no reason to exclude hospitals, foundations, churches, and others because they benefit from government services just as taxed entities do. This proposal may generate discussion, although with gross receipts taxed some provision may be necessary for a company that loses, say, $2 billion on sales of $10 billion but would still owe a tax of 1 percent of $10 billion, or $100 million.

There has been a lot of coverage (a poll showed 72 percent voter support) about an amendment to the Constitution that would require any proposed national government tax increase to be subject to a nationwide referendum vote. In view of the size of the bag of tricks possessed by career politicians that help them get around any limits on taxation, this proposal probably has little potential. (This caveat applies especially if members of Congress or their lawyers draft the proposal.)

Another recommendation suggests an amendment to require a balanced national government budget. This one has limited utility for the same reason, although the requirements of accrual accounting, independent citizen audit, and absolutely nothing placed off-budget would help. The core of the problem of big government lies not in a balanced budget, but rather in the overall size of the budget.

Here is a thought that has potential. If the principle of federalism as described in Chapter 3 were applied, state governments would indeed be perceived as separate from the central government and would act accordingly. Therefore if the state governments were taxed to support the central government, the latter would face a challenge in trying to collect, because state governments would be far better organized than are individual citizens. Furthermore, state government officials generally live and work among their constituents and are thus more vulnerable to voter dissatisfaction than are their counterparts in Washington.

Under such a federalist tax system there would be only fifty well-organized taxpayers supporting the federal government instead of more than 150 million unorganized citizens and businesses. State officials would find it worth their effort to pursue abuse in taxation and rectify it. The people would watch their representatives, and these officials would closely watch those on Capitol Hill.

Such a system would help taxpayers keep their rights, which should include the right to determine their own tax burdens. Here is just one example of present central government power giving the average citizen no choice. In the inner cities poor women addicted to drugs quite often and sometimes repeatedly give birth to "crack babies." They are not in a position to pay the cost, which runs around $125,000 before the baby is even released from the hospital. Therefore the taxpayer pays. Should the little one survive past infancy, the subsequent taxpayer obligation cannot be estimated accurately.

A taxpayer might object to such women infringing on their right to property, not to mention the life and liberty of the little tyke. It might occur to a concerned citizen that a law could force these women to use a contraceptive such as Norplant. This has been suggested, but the American Civil Liberties Union has objected, claiming that such a law would restrict the rights of the women. It would seem, however, that the taxpayer has rights that deserve consideration.

Browne is a concerned citizen who is unhappy with the personal income tax: "[It] is the biggest intrusion suffered by the . . . people. It forces every worker to be a bookkeeper, to open his records to the government . . . to fear conviction for a harmless accounting error. Hundreds of billions of dollars are wasted on attorneys, accountants . . . other costs."[10]

He presented four suggestions for a good tax system:

> *(1) Prohibit any tax on incomes. . . . (2) Specify the taxes that are authorized . . . and set absolute limits on their rates; (3) Prohibit the government from spending more money than was received in revenue the preceding fiscal year; and (4) In case of emergency, Congress could override [this] . . . if approved by a 75% majority in both houses . . . [to] expire automatically in two years, requiring 75% . . . [to] reenact.*

There may be some potential here, although the Clinton administration hoisted a red flag by arbitrarily calling any expense that exceeds spending targets an emergency.

Richard Rahn wondered if complaints about the income tax are wasted energy.[11]

> *Computer technology is making many types of monetary transactions virtually impossible for IRS officials to track, and thus making tax payments far easier to avoid. . . . Assume you are a lawyer in New York doing work for a client in a jurisdiction without an income tax. You send the work to your client over the Internet (as e-mail). The client agrees to pay you in electronic money. As your bills become due, the client sends you the money over the Internet, and you download it into your computer. You, in turn, pay your bills by sending electronic money from your computer.*
>
> *The government can respond in two ways: It can try to know and control everything (the totalitarian response), or it can give up trying to tax income (the libertarian response).*

Rahn recommended promotion of honest and efficient government rather than an IRS "too terrible to imagine." This makes a lot of sense, in that some taxpayers' imaginings about the IRS are already very impressive. Should this feeling spread widely, the logical consequence would be a tax rebellion.

If alert citizens kept government at all levels to a minimum, an income tax on individuals and businesses would not be necessary. Rather, consumption could be taxed. When combined with low inflation, such a tax would encourage saving, thus doing much to improve the current low saving rate in this country. High inflation encourages borrowing as people think they can pay back debts with cheaper dollars, while low inflation reduces this incentive.

There are those who claim that a sales tax hits the poor hardest, because they spend a larger part of their income. This is true, but today there is such wealth in the country that the impact would be much less than when this argument was first raised about forty years ago. Today charities are in far better shape to help the poor than they were then.

The logical outlet for savings is investment. An increase in this activity makes more money available to businesses, which in turn triggers the law of supply and demand to lower interest rates and make it still easier to borrow for expansion or formation of new businesses. (Interest is the price of money.)

Today savings are also discouraged through double taxation of dividends from stock ownership. That is, a company that issues shares pays a tax on its income, and then often declares a dividend payment per share of stock to shareholders. Thus the same money is taxed again as income to shareholders.

This section concludes with an intriguing piece of irony. People can recall reading about the Boston Tea Party in 1773, when colonists dressed as Indians broke open cases of British tea on ships in Boston Harbor and threw the tea into the water. They were registering a complaint about a tax on tea. *The Economist* recently recommended: "If America truly wants a new way to pay, it should send its entire tax code—every last scrap—to the bottom of the harbor." This publication is a **British** newspaper, apparently recommending another dump into Boston Harbor.

Thoughts on Specifics

In 1817 President Madison examined a bill for construction of roads and canals. He vetoed it on constitutional grounds: "Such a view of the Constitution would have the effect of giving to Congress a general power of legislation instead of the defined and limited one hitherto understood to belong to them." The next president, James Monroe, acted from the same perspective in 1822, as he vetoed a bill for maintaining the Cumberland Road. Logic and economics would have those citizens who would benefit from the projects pay for them; therefore money should be raised where it will be spent. Such logic also serves the need for accountability in public expenditures.

Carson wrote:

> *A society that looks upon thrift and frugality as social virtues, that believes with Benjamin Franklin "if you know how to spend less than you get, you have the philosopher's stone," such a society cannot escape the rich rewards that come from capital formation. On the other hand, a society whose habits are not thrifty will soon be poverty-stricken. Work is not a curse; it is the only means to sustain and improve human life. Work, hard work, and long hours of work are the parents of prosperity.*[12]

Some would question whether this statement of the Protestant work ethic still applies today, yet there is some truth in it, especially for government.

Government policies discourage saving in at least two ways. One is taxation of dividends and capital gains from shares of stock; another lies in the current condition of the national social security programs. Apparently government wants citizens to spend money as it creates the illusion of prosperity.

Glassman injected some little-known truth into this issue.[13]

> *But even if today's young people do get that pension, it will be paltry compared with the money they've put in over the years . . . . as an investment to create a retirement nest egg, which is the way most Americans see it, social security has become an outright rip-off. The Tax Foundation calculates that a couple, currently ages 46 to 50 and making average wages, will see real . . . returns of minus 1.5 percent annually on the contributions they and their employers make over a lifetime of work.*

It was pointed out that within a few years of the 1935 formation of the Social Security trust funds, members of Congress began taking money from them and using it to buy votes. Later much more money was taken and spent as surpluses built up. This meant there was very little money invested, which could add interest income to workers' earnings and employers' deposits over the decades since 1935.

Glassman commented, "[A] low-wage worker born in 1950 will receive $631 a month in current dollars . . . at retirement. But if the retirement portion of payroll taxes went instead into stocks, the worker would have an annuity yielding $2,490 a month. . . . Never in history have US stocks failed to beat inflation by at least a full point over a twenty-year stretch." Critics have referred to the stock market as a crap shoot. The reality is that gamblers, conservative investors, and in-betweens make up the 50+ percent of citizens who own shares either directly or indirectly through insurance policies and private pension funds.

Critics also argue that a worker would not know how to manage a private pension fund. "If Americans are allowed to opt out of the current system and put a mandatory 10 percent of their salaries into private plans instead, will they handle those investments wisely? The Chileans do; the British do. And . . . their populations were far less accustomed to stock market investing than Americans are today." Glassman did not mention additional benefits: pride in accomplishment as a worker sees a retirement nest egg grow, the option to augment that 10 percent later on when he or she is earning more, and a focus on long-term family well-being.

Very few people appreciate what is known as the miracle of compound interest; privatization presents an opportunity. To illustrate, a person might ask another how long it would take an investment yielding, say, 8 percent to double its value. At first blush, the answer would be 12.5 years, because eight times 12.5 equals a 100 percent increase, a doubling. The correct answer when the interest is left to accumulate and earn additional interest is only 9 years. This illustration involves only a one-time investment; with annual or monthly additions, the nest egg grows much faster.

Social engineering through government tax policies often distorts markets. For example, the home mortgage interest deduction, a darling of the multitudes, favors home ownership and therefore reduces worker mobility and economic efficiency. It is a lot easier to leave a rented apartment for a better job than to sell a house and buy another one. Furthermore, renters who cannot afford to buy do not appreciate subsidizing wealthier homeowners who get a tax break on their mortgage interest. Although indirect, here is another instance of transfer of wealth from poorer to wealthier.

Similarly, when bond interest is tax-deductible, companies tend to favor debt over equity finance. This makes them more vulnerable if they should get into financial difficulty, because interest on debt must be paid, whereas payment of dividends on shares can be deferred.

Bethell brought out a major national government abuse of the tax system.[14]

> *Consider the candidate for office who promises voters that he will dare to oppose new government spending. Elected, he arrives in Washington, and there he figures out something he hadn't foreseen on the campaign trail. If he votes "no" (e.g., on the highway bill), he will probably deprive his constituents of an opportunity to get back from Washington what they put into the $1.6 trillion common pool of the federal budget (in the form of taxes). But his "no" vote will not encourage a like restraint among other members of Congress. On the contrary, they will have more to divvy up among themselves.*
>
> *So instead of voting "no," he ends up . . . appropriating the money. Some of it is now earmarked for his district. Voters at home may think that he sold out. But it was the* ***institutional*** *arrangement of Congress that encouraged his change of heart. (emphasis added)*

The core of the difficulty is that there is no connection between the amount of taxes levied and what is spent in each district. "If the total dollars that a member of Congress votes to spend in the course of a year were tallied, and taxpayers in his or her district were 'billed' accordingly, with big spenders saddling their constituents with high taxes and low spenders rewarding . . ., the era of big government really would be over. In fact, it would end overnight." The whole issue therefore comes down to accountability and making those who will receive the benefits pay for them (and making politicians come clean about what they are doing).

The notion of a negative income tax for the poor has been floated. It has the merit of targeting the most needy of citizens, but the arguments against it include: (1) the difficulty of accurately measuring existing income to determine who the needy are (they avoid reporting some income); (2) poor people move into and out of poverty, sometimes as frequently as every month; (3) it requires a large bureaucracy to administer, so the program is inefficient; and (4) it is open to fraud.

Many economists and some politicians have pushed for what is called a flat income tax to replace the 10,000-page, 5.6 million-word mess that constitutes the current tax code. Incumbent politicians are not sincere in this because they profit mightily from selling tax breaks, credits, and loopholes, which can be hidden deep inside those pages.

A flat tax would exempt from tax the first sizable chunk of an individual's total income, which means the poor would pay no tax. The remainder would then be taxed at a uniform rate regardless of the amount. For example, the first $35,000 would be tax-free and the rest taxed at 17 percent; this would provide the national government enough revenue to operate as it does today. There would be no additional exemptions, no deductions, no tax credits, and no adjustments whatever. Finally, it would conform to the uniformity clause in the Constitution: equal proportionate burden for nearly all.

The Economist showed an advantage of the flat income tax: "What is fair? . . . the case for redistributing income through the income tax has an even more devastating flaw. In practice, Robin Hood almost always robs from the rich and gives to the middle classes."[15] This position is based on the reality that government programs that ostensibly help the poor route most of the money to contractors and other middle-class people who work on projects that presumably help the poor (and they kick back some of the money, as Chapter 10 showed).

"This points to what is perhaps the flat tax's greatest advantage. It can be used to focus efforts to redistribute income precisely where they belong: on the poor. A flat tax that allowed an exemption for a big slice of wage income and levied a single tax rate on everything else would force all of society to pay for whatever level of public charity it deems appropriate." Another advantage of the tax is elimination of the IRS, because agents would no longer need to pry deeply into people's personal financial affairs in search of tax evaders. And the annual forced and unpaid taking of up to a billion person-hours (devoted to tax preparation) away from productive activities would be eliminated.

The conclusion is that if citizens want a tax on income, a flat tax is probably fairest and most efficient. Measuring it against Smith's four criteria for a good tax it is fair, easy to collect, and it does not seriously distort the economy. (The fourth criterion, evasion, remains an important issue.) However, the great weight of history demonstrates that any direct tax (on income) has within it the potential for tremendous abuse. Politicians are limited only by their imaginations as they figure out ways to deviously increase the take.

In Europe the value-added tax (VAT) is popular and established in many countries (it runs about 18 percent in England). *The Economist* noted: "In many ways, VAT is a consumption tax akin to a general sales tax. In particular, consumers end up paying it."[16] Actually, consumers pay practically all taxes; there is no other main source. "Everybody in the production and distribution chain has a financial incentive to participate: only by doing so can producers, in effect, claim back the VAT they have paid on their inputs."

This statement pertains to the often lengthy and intricate process of creation and movement of raw materials and semi-processed goods, which precedes display of a product in a retail outlet. For example, a plant manager may buy, say, a ton of raw rubber for tire making, on which he pays a VAT to the supplier. Later he sells however many tires that ton of rubber can make, and then he collects VAT on those sales. Eventually a business or individual buys a set of four tires and pays VAT on that sale. This means double recording of every transaction, which reduces the opportunity for cheating.

The Economist continued:

> *America is the only rich country that has no national sales or consumption tax. Its direct (income) taxes therefore make up over seventy percent of its overall tax revenues, more than in most West European countries. This is a bad thing for two reasons. First, because the tax base is needlessly narrow, tax rates have to be higher than they otherwise would be in order to raise any given amount of revenue.*

This fact suggests that unless citizens demand a change, the total tax load will not diminish, although with VAT the burden would be spread wider and income tax rates could be reduced. Measured against Smith's four criteria, this tax is fair, easy to collect, and difficult to evade. (The amount of distortion of the economy is difficult to estimate.)

Adams suggested some legislation that goes "to the root of the problem" but at present would never get through Congress.[17] There is some learning value in the seven items.

1. "Establish a crime for tax extortion as well as a civil action for damages.
2. ". . . damage for tortious tax administration . . . It has now come to light that the executive branch . . . has used the IRS to harass, punish, and even

destroy businesses, prominent individuals, unpopular political organizations. . . . Presidents, including Roosevelt, Kennedy, Johnson, and Nixon, are among the most conspicuous abusers. . . . Our tax law is so complex and so screwed up . . . anyone with complicated financial affairs can be indicted easily.

3. "Have all federal tax districts coincide with congressional districts and provide for the recall of district directors. . . . Make tax chiefs responsible to the people they tax.
4. Adjudicate tax disputes like any other debt. It is time to . . . end special laws giving . . . powers to tax men. . . . People are often dumbfounded to learn that in a tax dispute, taxpayers who want to go to a regular court have to pay the tax debt and then sue to get their money back. "[In effect this policy is guilty until proven innocent, which is prohibited by the Constitution.]" Bankruptcy offers no relief as it does for ordinary debts. On top of all this there are over 150 penal provisions to trap and punish you for just about any error. . . .
5. "Decriminalize the tax law. . . . Everyone is in a constant state of illegality, arrestable at any time for a "felony" manufactured by the state. The ultimate means of political control by all totalitarian states. . . . The intimidation and resulting fear give the government the power of easy extortion.
6. "Make congressmen and federal judges immune from the IRS" [Adams believes they, too, can be harassed by the agency, although this surely seems unlikely today.]
7. "Make our federal tax system indirect as much as possible."

This chapter has presented the issue of tax systems in its great complexity, which does not for a minute mean that a citizen-created tax system must be complex. If citizens want it simple they will make it that way, although they would be well advised to consider some of the useful guidelines presented here.

Because the greatest abusers of the current tax system are members of Congress, the following hypothetical system attempts to eliminate that branch of government and get citizens more involved in taxing themselves. Admittedly, to have merit it needs refinement.

1. The executive branch presents an outline of a biennial central government budget with several broad categories of proposed spending at least six months before the end of the fiscal year. Copies are sent to all of the thousands of local precincts electronically.
2. Precinct captains hold meetings until they obtain a position on each category: okay as is, reject category, reject as too much money, reject as too little money, want more information. This feedback goes to Washington within ninety days.

3. The executive publishes the results of voting, acts on directions, makes revisions, and resubmits electronically with comments for a second round of discussion and voting. (This step is restricted to categories that generated controversial or less than clear results.)
4. Precincts act on this information and pass results along to the executive, together with preferences concerning how the agreed amount of money should be raised and collection procedures as appropriate. (It is the citizens' money, so they should be given a choice.)
5. Executive prepares final budget and circulates a copy together with projections of cash flows to each precinct. Tax laws are then repealed, updated, and passed in accordance with the public will. (At the beginning these revisions and new laws should be submitted for public approval. Later the citizens may agree that this would be done only by request.)
6. Executive submits monthly progress reports, with explanations for any deviations from budgeted amounts. He or she continues to be receptive to any comments from precincts on these reports. He will amend the plan if a groundswell of public opinion so indicates. Enlightened media will help with the vital tasks of dissemination of information and constant vigilance.

At first glance this seems utterly unworkable in view of today's tax code with its nearly 200,000 separate accounts. But in cutting the federal government down to a more manageable size, the citizens would drastically reduce that number.

This scheme provides the essential separation of the taxing and spending functions, and it also puts first responsibility for taxation solidly with the citizens. Because people support what they help create, citizens are very likely to be honest with paying taxes. Furthermore, with a continuing dialog between president and the people, responsibility for mistakes would be placed where it belongs.

Again hypothetically speaking, a severely downsized central government might be operated on an average annual budget of, say, $100 billion. Today's Capitol Hill costs taxpayers more than $2 trillion, or twenty times as much, and that is only what actually shows in the budget under the system of cash accounting. Off-budget expenditures and accumulated contingencies are something else again. Over a period of years the national debt could be retired, and a $1 trillion reserve accumulated on the plus side to deal with recessions and citizen-approved unanticipated major expenses. The money would be invested worldwide in offshore mutual funds, where professional money managers invest it in foreign companies that they believe will do well in the future.

Conservatively speaking, a wise investment portfolio for the reserve would yield an average of 6 percent, or $60 billion annually. This would leave $40 billion to be raised through taxation. With about 200 million future taxpaying citizens, the average annual federal tax burden on an individual would be $200. Today the bite is more than $4,500 in income tax only.

Notes

1. Charles Adams, F*or Good and Evil: The Impact of Taxes on the Course of Civilization.* Madison Books, 1993.
2. Hans Sennholz, introduction to *Taxation and Confiscation.* Foundation for Economic Education, 1993.
3. *The Economist,* "America's Tax Revolution." January 13, 1996, p. 15.
4. Harry Browne, *Why Government Doesn't Work.* St. Martin's Press, 1995.
5. John Locke, quoted in Jim Powell, *The Triumph of Liberty,* Free Press, 2000, p. 2.
6. Jim Powell, *The Triumph of Liberty,* Free Press, 2000, p. 135.
7. Adams, *For Good and Evil.*
8. Thomas Paine, *Rights of Man.* Knopf, 1915.
9. Ridgway K. Foley Jr., "The Elements of a Fair Tax System." In *Taxation and Confiscation,* ed. Hans Sennholz. Foundation for Economic Education, 1993.
10. Browne, *Why Government Doesn't Work.*
11. Richard W. Rahn, "E-money; Logical End of the Income Tax?" *News and Observer* (Raleigh, NC), April 1999 column.
12. Clarence B. Carson, "The General Welfare." *Taxation and Confiscation,* ed. Hans Sennholz. Foundation for Economic Education, 1993.
13. James K. Glassman, "Do-it-Yourself Social Security." *US News,* October 6, 1997, p. 50.
14. Tom Bethell, "Big Government: The Perpetual Motion Machine." Introduction to the *Hoover Digest* 1998 [booklet], p. 12.
15. *The Economist,* "America's Tax Revolution."
16. *The Economist,* "The VAT Man Cometh." April 24, 1993, p. 17.
17. Adams, *For Good and Evil.*

CHAPTER SIXTEEN: LEADERS AND GOOD IDEAS

I use not only all the brains I have, but all I can borrow.
—Woodrow Wilson

During World War II there were two sailors in the crew of a battleship. As they walked on the deck one day they passed an officer whom they both knew. Both saluted him as they were required to do, and the officer returned the salutes. After the officer had passed out of hearing, one sailor turned to the other and asked, "Did you salute the stripes or the man?"

This story illustrates a significant aspect of the difference between leadership of that era and what will prevail in the Age of Reason. In those days authority in the military and elsewhere was delegated from above, and most (though not all) salutes were aimed at the stripes. Today's trend has authority conferred from below; thus, the man. The current trend ties in with the positive incentives of human nature, in that respect is not commanded as in countries ruled by bloodlines or dictatorships. Rather, it must be earned, as in countries with democracies. It follows that a leader who has earned the respect of the people does not need tons of money to get elected to public office.

Before the Industrial Revolution seniority almost invariably placed older people in positions of leadership because they were believed to be wisest. This system worked quite well because there were few major technology-driven changes in the society. Young people who dared question authority were rare, and they were quickly put in their place in a hierarchical culture.

Many wrenching changes occurred in society after the Industrial Revolution. Expertise in science and other disciplines undermined the seniority system. Today adult education classes in computer technology often have instructors who are younger than most of the students.

But there is a flip side to this development, of which few people are aware. It rises from a combination of youth, ambition, and lack of a solid general education. This combination causes young people with leadership potential to embark on what is known as the fast track upward in an organization. On the way up the young executive learns rapidly, but allows no time for reflection on that learning.

Furthermore, without a good general education he or she lacks the ability to integrate into his own operation the impact of actions taken by other components of the organization. The ultimate result is often a rapid rise to what Lawrence Peter in his book *The Peter Principle* called a level of incompetence.

If the organization still subscribes to the seniority system, the person could stay at this level until retirement. This system guides the operation of Congress, because it is well suited to the ambitions of career politicians. Today political "leaders" are actually followers. They follow poll results, consensus on policy, and even editorials.

What they do not follow is the opinions of citizens, ample and amplified rhetoric to the contrary notwithstanding. To the extent that the people are forced to follow laws not made by themselves, they appear to delegate authority to their representatives in Congress. But this is not really delegation; the reality is that between Congress and the citizenry no authority is delegated and none conferred. What is "delegated" is mutual alienation and contempt.

This chapter will describe in detail the character and abilities of an effective leader in the Age of Reason, and it will show how he or she exercises that leadership. Stress is necessarily and properly put on open dialog, as opposed to barking commands. If the people are to govern themselves there is no other way.

The Ingredients of Effective Leadership

In his book *On Becoming a Leader*, Bennis revealed some important differences between a manager and a leader.[1] These differences emphasize the fact that organizations and institutions should be living, vibrant entities, so they can adapt to a rapidly changing society.

The manager administers; the leader innovates.
The manager is a copy; the leader is an original.
The manager maintains; the leader develops.
The manager focuses on systems and structure; the leader focuses on people.
The manager relies on control; the leader inspires trust.
The manager has a short-range view; the leader has a long-range perspective.
The manager asks how and when; the leader asks what and why.
The manager keeps an eye on the bottom line; the leader watches the horizon.
The manager accepts the status quo; the leader challenges it.
The manager is a classic good soldier; the leader is his own person.
The manager does things right; the leader does the right thing.

The accent is clearly on flexibility and long-range vision. The two work well together. Without a long-range vision, flexibility creates chaos, but vision without flexibility will eventually bury the organization due to lack of ability to adapt to a changing environment. The logical conclusion: Organizations need both managers and leaders.

Bennis presented a general description of effective leaders:

> *They know who they are, what their strengths and weaknesses are, and how to fully deploy their strengths and compensate for their weaknesses. They also know what they want, why they want it, and how to communicate what they want to others, in order to gain their cooperation and support. Finally, they know how to achieve their goals. The key to full self-expression is understanding one's self and the world, and the key to understanding is learning . . . from one's own life and experience.*

His description appropriately emphasized education, but if self-knowledge is the objective then general education must be a part of the learning experience. This requires extra effort in an age of specialization.

Bennis indicated some ingredients of effective leadership: a guiding vision, passion for the work, integrity, self-knowledge, candor, maturity, curiosity, and daring. A leader reaches out to the unknown while staying secure in his or her ability to recover and learn from mistakes.

Bennis believed that "writing is the most profound way of codifying your thoughts, the best way of learning from yourself who you are and what you believe." Writing greatly helps get thoughts organized, and then it utilizes them as springboards toward the original thinking necessary to develop vision. Furthermore, reading has the advantage of leisure; a reader has the opportunity to read a serious passage, reread it, reflect on the content, criticize it, and even elaborate on it and carry it forward through his or her writing if sufficiently interested. All of these activities involve learning.

The merit of print has become manifest in an unexpected place. *The Economist* interviewed Dmitrij Rupel, foreign minister of Slovenia.[2] Slovenia is scarcely more than ten years old, and a comparison with the infant United States is appropriate: a blank political slate on which to write when forming a government. "Mr. Rupel boots it up and shows off a software system that allows him access to almost everything and everyone he needs in the Slovenian government."

"His office, like those of other Slovenian ministers, is almost paperless. Every official document comes to him electronically." This may suggest an existence without printed words, but no minister could thoroughly understand the content of an important document unless he or she printed a copy and studied it in depth. The important point to make is that he can do this at a time during the day when he is free to reflect on these messages.

Most cabinet meetings in Slovenia take place online. Ministers vote by clicking buttons, attaching notes of explanation whenever this is deemed necessary or appropriate. However, not all is sweetness and light, as *The Economist* continued: "It is a grind: ministers feel obliged to log on and vote in e-cabinet sessions even when on holiday. No more waffling either. In the good old days of paper, a flustered minister could claim not to have received the relevant document. Now the all-knowing system records exactly which files ministers receive . . . and when and whether they open them." There is apparently no place to hide.

According to Bennis,

> *Trust lies squarely between faith and doubt. The leader always has faith in himself, his abilities, his co-workers, and their mutual possibilities. But he also has sufficient doubt to question, challenge, probe, and thereby progress. In the same way, his co-workers must believe in him, themselves, and their combined strength, but they must feel sufficiently confident to question, challenge, prove, and test, too. Maintain that vital balance between faith and doubt, preserving that mutual trust, is a primary task for any leader.*

Faith means the leader may not always appreciate what a co-worker says or does, but that worker knows the leader will always have faith in him or her. In a climate of mutual trust and confidence, doubt can play an important role in that the people can freely provide and accept constructive criticism aimed at improving the operation. No one treats criticism as a personal affront.

This is the type of climate in which teamwork attains its full potential; members of any championship sports team would agree. Team members will at one time be working on the faith side of the balance, and at another on the doubt side. Too much faith, and the organization blindly leaps into the abyss. Too much doubt, and nothing ventured nothing gained.

Carter offered several qualities of leadership.[3]

1. "Admiring Commitment . . . willingness to take risks for a cause."
2. "Admiring Forthrightness . . . we can trust them to say what they truly think, even at risk to themselves." Carter referred to Mahatma Gandhi and Martin Luther King, Jr. as examples. He also included a willingness to admit error.
3. "Admiring Steadfastness . . . Only a person who has done the hard work of discernment can stick to the course in the face of criticism and difficulty." Discernment is thinking hard about a controversial issue and arriving at a morally correct position on it.
4. "Admiring Compassion . . . Sympathy for the unfortunate is an important part of being human."
5. "Integrity and Promise . . . The notion that compromise is inimical to integrity is as common as it is wrong." Carter suggested that there are occasions when one desirable goal must be temporarily set aside in the interest of a more important long-range goal. He referred to Washington's and Jefferson's handling of the slavery issue as examples.
6. "Admiring Consistency . . . Bush's 1992 pardons of several former Reagan administration officials who had been accused . . . [in the] Iran-Contra [scandal].." Carter claimed that Bush was inconsistent in that when he

complained about the special prosecutor law he did not pardon all those convicted under it.

The ingredients of effective leadership could be more simply listed as wise vision, courage, persistence, sales ability, and openness to criticism. The first is necessary to know in which direction to guide the organization; when the occasion arises the second enables a leader to tell the people what they do not want to hear; the third is needed to keep telling it even when a leader is clearly swimming upstream; the fourth helps a leader convince the people that certain citizen-initiated ideas and recommendations are good ones; and the last helps ensure that suggestions for changes are heard, discussed, and acted on.

Vision is not clairvoyance, or the ability to see into the future what others cannot see. The best crystal ball or ouija board says nothing about what **should** occur in the future or what a leader should strive to attain. Timing enters into consideration. The idea would not show up in opinion research, but once it is put into motion a majority feel that this is what they have wanted all along. Indeed, when a visionary first mentions an idea, he and others may think he is swimming upstream; only later comes the realization that the direction of the current has changed. Reflection plays a very important role, because there may be little or nothing on record anywhere that even indirectly suggests what should occur. Put another way, original thinking does not exist until it appears in someone's brain.

Courage of convictions is a valuable leadership trait. However, if the conviction is not right courage quickly turns into bull-headedness. Courage and persistence in leaders were very effectively highlighted in 1995 when Israeli prime minister Yitzak Rabin and Palestine's Yasser Arafat kept working for peace as the current against them grew stronger. They were pursuing a shared vision. A short while later tragedy struck, as Rabin paid for his courage with his life.

Shortly after the French Revolution (1789) the British threatened France once again. Citizens of the United States became angry. Passions overruled reason and a majority in the United States was ready to declare war on England. The steady voice of President George Washington courageously spoke out against war, pointing out that the people were citizens of an infant nation and they had other things to do that would mean far more for them in the future. He, too, swam upstream. He persisted in his position to the point where he risked losing the only reward he truly valued: the love of his countrymen. Still he persisted.

Later the situation changed, in large part because over time passions always cool enough to allow reason a foot in the door. When sufficient time had passed the people came to realize that their president was right. Washington's courage, persistence, and willingness to risk the love of his compatriots had saved the country from the scourge of war. (It is disturbing to observe the behavior of recent presidents, as they seem to ask for conflict by sending soldiers, weapons, and military advisors and training overseas to myriad destinations, and occasionally even use them to kill, maim, and destroy. See Chapter 21.)

The accomplishment of consensus suggests the presence of a leader with sales ability. Having enlisted the assistance of various resources, including his people, he reflects on what he has learned and arrives at a conclusion that he knows the people want. Then his task is to convince the skeptics in the group of its merits. In this way the coordinated efforts of the entire team can be brought to bear on the project. An effective leader is self-confident because he is not self-contained. Available resources are limited only by the user's imagination: books, magazines, experts, consultants, computer storage, employees, customers, directors, online information, and so on.

It is important to utilize resources in this process; otherwise there is a real risk of selling the wrong course of action. This happened in Germany during the years 1933–39. Adolf Hitler was one of history's most accomplished salesmen, but he sold the wrong (top-down) product.

Early in Hitler's career, some Germans attempted to question what he was selling, but he did not listen. With benefit of hindsight, he surely should have. Listening is a very important skill in nearly every effective salesperson, and leaders are no exception. When a leader truly listens to a co-worker and that worker perceives the listening as genuine the leader **sends** a vital message: "I care about you as a person. The company values your contributions, not just technically but also your thinking concerning the whole company or section. I recognize your expertise in this part of the business, and we look forward to further contributions in the future." (A closed mouth gathers no feet.)

This is not easily done; few leaders or managers are good listeners. Why? Because engaging in this type of listening opens the listener to the possibility of having a cherished position on an issue changed. This is where self-confidence enters in: A self-aware leader does not fear such an instance. He or she looks on change as opportunity, whereas a poor leader perceives change as a threat. This is why national "leaders" in Washington worship the status quo.

Thomas Paine was born in England, but in the United States he served in public offices and considered himself a citizen.[4] He began his book *The Age of Reason* with the following salutation.

> *To my Fellow-Citizens of the United States of America: I put the following work under your protection. It contains my opinions upon Religion. You will do me the justice to remember, that I have always strenuously supported the Right of every Man to his own opinion, however different that opinion might be to mine. He who denies to another this right, makes a slave of himself to his present opinion, because he precludes himself the right of changing it.*
>
> *The most formidable weapon against errors of every kind is Reason. I have never used any other, and I trust I never shall.*

Deeply religious people were shocked and outraged when they read Paine's book. He wrote the above passage knowing that this reaction would be provoked, yet he did not flinch as reason guided his pen.

An elected public official actively solicits ideas, criticism, and recommendations from constituents, because otherwise he or she is not doing the job. How else are the people to keep an official informed concerning what they want him to do? If wisdom is challenged often enough, it will not have the opportunity to become conventional.

Tocqueville was impressed by what he found in this country: "In a democratic country such as the US a deputy hardly ever has a lasting hold over the minds of his constituents. However small an electoral body may be, it is constantly changing shape with the fluctuations of democracy. It must therefore be courted unceasingly."[5] Immediately on election a public official should initiate an open dialog with the people, and he or she should sell them on playing their part in maintaining it. He knows that when he talks he is only repeating what he already knows, but when he listens he can learn something. Without this dialog, self-government is impractical.

An effective leader develops a following, but it is a critical following or an active followership. Followers frequently question the decisions and actions of their leader, demanding justifications, convincing arguments, and explanations why other courses of action were rejected. The leader in turn questions the constituents, and they do likewise among themselves. In this way a collective wisdom is generated, which is the best vehicle in which to pursue truth. Leadership is the management, not of the supernatural, not of weapons, not of wealth, but rather of information, knowledge, and wisdom. This is leadership in the Age of Reason.

Powell was impressed with what Samuel Smiles wrote concerning leadership:

> *He wrote* Character *in 1871. "Truthfulness is at the foundation of all personal excellence," he wrote, "And a man is already of consequence in the world when it is known that he can be relied on—that when he says he knows a thing he does know it—that when he says he will do a thing, he can do it, and does. . . . It is the individual men, and the spirit which actuates them, that determine the moral standing and stability of nations. The only true barrier against the despotism of public opinion, whether it be of the many or of the few, is enlightened individual freedom and purity of personal character. Without these there can be no vigorous manhood, no true liberty in a nation."*[6]

Smiles's reference to a leader who when necessary will confront "the despotism of public opinion" is noteworthy. A leader and constituents share a joint responsibility: keeping one another alert and focused.

Collective wisdom has potential for predicting future events. An analogy can be found in the stock market, the function of which concentrates thousands of minds on one objective, which is some combination of money income and growth of capital. History has shown that the market can err; 1929–30 is a classic example. History has also shown that a large group of investors and analysts can predict its aggregate behavior remarkably accurately when reason prevails over passion during analysis and interpretation of the data that it yields in profusion. Collective wisdom is thus built into the price of a company's stock. This explains why no one can consistently beat the market by picking individual stocks.

A leader during the Age of Reason is unimpressed with titles, prestige, the big player, connections with the high and mighty, whom you know, and whom you can manipulate or deceive. Rather, he or she believes in what you know and in the strength that lies in good ideas and recommendations. In this way he draws forth the real strength in ordinary people, and through continuing dialog a virtuous circle is perpetuated.

As strong and relevant as it is, collective wisdom will occasionally err. A leader does not point a finger when something goes wrong; he knows where the buck stops. A leader with self-confidence and an active followership can recognize error and learn from it. A good team will immediately set to work correcting the error, and it will be achieved quickly and simply, in part because the action was kept simple during the planning stage. A recurrence of the same or a similar error is thus rendered unlikely.

In today's society, a habit that has been handed down from time immeasurable has been discarded. This habit is reflecting on experience. Bennis wrote, "Your accumulated experience is the basis for the rest of your life, and that base is solid and sound to the degree that you have reflected on it, understood it, and arrived at a workable solution." He argued that leadership without perspective and point of view is not leadership. But regular practice of this habit in a fast-paced society requires self-discipline; this in turn relates back to education for self-knowledge. Regular practice also requires faith and persistence, because very probably the first few sessions will bear little obvious fruit.

Johnson remarked on the only known modern president who believed in reflection: "Yet if [Calvin] Coolidge was sparing of words, what he did say was always pithy and clear, showing that he had reflected deeply on history and developed a considered, if somber, public philosophy."[7] Johnson continued, "There were very severe limits to his political ambitions, just as (in his view) there ought to be very severe limits to any political activity."

Democracy has citizens rejecting the immature temptation to look to Capitol Hill for authority, for guidance. It means seizing the initiative, taking the bull by the horns. During the 1992 election campaign *Time* magazine published a feature article that described Ross Perot as the nation's savior. This is misleading in that it suggests a perception of the office of the president and its incumbent as a heaven-sent authority figure to be admired and blindly followed. But acting on this belief is saluting the stripes and not the man.

Bennis summarized, "I believe in helping people to identify what they can do well and releasing them to do it. In such leaders, competence, vision, and virtue exist in nearly perfect balance. Competence, or knowledge, without vision and virtue, breeds technocrats. Virtue, without vision and knowledge, breeds ideologues. Vision, without virtue and knowledge, breeds demagogues." In the end it comes down to exercise of mature judgment, variously in various situations, while not losing sight of a distant beacon.

Political Power Placed in Good Ideas

Biographer Isaacson commented on Henry Kissinger's personality:

> *He was particularly comfortable dealing with powerful men whose minds he could engage. As a child of the holocaust and a scholar of Napoleonic-era statecraft, he sensed that great men as well as great forces were what shaped the world, and he knew that personality and policy could never be fully divorced. Secrecy came naturally to him as a tool of control. And he had an instinctive feel for power relationships and balances, both psychological and geostrategic.*[8]

Kissinger served the nation as a statesman, but his approach to personal power seeking epitomized that of the career politician. The only difference was that he flexed his muscles primarily in international affairs, but his need for secrecy was typical of the politician who had to face the voters.

As he described the workings of Congress, Greider quoted representative Byron Dorgan: "You have a bill that's ninety-six pages long and with 140 different tax changes which are all little pockmarks on the tax code. If my provision is number eighty-nine on the list and it's not very clearly described, it's likely you can get it passed with about seven and a half seconds of discussion. . . . Ideas are the enemy of progress here. At least to some extent, that's true."[9] Greider continued: "The most pernicious effect of campaign money is probably not on the legislative roll calls, but in how money works to keep important new ideas off the table—ideas that might find a popular constituency among citizens, but would offend important contributors." Greider argued that dirty money not only causes immoral and corrupt behavior but also stifles progress.

Bennis said: "As you may have noticed, I've excluded politicians, because candid politicians are in very short supply, and I was more interested in ideas than in ideology."[10] Fresh ideas are a threat to career politicians because they have little contact with real people and so they do not know how expression of such an idea will be received. It is much easier and safer to mouth sound bites on television and say what the polls indicate the people want to hear. However, once the election has passed and they are home free, there is practically no intent to follow up on what they said. After all, their primary and often only objective has been accomplished and they are free to begin thinking about (and raising money for) the next election.

In politics a driven person can attain the top, assisted by an imposing staff of spin doctors, speechwriters, media merchants, and special interest money. This is surface success, in that it lacks an anchor in principle. John F. Kennedy had charisma, but he was not a leader. His father may have bought his nomination at the Democratic convention in 1960, and he apparently won the election by projecting a more attractive image in the first televised presidential debates than did his opponent, Richard Nixon. Then he proclaimed that the nation had finally arrived at Camelot, after twelve years of arguably the most problem-free period in US history. (Not to overemphasize Kennedy; similar stories can describe the ascensions of most of the presidents since Truman and Eisenhower).

Bennis wrote, "Leaders have no interest in proving themselves, but an abiding interest in expressing themselves. The difference is crucial, for it's the difference between being driven, as too many people are today, and leading, as too few people do. Something else they have in common is that each of these individuals has continued to grow and develop throughout life." Driven suggests personal power seeking, whereas leading is seeking, facilitating, and coordinating the ideas and efforts of others. That is, the team wins it while the coach salutes its accomplishment. If there is a limelight the basking goes to the team, in stark contrast to George Bush Senior's demeanor while welcoming Gen. Norman Schwarzkopf back to this country as the hero of the Gulf War.

The presence in today's media environment of breaking news often gets in the way of the main business of today's government: fund-raising. Fallows talked with presidential aide David Dreyer.[11] "By the time the working day began, he said, the president and his staff felt that they had fallen half a cycle behind in the race to cope with breaking news and answer their opponents' criticisms."

This is not leadership; it is not even management. It is coping, or fire fighting (Bennis's shock learning). What is even more discouraging about this situation was illustrated in Chapter 10: Most of the quarreling is faked or staged. Also, the criticism is aimed at personalities and power seeking; there are no new ideas presented, which is typical of constructive criticism. Finally, and in the end tragically, there is no intent to offer this type of criticism.

Victor Hugo wrote, "An invasion of armies can be resisted, but not an idea whose time has come." Shevardnadze noted: "Born in great minds, great ideas long await their hour. Sometimes the wait goes on for centuries. But the hour chimes sooner or later. A new idea by itself, after all, is nothing but words if it does not capture the minds of the majority and at the same time provide motivation for practical behavior."[12]

A great idea is born in a mind that is great or can become so if the idea benefits from extensive discussion and criticism. It is through this process that the mind also acquires the motivation mentioned by Shevardnadze. Absent this process, which is the democratic process, and the idea remains only words. It will eventually die for lack of nourishment, possibly to be resurrected years later.

Ayn Rand, in *The Fountainhead,* quoted hero Howard Roark: "The great creators—the thinkers, artists, the scientists, the inventors—stood alone against the men of their time. Every great new thought was opposed. Every great new invention was denounced. . . . But the men of unborrowed vision went ahead. They fought, they suffered, and they paid. But they won."[13]

The courage of conviction was admirably displayed by antislavery crusader and publisher William Lloyd Garrison on the occasion of the first edition of his newspaper *The Liberator:* "I will be as harsh as truth, and as uncompromising as justice. . . . No! No! Tell a man whose house is on fire, to give a moderate alarm; tell him to moderately rescue his wife from the hands of the ravisher . . . but urge me not to moderation. . . . I am in earnest—I will not equivocate—I will not excuse—I will not retreat a single inch—AND I WILL BE HEARD."[14] Truth may be harsh indeed, but once identified, it also breeds courage.

It is equally important that the idea be kept separate during discussion from the personality of the person presenting it, elaborating on it, or arguing for or against it. Personal power seekers are easy to identify: What they are speaks so loudly that it is difficult to understand what they are saying. In 1992 Massachusetts senator Paul Tsongas ran for president. He was widely quoted as saying, "If the message is right it matters not who is the messenger." Lincoln said, "I have never professed an indifference to the honors of official station; and were I to do so . . . I should only make myself ridiculous. Yet I have never failed—do not now fail—to remember that in the republican cause there is a higher aim than mere office." A career politician cannot hear these words.

In the early years the republic was in an experimental stage, and public officials often had limited understanding of its nuances. During the 1800 presidential election campaign Jefferson ran against the incumbent, John Adams. Jefferson said,

> *I called on Mr. Adams on some official business. He was very sensibly affected, and accosted me with these words: "Well, I understand that you are to beat me in this contest, and I will only say that I will be as faithful a subject as any you will have." "Mr. Adams," said I, "this is no personal contest between you and me. Two systems of principles on the subject of government divide our fellow citizens into two parties. With one of these you concur, and I with the other."*

Adams's philosophy of government was related to monarchy; hence his reference to a subject. But Jefferson recognized the reality of democracy and its relation to principle: Minds may differ, but hearts can remain united. This was especially important to him, as the two friends had recently had a falling out when this conversation took place. (Their hearts were reunited later.) Jefferson continued: "Were we both to die today, tomorrow two other names would be in the place of ours, without any change in the motion of the machinery. Its motion is from its principle, not from you or myself."

Winston Churchill was arguably England's greatest leader and probably its greatest mind. Biographer Gilbert wrote: "Of the many eulogies, Lord Chandos: 'He enjoyed a conflict of ideas, but not conflict between people. His powers were those of imagination, experience, and magnanimity. Perhaps not enough had been made of his magnanimity. He saw man as a noble and not as a mean creature.'"[15]

From George Orwell's famous book *1984* (published in 1949): "If liberty means anything at all, it means the right to tell people what they do not want to hear. The common people still vaguely subscribe to that doctrine and act on it. . . . It is the liberals who fear liberty and the intellectuals who want to do dirt on the intellect." Modern liberalism had its start during the Franklin Roosevelt administration (1933–45). These people and the intellectuals sought personal power to do many things. In the process they infringed on the freedoms of individuals.

In a democracy ideas form the basis for creation of laws and for their revision to accurately reflect changes in the society. A slogan seems to capture the essence of democracy: Power in ideas; government by laws. The citizen who generates an idea that stands up well under withering debate and criticism feels a sense of accomplishment. He or she has made a significant contribution to good government in his neighborhood or community. If given appropriate recognition for the contribution, he will be motivated to generate another idea and another (see Chapter 18).

On the other hand, if the idea wilts under criticism and a leader summarizes the discussion by separating the citizen's persona from the idea and thus reassuring him of his worth to the neighborhood as a citizen, he, too, will be motivated. Once rejected, a poor idea indirectly contributes to good government, because no additional time need be wasted in discussion. A later time may prove its worth.

If power resides in ideas it will be widely dispersed, simply because any citizen may contribute. Just as Paine demonstrated in the case of wisdom, good ideas are not the sole province of the intelligent or the wealthy. Therefore keeping power in ideas contributes to deterring it from concentrating in one place. This is important, as it was shown that power tends to concentrate due to actions based on the negative side of human nature. This is the way good leaders help citizens keep a society moving in the right direction. When good government becomes a habit, institutions have no opportunity to become bloated, stagnant, irrelevant, and corrupt.

The conclusion is that "career politician" and "leader" make up a contradiction in terms. Jefferson commented,

> *An honest man can feel no pleasure in the exercise of power over his fellow citizens. And considering as the only offices of power those conferred by the peo-*

ple directly, that is to say, the executive and legislative functions of the general and state governments, the common refusal of these, and multiplied resignations, are proofs sufficient that power is not alluring to pure minds, and is not, with them, the primary principle of contest.

How Good Leaders Work with Citizens to Identify Good Ideas

Democracy is only an idea. Ideas are everywhere; they are truly a dime a dozen. However, good ideas are rare. What makes democracy a good idea? Wrong question. Correction: **Who** makes democracy a good idea? The answer to that question must lie in the citizenry; a good leader must approach the task of government from a bottom-up orientation. He or she must utilize the constituents as the most valuable among many available resources, to get direction and to carry out the task of governing (not ruling). Democracy is a challenge to be met by a team, so cohesiveness is paramount.

Jefferson understood leadership, as reported by Powell:

He affirmed that all people are entitled to liberty, regardless of what laws might say. If laws do not protect liberty, he declared, then the laws are illegitimate, and people should rebel. Although Jefferson did not originate this idea, he put it in a way that set afire the imagination of people around the world. Moreover, he articulated a doctrine for strictly limiting the power of government, the most dangerous threat to liberty everywhere.[16]

Top political leaders of that time habitually stayed in hotels or boarding houses, as there was not enough money to put them up in any kind of splendor. Thus it was that a visiting Englishman, Thomas Twinning, was staying in the same hotel as John Adams (vice-president and head of the Senate).

I was always glad (he wrote years later) when I saw Mr. Adams enter the room and take his place at our table. Indeed, to behold this distinguished man. . . . Occupying the chair of the Senate in the morning, and afterwards walking home through the streets and taking his seat among his fellow citizens as their equal, conversing amicably with men over whom he had just presided . . . was a singular spectacle, and a striking exemplification of the state of society in America at this period.[17]

People are more intelligent than politicians who rule by the PANG principle (People Are No Good) believe. They need only the opportunity to prove themselves, but this means a leader who is oriented to the positive incentives of human nature. This means keeping an enlightened faith in people, even when turbulence appears and they seem to be incapable of controlling it.

Once in place and functioning, democracy obliterates the NIHS, or not-invented-here syndrome. If a person spends much of his or her working life in a specialized occupation, he is likely to be subject to the NIHS. But in these times nearly everything changes, and this person should be receptive to suggestions from others concerning how an institution may be modernized and improved.

A leader can prove his value to government many times over by developing the skill of helping citizens distinguish between weak ideas and strong ones. Effectively led, constructive criticism and debate will add muscle to a potentially good idea, just as it will provide a soft landing for a poor one. A leader will teach the people how to criticize an idea by speaking so as to separate the idea from the persona of its originator or supporter. In such a discussion a polite person plays the devil's advocate. Decorum is important for maintaining a political environment characterized by mutual respect, trust, and confidence.

A potentially good idea may lie hidden in a reticent citizen. A good leader will develop a nose for such an idea and will help the person to present it to the group, either in written or oral form. Or an idea may come to someone, hang around for only a few seconds, and then fly away. A leader will encourage reflection by the people, as a pause may be all that is necessary to capture that idea long enough to reduce it to writing. After discussion a good idea may take the form of a resolution, a recommendation, a plan of action, or a law, or it may be handed on to a different level of government for consideration.

If a salesperson is not himself sold on a product he or she will have great difficulty in selling it to someone else. A leader has sold himself on ideas; it remains only to test-drive each one for quality. Hyman Rickover was a brilliant admiral in the US Navy, serving about sixty years before retirement. He said, "Great minds discuss ideas; medium minds discuss events; small minds discuss people."

If citizen vigilance does not remain constant, conventional wisdom can become entrenched. An excellent example exists today; it is called the cold war mentality. The cold war began in 1947 when differences in viewpoints between government officials of Western World War II allies and those of the Soviet Union became more serious. NATO and the Warsaw Pact were formed, and for the next forty-two years both sides concentrated on building bigger and more destructive armies and weapons. Near the end of the cold war a chillingly appropriate acronym was coined: MAD, or mutually assured destruction.

Millions of military men and officers built their careers around the cold war. Government officials also built careers, as politicians directed more and more taxpayer money to weapons construction and international trafficking, and defense contractors kicked back some of their planned fat profits into reelection campaigns. The news media cooperated, keeping ordinary citizens in most countries of the world fearful of a nuclear holocaust. The external threat theory flourished: MAD = panic.

Suddenly, in 1989 the cold war was over, as indicated by bloodless revolutions among Soviet satellite nations. The time was right for advanced countries to seize the initiative and lead the world into the Age of Reason. It did not happen because those officials who were responsible for providing leadership lacked the necessary vision, courage, persistence, and sales ability to change the direction of events. Furthermore, political and financial arrangements created and maintained over forty years were comfortable and lucrative. Therefore public officials were disinclined to listen to citizens expecting real change. Bennis briefly replayed: "The manager accepts the status quo; the leader challenges it. The manager does things right; the leader does the right thing."

Even today the news is full of attempts to convince the people of the imminent danger of some terrible threat from another country. However, when there is no enemy within sight, real or imagined, this product is difficult to sell. But warriors know little about doing anything other than war or preparing for it, and it was shown that career politicians are not leaders.

These people do have persistence, but it is the wrong kind: the belief that they can go on fooling the citizens indefinitely. The conclusion is this is a very expensive piece of conventional wisdom that needs to be challenged, even if thousands of high officials in the military, government, and the private defense industry do not want to hear it (Chapter 21 elaborates). Courage is needed to swim upstream.

Conventional wisdom will not become entrenched unless it develops in the absence of effective leadership. If it remains in this condition for as long as forty years or more, any force for change exerted within the organization is predestined to fail.

The last major change in the system of government in this country occurred in 1933, when the society was mired in the Great Depression. Since then public officials have had ample time to pile on layers of conventional wisdom. This means that the impetus for the necessary major change must originate from outside the system. Within it there are far too many vested interests, far too much turf to protect and butts to cover, and far too many habits ingrained for any impetus to gain the necessary momentum. And then there is the money.

Harris argued that people must work through reality to create a thriving community.[18]

> *Reality, understood through the study of history and the observation of man, is . . . the tool by which we construct a valid ethical system. We are not reasonable, however, if we assume that the only reality about man is that within our own personal experience or comprehension. We can spend a lifetime digging through the bones of past experience, as if this were the only place reality existed, and completely ignore other compelling realities. One such reality is the need for and existence of a system of moral values.*

He suggested that such a system could be acquired through interactions with other people and hence the generation of a collective wisdom.

A Native American chief once said, "Do not judge a man until you have walked a mile in his moccasins." This provides an effective guide for the process of constructive criticism, which is an art in itself. The critic must first listen carefully and without bias for understanding, asking questions as appropriate for clarification. Then he or she should reflect on what has been learned, conclude that the idea or proposal has weak points, and assemble a rejoinder. Then he is ready to speak. First the critic summarizes the idea's strong points, as this prepares the originator's or supporter's ego and thus enables him to listen to what is coming next. Finally the critic refers to the weak points and moves forward to contribute suggestions for improvement or rejection of the idea.

Public officials can and should generate ideas, but when these come to citizens from a position that might be interpreted as authoritative, extra effort must be made to avoid giving them preference over ideas that come from ordinary citizens. Above all these officials must open their ideas to criticism, and the people must understand that an idea rejected involves no loss of face under any circumstances. Public officials should always bear in mind that he who pays the piper calls the tune.

Alexander Hamilton wrote,

> *It is a just observation that the people commonly intend the PUBLIC GOOD. This often applies to their very errors . . . and the wonder is that they so seldom err as they do, beset as they continually are by the wiles of parasites and sycophants, by the snares of the ambitious, the avaricious, and desperate. . . . When occasions present themselves in which the interests of the people are at variance with their inclinations, it is the duty of the persons whom they have appointed to be the guardians of those interests to withstand the temporary delusion in order to give them time and opportunity for more cool and sedate reflection.*[19]

In situations like this a leader courageously speaks against the flow of opinion and persists as long as is necessary. At the same time the leader urges caution, reason, and reflection, because he or she knows that these assist in the quest for truth and are fully as important as debate and criticism. Spirited engagement in the latter two increase the risk of the triumph of passion over reason; pause to reflect, and a vital balance has been restored. Hamilton said, "[It] has procured lasting moments of their gratitude to the men who had courage and magnanimity to serve them at the peril of their displeasure."

If a community will discuss and agree on an objective, a potential leader or two will emerge from the discussion. However, analyses of both content and delivery of the remarks should occur before a leader is elected. Considering the former, a candidate may have excellent ideas for governing but his or her ability to communicate them is limited. Conversely, a candidate may have poor ideas but an impressive gift of speech. The best candidate possesses a combination of the two, but it will often require some effort to identify this person. He will have his own ideas because he has been open to others and has done some thinking, but he will also have the ability to encourage development of others' ideas. People have respect for his accomplishments and then affection; the heart follows the mind.

Gardner commented, "A society is being continuously re-created, for good or ill, by its members. This will strike some as a burdensome responsibility, but it will summon others to greatness."[20] This observation implies the famous 20-80 rule, wherein most organizations 20 percent of the members do 80 percent of the work. However, a leader who is painting a political landscape knows the value of offering a paintbrush to everyone, thus encouraging all to participate. An effective leader will strive to beat that 20 percent limit by a wide margin.

Bennis argued for what he called a learning organization. He claimed that a true leader remains sensitive to opportunities to rock the boat, that is, to introduce new and different ideas for consideration by his or her constituents. Democracy is dynamic; without it institutions stagnate and grow into monsters. "There are ten factors, ten personal and organizational characteristics for coping with change, forging a new future, and creating learning organizations." (Eight of them are listed here.)

1. "Leaders manage the dream. All leaders have the capacity to create a compelling vision, one that takes people to a new place, and then to translate that vision into reality."
2. "Leaders embrace error . . . [and] create an atmosphere in which risk taking is encouraged."
3. "Leaders encourage reflective backtalk . . . . [by] having someone in his life who would tell him the truth." During the era of conquest and plunder a king permitted no criticism, constructive or otherwise. Therefore the responsibility for criticism fell to the court jester, and often the message did not filter through the fog.
4. "Leaders encourage dissent." Dissent should be interpreted as constructive, not simply finding fault.
5. "Leaders possess the Nobel Factor: optimism, faith, and hope." The obvious tilt is toward the positive side of human nature.
6. "Leaders understand the Pygmalion effect in management. . . . . Expect the best of the people around them. Leaders know that the people around them change and grow. If you expect great things, your associates will give them to you." This means a deeper concern with what a citizen can give to government, rather than what he is getting from it.
7. "Leaders have what I think of as the Gretzky Factor, a certain 'touch.' . . . [It is] not as important to know where the puck is now as to know where it will be.
8. "Leaders see the long view."

Minds must be free, so their thoughts can range far and wide. Jefferson understood this: "For I have sworn upon the altar of God, eternal hostility against every form of tyranny over the mind of man."

Notes

1. Warren Bennis, *On Becoming a Leader.* Addison-Wesley, 1989.
2. *The Economist,* "Brave New World." October 20, 2001, p. 53.
3. Stephen Carter, *Integrity.* Basic Books, 1996.
4. Thomas Paine, *The Age of Reason.* Gramercy Books, 1993.
5. Alexis de Tocqueville, *Democracy in America.* Knopf, 1972.
6. Jim Powell, *The Triumph of Liberty.* Free Press 2000, p. 170.
7. Paul Johnson, *Modern Times.* Harper Collins, 1991, p. 229.
8. Walter Isaacson, *Kissinger: A Biography.* Simon and Schuster, 1992.
9. William Greider, *Who Will Tell the People: The Betrayal of American Democracy.* Simon and Schuster, 1992.
10. Bennis, *On Becoming a Leader.*
11. James Fallows, *Breaking the News: How the Media Undermine American Democracy.* Pantheon Books, 1996, p. 76.
12. Eduard Shevardnadze, *The Future Belongs to Freedom.* Free Press, 1991.
13. Ayn Rand, quoted in Jim Powell, *The Triumph of Liberty,* p. 62.
14. William Lloyd Garrison, quoted in Jim Powell, *The Triumph of Liberty*, p. 49.
15. Martin Gilbert, *Churchill: A Life.* Henry Holt, 1991.
16. Powell, *The Triumph of Liberty,* p. 32.
17. David McCullough, *John Adams.* Simon and Schuster, 2001.
18. Thomas A. Harris, *I'm Okay; You're Okay.* Avon Books, 1973.
19. Alexander Hamilton, Federalist Paper No. 70, *The Federalist Papers.* Mentor, 1961.
20. John W. Gardner, *Self Renewal.* Norton, 1981.

Part IV: Concerned Citizens Seize the Opportunity

We find comfort among those who agree with us; growth among those who don't.
—Frank A. Clark

Part IV transforms theory into practice. This is important, as it has been truly said that there is nothing so practical as a good theory. Theory is little more than a tentative explanation of an observed phenomenon. It acquires utility only if and when it can withstand testing and criticism. Theory is especially applicable to democracy, because true democracy is an experiment yet to be tried. Today the timing for a trial is good, as the world leaves behind conflict and destruction and moves forward into the Age of Reason.

In a democracy free and diverse individuals discover that they share an interest in good government. Therefore they freely choose to come together and apply their talents and efforts toward that objective. They do this because, having been finally enlightened concerning the nature of good government, they perceive benefits in it to themselves and their families. Furthermore they see in this a legacy that will enhance the happiness of their children, grandchildren, and generations to come. Their progeny will continue building on the practice of democracy while utilizing as a sound base the accomplishments of their ancestors. In this way the future stands on the shoulders of the present.

Chapter 17 promotes the attraction of civic pride to citizens and argues that a true democracy can work in today's information and technology environment. A scenario suggests how high-tech equipment might make political meetings more efficient, effective, and interesting. Experience will show the best way to recruit concerned, contributing citizens and put these talented people to work. Placed in the hearts and minds of moral and responsible people, truth can be such a mighty weapon as to subdue an army.

Chapter 18 suggests that people who volunteer their time, talent, money, and efforts tend to feel good while doing good. Because time is largely a matter of priorities, good feelings will cause people to revise their priorities in favor of volunteering. They will seek opportunities to help others, more so when overbearing big government is restrained from interfering. As for money, citizens will restrict their government at all levels from forcibly taking more than a minimum from them. They will have more money available, and with volunteerism they will enjoy freedom of choice concerning where, when, and how to donate.

Chapter 19 demonstrates how a family can take back responsibility for its health and future from big government. When people have the opportunity to mature into healthy and fully functioning adults they will not only raise their children more effectively, they will also look forward to contributing to good government and also to voluntary organizations.

In a democracy citizens will become involved in building institutions that will spread incentives based on the positive side of human nature. Equally important, people will exercise continuing vigilance so that institutions will be modernized to keep pace with a constantly changing society. Finally, people will take pride in their accomplishments and in their neighborhood and community. They will earn the respect of others, including their children.

Chapter Seventeen:
Creating Participating Citizens and Putting Democracy into Practice

Never mistake knowledge for wisdom.
One helps you make a living; the other helps you make a life.
—Sandra Carey

In her powerful book *The Discovery of Freedom,* Rose Wilder Lane argued that men and their energies are free by nature. She also demonstrated conclusively that for 6,000 years of history other people have consistently sought to undermine that natural freedom. Therefore it behooves contemporary man to exert some thought and effort to protect his God-given freedoms from the clutches of those who would take it from him, however gradually and insidiously.

Thomas Paine elaborated on this freedom by differentiating between natural rights and civil rights, the latter restraining exercise of an individual's natural rights via consideration of the natural rights of others.[1] Honesty in government should be considered a civil right by the people, who must restrain it lest public officials infringe on citizens' natural rights. In 1843, the *Edinburgh Review* added an important dimension: "Be assured that freedom of trade, freedom of thought, freedom of speech, and freedom of actions, are but modifications of one great fundamental truth, and that all must be maintained or all risked; they stand and fall together." Adversaries can be depended on to find the weakest point and begin nibbling at individual freedoms. Because some of these people occupy positions where they can exert force on citizens, they have a unique opportunity to do this.

Citizens in this country today face a major challenge, in that if the system is to make a vitally necessary sweeping change so also must their attitude toward government. This attitude must change from one of rolling with the punches administered by a top-down, paternalistic big government to one of courage to seize the initiative within a shared common interest in good government. Furthermore, it is known that attitudes based in the mind can change more readily than can those based in the heart.

When questioned, attitudes based in the heart are likely to bring on an ego-defensive reaction. This is one reason why Capitol Hill and its lackeys in the media appeal to people by arousing emotions instead of intellects. (Reagan's "feel-good" politics is an example. It was not designed to stimulate thinking about government.) Tabloid journalism tends to create tabloid citizens; this suits public officials, who want to keep the peasants dumbed down.

Today people do not trust one another. The practice of democracy will restore mutual trust, and from this will grow a faith in people's capability to solve their problems, both individually and through their collective wisdom. But this should be an enlightened faith: This is a faith in one another to keep commitments once made, and also a skepticism of commitments made by public officials. The main reason for this skepticism lies in the fact that they have been entrusted with temporary control over someone else's money, and money is a proven temptress.

There is a fortuitous element of timing in the proposed major change in government. Phillips commented: "The millennium should involve a great sense of discontinuity. Powerful forces for upheaval are converging. Popular willingness to accept far-reaching change should be unusually high."[2] It is quite possible that the new millennium will generate momentum for a sweeping change in government, which will receive the support of all concerned citizens.

This chapter will move democracy into the household for reflection and discussion. Then it will encourage enlightened citizens to the local meeting hall.

Pride as the Prize

Tocqueville remarked on civic pride during his 1830 visit to the United States.[3]

> *Picture to yourself . . . a society which comprises all the nations of the world—English, French, German: people differing from one another in language, in beliefs, in opinions; in a word a society possessing no roots, no memories, no prejudices, no routine, no common ideas, no national character, yet with a happiness a hundred times greater than our own. . . . How are they welded into one people? By community of interests. That is the secret!*

In those days a political leader tapped into diversity as a necessary group of resources. He knew he needed all resources to help his constituents mold civic pride. During centuries of European history up to that time, the English, French, Dutch, and Germans had fought each other repeatedly. But here in the United States they and others worked together. Therein lies much of the beauty of bottom-up government.

Later in the nineteenth century an English gentleman named Thomas Macaulay called "not for more philanthropy, but rather for more respect for the dignity of human life, and more faith in its ability to work out its own salvation."[4]

He continued: "The system has created its own dependent population." This country has recently moved away somewhat from this situation, affording a little momentum to help address the need for respect.

Late-twentieth-century poll results in the seven most advanced countries revealed fear among the people as welfare rolls expanded that societies were falling apart. The results also showed a clear disdain for political leaders and their parties. An interpretation of these results suggests that attitudes in favor of a sweeping change in systems of government may be gradually forming. Because people naturally tend to come together in shared activities when this coming together is motivated by a shared interest in good government, the way would open for restoration of civic pride. Furthermore the positive side of human nature would come into full play.

John Galt is the hero of Ayn Rand's powerful novel *Atlas Shrugged.*[5] He engineered a brain strike, in which he led all productive men away from a decaying society. In a lengthy radio speech he thoroughly castigated a paternalistic big government that public officials had gradually transformed into a police state. "Man must obtain his knowledge and choose his actions by a process of thinking, which nature will not force him to perform. Man has the power to act as his own destroyer—and that is the way he has acted through most of his history." His remarks very capably illustrated the devastation within man wrought by allowing the negative side of human nature full play.

Galt continued:

> *No, you do not have to think; it is an act of moral choice. But someone had to think to keep you alive: if you choose to default, you default on existence and you pass the deficit to some moral man, expecting him to sacrifice his good for the sake of letting you survive by your evil. No, you do not have to be a man; but today those who are, are not there any longer. I have removed your means of survival—your victims.*
>
> *Thinking is man's only basic virtue, from which all the others proceed. And his basic vice, the source of all his evils, is that nameless act which all of you practice, but struggle never to admit: the act of blanking out, the willful suspension of one's consciousness, the refusal to think—not blindness, but the refusal to see; not ignorance but the refusal to know.*

As Rand's novel goes, shortly after Galt's speech the society completely and utterly collapsed. The main point that Galt sought to make is that a person does in fact have a choice, but some courage is needed to make the right choice and to follow through on the resulting commitment. That choice is the moral choice, and when many people make it a society that has been ravaged by negative thoughts and actions will acquire a solid morality.

Lance Morrow reviewed Bennett's *Book of Virtues:* "The American challenge now is not to pay homage to every cultural variation and appease every ethnic sensitivity, but rather to encourage universally accepted ideals of behavior: self-discipline, compassion, responsibility, friendship, work, courage, perseverance, honesty, loyalty, and faith. Those qualities, in that order, are the 10 sections in Bennett's 831-page volume."[6] Bennett quoted: "We must not permit our disputes over thorny political questions to obscure the obligation we have to offer instruction to all our young people in the area in which we have, as a society, reached a consensus: namely on the importance of good character."

Both Galt and Bennett addressed the crucial inside of a person, the self-worth of the individual. Good government relies on that self-worth, because with it a citizen is aware within him or her of the courage necessary to reach out and cooperate in the vital joint endeavor known as government. Education and reflection are of the utmost importance in acquiring this courage. When they are present there will be teamwork, and the American dream can be finally realized—the "dream team," as it were.

During the 1960s a popular joke had someone asking how many Californians were required to change a light bulb. The punchline was five: one to change it, three to share the experience, and one to reflect on the implications. Acquiring courage of heart through education and reflection can help to change attitudes toward the self, others, and government. "Others" will include people who look, act, speak, and believe differently.

Civic pride transcends ethnic divides; it encourages people to ignore these barriers, and eventually they simply fade into the ether. Then children will have no opportunity to learn about interethnic jealousy. Each will have less excess baggage to tote throughout his or her adult life.

Democracy and the resulting civic pride are dynamic concepts—always changing, always building. Older citizens would retain something meaningful toward which to look forward. Without these they tend to look backward toward their diverse backgrounds, but this causes feelings of fragmentation because there is no cement present today to hold history together. Enlightened seniors prefer to look forward, and participation in democracy provides an excellent opportunity to utilize their considerable talents to help shape the future of their neighborhood or community. A side benefit lies in the respect that they would earn, especially among members of their extended families.

Another recent trend seems to be going in the right direction: Land developers are again emphasizing front porches and walking instead of always driving. Some planning includes small convenience stores liberally sprinkled in neighborhoods. As democracy gains momentum there will emerge reasons to make contact with neighbors hardly known to today's citizen. No matter how different in word, appearance, and deed, neighbors share an interest in a good life and government affects life. They will see the value in good government. In the initial stages a citizen who reaches out to a neighbor will be surprised to make this discovery. As the positive side of human nature motivates more such behavior citizens will overcome any insecure feelings.

Today's neighborhood culture is oriented to the automobile. An overemphasis on materialism tends to make for long commutes to work to maximize income. Children are sometimes bussed far away to big schools because this policy is perceived as more efficient than small, neighborhood schools. Frequently both parents work, perhaps at distant locations. The result of all this is a lack of neighborhood and community solidarity or pride. Furthermore, these conditions do not conduce to its attainment.

In the future many citizens will reflect on their present biases. A substantial number will put less emphasis on maximum material wealth. Cyberworkers and telecommuters will stay in or near their homes as power is dispersed both in government and in the private sector. Small, local schools will evolve in response to demand from parents who desire to be active in their children's education. Neighborhood convenience stores and multipurpose centers will reduce the demand for automotive transportation. People will reawaken to the virtue of walking. They will bring about changes in conditions, to facilitate reaching out to others in a shared interest in good government. Civic pride will follow naturally.

Pride in neighborhood is an attitude based on positive feelings. Naturally, it should be earned and encouraged, but at the same time an openness to ideas from elsewhere is advisable. All available resources should be utilized. There are people with incredibly varied skills, and all can be motivated to contribute. Frequently there is uniformity within a neighborhood, and some sense of solidarity in spite of the inroads of cars and TV. If one neighbor upgrades his property, others are likely to follow and the result will be a general improvement. However, with civic pride this tendency generalizes beyond the limits of neighborhood, uniting citizens throughout the community in a common interest that does not stop at residential improvements.

Epstein enlarged on the notion of the whole individual joining others for their mutual benefit.[7]

> *This theory of individual self-interest is not only a theory of conflict and competition; it is one of cooperation as well. The organism that goes it alone has no allies . . . when things go bad, and is blocked from engaging in any projects that require the coordination of two or more actors. The logic of self-interest does not . . . ignore the gains from cooperation in order to maximize only those gains from competition and aggression. With any foresight . . . [a democracy] encourages voluntary arrangements.*

In a democracy it is necessary to put stress on **voluntary** agreements, because this maximizes freedom of choice. For example, there was a fire on a national forest that burned very close to some farmers' private lands. Several farmers turned out and helped US Forest Service fire fighters contain and extinguish the fire. Later a ranger brought paychecks to the farmers as compensation for helping reduce damage to public lands. They refused to accept the checks, explaining that because it was their own land they were saving they would have done so without payment or the prospect of the same. The task brought together individuals of different backgrounds in a joint effort, working toward a common objective. If it had any impact, the money was probably perceived as a barrier thrown up between good neighbors.

The basic rights of citizens are God's grant to them; they predate and transcend any other rights that connect to government. Pemberton drove this point home:

> *Your Congress has been watchful, yet not of the encroachments of the other two branches, but for opportunity to gain influence by purchasing your favor with your own money. . . . You are not the slave of government at all, but because you think so, you may as well be! Nay! The Constitution is your servant and the master of your government. It is not the Constitution of the US, it is the Constitution of the people, and for the United States! It is not only the law by which you are governed, it is the law by which you may govern your government! It is not the law by which high-handed politicians may impose their collective will upon you, it is for you to impose upon them! It does not belong to the government, it belongs to you! It is yours! It is yours to enforce upon your government! It is yours to read to those self-wise do-gooders; and if you will hold it high in your hand, they will quail and flee before it like the cowardly knaves they are, while those who are your true friends will rejoice in your new commitment.*[8]

No further comment seems necessary.

Participation Perceived as Opportunity

Pericles was a prominent leader in Athens during the fifth century B.C. "We do not say that a man who takes no interest in politics is a man who minds his own business; we say that he has no business here at all." He thought each citizen should pull his own weight in helping all citizens govern themselves in that ancient democracy. Tocqueville found citizens very busy when he visited this country in 1830, but nevertheless they took time to participate in government.[9]

People enhance their dignity through participation in government. The denial of the opportunity for participation is worse in a citizen's perception than receiving taxpayer-financed benefits for no work performed. The frequent result is societal unrest caused by abuse of drugs and crime. Today government denies citizens a lot of activities: the minimum wage denies many poor young people employment; welfare traps others in poverty; licensing restricts entry into a variety of occupations; and so on.

Over three-fourths of the states have passed what is called preemption legislation. This stops communities from regulating gun ownership on their own. The intent may be good, but the method is wrong, because each community has its own unique crime problem and hence gun problem. For control to be effective concerned and participating citizens must address the matter as a local issue.

Participation in government takes time, and it surely seems that nearly everyone is extremely busy. However, a little reflection will reveal that a substantial amount of time each day is devoted to working around, through, under, and over the system. (In the Soviet Union the system ground people down to near-despair; simple survival occupied most of each day.) Admittedly this comparison is difficult to quantify, because historical experience with true democracy is all but entirely missing. It is quite probable that once democracy is up and running, time spent in active participation in government will be less than the amount of time spent today in fighting the system.

Tocqueville was moved to compare the life of a US citizen with his or her counterpart in Europe. "Shaken by the tumultuous passions which have often troubled his own house, the European finds it hard to submit to the authority of the state's legislators. When the American returns from the turmoil of politics to the bosom of the family, he immediately finds a perfect picture of order and peace." It is true that democracy is inefficient, but the founding fathers believed that the game was worth the effort. The century that followed the creation of the Constitution amply vindicated their faith in the morality of humankind.

Good government not only protects citizens' rights but also enables them to move efficiently toward their chosen destinies. It does this through discipline forced on it by actively participating people, which in turn liberates them. Honesty and truth play vital roles. "You shall know the truth, and truth shall make you free."

Today's public officials cannot be trusted, so they must be forced to act to protect and enable. Arblaster commented on participation today:

> *Nor is making a show of consultation and participation, when what is being looked for is essentially a ratification of decisions already taken. This is the appearance of democracy without the substance. The substance is the power of peoples to make governments, and make their representatives, accede to the popular will and to popular demands. Democracy involves debate and discussion, but these are not enough if they remain inconclusive and ineffective in determining actual policies.*[10]

In this country (Arblaster is from Britain) there may be a show of consultation, but it is often faked through rigged poll results, staged political debates, and the activities of influence mongers (Chapter 10).

In a democracy a public servant is a **servant**, and not just in name. There are only two differences between a butler and a public official. One is the public official has many more bosses, and the other is the public official has frequent occasion to handle other people's money. Both are on call at specified times, and both respond to requests or demands. If the head of the household is a taskmaster, the butler may be fully as challenged to do the job well as is the public servant.

Because there are so many prospective bosses for the public official, an election is organized to make the several candidates known to the public. Members of that public would sharpen their evaluations if campaign messages were made available only in print form. This is advisable, because with print there is available the resource of leisure for evaluation, and it is more amenable to discussions with others: a flyer or booklet can be carried about to stimulate discussions.

If a public official opts to be the chair at a political meeting he or she should constantly bear in mind the question: What can I do to help you govern yourselves more effectively? Such a leader should strive to ensure (insofar as possible) that a paintbrush is placed in every hand; he knows that people support what they help create. An official should also know that the law of supply and demand works as well with words: The more he speaks the less weight assigned by listeners to each word. Jefferson noted, "Speeches that go on by the hour die by the hour." It is far more important that the leader listen. With this in mind, he may ask another capable citizen to chair the meeting.

A citizen who takes a risk in the marketplace and becomes successful will not just hold his or her head higher. He may also feel a measure of gratitude for the healthy community that provided the quality institutions that helped him succeed. Therefore, future participation in government is likely to increase, no matter how busy he may be with business. The citizen wants others to have opportunities similar to his, and their success will probably mean more business for his company. Finally, a citizen wants his family to continue to enjoy life in a democratic community.

At the beginning many citizens will feel uncomfortable in participating among mostly strangers. They may need a helping hand, so to speak. One remedy that might be helpful is to write a brief script concerning an issue for role-playing. Present only a part of it and invite citizens who have previously had some background to play the roles to their own conclusions. Schedule a short debriefing session immediately afterward. Some of them will enjoy the experience and will promote it to others. This is selling people on participation, just as a car salesperson may hand the keys to a prospective buyer for a test drive.

Citizens have essentially five roles available to them during a political meeting.

1. Originator or change agent. During private reflection a thought pops into his head and he writes it down immediately. Further reflection is aimed at elaboration and preparation for introduction at a meeting; he works on content of the idea, and also how he will present it (content and delivery). He tests it with a spouse and some neighbors, making revisions as he sees fit. Then he is ready to present it.
2. Elaborator or developer. This person gets interested in the idea during the meeting, so she helps add flesh to the skeleton and clarify the delivery. She is a logical member of a committee to investigate the idea further, should this be requested by those at the meeting.
3. Cheer leader. He contributes support and arguments and persuades others who were not present at the meeting.
4. Critic. This person constructively attempts to separate good ideas and recommendations from weak ones. Effective criticism adds muscle to good ideas, thus recruiting others in support.
5. Devil's advocate. She argues to discourage further development of the idea being discussed and recruits others to her position.

A particular individual will naturally gravitate to one or two of these roles. However, he may at times move into a different role as he may freely choose. From this it becomes obvious that a competent public official needs participating citizens, just as they need a good official who will listen to arguments, help meetings to conclusions on issues, and act to carry out the public will on each.

People will appreciate the opportunity to contribute their thinking toward a better neighborhood or community. They will phase back on activities such as working around the bureaucracy, watching TV to avoid real communication, running away from themselves, and being rude to others. As they acquire a strong system of values they will spread their influence, and this will combine with others' efforts to develop a sound morality in the community. The feeling of participation will be highly valued. Laws made will be obeyed. Taxes may even be paid with enthusiasm.

A wealthy country can have both capitalism and a democracy, but only if the masses are involved in continuing dialogs. Far-reaching dialog spreads truth. When the people do not know what is really going in their government they begin to believe, accurately, that it is no longer their government. The result is fragmentation between groups of citizens, and alienation from government. If politicians are in charge of government there will be inadequate leadership, and the situation can only deteriorate further.

On the other hand, a worker in a job that does not tax his or her talents will often find fulfillment in a stimulating hobby. Frequently in a man there occurs a tendency for aggression, which can probably be traced back to the hunter-gatherer era. Some men satisfy this urge through hunting and fishing or through competitive sports. Another outlet can be found in the intellectual combat that is democracy, as Tocqueville noted. There is no reason why this stimulating hobby cannot also be rewarding.

Lapham wrote,

> *What joins the Americans one to another is not a common nationality, language, race, or ancestry (all of which testify to the burdens of the past) but rather the participation in a shared work of imagining the future. The love of country follows from the love of its freedoms, not from the pride in its armies or its gross national product. Construed as a means and not an end, the Constitution stands as the premise for a narrative rather than as a plan for an invasion or a monument.*[11]

Lapham is quite correct. The Constitution is a means for preserving citizens' freedoms, but only if said citizens actively participate in guarding them. Lapham's "narrative" is the continuously unfolding story of the democratic process. Citizens will be thrilled to watch this unfolding, especially as they combine their talents, time, and commitment to themselves and their children to make it happen.

The Potential of Direct Democracy

The founding fathers in 1787 created the Constitution, which provided for a republic in the new nation. In a republic the people govern through representatives, which in Congress are called representatives and senators. With direct democracy there is no middleman; the people govern themselves directly. The Constitution's original intent was to have direct democracy operate for the vast majority of issues relevant to citizens' daily lives. Citizens would govern through representatives at state and national levels for the few general issues that they either could not resolve by themselves or chose not to do so (national defense, for example).

Over the past two centuries the government has assumed power over myriad previously local issues, thus creating the huge, paternalistic government that is today a plague on the people. The Tenth Amendment to the Constitution, which was intended to keep most issues local, has been widely ignored and violated on Capitol Hill.

Beedham said, "The places that now consider themselves to be democracies are with a handful of exceptions run by the process generally known as 'representative' democracy. That qualifying adjective should make you sit up and think. Our children may find direct democracy more efficient, as well as more democratic, than the representative sort."[12] He reported that ordinary people given freedom of expression often surprise politicians with their intelligence and wisdom.

In 1787 the founding fathers believed in direct democracy but thought it impractical at that time due to the primitive nature of travel and communications. Much has changed in the intervening two centuries. The following presentation will argue that recent developments in communications technology have made direct democracy a concept worthy of discussion.

Phillips questioned the current viability of political parties.[13] "And exhausted parties are the easiest prey for special interests, because there is little heartfelt belief to get in the way. Scandal has also taken a toll." Campaigns fought on TV have helped create money-driven politics. Special interests bring ever larger amounts of money to Washington, politicians and bureaucrats rig laws in exchange for it, and parties use it to help reelect cooperative politicians. In this way government has gradually become a closed system catering to the whims of the elite class.

"Meanwhile, computer executives, teleconferencing consultants, and their like properly doubt that political parties will keep their role in the high-tech communications or information age." No institution can remain relevant indefinitely. Parties came into prominence in this country in the middle of the nineteenth century. By the 1890s they were active in citizens' lives.

But "no longer. Voter turnout in today's media age is a remnant of these former enthusiasms. Parties are less necessary and less liked. Much of what they and their interest groups now mobilize is voter contempt, not voter participation, and there is good reason to assume that party functions will be at least partly replaced by some new communication forms or institution. Direct democracy could take hold through a version of telepolitics, instant referendum, or national town meeting. That change is probably underway."

Today's parties do little more than raise money and stage empty conventions. People don't vote, because they know that dollars do. If political parties were relegated to history few citizens would miss them, because their functions no longer connect to people's immediate concerns.

The next logical focus of discussion is the need for a Congress in Washington. Were it feasible to eliminate that body, away with it would go decades of rampant abuse of citizens' trust, elitism, irrelevancy, waste, corruption, and outright thievery (Chapter 10). If the national government were reduced to a minimum size commensurate with its necessary functions, it is quite possible that the executive could respond directly to initiatives from citizens in making, updating, revising, and (what is seldom done today) repealing laws.

Watched closely by skeptical citizens, the president would also help them enforce the few laws that would be needed at the national level. There would be no money paid out by that government to individual citizens, and there would be no competition among states for federal largess.

If the founding fathers could read this, they would probably be concerned because the proposal flies in the face of their doctrine of separation of powers in government (which guards against one of the three branches of government acquiring too much power over the other two). However, if the executive's actions in the open society (Chapter 14) were made transparent by the citizens, they would need to closely watch only one person instead of 535 (both houses of Congress combined) who are today concerned with buying votes and keeping what is really going on hidden from the riffraff.

In practice, either the executive or the citizens could initiate consideration of an issue. Then time would be scheduled for discussion and debate by citizens at the neighborhood level. Next, an electronic dialog would ensue between the executive and the thousands of precincts, until the proposal would be either discarded or crystallized into a form suitable for a vote. Citizens might even put in place a mechanism for recalling their president before the end of the term of office, if they were sufficiently unhappy with his or her performance. This mechanism could apply to state and local officials as well, and probably should (see the appendix).

The next ninepin to fall would be the electoral college system, as discussed in Chapter 4. Eliminate the Congress, and this institution would vanish with it.

Phillips's 1994 book *Arrogant Capital* is in part about nonviolent revolutions in this country. He thinks one is seriously overdue today. "For any national political revolution of the Jeffersonian and Jacksonian sort to take place at the ballot box during the 1990s will require a new premise. No candidate can implement outsider changes through the current two-party system. It may even be necessary for any serious outsider seeking the presidency to assault that two-party system and its interest-group linkage."

The core of the difficulty is that in practice it is not a two-party system. If it were, the party out of power would form a loyal opposition and create a genuine political conflict during an election campaign. The reality is a one-party system catering to special-interest money, faked conflict, and no real choice for voters. Furthermore, even if an independent candidate were to win the presidency, he would be just one person of limited political power. He would be obliged to fight against the might of a deeply entrenched oligarchy, which had long ago precluded any opportunity for concerned citizens to rally to his support.

"Which brings us to the critical question: what form must any potentially successful neo-Jeffersonian revolution assume?" Phillips avoided specifics in his response to this question, but he did present an important point: "Bloodless political revolution must be on ways of displacing the outdated party system with the emerging technology of direct democracy." Then he generalized on this argument to state: "No North American political revitalization can succeed without greater emphasis on direct democracy." Since 1994 progress in information technology has been explosive. The timing is right as the new millennium unfolds.

Phillips thought that the people would have the courage to step forward and take back the genius of self-government that they had lost. "We can readily imagine, in the US of 2015, thirty to forty percent of the eligible citizens signing in on their home computers to vote during a 48-hour open period on a statewide ballot initiative." However, he warned against a referendum formulated by insiders and presented to the people, because this would likely be cleverly worded to favor the elites. Rather, the people should initiate a referendum. A computer today is not necessary in the home; a touch-tone phone can be used, at least for voting ("To vote yes, press one").

Phillips concluded:

> *Would it be revolutionary? Yes. Is it far-fetched? No. The technology is a snap. The core of the debate will involve the philosophy; should ordinary voters rule? . . . The absurdity of leaving serious tax decisions to the untutored will be proclaimed in mahogany-paneled executive suites from Back Bay to Beverly Hills, despite evidence that the Swiss electorate has been a model of seriousness in making sophisticated fiscal choices in nationwide referendums.*

Switzerland has been operating its government based in part on referendums for over 100 years. By collecting a specified number of signatures, citizens can insist that a proposed law be brought to a vote. By collecting additional signatures they can insist on a vote even when Parliament is against the proposal. The system has proved imperfect, but obviously quite workable.

The Economist wrote,

> *"Electronic democracy" is inspired by two overlapping dislikes—of bureaucrats and of politicians—and by two ideas for making these groups more likable. The first conjures up a world where the grumpy civil servant behind a counter is replaced by an easy-to-follow screen that makes all the government's information available at the touch of a button. The second idea wants to make politicians as answerable and accessible to their constituents as Pericles was to the tiny Athenian democracy.*[14]

There occurred a trial of the second idea on a TV quiz show. The response overwhelmed the digital technology available, because those who installed it seriously underestimated the number who wanted to participate. Fifteen Info/California machines operated for two months on a trial basis, and 36,000 people used them. Santa Monica tried a Public Electronic Network. There were minor difficulties with electronically windy citizens, but it reinforced other results: People are interested in participating.

In view of developments in computer deception and crime, a caveat is in order. It may turn out that the best political meetings are those in which participants are there in person. This is because in interpersonal communication messages are often sent in nonverbal form. For example, the look in a person's eye, gestures, one's body leaning forward to emphasize a point, and other clues all contribute to effective dialog. However, secure systems can be devised for sharing the results of deliberations and voting. Finally, a citizen given a salute from the group for a particular job well done will derive more benefit if he or she receives it in front of the group instead of over a phone line.

It may be practical for a shut-in citizen and others who cannot attend a meeting to participate through teleconferencing. He or she could see the meeting, hear the dialog, electronically ask to speak, and be heard by the group. An able-bodied but reticent citizen given such an opportunity may become interested enough to begin attending meetings (another paintbrush in hand). There is much to be said about the physical presence of an adversary during a debate.

Hempel commented on this issue: "Some say it's a network of networks . . . that functions as a vast community, or even a series of neighborhoods. Others say it merely masquerades as community, that it can't compare or even compete with the real thing."[15] Today this comparison is difficult to make because citizens have lost their basis for comparison—civic pride.

But craving for community is a part of human nature. When a person attempts to fulfill this craving online, "the freedom to embellish a touch, or fib a little . . . the mix of truth and fabrication jumbled together so seamlessly that the recipient can't tell the difference." When two Arab men are negotiating face-to-face, one will frequently place a hand on the other's knee and stare unblinkingly into his eyes. Over centuries members of the Arab culture have learned that this practice reliably brings forth truth. In any society the pursuit of truth clearly needs to employ every helpful resource, because lack of truth is a problem that looms large.

Phillips pointed out that members of Congress are less than enthusiastic about electronic government. With widespread public discussion, people would expect them to stay home a lot more and listen to the citizens as they expressed their concerns. Small wonder they do not like this prospect: They would be very uncomfortable staying home with the rabble when they very much prefer living in Washington and schmoozing with the glitterati.

Referendum votes have some difficulties, as Arblaster indicated: "They have been staged, and the issue presented, in such a way as to produce the outcome wanted by the government which initiates them. They have, in other words, been gestures in the direction of popular consultation rather than anything more substantial."[16] A recent proposition in California was drafted by the tobacco industry in such a way as to fool many antismoking citizens into signing the petition; enough signatures were collected to get it on the ballot. However, an honest executive in Washington would not have a political ax to grind, so with proper precautions, adequate citizen discussions, and sound organization the referendum has potential.

Epstein referred to a study by John Rawls that showed that when deciding on a rule a local citizen does not know how that rule will possibly affect him or her in the future when he may be involved in a dispute on which that rule would bear.[17] Therefore a person will tend to argue for a position that works to the long-term advantage of all members of the community. This seems to be another way in which individuals come together in a shared interest in good government.

Lawyer Epstein also said, "Law has much to learn from medicine; first, do no harm." Law made by citizens has already learned that lesson.

A career politician will never recommend that a line labeled NOTA, or none of the above, appear at the bottom of each list of candidates' names on a ballot. This line gives a voter the opportunity to reject a whole slate of candidates, and it might force another election with different candidates standing. A candidate running unopposed could be rejected. This scheme broadens citizen choice in a country that presumably emphasizes freedom of choice, so it is easy to see why career politicians hate it. The Constitution emphasizes what government may not do, but not what citizens may not do.

There are many instances of desired behavior that can be enforced through moral suasion, which has been in turn established by custom and common usage. If a neighborhood or community has acquired civic pride, such pressure can be very effective. This is a good thing because it reduces the need for legal enforcement, as by definition government is force and so it undermines individual liberty. People are not likely to feel harassed by a deviant in the neighborhood if they are occupied with participating in government. They may invite him or her to participate, as the person may have some good ideas. (If he needs professional assistance, concerned citizens would help find it.)

In a community with civic pride, citizens would goad the media into spreading truth about the proceedings in political meetings. If desired, minutes of such meetings could be published regularly for serious study. The media would be no one's lackey; rather, they would be concerned with constructive criticism of government. If the people become deeply interested in an issue and government does not seem to be cooperating, the media would adopt the "bull terrier" tactic: grab hold and don't let go until appropriate action is taken. Citizens would force creation of a media institution that is vastly different from the sorry excuse that bombards their sensitivities today.

A recent incipient trend in the media prompts some speculation. They have recently become a little more critical of government, especially the one in Washington. But today's media are run by business managers, not journalists. If they see customers as wanting tabloid news (sex, violence, tragedy, war, and so on) this is what will predominate in media time and space. This is also done because managers know the competition is doing it and they dare not lose out.

However, they must also keep their antennae aloft. If they should catch even a faint whiff of change in the air, each will try to react quickly, before the competition gets wind of it. In this way a news medium can promote itself as on the cutting edge of change in the community, state, or nation. A particular medium would capture many forward-looking customers, and then struggle to keep them as the competition see its success and responds accordingly.

Speculation comes in when three different blips on the radar screen present themselves for reflection. One states that there is nothing in the air. The economy is basically solid, consumer confidence is high, and people will continue as usual consuming their customary tabloid news diet. A second suggests that managers of news media realize there is a trend in society of increasing disgust with corrupt government and contempt for politicians. Therefore they have increased their criticism just enough to convince most citizens that the media are exposing nearly all the skullduggery going on in Washington, whereas in fact they are barely scratching the surface. The media remain the lackeys of big government as citizens continue to remain well and artfully deceived.

In a country with an ostensibly free press, deception of the public can continue to work only with news media that cooperate in the grand deception. But as officials in big government continue to move the regime toward a police state it becomes more difficult to keep the deception hidden (in which case it is no longer deception). Therefore the third blip has managers sniffing a major change in society and in citizens' attitude toward government. In this case each group of media managers would work hard to divine the timing of this shift, because they want their publication to be on top of it when it comes and not be caught pandering to a government on the way out. Such is the market when there is competition.

THE ACTIVE PRACTICE OF DEMOCRACY

Over the past fifty years TV has slowly and insidiously created a passive culture. Today people would rather go to and from their homes in cars and be entertained while at home instead of visiting with neighbors about what is going on in their communities. The sad result is the people's loss of citizenship and civic pride, often without fully realizing what has been lost. On the other hand, active citizenship will not only create civic pride; it will also forge a **united** United States of America. (Then the problem becomes how to keep it that way.) Citizenship is not a spectator sport.

In his book *Integrity,* Carter pulled no punches.[18]

Edmund Burke warned, famously, that all that is needed for the forces of evil to triumph is for enough good people to do nothing. When we retreat into cynicism or fatalism, we fertilize the ground from which evil springs. . . . If we do not demand of our politics sufficient integrity to keep evil at bay, we will wake one horrible morning and stare the triumphant evil in the face—in the mirror.

Carter showed courage in that he dared to write what people do not want to read, and he continued to hope that his book would sell.

Zoning laws in cities and towns were formulated with cars and TV in mind because those two products occupied a lot of time in the average family. Developers built big shopping centers with huge anchor stores, which big chain retailers occupied. The corner store, cafe, tavern, and coffee shop nearly disappeared, often pushed out by zoning laws favoring strictly residential occupancy. Increased wealth contributed its influence, as people bought bigger houses spaced farther apart in quiet, leafy surroundings.

These trends segregated the unwashed; that is, the wealthy congregated in their place, the next tier in theirs, and so on. Nevertheless, in cities today may be found urban ethnic neighborhoods where people live in old buildings with limited parking, noise, and lower-quality services because they are stimulated by all the activity going on around them (or nearly all). It has been said there is a flip side to wealth, and so adjusting to it is not automatic (Chapter 4). It is human nature to reach out and bond with people outside of family; apparently the wealthy are constraining themselves, maybe without realizing it.

As more and bigger vehicles crowd limited roads, commuters grow frustrated, and road rage becomes endemic, telecommuting may become only a partial solution. Walking and biking should become more popular.

In 1992 the prominent author of a book on elitism wrote: "In every democracy, public opinion judges incumbent political elites on their handling of issues, and especially on whether they provide answers to issues." This observation dramatically shows, even among intellectuals, how few people today understand what is democracy. In a democracy there are no political elites; rather, officials are public servants. Also, in a democracy the citizens resolve issues of their own choosing and then order their servants to do their bidding.

In 1788 citizens were teaching themselves about democracy. Paine reported on the scene:

It was the political bible of the state. Scarcely a family was without it. Every member of the government had a copy; and nothing was more common when any debate arose on the principle of a bill, or on the extent of any species of authority, than for the members to take the printed constitution out of their pocket, and read the chapter with which such matter in debate was connected.[19]

Today booklets can be printed in their millions for people to read at their leisure and reflect on the messages. These can be put in pockets and purses, to be kept ready for discussion on the job, in church, at the laundromat, a family gathering, tavern, and so on. Publius II's pocket gofers were written for just this purpose. This will be excellent practice for criticism and debate at political meetings. Famous American Revolution orator Patrick Henry said, "Sir, I heard what you said, I understand it, and I am in complete disagreement with it. But I will defend unto death your right to say it."

At such meetings citizens would discuss issues and formulate rules. Furthermore, they would obey them, simply because people support what they help create. Lane argued that public officials who believe that force can improve citizens' morals are stupid. Simple passage of a top-down law intended to stop a certain action will often fail to stop it. But when laws are made by the very people whose behavior will be guided by them, the situation is vastly different.

It will be good for managers of a business to encourage and reward employees who participate in government. Benefits include public relations and publicity as news media cover meetings and report on proceedings. Also, when a project to benefit the community is proposed, the business will be in it at the beginning. Moreover, a business may propose a project and then, if approved, remain active during the implementation phase, just as did prominent citizens in ancient Athens.

Political meetings will be held in a place that is convenient, and probably with a facility for childcare. Advance notice will be widespread and well timed. Vans will be available to bring people who do not drive. The person who coordinates a meeting as chairperson will have had some training and experience in conducting meetings, cross-cultural communication, and listening. He or she will be especially patient in drawing out citizens who desire to participate but are reticent. Participants should have some background in the mechanics of debate and critique.

Due to lack of experience in operating a democratic meeting, the following must be speculation. Included are only suggestions, as experience will show what is useful and what is not. Rapidly evolving technology will bring changes as resources are developed specifically for political meetings.

The meeting is brought to order by the chairperson with, say, 200 people attending. Floor assistants equipped with radio microphones and laptop computers circulate among the participants. The secretary reads the minutes, and any additions and corrections are recorded. After each committee report, the chair opens the floor for discussion. A summary of the report is displayed on a large electronic screen located behind the chair. Posted messages can be conveniently read by everyone at the meeting.

Some participants might have prepared brief written summaries of what they want to contribute; they are called on first. Then the chair indicates that ten minutes are available for oral criticism and debate. Floor assistants respond to requests for help in putting ideas and criticisms into words; this is done on a computer. When a participant is ready to talk he or she signals the chair, rises, and takes the mike from the assistant. Having first written what should be said, he or she will say it better and use fewer words.

The chair will exert great efforts to keep the discussion on an intellectual plane. The key point lies in separation of the persona of the speaker from the idea, argument, or recommendation. To the extent the chairperson is successful in this, he or she will encourage future participation by everyone, including those whose ideas do not win favor with the group.

Every participant has a remote signaling device that is similar to those used for home TV. These are used for choosing whether to call for a vote on the issue, continue discussion, or refer the matter to a committee for further analysis and later reporting back to the meeting. The results of their button pushing accumulate on the large screen.

They also can be used to help those attending to gently discourage a citizen who talks too long. As time passes a few participants think they have heard enough, so they push a button on their remotes. Later more do so, and a green light on the screen gradually changes to yellow. More such votes and the color phases into red. If the speaker has not yet taken the hint, a bell rings to tell him or her to finish immediately.

Democracy can be inefficient as citizens work to govern themselves. The mechanism described here constitutes a gentle and nonthreatening way of maintaining some efficiency without losing valuable inputs to discussion.

The meeting continues with additional committee reports, old business, and new business. Experience will tell citizens how long a typical meeting should last. Remotes could also be used to steer a meeting toward adjournment. After a meeting there should be an informal gathering, where people can interact directly in addition to the formal meeting environment. Refreshments might be served.

Minutes will be disseminated as widely as possible, utilizing email, Web site, mail, radio reports, newsletters, and so on. Major proposals will be prepared in booklet form to facilitate daily discussions. Information about issues relevant to government at other levels will be shared, and recommendations will be forwarded to the appropriate governing entities.

Extra effort is needed to convince an ordinary citizen that his or her thinking is as valued as highly as that of a prominent citizen. This is especially important when it is noted that over the past sixty years people have endured top-down government, and so many of them have been programmed to look up to others rather than to express themselves as individuals.

Active listening has great potential for accomplishing this vital transition, but it is a skill that does not come naturally to most people. Ultimately the issue comes down to faith in people, faith in the disheveled worker who has come directly to the meeting from the field without any opportunity to clean up and change clothes. As Paine said, wisdom pops up in places and times that cannot be predicted. The active listener will tap into more resources than will someone not so well versed.

Every participant in a meeting must be encouraged to maintain an open mind. Were there no opportunity to change minds there would be no need for criticism and debate. If minds are to remain closed there is no place for democracy, because debate and criticism would only harden minds in their previous positions. A citizen on the losing end of a vote would return home in a foul mood. This would be unlikely to happen if the citizen gave voice to an issue **and was heard**, because the resulting feeling phases into a belief that he or she had a bona fide opportunity to change minds even if he had been unsuccessful. He would be better prepared at the next meeting.

Neighborhood and community governments will operate directly beneath the noses of their constituents. Little will go unnoticed, and if a person should see or hear about something illegal he is likely to report it. After all, he helped make the law being violated. Some people might argue that if a low-paid worker discovered something amiss he would ask for a piece of the action rather than report the incident. But in a healthy, thriving community civic pride will goad a person to reject a temptation to acquiesce in crime. He would value more highly his own contribution to the community.

News media would present both sides of every controversial issue, and these presentations would be balanced even though everyone admits this is not easy. Bulletins would also be organized to stimulate discussions among citizens. The media would also criticize the speech and actions of public officials and publish learned criticisms written by citizens. When people demand this of their media, there will be far less tabloid journalism (and what there is will be relegated to bottom-feeding media).

Print media should be much preferred during election campaigns. An independent commission could prepare a pamphlet for publication on behalf of each candidate who qualifies through bona fide petition, at taxpayer expense. Furthermore, citizens should require that candidates repeatedly appear in person before groups of them to engage in debate and answer questions.

Citizens themselves can initiate new and different media for communication. These could be electronic chat rooms, coffee klatches, or email. The proprietor of a small neighborhood store might set aside some space for a couple of small tables and a coffee pot. The extra store traffic so generated may more than offset the sacrifice of selling space.

Once participatory democracy is in place, some citizens will be tempted to relax and let others handle it. But like a delicate blossom, democracy must be constantly nurtured by all or nearly all citizens. Therefore citizens might agree to be taxed to support a trained group of itinerant "preachers," who will visit neighborhood meeting halls and present stirring fifteen-minute talks on aspects of democracy. After giving the talk the visitor would attend the meeting, listen carefully to deliberations, and offer constructive criticism afterward both on the conduct of the meeting and on the theory of democracy. These Jeffersonian vagabonds might travel the circuits for free.

Democracy is forever building, changing. There never is a final result on which public officials can be judged. However, people can judge them on intangible traits like honesty, industry, trust, listening, reliability, commitment, and consistency. Campaign promotions should be limited to print. This would cut down considerably on image merchandising, and it would deemphasize charisma and power politics. Furthermore, people would have something tangible in their hands on which to ponder the implications and to use as guides to discussion.

A citizen's life is God's gift. What he does with that life is his own gift to God and his progeny. Opportunity knocks.

Notes

1. Thomas Paine, *Rights of Man.* Knopf, 1915.
2. Kevin Phillips, *Arrogant Capital.* Little, Brown, 1994.
3. Alexis de Tocqueville, *Democracy in America.* Knopf, 1972.
4. Thomas Macaulay, in Murray Rothbard, *For a New Liberty.* Fox and Wilkes, 1973.
5. Ayn Rand, *Atlas Shrugged.* Penguin Books, 1992.
6. Bill Bennett, *The Book of Virtues.* Simon and Schuster, 1993.
7. Richard A. Epstein, *Principles for a Free Society: Reconciling Individual Liberty with the Common Good.* Perseus Books, 1998.
8. Jackson Pemberton, "A New Message on the Constitution." In *The Foundations of American Constitutional Government,* ed. Robert Gorgoglione. Foundation for Economic Education, 1996.
9. Tocqueville, *Democracy in America.*
10. Anthony Arblaster, *Democracy.* University of Minnesota Press, 1987.
11. Lewis H. Lapham, *The Wish for Kings: Democracy at Bay.* Grove Press, 1993.
12. Brian Beedham, "Full Democracy." *The Economist* Survey, December 21, 1996.
13. Phillips, *Arrogant Capital.*
14. *The Economist,* "The PEN Is Mighty." February 1, 1992, p. 96.

15. Carlene Hempel, "E-Motional Distance." *News and Observer,* February 14, 2000, p. 1D.
16. Arblaster, *Democracy.*
17. Epstein, *Principles for a Free Society.*
18. Stephen Carter, *Integrity.* Basic Books, 1996.
19. Paine, *Rights of Man.*

CHAPTER EIGHTEEN:
VOLUNTEERING AND MAKING A CONTRIBUTION TO GOOD GOVERNMENT

It is one of the most beautiful compensations of this life that no man can sincerely help another without helping himself.
—Ralph Waldo Emerson

In his observation on human nature, Emerson spoke to the positive side; this chapter will accentuate the positive. With adequate faith in humanity, a citizen believes that even the most devilish among people have a good streak within them. It remains only to arrange institutions and events to bring forth this good.

For fifty years Friedrich Hayek argued that this desire to reach out to others could work well only in relatively small groups. Whenever a social system grows beyond a limit, voluntary cooperation between people will break down. (He also said that limit varies among cultures.) This means that for socialism to work for a country a top-down, oppressive big government is required. In turn this means there is no place for democracy.

ADVANTAGES OF VOLUNTEERISM OVER GOVERNMENT BUREAUCRACY

Bastiat wondered, "Is there in the heart of man only what the legislator has put there? Did fraternity have to make its appearance on earth by way of the ballot box? Are we to believe that women will cease to be self-sacrificing and that pity will no longer find a place in their hearts because self-sacrifice and pity will not be commanded by the law?"[1]

A capitalist, free-market democracy with minimum intervention in private lives by government is (probably) a very nice way to live. However, no matter what kind of government a society may select (or, more likely, have imposed on it) there will always be at least a few people who adjust poorly to their surroundings. This book has shown that a democracy when combined with free markets creates a maximum of winners and a minimum of losers. Furthermore, a loser need not remain so, especially if a minimal government places few barriers between him or her and opportunity.

From the producer or winner's viewpoint there should be as few as practical who require assistance. Under these conditions producers will **voluntarily** support the failures, but only if convinced that each able poor person is striving to once again become a producer. In an institutional environment created by paternalistic big government, bureaucrats constantly expand their turf by recruiting more clients among the poor. This means that producers will no longer voluntarily contribute, because no efforts are being made to minimize the number of clients. In such a society the government must exert force on producers through taxation.

Included among producers are those who may not be in paid employment at a particular time but are still capable. Examples are owners of producing assets, such as stocks, bonds, and other investments. A spouse who remains at home to care for children is a producer, because a working asset is receiving valuable assistance. It is equally important to provide for loving preparation of future working assets. Finally, the elderly who are not wealthy are also producers when they contribute their time, talents, and wisdom to family members, the neighborhood and community, and beyond.

Friedman showed how free markets work to enhance volunteerism.[2] "It is noteworthy that the heyday of laissez-faire, the middle and late nineteenth century in Britain and the US, saw an extraordinary proliferation of private eleemosynary organizations and institutions. One of the major costs of extension of governmental welfare activities has been the corresponding decline in private charitable activities."

During the nineteenth century millions of Polish, German, Italian, Irish, French, and Dutch people (and others) came to this country. Many brought little with them except the clothes on their backs and a desire for self-improvement. They built this nation, without welfare. There was no need for big government as they forged their own variety of paternalism. Pride welled up in their breasts as they watched their adopted country reach for glory.

Epstein wrote about charity in the nineteenth century: "Unlike contract and tort disputes, charitable organizations were not subject to legal sanctions, but extensive social norms guided their day-to-day operations."[3] Therefore they "were entitled to deny services to anyone as of right, no matter how great the need." Charities were also not held liable for ordinary negligence in rendering services. "Against the few individuals who suffered the sting of exclusion or malpractice, we must consider the tens and hundreds of persons whose access to care was promoted precisely because charitable institutions were untouched by any onerous regulation or liability." Today big government has regulated child care to the point where it is priced beyond the means of many parents with moderate incomes.

Caregivers quickly learned that blind trust was not a good idea.

> *Religious groups provided direct assistance in religious environments, where they could monitor the behavior of their recipients, a prospect that leaves many well-intentioned people uneasy today. Similarly, charity was never given as a cash grant. . . . recipient had to consume the food and service provided in plain view of the charitable provider.*

Close monitoring not only provides accountability; it also provides needed bonding between voluntary giver and recipient.

There were poor farms and county homes for those who fell on hard times. Churches supported orphanages. Families often took in poor relatives, who would do farm work for bed and board. Although far from perfect, the voluntary system worked quite well. Few citizens were left destitute, there was no government bureaucracy, there was little drug addiction, and there were very few broken families.

Living conditions on poor farms and in county homes were intentionally terrible in order to provide a strong incentive for occupants to get back on their feet. There were few formal attempts to counsel people who needed psychological help, but there was caring, and this is an important point as the need for caring is embedded in human nature.

With some changes, this system was still in place in the 1930s; government had made few inroads into charitable work. Then in 1930 the country was plunged into the Great Depression. Unemployment approached 25 percent, factories and banks failed by the thousands, and no one had any money. Churches and other charities were overwhelmed. Something had to be done for thousands of defeated people, so the government moved in with a variety of social programs intended to help the poor. So began the rapid and continuing growth of the welfare bureaucracies.

Epstein ably described the process.

> *The life cycle runs this course: The individuals who launch a new program, board, or commission may be filled with idealism—dedicated to making the program work. . . . Once . . . in place, its day-to-day administration falls into the hands of a professional cadre besieged by powerful interest groups whose influence grows as public interest wanes. Small "technical" changes in the rate of payout—in the findings needed to sustain an administrative ruling . . . can exert—far removed from the public scrutiny that gave birth to the program in the first place—enormous subterranean influences over its size and direction.*

At this point there is no discussion in government concerning whether the program has served its original purpose or even whether it is still relevant in a changing environment. Rather, discussion is limited to how much to increase the budget for the coming year.

Benefits dispensed are to a selected group of clients and are politically visible; politicians spread the word about the wonderful things they are doing for the poor. But the costs are dispersed among millions of taxpayers, and they are kept hidden, showing up only in the future. This means the social cost-benefit comparison is not only difficult to make; not far into the future it turns decisively negative due in large part to bureaucratic irrelevance and loss of sight of its original purpose.

There exists deep within the human psyche a feeling of sympathy for those who try hard to adjust to society but do not quite bring it off. Offsetting this feeling is the realization that there are people who will take advantage of others' generosity if they can get away with it. The line of division between these two categories of people is poorly drawn. Because private philanthropy sometimes errs in this area it is not difficult to imagine what happens when government gets involved. Furthermore, when various private charities must compete for donor dollars and talents they are more likely to improve their operations.

Government bureaucracies sometimes directly prevent private efforts. In 1995 Teen Challenge, a religious-based drug treatment program with a record of success since 1969, ran up against government. The Commission on Alcohol and Drug Abuse told managers that they must hire credentialed counselors or face fines and imprisonment.

This looks like a government agency dictating policy to a church. The First Amendment to the Constitution reads in part: "Congress shall make no law respecting an establishment of religion, or prohibiting the free exercise thereof." Teen Challenge sometimes uses noncredentialed counselors who are former addicts. People who have been there are often very effective counselors, and sometimes they are eager to give something back to the organization that helped them.

Although today's citizens are giving record amounts to charities, these organizations are not doing the job as well as they once did. Part of this deterioration is due to interference from government, but also most of them have organized themselves in a way similar to government agencies. That is, they have become top-down entities, utilizing the services of expert public relations people and telemarketers to appeal for donations. They then skim 30 percent off the top for administration and route the rest to the field, where there are more experts.

The result is like government agencies in that gaps have been opened between donors, managers, and recipients. Put another way, private philanthropy has gone big, centralized, and impersonal, whereas it once was local, dispersed, and personal. The overemphasis on solicitation of funds in effect denies donors the option to give their time and talents on a part-time basis, thus making the institution still more impersonal.

There has been some progress recently in the right direction concerning national government welfare. The first effective initiative was taken by the state of Wisconsin. *The Economist* reported:

> *The scheme is called "Wisconsin Works," or W-2. . . . [It] starts from the premise that the poor should no longer be entitled to benefits. The state made history by negotiating with the federal government to end the right to AFDC [Aid to Families with Dependent Children], and it was given a waiver to do so before the reform of 1996 ended the federal entitlement to welfare.*[4]

Each client is presumed to be capable of some type of work.

> *Even a junkie is expected to spend 28 hours a week. . . . These ferocious rules are intended to make benefits feel as much like work as possible. Pay is docked for failure to appear because that is what an employer would do; benefits do not vary with family size, because neither do wages. . . .*

"Is this too stern? 'The message we were sending to these families before,' says Jean Rogers . . . was, 'We think so little of you, we don't think you can cope in the workforce.' The number of critics has fallen precipitately as the predictions of tragedy have proved wrong."

Just like others more fortunate, these people feel a need to hold their heads high. A message like this denies them a desperately needed opportunity, but this is the nature of a bureaucracy whose members are interested in increasing the number on welfare.

Wisconsin agencies handed out benefits, but for the first time they asked something in return: recipients' children had to stay in school. Asking nothing in return for a handout robs a recipient of dignity. In fact, welfare reform today is not what the news media report, in that much of the tax money still gets routed through Capitol Hill and sent back out to the states. But at least recent developments represent a step away from top-down and toward bottom-up.

Caring citizens want to help, and recipients want to receive help from caring citizens. The way should be cleared for this to happen far more often than it does today. But the problems of needy poor children and seniors, drug addicts, and criminals require volunteers willing to work one-on-one with recipients. When the locations where assistance is rendered closely resemble war zones, recruiting volunteers is understandably difficult. One experienced volunteer described the result: "Give money to people you've never met, in places you've never been, with results you've never tried to measure."

As a result, successfully communicating caring in today's charity environment is a challenge, which private organizations meet more effectively than do public ones. They would do more good if public agencies were to leave the scene. Frank Reed was a hostage in the Middle East for forty-four months: "As a hostage, I learned one overriding fact: caring is a powerful force. If no one cares, you are truly alone."

THE "WHAT-CAN-I-CONTRIBUTE?" MENTALITY

The Scottish historian's observation (Chapter 2) bears repeating here. "Democracy cannot last indefinitely. It can last only to the point where the majority discover they can vote themselves largesse from the public treasury." Society in this country today is aging, and young people no longer vote frequently. In terms of numbers of voters, the elderly may soon be nearly a majority. Furthermore big government has over the past fifty years created a "what's-in-it-for-me?" mentality among citizens. Only a little reflection is necessary to appreciate the implications.

In the early days of the republic there were many instances of citizens helping citizens, and the desire to help was not restricted to family and church. With a community spirit that pervaded individuals' thinking, people pitched in and got the job done, whatever it was. The fable of the Little Red Hen was written about that time, but its modern version, "Not in my job description," had yet to become popular.

Today there are many more large cities and greatly increased occupational and daily mobility. People do not spend as much of their lives in one neighborhood, and so their loyalty wanes accordingly. Each person feels he or she has a lower stake in what happens in the community. If it deteriorates and he becomes discouraged he simply leaves for a second home or a favorite resort, returning later refreshed and ready for the rat race. There is no felt need to make any changes in the neighborhood to adjust to the changing needs of its residents; a person can simply move on.

Accomplishing change by the democratic process is risky; a citizen might alienate others if he were to stand up and argue a point. It is easier to just cut out. But on reflection it becomes obvious that this action is less cut out than cop out. This partially explains the presence of difficulties in neighborhoods and communities across the land. Good citizenship is a privilege, but it must be earned through discharge of obligations. No neighborhood can have its cake and eat it, too.

Today's young children lack yesterday's opportunities to contribute, which causes a lag in their maturation process. This process involves a move away from "what's-in-it-for-me?" to "what-can-I-contribute?" Years ago children could go many places on foot or by bicycle, and there were local stores on streets with light traffic. Parents felt secure in sending their children on errands. When youngsters made trips to the bakery, the grocery store, or the post office at their parents' request, they contributed to the family's well-being. What is more important, they felt a sense of contribution. Today's children must be taxied by car wherever they want to go.

Concerned citizens' antennae perked up in 1961 when President John F. Kennedy famously proclaimed: "Ask not what your country can do for you; rather, ask what you can do for your country." But then he authorized still more welfare and entitlement programs. These actions reinforced the nanny state, which had previously been given a tremendous boost by Roosevelt. Kennedy's proclamation quickly ran out of steam.

The nanny mentality infected new congressmen entering government service. They came to that city excited about making some needed and sweeping changes. They swept into government bearing a "what-can-I-contribute?" mentality. But this mentality promptly went up against a deeply entrenched "what's-in-it-for-me?" political environment. The positive side of human nature confronted the negative side. The young politician soon realized that to make any real change he had to attain a position of high personal power, but after some twenty years of struggle to attain that position he had lost his original impetus. He had many friends to whom he owed favors, and the money was just too good.

Eventually, the system captures every soul. Today the reality is there is almost no contributing going on in Washington except political money, and even that is taking on the trappings of extortion.

Alienated citizens cannot contribute even if they wish. Greider wrote,

> *Government responds to the public's desires with an artful dance of symbolic gestures. . . . Disconnected . . . people can neither contribute their thinking to the government's decisions nor take any real responsibility for them. Elite decision makers are unable to advance coherent governing agendas for the nation . . . since they are too isolated from common values and experiences to be persuasive. The result is an enervating sense of stalemate.*[5]

This reality stimulates the thought that perhaps people are so frustrated as to say to government, "All right; so you don't want us to help, and you know our problems and how to solve them. Okay, so deliver!" (Or, they might say that if they thought anyone in government would listen.)

Harris quoted Erich Fromm's interpretation of the "what-can-I-contribute?" mentality:

> *The most widespread misunderstanding is that which assumes that giving is 'giving up' something, being deprived of, sacrificing. People whose main orientation is a* ***nonproductive*** *one feel giving as an impoverishment. . . . Just because it is painful to give, one should give; the virtue of giving, to them, lies in the very act of acceptance of sacrifice. . . .*
>
> *For the* ***productive*** *character giving has an entirely different meaning. Giving is the highest expression of potency. In the very act of giving I experience my strength, my wealth, my power. . . . [It] fills me with joy . . . overflowing,*

spending, alive, hence as joyous. Giving is more joyous than receiving, not because it is a deprivation, but because in the act of giving lies the expression of my aliveness.[6]

Today's society has lost something meaningful and important. Evans and Boyte commented: "When people begin to see in themselves the capacity to end their own hurts, to take control of their lives, they gain the capacity to tap the democratic resources in their heritage."[7] Russia is a beautiful country whose image has been sadly distorted by decades of government-inspired news media hype. After the fall of the Soviet Union a paternalistic (communist) Russia began a monumental effort to adopt democracy as its government. One woman was quoted: "Who is in charge of my life now; who?" The answer to her question is, of course, herself. However, that response would surely come to her as a severe shock.

Goldfarb said, "There is a general sense that education is only a means to an end, not very valuable in itself. Money and power are the ends."[8] Whom you know is more important than what you know. In a democracy these statements are false, as a good education is in fact an end. That end lies in self-knowledge, self-worth, and self-actualization. With these traits internalized, a person feels no limits to what he or she can do, where he can go and when. For this person, money and power are just money and power. That is but one way to go among many, and he knows it probably will not deliver what he wants. What he truly wants is more likely available through making a contribution, by helping others.

Young people can contribute by completing high school and continuing their learning afterward through utilization of a variety of resources. When he was governor of Arkansas, Bill Clinton said that high school dropouts cost more to society than they contribute. They are more likely to cause trouble, go on welfare, and go to prison than are graduates. This is largely because they do not understand themselves, and this makes it difficult for them to integrate fully into the society as contributing adults.

Today African Americans are thinking more about what they can contribute than about what's in it for them. Enlightened leaders are working at convincing them to think in terms of individual effort instead of demonstrations, get out the vote, and petitions. They are emphasizing hard study to improve their ability to contribute.

Latinos may be just ahead of blacks in this massively important trend of political awareness, as Broder reported: "Door-to-door canvassing in the barrio neighborhoods of Los Angeles, confronting their neighbors with a forceful warning that unless they vote, they can forget their dreams of a living wage, health insurance protection and better schools for their children."[9]

Most Latinos are younger and more ambitious than those left behind in the Old Country. They deeply appreciate having a job (all but lacking back home);

therefore they are oriented to contributing to their families and by extension to their newly adopted community and country.

An intriguing irony presents itself. The authoritarian government back home did not provide such "dreams." Rather, it only took from families in the form of often vicious taxation. This means the worker and his or her family were on their own as they struggled against an overbearing top-down government.

This attitude of self-reliance does not connect with voting for government-provided benefits. Based on grisly experience, they don't trust the government to provide what they believe they themselves can provide, and by doing a better job to boot. Put another way, they came to the United States with a what-can-I-contribute? mentality. Small wonder the canvassers in the barrios are having a rough go of it. (What is amazing is that so many native-born US citizens continue to trust their authoritarian government.)

Rothbard commented on one of President Clinton's favorite themes.[10]

> *In fact, soaking the rich would have disastrous effects, not just for the rich but for the poor and middle classes themselves. For it is the rich who provide a proportionately greater amount of saving, investment capital, entrepreneurial foresight, and financing of technological innovation that has brought the US to by far the highest standard of living—for the mass of people—of any country in history. Soaking the rich would also be profoundly immoral, it would drastically penalize the very virtues: thrift, business foresight, and investment, that have brought about our remarkable standard of living.*

Taking from the wealthy by force tends to deny them the privilege of voluntarily giving to those organizations that in their judgment most deserve help. With occasional exceptions, surely they have earned the right to exercise this judgment. Furthermore, the government is likely to either waste what officials take, spend it on vote buying, or actually steal it.

In a democracy there are opportunities for the occasional brilliant achievement, mostly in the private sector. But more important is the habit, dispersed throughout the neighborhood, of doing small favors, little services, and obscure good deeds with no expectation of compensation. Civic pride in community encourages development of this habit. It also works to put a paintbrush in every hand, so that everyone perceives an opportunity to contribute in some small way. These people are limited only by their imaginations. When Sir Robert Baden-Powell founded the Boy Scouts in 1907 he coined their slogan: Do a good turn daily. Nearly 100 years later this slogan still guides boys' behavior.

Within the home it is also important to encourage development of this mentality. A father gathers tools together to make a small household repair. His five-year-old son notices this and asks, "Daddy, can I help?" Father immediately sees that an acceptance of his son's "help" means the job will require twice as much time as he had originally estimated. Therefore his first impulse might be to say,

"Sorry, son, you will just get in the way." But a second thought goads him to say, "Sure. I could use some help on this job."

Father realizes that he will not be able to watch the first quarter of the afternoon's football game on television, and his favorite team is playing. But next day in school his son is everywhere, boasting "I helped my dad fix a faucet!" There will probably be several missed first quarters in the future, but Father knows he and his wife are preparing a future contributor. Citizens throughout the community will appreciate their efforts, not to mention the young man himself (Emerson would approve).

"What-can-I-contribute?" will unite neighborhoods, which will unite communities, which will in turn unite states. The beginning of the development of this mentality must rest in the neighborhood, as democracy is bottom-up government. In the future the little boy mentioned may become a father himself, in which case he and his wife are very likely to carry on what has by then become a tradition. It means limited government, especially at state and national levels, as this in turn limits opportunities to exert top-down personal power and to fragment the society.

Today the excess parasitic baggage in Washington includes huge masses of excess politicians' staff, lobbyists, consultants, lawyers, bureaucrats, influence mongers, pundits, and spin-doctors. Citizens will demand that they leave town, go home, and start making contributions toward a better society. This action will at first cause thunderous outcries, as insiders realize they are being forced to confront reality. However, later on most of those who make the transition will be amazed at how much better they feel about themselves even if their wallets are somewhat thinner (though they need not be).

There is a story about a dedicated employee in a business who reluctantly agreed to talk with an organizer who wanted him to join a union. He told the organizer, "I think we are wasting our time, but if you want to talk I will listen." Twenty minutes later the organizer had finished his pitch. The employee uttered just one sentence in response, whereupon the organizer immediately stood up, said, "You are right; we are wasting our time," and walked out. What was that one sentence? "I am far more concerned with what I can give to this company than I am with what I am taking from it."

In a recent *Parade* article, Michael Ryan presented an excellent example of what-can-I-contribute.[11]

> *Schwartz and Shubin are among the group of volunteer physicians, nurses, social workers, and others who run the Samaritan House clinic, a cramped but joyful center in San Mateo, California, that offers free medical care to 500 patients a month. "This is medicine the way it should be," says Karla Petersen, 25, a medical student at UC San Francisco and a clinic volunteer. . . .*

> *Says Dr. John Sarconi, 65 . . . "I retired earlier than I would have, because I felt I was running on the wrong road. Internal medicine is a field where you need to spend time with people and get to know their needs. I felt that the time pressures had turned it into a conveyor belt."*
>
> *When Schwartz and his co-founders began to recruit retired doctors and other professionals in the area to staff the clinic, the response was overwhelming. . . .*
>
> *At any given time, about a dozen physicians and dentists still in active practice also volunteer at the clinic. "I work in one of the most efficient practices around," says Dr. Subha Aahlad, 39, a pediatrician, "and it takes two people working full time to do the paperwork. As for the hours I have to spend filling out forms—you don't want to go there. Here, I take care of patients and don't fill out forms."*

The article didn't say how patients are screened in advance; for a free good demand is infinite. Nor did it indicate whether some form of payment is expected. Nevertheless, a point was clearly made.

The Right Kind of Feel-Good Government

Haynes Johnson wrote a book called *Sleepwalking through History* about the Reagan years.[12]

> *He governed through the eye of the camera and by using devices of the entertainer. His, quite naturally, was a presidency of pictures, symbols, and staging. Every public act of his presidency was planned by his media experts for its maximum impact through television. Every word he uttered, either to welcome a visitor or to address a group, was scripted for him. Although to the press he was the least accessible president since the twenties, to the public his daily media event and photo opportunity made him the most familiar chief executive.*

A viewer of TV at that time might envision Reagan appearing in the program called "To Tell the Truth" and seeing members of the blindfolded panel guessing who is the real Reagan just before the MC asks, "Will the real Ronald Reagan please stand up?" They would probably guess wrong, as Johnson's observation above gives no clue whatever as to the real man behind the image. But this reality did not cause a moment's hesitation among Reagan's media spin doctors. For the viewing public his "It's morning in America!" communicated the message of feel-good government. Ron was in charge, and there was no cause for worry.

Eight years later the national debt had nearly tripled. Johnson:

> *Bush took office against a backdrop of an America conditioned during the Reagan years to think of addressing personal opportunities instead of national problems. For most of the decade, president and Congress had avoided acting on many difficult issues. Precious time and opportunities were squandered as prob-*

> *lems were allowed to fester. That was the case with, among others, the budget and trade deficits, the S&L debacle, the nuclear plants, the infrastructure, and the third world debt crisis that continued to mushroom, threatening international economic stability.*

A leader can listen to bad news, and he has the courage to tell people what they don't want to hear.

"Bush had another problem. It was his fate to follow . . . [the man] who, for eight years, escaped the blame for creating new problems or the responsibility for failing to solve old ones." During that time period, King Ron was transformed into Teflon Ron. His spin-doctored silver tongue had separated the society from reality, just as the motion picture industry often does.

Schulman wrote,

> *Over the past seven years, President Clinton has traded in the bully pulpit of the presidency for the roast-master's podium at the $5,000-a-plate dinner. Since January 1997, Clinton has spoken at more than 350 fund-raising events. . . . Fund-raising has become so all-consuming because governing itself relies heavily on paid political advertising.*
>
> *The genius of Clinton's predecessors was to harness the symbolic powers of their office to serve concrete political aims. Their words led the nation toward war and peace, new initiatives and ancient verities. By becoming fund-raiser in chief, Clinton has dissipated that legacy. His own reputation, and the presidency, will suffer for it.*[13]

When history evaluates the Clinton era, it may find that he engineered a new incarnation of phony feel-good government.

Today concerned citizens feel a need to learn more about reality, but they continue to find in Washington a poor resource for learning. Other sources are apparently affected by this lack of candor: The International Encyclopedia of the Social Sciences includes seventeen volumes, but there is nothing in it that delves into any detail concerning citizenship.

Lawyer Epstein wrote of laissez-faire economics, or free markets: "Harms by aggression and harms by competition are too easily treated as parallel violations of the single prohibition against harm to others; and their profound differences are not grasped solely by reference to the fate of the immediate parties to any dispute, but by their overall social consequences."[14] Harms by aggression destroy, whereas someone harmed by competition has often learned something from the experience that will be useful when he or she is ready for another try.

"But once we recognize that laissez-faire is not wedded to any notion of unbridled self-interest, we can see how laissez-faire supports a social norm of **voluntary** redistribution from those with plenty to those in need" (emphasis added). Competition and a law protecting the sanctity of contracts provide the bridle, and free markets provide the freedom for those with plenty to decide how to make contributions as they see fit. Top-down, paternalistic, one-size-fits-all programs force everyone to support what they did not create and probably don't believe in. Voluntary is bottom-up: neighbors helping neighbors throughout a typical community.

Fukuyama commented: "To a greater degree than many other western societies, the US has a dense and complex network of voluntary organizations: churches, professional societies, charitable institutions, private schools, universities, and hospitals, and, of course, a very strong private business sector."[15] He found these institutions in this country to be relatively strong in spite of inroads of big government.

But the key word here is *relatively*; big government's inroads have become even deeper in other Western countries. This fact would seem to suggest that one of the others, say, Germany or France, should seize the initiative in this matter. However, the United States was an effective world leader through World War II, and much of the world still perceives this country in those terms. Citizens here believe there remains a real potential in this country waiting to be tapped. Fukuyama apparently saw this potential.

In 1998 citizens gave $175 billion to nongovernmental organizations helping the poor. It seems that people want to help, but they are unsure how to put their time and talents to work, so they donate money. What they are sure of is that by contributing they enhance their sense of personal worth.

However, writing a check is private, and many people want others to know they are giving of themselves. This illustrates the potential of democracy, when people can make a contribution to good government by working with and through others. This is the real feel-good government that people are seeking, and it is infectious.

Betty Friedan's book *The Feminine Mystique* was hugely popular during the 1960s. Thirty years later she wrote a book called *The Fountain of Age,* which has a message for the traditional movement that she had a hand in starting. "The movement that flows from the Fountain of Age cannot be a special interest group. It would be a violation of our own wisdom and generativity to empower ourselves in age only for our own security and care." Friedan suggested that older people have much to contribute to their communities and their governments. If they would reach out with open hearts they would find any preoccupation with taking swamped by a preoccupation with giving.

Recently former chairman of the Joint Chiefs of Staff Colin Powell used his high public profile to make a contribution to children.[16]

> *Every child needs a caring adult role model . . . a safe place to learn and grow; a healthy start. . . . As chairman of America's Promise—The Alliance for Youth, I am currently leading a national crusade to help meet all these needs, and one more: the need to give back through service to the community. Young*

people need to learn the paradox of giving—that when we help others, we get back far more than we contribute. . . . They learn to value themselves by a more mature standard.

Here is a former career soldier and top bureaucrat who did not want to retire. Friedan's wisdom and generativity have influenced this man. Today Gen. Powell is Secretary of State. He plans to remain active in America's Promise.

President Clinton suggested that everyone ready to graduate from high school be required to do community service, as he apparently believed that this experience helps the maturation process and sets in place a pattern that will influence future participation. But this suggestion is misguided, because required community service would obviously not be voluntary.

Marvin Olasky is a top thinker on charities. He argued that charity fails when it does not ask something in return for help extended. "For compassion to be effective, it needs to be challenging, personal, and spiritual. Federal government programs have provided entitlement, bureaucracy, and an attempt to banish God."

Mormons (Latter-Day Saints) have traditionally had a strong sense of community. They support the poor within these communities. Fukuyama wrote, "Welfare support from the church is coupled with a requirement that recipients work in return, and the latter are encouraged to look after themselves as soon as possible. There is an intrusive early detection system that tries to prevent individual families from sliding into poverty."

Many of the thousands of charities are fakes. Organizations such as the Better Business Bureau and National Charities Information Bureau help donors avoid phony charities and make the best decisions concerning where to donate money. These organizations carefully check the name of every charity, as con artists often use names very similar to reputable organizations. The American Institute of Philanthropy has records on many charities that include percent of receipts spent on actual charitable work, the cost to raise $100, salaries of top officials, and a letter grade varying from A to F. Also, people who have received a solicitation that looks worthwhile can view a Web site called Guidestar (www.guidestar.org) and obtain useful information.

Nobody spends someone else's money as carefully as they spend their own. For this reason it is important to be free to choose whom to support. When a citizen is taxed the same truth stated here is applicable, but there is no choice. The situation today is taxation without representation. (In 1775 colonists were similarly put upon.)

Managers of charities know that donors have choices and that this means competition, so they strive hard to do a good job and to get the word out about the job they are doing. They welcome evaluating organizations such as those mentioned, because they want not only a good report published but also an opportunity to see where they can improve their operations. Internally, managers must coordinate the activities of donors, recipients, paid staff, and volunteers. This is always a challenge, but when it is successfully met the organization will accomplish its objectives.

It is interesting to observe that a private nonprofit organization called the March of Dimes began its existence to eradicate poliomyelitis. Years later it had accomplished its objective, so it switched gears and went after birth defects. Public agencies don't switch; they only expand their operations.

A citizen who wishes to make a contribution to a local charity has choices concerning where to direct money, time, talents, or some combination thereof. When the organization is local he or she can personally check to see whether a good job is being done, and if not, he is free to go elsewhere. This fact is not lost on the manager, who will strive to keep the charity shaped up. Money is raised where it will be spent, so the question of accountability is resolved far more easily than when tax money goes to Washington.

Many young Internet workers and computer geeks have quickly amassed sizable fortunes. Following Bill Gates's lead, they are looking for opportunities to donate to charities. Most are rejecting the tradition of simply sending a big check to a major charity without knowing precisely how the money will be used. They are making the effort to target their giving. It is not always money: Some are donating computer equipment, a Web page, or training in use of software.

Another argument for localized action is that recipients of aid can personally thank volunteers and sometimes donors for often desperately needed assistance. This means both giver and receiver receive; this reality connects to Fromm's definition of giving, as already mentioned. Furthermore, recipients will often return periodically to share their success. Some of them will want to work for the charity as a volunteer, because this is an opportunity to give back some of what they received. Often these people are especially effective as volunteers; they have been there and can relate strongly to recipients.

When neighbors help neighbors the action is not limited to charities. With minor adjustments, what has been shown also applies to good government. The important point to remember is that by nature the human animal is social; there exists a need for interaction with others working toward a common objective. Today there are many organizations that function in this way while working around government impediments. What is sadly missing are institutions of government that activate the positive side of human nature.

A person whose job is to guard a warehouse full of valuable equipment and supplies has a difficult job. He must spend up to 99 percent of his time fighting crushing boredom; the other 1 percent may involve confronting real danger. But the task of guarding democracy, though not boring and dangerous, is equally difficult. The thing being guarded is intangible, and because artful politicians are tempted to mislead their constituents it is very difficult to determine when democracy is slipping away. When citizens awaken years later to discover that they have lost the prize its retrieval is more difficult than was establishing it in the first place. The reason for this difficulty lies in vested interests and personal power, which privileged elites hang onto at all costs.

Democracy in the form of a republic began in this country only after a war in which gallant men fought against great odds for an idea. Now the aftermath of President Reagan's feel-good government weighs heavily on citizens, and the feeling of frustration is similar to that borne by the colonists in 1776.

However, there are at least three major differences. One is that the oppression has not yet reached the intensity of that felt by the colonists. Another is that today there is wealth, which tends to ameliorate the misery. A third difference is that the advanced world is entering the Age of Reason, when war will no longer be feasible as a means of resolving disputes (see Chapter 20).

This is not to minimize the magnitude of the task ahead. But the right kind of feel-good government lies within the grasp of the citizenry, provided that **they have the will to act.**

From Ben Franklin's *Poor Richard's Almanac* comes good advice: "When you're good to others, you are best to yourself."

Notes

1. Frederic Bastiat, in Jim Powell, *The Triumph of Liberty.* Free Press, 2000, p. 256.
2. Milton Friedman, *Capitalism and Freedom.* University of Chicago Press, 1982.
3. Richard A. Epstein, *Principles for a Free Society: Reconciling Individual Liberty with the Common Good.* Perseus Books, 1998.
4. *The Economist,* "Where Wisconsin Goes, Can the World Follow?" November 1, 1997, p. 25.
5. William Greider, *Who Will Tell the People: The Betrayal of American Democracy.* Simon and Schuster, 1992.
6. Thomas A. Harris, *I'm Okay; You're Okay.* Avon Books, 1973.
7. Sara M. Evans and Harry C. Boyte, *Free Spaces: The Sources of Democratic Change in America.* University of Chicago Press, 1992.
8. Jeffrey C. Goldfarb, *The Cynical Society: The Culture of Politics and the Politics of Culture in American Life.* University of Chicago Press, 1991.
9. David Broder, "On the Move toward Stronger Democracy." *News and Observer* (Raleigh, NC), February 23, 2001, p. 19A.
10. Murray Rothbard, *For a New Liberty.* Fox and Wilkes, 1973.
11. Michael Ryan, "This Is Medicine the Way It Should Be." *Parade,* October 29, 2000, p. 18.

12. Haynes Johnson, *Sleepwalking through History: America in the Reagan Years.* Norton, 1991.
13. Bruce J. Schulman, "Sadly, Clinton's Story Hasn't Been Oratory." *News and Observer,* June 2000.
14. Epstein, *Principles for a Free Society.*
15. Francis Fukuyama, *Trust.* Free Press, 1995.
16. Colin Powell, "Learn the Joy of Serving Others." *Parade,* April 11, 1999, p. 5.

Chapter Nineteen:
Retrieving the Importance of the Family and Guiding Its Future in a Democracy

The first half of our lives is ruined by our parents and the second half by our children.
—Clarence Darrow

The Industrial Revolution (1750–1850) brought on the machine age, and worker productivity was dramatically increased. This meant a worker could produce much more with the same amount of effort and therefore could be paid more. With more money in his pocket he could buy much more; his living standard rose accordingly.

When Tocqueville visited this country he noticed several contrasts with his native Europe.[1] In the Old World, marriages among aristocrats were generally to unite property rather than hearts. However, in this country he found a unique equality between partners in marriage. "Americans constantly display complete confidence in their spouses' judgment and deep respect for their freedom. They hold that woman's mind is just as capable as man's of discovering the naked truth, and her heart as firm to face it."

From 1870 to 1940 there occurred mass migrations from mechanized farms into cities in search of wage labor. Later increases in daily mobility due to the popularity of the automobile created what William White in his postwar book *The Organization Man* called "bedroom communities." Husbands and fathers commuted downtown to work while their wives and children lived and went to school in newly created suburbs. Women with children formed the habit of attending a coffee klatch two or three times a week. About ten in the morning they assembled with their babies and small children.

The invention of household labor-saving machines had given women much-deserved free time. Men thought their wives were wasting their time in klatching, but they were wrong. The reality was that school was in session, especially for the younger moms. There was much to learn from older mothers about care of babies, children, husbands, other family members, as well as about current events.

Grandparents were still active as teachers and mentors, but increased occupational mobility meant that they were less available.

After a long day in factory/office and home and after the children had gone to bed, evenings were relaxing and bonding. There was time for each parent to attend a meeting or other event outside the home once or twice a week. These included political meetings, so that a good family was also a good citizen. Few people turned on the TV, simply because that household appliance was not yet widely available.

World War II permanently changed the family lifestyle. Most of the men had gone overseas, and so it was up to the women to fill in with factory jobs producing what their men needed for combat. Tocqueville was right: Their hearts were just as firm when it came to facing grim reality, and they responded in great numbers with dedication and drive. Ditto for grandparents, aunts, and uncles, as they filled in behind working mothers in performing household tasks, including child care.

The big war won, those men who were still alive came home to a stupendous welcome. The war had caused productive capacity and worker productivity to increase tremendously. Women had extra money in their pockets, and after many factories had converted back to producing consumer goods productivity and money united to bring on what has been called the affluent society.

Having become used to earning money outside the home, women soon reentered the labor force. The economy was expanding so rapidly that new jobs could absorb returning servicemen and also the women who wanted to remain in the workforce. After the invention of the credit card, people often spent more than they should. Many men and women adjusted poorly to the sudden increase in wealth; they got themselves into financial difficulty. This problem affected other components of a typical marriage, and correlated with an increased incidence of divorce.

Before World War II there was far less wealth, and life was generally more difficult. Families stuck together from grim necessity. With the arrival of wealth, the heritage of a tough, pioneer spirit faded. People's resolve to succeed in marriage weakened, and lack of time due to the two-income family exacerbated the trend.

Marriage was not the only institution that was weakened. Churches, schools, and civic organizations also became less effective as support systems for families.

Families Taking Charge of Their Own Health

The Economist noted: "The World Health Organization rates France's health-care system first among the 191 countries in its latest survey: not bad, given that France spends a bit under 10% of GDP on health, whereas the US spends almost 13% and comes 37th."[2]

Before the Industrial Revolution, the United States had an agrarian economy, where hard physical labor was the order of the day both inside and outside of the home. Over thousands of years people had evolved to adapt their bodies to a demanding physical regimen. Back then mothers knew best, and nature did the rest. (Or most of it. Perfect health was rare even then, and ability to treat a severe illness or injury was limited.)

Migrants to cities and towns and factory work found a different existence: As time passed machines became more capable of doing the hard physical work. People used muscles less and brains more. In terms of evolution, muscles have limited capacity to adapt to limited use, whereas the brain has always been and remains infinitely adaptable. In cities the density of living was much higher, making it easier for disease to spread. Even today a flu bug can cause widespread misery. This development combined with less active bodies to cause a further loss of health.

More and more people spend the day sitting in offices, airplanes, cars, and at home, tending machines or watching computer screens. Their bodies cannot easily adapt, but nevertheless this is the way of work in the postindustrial era. Poor adaptation causes stress, which becomes manifest in the form of headaches, heart disease, ulcers, obesity, overuse of tobacco, and so on.

The current delivery system for what is called health care is not designed to meet the current need. The core of the problem comes down to a system that is mislabeled; **it does not deliver good health**. Rather than preventing illness, its primary focus is on curing of illness and repair of injuries. The "health care" institution spends $1 trillion annually; as currently designed it cannot deliver health. This section will demonstrate the truth of this argument, and it will present a recommendation for a different system that is based on current trends in the field.

Before World War II most minor ailments and injuries were treated at home. A doctor was needed only rarely, and he often made house calls. He came to know his patients personally and could sometimes recommend healthful changes in lifestyle based on firsthand observation. He knew that every **body** is different from every other, so by getting to know a patient he could adapt his treatment to a unique set of needs. That was then, before the government became involved.

Today medical people operate mills. Patients go to the doctor, not the reverse. They talk briefly with several medical people, none of whom has opportunity to get to know them. Patients come out the other end with a piece of paper that suggests the use of a chemical that has been tested on several hundred people and several thousand mice, none of whom has a body exactly like that of the patient. The result is a temporary cure of an ailment with very little research into what aspect of a patient's lifestyle may have contributed to the condition. This means that another trip to see the doctor is probably not far off.

The health insurance industry is also not oriented to health. When someone else is paying, a patient or doctor might order tests and procedures over and above what would reasonably be judged as necessary. A doctor will also order extra tests to protect him- or herself in the event of a lawsuit.

The original idea behind insurance was that an individual, family, company, or other organization would have protection from some terrible catastrophe that could not be anticipated and could not be paid for out of available resources. Everyone insured would make regular payments into a pool, and the money would be invested to increase the amount. On the occasion of a serious accident or illness, the money would be available.

This is the way insurance generally works, but not in health care. In this business practically every routine activity and purchase is covered. "Mother knows best and nature does the rest" has all but vanished. This penetration into every aspect of an individual's private health is horribly expensive, primarily because it is so inefficient and wasteful. In every routine doctor visit 20 percent of the cost is skimmed off by the bureaucracy; this money provides little benefit to the patient. Medicare is a $280 billion a year business; bureaucrats and their assistants annually process 800 million claims. Various forms of fraud drain $80 billion a year from the Medicare and Medicaid programs, mainly because it is impractical to maintain control over mountains of money, especially when there is no competition in the marketplace.

Big government has responded to citizens' concerns with ever-expanding health programs. Politicians have largely convinced people that they have a right to health care. The reality behind this right is government exerting force on some people so that others may have a level of care that they cannot afford on their own. There is no provision for the irresponsible person who squanders money on other things, and therefore has no money when he or she gets sick. "Cannot afford" is broad-brush treatment of a complex issue. Furthermore, government is force. If citizens want to live in a free society they must limit government, or surely it will use that force to severely limit citizens' freedom.

Some people are generally healthy, and others are more often sick or injured. If an insurance company in a free market tried to charge both groups the same premium, the healthy people would go to competing companies who can charge less because they accept only relatively healthy customers. They will do this as soon as they realize they are indirectly subsidizing part of the sick group's premiums. This situation can continue: one company charges somewhat higher premiums to cater to not-so-healthy customers, whereas the other sticks to the healthy variety. This provides incentives for relatively sick people to improve their lifestyles, just as threatened increases in car insurance premiums encourage safer driving habits.

But socialized insurance as done by law does not allow a healthy worker this option; it requires one premium for all. Epstein provided some other ramifications:

> *Want to hire your own physician on a fee-for-service basis? Can't do it, given harm to others. Only healthy people will opt for this alternative, thereby causing an increase in the costs to the remaining . . . population. Want to do without insurance altogether? Again a wrong: same reason as above . . . forcing up rates for those at greater risk. Want to purchase group insurance with high deductibles? Sorry, offering that policy is a way of signaling insurers that one anticipates lower utilization of the services, and thus should be charged lower rates. This new definition . . . allows the most massive form of regulation from the cradle to the grave.*[3]

Recently there was an actual instance when some senior citizens wanted extra services not covered by Medicare and were willing to pay for them. But the law said no, because that would not be fair to others who would be denied the same opportunity. It seems strange that seniors who saved extra money throughout their working lives must go underground to purchase a legitimate service.

Epstein continued: "[The] 1986 passage of the Emergency Medical Treatment and Active Labor Act (EMTALA), which . . . requires a hospital to admit, regardless of ability to pay, all persons who arrive in its emergency room in active labor or in need of emergency medical treatment. For such cases, a hospital has lost its power to decide whom to admit." The clear implication is that many more people might live more recklessly, knowing that in any emergency they can get hospital treatment for free. One of those unfortunate people who live life on the edge might sustain an injury during a family fight. He can cool his temper overnight in a free accommodation courtesy of the taxpayer.

> *Under the old . . . system, a hospital did not have to shrink the size of its emergency facilities to reduce its potential legal liability. Under the modern legal rules, it will do just that, even though that will result in less care for all. Hospitals are forced to cut out care to the deserving poor and their paying customers (not all of whom are rich) in order to fence out the high-risk cases that could spell their financial doom.*

Here is but one more instance of the perverse results whenever big government officials distort the market while trolling for votes.

Scarcity cannot be eliminated. Therefore the question comes up: How much medical care should be made available to each citizen? This seems to be a simple question; the logical answer is "as much as each one needs." But need is like beauty in that it exists in the eye of the beholder. Just as some people are more beautiful than are others, some will need more medical care. Today the issue will always be resolved by government determining who gets how much of what kind of care.

This means public officials, the wealthy, and celebrities will get more, of course. Just as scarcity cannot be eliminated, neither can human nature.

The "right" to health care is not a natural right as discussed previously (Chapter 3). Rather, it is an economic right, which means the question of who decides who gets how much can be resolved only through the use of force. Natural rights are negative, in that their realization requires only restraint by others, including government, from infringing on those rights held by an individual. On the other hand, a positive right is unearned, and it requires that force be exerted against others to provide it.

For example, Worker A works hard, saves some of his money, and accumulates wealth. If he knows his property will be taxed to support Worker B, who spends his wages in riotous living and is often sick, will Worker A continue to work hard, save, and invest? He might well slack off, because his freedom of choice is being undermined along with his ability to pay tax to support Worker B. From this it is obvious that a government that avoids exertion of force on its citizens can guarantee only negative rights (protection from exertion of force or fraud by one citizen or group upon another).

Broder commented on government involvement in health care: "The key dimensions of a realistic discussion are three: cost, coverage, and quality. All three are inextricably linked. But Washington has chosen to deal with them one at a time . . . and by doing so, has almost guaranteed that realistic solutions will not be found."[4] Washington has little interest in finding a solution. The real intent is to convince voters that members of each party are striving mightily toward a solution, each furiously one-upping the other in search of votes. This perennially hot issue can be counted on to arouse emotions; the news media hunt for medical horror stories to enhance health care's vote-buying potential.

Even though organized poorly as described, before 1993 insurers and health personnel managed costs better than today. Then along came the Clintons with their focus on coverage. Of course, if enacted their proposal would have made the already horrendous cost of health care still higher. By 1998 the main focus was on quality, but this too increases costs.

Medications are regulated by the Food and Drug Administration (FDA), but this agency's approach requires rigorous testing on animals and humans to approve a drug for use with an acceptable safety profile. As an educated person gets better acquainted with his or her body over time, he gains insights into what helps him recover from illness and how to stay healthy. But if he discovers a use for a prescriptive medication that is not approved by the FDA for that use (known as off-label indication) and puts it to work on his own behalf, he is technically acting illegally. A citizen should have something to say about how to treat his or her own illness, and today the medical community is slowly coming to agree with this right.

Having discussed coverage and quality, the next topic is costs. It is human nature to look askance at any innovation, but in the case of health maintenance organizations (HMOs) the reaction has been sadly overplayed. The notion of managed care has been around for some sixty years, but its popularity rapidly increased only recently in response to skyrocketing costs of medical care. In fact by 1996 HMOs had all but stopped a former average 12 percent annual rise in costs that had been going on for years. At this rate the cost of medical care nearly doubles in six years.

But then the news media began bashing HMOs. Every health care institution, no matter how organized, consists of people, and now and then people make mistakes. The news media publicized some of the more serious mistakes by HMO personnel, and politicians of course became involved as soon as they smelled votes in the issue. Today the big push is for regulation of these facilities. Complying with regulations will force costs upward, and thus defeat the purpose for which HMOs grew popular.

Journalists have argued that managers of HMOs reward doctors for denying care rather than providing it. They claimed that referral to a specialist or a hospital stay causes an HMO to lose money. But if doctors and other medical personnel are on salary there is little incentive to treat too lavishly or too miserly. Although a doctor will be expected to listen to a cost-conscious manager, if both maintain open minds diverging perceptions can be easily reconciled. Should the doctor win too many, costs rise and the company becomes unprofitable. Should the manager win too many, quality of care suffers and customers will choose to go to a competitor (and there may be a lawsuit). This is how good quality care can be provided at a reasonable cost. It is also good management.

Some HMOs plans pay a doctor a fixed annual fee per patient, say $150. If the doctor and a patient cooperate to keep the patient healthy, most of the money is free and clear. On the other hand, one serious illness would cost many times that much money, and it would come directly from the doctor's pocket.

The Economist commented:

> *American medical technology is the best on earth, but its health-care system is the most wasteful. . . . Sadly, most of their politicians have misdiagnosed the ailment and are proposing a battery of quack remedies. Bill Clinton seems to believe that the problem is not waste, but frugality.*
>
> *HMOs are hugely unpopular, so Mr. Clinton is politically astute to attack them. But he is wrong. The evidence shows that managed care has curbed medical inflation without compromising the quality of care.*[5]

Political expediency often overrules economic logic, and not just in medical care.

> *Managed care cuts costs in several ways. First, big HMOs have the bargaining power to squeeze discounts from their suppliers, whether hospitals, drug firms or doctors. All three have long been dearer in America than anywhere else*

in the world—doctors' fees ruinously so. Second, they have cut the number of unnecessary tests, operations and days spent expensively languishing in hospital. Third, they focus more on preventive care, which may save money in the long run. Fourth, they make better use of information technology to crunch reams of data about patients in order to discover which treatments work best and which are the most cost-effective.

Health is an emotional issue, so politicians and their journalists lock onto it. The especially sad aspect of this lies in the ability of activists and the media to mislead the public through perpetrating a continuing avalanche of negative publicity. The results cited here come directly from the application of sound, rational management principles to medical care: effectiveness and efficiency. The former provides good service for customers, and the latter provides it at minimum cost. This is nothing more or less than the objectives of every business.

There is an important lesson here, to be learned by both politicians and the media: **Give the market a chance**. For years there has been expressed a deep concern with the spiraling costs of medical care. Along comes an institution that has proven ability to stem the apparently inexorable rise in costs, and it is promptly undermined by powerful people who are ignorant of its potential for minimizing a trillion-dollar problem.

Any innovation will take a while to find its place in the economy, especially if it is a major one. During the integration process there will be errors; new computer programs often have glitches in them that slip through premarket testing. Government has seen fit to avoid regulating these new programs, but not for HMOs entering the market, as short-term political imperatives overrule long-term economic benefits.

The predictable happened. Health premiums began to rise rapidly in the late 1990s, increasing by more than 8 percent in 2000 while inflation caused a general increase in prices of only 3 percent. Needless to say, the outlook is for more of same as the nation regresses to its pre-HMO price spiral.

Bergland argued against restrictive licensing in medical care:

The medical monopolists cloaked their true motivation in public interest language. "We must protect the ignorant public from quacks and charlatans without proper medical training or a sense of ethics." The government medical bureaucracy makes the same argument. It is a lie. Medical licensing has little to do with quality medical care. It has everything to do with limiting and controlling the people offering health advice and care.[6]

The law of supply and demand dictates that limiting supply without changing the level of demand will drive up the price.

Licensing has a place in consumer choice—ownership of a license constitutes independent evidence that suggests a degree of expertise possessed by its owner. This provides useful information to a customer seeking assistance. Seeking help from a practitioner without a license involves a greater risk because this information is absent. However, that practitioner may have an excellent reputation, and his or her prices are probably lower. The crux of the argument in this issue lies in increased consumer choice in a free market.

A similar argument is applicable to medicines. If a new medication shows promise but lacks a record of extensive testing, some patients may ask for it anyway. A doctor may agree to this, but lacking hard evidence, he or she may ask the patient to sign a waiver of liability. This situation applies to AIDS patients whose lives are in jeopardy.

But the FDA will not permit this; the bureaucracy requires extensive and extremely expensive testing before it will grant access for a new drug to the market. Bergland continued: "If government were to leave the field, existing information-providing businesses would expand to provide medical consumers with all necessary data. All you and I need to do is be responsible patients and make intelligent use of the available information." Drug companies are not interested in killing or harming their customers. They would cooperate with information companies.

People naturally tend to look after their own health, in economic terms as well as biological. "Millions of people have no medical insurance. . . . Many others make the rational choice not to buy medical insurance because it is too expensive, particularly if the expense is not tax deductible. They choose to be 'self insured.'" The news media keep the public in the dark about the number of these relatively healthy and wealthy people. They are lumped in with the others who lack coverage to inflate the total number for greater political impact. The media also choose not to mention that when the healthy and wealthy abandon the bloated health insurance market this causes premiums for all those still in the market to increase more, because if the healthy were included their premium money would subsidize those who are heavy users of medical services.

Bergland described a new idea called "medisave." A law would allow a worker to put tax-free money into a medical savings account; withdrawals would be limited to catastrophes that cannot be anticipated and that the worker cannot finance out of ordinary income and savings. The worker would meet routine expenses out of pocket, so this scheme removes health insurance companies from their current deep and wasteful involvement in customers' medical affairs.

In 1996 Congress passed a bill creating something similar although not identical: tax-free medical savings accounts (MSAs) for the self-employed and small businesses. This scheme provides an account that pays for routine care, plus an insurance policy that pays any large bills. Participants have unrestricted choice of doctors and can annually deposit a maximum of $3,375 for a family and $1,462 for an individual.

Workers in both schemes can keep any money not spent, so they have an incentive to shop around for good and inexpensive care. More important, there is an incentive to get and stay healthy.

Critics have argued that chronically sick people will have more difficulty in getting coverage, and it will cost more. But in the interest of fairness, it should. Such people would feel a strong incentive to keep their disease in remission. (The volunteer sector, described in Chapter 18, would help those who are seriously ill through no fault of their own.)

Critics have also argued that another incentive will operate: People will avoid routine visits to a clinic or doctor to keep more money in the MSA. But thinking people will soon realize that this is probably false economy, as the risk of the condition escalating into something really expensive increases. Thus both overuse and underuse of medical facilities works to the disadvantage of the customer.

The combination of the availability of HMOs, MSAs, and the current trend toward increased fitness provides an appropriate introduction to the recommendation contained below. It is a health care system that provides for health and fitness, which is, after all, what practically everyone wants from such a system but which the current system cannot deliver.

Begin with an individual who is willing to assume responsibility for his or her own health and fitness. He realizes that over the past few centuries medical people have utilized technology and tendencies inherent in human nature to gradually acquire control over his health. This has been done with titles, letters after signatures, language not understood by ordinary people, and media-hyped "miracle" breakthroughs in research. All these factors have created a mystique that surrounds today's health care industry. Mere patients have been expected not to question it, just to go on paying for it.

But an educated individual can see through this mystique, so he need not continue to blindly accept it. Having become familiar with his body and what it needs for health and fitness, he will utilize medical and fitness resources if and when he determines a need. "An apple a day keeps the doctor away" goes the old saw. Eating an apple a day symbolically illustrates the act of seizing the initiative for health and fitness. It is this initiative that drives the individual toward his objective.

Resources developed in the free market in response to demand will include health consultants, classes, Web sites, online chat rooms, videos, books, exercise facilities at home and work, sports, and other outdoor experiences. There will be computerized databases, which an individual can peruse for information that has worked well for others similar in age, gender, and lifestyle. Medical personnel will also be available. As the new system works out the glitches (give the market a chance), other resources will spring up as demand dictates. There will be no mystique because it will be an open system.

As indicated, the new institution will center on the individual, just as did the recommended education system center on the student (Chapter 13). Resources will be organized around a general health and fitness resource company. Discussion to follow will be split into two parts: internal and external management. This arrangement follows the usual pattern for a business: internal involves employees, materials, equipment, and cost control; external involves relations with suppliers, customers, and competitors.

Because a customer naturally wants to "keep the doctor away," the primary institutional emphasis is on prevention—good health and fitness. Resources available in the home will focus on this objective. Minor ailments and injuries will be treated in the home using in-home resources. These will include education aimed at maximizing occasions for in-home treatment, because this operates to the mutual advantage of both company and individual: less expense for the former and less inconvenience for the latter.

A general health company will have under contract or ownership satellite clinics located in neighborhoods, where they are handy for pursuit of health and fitness and for simple medical needs that are not treatable in the home. A person actively engaged in the search for health and fitness will find consultants in these facilities, along with medical personnel. Consultants will inform customers about a great variety of resources, and discussion with the customer will enable him or her to make decisions about which are best for him and the best conditions for use. No one will decide for the customer. Because a person's body changes with age and new resources are constantly becoming available, periodic visits with a consultant will keep him on track toward the objective.

Consultants will provide information concerning holistic health, or the coordinated involvement between the body, heart, mind, and spirit in the interest of general wellness. Many of today's medical people are so specialized that they don't understand the interaction between these four key components. Medical people will have knowledge about and respect for a variety of resources in alternative medicine, such as acupuncture, chiropractic, yoga, meditation, and so on.

A general health company is like a general contractor, who contracts with suppliers as well as satellite clinics in the interest of customer wellness. The company competes with others in recruiting and keeping customers and suppliers, keeping shareholders satisfied, and recruiting, developing, and retaining the best people for its staff. Like any other, the company is interested in making good profits. It does this by minimizing its costs while providing excellent services to its customers at a price that is mutually agreeable. Competition will keep prices from rising rapidly (a major problem in today's health institution).

The person in charge of a general health company will be educated and experienced in both health and fitness and in business management. He or she will himself practice what he "preaches" and will encourage members of the staff to do likewise. He will know that if employees are not presold on a product they cannot effectively sell it to customers. For this reason the company will also help train personnel in satellite clinics. Because consultants and other staff members in satellites will know each customer personally, they will be in position to offer useful suggestions.

Marketing consists of developing products that people want, making them conveniently available, pricing them right, and informing people about them. A customer under contract to a general health company will have the option of choosing among two or more satellites, and each of these may be under contract with more than one general company. Independent firms will be organized to provide information useful to a prospective customer when deciding which company a person will use to help him or toward his or her health goal.

A general health company will provide a competitive bid for services at the request of any prospective individual customer, family, or small business. The customer will shop around for the best deal. After a trial period, a contract will run for a fixed time, perhaps five years. On or before contract renewal time, customers will have the option of changing suppliers.

Each individual or family will pay a fixed, negotiated monthly fee, and there will be no problem whenever a change of job occurs. Companies will have facilities or links to others nationwide, so even if a job change involves a long-distance move there would probably be no interruption in service. Dissatisfied customers will change providers; this threat is not lost on managers. They will exert great efforts to keep them satisfied.

Problems that a satellite clinic cannot handle will be referred to the company's general hospital. Rarely will an illness or injury be so severe as to require assistance that is beyond the capability of a general health company. For these instances, a company will have a contract with several major hospitals, each of which specializes in treatment of certain serious problems. There are a few available today.

The Economist noted:

> *Americans rank hospital services lower by value for money than anything else they buy, including legal advice. . . . Hospitals that earn praise from their patients have one thing in common; a limited menu. An example is the Shouldice Hospital in Toronto, which treats nothing but abdominal hernias . . . charges $2,000 for an operation that can cost far more at other Canadian hospitals and up to $15,000 at some American ones.*
>
> *At the Texas Heart Institute . . . [one can receive] bypass surgery for $27,000, roughly $16,000 cheaper than the national average. Dr. Cooley and his fellow surgeons achieve such startling economy through practice—he has led over 80,000 open heart operations—and by attention to detail: the institute's surgical teams strive constantly to simplify procedures, and to replace expensive bits of equipment with cheaper ones. None of this compromises effectiveness. At*

92%, the five-year survival rate for . . . bypass patients is above the national average.[7]

Chronic ailments require maintenance to keep them in check as far as practical. Those who cannot afford continuing care would be helped financially by churches and private foundations organized for this purpose. General health companies will form associations to carry on research aimed at prevention or cure of these and other diseases. If two or more research facilities do similar work, the one that gets results will receive more money. Today's government-financed research is tainted with politics by its very nature.

Profit is the reward for accepting risk. If the risks are high, so must be the projected profit in a venture, or no one will assume the risk. There is always the possibility of loss and failure. The illegal drug business conforms to the definition of profit. Obviously the risks are high—getting caught means prison. So are the possible profits, or no one would enter the business. In today's fee-for-service medical care, complete with its mystique, there is very little chance of failure. In spite of low risk, fees are very high, and customer-financed insurance companies pay them. Therefore the industry does not conform to the definition of profit; this means there is almost no free market in health care.

PR = R – C, or PROFIT equals REVENUES minus COSTS. A glance at this formula reveals that increasing revenues, decreasing costs, or some combination thereof will increase profit. Even when both increase, if revenues outpace the rise in costs profit will be enhanced. This result describes a growing organization, which is frequently an objective of management. It applies to a general health company as follows.

If the job is done right, customers are successful in maintaining health and fitness. There will be fewer visits to satellites and also to the general company. Furthermore, many (if not most) people will pass an entire lifetime and never go to a major hospital as a patient. Highly trained staff people will find they have time on their hands.

Obviously, this situation suggests recruiting additional customers, and therefore revenues will increase. Because few additional resources will be needed to serve the new arrivals, costs will increase only a little, and so profit increases. Managers and all employees can be paid more, which will make it easier to attract top talent and keep it away from competitors. Bonuses can be given to outstanding staff members. Shareholders can enjoy bigger dividends and capital appreciation. These are the results of excellent practice by effective management.

On the other hand, government medical programs have bureaucrats running them. Because these people have no competition there is no incentive to minimize costs. Because they thrive on problems and not solutions, they constantly try to expand programs and thus justify more taxpayer dollars for their programs (and themselves). They don't want customers who are healthy, because this cuts into "business." When Medicare was established in 1965, Congress projected program costs in 1990 at $12 billion. The actual cost to taxpayers in 1990 was $98 billion. Today the tab is up to around $280 billion, and there is no end in sight.

Seriously handicapped, unemployed, and poor persons could be cared for by the volunteer sector, as described in Chapter 18. Some of the staff members who retire from the system outlined above will want to serve on a part-time or voluntary basis, so their talents will be made available to the indigent.

A thought on aging and health is in order. As people age they gradually become aware of their own mortality. This feeling tends to cause minor aches and pains, previously ignored, to become matters of concern. In a "health care" system where someone else is paying, economists tell us that medical facilities will get more intensive use than otherwise.

The generation gap could exacerbate this tendency; the elderly quite naturally feel lonely. A visit to a medical facility, therefore, may be the only chance for interaction with people for days on end. These factors combine to dramatically increase use, and indirectly suggest that "old means sick."

In a society where health is promoted (instead of curing sickness) people feel healthy because they take personal responsibility for their health. Furthermore as a result of continuing learning, they know their bodies, and so they know when a particular ache is nonthreatening and will pass quickly. They also know when a medical person should examine a condition.

The feeling of wellness can persist into advanced old age. People will feel useful to family and community as they share wisdom based on long experience. They will change today's definitions of "aging" and "elderly."

The proposed system has been designed to cater to individuals and families who are able and willing to seize the initiative for their own health and fitness. It ties in well with bottom-up democracy, where citizens seize the initiative in working toward good government. It acknowledges the reality that a particular individual is the only person who knows what is best for him or her. No amount of government, however organized, can cancel this truth.

Finally, the new system facilitates fulfillment of man's inherent desire to improve his lot in life. When he is healthy and fit, additional opportunities will open up.

Families Taking Charge of Their Own Destiny

Generations ago, extended families frequently stayed intact in spite of major challenges coming from both inside and outside the home. Before World War II there was less wealth and less occupational mobility; these combined to keep divorce rates relatively low. After the war, a new social force made its presence known. Powered by the career politician, it connected to the negative side of human nature. This force caused a previously expanding national government to dramatically accelerate its growth, and this development was not healthy for individuals or families.

Carbone reported that today 28 percent of young children live with only one of their parents.[8] They have a 77 percent greater chance of being physically abused when compared with children who live with both parents. Fatherless children are twice as likely to drop out of school and five times as likely to suffer poverty. Teenage suicide is far more likely in single-parent households. Finally, children in families with a step-parent have as many behavioral difficulties as those in single-parent households.

It is unlikely that this deterioration was caused only by increased wealth and mobility. The evidence that big government is in large part responsible is impressive. First, no-fault divorce has in effect reduced marriage to the status of an unenforceable contract. Second, poor families have been ruined by public welfare. There exists a large group of people in inner cities who do not even know anyone who is married. Then there is the marriage tax penalty, which tends to force women into the workplace when they might prefer to be home raising and loving their children. Fourth, teaching sex education and distributing condoms in schools have taught children there is nothing wrong with premarital sex. Fifth, by providing child care the government has weakened the bond between parent and child. Finally, the news media report on public figures who repeatedly break their marriage vows with apparently little ill effect. This litany of problems leads people to conclude that marriage in the United States is not the strong institution it once was.

Demographers attempt to track long-term trends in marriage. Although divorce is down slightly from its peak in 1980, more than one third of new marriages today will fail. Besharov reported that if citizens aged twenty to seventy-four are included, only 64 percent of women were currently married when surveyed in 1996, whereas in 1960 76 percent were married.[9]

Columnist George Will noted in January 2002: "In 1958 the percentage of children born to unmarried women was 5; in 1969, 10; in 1980, 18; in 1999, 33. The especially chilling number: in 1999 almost half (48.4 percent) of all children born to women ages 20–24—women of all races and ethnicities—were born out of wedlock."[10]

In another column Will argued that the parenting crisis includes three parts: widespread divorce, illegitimacy, and the entry of women in the labor force (including those with young children).[11] "For decades more and more parents have been spending less and less time at home, and many measurements—those pertaining to mental problems, child sexual abuse, drug and alcohol abuse, educational backwardness and more—show that child well-being is in 'what once would have been judged scandalous decline.'"

Will was not through yet. "In 1994 the census bureau estimated that about one-fifth of children age 5 to 14—4.5 million of them—were 'latchkey children,' defined as those who 'care for self' outside of school.' One study finds that children home alone for 11 or more hours a week are three times more likely than other children to abuse alcohol, tobacco or drugs." From 1960 to 1990 the rate of suicide among teens tripled.

Textbook writers are not helping the situation, and Will thoroughly castigated them.[12] One college text states: "Marriage has an adverse effect on women's mental health." Another dismissed the results of a survey that showed a majority of wives saying they were happy: "Happiness is interpreted by wives in terms of conformity. Since they are conforming to society's expectations, this must be happiness." And a third reported that the 1950s "brought only a flicker of contentment to a minuscule number of white, middle-class, suburban US families." These statements are only a small sampling of many. One logical conclusion is that if a typical marriage expert does not portray the family as dysfunctional he or she may be out of a job. A concerned citizen would suggest that the writers address the litany of problems mentioned, rather than attack the institution of marriage.

About 1845, former slave Frederick Douglass wrote: "Knowledge, wisdom, culture, refinement, manners, are all founded on work and the wealth which work brings. . . . Without money, there's no leisure, without leisure no thought, without thought no progress."[13]

In 1989 Schumacher commented on the subsequent advent of wealth: "The cultivation of needs is the antithesis of wisdom. It is also the antithesis of freedom and peace. Every increase of needs tends to increase one's dependence on outside forces over which one cannot have control, and therefore increases existential fear."[14]

His comment resonates with Walter Kerr's argument in his book *The Decline of Pleasure.* Kerr argued that there comes a point in the economic life of a family when members cease to own their myriad products, and the products begin to own them. There is a loss of control. To regain it, a logical conclusion points away from loving things and using people, and toward loving people and using things.

The present loss of control stems in part from an overbearing and deceptive government, whose officials don't want to encourage good education. Thus, without Douglass's "knowledge," people cannot appreciate the value of leisure and introspective thought. They become trapped into believing in things rather than in people and values.

This loss of control generalizes to relationships in a family and in school. Parents today do not discipline children as previous generations of parents did. This is frustrating to the young, as they need to test their behavior against firm rules as part of the maturation process. Children need discipline fully as much as they need love. There is a reason why the 1960s Beatles song "Money Can't Buy

Me Love" was so popular. The offspring of history's first affluent society parents were teenagers then; a pause to reflect on this development might yield an insight.

A prominent columnist recently went so far as to argue against truth.

> *Our national divorce rate is already too high. But think of what it would be like if husbands and wives told each other nothing but the truth. "So, how did things go at the company convention?" "Oh, the meetings were kind of dull. But I met a cute little bimbo from marketing at the hotel bar, we got half loaded and ended up in the sack. So how are the kids and what's for dinner?" . . . So let us give lying the respect it deserves.*[15]

In Chapter 14 this book argued for a society based on honesty and mutual trust. The above passage actually supports that argument indirectly, as reflection reveals that otherwise there can be no society. Chapter 9 showed that people in government frequently lie; this has become generally accepted practice on Capitol Hill. It is logical to conclude that many families perceive "leaders" in government as examples and guides for behavior, but this does not make lying right.

Other statistics indicate that close to 75 percent of second marriages fail, and almost 90 percent of third marriages suffer the same fate. Furthermore, after a divorce people are more likely to end up on welfare. The impact on children is not just economic; they pay a heavy emotional price, as often they are either not strong enough to handle it or too young to understand the forces involved.

Promotional messages by the thousands daily bombard the family. If strong bonds between members are lacking, they will be more vulnerable to these blandishments. Even if (and often because) there are two breadwinners in the family, financial management is weakened and trouble lies ahead. This causes a short-term orientation; a family lives hand-to-mouth. But children are a long-term investment and they are easily confused, especially when management of time suffers along with management of money.

Raspberry reported on "a fledgling national program called Marriage Savers, which helps local churches organize to create a 'community marriage policy' that includes intensive premarital training."[16] This is surely a sound approach, as the old saw about an ounce of prevention being better than a pound of cure is perhaps more appropriate to the institution of marriage than almost anywhere else. "Divorce rate in Modesto, California, which adopted the first . . . policy, fell by 35 percent between 1986 and 1997 . . . while the national divorce rate was dropping by just 1.3 percent." There are other examples with almost as impressive numbers.

The key seems to lie in specially trained mentoring couples who have been married for around thirty years. They spend up to four months intensively engaging young couples on every aspect of marriage. "It stresses the spiritual importance of commitment, and it offers time-tested how-to's. As Harriet McManus put it:

'Before you tie the knot, let us show you the ropes.'" This program seems to have good potential; surely it answers a need.

In an August 1997 column, George Will reported on a study by Chris DeMuth, which argued that economic equality is increasing.[17] Notwithstanding years of news media hype about the growing gap between rich and poor, this gap has been getting smaller. "People who deny that equality is increasing are fixated on the recent small increase in income inequality. That increase is, DeMuth argued, a small incongruity in the long-term 'leveling of material circumstances' that has been under way for three centuries and is accelerating." Although economic statistics going back that far may be less than reliable, the theory of capitalism suggests that this leveling is to be expected in the long run.

Money income, DeMuth argued, is becoming a less informative measure of individual welfare, as this fact shows: Western democracies have become so wealthy that, for the first time, "voluntary reduction in time spent at paid employment has become a major social and economic phenomenon." . . . He estimated that since 1880, the time devoted each week by the average American male head of household to nonwork activities has risen from 10.5 hours to 40 hours, while time at work has been cut nearly in half, from 61.6 to 33.6 hours. Income inequality has widened as social equality has increased. It has widened, in part, because of people's ability to choose to substitute leisure for income-producing work.

Some families have recognized the presence of a trade-off due to increased wealth and hence freedom of choice. Note how this choice ties in to human nature: the negative side tugs toward buying more; the positive side tugs toward increasing leisure and (presumably) happiness.

For many the pressure to buy is out of control; it remains for each citizen to realize this and act on that realization. One theory has today's people and families less educated than their grandparents in spite of more resources poured into public education and higher median levels attained (see Chapter 8). Therefore they are not sharp enough to see through the blandishments of professional marketers (or those of big government).

Advocates of simple living suggest that families slow down, smell the roses, and spend less. One option is to emulate the hippies of the 1960s and drop out of society. However, the more realistic option for most families is to reflect on their lifestyles and select pieces to eliminate or reduce that will enhance their happiness. A promotion on the job may be refused in the interest of quality family time. Dick Roy is a cofounder of the Northwest Earth Institute: "It's a practice of people who find their lives are enriched not by what they buy but by the passion they bring to the day." Carpe diem!

Ann Smith interviewed the authors of *The Millionaires Next Door: The Surprising Secrets of America's Wealthy.*[18]

How do millionaires get to be that way? By questioning the conventional wisdom. . . . But you have to understand that there's a big difference between income and wealth. You have to realize that while you can play great offense in order to make money, you need to put together a good defense in order to accumulate it. What's the best defense? Living below your means. The median annual income for the millionaires we studied is $131,000. But . . . a whole lot of millionaires in this country live on $60,00 to $80,000 a year.

Here are some people who have actually found Ben Franklin's philosopher's stone.

If a family wants to be a millionaire by age 55, say, they should save at least 15 percent of their income each year. Begin with 5 percent and work up to 15 by the late 40s, and put the money where taxes are not due immediately, such as real estate, stocks or a business. One of the authors, Thomas Stanley, provided a chart showing what happens when a 25-year-old invests . . . 5 percent of a $30,000 annual income, upping . . . to 10 percent at age 35 and 15 percent at 45.

This example assumes a 4 percent average annual raise in salary and a 9.6 percent annual return on the money.

Note the miracle of compounding:

Age (years)	Net Worth ($)
25	1,644
30	13,737
35	37,709
40	92,607
45	190,170
50	373,953
55	680,456
60	1,200,000
65	2,000,000

Stanley elaborated on the defense.

Spending a lot on things that have no value—clothing, eating out, dry cleaning . . . If you're a doctor . . . MBA, whatever, there's a certain standard of living you think you have to be associated with . . . live in a particular neighborhood, drive a particular car. . . . How much is a $2,000 suit worth after you walk out of the store with it? How much can you sell it for at a garage sale? . . . Half the millionaires . . . live in middle class, blue collar, or rural areas, like one guy we interviewed who defied us to find a suit in his closet . . . drove a 10-year-old car and wore cowboy boots.

Over the decades since World War II new wealth has bought a great variety of technology in the form of household labor-saving products, to which members of a typical household have adapted readily. Today in many instances each child's wired bedroom includes a beeper, a phone, CD player, TV, VCR, and computer. These gadgets enable a child to isolate him- or herself for hours at a time from any interaction with other family members. Some of them even eat in their rooms.

Hafner recorded an observation of a teenage expert at "multitasking."[19]

> *While working on a paper for a class on state drug laws, a project that involved not just writing but searching the Web for information, Colleen checked her e-mail on a running basis and kept up to eight Instant Messenger screens running, engaging in bursts of online conversation with friends about weekend plans. All this while listening to Faith Hill on her MP3 player and burning a CD with songs from The Corrs, a new favorite band.*

Psychologists point out that the normal human brain cannot focus on more than one task simultaneously. Although the example here may be slightly overdone, a thinking citizen might wonder if today's parents are raising a nation of scatterbrains. Will these teenagers express themselves in the future, or will they become as malleable as their elders?

These electronic gadgets are things. Human behavior has changed, but human nature has not. Today's children need fully as much love and discipline as did their counterparts two or three generations ago. Many parents tend to assume that their children's basic needs change along with major changes in household activities. Parents need to realize that no amount of electronic gadgetry can compensate for a lack of love and discipline. Nor can online relationships or Web sites fill the gap.

These products may well cause fragmentation in a family. A little creativity could co-opt this situation and turn it around. For example, each family member could be given information on several alternative trip destinations, sent via e-mail and including references to Web sites for additional information. Then each would select the one preferred, develop arguments in favor of that one and against the other alternatives, and send this message into "central computing." Each would then receive a copy of all inputs, and the process could recycle two or three times before the family assembles at a prearranged time and place for discussion and a final decision.

Or, one child in a geography class might be studying the Galapagos Islands while another is studying math. An exercise would have them estimate the population of great frigate birds on the islands based on a sample drawn from just one island of a specified size. A member would then check estimates against the record in an encyclopedia, and a prize would be ceremoniously awarded to the winner. All family members could join in this exercise.

Other exercises could focus on physical activity, such as sports, and spiritual nourishment. As time passes and children become accomplished at these activities, one or more might begin creating original exercises. (As indicated in Chapter 13, Maria Montessori would approve.)

These are examples of participatory democracy in microcosmic form. Through them a maturing child acquires a feeling of choice, or power over his or her own destiny. Next comes a feeling of control over his life, and it can spread beyond the family as he contributes toward good government in the neighborhood. A person may do this as a citizen or as a public servant, as an example of leadership for his family. With a tradition of active participation in family decisions and activities a healthy relationship is likely to persist even after a child has left the home. The implications for the generation gap are obvious.

The following discussion presents a chronology of a hypothetical family of the future in a democracy. It is potentially useful only as a guide, and it emphasizes free choices throughout the life cycle. There is no intent to offer a cookie-cutter prescription.

Whenever two young single people of opposite genders meet and like what they see, two selling processes begin. The amalgamation may move forward, and it may stop after a while. If it continues forward the couple will make plans for marriage.

Once the honeymoon is over most couples conclude there is little additional selling needed—the knot has been tied. But here is where the selling task takes on increased importance, just as the fantastic thrill of new romance begins to fade. This means the major challenge lies in postmarital selling, because it must transcend a thousand annoyances. The use of experienced consultants, references, and other resources enables a couple to anticipate many of these and plan for them. Done properly, it makes the later selling task more manageable, perhaps even fun.

Imagine a young man and woman who have fallen in love. The immediate challenge, addressed only infrequently, is to make long-range plans while swept up in the fantastic thrill of romance. This thrill is very often described as fantastic, but two definitions of the word apply: the contemporary, which also means great, all-pervasive, enchanting, and so on; and the traditional definition, which means unreal. It is far too tempting to ignore the latter definition until after the honeymoon, when grim reality gradually makes its presence felt. By then it may be too late.

Married family and friends all too frequently tend to relive their own past romances during wedding preparations, so they are reluctant to say anything to the young lovers about that reality. If adequate long-range planning precedes the marriage ceremony, later reality will probably be far less grim (but not absent). During this planning phase someone should tell them that "and they lived happily ever after" is the stuff of fairy tales.

Today's woman is financially much more independent than was her grandmother, and so she might tend to put relatively more weight on the romantic aspects of marriage. Generally speaking, this is unreal. However, this is not to say that as time passes it is not appropriate and much appreciated for a spouse to do little romantic things for a partner now and then. If this and other constructive behavior should become a habit, the odds of long-term success in the venture will be enhanced. For the truth is that almost anyone can get married; sustaining a happy marriage constitutes one of life's greatest challenges. Romance can and should be a part of it.

Peter and Joan may agree to delay marriage for a while so they can get to know each other better and also complete their college educations. As they plan they will consult various resources, both human and otherwise. An older family member or friend may share with them a vital truth (as discussed in Chapter 13): a person must know him- or herself before he can truly come to know another. He must love himself (self-esteem) before he can truly love another. In addition, a good higher educational experience that includes some liberal education and reflection will help the couple along the road to true and lasting love.

An equally important side benefit lies in the acquisition of insights into human nature. Yet another important benefit is the discovery that learning can be fun; this revelation stimulates formation of the habit of continuing learning throughout life. This in turn enables a person to stay acquainted with him- or herself as the self changes with advancing age. First mentioned in Chapter 13, this conclusion applies as well to a marital relationship.

Belief in the truth of these observations makes for orderly development of the mind and heart toward full adulthood. This means that both resources remain honed to provide service to others, including children. Peter and Joan are also well advised to consider alternatives for maintaining their health and fitness, in both body and spirit. In this way the four vital components of life—heart, mind, body, and spirit—become integrated into one holistic entity oriented toward the pursuit of happiness, as mentioned in the Declaration of Independence.

Any recently discovered need for additional formal education should probably be filled before children arrive. Peter and Joan agree that they want two children spaced about three years apart, and they plan to have the first one after five years of marriage. This delay will permit each to get to know the other better, to accumulate the accouterments of a household, purchase life insurance, and save some money as both continue to work. The money saved will be divided into three general categories: down payment on a home, retirement, and to absorb the switch from a two-income family to a single income when children are born. The proportion devoted to each category will change with time.

They decide that one spouse will remain in the home with the children as they grow. If Joan wants to nurse their babies, she will be the homemaker, at least in the early going. The purpose for this is obvious: bonding with the children. Yet in today's race for the riches this need is often short-changed. Centuries ago during the agrarian era this was not a problem, because both parents were never far away from the children. But today the situation is far different; the full implication of this difference should be appreciated and acted on.

Because the reduction in income was anticipated, the adjustment is made relatively easy. As mentioned earlier, money management is a two-way process. The home spouse will become an expert in "consumership," or putting together a good defense. More time will be devoted to be sure of a good buy. The family will buy less and is less likely to be cheated.

A change to a one-car family saves money in payments, operating costs, insurance, taxes, depreciation, maintenance, tolls, and parking fees. Expenses for clothing and income taxes diminish. Day care is not necessary, and the family does not eat out as often. (Good-quality day care can cost $700 per month.) When these savings are combined with expertise in shopping, Peter and Joan may discover that the financial sacrifice connected with having children and bonding with them is not all that much. In fact, they may be better off.

When the young ones are in school the home spouse can take on part-time work, often in the home. This will probably trigger a change in the previous savings pattern. About now the purchase of a house is probably feasible, but the temptation to buy the most expensive affordable should be resisted. This act would render the family vulnerable in the event of an unanticipated occurrence. There is time, and patience is a virtue. Furthermore, the chart above shows impressive numbers; this means a little restraint now pays great dividends later on.

Children may not be able to say it outright, but in their natures they prefer parental love and companionship over extra batches of toys and video games. If Peter and Joan do well, when they are grandparents their children will reach out to maintain healthy relationships with them. "Happiness is being a grandparent" will contain more meaning than just a bumper sticker platitude. Family trips and other activities will also enhance the bonding process.

Older folks attend church frequently. They vote a lot, both for church policy and in the voting booth. Because they contribute more money to the church or synagogue, these facilities tend to maintain conservative policies. Government does not change much either as powerful senior politicians worship the status quo.

Seniors don't appreciate the generation gap. Even their own adult children often put them out to pasture (retirement communities) tucked securely away from the hullabaloo of modern society. Exploding technological development and society's response to the resulting blizzard of information often confuse the elderly and exacerbate feelings of separation from their progeny. They miss seeing grandchildren growing up.

Enter continuing learning (Chapter 13). Schooling under the new system will demonstrate to children that learning can be fun. Parents, teachers, and enlightened clergy will help. Then older folks would enjoy keeping up with the blizzard of information; indeed, they would not see it as so. Intergenerational communication would remain open, so there would be far more frequent visits with children in both directions. Furthermore seniors would be anxious to make their influence known in community organizations, including government. Both church and government would become dynamic. The community's mature citizens' mentalities would change from What's-in-it-for-me? to What-can-I-contribute?

There is another important aspect of marriage that deserves discussion—sex. With many other aspects of the relationship made healthy, the sexual one will only get better. Both spouses will come to believe it cannot be any better elsewhere, and this may well eliminate a major cause of marital failure.

There will be rough spots. Helpful resources include family, friends, books, therapists, prenatal counseling, parenting guidance, and others. Due to their education Peter and Joan know when and how to utilize them. They can tap into the wisdom often found in older people, who will be very pleased with the opportunity to help. The initiative should come from the younger people, because in their wisdom seniors know the value of unsolicited advice. The young should understand that even though society has greatly changed since the old were their age, even the less educated elderly can share valuable insights into human nature.

With love and bonding must come discipline, and children also need this. Parents should agree on a policy that will cover all anticipated instances. There will be unanticipated occasions of course, but with a policy in place they can be handled fairly easily. Punishment should be swift, fitting, sure, relatively mild, and administered with love. To the extent feasible, the policy should be coordinated with those in school, sports, and religious organization. Therefore channels of communication with these facilities should remain open.

In late 1994 President Clinton jumped into the great family values debate with both feet. This action suggested that the government was interested in the welfare of families. The reality was, as usual, votes rather than genuine interest. The elites look after their own families, but they care little for those in the hinterlands unless there are votes to be mined. Furthermore, it is surely a stretch to believe that Washington can preach values to anyone.

Ada Tredwell's father had been a Southern sharecropper before coming North to work in a meat packing plant. Her conclusion displayed a rare wisdom.[20]

> *The way values keep changing, young people don't know what the rules are. There was a time when, if a boy got a girl pregnant, he had to marry her. That was the way we were brought up. Now you look at television and say, "Hey, that's okay. This is okay." And you find yourself changing your life, your standards, your values. It keeps getting foisted on you. You see it enough times, you keep seeing it over and over. And you think: what's wrong with that? So we accept it. There was a time you protested, "Oh, I think it's terrible these kids are getting pregnant or these babies are having babies." Now people criticize you for*

even objecting. And naturally, the more you accept it, the more acceptable it becomes. And you lose your values. That's what happens.

What does big government have to do with this deeply disturbing trend? Hard proof is elusive, but it can be argued that if "leaders" in government practice an immoral existence and the people continue to look to their leaders for guidance the trend can only be expected. Whenever Hitler rose to speak, too many Germans who did not agree with his values remained silent. The few who spoke out were shouted down. There is a lesson in this.

There will be young people who elect not to go to college. A possible difficulty here lies in probable failure to appreciate the value in learning, and hence a lowering of attention to this vital habit in the future. But blue-collar workers and their supervisors have always contributed greatly to society and to its economic development, and this will continue in the future. The only suggestion is to keep sensitive to opportunities for additional learning. This sensitivity is more easily acquired today, as learning resources are ubiquitous. Future employers will encourage learning so that more workers can contribute ideas along with muscle.

Some thoughts about retirement are in order. *The Economist* added perspective to the subject as discussed in Chapter 5.[21]

> *. . . same principle as the Ponzi scam. America's Social Security scheme is the pay-as-you-go sort in which today's workers pay for today's pensioners. The first few generations of pensioners received much more . . . [than they] had paid in. . . .*
>
> *[The] return from this kind of pension comes from the growth in the workforce and its real earnings. But in the 1970s, the post-war baby-boom gave way to a baby-bust which put an end to the indefinite . . . "more youths than old folks." Besides, those "old folks" were living longer.*

The Social Security retirement system has been horribly politicized, as *The Economist* continued: "Imagine a world where you had no direct property right to your most important financial asset, probably worth more than your house; where the value of that asset bore no direct relationship to what you had put into it; and where that asset, and the return on it, was often assigned to you arbitrarily and unfairly."

In the early 1980s a law started what is known as a 401(k) pension plan. This law permits employees to make voluntary contributions that are partially matched by employers. Ownership and control have been thus clarified. This substantial improvement is long overdue, but it is far from an instant solution. Therefore the following commentary refers to the distant future; what irresponsible career politicians have done to the country's young people will not go away soon.

Genetski's figures nearly mimic those of Thomas Stanley.[22] If a young worker currently earning $500 a week were to set aside 10 percent of his or her wages toward retirement in a private pension fund; received annual 2 percent raises; the retirement fund earned 6 percent annually in a free market without government interference and with healthy economic growth; he or she would retire with a million dollars in assets.

In terms of building value over a long period of time, private pensions have repeatedly outdone public ones, especially when, as in this country, the latter are annually plundered and the money spent by public officials to buy votes. Britain has almost wholly converted to a private pension system, which today exceeds $1 trillion in asset value.

Genetski is an economist, but he also offered an observation based on psychology: "As workers see their retirement accounts grow, a sense of pride and accomplishment develops. Individuals recognize that they alone are responsible for their retirement. The relationship between a lifetime of work and economic security . . . becomes more apparent than ever before." This is important. As Frank Sinatra sang so often, "I did it my way."

Thoughts of institutions positively affecting human nature come to mind in Genetski's conclusion. "Imagine the social and economic implications of allowing low-income workers to accumulate hundreds of thousands of dollars. With enormous visible rewards for legitimate work, the nation's moral and social structure would change dramatically." However, this delightful scenario depends on two very important assumptions: self-discipline within workers and a government that does not meddle in the economy. (Chapter 11 showed that these two assumptions are really only one: if a citizen can discipline him- or herself, he will discipline the government.)

Finally, regardless of what happens, the future will be no utopia. People are people, and as such they are prone to mistakes and misbehavior. As family members build and enhance democracy and its accompanying personal freedom they need to be constantly aware that others are nibbling at their freedom. These people should be sought out and restrained, as in politics and government an ounce of prevention is worth more than a pound of cure.

"There is nothing nobler or more admirable than when two people who see eye to eye keep house as man and wife, confounding their enemies and delighting their friends," noted Homer.

Notes

1. Alexis de Tocqueville, *Democracy in America*. Knopf, 1972.
2. *The Economist*, "Under a Financial Anaesthetic." January 12, 2002, p. 47.
3. Richard A. Epstein, *Principles for a Free Society: Reconciling Individual Liberty with the Common Good*. Perseus Books, 1998.
4. David Broder, "In the Health Care Furor, Amnesia is Epidemic." *News and Observer* (Raleigh, NC), July 1998 column.
5. *The Economist*, "Patients or Profits?" March 7, 1998, p. 23.

6. David Bergland, *Libertarianism in One Easy Lesson.* Orpheus, 1997.
7. *The Economist*, "Hamburgers and Hernias." August 9, 1997, p. 55.
8. Leslie Carbone, "Being Faithful to America's Families." *News and Observer* January 31, 1999, p. 27A.
9. Douglas J. Besharov, "Marriage Retreats, and Adapts." *News and Observer*, July 1999, column.
10. George F. Will, "Lessons Unlearned in School Bill." *News and Observer*, January 6, 2002, p. 23A).
11. George F. Will, "Parenting's Crisis Is Home Alone." *News and Observer*, June 7, 2001, p. 19A.
12. George F. Will, "Marriage in Chapter and Verse: The Texts Get it Wrong." *News and Observer*, November 1998.
13. Frederick Douglass, quoted in Jim Powell, *The Triumph of Liberty*, Free Press, 2000.
14. E. F. Schumacher, *Small Is Beautiful: Economics as if People Mattered.* Harper and Row, 1989.
15. Mike Royco, "Little Lies and Whoppers Keep the World Spinning." *News and Observer.* January 20, 1996, p. 13A.
16. William Raspberry, "Serious about Marriage." *News and Observer*, February 1999.
17. George F. Will, "The Leveling of Society." *News and Observer*, August 1997.
18. Ann Kates Smith, "$1 Million Worth of Secrets." *US News*, June 9, 1997, p. 90.
19. Katie Hafner, "Teens' Minds: Digitally Divided." *News and Observer*, April 16, 2001, p. 1D.
20. *The Economist*, "The Price of Perjury." November 28, 1998, p. 32.
21. *The Economist Survey*, "Time to Grow Up." February 16, 2002.
22. Robert J. Genetsky, *A Nation of Millionaires: Unleashing America's Economic Potential.* Heartland Institute, 1997.

Part V: Thoughts on a New World Order

Freedom is not the right to live as we please, but the right to find how we ought to live in order to fulfill our potential.
—Ralph Waldo Emerson

After thousands of years of warfare it surely seems that the world deserves a break.

In 1989 there were bloodless revolutions in several satellite nations of the Soviet Union, and thus began serious talk of a new world order. In 1991 the Soviet Union itself collapsed, signifying the official end of the cold war, and there was more talk of a new world order. No one in authority defined in detail what was meant by this term, which leads to today's conclusion that these discussions were mostly political hype. There was no serious intent to make a sweeping change in the way governments of advanced countries governed, even when a historic opportunity had plunked itself into their midst.

At first glance Part V lays out an impossible agenda: a world free of the scourge of war and a switch in emphasis to free trade, which will in the long run provide great benefits to rich and poor countries alike. However, in view of what has gone before a convincing argument can be advanced that the transition to such a world can and must be accomplished. This part provides that argument.

Chapter 20 demonstrates that today's international political and military tensions and conflicts are more fabrications of cold warriors and their politicians still hanging onto power positions than they are of today's reality. The negative tugs of human nature still prevail. Therefore this chapter peels the wool aside and reveals the potential for a world at peace based on contemporary reality: the advancement of the Age of Reason.

Chapter 21 discusses the contrast between the world role played by the US government in today's fabricated strife and that available to government and citizens under the new world order, which will emphasize peace and the positive side of human nature. As a large nation the United States would retain an important leadership role, but it would be constructive rather than destructive.

Chapter 22 presents a brief history of the United Nations, stressing the difficult nature of its task during the first fifty years of its existence. It is not entirely its own fault that it is so plagued by difficulties today. The chapter finishes with a brief but sweeping recommendation.

The year 1776 was a pivotal year in the New World, as colonists struggled with the fateful decision whether to cave in to the British crown or fight for independence. Thomas Paine struggled to save enough money to publish a pamphlet called "Common Sense," in which he implored the colonists to stiffen their backbones and fight, lest the situation only grow worse. "There hath not been such an opportunity since the time of Adam. We have it in our power to make a new world!"

The miracle of today lies not just in the presence of a similar opportunity, but that it may be seized without bloodshed.

Chapter Twenty:
On War Becoming Peace

Violence is the last refuge of the incompetent.
—Isaac Asimov

Thomas Jefferson wrote: "but sound principles will not justify our taxing the industry of our fellow citizens to accumulate treasure for wars to happen we know not when, and which might perhaps not happen but from the temptations offered by that treasure." History has demonstrated time and again that a government's preparation for war does not stop with attainment of peace. This explains how over the several centuries prior to 1900 the countries of Western Europe got themselves into such deep cultural and economic difficulty: temptations offered by treasure won through oppressive taxation, conquest, and plunder.

Note the operation of negative forces discussed previously: personal power, external threat, and passion. Because they connect to human nature they have been around for a long time. Kings and dictators are human beings, and it is in human nature that passions occasionally displace reason. Because most of these people were egomaniacs, war happened more often than occasionally.

This chapter will build arguments for peace around a unique coincidence of such towering importance as to overshadow all history of war and conquest. Man is the only higher animal who routinely kills its own kind. This condition was created and sustained because humankind had no natural enemies, and so this was the method by which world population growth was controlled over the millenniums of human existence.

But today there are a variety of techniques for controlling the growth of world population without wars. This technology has seen fit to make its entrance at a time that coincides with development of another technology: weapons of such awesome destructive capacity as to threaten the very future of mankind. Is the confluence of negative impulses in the nature of man and the development of birth control technology just a miraculous coincidence? Perhaps a divine Being had a hand in this. Either way, people and public officials are surely well advised to ponder the implications in terms of war and peace. It is entirely possible that mankind is poised on the threshold of a totally new era, which has been called the Age of Reason.

The positive side of human nature yearns to assert its presence in today's world. Psychologist Carl Rogers spent some fifty years studying and counseling people. He concluded that people are basically good and want to do good. The original threat suggesting that people are by nature sinners and they can be saved from eternal hell only by repentance was very possibly an artifact of priestcraft. In prehistoric times people knew practically nothing of science, so they knew little of their surroundings. Therefore they were vulnerable to the preaching of mystics and shamans who professed to understand these surroundings. The priests soon learned that to keep their flocks in line they had only to keep constantly before them the threat of eternal damnation and the people would do their bidding.

This observation is not an argument for ending religion; that would be Marxist. Rather, the emphasis is on freedom of choice. The assumption persists that people need some manner of spiritual nourishment to become whole.

The threat of hell worked for thousands of years. There are many places where it still works. But today, due to advances in science, mathematics, and other technologies people understand far more about their surroundings. Therefore the advanced world (at least) stands at a point in time when citizens can finally admit to its proper place the positive side of human nature. This could well become history's first true worldwide liberation of man's intellect and energies. The implications are mind-boggling.

The desire for revenge suggests, "Don't get mad; get even." But this saying is misleading, in that the seeking of revenge for wrongs real or imagined is all passion; it is madness. The reason for this lies in the sad truth that there is no end to this seeking; enemies never agree on what is "even." A Bosnian refugee was quoted: "They killed my husband and son. They burned our home. But they can never rest easy, because one day we will do the same to them, or worse. My children will get their revenge, or their children." The terrible situation in Bosnia and in other Balkan countries can be traced historically to a battle fought in 1221. There is apparently no end to the misery as long as revenge-seeking passion overrules reason.

Any peace at the end of armed conflict is not a genuine peace, as long as one side is plotting revenge. Unless the courage can be found to break out of this rut, a grim destiny awaits. Today the cold war is over and there exists an opportunity to break this vicious circle for as far as anyone can see into the future. But from where will come the necessary courage?

Chapter 4 showed that looking to career politicians for this trait is an exercise in futility. This book will argue that, paradoxically, consulting career warriors will yield a similar result. For a different reason they too are not interested in peace.

The Age of Reason does not mandate the end of empire, but it does suggest that an empire can end without violence. An example was set for the world in 1989, when the Soviet Union's Mikhail Gorbachev permitted several satellite countries to break away from the Warsaw Pact, and there was almost no violence involved. This act required courage, because at that time most of the Soviet Union's top leaders and generals still believed the West was poised to attack their country and was just waiting for the right moment. The act of letting their buffer states go free would make the country more vulnerable to an attack.

It is interesting to note that as these bloodless revolutions unfolded the US news media said little or nothing about Gorbachev's courage. This is because the oligarchy prefers to emphasize courage on the battlefield instead of the kind of courage that is required to step forward in the name of peace.

External Threats and Previous Wars

H. L. Mencken: "The whole aim of practical politics is to keep the populace alarmed (and hence clamorous to be led to safety) by menacing it with an endless series of hobgoblins, all of them imaginary." Reflection strongly suggests that there is truth to his observation. Further thought suggests in turn that practical politics is but a modern reincarnation of the gimmick employed so successfully by ancient priests and shamans during the era of priestcraft: fear of damnation.

But if people have been enlightened since that time, how can public officials continue to make this tactic work so well? The answer lies in artful politicians. Mencken saw through the subterfuge: "Wars are seldom caused by spontaneous hatreds between people, for peoples in general are too ignorant of one another to have grievances and too indifferent to what goes on beyond their borders to plan conquests. They must be urged to the slaughter by politicians who know how to alarm them."

Thousands of years ago as populations grew territory needed for hunting and gathering grew scarce, and conflict resulted. To be more successful in conflict people gathered into bands and later into tribes or clans. But external threats persisted, and chiefs quickly saw the advantage in keeping people in a constant state of anxiety. They and other elders created rites of passage into adulthood for boys that emphasized skill and courage in battle.

With the early beginnings of the nation-state the king gradually replaced the priest, but the same gimmick kept working just as effectively. The next logical form of organization lay in feudalism, where lords agreed to keep their serfs safe from marauding bands in exchange for labor. Much later there evolved the more complex concept of the nation-state. All the while top leaders continued to see advantage in keeping their "flocks" subservient through use of the same ruse.

In Europe the coming of the age of conquest and plunder made more real the external threat. For some 400 years alliances among European nations were made and broken by wars, remade, and again broken. The continent existed in a constant state of turmoil. In 1511 Erasmus wrote *In Praise of Folly*:

> *War is something so monstrous that it befits wild beasts rather than men, so crazy that the poets even imagine that it is let loose by Furies, so deadly that it sweeps like a plague through the world, so unjust that it is generally best carried on by the worst type of bandit, so impious that it is quite alien to Christ; and yet they leave everything to devote themselves to war.*[1]

This protracted tragedy impelled Jefferson to write, "Our first and fundamental maxim should be, never to entangle ourselves in the broils of Europe." (This sage advice appeared in an 1823 letter to President Monroe. It influenced the creation of the Monroe Doctrine, which kept this country out of wars for many years.) The conclusion is obvious: The external threat theory has been proven effective for so many centuries that it has become the conventional wisdom of today. Therefore no one questions it.

In *Federalist Paper* 6 Alexander Hamilton wrote of the negative force involved in the issue of war. "Men of this class . . . have in too many instances abused the confidence they possessed; and assuming the pretext of some public motive, have not scrupled to sacrifice the national tranquillity to personal advantage or personal gratification." Like uncertainty, national security cannot be measured, so Hamilton's observation is just as relevant today as it was in 1788. Today "men of this class" exert power, accumulate treasure, and react with passion to even the smallest slight.

Hamilton predicted today's predominance of the military:

> *The continual necessity for their services enhances the importance of the soldier, and proportionately degrades the condition of the citizen. The military state becomes elevated above the civil . . . frequent infringements of their rights, which serve* ***to weaken their sense of those rights****; and by degrees the people are brought to consider the soldiery not only as their protectors but as their superiors. The transition from this disposition to that of considering them masters is neither remote nor difficult; but it is very difficult to prevail upon a people under such impressions to make a bold or effectual resistance to usurpations supported by the military power. [emphasis added]*

In a country such as the United States, with a civilian in charge of the military (the president) this still happens, albeit at a slower and more insidious pace. Hamilton had great insight into human nature.

Tocqueville also accurately perceived reality: "All nations that have had to engage in great wars have been led, almost in spite of themselves, to increase the power of the government. Those which have not succeeded in this have been conquered. A long war almost always faces nations with this sad choice: either defeat will lead them to destruction or victory will bring them to despotism."[2] War has nearly always been a lose-lose phenomenon for the ordinary citizen, but the power of the negative aspects of human nature to regulate leaders' behavior has great strength. Those who argue that nobody wins a war have a point.

In 1848 John Stuart Mill declared that commerce was rendering war obsolete. In 1891 the populist politician Tom Watson

> *opposed a threatened war with Chile on the grounds that "it would arouse the military spirit everywhere" and argued on the floor of the House of Representatives that "the time is approaching . . . when wars—those barbarous settlements of disputes by appeal to arms—will be just as much a relic of the past . . . as are now the old, rude ways of trial by combat and dueling."* [3]

The time draws nigh.

Rose Wilder Lane commented. "War is caused by the ancient pagan belief that Authority controls individuals, and must and should control them. This belief is in individuals' minds. . . . War will end when a majority of men on this earth know that every man is free. Each person must see for himself."[4] She argued that it is in the nature of man to be free to utilize his energies as he sees fit and in respect of the next person. A central authority can harass a person, but it cannot control him or her. "So long as any large group of persons, anywhere on this earth, believe the ancient superstition . . . Authority . . . they will set up some image of that Authority and try to obey it. And the result will be poverty and war."

Barber also believed that war went against the nature of man: "Especially as weapons improved and bands of warriors increased in size, war required men to go against one of their deepest, most natural instincts: the instinct to run away from danger."[5] This fact made it necessary for military leaders to create a mystique around war: patriotism, heroism, glory. This was the carrot, but the stick was also necessary. "So the governance of the military emerged as an autocracy; power at the top forcing performance by those at the bottom. . . . War was not typically carried out by the consent of the governed but by the force of the governors." This is why nations having governments guided by even pseudo-democracies practically never fight one another.

This forced action can, over centuries, generate in young people a twisted mentality. Living in Europe during World War II, Rose Wilder Lane met such a man.

> *I was confused, myself, for like most Americans I had taken it for granted that no one wants war. My friend had the best European schooling, Italian, German, and English. He was widely and accurately informed; he was intelligent, open-minded, and eager to understand my puzzling country. The clue, he said, was in our attitude toward war. It baffled him. American patriotism is peculiar, he said. Americans never say "my fatherland," "my motherland." What a peculiar attitude toward your country, to call it Uncle Sam. . . . That is not the way in which a man speaks of his country. . . .*

One morning . . . He came in, excited. . . . "As you have said, Signora: Americans hate war because it kills men and destroys property. Suddenly, it comes to me. What are lives and property? Material things. All men die, time destroys all property. Lives and property have no value. The immortal value is the soul of a nation, and war regenerates the nation's soul. Americans cannot see spiritual values."

How can a citizen respond to this, except to take pity on this presumably intelligent young man? But in this mentality lies the explanation for a Europe torn asunder by war after war for several centuries.

A thinking citizen would ask how this mentality came to be, flying as it does in the face of Barber's natural human tendency to flee from danger. The only answer is that it was imposed on that era's citizens by Lane's "Authority."

Lane continued:

History is a spectacle of billions of human beings. . . . Not one of them could live if human energy did not ceaselessly attack this indifferent and dangerous earth; not one could live without the help of his kind. Yet they always use their energy to kill their kind and to destroy the food and shelter upon which human life depends. This is suicidal. War does not only kill individuals; it attacks the very root of human survival.

With the invention of new weapons of ever greater destructive powers, whither civilization?

Lane wrote *The Discovery of Freedom* during World War II.

The caterpillar tractor that Americans invented to plow the peaceful fields and multiply the farmer's productive energy as if by magic, now armored and armed it charges in battalions of tanks over the bodies of men. The submarine, that an American invented to rescue a broken man from imprisonment on St. Helena, now it lurks hidden under all the seas to kill men. The machine that two brothers invented in their bicycle shop, to give all men wings, now it makes the moonlit sky a terror that drives men underground.

She argued that the American Revolution, which for only the third time in history gave true freedom to people, was being stolen by despotic war mongers.

Bernard Grady fought in the Vietnam War.[6]

This most powerful nation, which proclaims "In God We Trust," does not trust its God to rightfully settle a dispute among men. The nation that purports to follow the commandment "Thou shalt not kill," is doing just that. Therefore, the chaplain is required to legitimize the violent death, to vest mayhem with righteousness, to connect death with truth and goodness. He is there, in part, to remind us that we are The Good. The enemy, the Communist and therefore the Godless, is The Evil. Remorse at having killed is, thereby, rendered unnecessary; death at the hands of the enemy has a purpose, is given worth.

Grady was obviously among the many in Vietnam who devoted some serious thought to what they were doing and why. This development was disturbing news for Washington's warriors, not to mention the greater public who were not consulted before the decision to go to war was secretly finalized. "Deriving their just powers from the consent of the governed" is an excerpt from the second paragraph of the Declaration of Independence. But the elite class knew better than to adhere to this tenet; consent would not be forthcoming.

Grady found a mortally wounded enemy soldier whose comrades had left him with only a photo of his wife and four-year-old daughter.

> *A medic shot him with morphine to ease the pain, and he took the photo for a look. The man was crying, not in pain, but he wanted the photo back. He got it just before he died. The first sergeant, who fought in World War II and Korea, came to attention and paid his respects to a fellow soldier with a salute. That old warrior had seen too much . . . and who himself . . . would be just a memory in the minds of his wife, son and two daughters . . . asked the heavens as he walked away, "God, isn't there a better way?"*

Powell capably summarized the mayhem and tragedy of war:

> *Throughout history, governments have killed more than 300 million people. During the 20th century alone, government killed some 170 million. . . . Only about 38 million were battle deaths. The great bulk . . . [were] mass murder in the name of political, ethnic, racial, or religious doctrines. These crimes were committed by some of the most astute political thinkers, who deserve to be better known.*[7]

The news media persist in hyping all external threats, real and imagined. These actions keep the populace hunkered down and in a continuing state of panic. If asked, media managers might respond that should the almost impossible actually happen and someone actually fires a missile at this country, they cannot afford to be caught out. But this gutless policy only panders to the negative incentives that operate on the elite class, whose members know that if the media do not cooperate their dirty secret will be revealed.

Leach commented on the knee-jerk policies of the news media.[8]

> *Within minutes of the horrific attack on the World Trade Center, Tom Brokaw of NBC News was declaring war on terrorism. On almost every TV channel, references to Pearl Harbor were flying even before the Center towers collapsed. . . . Some people in the media seem eager to turn in their first draft while events are still going on. This is irresponsible reporting and dangerous history.*

Recall that after the cold war the oligarchy furiously searched the world for an ogre that seemed tough enough to replace the Soviet Union, and largely in vain. Small wonder it sprung like a cougar on this one.

Leach moved backward nearly a century to record a presidential warning:

Privately, Wilson had darker thoughts about the costs of WWI. The night before he delivered his war message to the Congress, he told a newspaper editor: "Once lead this people into war, and they forget there ever was such a thing as tolerance. To fight, you must be brutal and ruthless, and the spirit of ruthless brutality will enter into the very fiber of our national life, infecting Congress, the courts."

Lacking self-discipline and having succumbed to the negative tugs of human nature, politicians and analysts have allowed themselves to become war criminals. Some may believe this is an overly strong indictment. But in 1900 one in ten casualties in war was a civilian. Today it is nine of every ten, as bombs and missiles fly hundreds and thousands of miles and land who knows precisely where? During the Kosovo conflict NATO spokesmen papered over the killing of hundreds of innocent civilians, calling it "collateral damage." If asked, surviving family members of those killed would surely describe the slaughter in different terms. But the news media apparently did not see fit to ask.

While on trial for the Oklahoma City bombing, Timothy McVeigh learned of the dozens of children that he had killed. He called that tragedy "collateral damage," but the news media hushed that one. Had it been properly informed, the public would have been expected to believe that killing Kosovar children is good collateral damage, whereas killing US children exemplifies the bad variety. The government may have thought that even gullible citizens might start wondering about what actions they are paying for.

Right after the end of the cold war the military became alarmed, because it seemed there was no longer an enemy to threaten citizens and make them willing to be heavily taxed to support the world's mightiest war machine. A top military leader delivered a speech in which he argued that at present the citizens' greatest fear was uncertainty.

The difficulty with this argument lies in inability to measure uncertainty, and also in the fact that uncertainty is inherent in every society. This constant presence and inability to measure combine to justify almost any price for national security, and so the speaker, a career military man, attempted in his speech to guarantee a lush future for the military at taxpayer expense.

Recently a high-level officer in space command castigated the Canadian government for its disapproval of the proposed National Missile Defense project (commonly called "Star Wars"). He warned Canadian officials that the United States would feel no obligation to defend their country against a missile attack. The officer attempted to provide some diplomatic cover for a project that breaks the 1972 START II treaty, is technologically questionable, and of which the Russian and Chinese governments strongly disapprove. (The Canadians were not buying, either.)

No one claims that swimming upstream is easy. With no enemy in sight, finding justifications for continuing to annually spend up to $400 billion of taxpayer money has indeed become a major challenge. As this is being written President Bush's "axis of evil" is losing its appeal as suspicions continue to grow.

The external threat supports strong arguments for preserving NATO, which was formed in 1947 by Western European countries and the United States solely to counter a perceived threat from the Soviet Union. The same rationale has recently been stretched to justify expanding the organization. The threat, if it ever truly existed, is gone, but NATO grows bigger anyway. What would Jefferson say?

When examining the rationale for expansion of NATO, it is instructive to seek commentary from a man who could be described as foreign policy's modern Jefferson. As part of his developing expertise on the Soviet Union over a fifty-year period, George Kennan became an expert on NATO.[9] When interviewed in 1998 the man was visibly upset.

> *The view, bluntly stated, is that expanding NATO would be the most fateful error of American policy in the entire post-cold war era. Such a decision may be expected to inflame the nationalistic, anti-western, and militaristic tendencies in Russian opinion; to have an adverse effect on the development of Russian democracy; to restore the atmosphere of the Cold War to East-West relations, and to impel Russian foreign policy in directions decidedly not to our liking.*

These are powerful arguments. He concluded that there was a "total lack of necessity for this move." This move creates the fervent hope in the breasts of millions of thinking citizens that the ultimate result is not a throwback into the previous European history of 400 years of nearly constant warfare. Short-term political imperatives should not swamp important long-term considerations, especially when the stakes are of such size as described here. Thomas Friedman's column indicated that the public relations campaign for NATO expansion was funded by lobbyists representing international arms merchants.[10]

This business must surely be lucrative in the extreme, as fiscal year 2003's "defense" budget has risen to $380 billion. Bush and his mandarins in Washington must believe there is no end to taxpayers' generosity (or fear of some imaginary threat).

In May 2002 *The Economist* believed that NATO figures into the government's stupendous ambitions.[11] "The NATO alliance has until its November summit in Prague to decide what it is for." After the Soviet Union collapsed in 1991 that newspaper posed a question on one of its covers: "Staying On?" The only purpose for which NATO existed had vanished, so the question reeked of pure logic. The fact that the organization is not only still around twelve years later but is expanding is grim testimony to the staying power of a huge bureaucracy. Today the question of purpose is still trolling for an answer.

"Mr. Bush called on NATO to be ready at Prague to issue as many new invitations as possible." This is understandable. New member nations will need to gear up for mortal combat so that their arsenals' destructive capacity will dovetail into those of existing members. They will need massive quantities of weapons. It is no coincidence that Mr. Bush presides over the world's foremost international weapons trafficker. Business will pick up commensurately with the number of new member nations brought under NATO's wing.

"NATO must be ready to act where its vital security interests are at stake, whether in Europe or some other corner of the world." Ergo, just as Bush indicated, it will be carte blanche. Any top warrior can define the organization's vital security interests to include whatever tickles his fancy, and there is clearly no problem with money. If this policy is pursued to its logical conclusion the entire advanced world economy will be set back who knows how many decades. At the end of World War II some wag said he didn't know what types of weapons will supply World War III, but he did know those that will be used in World War IV: stone axes and clubs.

It seems that a vital message has been smothered, probably by military leaders who see their careers placed in jeopardy. Wilson pointed out that before Europeans came to New Zealand the Maori were extremely aggressive.[12] There were forty Maori tribes, and strife was constant. "[They] acquired guns of their own. . . . Other tribes rushed to arm themselves in order to regain parity in the escalating hostilities."

> *The arms race soon became self-limiting. Even the victors paid a heavy price. To obtain more muskets, the Maoris devoted inordinate amounts of their time to producing flax and other goods that could be traded to the Europeans for guns. And in order to grow more flax many moved to the swampy lowlands, where large numbers died of disease. During the approximately twenty years . . . fully one quarter of the population died . . . related to the conflict. By 1830 the Nga Puhi had begun to question the use of fighting in revenge; the old values crumbled soon afterward. In the late 1830s and early 1840s the Maoris as a whole converted . . . to Christianity, and warfare among the tribes ceased entirely.*

This example indicates that, with courage, effort, and faith in the positive side of human nature the external threat and the propensity to seek revenge can be halted. Political leaders in the Middle East, the Balkan countries, Northern Ireland, and other places might learn something important from this rare example.

Prehistoric humans developed hunting skills to survive, and these skills were used in fighting when necessary. However, warfare was never a basic survival skill. Rather, it evolved in primitive eras when little was known about effective leadership. Today the situation is different, but the historical pattern has been deeply ingrained.

During the cold war the arms race was promoted by the military-industrial complex as maintaining stability in the world, but the reality was destabilization. Whenever public officials in one nation saw weapons being made or purchased by a neighbor of questionable integrity they became nervous, no matter how many weapons they already had in stock. Other emotions included fear and resentment.

These negative emotions are not conducive to stability; it is highly probable that officials will act on them and order more weapons. They will consult their resident warlords concerning what and how much to buy; in this way generals and admirals acquire greater personal power and influence in many countries (just as Hamilton argued). Because war and preparation for it is their bread and butter, they are not likely to be bashful in their recommendations.

The world's chief international traffickers in weapons explain their behavior in terms of a balance of power, which presumably results in stability. But the notion of a balance of military power is perceptual; that is, a balance in the eyes of top leaders in one country will certainly be seen as an imbalance in the perceptions of leaders in several or many other countries. Each of these will then scurry to right the imbalance by acquiring additional weapons and training additional soldiers. This in turn will cause still others to move toward righting what **they** see as an imbalance.

An arms race takes off, politicians add credibility to their posturing about the external threat, defense contractors make piles of money, and some of this loot is kicked back into congressional reelection campaigns. Taxpayers may not like this racket, but they have little to say about it.

In poor countries the situation is far worse, as they have little wealth available to build their economies, and what they do have their top leaders squander on products that destroy economies. (The same actions created centuries of strife in Europe.) A vice president of Iran said, "Since Israel continues to possess nuclear weapons, we, the Muslims, must cooperate to produce an atom bomb, regardless of UN attempts to prevent proliferation."

Ever since World War II the military imperative has been a balance of power. Mueller criticized generals who emphasized numbers while arguing for more resources: "Some western intelligence estimates in the late 1940s concluded that the Soviets could sweep to the English Channel and to the French-Spanish border in a matter of weeks. They calculated that arrayed against less than 20 western divisions were some 175 Soviet divisions plus 75 more from East Europe."[13]

This was a clear reference to the imperative. A study was done that attempted to connect these numbers to effectiveness as fighting forces. "The number of Soviet troops actually available for attack was probably not much greater than the West had for defense. Furthermore, the Soviet troops had morale problems, were ill-equipped for rapid thrusts, and were backed by primitive transport, communications, and logistic systems."

Stalin probably encouraged such counting to discourage any Western thoughts of attacking the Soviet Union. He knew his military force had been all but destroyed during World War II, and that the economic wherewithal to rebuild it did not exist. A division typically consists of about 15,000 soldiers. Because the Soviets lost 20 million young men during the war (10 percent of the entire population), belief in the existence of 175 combat-ready divisions would require an improbable stretch of imagination.

Intelligence, or spying, agencies rely on exaggeration and scare tactics for their bread and butter. Western analysts at the time knew that it would be very difficult for the Soviets to mount a massive attack, in large part because they could not quickly bring supplies to the front. The reason for this handicap goes back to some time after Napoleon's armies moved into Russia (1812), when the railroad track gauge was widened beyond standard width to make it difficult for foreigners to invade the country. (Russia never had and still does not have a motor highway system worthy of the name.)

Thousands of tons of war equipment and supplies would need to be transferred from railroad cars on one gauge track to cars on the other; either that or each car must be jacked up to install a different set of wheels. Such transfer points would be obvious and easy targets for Allied bombers.

During the late 1940s and 1950s this situation made it very difficult for either side to wage war in Europe. But it did little to deter warriors in Western nations from starting a cold war, forming NATO, and starting a massive arms race in the interest of preservation of a balance of power. Generals and admirals do not like peace, although it is unlikely that anyone will hear them say this. If the public is kept uninformed or given disinformation (Chapter 10), the warriors are free to spend taxpayer money almost as if they were handed a blank check.

The unavoidable conclusion is **there is no such thing as a balance of power**. The expenditure over the past fifty years of untold trillions of dollars has created turbulence in international relations, not stability. For roughly that same period of time the Middle East has had the world's highest concentration of weapons, and it has for that long been the most unstable region in the world. Seeking a balance has therefore involved a stupendous effort aimed at an impossible objective. The reality is that the warriors of the world have been working toward a different objective—personal power—and they have been getting away with it.

Between 1988 and 1992 the world's six largest exporters shipped the equivalent of $133 billion of weapons across national boundaries. Five of these huge merchants of death are the biggest suppliers of weapons to poor countries. They are also the five permanent members of the UN Security Council: the United States, Russia, France, China, and Britain.

Now, the sole purpose of establishing the United Nations in 1945 at the end of the horror of World War II was to **prevent** future wars. In 1996 worldwide military spending was estimated at $811 billion. The peacekeeping budget in the UN that year was $1 billion. Apparently the leaders of that organization are bent on undermining its main purpose.

The UN Development Program reported that in poor countries the chances of dying from malnutrition or disease are thirty-three times greater than the chances of dying in a fight with a neighboring country. There are two reasons for this: One is much greater use of imported weapons by dictators to oppress their own people rather than waging international conflicts (diverts scarce resources away from health care); and other lies in the fact that on average such countries have twenty soldiers for every doctor.

It's no small wonder these countries are desperately poor. Weapons and soldiers do not build economies; they destroy them. Where can be found foreign businesses that are interested in trade and in risking investment capital in these countries? Unless something is done, their only logical future destiny has dictators asking for more foreign aid, and then using it to either enrich themselves or squander it on weapons.

Dictators in poor and nonpoor countries are human, and they get angry now and then. Any individual who is sufficiently angry loses control of his or her behavior; if there is a weapon handy it may well be used. Proof of this truth can be found in inner cities of dozens of countries.

But angry and paranoid dictators have much bigger guns and whole armies to shoot them. It is interesting to note that countries often create barriers to trade in products, and there are periodic media-hyped attempts at nonproliferation in the weapons trade. But the barriers to cross-border movement of peaceful products are real, whereas those for weapons are often illusory. Politicians' rhetoric does not match the reality.

Warriors and their politicians will often defend their actions by saying that weapons are sold only to friendly foreign nations. There are two problems with this. One is that over time a friend might turn into an enemy: Iraq and the United States had good relations until 1990, but during the Gulf War some US-made weapons were fired by Iraqis at US soldiers. The other problem lies in the fact that almost all weapons are durable and can easily be sold on to renegade dictators whenever the cash account needs an infusion. (Israel has sold US-supplied weapons to questionable nations.) Some high-tech weapons may become obsolete, but this problem would be limited to high-tech countries. They are still marketable to poor countries.

In 1989 the news media blitzed their customers with variations on the headline "We Won the Cold War." The truth is that neither the United States and the West nor the Soviet Union won it. There has always been a trade-off between economic development and military strength. During the cold war the United States and its allies devoted 4–6 percent of their national budgets to defense, and the

Soviet Union, with a much smaller and poorly developed economy, devoted around 25 percent.

Combine this with the fact that single-party socialism utilizes an extremely inefficient method of allocating economic resources, and it becomes obvious that the West did not "win"; rather, the Soviets lost it. Alexander Hamilton knew what he was talking about when he said, "No nation, however strong, can afford to maintain a standing army in peacetime." The West was lucky in that the other side deteriorated more rapidly.

After the cold war thousands of frustrated resentments and desires for revenge suddenly became free. In the presence of huge stocks of weapons widely distributed by both sides during the war, the result was predictable. By this time many poor countries were in sad economic shape, in part through working the wrong side of the trade-off between economic development and overemphasis on the military. Predictable eruptions of hostility only made the situation worse.

All this leads to reflection and some speculation. The Soviet Russians never occupied a country that did not share a border with the USSR; this suggests that officials were primarily concerned with buffer states as components of a defensive posture. The Russian bear did indeed snarl and bare his claws, but this could have been an attempt to divert Western attention from the fact that the Russians had only a poorly industrialized economy going into World War II. Furthermore they came out of it with their economy utterly devastated and minus 20 million men. Years later the Soviet Union became known as the "grandfatherless society."

Just before and during World War II the US defense industry had grown tremendously, and the business paid very well. Even though spy agencies were not very effective, public officials knew that during the war the Soviet economy was suffering, and at the end there was little left of it. If a strong postwar leader had emerged and responded to the public will by sharply reducing the size of the military-industrial complex, several terrible things probably would not have happened:

1. the cold war.
2. the arms race.
3. development of far more devastating nuclear weapons and thousands of intercontinental ballistic missiles.
4. massive international trafficking in weapons, which made poor countries much poorer and more miserable.
5. the monstrous cash drain of having thousands of US military bases abroad (many still there today).
6. quite possibly the lost lives of around 100,000 US soldiers, twice that of enemy soldiers lost, and a million civilians in Korea and Vietnam.

The leader would have counseled patience: Give communism time and it will bury itself. Economists were around at the time who could have informed political and military leaders of this outlook, if any had listened. But as Chapter 4 showed, the career politician needs high drama, excitement, and war to exert personal power and to collect a maximum of votes from a cowed constituency.

If President Kennedy had agreed with Eisenhower's defense policies, which came from a career as a soldier, the Vietnam War might have been avoided. When Kennedy proclaimed, "Bear any burden!" this indicated that maybe he was not aware of the arms–economic development trade-off. Once built, weapons do nothing to expand an economy even if not used; rather, they act as a drag, and if used they destroy an economy.

The end of the cold war came as a surprise to policy makers, although this would not have been so if US and Western spy agencies had been doing the job. When the Berlin Wall was hauled down on November 9, 1989, it came as a rude shock to thousands of people on both sides of it.

Immediately a crash program aimed at finding a replacement enemy was launched; Lapham noted: "As the cold war faded into the mists of warm and nostalgic memory, the war on drugs provided the rubrics of constant terror and ceaseless threat under which the government could subtract as much as possible from the sum of the nation's civil rights and impose de facto martial law on a citizenry that it chooses to imagine as a dangerous rabble."[14] Mencken must have chuckled in his grave.

Democracy is an uneasy existence for the aspiring career politician because to serve as long as he wants he must provide leadership and sincerely act on the public will. If a person pursues the democratic way he never knows whether and when another candidate will beat him, and there goes his soft job with perks, junkets, rubbing shoulders with powerful people, and so on. The external threat comes close to a failsafe system for remaining in office. Keeping the exact nature and severity of a threat secret makes it easier to fool the public into believing the worst possible scenario, and he is home free. He looks to the next election as only a minor inconvenience.

Even if the cold war had begun in spite of good leadership, surely there would have been plans for a new world order on the shelf long before the war ended. Come the event, there were none. This planning vacuum suggests that, in spite of all the rhetoric about world peace there was no intent to move past the external threat theory and into the Age of Reason. There was, and is, simply too much money in the current arrangement for career politicians, public officials, lawyers, lobbyists, and others who are feeding at the public trough.

Harris argued that a person consumed by fear cannot complete development into an adult.[15] "When fear dominates his life, there is no possibility for the kind of precision data processing which can make possible a position of cure—I'M OKAY—YOU'RE OKAY." With the cold war over and concern about illegal drugs fading, the push today is toward terrorism.

Public officials understand that there is no end to the seeking of revenge, so instead of working to discover the cause of terrorism and formulate a policy that addresses that cause they arrange to fight it. A belligerent policy ensures its continuation. There are hundreds of bureaucrats who have staked their careers on this continuance.

Rothbard noted, "War has always been the occasion of a great—and unusually permanent—acceleration and intensification of State power over society. War is the great excuse for mobilizing all the energies and resources of the nation, in the name of patriotic rhetoric, under the aegis and dictation of the State apparatus."[16] This explains why so much of world history has been infused with the scourge of war. But today that scourge has assumed the status of potential Armageddon; it is urgent that thinking citizens of the world and their public officials enter into the Age of Reason.

Are these officials learning anything important from thinking about this grim world destiny? Rennert's January 2000 column suggests not:

> *The next president can look forward to rocky relations with Russia and China, missile threats from rogue states such as North Korea and Iran, a defiant Saddam Hussein astride Iraq, terrorist groups on the prowl against US targets and simmering ethnic conflicts in the Balkans. And that will be just for starters as the new leader of the world's only superpower confronts the full range of daunting challenges to US security, interest and values on his four-year watch.*[17]

It looks very much like business as usual in Washington.

Weapons and "Leaders" of Poor Countries

It has been argued that the arms race caused no wars; therefore it encouraged stability. But this position is inaccurate in that it applied only to big countries. The distribution of mountains of weapons to small countries caused no end of trouble. The original intent behind this distribution was to line up small countries on one side or the other during the cold war. But this was in turn connected to the necessity for a cold war, and this conventional wisdom has apparently never been questioned, even to this day.

Mueller noted, "As Nikita Khrushchev remarks in his memoirs, 'Our military objectives have always been defensive. That was true even under Stalin. I never once heard Stalin say anything about preparing to commit aggression against another country. His biggest concern was putting up antiaircraft installations around Moscow.'" Khrushchev had the opportunity to get to know the ruthless dictator. Brute that he surely was, Stalin's cruelty was limited to his own people and to a lesser extent those in satellite countries. His hegemony was an artifact crafted by Western warriors whose bread and butter is war and preparation therefor.

The notion, then, was that while holding the capitalist world at bay by defensive military preparations and ingenious political maneuvers, the Soviets would aid and inspire subversive revolutionary movements throughout the world. With luck, capitalism would lurch to its inevitable demise without ever getting around to invading the "Socialist Fatherland." Aggressive, conquering Hitlerian war by the Soviets themselves would foolishly risk everything; it does not fit into this scheme at all.

The thought that the horrendous expense, small conflicts, and widespread misery that were the grisly results of the cold war might have been avoided with better leadership is as intriguing as it is disturbing.

George Kennan became an expert on the Soviet Union during the late 1940s, and remained so during the next fifty-plus years. In 1949 he concluded that there was a strong possibility that Soviet power "bears within it the seeds of its own decay, and that the sprouting of these seeds is well advanced."

The nature of the primarily Western interpretation of the cold war required that every nation take sides. There was little opportunity to remain neutral, even though the reality as usual included shades of difference and similarity. Every country caught up in the dichotomy accepted thousands of tons of advanced weapons and often training in their use to be ready for the biggest and bloodiest showdown in history.

This explains why Somalia's economy is today a basket case: the poor country had the bad luck to be located on the strategically vital Horn of Africa, so both major powers sent in weapons by the shipload. Somalis are culturally very similar, and they share the same language. Historically they have been generally peaceful, but the presence of mountains of weapons eventually aggravated tensions between clans and their warlords that otherwise might have remained latent. In 1993 the media played up the loss of 18 gallant US soldiers, but simultaneously played down both years of innocent citizens killed by US-made weapons and around 200 people killed immediately after the loss by helicopter gun ships firing indiscriminately into houses.

A few days after the terrorist attacks on September 11, 2001, *The Economist* provided some thinking.[18] "In its understandable rage for justice, America may be tempted to overlook one uncomfortable fact. Its own policies in Afghanistan a decade and more ago helped to create both Osama bin Laden and the fundamentalist Taliban regime that shelters him." The writer added: "[This] terrible legacy . . . left [the country] awash with weapons, warlords, and extreme religious zealotry." Rage is passion. Fact is reason.

Top leaders of poor countries were (and still are) generally egomaniacs. That is, they were avid seekers of personal power over others. Suddenly, here came thousands of guns and other weapons, almost like manna from heaven. The gentle hand of leadership became ham-fisted oppression; whenever the natives got restless government thugs would simply torture or kill them.

Torturing is counterproductive for two reasons. A weak person is not a threat to the regime, so torturing only feeds the sadistic nature of the oppressor. Torturing a strong person only poisons his or her mind and strengthens resolve to wreak revenge in the future. If he is killed afterward and others find out, the poisoning is only multiplied.

Because violence only begets more violence, these countries became extremely unstable. Leaders proclaimed themselves president for life. Presidents they were not, but assuming the title helped convince donors of aid and weapons that they were presiding over democratic/socialist governments that had to be defended.

A despot is always condemned to hang onto power until death. If he leaves office for whatever reason he loses control over both information and citizens. He knows that if they don't already know they will soon learn what he has done to them, and there is no longer a regiment of thugs to protect him. Therefore while in office he leads the life of a paranoiac.

Any disturbance, however slight, was immediately interpreted as subversive; this kept the superpowers pouring in weapons. Stronger power was centralized in governments and citizens enjoyed fewer rights (which caused more disturbances). But then, it was shown above that this is the type of regime most suited to warfare. Nations in the third world asked for money to build transport and communications infrastructure, but they also spent $180 billion a year on weapons.

Rhetoric notwithstanding, international trafficking in weapons creates instability, as those without see others acquiring bigger and more effective killing machines. Some of them react to this development, and this creates more instability. In response to this, orders for still more weapons are sent on, and the result is a vicious and deadly circle.

With the cold war over, hopes rose, but only briefly. *The Economist* reported: "The recently signed peace agreements in Congo and Sierra Leone may make immunization easier in those countries. But both places share the curse that fuels so many civil wars; vast mineral wealth. In too many countries, oil, diamonds, and various types of ore keep soldiers equipped and their leaders eager to fight on, so that they can loot on."[19] Most of Africa's grim legacy of interminable conflict is internal within nations (although soldiers of fortune often cross borders if the price is right). With that legacy reinforced by the cold war experience, it is not difficult to understand why there is apparently no end to it.

"For the polio virus, war is the last safe haven. Protecting the virus is one of the few ways that forgotten conflicts threaten the rest of the world. So long as polio still exists somewhere, it can always spread." Aid workers and medical people have great difficulty in getting around to immunize widely scattered citizens, when roads are often all but nonexistent and bullets are flying.

Over the decades technology has created near-miracles by the score in advanced countries. Free competition in high-tech industries has spurred development of more powerful, smaller, and cheaper products. Unfortunately, this trend applies as well to weapons: Many are getting smaller, cheaper, and more destructive. Shawcross noted:

> *It is impossible to exaggerate the importance of light weapons in the wars of today. They are far more deadly than tanks, warplanes and warships. Of the 49 conflicts which broke out between 1990 and 1997, light weapons were used in 46.*
>
> *Many of these weapons flood across the world from armaments factories in Eastern Europe, now deprived of their traditional Cold War markets. Others are detritus from the Afghanistan war, into which the CIA piled some three million AK-47 assault rifles to enable the mujahideen to resist Soviet occupation. Now the surplus killing power of these weapons has spread through Africa.*[20]

Some day in the not very distant future a man will hold in his hand a weapon capable of completely destroying a village and all its inhabitants. And it may have been purchased with the pooled resources of several of his friends.

By the mid-1990s there were fifty-six wars going on around the world. The Red Cross concluded that these were combining with natural disasters to overwhelm agencies' abilities to respond.

The Economist brought a different slant to discussion of small states.[21]

> *in the ancient world . . . choice was between order and chaos, and order meant empire. . . . To be within the empire was to have law, culture, and civilization; to be outside was to endure disorder and barbarism. But empires are ill designed for promoting change; their preoccupation is to hold together, an imperative that tends to need authoritarianism. Innovation, and ultimately world leadership for Europe, came with Europe's unique contribution, the small state.*

It is possible that some potential leaders became disillusioned with authoritarian government, left it, took their chances with the barbarians and eventually emerged in charge of these small states.

"Small states brought competition, and all its benefits, but also war, because these states were intermittently, if not permanently, aggressive." The writer suggested that this trend began in 1648, with the end of the Thirty Years' War. The cycle of alliances made and broken was formalized at about this time, the objective being accomplishment of a balance of power such that one state could not dominate many others.

However, "the power-balancing system would have been in trouble even without the unification of Germany (1871), . . . because the price of war—and **war was inherent in the system** [emphasis added]—was by the beginning of the 20th century being transformed by technology to levels that were unaffordable."

Because the imperative of war required establishment and maintenance of oppressive regimes against which thinking citizens rebelled, the result was a continuing string of armed conflict, either among or within nations—a Europe in constant turmoil. It was this misery that pioneers abandoned when they dared cross a dangerous ocean in small sailing ships to settle in a land about which they knew very little.

Reflection on this protracted turmoil suggests that in both large and small states war and the preparation for it require the existence of oppressive regimes of government. Top leaders respond to negative tugs of human nature, in direct contrast to the desires of people motivated by positive tugs. This is the reality.

Negative tugs impel the elite class in government to seek out crises for their value in the acceptance by naive citizens of still greater increases in personal power over them. The presence of a crisis cows the populace and thus permits massive increases in money spent for presumably defensive war and preparation for it.

As if this is not abusive enough, when the crisis is over officials no longer relinquish their newly acquired power, as used to be done in several instances. Quite the opposite—they strive to keep a crisis going indefinitely, all the while searching for others to keep in the bullpen. Lacking this, officials are not above sending troops and weapons abroad to create such a situation. This text is being written eighteen months after the September 11, 2001, attacks. The Bush administration is playing this one out precisely in accordance with the script outlined here, even as a worlwide anti-war groundswell gathers momentum.

It is not difficult to learn from where come the mountains of weapons that cause such massive destruction, death and misery in poor countries. Molly Ivins, in a 1996 column, wrote: "The US spends more than $450 million and employs nearly 6,500 full-time people to promote and service foreign arms sales by US companies. The Pentagon has an arms sales staff of 6,395."[22] Hard proof is lacking, but it looks very much like the taxpayer is underwriting this expense. This money is not for weapons, only promoting sales of killing machines, many if not most of them to governments of poor countries.

> *Since you've never heard anyone running for office say, "Vote for me, and I'll use your tax dollars to subsidize weapons manufacturers," you may wonder how this charming arrangement came about. And you will not be amazed to learn that major weapons-exporting firms contributed $14.8 million to congressional candidates from 1990 to 1994.*

Here is another example of loosely bid contracts with kickbacks built in, as discussed in Chapter 10. Poor governments cannot pay very much for weapons, so the US taxpayer apparently makes up the deficit, to such an extent that defense contractors, their lobbyists, and congressmen make out very well. There is evidence that some "defense" contractors have entered the business of repairing damage overseas that their weapons have caused. In this event, the more destruction the better for business.

Ivins continued: "The sheer stupidity of this piece of lunacy is nicely illustrated by the last five times we have sent our troops into conflict situations . . . Panama, Iraq, Somalia, Haiti, and Bosnia. In every case, the forces on the other side had access to US weaponry, training or military technology. Does the word 'self-defeating' ring any bells?"

There is an important oversight in this argument and that below; it lies in the use of the word *we*. That is, citizens had nothing to say about entering any of these conflicts, so a correction would be "*the government* has sent our troops."

This of course does nothing to lessen the stupidity, as Ivins completed her devastating argument:

> *The World Policy Institute study clearly demonstrates that many of the weapons proliferation threats cited by the CIA and our military intelligence agencies as rationales for increasing US military spending have been exacerbated by our own weapons sales. In other words, we have to spend more to defend against dangerous situations we ourselves have helped create. Does the word "dumb" come to mind?*

Not to the mind of a politician: In 1992 President Bush (Sr.) was campaigning for reelection. He authorized the sale of $6 billion of fighter aircraft; shortly thereafter he went to the Texas factory where these killing machines are made and spoke to employees in front of a huge sign: "JOBS FOR AMERICA—THANKS, MR. PRESIDENT," while the cameras rolled. Candidate Bill Clinton instantly approved of the sale, and after he took office he promised a policy review of the international weapons trafficking business. To date there has been no such review.

Poor countries are not necessarily small ones. Eduard Shevardnadze served as the foreign minister of the Soviet Union, and he is today president of the republic of Georgia. His book, *The Future Belongs to Freedom*, contains many insights.[23] In one statement he referred to nuclear weapons:

> *I want to note a particular subtlety here: They were used not only against the Japanese, but against the Soviet Union. First, by sowing in our hearts the seeds of alarm, it engendered a striving to create the means for atomic self-defense and an adequate nuclear arsenal. In other words, the first explosions of American bombs also exploded the strategic stability and sparked the nuclear arms race.*

When she was prime minister of Britain, Margaret Thatcher said, "Nuclear weapons are a blessing." During her eleven years in office she showed impressive leadership in several areas, but in this one she was wrong. When one nation acquires nukes it sows "the seeds of alarm" elsewhere, and it causes expensive crash programs aimed at restoring a nonexistent balance of power. Multiply this imperative by approximately 180 nuclear have-not nations, and the problem magnifies beyond comprehension. (It has been said that the basic design for an atomic bomb can be found on the World Wide Web.)

Shevardnadze continued: "Nuclear weapons . . . encouraged bullying on the part of members of the 'nuclear club.' This in turn fostered bullying and lawlessness by some of the nonnuclear countries, who tried to protect themselves from nuclear blackmail by developing their own nuclear capability." The spreading of this propensity cannot be stopped, short of acquiring the courage to insist on the Age of Reason. Fear is a very real emotion, and it occupies a central position in human nature.

The author next addressed the external threat theory. "Some people must find it hard to breathe when there are no longer any enemies around. The maintenance of excessively large armed forces and weapons stockpiles will inevitably push a country backward and make it worse off than its competitors who do without such military budgets."

This observation is reminiscent of Hamilton's argument that no nation can afford to maintain a standing army in peacetime. The small Central American country of Costa Rica disbanded its army in 1948. Since then it has existed free of armed conflict, while its neighbors have suffered from recurrent strife.

Developments in international law have made some progress in holding dictators accountable for their crimes against humanity. *The Economist* in 1999 noted:

> *On April 29th, a federal judge is expected to endorse an unprecedented $150m settlement between the estate of Ferdinand Marcos, former dictator of the Philippines, and thousands of victims of human-rights abuses committed by his regime. . . . A string of similar cases has resulted in about $2 billion in damages being awarded to victims of other foreign torturers and murderers, but, until the Marcos settlement, a mere $460 had been collected. Still, the ability to sue foreigners in American courts . . . is a weapon that human-rights campaigners consider increasingly valuable.*[24]

(Courts in poor countries are frequently so corrupt that lawsuits there accomplish nothing.)

Many dictators, realizing that their own countries are poor places to invest looted cash, ship it to places with strong economies like Switzerland and the United States. As the ability to sue expands, this money becomes available to pay damages; this should provide an additional incentive to amend previously abominable behavior. A world criminal court has recently been established in The Hague. It is being developed as an additional deterrent, aimed at capture and imprisonment.

Dyson reported that a large element of the clergy has joined scientists in speaking out against weapons proliferation.[25]

> *Scientists have written a great deal about nuclear strategy, but nothing we have written is as thoughtful as the Pastoral Letter on War and Peace, "The Challenge of Peace: God's Promise and Our Response," which the Catholic bishops of America hammered out and issued to the world in 1983. That letter is indeed a challenge, a challenge to us scientists as well as to everybody else. It expresses a* ***fundamental rejection of the idea that permanent peace on earth can be achieved with nuclear weapons.*** [emphasis added]

Shevardnadze completed his argument: "In our century, security is gained not by the highest possible level of strategic parity, but the lowest possible level, and nuclear and other weapons of mass destruction must be removed from the equation." His point is an indirect appeal to human nature: regardless of the type of weapon (nuclear or otherwise) whenever passion overrules reason a weapon will be used. In the Age of Reason there will be no need for any weapons of mass death and destruction, and no exceptions anywhere, anytime, forever.

This means the lowest level of weapons that Shevardnadze recommended is zero, which on the surface does not seem feasible. But if only 5 percent of the $800 billion or so annually squandered on war were devoted to research on systems that detect clandestine weapon construction and every thinking person in the world cooperated, zero would become not just feasible but probable.

Cell phones will soon be everywhere, and this is just one piece of high technology that could be brought to bear on the problem. Anyone who spots something suspicious could uplink a cell phone to a satellite and the word would be out, probably without those involved even aware that they are being observed. Knowing this, they would probably not get involved.

Perhaps inadvertently, the United States has made a beginning in this new technology. Its Nuclear Emergency Search Team (NEST) has ultra-sensitive detection equipment and sophisticated technology for disarming any nuclear weapons that may come to its attention. Over the past twenty-five years the team has responded to a large number of alarms concerning lost, stolen, or homemade weapons, although members have yet to find one.

No Longer Feasible, Just Politically Expedient

Jefferson said, "As to myself, I love peace, and I am anxious that we should give the world still another useful lesson, by showing to them other modes of punishing injuries than by war, which is as much a punishment to the punisher as to the sufferer." Evidence abounds that neither the United States nor any other country has provided that lesson to the world.

During World War II the productive capacity of this country multiplied, the economy roared ahead, and ordinary people rose from the misery of the Great Depression to the elation of final victory. This great momentum distracted citizens from serious thinking concerning their high tax burdens, and this vital fact was not lost on politicians of the time. Thus were planted the seeds of corruption, along with the invention of the theory of accumulation of money.

During the war a crash program to develop a nuclear weapon formed the background for additional research into the relationship between mass and energy based on Einstein's theory of relativity. A short while later, when relations between the West and the Soviet Union became sticky, the emphasis of this research switched away from constructive uses back to destructive. The negative side of human nature asserted its presence once again.

The discipline of nuclear physics was nearly brand new, which meant a vast unknown and a broad-based cutting edge of knowledge for scientists. Furthermore, there was plenty of money, which enabled these scientists to pursue a great variety of research tracks. The combination of newness, money, a perceived (and media-hyped) huge ogre offshore, and excited scientists led the Department of Defense to offer loosely bid cost-plus contracts for development of new weapons of awesome destructive capacity.

Cost-plus means the initial cost of the research is a minor consideration in the relationship between defense contractor and customer (the government), primarily because no one knows in which direction the research will go and how much it might cost to get there. Therefore the really big money is awarded later, in captive negotiations with just one supplier instead of several competing for the business. To repeat: There was no problem because lots of taxpayer money was available.

Savvy defense contractors knew this, and so their cost accountants became adept at padding existing and projected expenses to justify large additional injections of taxpayer money with each instance of renegotiation. Defense officials in government saw no reason to be hard-nosed during these negotiations, and in fact they were restricted anyway due to a lack of alternative suppliers (data collected were understandably not shared with other defense contractors).

It did not take long for politicians to see the potential benefits for them and to tap into this mother lode for their reelection campaigns. Members of Congress had to approve contract awards, so some of the extra money was routed to their campaign war chests in the form of kickbacks. This business quickly expanded. The end result today has taxpayers subsidizing immorality and occasionally outright thievery.

Nuclear weapons do a lot of damage even when they are not detonated. They contaminate the environment and undermine people's health. Land and water have been fouled in Georgia, Idaho, Kentucky, Ohio, South Carolina, Tennessee, and Washington. The estimated cost of clean-up is $300 billion, if in fact the job can be completed at any price. Government officials see fit to pass many laws and regulations intended to force compliance in cleaning the air and water in this country, and in effect they force the media to avoid informing the public that the government itself is by far the nation's biggest polluter.

What is really discouraging is that there is no need for this expensive and tawdry business. Generalizing beyond nukes, this country's government today spends twice as much on "defense" as its ten biggest remotely possible enemies combined, and it is highly unlikely even in the Pentagon that two officials can be found who would provide the same ten country names if asked. The external threat theory continues to work, but with increasing difficulty as Congress and the Pentagon furiously scramble to identify and hype the necessary terrible enemy. (As this is being written some 200 inspection trips in Iraq have uncovered zero weapons of mass destruction.) Chapter 21 discusses foreign adventurism by the military, which helps reinforce the theory by creating enemies where they did not previously exist.

The Economist does not always get it right. "In an imperfect world, nuclear weapons still deter."[26] They do not deter, and they never did, as Shevardnadze convincingly showed (and North Korea is showing). The notion of deterrence is based on reason, whereas the attitude toward the prospect of nuclear war, fear, is based on passion.

Keeping the country on a war footing is a major part of the business of today's Capitol Hill as it generates all but unlimited money, burnishes insiders' macho credentials, and gets politicians reelected. This fact became even more obvious to thinking citizens during the Vietnam War, when enemy body counts were exaggerated to suggest imminent victory and discourage opposition to the conflict. But the war dragged on, and in the end the cumulative total of body counts exceeded 1.5 times the entire population of Vietnam, both North and South. But of course this statistic was kept from the public.

The world has moved far beyond the point where war can solve any international dispute, and it is losing its effectiveness in resolving domestic difficulties. The United States and a few allied soldiers fought in Korea in 1950–53. Fifty years later the question remains, What problems have been solved? What problems in Vietnam were solved? (These questions mean to take nothing away from the valor of those who fought in these wars.) There are also the Dominican Republic, Panama, Lebanon, Tripoli, Israel, Nicaragua, Guatemala, Angola, Afghanistan, Iraq, Somalia, Haiti, Bosnia, Kosovo, and others, where the United States supplied weapons, training, troops, or a combination thereof. It is hard to see where problems in any of these countries were solved by these actions. It is easier to see how the business has enriched selected members of the elite class in Washington.

Isaacson noted:

> *An escalating arms race between the US and the Soviet Union served the national interest of neither country. Throughout history, each addition to a*

nation's arsenal could readily be translated into increased global influence. But the 1960s brought the great irony of the nuclear age: the quantum leap in military force made incremental additions to each side's military less meaningful. [27]

Applied to early history, Isaacson's argument lacks credibility. But this does not detract from the point that once officials' focus had centered on nukes and a balance of terror, the conventional weapons business assumed a lesser importance in terms of relations between superpowers. However, this development apparently did little to slow down the existing business in conventional weapons; poor country public officials, who saw little chance of developing their own nuclear capability, continued to snap up these killing machines.

In January 1981 Ronald Reagan was inaugurated as president. The man chose to perceive the cold war in good/bad terms, with no room for shades of gray in spite of the fact that both communism and democracy existed in great variety. Reagan perceived the West as composed exclusively of good guys, and the communist bloc contained only bad guys. Enormous amounts of borrowed money combined with tunnel vision to vastly accelerate the arms race. This monstrous build-up created a legacy that today fulfills Hamilton's prediction: The military prevails over civilian concerns in Washington. War prevails over peace.

Rothbard commented:

It is particularly ironic that conservatives, at least in rhetoric supporters of a free-market economy; should be so complacent and even admiring of our vast military-industrial complex. There is no greater single distortion of the free market in present-day America. The bulk of our scientists and engineers have been diverted from basic research for civilian ends, from increasing productivity and the standard of living of consumers into wasteful, inefficient and nonproductive military and space boondoggles.[28]

This irony is easily explained: conservative politicians love money fully as much as do liberals. In fact it is this love that, as Chapter 10 showed, unites members of the two major political parties in a common cause: fleecing the public.

During the election campaign of 2000 President Clinton turned away from his party's seventeen years of opposition to a ballistic missile defense to promote it on a trip through Europe. He himself objected to this project on moral grounds, but he felt the political imperative of providing Al Gore with cover on the issue to fend off Republican charges of being soft on defense. Politics displaces morality whenever any government becomes politicized.

The National Missile Defense is an exceptionally bad policy for at least four reasons. First, leaders throughout the world are against the project, because they believe its development will surely restart the arms race. (They perceive the US defense as offense, and the record certainly agrees with them.) Second, after more than $60 billion of taxpayer money there is still nothing available that works, and dozens of top scientists have agreed on a prediction that there will not be anything in the future. (But an open-ended project like this one is a mecca for distributors of pork.) Third, because both major political parties have united with the military-industrial complex in the joint effort of draining money from citizens' pockets, it makes no difference whatever who is soft on defense. Finally, there is no enemy, real or imaginary. (As this is being written, North Korea seems to be building nuclear bombs, but that dirt-poor and devastated country was and is no real threat to the US.)

Rothbard wrote,

> *Politics, in field after field, has replaced economics in guiding the activities of industry. Furthermore, as entire industries and regions of the country have come to depend upon government and military contracts, a huge vested interest has been created in continuing the program, heedless of whether they retain even the most threadbare excuse of military necessity.*

Congressmen long ago strove to ensure that at least one military facility existed in each of the 435 congressional districts. Today there are around 3,500 of these facilities, and there is strong resistance within Congress against reducing that number. They provide many jobs and votes.

Using dollars adjusted for inflation, between 1945 and 1989 the price of a destroyer increased 90 times, and that of a fighter airplane 290 times. The corresponding figures for cars and cameras are eight and four times, but of course these products must compete in a free marketplace for customers, so companies cannot sell them unless they hold down price increases.

Someone who is involved in the military-industrial complex might argue that there is relatively much more high technology installed in destroyers and fighters than in cars and cameras. But older citizens, who can accurately recall the primitive nature of cars in 1946, will assert that improvements since then have been equally dramatic, and cars and cameras are not designed to kill people.

After the Gulf War the government put $15 billion "off-budget" for the military, so the fiscal deficit for the year 1991 would not look so bad. Taxpayers must cover this, of course, because the money was spent just as if it were in the budget. This gimmick for deceiving the public has been utilized many times.

Members of Congress from Rhode Island rammed through that body legislation authorizing the manufacturing of two additional new Seawolf class nuclear attack submarines (later increased by President Clinton to three) at around $3 billion a copy. No one knows what these killing machines will be used for, but building them provides thousands of jobs in Rhode Island and Connecticut.

Why did other members of Congress approve this expenditure? The explanation lies in the nature of pork-barrel spending: in exchange for support of this project, congresspeople representing Rhode Island and Connecticut pledged to strongly support any expensive boondoggles that are dreamed up in other congressional districts nationwide. Any confusion about this arrangement centers on the role for taxpayers, besides paying for the submarines and other boondoggles.

Alterman's 1993 book underscores the arrogance that pervades Department of Defense dealings.[29] "The Pentagon leaked a draft 'Defense Policy Guidance' report calling for the investment of yet another $1.2 trillion over the next five years to ensure, virtually unilaterally, that the US be able to defeat not existing adversaries, but 'potential competitors,' lest they 'aspire to a larger regional or global role.'" Apparently there was no felt need to accurately identify these "potential competitors," probably because this action would expose at least part of the report as a sham.

For politicians who at least theoretically must cooperate with the president in approving any international conflicts, the foreign policy is as follows. Be late in moving into a high-tension area of the world with diplomacy, in hopes that the situation will deteriorate into armed conflict before diplomacy can resolve a dispute.

Due to previous international trafficking, most of the necessary weapons are already there, so the stage is set for armed intervention. Conflict uses up weapons that dictators will surely want to replace. (Diplomacy plods, and so it makes poor copy for media oriented to high drama and conflict.) Keeping the United Nations poor by not paying dues also enhances the effectiveness of the strategy, as this means there is very little money available for peacekeeping.

Secretary-general of the United Nations Kofi Annan wrote: "Time and again, differences are allowed to develop into disputes and disputes allowed to develop into deadly conflicts. Time and again, warning signs are ignored and pleas for help overlooked."[30] So intense and blinding is the love of the US military-industrial complex and its lackeys in Congress for money that they ignore the lost lives, maimed children, and massive destruction that always accompany armed conflict. Morality has vanished altogether.

> *There are, in my view, three main reasons for the failure of prevention when prevention so clearly is possible. First, the reluctance of one or more of the parties to a conflict to accept external intervention of any kind. Second, the lack of political will at the highest levels of the international community. Third, a lack of integrated conflict-prevention strategies within the UN system and the international community. Of all these, the will to act is the most important.*

The explanation of this lack of will is difficult for a concerned citizen to accept.

The Economist also complained about the lack of political will (July 2001).[31]

> *Just about everyone bar the culprits agrees that the spread of nuclear, chemical and biological weapons, as well as missiles to deliver them, will pose the biggest threat to international peace and security in the 21st century. . . This weekend . . . China and Russia will sign a new friendship treaty; next weekend*

Russia joins the US, Canada, Japan and the bigger Europeans for their annual G8 summit. Yet non-proliferation is top of neither agenda. This is a pity."

By now no thinking citizen can remain unaware of the reason for this amazing ability on the part of the world's top leaders to look the other way: money. The million-dollar question is how much longer these people and their mandarins in government and defense companies can continue to get away with this egregious corruption.

In his book *Parliament of Whores,* acid-tongued commentator P J O'Rourke went after the Department of Defense.[32]

Even if defense spending were managed by honest, clairvoyant geniuses (and this is not the case), it would still be immensely wasteful. All forms of defense—national, personal, and even biological—are wasteful. The body's immune system is a real waste—big sprawling old white blood corpuscles floating around all over the place doing absolutely nothing to earn their keep . . . until the body gets sick. By the same token soldiers and weapons do nothing unless there's a war.

There is an important difference, in that most people know that maintaining a healthy diet, exercise, and rest is not very expensive, and through these practices the body stays almost free of disease and it feels good to its owner. But to maintain fighting forces in trim it has been deemed necessary by those in charge to give them something to do besides drills and exercises. That is, these forces apparently must keep in shape through horribly expensive and destructive warfare. If citizens were in charge, the situation would surely be different.

O'Rourke continued: "But the best and final argument against cutting defense spending cannot be put into words. It's visceral, hormonal. It is that excitement in the gut, that swelling of the chest, the involuntary smile that comes across the face of every male when he has a weapon to hand."

Observant citizens who watched President Bush's first speech after the 9/11 attacks could see his chest swell as the audience cheered his declaration of war on terrorism. As commander-in-chief of the armed forces this man has history's most stupendous collection of weapons to hand, together with an overwhelming incentive to use them.

Acting on this propensity in human nature kills people, intimidates the small person/nation, feeds the desire for revenge, and makes it difficult for poor families to feed their children. The average family in the third world will suffer the brunt of almost any war, as it is the most defenseless. (All but one of the fourteen countries listed previously that have been the objects of US military intervention are in the third world.) This is the type of ego trip on which the military-industrial complex congratulates itself, even as the rhetoric keeps trumpeting elaborations on the external threat theory.

After the 1995 conflict in Bosnia-Herzegovina, Western allies decided that the best way to preserve the peace in that strife-torn country was to even the distribution of weapons and training among the Muslims, Croats, and Serbs. This policy would keep the powers balanced. The policy has not worked, but it has been very good for the weapons business because many of these were delivered (mainly to Muslims). It is logical to conclude that this was the original intent.

During his 1988 presidential campaign, George Bush (Sr.) stated that power and the willingness to use it helps bring and keep peace. He was far from alone in this; many presidents before him apparently believed in the same myth (peace through strength). They preached restraint in weapons development and distribution while simultaneously authorizing enormous overseas shipments of weapons. Citizens and leaders of other nations readily see through this hypocrisy.

All this has worked wonderfully well for public officials; the government recently had a whopping 70 percent share of the international weapons trade. But this practice causes instability, resentment, and desire for revenge, none of which are conducive to peace. The Middle East has perennially been the world's most unstable region, and here may be found the highest mountains of weapons. Bush's Secretary of State James Baker admitted the truth of this argument on national TV. Small wonder that people in the Middle East call the United States nasty names like the "Great Satan."

The European Union is a group of fifteen countries whose primary objective is economic development and hence increased living standards for citizens of those countries. The original impetus for this organization formed in 1950. Although it has taken a long time to attain its present healthy status, its accomplishments are impressive in view of the many different cultures that are represented. The European Union believes in peaceful development.

Or, does it? *The Economist* published a shocking report: "The European Union's military ideas are getting bigger."[33] As if this were not enough. "Britain's defense minister Geoff Hoon, said that his understanding of the Petersburg tasks would include something like the current bombing of Afghanistan, which would fall under the heading of 'peacemaking.'" It seems hard to believe that anyone can make peace with bombs, and surely not a pacific organization like the European Union. Furthermore jurisdiction over military affairs was claimed by NATO many years ago.

NATO was organized in 1947 and was powerful almost from the start. Its sole purpose for existence was to counter a perceived military threat coming from the Soviet Union. Thus the reason for its existence may be directly traced to the external threat theory.

Against this background it is truly amazing that, now that the Soviet Union no longer exists, not only does the organization still exist but it is expanding. This example dramatically underscores an ironclad rule for bureaucracies: They do not die with the purpose for which they were organized; rather, they can only grow. The motivation is political, as shown by the recent Secretary of State Madeleine

Albright, who responded to an invitation from *The Economist* to write: "but dangers remain: from Bosnia to Chechnya . . . From Serbia to Belarus, reminders are appearing that Europe's democratic revolution is not complete."[34]

It is hard to imagine severe and imminent danger to anyone being caused by these countries, whose governments and citizens are preoccupied with the imperatives of simple survival. Which member or members of NATO did she have in mind as potential victims of aggression?

"But it is NATO . . . principal mechanism of American involvement in Europe, that is playing the leading role in bringing Europe together." It is true that Europe appears to be coming together in spite of its grim history of nearly constant warfare, and this is wonderful news. But this pleasant development cannot be attributed to any organization that is designed to wage war; credit should logically go to the European Union.

"[NATO was founded to] contain the Soviet threat. But that is not all it did. It provided the confidence and security shattered economies needed to rebuild themselves." This remarkable postwar rebuilding was done through aid organized through the Marshall Plan and not NATO. During the immediate postwar period, the last thing on the minds of citizens and officials in defeated and devastated countries was starting another war. There was surely no need for NATO to provide any security. This line of thought applied as well to the Soviet Union, whose economy was also in shambles.

"Now the new NATO can . . . vanquish old hatreds, promote integration." An organization geared for war does not vanquish hatreds; it feeds them. "Countries aspiring to membership will have to modernize their armed forces." Here Albright inadvertently revealed the hidden agenda behind US policy toward NATO. New members Poland, Hungary, and the Czech Republic will need lots of sophisticated weapons and training. With over 50 percent of the market in international weapons trafficking, defense contractors and their members of Congress are ready and waiting for multibillion-dollar orders. This is the real security that Madame Secretary was promoting.

"It requires abandoning cold war stereotypes." She may not have thought this statement through, because if this were to actually happen NATO would vanish. Here is a bit of idle speculation: If US citizens were to force passage of a law that requires the offspring aged 18–35 of all public officials in the elite class who cling to a war mentality to serve out the duration of any armed conflict in combat, perhaps officials' persistent refusal to welcome the Age of Reason would change.

In November 2000 Russia's President Vladimir Putin promulgated his fervent desire that both of the leading nuclear nations drastically reduce stockpiles of nuclear weapons. His country simply could not afford to maintain its thousands of missiles, and top officials anyway saw little point in doing this.

But a thinking citizen will not be surprised if Congress and the Pentagon drag their feet; those lobbyists come by frequently, and they always bring lots of money with them. Not only this, but President Bush is again pushing a national missile defense program. Possibly excepting Britain, no other country in the world approves of this rash and technologically infeasible venture. When negative incentives govern behavior, it is truly amazing how billions of dollars impel public officials to ignore the rest of the world.

The military-industrial complex has relied in part on inertia as it continues to live high and largely at taxpayer expense in spite of the lack of a credible enemy. Harris said, "It takes only one generation for a good thing to become a bad thing, for an inference about experience to become a dogma. Dogma is the enemy of truth and the enemy of persons."[35]

Picture a war today, when a few fringe elements of the press refuse to cooperate in the deception of the public. Reporters, correspondents, and stringers would circulate along the boundaries of the conflict, distributing cell phones with satellite uplinks to local people (who have no interest in being swept up into a conflict). Each possessor would have a personal code by which newsrooms could identify the source of a bulletin. Any dispatch used would mean a generous reward for the source.

These fringe elements could be based in any country. They would exist at risk of discovery by governments who would control information flows. If caught these people would be prosecuted, even though in any country there may ostensibly be a free press.

Why would these businesses be organized and operated? There would be a need for reliable information and someone would find a way to fill it, and with high risk there would be serious money in the venture. Risk and reward go hand in hand, regardless of which government officials call a venture illegal and exact severe punishment for offenders.

Concerned citizens learned about the reality of the Vietnam War without benefit of uplinks, but it took a long time and many lives wasted (and not only those who were killed). But today truth about war would be extremely difficult to hide, because an enlightened public would see through the smoke and mirrors.

The Merchant Replaces the Warrior

Thomas Jefferson wrote,

Never was so much false arithmetic employed on any subject as that which has been employed to persuade nations that it is in their interest to go to war. Were the money that it has cost to gain, at the close of a long war, a little town, or a little territory, the right to cut wood here, or to catch fish there, expended in improving what they already possess, in making roads, opening rivers, build-

ing ports, improving the arts . . . it would render them much stronger, much wealthier and happier. This I hope will be our wisdom.

Thomas Paine wrote in 1792:

> *On this question of war, three things are to be considered. First, the right of declaring it; secondly, the expense of supporting it; thirdly, the mode of conducting it after it is declared. The French Constitution places the right where the expense must fall, and this union can be only in the nation. The mode of conducting it after it is declared, it consigns to the executive department. Were this the case in all countries, we should hear but little more of wars.*

If widely followed, this policy would also have precluded any thoughts of terrorism.

Jefferson and Paine utilized different rationales in their arguments, but they were of one mind regarding the objective. It is not only logical but morally imperative that those who must finance a war and send their young people to fight it and perhaps sacrifice life and limb should have much to say about declaring it. Also logically, this dictum applies to conflicts not officially declared as war (as this is a dodge); in terms of the horrendous expense and the sacrifice of young people, the argument holds as well for any armed conflict. If President Johnson had called for a referendum on escalating the war in Vietnam, what could have been the result?

As time passes and people become more educated and reflect on their learning, thoughts such as these will become more prevalent. If discussion with other citizens were included, the door would open to the Age of Reason. By 1792 Thomas Paine had witnessed two revolutions against tyranny (the American and the French), and his reflection led him to conclude that this age was about to dawn. Unfortunately, he underestimated the staying power of personal power seeking.

In 1904 Churchill said "that capital shall be made the servant and not the master of the State, and . . . true happiness of nations is to be secured by industrial development and social reform at home, rather than by territorial expansion and military adventures abroad." Eisler added a feminine slant on the issue: "There seems little question that from the very beginning warfare was an essential instrument for replacing the partnership model with the dominator model. . . . At the core of the invaders' system was the placing of higher value on the power that takes, rather than gives, life."[36]

Schumpeter commented,

> *Success in industry and commerce requires a lot of stamina, yet industrial and commercial activity is essentially unheroic in the knight's sense—no flourishing of swords about it, not much physical prowess, no chance to gallop the armored horse into the enemy, preferably a heretic or heathen—and the ideolo-*

gy that glorifies the idea of fighting for fighting's sake and of victory for victory's sake understandably withers in the office among all the columns of figures.[37]

Writing in 1942, Schumpeter argued that if capitalism were allowed full play its players would be far too busy to think about wars and fighting. Note how this argument ties into Paine's point above. Removing the decision to declare war from the public sector—government—and placing it in the private sector—where reside the citizens who must finance it and sacrifice their youth—would go far toward "we should hear but little more of wars."

Chapter 14 argued for the coming open society, in which human intercourse would be guided by honesty and openness. If this were the case, public officials who plan a war when they know the citizens would not approve would be discovered by vigilant constituents. Knowing this, they would be strongly deterred from such a decision irrespective of any negative or macho propensities that might be influential in any such instance. Put another way, they would be accountable to their bosses, the citizens.

This sounds encouraging, but surely skeptics will ask how to control the urges of a foreign dictator who is armed to the teeth and ruled by passion. But in an open society it will be extremely difficult if not impossible for such a leader to accumulate an arsenal without someone finding out about his plans early on and exposing them. For example, there are satellites aloft today that can read the headline on a newspaper on the ground, and this is just the beginning. Soon there will be communications satellites covering every square kilometer on the face of the planet, so that anyone with a cell phone can report any suspicious activity observed while remaining unobserved.

Satellite imagery is becoming more important in verifying arms control agreements. When each side can see what the other is up to, tensions tend to relax. A company called Public Eye recently bought several one-meter-resolution "ikonos" satellite images of North Korean and Pakistani weapons sites, and handed them over to the press. This development raises a question that concerns the Senate Foreign Relations Committee, of which North Carolina Senator Jesse Helms is chair (Helms is stepping down in 2003). How can the committee reject the most recent arms control treaty on grounds of difficulty in verification of good faith in compliance?

The private sector will combine with democratic, bottom-up government to eliminate war. For the first time in history some country will soon install a nearly pure democracy. Other countries will follow. Mueller wrote: "When the notion of war chiefly inspires ridicule rather than fear, it will have become obsolete. Within the developed world at least, that condition seems to be gradually emerging. Perhaps we are growing up at last."[38]

Reported in his book *On Human Nature*, Wilson's research spanned thousands of years.[39] "Although the evidence suggests that the biological nature of humankind launched the evolution of organized aggression and roughly directed its early history across many societies, the eventual outcome of that evolution will be determined by cultural processes brought increasingly under the control of rational thought." As pointed out previously, the oppression of people by priestcraft and conquest and plunder was promulgated through passions, whereas the Age of Reason appeals to a much further developed intellect.

Alterman's report on the transformation of Edward Luttwak's thinking is very interesting.[40]

> *Once prized by the Reagan punditocracy as the most creative mind in its consensus of belligerence, Luttwak became during the prelude to the [Gulf] war the most eloquent American voice of the new—geoeconomic—world order. As Luttwak explained to a shocked Senate Armed Services Committee: "The great questions to be resolved in the main arena of international life have not been changed at all by Iraq's invasion of Kuwait: who will develop and market the next generation of computers, civilian aircraft, advanced materials, and other high added-value products. For that it is not expeditionary armies that are needed but abundant, patient capital, not impressive warships but educational investment in a highly skilled labor force.*

Senators on this committee have by definition a warrior mentality, so they did not want to hear any talk that advocated the end of warfare.

At the end of World War II the Allies put into force a policy of indefinite duration that forbade Germany and Japan to develop any significant amount of weapons and training of soldiers. In fact, the Allies installed hundreds of military bases on the soil of these two countries and manned them at great and continuing expense, ostensibly to guard against any resurgence of belligerence by these countries (and communist hegemony). Thus freed of the need to develop massive and sophisticated war fighting machinery, these two countries rebuilt their war-destroyed economies with impressive rapidity. The projected 2000 gross domestic product (GDP) per person for Germany in US dollars was $27,337, and the figure for Japan was $30,720. (GDP per person is considered a rough measure of a country's wealth; the corresponding figure for this country was $33,946.)

Ralph Waldo Emerson noted,

> *The philosopher and lover of man have much harm to say of trade; but the historian will see that trade was the principle of liberty; that trade planted America and destroyed Feudalism; that it makes peace and keeps peace, and it will abolish slavery. We complain of its oppression of the poor, and of its building up a new aristocracy on the ruins of the aristocracy it destroyed. But the aristocracy of trade has no permanence, is not entailed, was the result of toil and talent, the result of merit of some kind, and is continually falling, like the waves of the sea, before new claims of the same sort.*

This insight into the nature of commerce has not received the exposure that it would enjoy in an open society. Production and trade, both domestic and international, are what built this country. Emerson's observation ties in very closely with the main theme of Schumpeter's book *Capitalism, Socialism and Democracy*; Schumpeter called the phenomenon "creative destruction." The evidence of its existence today may be found in a glance at the number of companies, both small and large, which seemed to dominate their industries, say, forty years ago and do not exist today. Both capitalism and democracy are dynamic concepts. As companies rise and fall, so do policies and public servants as the nature and consequent needs of the society change.

Even a world governed by economic and commercial interests and free of war is not a perfect world. As international trade has burgeoned (globalization), national governments have seen fit to increase the number, variety, and intensity of previously established barriers to trade. On the surface, these actions are designed to help companies compete in the international marketplace through discouraging the importation of foreign products and services. This is the political imperative, but these barriers reduce economic benefits to the people.

In the 1840s Englishman Richard Cobden showed how free trade would benefit his country, especially for poor people who needed access to cheap food. This benefit applied even when other countries kept their barriers to free trade, and by taking the politics out of trade it reduced chances of disputes escalating into open war.

The democratic principle of private property stipulates that a legal owner may dispose of his or her property in any legal way he may see fit. This includes selling it to a willing buyer who happens to be located in another country, freely in terms agreed to by both parties to the transaction, and without interference by any government. Untold billions of such transactions over centuries have combined to build today's national economies.

A popular example of a trade barrier is a **tariff**, usually a percentage added onto the price of an imported product, which the government takes as a tax. If a consumer must pay 40 percent more for an imported product than for a product without a tariff, that portion of the free market price of the product is lost to the buyer; he or she must forgo the opportunity either to save that money or spend it on something else. In this way, his living standard is reduced by that much money. Therefore perhaps one should "buy American," but this does little good because the maker of the domestic product may have already realized that they can raise the price by around 40 percent (to equal the imports) and still sell the same number of products. The presence of the tariff allows the maker to do this. The only immediate disadvantage lies in the tiny portion of that 40 percent that the industry's lobbyist had to spend to buy the tariff law.

Does this mean that domestic companies make extra profits, which they can invest in improving their products? Very often, no. The domestic makers are less efficient than are their overseas competitors, which is why the industry lobbied for the tariff in the first place. Therefore those extra "profits" were squandered before they became profits, in inefficiency. Generalizing, the end result of tariffs is smaller rises in living standards for consumers and lower wages paid to workers because the resulting inefficiency cuts into a company's ability to pay well.

Government farm support programs in advanced countries are a disgrace. *The Economist* reported that the tariff on imported rice in Japan was recently elevated to close to 1,000 percent.[41] "Within the OECD [Organization for Economic Cooperation and Development, or the twenty-five richest nations], annual state payments to the agricultural sector exceed Africa's entire GDP And domestic support in America, Europe, and Japan accounts for about 80% of the world's total." Farmers in poor countries generally have no chance of penetrating export markets. "If rich countries were to remove the subsidies that create these price differences, poor countries would benefit by more than three times the amount of all the overseas development assistance they receive each year."

A similar problem develops whenever a government imposes import **quotas** (a second example), which allow only a specified maximum number of, say, cars to be imported. The Reagan administration did this to Japanese automakers, calling these quotas "voluntary import restraints." There was nothing voluntary about them, but calling them that made better copy. The result was buyers of imported new Japanese cars were paying up to 20 percent higher than sticker price; over a four-year period they paid $26 billion over and above what they would have paid without quotas. Spent elsewhere in the economy, that money would have raised consumer living standards and provided thousands more jobs. Instead, it went to Japanese companies.

The Economist showed that when advanced country governments **subsidized** (a third example) their farmers' exports farmers in poor countries suffer.[42] "Farmers in poor countries struggle to compete with heavily subsidized farmers in Europe and America—and even see their own market destroyed when food surpluses are dumped. Lost trade costs poor countries an estimated $700 billion each year, says the United Nations, a figure that dwarfs aid spending." (Total aid to poor countries in 1997 was estimated at $187 billion.) Trade, not aid, is a better deal for practically everyone.

The issue of globalization has been generating controversy recently. This process had its origin before the time of Marco Polo (thirteenth century). During the second half of the nineteenth century, growing free trade spurred the most rapid economic development worldwide in history. Today globalization continues to help increase living standards for all of the world's people. Although the process is not perfect, the good far outweighs the bad, as Crook cogently argued in considerable detail.[43]

> *"Trade policy" should ideally be abolished outright: governments have no business infringing people's liberty to buy goods where they will, least of all when the aim is to add to corporate earnings. . . . Governments should hold themselves accountable to voters at large, not to companies, industry associations, special interests or indeed to any kind of non-governmental organization, whatever its ideology or dress code. [The business of government is not the government of business; see Appendix.] Worst of all, governments everywhere deny responsibility when they explain broken promises, failures of will or capitulations to special interests as the unavoidable consequences of globalization. That is not harmless evasion, but a lie that rots democracy itself.*

Crook continued: "Globalization is a great force for good. But neither governments nor businesses . . . can be trusted to make the case." Invented in antiquity and given a tremendous boost during the Industrial Revolution, capitalism is the only known nonviolent method for creating and accumulating wealth. The pity is that so few people can see and appreciate this great reality.

But the grim reality of today has public officials being manipulated by lobbyists for various special interests, including business. However, if officials in this country and elsewhere were to act as the US Constitution specifies—as agents of the citizens—then their actions would respond to the public will and not to that of the lobbyists (and their money). Private capital needs unfettered movement worldwide so it can find its most efficient use to benefit the people. Profits cannot be placed before people if they think about where they are putting their money. Business fully understands this position; without customers they cannot make profits. The competition forces a company to be efficient along with effective in serving customers: The former minimizes costs and the latter maximizes consumer satisfaction. Neglect these imperatives and thinking customers vanish quickly as they migrate to the competition.

Critics ask what about the worker in a poor country. The same critics are unlikely to ask a few of these workers about their work. If asked the response would be they prefer to have jobs at $3 per day under tough working conditions than no jobs at $25 per day. To a westerner, $3 per day is surely thin gruel, but it puts money into pockets where none existed before (there is no unemployment insurance in most poor countries). This money will be spent to increase workers' and their families' living standards through purchases of goods. But who will make these extra goods? Workers will, but this requires more jobs.

The flip side of this issue has governments forcing companies to pay more and provide better working conditions. This distorts the labor market in a poor country, because with freedom of hiring $3 per day just clears the market. Not enough workers will choose to work for less than $3 and paying more than $3 generates a flood of applicants, so a company sees little point in paying more.

If government were to horn in anyway, factories will either go out of business or move elsewhere, and there would go the employment. Thus the critics win—or do they? If the market is denied, poor consumers will be forced to pay more and in many instances will be simply priced out of the market.

Critics also argue that many workers in rich countries lose their jobs when a company moves its operation offshore. Most will find other work, probably paying less than they were earning beforehand. This situation opens the door to special interest politics. President Bush recently granted the steel industry tariff protection from imported steel. But this is groupthink, as discussed in Chapter 7. Democracy is individual rights, so in this instance a skilled and conscientious steel worker would have seen the writing on the wall and therefore long since made plans for alternative employment. Were he really good he would find employers very interested in hiring him, and one could be found that pays as well or nearly as well as in his steel job.

But the career politician has a different take on the trade issue; steel industry lobbyists frequently come to Washington and they always bring lots of money. *The Economist* fired a broadside:

> *An ailing industry, a case of unfair trade before America's International Trade Commission and a president mulling sanctions. No, this is not 2002, but 1976, when Gerald Ford was in the White House and America's sickly steel companies were clamoring for import protection to help them back on their feet. Twenty-six years later, the same steel makers are still flat on their backs. . . . Amid widespread groans, on March 5th . . . Bush slapped tariffs . . . for three years—a period of time, ventured Mr. Bush's trade representative, Robert Zoellick, "that will give the US steel industry the opportunity to get back on its feet."* [44]

European steel companies are boiling mad. These barriers will add 30 percent to prices of over a $1 billion worth of their exports to this country, and their own markets will be inundated with steel that would otherwise have been routed to US markets.

> *This steel-tariff plan, it is important to remember, lies well outside the ordinary run of bad economic policy: it is so wrong it makes other kinds of wealth-destroying intervention feel inadequate. And was it really politically inescapable? What a depressingly feeble excuse from a president who has promised, and shown, strong leadership in other respects, and who had claimed, by the way, to be a champion of liberal trade. Mr. Bush and his advisers should be ashamed. . . .*
>
> *[It] will make most Americans worse off, by forcing them to pay more for their steel (in products). Except in the short term it will also do little to help the*

people it is intended to help . . . namely, workers in the parts of America's steel industry that cannot compete with foreign suppliers or with America's own more productive mini-mills.

Mini-mills utilize scrap steel, so they can make steel much cheaper than can the old-style blast furnaces (which companies supplied the lobbyists with tainted money). *The Economist* predicted that the old companies will eventually fold their tents anyway.

Will questioned whether there is an end to politicians' distorting international markets.[45] "The United States has asked for and received extraordinary help from Pakistan in the war on terrorism. Now Pakistan has asked for something from the United States."

Pakistan (per capita income: $470) has asked this mighty republic (per capita income: $26,503) . . . to remove the quotas on imports of Pakistani pillows and sheets. It also asked . . . [to] permit 50 percent increases in quotas for pajamas, towels, underwear and some other apparel.

But the United States . . . nevertheless ***flinches from some threats****, and one of them is a potential torrent of inexpensive Pakistani pajamas. [emphasis added]*

(The government offered 15 to 20 percent increases in some quotas.)

Firing another broadside, *The Economist* commented:

Opponents of globalization claim that poor countries are losers from global integration. A new report from the World Bank demolishes that claim with one simple statistic. If you divide poor countries into those that are "more globalized" and those that are "less globalized"—with globalization measured simply as a rise in the ratio of trade to national income—you find that more globalized poor countries have grown faster than rich countries, while less globalized countries have seen income per person fall. . . .

Manufactured goods rose from 25% of poor-country exports in 1980 to more than 80% in 1998. This integration was concentrated in two dozen countries—including China, India and Mexico—that are home to 3 billion people. Over the past two decades, these countries have doubled their ratio of trade to national income.[46]

In most African countries, the ratios of trade to national income have fallen and the number of people in poverty has risen.

The paying of "grease," "baksheesh," "mordida," or bribes to get around trade barriers or simply to do business has a long tradition in world trade. Local bureaucrats, especially in poor countries, are paid next to nothing with the understanding that they can supplement their incomes through soliciting bribes. Over the past several decades the tradition has become so deeply ingrained that most businesspeople have given up trying to eliminate it or even minimize it.

The Economist for the first time reported on some progress.[47]

Economists have been totting up the terrible costs of corruption. Organizations like Transparency International have borrowed some of the passion that animates campaigns for human rights. And multilateral lenders like the World Bank and the IMF [International Monetary Fund] have joined the battle. Next month an international convention making the bribery of foreign public officials a crime—the first to do so outside America—goes into force. . . . Liberalism begins with the assumption of equality . . . no person or group should start with inherent advantages. . . . Corruption offends that aim by injecting private preferences into public dealings.

A pioneering paper by Paolo Mauro, an economist at the IMF, showed that countries with a lot of corruption have less of their GDP going into investment, and lower growth rates. His later work has suggested that corrupt countries invest less in education, which pays big economic dividends but small bribes, than clean countries do.

Neglect of education, especially at elementary level, keeps poor countries poor. And paying bribes only exacerbates the problem. "A 1996 study found that, the more Ukrainian businessmen paid in bribes, the more time they then spent with palms-out bureaucrats."

Meuller noted that on May 15, 1984, "the major countries of the developed world had managed to remain at peace with each other for the longest continuous stretch of time since the days of the Roman Empire." A citizen could make a comprehensive search of all news media for that date and find not a word of coverage. War makes better headlines than peace does (as long as it is over there). News about the coming Age of Reason gets practically no play for the same reason. The people obviously want peace, but Chapter 9 showed why the media do not cooperate.

Giving aid to poor countries and simultaneously selling them weapons is counterproductive. Their economies cannot grow if parts of them are destroyed as quickly as they are built. This means demands for more and more aid instead of encouraging economic development and formation of active trading partners that benefit all, including advanced countries. Because much of the aid finds its way into the pockets of government officials, it is far better for policy to act on the slogan, "Trade, not aid." Today's policy helps inefficiently while destroying horribly efficiently, and everyone is losing.

The Economist saluted the late economist Peter Bauer:

After the second world war a new "development economics" came to dominate policymaking in poorer countries. . . . It argued that poor countries were victims of a vicious circle of poverty, doomed to remain poor because they lacked the income that provided savings which, when invested, generated economic growth. The answer? Rich countries should provide the capital, in the form of foreign aid. To use the capital efficiently, poor-country governments should plan

> *their economies and create new industries to substitute for foreign imports. And to give these nascent industries a chance, competition should be restricted through monopoly rights and barriers to foreign trade.* [48]

Lord Bauer was appalled. "[In] his studies . . . there could be wealth creation, even in subsistence economies, if only market forces were allowed to work. Trade barriers and monopolies merely destroyed entrepreneurialism." Even though big government has seriously distorted markets in the United States, the country continues to provide relatively good opportunities for risk-accepting people to start businesses.

> *All countries had started poor, he argued. If the vicious-cycle [sic] theory were true, mankind would still be living in the stone age. Opportunities for private profit, not governments' plans, held the key to development. Governments had the limited though crucial role of protecting property rights, enforcing contracts, treating everybody equally before the law, minimizing inflation and keeping taxes low.*

This is the usual prescription, well known to economists nearly everywhere even if not publicized (see Chapter 9).

> *Above all, Lord Bauer argued, there would be no concept of the third world at all were it not for the invention of foreign aid. Aid politicized economies, directing money into the hands of governments rather than toward profitable business. . . . aid had proved "an excellent method for transferring money from poor people in rich countries to rich people in poor countries."*

Here is apparently yet another example of transferring wealth from nonrich to rich.

The Economist studied the 2001 World Development Report.[49]

> *The study, which gathered existing research and added a survey of around 100 countries, found that economies that allowed open flows of information to as many people as possible (with free, competitive media), good protection for the property rights of the poor (especially over land and the efficient collection of loans) and broad access to judicial systems (even for illiterate peasants or people who cannot pay high legal fees) were most likely to be competitive, and to develop.*

This makes far more sense than does international trafficking in weapons.

Peruvian economist Hernando de Soto has demonstrated the awesome potential for development in poor countries that is locked up today in the lack of legal title to land.[50] Property in third world and formerly communist countries so encumbered is estimated to total $9.3 trillion. "In the midst of their own poorest neighborhoods and shanty towns there are trillions of dollars, all ready to be put to use if only the mystery of how assets are transformed into capital can be unraveled." Benefits include land as collateral for loans for improvements, defense against rich rogues with contacts in government who may arbitrarily seize land held for generations by peasant families, freedom to sell land or other assets no longer needed, freedom to allow others to invest in expansion of any operation, freedom to give assets to children and other family, and freedom to do business with strangers.

It is hard to understand how government officials of countries that export weapons can preach to other nations regarding human rights. Weapons do not protect human rights; they take them away. In Cambodia the average age of a citizen is eighteen years because there are many children. That poor country suffered through a terrible civil war for years during the 1970s, when up to 2 million (mostly adult) people were killed. Since that time 200,000 children have stepped on land mines and have either been killed or had parts of their bodies blown away. The conflict has long since finished, but weapons are durable. Today around 300 children each month step on one of these killers.

Estimates are that anywhere from 4 to 10 million of them remain distributed worldwide, each one patiently waiting for the next innocent child. Jody Williams has been deeply concerned about this tragedy. She received the Nobel Peace Prize for her efforts aimed at removing land mines from anywhere in the world that they threaten life and limb.

It is quite possible that weapons merchants will eventually drive themselves out of business. Suppose that the present trend continues, and more destructive weapons continue to be developed and sold. They will be sold to almost any nation, with rare exceptions. Arms suppliers apparently do not need consciences. They predictably argue that if they do not sell them someone else will. But this argument lacks even a shred of morality. Suppose in addition that in the open society the media function as they should: providing truth and exposing skullduggery by public officials. As weapons continue to grow ever more horrible, an aroused public will at some point force the merchants of death to cease production.

The correct and sought-after approach to international relations is to emphasize companies, not countries, because "when goods don't cross boundaries, armies will." When hegemony takes on economic trappings there will be no need for this or any other country to remain a superpower, especially in the military sense as it is perceived today. A company may rule the roost in an industry, but experience has shown that this hegemony is for a limited time only. Also, a company who does business worldwide may eventually lack a recognizable base of operations in any one country. If this becomes a common practice, what is today known as negatively inspired nationalism may fade into history.

Even today the issue of moving manufacturing operations offshore involves more than meets the eye. What meets the eye (media hype) is loss of jobs at home, but the truth is either a shifting of job locations and skills with no loss or a net increase in jobs. If a factory moves overseas its operations create jobs for thousands of people. These people will have new money in their pockets and will be in the market for a variety of goods, some of them produced in the country from which the factory relocated. This increase in demand must be met through gearing up production, and therefore hiring additional workers and managers.

Cheap, exploited labor is not nearly as often the primary reason for moving a factory offshore. For example, if workers in a poor country make only one-fifth as much as workers doing a similar job in an advanced country, on the surface this looks like exploitation. However, if the uneducated poor worker is only one-sixth as productive, is less trainable due to lack of education, and other considerations are about equal, the company probably will not move the factory.

Some conclusions are in order.

1. Belief in the external threat enables elite classes to maintain top-down control over citizens.
2. Warriors claim that conflict and tensions generate a demand for weapons and training of soldiers. The reality is the reverse. Once weapons are in place, the temptation for egotistical leaders to use them whenever passion overrules reason is too great to resist, especially when they are not accountable to their people.
3. When such weapons are used, they do not make peace. Rather, their use causes resentment, hatred, and unending desire for revenge.
4. Dictators in poor countries often use imported sophisticated weapons, not to preserve stability but to quell unrest among their citizens through brute force.
5. There is an unavoidable trade-off between production of weapons (and the resulting conflict) and economic development.
6. Irresponsible and egotistical top leaders make war. Citizens do not, because they realize that they must finance it, fight it, and die in it.
7. International trafficking in weapons creates widespread instability, primarily because there is no such thing as a balance of military power.
8. Politicians who preach world peace while buying votes through domestic manufacture and foreign sales of weapons are hypocrites, not leaders.
9. Have-not countries will always strive to equalize with the have countries, unless an organized, bottom-up, citizen effort is mounted to rid the world of all weapons of mass death and destruction. No exceptions anywhere, any time, any way, ever.

Due to the development of guerrilla tactics, even "small" conflicts have no victor. Wars in Sudan, Myanmar (Burma), Chechnya, Sierra Leone, Northern Ireland, Columbia, and the Middle East have, perhaps with occasional pauses, ground on for thirty years or more. Guerrilla tactics include hiding out, usually in mountains that they know far better than the enemy, moving in secretly, striking hard, and moving quickly away before the enemy can react. The development of lighter, cheaper, more easily concealed, destructive weapons favors the guerrillas over a regular army, even a large one. Resentment, hatred, and desire for revenge provide the fuel to keep such conflicts going indefinitely.

This grim reality means a life of fear, grief, and continuing misery for millions of noncombatants, each of whom wants only to go about his or her daily business in peace. This desire seems not unreasonable. A pair of Serbs was interviewed after the siege of Sarajevo, in which Serbs, Croats, and Muslims together endured months of hell raining from the skies. "We lived in this town. We loved in this town, we dreamed in this town . . . many beautiful nights. If there is a victory, it is simply that we are alive."

If a foreign conqueror is to rule a country successfully, its leaders must utilize a very strong, centralized bureaucracy that is composed of well-established institutions of personal power. Examples of key parts of this bureaucracy existed in the Nazi Gestapo and the Soviet KGB. This bureaucracy has been proven to be absolutely necessary, simply because without it conquered citizens will not accept oppression.

But in a democracy established and maintained during the Age of Reason personal power would be dispersed in a thousand directions and kept that way. The institutions needed for oppressive rule over the population would not exist, and it would take years of top-down effort to firmly establish them. In the meantime the conqueror must fight a thousand insurrections emanating from dispersed power centers throughout the land. Preoccupied with these continuing guerrilla battles, the task of establishing institutions of oppression would become impossible. In the open society a potential conqueror would know this, so no attack would be forthcoming.

It is interesting to observe that in this respect Al Qaeda operates a democracy. Power is dispersed outward to cells in various countries around the world, and although all share a common objective, each operates independently of the others. There is no way for anyone to predict when, where, and how a particular cell will strike, unless the necessary institutions for oppression are established throughout the world. This truth explains why the Bush administration's "war" against this organization cannot be won, even though for political reasons a victory may someday be declared.

And with the Age of Reason would come world history's **final and overdue burial of the external threat theory**. Career warriors would be dragged, kicking and screaming, into the new age. However, once reason has had time to develop, nearly all would happily change their stripes.

Douglas Casey imagined an island continent consisting of two countries of about the same size, economy, and life style separated by a mountain range.[51] Democracy and free markets prevailed and nearly everyone was very happy with the arrangements. Then a citizen in Country A returned from a trip and said he had a plan to make things still better; it would emphasize the "public good" over "private interests." He hired thugs to collect the needed additional taxes, and because the government knew better than citizens what was good for people, it passed many laws and regulations. There was something in them for everyone, and taxes took only from those with ability to satisfy those in need.

As time passed the government of Country A noticed that producers were not paying taxes, so it rewarded other citizens who informed on these people. But there was even less money coming as more people evaded ever-increasing taxes, so the government solved that problem by simply printing more money. But this brought on inflation, and the money lost value. To get cooperation from citizens it was necessary to assign still more personal power to government. Good citizens emigrated across the mountains to live in Country B, which still enjoyed prosperity. The government saw an opportunity to improve its and the country's situation by conquering Country B, so it organized an army and invaded.

Country B had no army, so citizens just watched as Country A's army came into their country. But the soldiers liked what they saw in Country B, so they deserted and joined the other side. Eventually government officials in Country A conceded defeat.

A 1960s flower child said: "Suppose they gave a war, and nobody came."

Notes

1. Desiderius Erasmus, in Jim Powell, *The Triumph of Liberty*. Free Press, 2000, p. 74.
2. Alexis de Tocqueville, *Democracy in America*. Knopf, 1972.
3. Tom Watson, quoted in Sara M. Evans and Harry C. Boyte, *Free Spaces: The Sources of Democratic Change in America*. University of Chicago Press, 1992, p. 174.
4. Rose Wilder Lane, *The Discovery of Freedom*. Fox and Wilkes, 1993.
5. James D. Barber, *The Book of Democracy*. Prentice Hall, 1995.
6. Bernard E. Grady, *On the Tiger's Back*. Biddle, 1994.
7. Jim Powell, *The Triumph of Liberty*. Free Press, 2000, p. 335.
8. Eugene E. Leach, "Resisting the Blind Rush into War." *News and Observer* [Raleigh, NC], September 14, 2001, p. 21A.
9. George Kennan, "Why Is Expanding NATO a Done Deal?" *News and Observer*, February 6, 1997, p. 19A.
10. Thomas L. Friedman, "Expand NATO? The Answers Aren't There." *News and Observer*, March 4, 1998, p. 15A.
11. *The Economist*, "A Moment of Truth." May 4, 2002, p. 23.
12. Edward O. Wilson, *On Human Nature*. Harvard University Press, 1978.
13. John Mueller, *Retreat from Doomsday*. Basic Books, 1989.

14. Lewis H. Lapham, *The Wish for Kings: Democracy at Bay*. Grove Press, 1993.
15. Thomas A. Harris, *I'm Okay; You're Okay*. Avon Books, 1973.
16. Murray Rothbard, *For a New Liberty*. Fox and Wilkes, 1973.
17. Leo Rennert, "What in the World?" *News and Observer* [Raleigh, NC], January 30, 2000, p. 19A.
18. *The Economist*, "A Bitter Harvest." September 15, 2001, p. 19.
19. *The Economist*, "How Angola's War Protects Polio." July 24, 1999, p. 61.
20. Willliam Shawcross, *Deliver Us from Evil: Peacekeepers, Warlords and a World of Endless Conflict*. Simon and Schuster, 2000.
21. *The Economist*, "Not Quite a New World Order, More a Three-way Split." December 20, 1997, p. 41.
22. Molly Ivins, "That's Some Arms Trade for Us." *News and Observer*, August 1996 column.
23. Eduard Shevardnadze, *The Future Belongs to Freedom*. Free Press, 1991.
24. *The Economist*, "To Sue a Dictator." April 24, 1999, p. 26.
25. Freeman Dyson, *Infinite in All Directions*. Harper and Row, 1988.
26. *The Economist*, "Don't Ban the Bomb." January 4, 1997, p. 15.
27. Walter Isaacson, *Kissinger: A Biography*, Simon and Schuster, 1992.
28. Rothbard, *For a New Liberty*.
29. Eric Alterman, *Sound and Fury: The Washington Punditocracy and the Collapse of American Politics*. Harper Collins, 1992.
30. Kofi Annan, "Preventing Conflict in the Next Century." *The World in 2000* (*Economist* booklet), p. 51.
31. *The Economist*, "A Proliferating Problem." July 14, 2001, p. 12.
32. P J O'Rourke, *A Parliament of Whores*. Atlantic Monthly Press, 1991.
33. *The Economist*, "If Only Words Were Guns." November 24, 2001, p. 47.
34. Madeleine Albright, "Why Bigger Is Better." *The Economist*, February 15, 1997, p. 21.
35. Harris, *I'm Okay; You're Okay*.
36. Riane Eisler, *The Chalice and the Blade: Our History, Our Future*. Harper Collins, 1988.
37. Joseph A. Schumpeter, *Capitalism, Socialism and Democracy*. Harper and Row, 1942.
38. Mueller, *Retreat from Doomsday*.
39. Wilson, *On Human Nature*.
40. Alterman, *Sound and Fury*.
41. *The Economist*, "Patches of Light." June 9, 2001, p. 69.
42. *The Economist*, "The Poor Who Are Always with Us." July 1, 2000, p. 46.
43. Clive Crook, "Globalization and its Critics." *The Economist Survey*, September 29, 2001, p. 3.

44. *The Economist*, "George Bush, Protectionist." March 9, 2002, p. 13; and "Rust Never Sleeps," p. 61.
45. George Will, "Free Trade Phobia Is Spreading." *News and Observer*, April 14, 2002, p. 29A.
46. *The Economist*, "Going Global." December 8, 2001, p. 67.
47. *The Economist*, "Stop the Rot." January 16, 1999, pp. 19 and 22.
48. *The Economist*, "A Voice for the Poor." May 4, 2002, p. 76.
49. *The Economist*, "Now, Think Small." September 15, 2001, p. 40.
50. *The Economist*, "No title." March 3, 2001, p. 20.
51. Douglas Casey, *Crisis Investing: Opportunities and Profits in the Coming Great Depression*. Stratford Press, 1980.

Chapter Twenty-One:
On the Neighborhood Bully Becoming a Citizen of the World

To educate a man in mind and not in morals is to educate a menace to society.
—Theodore Roosevelt

This chapter investigates the notion of selective perception as it affects relations between the US government and those of other nations in the world. The meaning of the notion can be illustrated in sayings such as "Beauty lies in the eye of the beholder" and "One man's meat is another man's poison." That is, two different people or groups can experience the same phenomenon, and their conclusions may differ greatly. Baseball fans are familiar with the notion: The pitcher throws a fastball and the umpire calls it a strike, but the batter, manager, and his teammates vehemently disagree. All saw the same pitch, but selective perception follows psychological tendencies and hence the different conclusions. Of course these tendencies increase when it is the bottom of the ninth inning, a runner on base, and the score is tied.

The same tendencies apply to international relations. Well after the end of the cold war government officials continue to push for a balance of power among nations, because this has been their strategy for fifty years and it pays very well. Along with this "balance," officials push democracy on cultures that they see no need to understand.

This strategy works poorly if at all, and for several reasons. Besides lack of understanding, by its definition democracy is free choice among citizens. Therefore it cannot be imposed, certainly not by some huge and unpopular foreign power. Also, if US public officials are not sold on democracy how can they effectively sell it to other governments? Finally, psychological tendencies (negative and positive) rest in human nature. If there is a negative motivation in any instance it is not likely to go down well with people who naturally hope that their lives will improve.

The seeking and holding of personal power has no place in a democracy. But this is the hidden agenda behind the rhetoric defending democracy. This agenda is understood by foreign public officials, but generally not by their citizens. Therefore officials feel a need to withhold information from the masses.

MIGHT MAKES RIGHT, FOR SOME PEOPLE

Thomas Paine wrote,

The spectacle at present afforded by the English government is sufficiently strange: it perceives that the ill feeling which once existed between the French and English peoples, and which brought poverty and misfortune to both, is gradually fading away, so now it is looking in other directions for an enemy, because it will have no excuse for its enormous revenue and taxation, except it can prove that, somewhere or other, it has enemies.[1]

The government had previously sought and achieved personal power over people through warfare and exploitation of the external threat. The worry was that people's natural tendency to look on the bright side was causing the loss of some of this power. It is no different today in this country.

Madison spoke to the negative tendency of power-seeking officials.[2] "So strong is this propensity of mankind to fall into mutual animosities that where no substantial occasion presents itself the most frivolous and fanciful distinctions have been sufficient to kindle their unfriendly passions and excite their most violent conflicts." Long after the cold war, saber rattling continues.

Charles Adams showed that the US Constitution restricts warfare, stating that tax money could be used only for defensive conflicts.[3] The president and Congress can wage as much offensive war overseas as they want to, but not with citizens' money. Selective perception enters into this issue, as the government and the defense establishment call these many conflicts "forward defense" or "forward deployment." A thinking citizen might complain about this distortion of fact, but his or her voice would be overwhelmed by the prevailing perception (conventional wisdom) couched in the external threat theory. So he continues paying taxes to support a bloated military budget that takes up to $400 billion a year from the people. After the terrorist attacks of September 11, 2001, there is apparently no limit to citizens' gullibility.

Originally the government was small and weak, so citizens necessarily relied on their own courage and initiative to survive and get ahead. They set up a republic with few restrictions on the free market, and after the Industrial Revolution the economy sped forward. Tocqueville noted:

I have come to the conclusion that all the causes tending to maintain a democratic republic in the US fall into three categories: The first is the peculiar and accidental situation in which Providence has placed the Americans. Their laws are the second. Their habits and mores are the third. . . . They have also hardly anything to fear from something else which is a greater scourge for democratic republics than all these others put together, namely, military glory.[4]

In his first category Tocqueville referred to early America as an untamed and unpoliticized wilderness. At that time there were **few laws**, and through local discussion and actions the citizens made most of them. Under these conditions, they were able to establish a **sound morality** to guide their daily living.

After the end of World War I, Lenin and the Bolsheviks adopted a policy of peaceful coexistence with other nations. This conclusion was thoroughly based in the reality of that time: The country was utterly devastated, and therefore any thoughts of foreign adventurism were considered foolhardy.

After World War II Soviet Russia confronted the same dire situation. Because Lenin's influence was still strong, the tendency was to avoid conflict under any circumstances. In spite of their difficulties the Soviets refused to accept aid that the United States offered under the Marshall Plan, because they believed that strong pressure to adopt capitalism would accompany the offer. They also believed that, in accordance with the teaching of Marx, capitalism would eventually collapse. Hence the Soviets' defensive posture during the cold war (as will be demonstrated).

Afraid of Western (especially US) armed might, the Soviets closed their economy to outside influence and visitation. They did not want to let the Western world know the extent of their weakness. In addition, brutal dictator Stalin maneuvered himself into the Communist Party Secretary position on Lenin's death in 1924. He immediately saw the problem, so he began acting the "tough guy" role to distract attention from the country's plight. He continued with this tactic up until his death in 1953.

This was all the US military-industrial complex needed. Stalin had provided a perfect cover for the external threat theory to reassert itself, and in 1947 the cold war took off. Every time the Russian bear growled the thickness of the cover increased. This bluffing posture justified maintaining the high tax rates that were needed during World War II, and so for years big money poured into Capitol Hill. Government expanded without restraint.

People tend to act on their perceptions. If their predominant perception in international relations is fear, they will permit incredible increases in taxes to beef up the "defense" establishment; just please keep that terrible ogre lurking offshore away from their children. This reality is not lost on public officials, so they stoke this fear at every opportunity.

The ogre need not be real; today the military-industrial complex is scrambling to conjure one where it does not exist. Recent alarmist news bulletins have focused on North Korea's presumed missile development even though its economy is all but nonexistent, its citizens are starving, and its army could not possibly mount a sustained attack, even on its neighbor to the south. But as long as people don't know the reality, these news bulletins will be perceived as truth. Because the

North Korean economy remains closed and the media don't cooperate, truth is hard to come by.

For fifty years (up until very recently) North Korea's government has been fiercely isolationist. The people have suffered horribly under an oppressive regime. President Kim Jong-Il is an experienced and astute proponent of the external threat theory. The constant presence of a huge military presence to the south conveniently enables him to keep the masses panicked and downtrodden. Another proponent of the external threat theory helps him tremendously: The US government maintains about 37,000 of its soldiers in South Korea.

The Economist commented on Kim's foreign policy.[5]

> *He insists he can sell his missiles to whomever he pleases. Rather than exploring the nature of the bribe he is demanding, America and its allies surely ought to be asking themselves whether the huge new sums in aid and investment already being talked about—for new railroads, bridges, harbors, and factories—should actually flow if North Korea continues its roguish behavior.*

The desperate leader of a wrecked country will always scrape the bottom of the barrel. For Kim the only way to obtain absolutely necessary economic development is through a threat to stimulate the arms race. Note that the writer omitted mention that the US government itself sells missiles to whomever it pleases, and the reincarnation of Reagan's Star Wars missile defense system also threatens to rekindle the arms race.

There is also an organized attempt by US officials to wring some modicum of credibility out of a threat from Iran, even as the people through their voting reject their militant Islamic government in favor of democracy. Career politicians and bureaucrats' imaginations know few bounds.

On this issue *The Economist*'s shortsightedness knows few bounds: "The world George W. Bush faces is one in which wars of intervention may be increasingly necessary. This calls for a new geopolitical outlook."[6] But the newspaper's recommendation is just for more of the same. "They are wars that are almost certainly going to happen; but a lot of people are still struggling to understand why and when it may be necessary to fight them. One big test of George Bush's foreign policy is whether he can see the growing case in today's world for what have come to be called 'wars of intervention.'"

The policy of the government, if there is one, could be called selective intervention. That is, ignore Chechnya (10,000 dead, with numbers still growing), East Timor (150–200,000 dead) and Rwanda (800,000 dead), but intervene in Kosovo, where a thoroughly despicable dictator was harassing some of the people. The news media can play this one up as justification for armed intervention in a province where about 250–300 civilians have been killed.

The basis of the principle of selective intervention lies in its lack of principle. It selects places to attack that the elites think will make the United States look like the good guys (the moral high ground), in which soldiers can earn a quick victory, and that will minimize loss of soldiers' lives. For military and career politicians, Kosovo turned out to be the perfect war: lots of weapons used up, but no body bags coming home. It is interesting to note that there is evidence that the conflict was started by Albanians, who make up 90 percent of the population of Kosovo, trying to throw out the few Serbs. But this news was smothered, as it did not fit into the grand plan. Today interethnic conflict persists, almost as if there had been no intervention. And it will continue.

A lesson in this? Tolerance and the Age of Reason must be an integral part of the United Nations' peacekeeping policy, and the United States and all other nations must actively support this policy (see Chapter 22).

The end of the cold war kicked loose a string of smaller wars. Violence only begets more violence; therefore it is only logical to break this vicious circle by bringing into the world the Age of Reason. Furthermore, there is not a single democracy in the world today, and only a few instances of approximations in small countries. Therefore intervening national governments are actually attempting to impose democracy on other countries by force. But democracy is by definition the absence of force. The unavoidable conclusion is that any government that promotes or attempts to force democracy by using violent intervention is not practicing what it preaches. These governments and *The Economist* both need to rethink this issue.

If a country is a military superpower in the world its government may see no need to think through the implications concerning its foreign policy. That is, might makes right. In his military memoirs, Colin Powell thought that discussions among the principals over this country's role in the world were not foreign policy making. Rather, they came across as group therapy.

The government favored Iraq during its miserable and senseless eight-year war with Iran (although defense contractors sold weapons to both sides). Experts thought this policy was well thought out. But then in 1990 Saddam Hussein moved his army into Kuwait. Suddenly the same experts switched gears without so much as a hiccup, because President Bush saw an opportunity to flex the country's muscles and thus regain lost popularity with his constituents.

This occurrence was not unique; for more than forty-five years the government has deployed to many places in the world soldiers, weapons, training, or some combination, stirring up trouble in the name of defending its interests. The intriguing aspect of this bullying is that apparently during all these years no one in Washington saw fit to check to see if the government's interests match those of the citizens who are paying for this foreign adventurism.

In 1770 lawyer John Adams agreed to defend several British soldiers who had fired on colonists during the Boston Massacre, even though he knew this act would be very unpopular.[7]

"The tragedy was not brought on by the soldiers, but by the mob, and the mob, it must be understood, was the inevitable result of the flawed policy of quartering troops in a city on the pretext of keeping the peace. . . . Soldiers quartered in a populous town will always occasion two mobs where they prevent one. They are wretched conservators of the peace."

Today the government quarters troops over much of the world, ostensibly to keep the peace. This is not always done in cities, but the effects are felt just the same. When such bases are terrorized, such as those in Lebanon and Saudi Arabia, no one should be shocked. But the news media have convinced the public that it should be shocked, and that retaliation in kind is in order. In this way violence is perpetuated.

A neighborhood bully is usually a big guy who thinks he is tough. He worries little about anyone who questions his status or policy of harassing smaller people. Anyone who goes around looking for trouble is sure to find it eventually; it is a self-fulfilling prophecy. The same propensity and result apply to international relations. The September 11, 2001, attacks dramatically and tragically testified to this truth.

In 1948 Albert Einstein believed the pursuit of national security through armaments was a dangerous delusion. About that time Winston Churchill suggested that nuclear weapons make war impossible. (A thinking citizen said it is hard to hug children with nuclear arms.) These two men were a great scientist and a great leader, respectively. "Leaders" in the US government listened to them until they said things that public officials did not want to hear. Their perception was influenced by the potential for personal gain through the external threat theory, not in world peace.

When he retired from the presidency in January 1961, Dwight Eisenhower, a career soldier, warned the country against allowing what he called the military-industrial complex to get out of civilian control. During eight years in office he fought tenaciously against its growth. But that institution was already huge, and people had enjoyed such prosperity under eight years of Ike's leadership that they did not hear the warning (or chose not to act on it). Today the citizen/taxpayer supports the institution, not the reverse.

Top officials in the Pentagon, defense contractors, congressmen, and other elites are nearly all of European descent. This means they continue to subscribe to Rose Lane's notion of Authority, where people were programmed on that continent for centuries to look to an Authority as direction for their lives. When that Authority takes on a military form, a lot of things happen. It has been shown that these happenings were not good: the era of conquest and plunder caused centuries of misery.

Ronald Reagan chose not to hear analyses from economists and political science experts suggesting that communism works poorly at best as a means of allocating economic resources in a nation. But he understood very well the external threat theory. Therefore he set his narrow sights on smashing the (perceived) terrible communist bear, and he spent close to $4 trillion of taxpayer money to be absolutely sure the job got done. Charles Adams noted, "If you leave it alone and don't pester it, in time it will die . . . like mercantilism did 200 years ago. By brooding over communism, by giving it undue attention, by being a bully and ganging up on it, and by fearing it and attacking it, we give it a power which it does not possess." A good example may be found today in Cuba.

The "geopolitical" mentality is deeply ingrained. Recently Russia cut its military spending by 80 percent; officials quite logically figured that the country could not afford to do otherwise. Under senior President Bush the government planned to cut its military spending by less than 4 percent, and the long-range plan called for an **increase** beyond 1997.

It's no small wonder the search for a credible monster has intensified. This search has not been limited to Mother Earth; Pentagon officials consulted astronomers to see if an asteroid might threaten the world in the foreseeable future (not for at least 100,000 years). The strategy was therefore to make a few token cuts to satisfy taxpayers who knew the cold war was over, and then pour it on later, when public concern can be diverted elsewhere. Absent an appeal to reason, the strategy is working.

The September 11, 2001 attacks caused a disturbing change in the younger President Bush's stance on foreign policy. Abandoning all thoughts of compassion, he adopted the typical bully stance. Krauthammer interpreted: "The new Bush doctrine holds that, when it comes to designing our nuclear forces, we build to suit. We will build defensive missiles to suit our needs. We will build offensive missiles to suit our needs."[8] One brief thought exposes the folly of this doctrine: What if every other nation built to suit?

Pundit Krauthammer was pleased with the doctrine. However, in March 2002 *The Economist* shared a deep and widely held concern:

> *For a president who a year ago set himself the laudable aim of reducing America's reliance on nuclear weapons for its defenses, George Bush has generated a lot of angry fallout. He stands accused by his critics of looking to America's security at the expense of others, or reducing to rubble the familiar landscape of treaties and agreements that helped manage past dangers. He is developing new missile defenses, giving notice of American withdrawal from the Anti-Ballistic Missile treaty. He has abandoned the quest for new treaty-limited weapons cuts*

with Russia in favor of unilateral ones. He refuses to ratify a nuclear test ban, accepting only a self-imposed (and more easily lifted) moratorium.[9]

The response is as predictable as it is frightening. "Those on Mr. Bush's worry-list have nuclear, chemical or biological weapons, or are trying hard to get them, despite treaty promises not to. All are building the longer-range rockets needed to deliver them." *The Economist* noted that "the *New York Times*, for one, compared the new plan to the action of a rogue state." It looks very much like once in a while a US news outlet feels that it cannot continue to avoid realistic commentary on foreign policy. Unfortunately, Texas gunslingers can't listen to criticism.

Krauthammer argued that the monstrous cold war stockpile of nuclear weapons was built to deter the Soviets "from launching a **conventional** attack on Europe." However, former Soviet foreign minister Shevardnadze wrote in his book, *The Future Belongs to Freedom*, that nuclear weapons do not deter. Quite the contrary, they spur crash programs aimed at parity or better. This explains at least in part the existence of a forty-year arms race and horrendous expense on both sides that need not have occurred.

Columns like Krauthammer's helped spur the Pentagon's bean counters. *The Economist* referred to the Quadrennial Defense Review (QDR), the every-four-years money grab based in large part on the external threat theory, in an article entitled "Don't Even Think about It."[10] After September 11, 2001, "The QDR concludes that America needs more of just about everything, especially communications and surveillance equipment, overseas bases, and long-range aircraft and ships." "Just about everything" is enough to scare the pants off any taxpayer.

The Economist delved deeper into the bully mentality.

> *The big question for the American contractors is how far the balance will shift away from traditional hardware to sophisticated new systems for fighting remote battles. . . . But that doesn't mean existing programs will be ditched. Boeing and Lockheed Martin still expect to hear . . . which of them has been chosen to lead production of the $200 billion Joint Strike Fighter [JSF]—the biggest defense project ever.*

The JSF has momentum and thousands of defense-related businesses are salivating, so it will not be terminated. Continuing: "[The JSF has the] ability to make precision strikes at enemy targets unseen. This has shifted defense procurement away from bigger and faster aircraft and towards advance electronics and software. There is even a proposal to develop an unmanned fighter aircraft." If the taxpayer mentioned above is still around he or she might be tempted to ask about the need for $200 billion spent on manned fighter aircraft if future fights will be without pilots. The nontaxpaying *Economist* was also moved to wonder, "But as the steady progress of the JSF indicates, none of this spells the end of either the manned warplane or the tank."

A researcher was quoted: "The US continues to spend money it does not have to buy weapons it does not need to fight enemies who do not exist." A Department of Defense spokesman was interviewed about the F-22 JSF plane program: "We're committed to it even though I can't project a threat right now that justifies it." The defense budget for fiscal year 2003 is $355 billion. This sets a new record by a margin of around $56 billion.

The notion of differential perception in international relations can be illustrated in real terms through holding up an imaginary mirror: (1) Iran sends a fleet of warships into the Gulf of Mexico; (2) Mexico agrees to provide training facilities for terrorists who would like to overthrow the US government; and (3) Libyan aircraft based in Cuba bomb Washington, DC. Any one of these would be enough to strike fear into the hearts of citizens. When the mirror is flipped to the reverse side: (1) The US government sent warships into the Persian Gulf; (2) US soldiers trained terrorists in Honduras to harass the government of Nicaragua; and (3) Reagan gave the order to bomb Tripoli, the capital of Libya.

There is no record of the reactions of ordinary citizens to these actual incursions, but it is reasonable to suspect that they were similar to those on the first side of the mirror. People have been programmed by media to accept almost any instance of foreign adventurism as necessary and appropriate. (Except for the Vietnam War; it is encouraging to know that there may be a limit to public tolerance of its government's bullying.)

The US government accounts for about 40 percent of the world's total military expenditures. This amounts to well over three times as much as Russia spends, and it is twice as much as Britain, France, Germany, and Japan combined. In 1996 William Kristol was editor of the *Weekly Standard*, and Robert Kagan was a former aide in the Bush administration. These men called for an additional $60–80 billion for defense. Good citizens will defend the right of people of this line of thought to speak out on an issue, but afterward they will not remain silent.

Bandow reported:

> *Such an enormous military buildup is necessary only to police the globe: to meddle in civil wars in distant continents, to restore order in chaotic societies and to extend American security guarantees, through NATO, right up to Russia's borders. The idea, in the words of Kristol and Kagan, is to establish a "benevolent hegemony" and to "preserve that hegemony as far into the future as possible." They argue that this is not a radical proposal, but it is.*[11]

"Benevolent" also exists in the eye of the beholder. From the perspective of leaders of the Third Reich, Hitler planned to set up a benevolent regime that would last for 1,000 years. Therefore Kristol and Kagan's proposal is not radical, but it is ridiculous and unworkable because those placed under the influence of this hegemony would not perceive it as benevolent. Over time human nature will cause the perceptions of benevoler and benevolee to diverge.

Isaacson reported on President Nixon's Secretary of State Henry Kissinger's belief.[12] "Fundamental to Kissinger's philosophy—and to the realist political tradition—was that diplomacy must be backed by the threat of force." In the perception of the other side this is not diplomacy; it is bullying. Frenchman Jean Monnet is credited with originally organizing the European Coal and Steel Community, which later became the European Union. He defined diplomacy as placing both negotiating groups on one side of the table and the problem on the other side. The contrast between the perceptions of Kissinger and Monnet is intriguing.

Isaacson continued (in 1970, when communist Salvador Allende took over Chile): "Kissinger had few qualms about meddling in Chile's internal affairs. As he told a meeting of the 40 committee, only half in jest, 'I don't see why we have to let a country go Marxist just because its people are irresponsible.'" At this time there was some talk in Santiago, the capital city of Chile, which played a similar theme: "I don't see why we have to allow the US to continue as capitalist just because its citizens are irresponsible."

Kissinger's realpolitik emphasized peace through a balance of military power, which meant that every nation in the world had to accumulate a stockpile of weapons and train soldiers to be prepared for war. But as has been shown, this creates an inevitable self-fulfilling prophecy.

Kennedy wrote:

> *As the recent Pentagon-sponsored Commission on Integrated Long-Term Strategy put it . . . "Defense planning in the US has centered for many years on a grand strategy of extraordinary global sweep. The strategy can be stated quite simply: forward deployment of American forces, assigned to oppose invading armies and backed by strong reserves and a capability to use nuclear weapons if necessary. Resting on alliances with other democratic countries, the strategy aims to draw a line that no aggressor will dare to cross."*[13]

There is in this a clear contradiction in terms: "defense planning" and "forward deployment." "One obvious consequence of this postwar transformation of the American strategic posture is that it has needed to allocate a far larger share . . . to defense." Kennedy went on to demonstrate the damage that this strategy does to the economy.

The British newspaper *The Economist* often has value for its objective view of US military policy, which is all but lacking in the domestic news media.[14] A 1997 article reported:

> *The news will surprise some of its members, but no one appointed the Congress of the United States as God. No, nor even as lawmaker, policeman, jury, judge, and executioner to planet Earth. Not even the American president, who at least heads, not just legislates for, the planet's only superpower, can claim as much. Yet between them—Congress more, Mr. Clinton less—they have been*

trying to play all these roles. And in so doing they have antagonized their country's friends without notably hurting its enemies.

Current foreign policy ensures the presence of enemies, as Washington elites need them to keep taxes high. But its implementation can create some pretty weird and tragic results.

Last year's folly was the Helms-Burton law. . . . This bit of extra-territorial arrogance has angered much of Europe and Latin America, without destroying Fidel Castro. Similar . . . Iran and Libya have not brought down, or even low, the ayatollahs or Colonel Qaddafi. Last year also [saw the]. . . "decertification" of Colombia . . . [in the] war against drugs. President Ernesto Samper . . . Has he gone? . . . He has not. . . . True, Colombia and Mexico are awash with drugs and drug traffickers. So, as both governments point out, is the United States—and with users too. But even if that riposte were unjustified, no country, however mighty, is entitled to write the laws of others. That, exactly, is what the US demands: they must alter their criminal codes and extradition laws."

There is talk around the UN headquarters in New York City that refers to the United States as "the big bully."

The Arab-American Research Institute in Washington, DC asked foreign citizens to do one thing: Describe America in one word. Thirty percent said "terrorist"; 28 percent said "superpower"; 21 percent said "oppressive"; 8 percent said "defeated"; and 6 percent said "country of freedom." What is appalling in this result is that a total of 79 percent of the responses were concentrated in just three words, and to an open question! Moreover, the connotations vary from negative to horrendous. A thinking citizen would conclude that something is out of synch.

Shevardnadze was appointed foreign minister of the Soviet Union under Gorbachev. He wrote, "We became a superpower largely because of our military might. . . . What kind of national security is this? It is not just immoral but politically dangerous to equate national security with tanks and nuclear warheads, while leaving out such 'trivia' as human life and welfare."[15]

Gorbachev brought this man in over experienced bureaucrats in the foreign ministry because he knew that the institution had become hidebound and needed to be shaken up.

States that rely mostly on military means of protection cannot consider themselves safe. They are in a no-win position, for the source of political influence in the world and the protection of national interest increasingly depend on economic, technological, and financial factors, whereas enormous arsenals of weapons cannot provide rational answers to the challenges of the day. These weapons cannot be used without risking the destruction of one's own country, its neighbors, and half the world.

This insight was echoed recently by Robert McNamara, who was Secretary of Defense during the Vietnam War (interviewed in *Time*, February 11, 1991). He said that during the cold war there were real threats. "But I suspect we exaggerated, greatly exaggerated, the strength that lay behind those threats, and therefore I think we probably misused our resources and directed excessive resources toward responding to those threats at considerable cost to our domestic societies." This is a rare instance of candor from a very high-ranking former member of the military-industrial complex.

> *We could have maintained deterrence with a fraction of the number of warheads we built. The cost is tremendous . . . not just of warheads. It's research, and it's building all the goddamn missiles. Over the past 20 years the unnecessary costs are in the tens of billions. Insane. It was not necessary. And moreover, our actions stimulated the Russians ultimately.*

Here McNamara referred to the other side of selective perception, which connects with Shevardnadze's arguments. This instance of leaders from both sides of the cold war agreeing with one another may be unique.

Especially for McNamara, it took courage to admit that after many years and a colossal waste of resources (including human), he could admit that his and the government's policies were wrong. A bully practically never does this.

Foreign citizens who feel resentment against the government's bullying have no outlet for their frustration, as they cannot directly retaliate. Most of them believe the rhetoric generated by US media that continue to describe this country as a democracy. Therefore they believe that the citizens consented to these bullying tactics, and so they are prone to harass and even attack citizens traveling abroad. Foreigners have no means of knowing that citizens in this country have no control over their government's foreign adventurism. Therefore what should be free travel in foreign countries is in effect restricted, and sometimes it is official policy.

In 1997 President Clinton reversed a long-standing ban on selling weapons to Latin American governments. *The Economist* commented: "Mr. Clinton's special adviser for Latin America, Mack McLarty, calls this a natural step from the fact that the region is run almost entirely by democratic, civilian governments. It 'deserves the same respect as the rest of the world,' he says."[16]

This argument reverses the thinking that went into the original placement of the ban in the first place: The presence of weapons drives conflict, so the fewer the weapons the fewer the conflicts. This policy had worked since the 1970s to reduce conflict and thus help establish the democracies to which McLarty referred. Therefore it truly strains credibility to sell weapons in the face of relative peace due in large part to their absence.

McLarty offered a timeworn rationale: If we don't sell, the rest of the world will. He offered no evidence that, during the ban, other international arms merchants leaped to take advantage of the opportunity. *The Economist*:

> *[It] outrages Latin America's Jimmy Carter, Oscar Arias, ex-president of Costa Rica. He sees no difference between pushing arms and pushing drugs. 'What if Colombia refused to crack down on its traffickers, saying that if they did not meet America's demand for cocaine, Peruvian ones would?' . . . Who needs this status, Brazilian officials ask tartly. . . . Latin America's wild inequalities of income call for spending on schools, they say, not jet fighters.*

Barber wrote: "For almost every one of the 45 years since the end of World War II presidents have ordered American soldiers into battle somewhere."[17] Surveys revealed that over half of this country's citizens were against the use of force in Iraq during the Gulf War; blood for oil did not make sense to them. But these results were ignored, because Washington's pundits were spoiling for a fight and President Bush needed to bolster his popularity rating.

The news media mention almost none of the widespread and fierce feelings of injury, frustration, and resentment that US foreign policy based on force has produced around the world. A thinking citizen might wonder why around 100 of the 170+ embassies abroad look like fortresses.

Hadar wrote in 1992:

> *Almost no one seemed to doubt the assumptions underlying Bush's decision to contain Iraq's moves in the gulf or that Washington should be committed to a combination of hyperactive diplomacy and military engagement in the Middle East . . . ranging from containing Muslim fundamentalism and Arab radicalism to making the Middle East safe for democracy, were raised as a way of justifying new military and diplomatic commitments.*[18]

This is just another instance of no one doubting conventional wisdom, as the government has intervened in the Middle East ever since 1948, frequently without so much as a by-your-leave. Middle East countries have had no experience with democracy and their governments neither understand nor care about it. Kuwait's government was antidemocratic, anti-Semitic, and anti-American, but these facts apparently did not cause Bush a moment's hesitation.

For decades the government has been in effect trading weapons for oil in the Middle East. Hadar referred to the 1973 and 1979 dramatic oil price increases:

> *[A] rise in oil prices . . . helped the Iranians and the Saudis to purchase huge quantities of American military equipment and increased the profits of the major . . . oil companies. Higher oil prices were . . . a form of taxation through which Americans helped to subsidize the gulf oil states . . . and through them the military-industrial complex in this country.*

There still is oil in that region, but the mountain of weapons has grown so high as to choke off serious economic development. Big oil companies, big defense contractors, and a wealthy Jewish community have all been heavy contributors to congressional reelection campaigns. The Gulf War was a handy training exercise for US soldiers, as the war-weary enemy guaranteed a victory with little loss of life. In fact, friendly fire killed about as many soldiers as did Iraqi troops, and the conflict generated lots of new orders for weapons.

Lapham commented:

> *The American army never had to go to the trouble of fighting a battle on the ground, and the American air force never came up against any opposition in the air. General [Norman] Schwarzkopf's forces conducted a kind of grandiose police raid. . . . But the country wanted to believe that the general had won a great and glorious victory, and the media staged a hero's welcome when he returned from the Persian Gulf in May to address a joint session of a grateful Congress. The politicians rose as one person to decorate the general with a standing ovation, and the next day on the White House lawn President Bush preened himself in the light of the general's celebrity.*[19]

Codevilla raised an interesting question.[20]

> *Perhaps the sturdiest kind of ignorance stems from disinterest. The most outstanding contemporary example is the contemporary western elites' lack of interest in religion. . . . How can anyone analyze data from the Middle East and remain ignorant of Islam? These ideas must motivate around 2/3 of all actions which run counter to the interests of the US.*

The answer is simple: There is no need for a bully to understand the motivations of the person or group being bullied. In fact, the very name Islam translates as "peace," but there may be no one in the Washington elite class who knows this. Or even cares to know, and therein lies a significant part of the tragedy of the Middle East (and September 11, 2001).

The "globocop" of the world lacked the money to put 500,000 soldiers into Saudi Arabia for several months in preparation for a ninety-six-hour "war" against Iraq; Ronald Reagan had previously spent too much. So Secretary of State James Baker made the rounds of other UN countries, hat in hand. A survey showed that 71 percent of citizens believed the US government plays the role of world policeman too frequently. In the end, selective perception again made its presence known: While Gen. Schwarzkopf basked in the hero's glow in this country the Middle East saluted Saddam Hussein as a hero for standing up to the Great Satan, and congratulated him for winning the "war." Apparently President Bush was not the only one who preened himself.

The Economist perhaps inadvertently revealed the public officials' tendency to govern by manipulating perceptions.[21]

> *America likes its enemies to look the part. In past confrontations. . . . Mr. Qaddafi wore dark glasses; that Fidel Castro and the Ayatollah Khomeini . . . [wore] beards; that Manuel Noriega was ugly. . . . Slobodan Milosevic has a brutal-sounding name, and that Radovan Karadzic is memorably hairy. . . . an enemy must not just present a clear and present threat, but a convincing image of one as well. Mr. Hussein is a demon from central casting. He has a Stalin-quality mustache; he has a Rottweiler sneer; his eyes are pure murder. . . . His name is excellent, too; the first part conjures up the damned, the second rhymes with "insane."*

Ogre du jour Osama bin Laden surely fits the mold. In a country like the United States, whose public officials emphasize personal power and empty perceptions over ideas and democracy, this overdramatized scenario is to be expected.

Terrorism is dramatic and often tragic, so it makes excellent copy for the media and tends to burnish the image of any government insider who speaks out against it. Hadar noted that

> *dividends include decisions on oil prices and military procurement and election to seats in Congress; intellectual prizes in the form of positive scores in the popular Washington war of ideas, op-ed pieces, and television news bites; and personal rewards such as professional advancement in the bureaucracy, consulting jobs, and research grants. Middle Eastern terrorism . . . has become a full-time industry for many experts and consultants.*[22]

It was shown previously that bureaucracies do not die, they only grow. Therefore, difficult as it may be for a concerned citizen to accept, here is another instance of bureaucratic growth. After the events of September 11, 2001, this must be the hottest bureaucracy in town. From the perception of the Washington elites it is counterproductive to ask what causes terrorism, discuss these causes, and arrive at a workable solution to the problem. What is truly sad is that apparently no one else asks, and so passion governs behavior.

In an accurate statement *The Economist* wrote:

> *Its economic sanctions and no-fly zones have not brought down Iraq's Saddam Hussein, but they have poured fuel on the anti-American fire. Its military bases in Saudi Arabia leave it seemingly cosy with an often brutal regime, while also offering opponents both of the West and of the Saudi royal family a useful cause. Its financial support for Israel gives it guilt by association in Arab eyes for Israel's occupation of Palestinian lands, without giving it any noticeable leverage. Its financial support for Egypt, designed originally to reward peace and establish some balance between Jews and Arabs, merely associates it with an authoritarian regime without persuading that regime to moderate the anti-western views that pervade even the state-controlled media there.*[23]

One would think that surely some rethinking is in order, but a bully sees no problems here.

Beeman's apt summary following the September 11 attacks focused attention on the root cause:

> *This event is not an isolated instance of violence. This is not an "act of war." It is one symptom of a cancer that threatens to metastasize. The root cause is not terrorist activity, as has been widely stated. It is the relationship between the US and the Islamic world. Until this central cancerous problem is treated, Americans will never be free from fear.* [24]

This argument directly suggested that the government's foreign policy has caused real fear in the populace; if it has not done this yet, it surely will.

What is especially galling is the fateful irony of the situation. Through stoking the external threat Al Qaeda has reinforced the government's argument for still more taxpayer money flung at the defense establishment. Not only this, by reacting to the terrorist acts with passion instead of reason, the world image of the United States as bully has also been reinforced. Beeman concluded: "Above all, Americans need to remember that the rest of the world has an absolute right to self-determination that is as defensible as our own. . . . If we perpetuate a cycle of hate and revenge, this conflict will escalate into a war that our great-grandchildren will be fighting."

Lack of concern for others can often cause a bully to shoot himself in the foot, as Thomas Friedman reported:

> *Congress spent its last week barring the president from signing any more free-trade agreements, barring the president from paying America's overdue UN dues—at a time when the US is trying to rally the UN to deal with Iraq—and barring the president from adding $3.5 billion to the IMF so that . . . [they] can better deal with global financial meltdowns before they hit America's shores. Both the IMF and UN payments are being held hostage by Newt Gingrich until Clinton gives in to demands of Republican anti-abortion fanatics.*[25]

The amazing inertia brought on by the cold war has been explained by the imperatives of the military-industrial complex. But recourse must be made to simple personal power seeking and holding to explain why the president of the United States still carries around the "football." (This is the term applied to the codes that when activated would launch intercontinental ballistic missiles from their silos in North Dakota, presumably aimed at the former Soviet Union.)

Even though the media persist in saying that the president has the "most powerful job in the world," the notion of "leader of the free world" has acquired a hollow ring. It would seem that retiring the man and the football would send a resounding message to the world: The cold war is in fact over, and the planet is ready for the Age of Reason.

But as Alterman showed, Washington's pundits were not ready to retire, as their principles were those of the high and powerful.[26] "Defining these principles for the powerful people who made them and the powerless people who fought and sometimes died for them was the essential business of the cold war–Washington pundit." In 1949 prominent journalist and analyst Walter Lippmann wrote, "My strongest impression is that the Russians have lost the cold war and they know it." At that time the punditocracy in Washington was just gaining its initial momentum.

Later Alterman added:

Analysts and academics . . . all published major works throughout the eighties delineating the collapsing economic position of the US and warning of the consequences of continued denial on the part of our leaders. But it was still "morning" in the punditocracy, and all opposing arguments sank from public debate without a trace.

In 1988 Paul Kennedy published a thoroughly researched book called *The Rise and Fall of the Great Powers*, which depicted the apparently inevitable fall of all the great empires of the past 500 years. Each government projected strong military power until eventually the overemphasis on the military undermined the source of its power—its economic base.

The book quickly entered both the *Washington Post* and *New York Times* best-seller lists and remained there for close to a year. The pundits gagged on it. Equally quickly, they harnessed their word processors to the task of reestablishing their personal power base. Eventually they emerged triumphant.

The end of the cold war could have been forecast by the CIA, or any one of twelve other cloak-and-dagger agencies financed by US taxpayers. The agency did not publish such a forecast, which means it did not do its job. But gathering intelligence on enemies is its reason for being, and jobs were at stake, so its members decided to hang on as long as possible. Due to inertia, personal power seeking and the notion of eternal bureaucracy the organization is still very much alive today. In 1989, the CIA reported that the economy of what was then East Germany was slightly larger than that of West Germany, and that was the year the Berlin Wall fell.

Daniel Heimbach is a Vietnam War veteran and a former Pentagon official.[27]

By leading NATO nations into the fight and sending military forces into combat, President Clinton has made Kosovo "our war." So, what should we think? . . . I think it is a monumental mistake. It violates the purpose of NATO, which was limited to defending . . . against invasion. . .. It has no clearly winnable objective. . . . What gives the president . . . moral authority to determine what citizens of another nation are allowed to fight over, and then to take NATO outside its charter to enforce? . . . As long as each side is determined to "cleanse" the other, how will a bombing campaign make them stop? For that matter, how will ground troops make determined "cleansers" stop . . . without taking independent governing control away from both sides? In my book, that's called "invasion to conquer."

Several years after the fact, most of what Heimbach argued has been borne out: No objective has been won, and the cleansers are still cleansing. Nevertheless the defense establishment liked the result, so members decided to utilize similar tactics during the next instance of foreign intervention, Afghanistan.

The only obstacle lay in veto votes in the UN Security Council, so Clinton simply ignored that organization and whipsawed NATO into backing his Kosovo caper. The fact that this armed force was being taken away from its home turf and being used to perpetrate an invasion of a sovereign country was also ignored. Also, all collateral damage (read: dead and maimed civilians) was ignored. These kinds of ignorance are not difficult for a bully; might makes right.

The nation's blind rush into war after the September 11, 2001, attacks left *The Economist* confused as to the real purpose of the war.[28]

Which are the most important of the multiple purposes of the American-led war effort in Afghanistan? Victoria Clarke, the Pentagon's chief spokeswoman, singled out two of them when she met reporters this week: "creating the conditions necessary for sustained anti-terrorist operations, and for the delivery of humanitarian aid."

Other American officials seemed to have a different emphasis: punishing the Taliban regime for its insistence on hosting Osama bin Laden and his al-Qaeda network of terror, and forcing it out of office. Others still . . . notably Colin Powell . . . focusing on something different again, though related: securing agreement on an acceptable form of government after the Taliban's removal.

Some agreement on objectives seemed necessary so that the many parts of the coalition can cooperate, but the difficult is that there is no objective on which all (or even most) can agree.

Although not publicizing their conclusion, members of the military-industrial complex are in complete agreement: Drop thousands of tons of bombs that will need to be replaced, and almost no body bags coming home. The whole thing was a replay of Kosovo.

The Economist saw fit to publish an argument by a Muslim:

Yusef al-Qaradawi, an Egyptian tele-sheikh and cleric who is a star on the Al Jazeera television network, epitomizes the moderate Arab view. He is scathing about the attack on Afghanistan, describing it as "the logic of the bully." Fighting terrorism by waging a huge war, he says, means using the same logic as the terrorists, punishing the innocent for the crimes of a few. The way to fight, he argues, is with ideas.

Were it possible for the sheikh to meet Thomas Jefferson, a citizen might believe the two men would get along very well.

Rania Masri probably disliked the Taliban as much as anyone.[29] "We recognize that it is immoral to slaughter thousands of American civilians to induce a change in US policy. It is no less immoral to kill thousands of Afghans to force the Taliban militia to change its policies." Figures for the second group of victims are not available, but a logical conclusion is that their numbers exceed those of the first group. Masri pointed out the next logical conclusion: "The insistence for respect for human life and civil liberties—at home and abroad—is the only path toward security, for us and all people on our small, interconnected planet. To achieve justice and national security, we need to employ the principles of human rights, and not the rhetoric of vengeance."

Shields not only agreed with Masri but also added a towering point:

> *From a humanitarian point of view, killing the people of Afghanistan is appalling. They lived through Soviet occupation and a war for independence; they have survived a civil war, a drought and countless attacks against civilians since the end of the Soviet era. They did not choose the Taliban; they have suffered from Taliban rule.* ***What horrible irony for the people of Afghanistan to be punished by the US for helplessly harboring the terrorists we helped to create.***[30] [emphasis added]

Her conclusion: "Bin Laden is the result of misguided US policies. New misguided US policies will create dozens, perhaps hundreds more bin Ladens." Practically no citizen will be safe.

Following the examples set in Iraq, Bosnia, and Kosovo, the government does not want the people who finance the war in Afghanistan to know what is going on over there. Perhaps officials are concerned lest the public disapprove of slaughtering thousands of civilians. Helm commented: "Reporters have been allowed only on an aircraft carrier where some bombers are based, and allowed to accompany only planes airlifting humanitarian supplies to Afghans."[31] The US Secretary of Defense Donald Rumsfeld "explained during a meeting with Washington bureau chiefs. He went out of his way to praise the media's role in a free society. . . . Then he made . . . clear that he wanted to control what information the media could have."

Helm continued: "The White House asked television networks not to air unedited videotapes of statements by Osama bin Laden and his key aides, saying the tapes could contain coded messages to his followers." Apparently the public is to hear only one side, which includes bombs striking their targets. But Soviet bombers had previously left the country a sea of rubble, so US bombs mostly just stir up the rubble along with killing civilians. (If anyone cared about informing the public, a code might be broken.)

But Helm was not yet finished. Writing in November 2001, "Last month the State Department tried unsuccessfully to prevent Voice of America . . . from broadcasting an interview with Mullah Muhammad Omar, the top Taliban leader. Department officials and conservative lawmakers said the interview would allow him to criticize the US." Perhaps officials thought that the First Amendment's protection of free speech does not apply to foreigners.

It is interesting to observe that the elite class sees no need to block publication and distribution in the United States of *The Economist.* This is a British newspaper that this book clearly indicates has an extensive editorial yen to criticize this country. The elites obviously provide ample grist for the mill, which helps fill the gap in coverage left by the US news media.

In an *Economist Survey* article of July 14, 1997, Charles Grant predicted the globalization of the defense industry as nations order missiles, warheads, and parts of these from suppliers located abroad. The whole idea is to make the world safe. But this grand idea is also a grand delusion; the future development of ever more terrible and destructive missiles and warheads will only preserve a balance of terror, in which the world's children will grow up into an adulthood plagued by passion and violence.

Today public officials manipulate information to keep the public quaking in fear. They also appeal to citizens' sense of patriotism, as Browne reported:

> *The politicians' stirring phrases . . . [suggest] heroic young men marching in parades, winning glorious battles, and bringing peace . . . to the world. But war is something quite different from that. It is your children . . . dying before they're even fully adults, or being maimed or mentally scarred for life. It is your brothers and sisters being taught to kill other people . . . and to hate people who are just like themselves and who don't want to kill anyone either. It is your children . . . limbs blown off their bodies.*[32]

Veterans of such battles are seldom interviewed by the news media, for two reasons. One is they do not want to relive the horror of their experiences, and the other is that the military-industrial complex simply does not want this kind of exposure.

Alterman referred to some of Washington's more powerful personages in his prediction:

> *Long after names like Krauthammer, Kondracke, and Kissinger have receded . . . scholars of the American past will . . . ask [why] . . . a nation so blessed with economic advantage, with such abundant natural resources, and with so sophisticated a guiding political class allowed itself to squander its national treasure and destroy the foundations of its prosperity . . . in pursuit of enemies that had long ceased to threaten it?*

A thinking citizen might wonder if persistent bullying on the part of the world's strongest nation actually serves to hasten the arrival of the Age of Reason. That is, other countries' citizens watch what is going on, think about it, and conclude there must be a better way to operate Planet Earth.

A small boy sits with his father in front of the TV. After a spirited argument the father admits to his son: "Okay. Except for low ratings, violence never solves anything."

THE UNMIGHTY SIDE OF SELECTIVE PERCEPTION

Projecting a vision and an appreciation of the other side of an issue on which a person has strong feelings is a challenge requiring thought and effort. However, a moment's reflection on the potential in terms of international relations is very likely to stimulate a thinking citizen to accept the challenge. The objective is empathy, which goes beyond sympathy for the other fellow's perception of the issue to vicariously experiencing that viewpoint along with him or her.

Tolerance is achieved through empathy, which is achieved in turn through thinking and making the effort to listen and understand the other fellow's viewpoint. This lesson is even more important today in the age of nuclear weapons.

When thinking about the "wrong" side of selective perception it becomes obvious that any **defensive** strategy employed by a have nation, such as a missile defense system, will be perceived as an **offensive** move by public officials in any potential target nation. People act on their perceptions, and so the logical reaction is to increase defensive armaments to counter a new external threat.

Because the US government has sent soldiers and weapons abroad to forty-five countries over the past fifty-five years, officials in lots of nations perceive their countries as potential targets. Most therefore perceive Star Wars as a threat. This condition is obviously great for the international weapons trafficking business, but it does little for world peace.

It looks like the so-called axis of evil is losing its punch as an external threat, so it becomes necessary for public officials to once again put their imaginations to work. They are intensively searching for a reason to continue with plans to build Star Wars. Here are six additional arguments in favor of scrapping the idea:

1. Russian nuclear weapons are deteriorating and there is no money available to maintain them;
2. In the long term there is an absolute necessity for eliminating all weapons of mass death and destruction;
3. The system has no reliable technology to support it, and a group of prominent aerospace scientists have asserted that the outlook for development of such technology is problematic;

4. There will surely be a huge and abominable waste of taxpayer money as pork is distributed throughout the nation to pay for the missile defense system;
5. Top officials in this country's allies don't want the system built; and
6. Even one of the country's most prominent cold warriors, Zbigniew Brzezinski, thinks it is a lousy idea.

Columnist Molly Ivins could not resist an opportunity to share a deep concern.[33]

> *I am informed by a source at Los Alamos that, as a rule of thumb, a defensive weapon costs at least seven times as much as an offensive weapon. That's why, in the history of warfare, it has always proved cheaper to build a lot of offensive weapons and thus overwhelm the defensive ones.*
>
> *However, there's another element to this. . . . building NMD [national missile defense] will cause China to "significantly accelerate its production of nuclear weapons beyond current plans, according to officials familiar with the document." . . . This is precisely what China and Russia have been telling us and telling us and telling us.*
>
> *You see, to them this does not look like a defensive weapon to protect us from nations formerly known as "rogue" and now known as "of concern." This looks to them like a clear case of us trying to get the capability for a first strike with no possibility of return damage, thus wiping out their nuclear deterrents, thus destabilizing the whole mess once again and setting off a fresh arms race.*

The evolution of warriors' buzzwords has now moved from Reagan's "evil empire" to "rogue nations" to "of concern," and now to "axis of evil." Apparently the citizens' state of panic needs frequent refreshment. The unmighty side sees the situation in very different terms.

The Economist wondered if the "defense" establishment's thinking has slipped a cog.[34] "The administration's broad hint that it would also understand if China—which, like America, has signed the Comprehensive Test-Ban Treaty but not ratified it—were someday to resume explosive nuclear testing. At this point America starts to look like a danger to itself." This implies that the government is granting carte blanche to China for weapons development. But the writer was far from through:

> *Mr. Bush has no intention of ratifying the test-ban treaty either. His aides argue that it does not stop new countries getting the bomb—which is the job of the Nuclear Non-Proliferation Treaty—and prevents responsible nuclear powers from ensuring the reliability of their weapons. Yet the US has other ways of checking its bomb designs. And the promise of a test ban helped win the indefinite extension of the non-proliferation treaty. If America walks away from the bargain, so can others that covet a bomb of their own. What folly for America*

to spend billions on missile defenses, while unraveling the rules which limit the weapons that may someday get through or around them.

An Iranian vice president stated that due to possession of nuclear weapons by Israel, his country was obliged to acquire them. Top US military officials argue that it is obvious that in acquiring nukes Iran has aggressive intentions. This must be true, as Iran is aiding terrorism in Israel. However, it seems that an empathetic citizen would perceive Iran's motive as helping defend fellow Muslim Palestinians against Israeli terrorism.

The vice president would immediately counter this argument by ticking off, one by one, those forty-five instances of foreign aggression perpetrated by the United States. Back would come the generals with, "Oh, but that is different!" They are right of course, in their perception. This hypothetical confrontation adequately illustrates both sides of selective perception; at the same time it argues that there can be no end to the arms race until all weapons of mass destruction are eliminated.

The navigator of the *Enola Gay*, the airplane that delivered the atomic bomb to Hiroshima that killed nearly 100,000 innocent civilians, stated that after the flight he "had a bite, a few beers, hit the sack." Furthermore, he claimed not to have lost a moment's sleep over the next forty years.

The Economist reviewed a book called *An Intimate History of Killing,* by Joanna Burke.[35] "Lieutenant William Calley seemed bewildered when he was prosecuted for organizing the massacre, accompanied by sadism and sexual violence, of about 500 unarmed civilians in the Vietnamese hamlet of My Lai in March 1968. 'I had killed, but so had a million others,' he wailed. 'It couldn't be wrong or else I would have remorse about it.'"

War understandably engenders strong negative feelings. This is the reality and the morality of war. Strong feelings become even stronger when a soldier finds his own life in danger: Passion overrules reason, and empathy has no place. But in the two instances mentioned above there was no immediate danger to life and limb, yet there was no remorse. There is an important reason for this: Were remorse a part of them, these men and "a million others" could not have wantonly killed innocent civilians.

Military trainers know this, so the training regimen must utilize brain washing to erase morality, and thus remorse after the grisly fact. Therefore the training must take away a vital part of a person's humanity. Small wonder that battle-scarred veterans often have great difficulty integrating back into a civilian society.

After World War II career politicians needed a surface rationale to present to the public who would pay the necessary continuing high price, so the Soviet Union was cast into the role of foreign bad guy. All that was needed was to misconstrue the Soviets' intention, so it was called hegemony. It was easy to fool the public, because Stalin kept his true intentions secret and growled at the West.

Having been active during the war, cloak-and-dagger agencies interested in continuing their operations leaped to feed the intrigue.

High officials in European nations readily cooperated; they looked back on a 400-year history of nearly constant warfare and concluded that the next chapter was imminent. In this way the cold war and its accompanying arms race were launched. Responsibility for the entire colossal waste of resources can logically be traced back to about 1947, when the US military was even more predominant than today over devastated armies and economies worldwide. That was the time when only a little courage was required to move the advanced world toward peace, and the rest of the world would have followed the lead. Formed in 1945, the United Nations tried to assume its rightful leadership role during the next fifty years, but career politicians in Washington would have none of it.

There is a tradition of peaceful resolution of quarrels, but the news media reveal few details due to their preoccupation with high drama and violence. Klohr commented:

> *Consider: In the past 15 years, nations comprising 1,782,000,000 people used nonviolent means to achieve major political changes beyond anyone's wildest expectations. Their opponents included dictators as ruthless as Milosevic. Going back another 40 years, more than half of the world's people have experienced major nonviolent social change. "All this in the teeth of the assertion, endlessly repeated, that nonviolence doesn't work in the real world" . . . to quote Walter Wink in his book* Engaging the Powers.[36]

Endless repetition is necessary to project error as truth, as Hitler proved so conclusively. However, public officials and others in the military-industrial complex who are gorging themselves at the public trough do not want to discourage conflict because there is practically no money for them in peace.

Klohr continued: "There are groups with at least 10 years of experience in nonviolent engagement of conflict. These include Peace Brigades International, Witness for Peace, Christian Peacemaker Teams, Peaceworkers, Quaker Peace Service." There are many more, including an organization of which many members have directly experienced the horror of war on the battlefield—Veterans for Peace.

"Every living Nobel Peace Prize laureate has signed an appeal 'for the children of the world,' designating the years 2000 to 2010 a 'decade for building a culture of nonviolence.' After much debate, the UN General Assembly unanimously approved the appeal." The groups mentioned above could provide essential resources for peace, but unless citizens demand publicity from the mass media few concerned people will be aware of them and their potential.

The Economist pointed out that Islam is a tolerant faith.[37] "Nearly all Muslims, almost all the time, lean to the softer meaning. They think of *jihad* as striving to perfect oneself." Later the writer observed: "More important, many of them are attracted by the idea of individual responsibility, the notion that each person has the right to think his or her own way through life's problems. The Muslim world, in short, may be starting to grope its way towards its own Reformation." There could be an important lesson in this for non-Muslims as they think through their life spaces and reflect on the proper role for government in the future.

In their desire to cooperate with the grand deception in Washington, today's journalists often mislead the public. Reeves wrote: "Since WWII, Americans have periodically deluded themselves into believing that because we have the power to disrupt normal life in most any part of the world, we therefore must have the power to stop or start ancient enmities we know little about . . . and that little is wrong."[38] Reeves's use of language leads the unthinking reader to believe that *we* have the power to disrupt, *we* have the power to stop or start. This predominant habit of thousands of journalists and columnists (not to single out Reeves and Ivins) suggests that in this country citizens actually have such powers, whereas the reality is that these negatively inspired powers control behavior by the government and not the citizens. Yet politicians persist in touting the wonders of democracy.

Seeing but one side of selective perception enables the government to cast any chosen country or person as despicable villain and get away with it. Retired army colonel Harry Summers pointed to the fact that the United States has "demonized" its enemies for decades. "It helps explain things to the American people. It always makes it easier to fight a war if you demonize people so that you're not killing human beings, you're killing the devil." But the flip side occasionally gets some ink: "America is the Great Satan."

A bully has poor listening ability. Several years ago, aging North Korean leader Kim Il-Sung was losing his grip on power, so he needed a strong credible external threat to regain it. He let it be known that he was developing a nuclear weapon and a missile. Right on cue the most credible external threat on earth chimed in: President Clinton flexed his mighty muscles and said that if such a weapon were fired it would be the end of Kim's country. There was apparently little thought of empathizing with Kim and his economic difficulties. Rather, the emphasis was on power seeking and an ego trip.

The explanation for terrorism may also be found in selective perception. Frank Reed spent forty-four months as a hostage in the Middle East. When questioned about sensitivities in that area of the world, he could not understand why anyone who opposes Israel is automatically labeled a terrorist. The reason may be found in policies of the news media, which reflect fifty years of lopsided US support for Israel: The Israelis are the good guys and the Arabs are bad guys. Arabs perceive those who sacrifice life and limb on behalf of their side of the issue as heroes or martyrs; Israelis are the terrorists.

The Economist provided an insight from the unmighty side:

A recent commentary in Al Ahram, an Egyptian daily, asserted that the war in Afghanistan was merely a test for the new weapons America will use to "enforce absolute sovereignty of the world at large." . . . American credibility is still so low that, in an Internet poll by the al-Jazeera TV channel, more than 80% of respondents thought the videotape released by the Pentagon which purports to show Mr. Bin Laden taking credit for the attacks on America was a fake.[39]

The US government's credibility in the eyes of its own citizens has diminished to the point where, especially when vital information is being withheld, a thinking citizen might also suspect that the tape was not genuine.

Former senator George Mitchell headed a committee whose report ties Palestinian violence directly to a long period of settlement building by Israel on occupied lands.[40]

The whole point of planting settlers in Israeli-occupied land was to make it hard ever to return this land. The settlers in Sinai were uprooted in the overwhelming interests of an Israeli-Egyptian peace treaty, but in Syria, the West Bank and Gaza they stay on, and are encouraged to multiply, even when peace with the true owners of these territories is being sought. This is a glaring contradiction that successive Israeli governments have declined to recognize. Now, to Israel's great dismay, the illogic is being hammered home to them, not by Syrians and by Palestinians, but by an American-led international committee representing a wide consensus.

During the Oslo Peace Process's seven years, the Israelis were supposed to be dismantling some settlements and consolidating others. However, the number of housing units grew by 50 percent, even though many already constructed remained empty. Shields revealed some thinking by empathic Israelis.[41]

Israel's Peace Now movement claims that, in the years since Oslo was signed, housing construction in the occupied territories increased by 52 percent, the number of Israeli settlers in occupied territories increased by 53 percent, and 740 Palestinian homes have been demolished. The Israelis imposed complete closure on the occupied territories for more than 300 days during those "peace process" years, closures that inflicted billions of dollars of losses on Palestinians.

Israeli writer Uri Avnery summed up the Israeli peace movement's view of [former Prime Minister Ehud] Barak: "While speaking about peace, he enlarged the settlements. Cut the Palestinian territories into pieces with bypass roads. Confiscated lands. Demolished homes. Uprooted trees. Paralyzed the Palestinian economy. Did not do a thing to put an end to the daily harassment of Palestinian civilians at the hundreds of army roadblocks all over the territories. Caused a huge accumulation of rage in the hearts of the Palestinians.

Conducted negotiations in which he tried to dictate to the Palestinians a peace that amounts to capitulation."

Shields went on to state:

Only in the US do we get an undiluted Israeli version of events, a narrative that makes the victims responsible for their own deaths. . . . Israelis advocating peace have long claimed that the US policy of unconditional support for Israel makes their work much harder. . . . Extremist groups . . . have until now received US aid despite their flagrant disregard of international law.

Siegman offered a rare published glimpse into the reality in the Middle East:

The real problem between Israel and the Palestinians is not the absence of a formal peace agreement. It is, rather, Israel's continued enmeshment in the daily lives of 3 million Palestinians. The late Yitzhak Rabin came to understand the need for "separation" between the two communities—a euphemism for finally getting Israel out of Palestinians' hair. . . . Israel and the US would do well to re-examine their long-held belief that Israel cannot withdraw from the west Bank and Gaza without first achieving an acceptable peace agreement. That notion, like the long-held notion that Israel cannot withdraw from Lebanon without an agreement, is false.[42]

Adams commented:

With the spirit of devotion of the Jewish people throughout the world as well as in Israel, with huge sums of financial support . . . the state of Israel should be the most prosperous country on earth. . . . The lure of their ancient homeland . . . has been overshadowed by the economic drag of the socialist policies espoused by all political parties. For the past decade, the net immigration of Jews to Israel is a minus.[43]

The government provides aid to this tiny country in the amount of $3 billion of taxpayer money annually. Shields pointed out that $1.8 billion of this is military aid.[44] "Our taxes are supplying the weapons and ammunition killing Palestinians. Solutions to this conflict cannot be accomplished as long as arms flows continue unchecked."

It will surprise some citizens to learn that Israel's lack of economic progress is due in large part to this aid money. This is not a paradox when people realize that this massive foreign infusion enables the government to continue its socialist policies, instead of permitting its citizens the freedom to develop the economy through risking capital and sweat in a free marketplace. Instead of promoting democracy, part of that $3 billion is subsidizing socialism.

Were the spigot turned off, both Israelis and Palestinians would benefit greatly because this would force the Israeli government to negotiate an end to the conflict under the guidance of UN Resolution 242 (trading captured land for peace) and on even terms with the Palestinians. Terrorism there would soon fade away, to be replaced by peaceful coexistence. Then the US government would need only to kick the oil habit by cutting off taxpayer subsidies to big oil, stopping shipments of weapons into the region, and cooperating with local citizens in getting rid of those already there. Eventually free trade would cause Arabs and Jews to come together for their mutual benefit. (Admittedly, this would require effective leadership and some time.)

Conflict only destroys, as it appeals to the negatives hidden in human nature, whereas commerce builds. This fact points to other serious mistakes by Israel. Ariel Sharon's high-profile visit in fall 2000 to the Temple Mount in Jerusalem was clearly done with malice aforethought. But this provocation will be erased in the memories of Palestinians and the world by the horror of the massacres in the Shatila and Jenin refugee camps.

The Economist reported on the feelings of those on the unmighty side: "Also in much of Europe, the uneven battles on the West Bank have encouraged demonstrators to burn the American flag on the streets, alongside the flag of Israel. But even before those battles, European politicians were lining up to denounce Mr. Bush's 'simplistic' foreign policy and deplore America's preponderance in the world."[45]

This newspaper stated that America was not responsible for the fighting, but this is incorrect. Weapons drive conflict, as was demonstrated in Chapter 20, and since 1948 the United States has poured millions of tons of weapons into Israel. Part of this outpouring enabled that country to respond with such fury to the Six-Day War in 1967 that it captured practically all of the land occupied by Palestinians outside neighboring countries. Not only this, Israel built hundreds of settlements with the clear intention of never giving back Palestinian land. There are around eight to ten Palestinians for each Israeli. Without weapons the Israelis and their government would have been required to maintain peace and tolerance of their neighbors in the interest of their own survival.

The Economist further observed, "In most of the world, ***but not America*** [emphasis added], pictures of the bulldozed Jenin refugee camp plaster the front pages. To an extent that Americans do not realize, being blamed for Israel's actions is ripping up the coalition Mr. Bush took such pains to knit together last September." Israeli soldiers denied wounded women, children, and elderly access to medical help. Many died slowly of their wounds.

Sadly, this is not the end of the story. "Some will cite the events there as evidence of the hypocrisy of a West which wants Serbia, as the price for economic aid, to co-operate with a war-crimes tribunal whose jurisdiction covers the 'wanton destruction of cities, towns or villages.'" A thinking citizen must wonder how the president can explain this one to the world.

When elder President Bush decided to fight a war in Iraq, he asked Germany and Japan to contribute soldiers, in part so that the operation would look more like a UN conflict instead of a purely US one. But officials in these governments explained to him that forty-five years earlier the US government had forced constitutions on the defeated Germans and Japanese that forbade them from deploying any soldiers beyond the borders of their countries (the US Constitution does not authorize this practice either). Germany and Japan could fight strictly to defend their homelands, but could not go offshore with their armies. In terms of selective perception, these two countries had formerly been listed among the bad guys and forty-five years later they were good guys, but apparently only in a limited sense.

Even in Iraq, with the media's demonization of Saddam Hussein, selective perception had its place. At the end of the war a medical team predicted that hundreds of thousands of children and old people would die as a result of stringent economic sanctions imposed by the United Nations. To date this prediction has been exceeded: half a million to a million have died and malnourished children are legion.

Markatos made a point concerning the continuing bombing:

> *[The] main accomplishment would be to squeeze several billion dollars more out of US taxpayers. Anyone who has thought about the suffering caused in Oklahoma City by a single bomb can see what a profane and despicable act it would be to heap additional suffering upon the people of Iraq. In this post cold war world, our biggest challenge . . . could be to learn how to restrain certain unilateral actions of our own government.*[46]

The United Nations imposed the sanctions, but the bombing is being carried out mostly by the United States.

Now it looks very much like younger President Bush will order the armed forces to have another go at Iraq. Shields was not happy with this prospect:

> *The notion that Iraq is a threat because it has weapons of mass destruction. Israel also has nuclear capabilities, but the US does not publicly pressure the Israelis to dismantle their arsenal. The argument that Iraq is a greater threat to the region does not pass muster with most Arabs, who can point to a long history of Israeli military attacks against Arab civilians.*[47]

The United States gave or sold nukes and tons of other devastating weapons to Israel, but the government apparently cannot abide the idea that Saddam Hussein has **any** kind of weapons of mass destruction. Sure, the government contends that he has used such weapons to kill not just Iranian soldiers but also thousands of innocent Kurds. But the Israelis have done similar mayhem to their own citizens (Arab Israelis), and when Palestinian deaths are included, about an equal amount of blood lies on their government's hands as on those of Iraq's ruler.

The Arab perception of the long-standing policy in the Middle East of trampling on Arab sensitivities came into stark focus when a bomb exploded on a US military base in Saudi Arabia and killed many soldiers. *The Economist*: "People speak . . . of a pax Americana; the US threw Iraq out of Kuwait; stayed on to protect the gulf states from Iraqi and Iranian troublemaking; guided Israel and the Arab states into, or towards, peace. But now, in Saudi Arabia, the kindly hand has been savagely bitten."[48] This report dramatically illustrates the lack of ability to empathize with the other side; from that perspective a "kindly hand" is a huge fist. A bully feels no need to investigate this matter, except to identify, hunt down, and punish the bombers.

The bully acted predictably when a sex scandal threatened his credibility and reputation. Clinton needed to distract his citizens from the scandal and to attempt to bolster his tattered leadership credentials. At the same time Hussein needed to solidify his position of leadership as his people starved. So Clinton and Hussein both needed a foreign ogre. Therefore the two men joined in service to a mutual need; they had by circuitous routes come to depend on one another.

The government's failure to anticipate the Kosovo tragedy was not surprising; this has been and is policy (to the extent that a foreign policy exists). The elites in the military-industrial complex wanted war to break out. This gave the military the exercise that it needed to remain in top fighting trim. More important, it used up expensive bombs and missiles.

The conflict generated a demand for more of these killing machines back home, and with practically no risk that any of them or any others would be thrown at or dropped on the United States. Ever since World War II, making weapons has been the bread and butter of the military-industrial complex; recently members have taken to slathering on the butter in great profusion.

That those bombs and missiles rained hell on innocent people seemed not to have entered the thinking of the elites in the oligarchy. The news media called the killing "collateral damage," presumably to distract members of their audiences from thinking about this indiscriminate slaughter.

Clinton explained that the bombing was intended to keep the conflict from blowing up and destabilizing small and poor neighboring countries due to large influxes of refugees. But the bombing caused these massive influxes. Citizens in the United States and elsewhere were supposed to believe that seventy-eight days of bombing would make peace in Kosovo, which lies in a region of the world that has been wracked by interethnic conflict for seven centuries.

At one point Clinton compared Milosevic's Serbia to Hitler's Germany. This careless remark rallied the Serbs around Milosevic, just when his leadership position was weakening. The external threat theory still works.

But this was most probably not careless rhetoric; more likely, it was by design. (Clinton may have been weak in many areas, but in designs he was well stocked.) The idea was to ramp up the war to maximize the use of weapons. This in turn ramped up the demand for replacements and for labor to make them. Taxpayer money was spent to keep lucrative jobs going in defense plants and hence votes, and also to provide lush kickbacks for congressional reelection war chests.

As policy this scheme will continue to work as long as the real agenda is kept hidden. If the public had realized that their tax money was being spent to kill innocent people and destroy an economy they would have put a stop to that lunacy. There was this danger, which was one reason why the whole catastrophe had to be pulled off quickly. It can credibly be argued that Milosevic is a bad guy. But imposing a bigger bully atop a smaller one only adds fuel to the fire.

The action to expand NATO right up to Russia's border through the addition of former Soviet satellite nations Poland, Hungary, and the Czech Republic has been severely criticized. During the cold war citizens of these countries existed primarily through gritting their teeth and bearing an oppressive regime. To maximize the oppression the Soviets needed a bad guy to keep the citizens in a constant state of panic, and the West conveniently provided one. Therefore it is interesting to observe their reactions as new members of NATO to that organization's bombing campaign against Kosovo.

First, the secretary-general of NATO criticized the Czech ambassador because his government tried to dissociate itself from the campaign. Then the Hungarian foreign minister said, "It would be unthinkable for Hungary to supply troops for a NATO ground offensive in Kosovo." After forty-five years on the other side these countries are today considered good guys, but they were apparently reluctant to blindly join other presumably good guys in attacking a sovereign nation. They had been there, and recently. (Soviet armies moved into Czechoslovakia in 1968, and into Hungary in 1956.)

In spite of several years of attempts by Russia and the West to unite in common interests Russians noted the advance of NATO, which was organized in 1947 only to defend against attack by the Soviet Union. They logically concluded that they are still considered bad guys. Jack Matlock is a former ambassador to the Soviet Union.[49]

> *The negative reaction in Russia to NATO's attack was predictable. After all, we had assured Russia during the debate on NATO enlargement that there was nothing to fear. NATO, we said, was a purely defensive alliance, constitutionally incapable of taking offensive military action. (We had earlier given Mikhail Gorbachev to understand that NATO's borders would not be moved further east if Germany were allowed to unite and stay in NATO.)*

Diplomacy aims to build mutual trust between nations.

For fifty years Russians and their government had perceived NATO as a terrible external threat. When it decided to come closer, even after the cold war, they found it difficult to immediately erase a perception of fifty years' duration. It was also very disturbing to have NATO renege on its promises. "Nothing to fear" must have been (selectively) perceived by Russians as empty rhetoric (which must be utilized frequently by officials in any country without an empathetic foreign policy).

Thomas Friedman interviewed fifty-year Russia expert George Kennan, still possessing a sharp mind at age ninety-four.[50] "'I think it is the beginning of a new Cold War,' said Kennan. . . . I think the Russians will gradually react quite adversely and it will affect their policies. I think it is a tragic mistake. . . . No one was threatening anybody else. . . . What bothers me is how superficial and ill-informed the whole Senate debate was.'"

Members of that august body saw no need for serious debate; a bully never does. Furthermore a genuine debate would have risked revealing the hollow reasoning which went into the decision to expand NATO, and this would have been embarrassing. Therefore the debate was only a showcase.

Kennan continued: "I was particularly bothered by the references to Russia as a country dying to attack Western Europe. Don't people understand? Our differences in the Cold War were with the Soviet Communist regime. And now we are turning our backs on the very people who mounted the greatest bloodless revolution in history to remove that Soviet regime." This is the same country that sacrificed 26 million lives during World War II, so that Western Europeans and other peoples and their progeny could live their future lives free from Hitler's Gestapo. At the end of the interview, Kennan said, "This has been my life, and it pains me to see it so screwed up in the end."

At this point taxpayers must believe they have been relegated to the wrong side of selective perception as they continue to be forced to pay for one baseless foreign conflict after another. Top brass in the army, navy, air force, and marines continue to carry on their traditional battles for larger pieces of the money pie, an ever larger portion of which must pay for bands of detectives constantly searching for the next enemy. These men spent their careers preparing to fight the Soviets, and after the cold war they probably felt cheated. Taxpayers must have similar feelings, although for different reasons.

Haque also joined in sounding the alarm: "Contrary to President Bush's assurances that America is not at war with Islam, the relentless bombing of Afghanistan is creating precisely that impression among many Muslims. And by no means is this the end of it. The American public slowly is being prepared for similar campaigns in Iraq, Somalia, Sudan, Kashmir, Palestine, and other places."[51] The writer might have embellished by naming so many places. But only a glance at the postwar record of foreign adventurism would convince a reader otherwise; Haque was only extrapolating a grisly past record into the future.

"America's overwhelming military response is bound to create more enemies in the future. This is a repeat of the same failed foreign policy Washington has pursued in the past, only now it has become markedly more belligerent. How long can the US deny that its own policies are partially to blame for this mess?"

In 1999, there occurred discussion aimed at determining where to wage the next war. Secretary of State Madeleine Albright published a paper entitled "Colombia's Struggles and How We Can Help: Supporting a Troubled Nation Means More than Drug Interdiction." President Clinton diverted $1.6 billion of taxpayer money to that country, in addition to about half a billion previously earmarked.

Albright's inference is about 2 percent correct; officials in Colombia's government would like to have done with a thirty-five-year insurrection. The other ninety-eight percent of Colombians would much rather live their lives in peace. They have learned over the years to hate war, but the news media have reported practically nothing about these feelings. However, there was coverage of US troops entering the country under the guise of stopping the flow of drugs into this country.

A couple of thoughts on the current direction of foreign policy cause consternation. The policy of unilateral foreign adventurism has been given increased legitimacy by Al Qaeda. At this point the administration and Pentagon need only say of any particular country: "It is believed to be harboring terrorists" or "It has links to Al Qaeda" and the UN-built diplomatic gate protecting this country from foreign intervention swings wide open. Put another way, suddenly and conveniently it is open season for additional US aggression. The end result is predictable: creation of hundreds of additional terrorists, increased foreign intervention, and a vicious circle of death, destruction, and misery.

If continued, this policy will create many more Osama bin Ladens. The inescapable conclusion is that any war on terrorism is unwinnable. Proof of this grisly outlook is arguably present today in Israel: Violence only begets more of same.

The next thought examines interior abilities to preempt and defend against this increase in terrorism. Here the outlook is equally dark. The FBI and other internal security agencies are largely bloated and stale and thus incompetent, as was amply demonstrated by their utter failure to anticipate and prevent the attacks of September 11, 2001. This operation was very elaborate, took many months to prepare, and involved detailed planning with perhaps hundreds of people. To summarize, the government has embarked on an extremely dangerous unilateral foreign policy. Not only do very few other countries approve of it, the policy puts citizens of this country into harm's way.

Sun Yatsen was an academic who organized the peaceful end to the last Chinese dynasty, the Qing, in 1911. One of his conclusions is offered here: "Well-organized nations count votes out of ballot boxes. Badly organized nations count bodies, dead ones, on the battlefields."

One Nation a Citizen among Many

On an individual basis a citizen owes allegiance to his or her nation and is lawfully entitled to protection from force that comes from afar. A person is a free, governing member of the nation, with the right to participate in the legislative and judicial functions of government through voting, engaging in discussions and debates and holding public office. He has either a direct or an indirect influence on how he and fellow citizens live and are governed. He lives by natural law with its basic human rights and by civil rights, which are his to the extent that in their implementation he does not infringe on the basic rights of another citizen.

The logical question then arises: Can nations live and be governed in this manner? The answer is yes, provided that every nation who is a member of a supranational group is willing to give up a specified degree of sovereignty that is through discussion and collective wisdom deemed necessary for the group to function effectively. In this country an analogy has citizens in a community giving up some of their sovereignty so that their state government can function effectively, and ditto at the national level.

This book has argued that the amount of sovereignty given up should be minimal and carefully measured, and constant vigilance should operate to ensure that what is handed to the larger span of government is not abused in its use. The term "span" is used here to avoid the assumption that just because a level of government serves a larger population it must be larger in size than a government covering a smaller population. It is important to question this assumption.

Tocqueville understood a democratic nation's role in the world even in 1830, long before there existed international alliances based on anything besides warfare.[52]

> *Do you set out to organize a nation so that it will have a powerful influence over all others? Do you expect it to attempt great enterprises and, whatever be the result of its efforts, to leave a great mark on history? If in your view that should be the main object of men in society, do not support democratic government; it surely will not lead you to that goal.*

The inference is that great enterprises can and should surely be attempted, but not by nations, because such actions would be sure to arouse envy, suspicion, and fear among others. These reactions are based on the negative components of human nature, and the grim results have been amply demonstrated.

Such great enterprises should be attempted by individuals, who will recruit the assistance of other people when needed. This is the impetus under which companies, foundations, religious entities, and other organizations are formed. The preferred way has individuals **voluntarily** banding together in a common interest, and it works as well in the quest for good government. As time passes, just as companies join with and separate from other companies and other organizations find it in their shared interest to merge or separate, so it can be with individual nations. All are groups of people.

There is a difference, however. In the private sector companies are formed, live, expand, wither, and die, but national governments last much longer. Therefore any world organization in which a nation wishes to actively participate as a citizen must be kept fluid and dynamic.

But then, so it is with democracy. Because democracy is free choice a country may also freely choose to leave the organization if its citizens see advantage in doing so. (If many nations leave, that says something important about how the organization is performing the job of governing.) Conditions of free choice and citizen assent to a minimum of coercive laws suggest that the Age of Reason has arrived.

The United States as a world citizen would feel and act as a warm and caring "person," anxious to participate in a shared and peaceful interest in improving humanity worldwide. People in other nations would be grateful, and they would encourage their governments to look for opportunities to return favors freely given. No one would keep score.

In this way mutual trust, tolerance of differences, and outreaching friendship would be established, maintained, and enhanced. Individual citizens as representatives to the world body would actively participate in discussions, criticisms, and debates and, having been heard, they would be more willing to accept decisions that do not go their way. Deliberations in the assembly hall would replace bombs and missiles in killing fields.

Efforts in this direction are under way, as are predictable responses: the Age of Reason has not yet been sold to public officials. President Clinton signed a treaty creating an International Criminal Court, whose task would be to seek out designated world criminals and bring them to justice. But he knew Congress would not ratify the treaty. Why? *The Economist* explained:

> *America's allies, including most NATO members, decided that such a body would be too open to political manipulation. They opted for a court largely independent of the Security Council, with universal jurisdiction and its own decision-making power. America balked at this, and then tried to win for its citizens an absolute exemption . . . its troops might be subject to prosecution.*[53]

This stance is tantamount to an admission that the administration orders armed forces to ignore human rights among citizens of foreign nations that they attack. If every nation in its guise as world citizen acted in this manner there could be no treaty.

The Economist continued: "Some 27 countries have ratified the treaty and others, including Britain, are due to join them in the next few months. Once 60 countries have ratified, the court will be born, despite America's best efforts."

Top officials know how much of the rest of the world feels about the long history of the United States government bullying other countries. Here comes an apparent opportunity for others to sets things right, hence US officials' reluctance to move forward. Many young men and women might be deterred from joining the military if they fear that following bullying orders from the top would result in their incarceration. It is interesting to observe that thinking young people might forcibly reduce the current oversized military, and this would indirectly expedite the arrival of the Age of Reason.

There would be differences of opinion, but the democratic process is far superior to conflict as a resolving influence. Chapter 16 discussed the importance of keeping separate the idea from the persona of its maker and advocate; this principle would guide discussion in the world arena as well. Of equal importance would be tolerance, because this assembly would be a forum where people of every hue and belief gather together. Empathy would play a vital role.

Colin Powell was a general and chair of the Joint Chiefs of Staff when Saddam Hussein moved his soldiers into Kuwait. He opposed the proposal of a Gulf War, suggesting sanctions instead. Were such sanctions imposed by a revamped United Nations (see next chapter) and not just by a couple of nations, they would have been far more effective. In 1995 Powell disapproved of bombing the Serbs: "Nobody really thinks (the West) has a vital interest (in Bosnia)."

Today Powell is Secretary of State. His attitude toward indiscriminate use of armed conflict to solve international disputes seems to tie in closely with the coming of the Age of Reason. Furthermore, he is in a position to exert some influence in this desirable direction.

Plato said,

> *The creation of the world is the victory of persuasion over force. . . . Civilization is the maintenance of the social order, by its own inherent persuasiveness as embodying the nobler alternative. The recourse to force, however unavoidable, is a disclosure of the failure of civilization, either in the general society or in a remnant of individuals.*

The United States was founded on the principle of persuasion in government. At the time the government was popularly referred to as the grand experiment, because nothing closely resembling its configuration had ever before been attempted. Much has changed since then.

Skousen noted: "Too often lawmakers resort to the use of force rather than the power of persuasion to solve a problem in society."[54] For public officials this method is much easier, provided that the necessary muscle to force public cooperation be kept near at hand. "They are too quick to pass another statute or regulation in an effort to suppress the effects of a deep-rooted problem in society rather than seeking to recognize and deal with the real cause . . . which may require parents, teachers, pastors, and community leaders to convince people to change their ways." It's easier to crack heads than ideas.

Public officials say, "People are not willing to pay for services themselves," so they force other citizens to pay for them. There is seldom any inquiry concerning whether citizens want government to provide certain services; rather, they just go ahead. Skousen pointed out that attitudes toward the different races cannot be changed through legislation. What increases tolerance of minorities is members of those groups improving their status through individual efforts.

> *Is competition from the Japanese, Germans and the Brazilians too stiff for American industry? . . . Just impose import quotas or heavy duties on foreign products and force them to "play fair." Is the use of mind-altering drugs a problem in America? Then let's pass legislation prohibiting the use. . . . People still want to use them? Then let's hire more police. . . . Surely that will solve the problem. Yet such laws never address the fundamental issue.*

They do address the fundamental issue, but only for lawmakers—votes.

> *Abortion is a troublesome issue. . . . So, for many conservatives the answer is simple: Ban abortions! Force women to give birth to their unexpected and unwanted babies. That will solve the problem. . . . We can solve the murder and crime problem in this country, they reason, simply by passing a law taking away the weapons of murder. No guns, no killings. Simple, right? Yet they only change the outward symptoms, while showing little interest in finding ways to discourage a person from becoming a criminal or violent in the first place.*

Rose Wilder Lane argued that passing a top-down law will not stop a particular human activity.

Skousen next argued from a different perspective. "There is little satisfaction from doing good if individuals are mandated to do the right thing. Character and responsibility are built when people **voluntarily** [emphasis added] choose right over wrong, not when they are forced to do so." The clear inference here is that force prevents people from maturing into fully functioning adults, as explained in Chapter 6. "As Sir James Russell Lowell said, 'The ultimate result of protecting fools from their folly is to fill the planet full of fools.'"

Skousen completed his interesting treatise: "I have a vision of world peace, not because the military have been called in to maintain order, but because we have peace from within and friendship with every nation." Concerned citizens of the world have been envisioning world peace for centuries; today the Age of Reason is at long last a real and attainable goal. There are but two requirements: truth in mind and courage of heart.

The reality today is that many warriors are still around even though the cold war is long over. A true leader in the White House would find a way to thank them for prior service and sacrifice dutifully rendered, and would wish them a pleasant retirement. A leader would not allow the military-industrial complex to run foreign policy; President Truman fired Gen. Douglas MacArthur when he tried to do this.

Career politicians often miss the whole point of free world trade, primarily because there is little money in it for them. As Winston Churchill argued, it is not a game, a battle, or a war.

> *Both the selling and the buying . . . were profitable to us; that what we sold . . . [gave us] profit . . . what we bought . . . [was] worth our while to buy, and . . . turn it to advantage. And in this way commerce is utterly different from war, so that the ideas . . . of the one should never be applied to the other; for in war both sides lose whoever wins the victory, but the transactions of trade, like the quality of mercy, are twice blessed, and confer a benefit on both parties.*

Few people, no matter where they live or whatever their work, fully realize that war is a lose-lose proposition, whereas free trade is a win-win proposition. Awareness is the key: Increase this sufficiently, add a generous measure of courage, and the pen would become even more mightier than the sword.

Churchill's observations are interesting, coming from a man who waged an all-out war in Europe. President Eisenhower was a career soldier, but he also had the wisdom to see the truth. Alsop commented on a similar insight possessed by Ike.[55]

> *Great reductions in the country's defense outlays were made. In taking a more cautious approach to military commitment and expenditure, the president, it is fair to say, viewed the effect of high budget deficits on the economy—and their potential, as he put it, to "destroy what we are attempting to defend"—to be of more importance than any immediate military threat posed to the US and her allies by the Soviet Union.*

Alsop himself disagreed with his president's position on this issue.

The debate continued, as Hadar observed: ". . . debate between those who advocated shifting economic resources from the military to the civilian sector so America could compete more effectively with Europe and Japan in the international market and those who supported a continued US global military role."[56] Today there is little room for debate. Members of Congress choose not to listen as they order the construction of more expensive weapons, which the Pentagon has said it does not want.

The nation has for years had a deficit in its balance of international payments: More money is going overseas than coming into the country. Were the military to retire, economic resources and expertise thus made available to the private sector would erase the deficit in quick order.

The US and other nations can sign as many arms control treaties such as NPTs, MTCRs, STARTs, and so on as they want. The officials who sign them are world "leaders," and they are mostly the same ones who have been stoking the arms race for fifty years. In the coming open society there will be no secrets except in some parts of personal finance, the voting booth, and the bedroom (Chapter 14). Therefore with the requisite political will it would be possible to rid the world of all weapons of mass death and destruction. It remains only that control be handed over to the taxpayers who are today forced to finance wars.

There is today a golden opportunity for the government to behave like a world leader instead of a bully. By seizing the initiative in seeking a total elimination of all weapons the United States would be leading, and would be perceived by other countries as leading, in the right direction. It is in the nature of people to cooperate in a worthwhile effort, and this one is surely worthwhile, especially when the alternative is considered. Citizens reclaiming their government would constitute an impressive additional benefit.

Furthermore, it is well known that democracies practically never shoot at each other. Chapter 20 demonstrated that to wage war concentration of personal power in large, strong central government institutions is necessary. Democracies work at dispersing power.

Officials in the government of every member country in the United Nations would be under great pressure to follow the lead. This pressure would come primarily from their own citizens, millions of whom have suffered on the unmighty side of selective perception. No rational person truly wants to fire a nuclear missile. These would be first to go, and elimination of other weapons would follow in time. (It is intriguing to speculate whether eliminating the international arms race would bring about elimination of arms races in inner cities.)

The open sore on the Korean peninsula that has festered for fifty years would heal quickly if the US government were to remove its soldiers and close their bases. Their presence has always evoked fear and resentment among officials in the North Korean government. Bases on Japanese, German, Italian, Spanish, Saudi Arabian, and other lands are tolerated through clenched teeth. Few citizens realize how many of these bases they are paying for, and there is surely no need for them after the cold war. Add the impacts of all these bases together and it is obvious that a lot of fear and resentment has been generated over the past several decades.

No one can make war in the name of peace and expect peace on earth and goodwill to all. Nuclear weapons have made big wars no longer feasible. Many examples have proven that small wars have no end, as guerrillas take to the hills with their portable weapons and subsist on the sympathies of local people. Desire for revenge pervades every breath they draw; passion rules their lives. Theirs is a miserable existence. The inescapable conclusion is that armed conflict cannot settle any disputes, international or domestic.

There is momentum today toward an economic world in the Age of Reason. Many supranational organizations are based on trade, such as the World Trade Organization, the North American Free Trade Association, MERCOSUR (an economic union of several South American nations), Association of Southeast Asian Nations, the European Union, and others. With greater support from the United States as leader and world citizen, these groups would flourish.

The doctrine of separation of church and state was a good idea in colonial times, as leaders of that time thought back to a long period when some of history's most horrible conflicts were fought due to different perceptions of how God (or gods) should be worshiped. Since then there has evolved a long secular trend, so that during the Age of Reason there is much less urgency attached to this separation.

There should be no reason why people cannot pray at public functions, such as sporting events or in schools. There will also be no further need for public officials in the courts to continue their strict interpretation of this issue, especially as the reality is that the only contemporary motivation for doing so is to fragment the society. Each community can formulate its own policy in this matter.

Lincoln said, "Let us have faith that **right makes might**, and in that faith, let us, to the end, dare to do our duty as we understand it." [emphasis added]

Governments make war. Only citizens can make and keep the peace.

Notes

1. Thomas Paine, *Rights of Man*. Knopf, 1915.
2. James Madison, *Federalist Paper* No. 10, *The Federalist Papers*. Mentor, 1961.
3. Charles Adams, *For Good and Evil: The Impact of Taxes on the Course of Civilization*. Madison Books, 1993.
4. Alexis de Tocqueville, *Democracy in America*, Knopf, 1972.
5. *The Economist*, "More Bribes for North Korea?" September 23, 2000, p. 24.
6. *The Economist*, "Wars of Intervention." January 6, 2001, p. 19.
7. David McCullough, *John Adams*. Simon and Schuster 2001.
8. Charles Krauthammer, "A Welcome End to Arms Control." *News and Observer* [Raleigh, NC], May 6, 2001, p. 33A.
9. *The Economist*, "Fission and Confusion." March 16, 2002, p. 15; and "What's New?" p. 35.
10. *The Economist*, "Don't Even Think about It." October 6, 2001, p. 33; and "The Defense Industry's New Look." p. 57.
11. Doug Bandow, "Why Pay to Defend an Empire?" *News and Observer*, July 9, 1996, p. 9A.
12. Walter Isaacson, *Kissinger: A Biography*. Simon and Schuster, 1992.

13. Paul Kennedy (ed.), *Grand Strategies in War and Peace.* Yale University Press, 1991.
14. *The Economist*, "Arm-Twisting in Latin America." March 29, 1997, p. 17.
15. Eduard Shevardnadze, *The Future Belongs to Freedom.* Free Press, 1991.
16. *The Economist*, "Your Friendly Neighborhood Arms Dealer." August 23, 1997, p. 25.
17. James, D. Barber, *The Book of Democracy.* Prentice Hall, 1995.
18. Leon T. Hadar, *Quagmire: America in the Middle East.* Cato Institute, 1992.
19. Lewis H. Lapham, *The Wish for Kings: Democracy at Bay.* Grove Press. 1993.
20. Angelo Codevilla, *Informing Statecraft: Intelligence for a New Century.* Free Press, 1992.
21. *The Economist*, "America's Demons." November 22, 1997, p. 34.
22. Hadar, *Quagmire.*
23. *The Economist*, "The Patient Accumulation of Successes." December 22, 2001, p. 9.
24. William O. Beeman, "Who He Is, and What he Wants," *News and Observer*, September 16, 2001, p. 33A.
25. Thomas L. Friedman, "Wise Up to the Economic Domino Theory." *News and Observer*, November 18, 1997, p. 11A.
26. Eric Alterman, *Sound and Fury: The Washington Punditocracy and the Collapse of American Politics.* Harper Collins, 1992.
27. Daniel R. Heimbach, "NATO's Unjust Balkan War." *News and Observer*, April 30, 1999, p. 23A.
28. *The Economist*, "Nation-Bruising, Nation-Building." October 20, 2001, p. 15; and "Uneasier, But Not Yet Explosive." p. 17.
29. Rania Masri, "Lead by Example; Let Law Rule." *News and Observer*, October 7, 2001, p. 25A.
30. Sarah Shields, "They're Bad—But War Isn't the Best Response." *News and Observer*, September 30, 2001, p. 31A.
31. Mark Helm, "Is it Your Right to Know?" *News and Observer*, October 28, 2001, p. 23A.
32. Harry Browne, *Why Government Doesn't Work.* St. Martin's Press, 1995.
33. Molly Ivins, "Firing Up a Renewed Arms Race." *News and Observer*, August 2000 column.
34. *The Economist*, "Defense Folly." September 8, 2001, p. 12.
35. *The Economist Survey*, "The Morality of Warfare: Is Closer Necessarily Worse?" July 17, 1999, p. 4.
36. Leo Klohr, "Instead of Peacekeeping, Try Peacemaking." *News and Observer*, May 7, 1999, p. 23A.
37. *The Economist*, "Enemies Within, Enemies Without." September 22, 2001, p. 20.

38. Richard Reeves, "Uncle Sam—Tempted Again by the World's Trouble Spots." *News and Observer,* January 1999 column.
39. *The Economist,* "The Liberals' Hour." December 22, 2001, p. 12.
40. *The Economist,* "Stop Building, Please." May 12, 2001, p. 15.
41. Sarah Shields, "Fundamentally Unfair to Palestinians." *News and Observer,* February 11, 2001, p. 29A.
42. Henry Siegman, "A State to End Mideast Stalemate." *News and Observer,* October 2000 column.
43. Adams, *For Good and Evil.*
44. Sarah Shields, "Aiding Israel's Excessive Force." *News and Observer,* October 5, 2000, p. 21A.
45. *The Economist,* "Friendly Fire." April 20, 2002, p. 9; and "Israel's 'War Crime.'" p. 10.
46. Jerry Markatos, "Don't Let Arms Sales Shove Us into War." *News and Observer,* February 5, 1998, p. 17A.
47. Shields, "Aiding Israel's Excessive Force."
48. *The Economist,* "The Bombing of Arabia." June 29, 1996, p. 39.
49. Jack Matlock, "Moscow is on the Road to Peace." April 1999 column.
50. Thomas L. Friedman, "And This Is Russia's Reward." *News and Observer,* May 6, 1998, p. 11A.
51. Ekram Haque, "Thwarting Islamic Aspirations." *News and Observer,* December 2, 2001, p. 31A.
52. Tocqueville, *Democracy in America.*
53. *The Economist,* "Sign On, Opt Out." January 6, 2001, p. 28.
54. Mark Skousen, "Persuasion Versus Force." 1997 pamphlet.
55. Joseph W. Alsop, *I've Seen the Best of It.* Norton, 1992.
56. Hadar, *Quagmire.*

Chapter Twenty-Two:
On the Old United Nations Becoming a New One for the Age of Reason

If a diplomat says yes he means maybe; if he says maybe he means no; but if he says no he is no diplomat.

—Author unknown

All too often a successful personal power seeker occupies the top position in a nation's government. This is a tribute, of sorts, to the negative tug of human nature. Once in power another negative influences his or her behavior: This is the fact that every human being occasionally takes offense at some event or remark uttered by another. Whenever this happens, passion dominates and displaces reason as the governor of behavior. Combine these tendencies with the presence and control of vast quantities of weapons of mass death and destruction, and the result is as tragic as it is predictable.

The above paragraph presents a summary of the motivations that originally brought on the age of conquest and plunder several centuries ago. A study of world history beginning with the Crusades in the eleventh century suggests that the entire age consisted of continuous wars and little else. There were a lot of wars, but historians tend to exaggerate their importance because few people could write during those times, and kings hired those who could to record their exploits on the battlefield. Therefore there exist few records of peace and tranquillity.

The twentieth century has seen development of weapons of such awesome destructive power as to be all but incomprehensible. With this trend has occurred a growth in the personal power of the warriors who supervise weapons development. As Alexander Hamilton warned over 200 years ago, the military mentality has become conventional wisdom. He predicted that citizens would gradually come to accept this situation and would go on paying for it without asking any questions. Especially in the United States, the military-industrial complex is slowly displacing economic development as a primary emphasis in the culture.

But the unavoidable conclusion is that weapons development and warfare cannot continue indefinitely, lest the world dissolve in flames and a mushroom cloud. However, generals and admirals who cut their teeth on warfare and preparation for the same and who have spent their careers in these occupations are understandably reluctant to admit that their services are no longer needed.

A new and different age must evolve; there is no other alternative. The end of the cold war in 1989 opened wide the door to a new age, but so far outmoded conventional wisdom has prevailed. This chapter continues to question this wisdom as it applies to roles of the United Nations in world politics and economics.

THE UNITED NATIONS' FIRST FIFTY YEARS

During World War II, President Roosevelt found time to think about a world after its end. He had seen the formation of the League of Nations after World War I and had shared people's disappointment when the United States did not join the organization. This time would be different.

Roosevelt had a vision, but it did not include the Age of Reason. Rather, he saw a United Nations with several policemen: big countries with awesome military power who would squelch incipient conflicts as they arose. (Perhaps it was fortunate that he did not live to see the formation of the new organization.) Foreign ministers of nations met at Dumbarton Oaks, outside Washington, D.C., in 1945 and agreed on a configuration that resembled democratic governments in several of these countries: a legislative General Assembly, an executive Secretariat (Security Council), and an international Court of Justice. A second meeting took place in San Francisco, California.

Preamble to the Charter of the United Nations

WE THE PEOPLES OF THE UNITED NATIONS DETERMINED

- To save succeeding generations from the scourge of war, which twice in our lifetime has brought untold sorrow to mankind, and
- To reaffirm faith in fundamental human rights, in the dignity and worth of the human person, in the equal rights of men and women and of nations large and small, and
- To establish conditions under which justice and respect for the obligations arising from treaties and other sources of international law can be maintained, and
- To promote social progress and better standards of life in larger freedom,

AND FOR THESE ENDS

- To practice tolerance and live together in peace with one another as good neighbours, and
- To unite our strength to maintain international peace and security, and
- To ensure, by the acceptance of principles and the institution of methods, that armed force shall not be used, save in the common interest, and
- To employ international machinery for the promotion of the economic and social advancement of all peoples,

HAVE RESOLVED TO COMBINE OUR EFFORTS TO ACCOMPLISH THESE AIMS.

Accordingly, our respective Governments, through representatives assembled in the city of San Francisco, who have exhibited their full powers found to be in good and due form, have agreed to the present Charter of the United Nations and do hereby establish an international organization to be known as the United Nations.

Strongly implicit in this preamble and in the charter that followed is the argument that the world is finally ready to enter the Age of Reason. Similarly implicit is the constraint that no international boundaries shall be changed through force. Also implicit is Lane's argument that man is by nature free, and Tocqueville's observation that when acting alone he owes an accounting only to his god(s). Finally, and explicitly, is respect throughout the entire membership for basic human rights and the promotion of social and economic rights. Morality and laws shall govern people and nations.

Although he was no longer prime minister of Britain at the time, Winston Churchill expressed the hope that the new United Nations would be "a force for action, and not merely a frothing of words." Albert Einstein's research led to the development of the atomic bomb: "There is only one path to peace and security: the path of supranational organization. One-sided armament on a national basis only heightens the general uncertainty and confusion without being an effective protection."

But almost immediately the reality of conventional wisdom and the external threat theory displaced a wealth of intentions based on the positive side of human nature. Even President Eisenhower believed in peace through strength, and so he continued the military draft long after the World War II had ended.

Young George Kennan was charge d'affairs in Moscow during the late 1940s, and over the next fifty years he became a world-renowned expert on the Soviet Union. Meisler wrote: "Kennan described a Soviet Union so fearful and insecure that it could not negotiate in confidence."[1] Stalin and other leaders perceived the outside world as evil and ready to pounce at any moment on their country, which had been utterly devastated by the war. It is a tribute to the longevity of the external threat theory that, forty years later, Ronald Reagan referred to the same country as the evil empire.

Soviet Foreign Minister Andrei Gromyko nominated the man who became the United Nations' first secretary-general, Norway's Trygve Lie. His leadership disappointed many warriors because he saw his job as exerting moral and not physical force in international relations. He recognized that violence only begets more violence.

The first major challenge for the infant organization was another infant: Israel. Meisler saluted the stellar contribution of a US civil servant to resolution of this prickly issue:

> *Ralph Bunche never rose to the higher ranks of American officialdom because he was black, and never rose to the highest position in the United Nations because he was American. Yet there is little doubt that he deserves acclaim as one of the great civil servants of the twentieth century, a man who helped infuse the United Nations for its first two decades with integrity, intelligence, and sensitive diplomatic skill.*

After World War I and the collapse of the (Islamic) Ottoman Empire, the British kept control of Palestine and promised its Jews the creation of a homeland. After the Holocaust in World War II the pressure increased. But Arabs stridently disagreed; they saw this creation as giving their land to Jews to assuage European guilt. There occurred conflict, and eventually the British grew weary of Jewish terror against Arabs and dumped the problem onto the United Nations. The Security Council favored the creation of Israel through partitioning Palestine. This plan was accepted by the General Assembly in November 1947; almost immediately there was war.

Thus the United Nations, whose charter aimed at an end to warfare, started off by causing a war. An armistice was signed in February 1949 due in large part to the efforts of Bunche. Today there remain thousands of Palestinian refugees who have lived in squalid camps since 1948, hoping to someday return to their homeland.

The first real test of the new United Nations began in June 1950 when the North Korean army crossed the 38th parallel of latitude and invaded South Korea. Secretary-General Lie strongly desired a key role in this conflict for the United Nations, as the Security Council had agreed that here was a clear case of foreign invasion. But the US military would have none of this; Pentagon officials accused the United Nations of meddling in their war. The fact was that under its charter this was a proper UN responsibility; therefore any meddling was done by the United States.

Not only this, but after the primarily US force had repelled the attack and chased the North Korean army back across the parallel, the Truman administration changed its objective in the war. Instead of simply repelling an invasion the military would continue north and eventually unite the two Koreas by force of arms. After being happy with the repelling of invasion, Lie was again deeply disappointed.

Chinese Premier Zhou Enlai had previously warned that if the 38th parallel were crossed, China would send troops. He was not bluffing: 260,000 of them crossed the Yalu River and attacked. Thus Truman's deliberate provocation caused the war to last two years longer than necessary. Realizing his tragic mistake, the president compiled a plan to settle the conflict. But this time he was one-upped as career warrior Gen. Douglas MacArthur issued an ultimatum to China to sue for peace or be annihilated. Later Truman had to fire his top general for insubordination. MacArthur had allowed his career warrior mentality to take him beyond his remit: the president is properly in charge of foreign policy.

Meisler commented: "The Trygve Lie era fostered a dangerous attitude in the US about the United Nations. Americans believed that the UN was strongest and most dynamic and most significant when it did America's bidding." This attitude has sadly persisted throughout the organization's history, and it became most apparent again during the Gulf War. (Meisler should substitute "American government" for "America" when he writes, until citizens' actions obliterate this distinction.)

The next secretary-general, Sweden's Dag Hammarskjold, is considered one of the two best people in the job. His first crisis took place in Egypt, where President Nasser had wanted the West to help him construct the Aswan High Dam. There were difficulties, and when he said he would get the Soviets to build it Western officials said go ahead. Passion then got the better of him, and he nationalized the Suez Canal, thus taking authority to operate it away from the British and French.

These two countries then got together with the Israelis and mounted a force aimed at seizing the canal. But neither the United States nor the United Nations was notified in advance. President Eisenhower was furious, and Hammarskjold was shocked. It is a tribute to his leadership that many ordinary British and French citizens believed in the United Nations more than in their own renegade governments. This conflict was stopped short of extensive damage. However, the Soviets took advantage of a distracted United Nations to move troops into Hungary. This incursion was ignored by nearly everyone except the poor Hungarians.

Meisler wrote, "The secretary-general now had enough prestige to lead the Security Council toward crises and deal with them by carrying out the council's resolutions in his own way. The Security Council could not micromanage him." The next major challenge occurred in the Congo in central Africa. This was a crucial turning point in that the Security Council authorized the use of weapons beyond self-protection.

For years Brian Urquhart had served capably and with dedication on the staff of the secretary-general. The weapons issue tormented him: "The moment a peacekeeping force starts killing people it becomes a part of the conflict it is supposed to be controlling and thus a part of the problem." Here is a strong argument for a preventive role for the United Nations, which will be discussed later in this chapter.

After twice losing elections for president to Eisenhower, Adlai Stevenson served with distinction as US ambassador to the United Nations. But after the

Cuban missile crisis he realized that he had no influence on foreign policy, so he simply kept the seat warm until he was replaced. During the crisis, Soviet Premier Khruschev said, "Only a fool would think we wanted to invade the American continent from Cuba."

The Soviet Russians faced thousands of missiles located in Western Europe and aimed at them. Quite possibly they wanted only for the United States to see how it felt to be threatened in this manner. Be that as it may, the external threat theory promptly preempted government officials' thinking.

Was the Soviet premier indirectly calling President Kennedy a fool? JFK had previously passed up no opportunity to remind him of America's superiority in nuclear weapons, and when Kennedy discovered missiles on Cuban soil he saw another opportunity to enhance his macho credentials. He probably knew the Soviets would not fire a missile from Cuba, but the urge to be perceived as a supreme leader by millions of subjects is often overpowering. Therefore the stage was set for an eyeball-to-eyeball confrontation.

Clashes of egos do little for effective leadership of nations. Predictably, the news media hyped the external threat for all it was worth. The Soviets removed the missiles.

Burmese Secretary-General U Thant sent a contingent of blue helmets (UN personnel) to the island of Cyprus. Even though Greece and Turkey were at loggerheads over this country the peacekeeping force was able to sustain an invasion by Turkey in 1974; today both countries are moving toward a resolution of their differences.

It is interesting to note that at present the incentives are positive, economic, and humanitarian. Turkey wants to join the European Union, which is an economic organization consisting of fifteen countries and adding more to its roster. Also, Turkey recently suffered a couple of devastating earthquakes, and EU member Greece sent large amounts of aid in addition to reducing its opposition to Turkey's aspirations to join. This has been at least a partial success story, and the most logical explanation lay in the fact that the United Nations moved in before the conflict flared up beyond control.

But Vietnam was a different story. The area that included Vietnam was known early in the twentieth century as French Indochina, but the French army left what is now Vietnam after suffering a defeat in 1954. U Thant had grown up in that part of the world (Meisler quoted him):

> *Even if the US were right politically, it was, in my view, immoral to wage a war of this kind. Military methods have failed to solve the problem. They did not solve it in 1954 . . . and I do not see any reason why they would succeed ten years later. As I see the problem in Southeast Asia, it is not essentially military, it is political; and therefore, political and diplomatic means alone, in my view, can solve it.*

But the prevailing attitude in the US government at that time was narrow-minded antagonism toward communism: "My mind is made up; don't confuse me with facts." Furthermore, the die had been previously cast regarding the attitude of public officials toward the United Nations. The fact that U Thant owned a perspective on the issue formed from a lifetime of experience in Southeast Asia apparently caused not a ripple. It remained for an enlightened public to bring the war to a close.

In 1967 the Arab-Israeli issue arose to bite the United Nations again. Meisler wrote,

> *For the UN, the Six-Day war was a devastating blow. The first UN peace-keeping force had stood on guard for a decade and then failed its terrible time of testing. "We all labored under a crushing sense of failure," Brian Urquhart wrote. "I believe that both U Thant and Bunche suffered irreparable psychological damage from this episode, and the physical health of both steadily declined after it."*
>
> *Shut out of most Cold War conflicts and now bereft of much of the Israeli problem—the kind of problem that Harry Truman once said we had the UN for—the UN entered an era that was surely the nadir of its first fifty years.*

The problems must have seemed intractable to nearly everyone.

With the organization under Austrian Secretary-General Kurt Waldheim, European countries with colonies in Africa pulled back and allowed them independence. All of these newly independent countries joined the United Nations and sent ambassadors.

Soon developing countries held an overwhelming majority in the General Assembly. These members quickly showed their frustration with US dominance by voting a seat for communist China and ousting Taiwan, and by passing a resolution that equated Zionism with racism. The latter was seen as a disaster by officials from advanced country governments, but Waldheim properly refused to condemn a democratically passed resolution. (It was revoked sixteen years later.)

The African nations were naturally deeply concerned with their poverty, and so they created a vast number of agencies. A typical example is United Nations Educational, Scientific and Cultural Organization (UNESCO), which was intended to educate peoples of the world in tolerance and hence avoidance of war. But the propensity for war lay not in the people but with egotistical government officials.

Due to the voting power of developing country ambassadors as they audaciously sought the end of poverty and socioeconomic equality with advanced countries, the entire UN organization eventually bogged down. In fact, its charter was undermined.

Meisler said,

The original charter, bolstered by Third World pressures, spawned an enormous number of agencies, programs, and special bodies with a dizzying array of acronyms that made up what bureaucrats called "the UN family." By the 1990s, the UN family had 19 specialized agencies (counting the World Bank and IMF), 15 programs, and seven smaller, "special bodies." The patriarch—the traditional NY-headquartered UN comprising the Security Council, the General Assembly, the Economic and Social Council, the secretary-general and his staff—was dwarfed in size and spending by all the other UN family operations.

The unbridled growth of bureaucracy and the proliferation of dead wood can be readily imagined. Absent accountability, human nature will have its way.

One of the results was a cry for what developing countries called a New World Information and Communication Order. There was justification for this movement as Western interests dominated the world's media, and this created a clear bias in reporting even as some of them strove to avoid it. The solution was not immediately apparent, for even if reporters were to actively solicit news and commentary from poor country leaders, what they would receive would surely be severely biased in the other direction.

While the "family" was expanding, Jeane Kirkpatrick served as ambassador to the United Nations: "The US sunk slowly to a position so impotent and isolated . . . that we could not even protect ourselves against the attacks of arrogant dictators who are dependent on us for help." Because the government paid 25 percent of the United Nations' total membership dues income, these instances of biting the hand that fed them understandably caused the United States to withhold dues and assessments right up to the present.

The United States also terminated its membership in UNESCO, followed by Britain and Singapore. Other countries promised the same if the fiercely autocratic Amadou-Mahtar M'Bow was given a third term as head of the agency. He was not, and the newly elected Federico Mayor performed a major overhaul.

In 1982 Peru's Javier Perez de Cuellar was elected secretary-general. He is considered one of the best in the job, along with Dag Hammarskjold. He soon issued a report on the state of the United Nations that pulled no punches. Meisler:

Yet Perez de Cuellar was so self-effacing as secretary-general that it has been hard to credit him with guiding the turn. Don Shannon of the LA Times, who covered the two terms . . . found him a well-meaning but ineffectual diplomat, a leader who so "lacked any kind of forceful personality" that he could never generate excitement for an issue.

This is precisely the type of leader who is needed at the helm of the United Nations, and of national governments who wish to practice democracy. Small wonder the man was successful in the job, and also small wonder that Shannon and many others failed to appreciate his effectiveness: they had all been programmed to expect the big wheel, the flamboyant, charismatic, and powerful big player at the helm.

Anyone with these traits will by definition work poorly with the egomaniacs who are found in top government positions in war-prone countries. Perez de Cuellar was just the type of diplomat who could slather it on, massage fragile egos, enlist cooperation through inductive ideation, and get things done. (Inductive ideation is selling an idea by subtly manipulating the discussion without lying, so that the customer comes to believe that he thought of the idea originally.) Stroking egos is a vital component of effective diplomacy.

Perez de Cuellar had been associated with the United Nations since 1946, so he had ample opportunity to develop his own diplomatic style. It is reminiscent of that of Frenchman Jean Monnet, who is considered the father of the European Union. Monnet never held public office, but he was widely known for his ability to work through the egos of top national leaders in order to get things done.

The Iran-Iraq war of the 1980s induced Perez de Cuellar toward innovation: He asked the "big five" permanent members of the Security Council (the United States, Soviet Union, the United Kingdom, France, and China) to meet privately and try to work toward a solution to the conflict. Previously such meetings had been public, which had led to much drama and posturing as delegates strove to prove to media audiences that they were powerfully advocating their country's interests. In the end a resolution was passed which authorized the use of force, but only if the two warring nations did not cease hostilities. Closed meetings became standard policy. (Iran and Iraq soon tired of fighting and stopped.)

Perez de Cuellar later sent the United Nations into Cambodia, a poor Southeast Asian country that had been wracked by civil war for twenty years and that had suffered horrible genocide at the hands of the Khmer Rouge rebels. An uneasy peace was negotiated, but the United Nations went beyond this and held a fairly free election in the interest of establishing a democracy. To do this agents had to educate Cambodians concerning what voting was, why it was important, and how to do it. Today the Khmer Rouge is a spent force, there is no conflict to speak of, and the outlook is encouraging even though UN officials have nearly given up trying to convince Premier Hun Sen to allow them to put Khmer Rouge leaders on trial.

The US government saw fit to maintain its arrogance and contempt for the United Nations. Alterman wrote,

> *The US was condemned by the World Court in June 1986 for its "unlawful use of force" in mining Nicaragua's harbors, supporting the Contras, and conducting illegal economic warfare there. The US vetoed the November 1986 Security Council resolution, passed 11-1 with 3 abstentions, calling on the US to observe international law in the case of Nicaragua, and then lost a 94-3 vote in the General Assembly calling on it to comply with the World Court's decision.*

> *In 1987 . . . the General Assembly voted 154-1 to oppose the buildup of weapons in outer space. It voted 135-1 against development of new weapons of mass destruction. The US provided the lone dissent in both votes. In the same session, the General Assembly passed a resolution condemning "Terrorism Wherever and by Whomever Committed." The vote was 153-2 this time, with Israel and the US in opposition.*[2]

In view of these developments, a thinking citizen might wonder about his or her government's as role world citizen.

The end of the cold war in 1989 was an historic milestone, but the government somehow managed to ignore this one. Alterman: "If, after more than a decade of contempt, George Bush had truly gotten religion regarding the UN's potential, he could have secured a resolution under article 43 of the body's charter, creating a true UN force with a UN military staff. Such a path would have helped spread international costs . . . evenly."

But it would also have restricted the president's freedom of action in exactly the fashion envisioned by the United Nations' founders. As such, it was never seriously considered. This lack of action left the door open for Bush to do pretty much whatever he wanted against Iraq. (Apparently his much-hyped pronouncements about a new world order were empty rhetoric.)

Within twelve hours after Saddam Hussein invaded Kuwait, the UN Security Council had a resolution on the books. It stated the right to impose economic sanctions after the incident and to use force if Hussein refused to pull back his army. The vote was 14-0, with Yemen abstaining; even Cuba voted with the United States and others.

President Bush (Sr.) ordered what eventually totaled 400,000 troops into Saudi Arabia, ostensibly to protect that country from aggression even though Hussein gave no indication that he intended to attack. Bush's real agenda was war against Iraq. The United Nations of course had no interest in a war, but this bothered Bush not at all. Even though his chief of staff Gen. Powell demurred, Bush ordered the Pentagon to prepare for war.

Soviet Foreign Minister Eduard Shevardnadze agreed with the resolution, even though Iraq was a friend of that country. When war came Bush wanted to fly the UN flag into battle, but Perez de Cuellar said no. He did not want another Korea, where the flag was flown but the United States tolerated no interference from that organization. Meisler noted, "The UN had no role in the war, but some UN officials and ambassadors hoped for a brief moment that they might bring it to a close in February and avert the carnage of an American-led ground offensive."

The Soviets had compiled a plan for withdrawal, which Hussein had approved. But, "Bush pre-empted any consideration of the plan by proclaiming an ultimatum to Saddam Hussein to start leaving Kuwait City within 24 hours or face annihilation."

It is ironic that Bush had previously been ambassador to the UN. Apparently that experience also did nothing to deter him. Later, without UN authority, he ordered troops into northern Iraq to provide relief to the Kurds from harassment by Saddam. Also later the U.S., British, and French figured they needed no approval from the UN when they established a no-fly zone in northern Iraq. Meisler: ". . . war solidified the American notion that the UN worked best when it did what the US wanted. . . .. Americans acted as if the UN were their UN." If the Age of Reason were to come into existence, someone apparently would need to have a serious word with the president of the United States.

THE UNITED NATIONS TODAY

The habit of unilateral action by the United States continued when on December 21, 1988, a bomb caused pieces of a Boeing 747 and its passengers to rain down over Lockerbie, Scotland. Britain and the United States did not wait for the World Court to act; they rammed a resolution through the Security Council that threatened economic sanctions against Libya if the government did not turn its two suspects over for trial. This impetuous action turned a legal issue into a political one, just as the World Court was becoming firmly established. It undermined the democratic process because it cast members of the Security Council in the roles of judges, policemen, and possible executioners.

The short-term result placed Libya's top leader, Moammar Qaddafi, into hero status in the eyes of millions of Arabs. This act of terrorism was done possibly in retaliation for bombs that President Reagan authorized to be dropped on the capital city, Tripoli, in 1986. (This act was surely perceived as terrorism by Qaddafi, and a bomb may have killed one of his children.) To bask in the hero's afterglow and tweak the mighty United States, he presumably waited for ten years before he turned over the two men.

In 1774 a man murdered a British subject in Massachusetts Colony. King George III demanded that the trial take place in England, which would have changed a legal issue into a political one: kangaroo court. The colonists refused to hand him over. Today the double standard persists: Arabs draw a stark contrast between the punishment meted out to Iraq for disobeying UN resolutions and the ability of Israel to avoid punishment for disobeying more resolutions for a much longer time.

During the cold war the United Nations was severely constrained in accomplishing its primary task of peacekeeping. Because the cold war lasted nearly fifty years, the organization had a long time to expand and become inflexible, as would any bureaucracy. Suddenly the big opportunity for which the United Nations was founded presented itself—the end of the cold war in 1989.

The response was less than impressive, for at least four reasons. One was the overgrown and ossified condition of the organization; a second lay in the continuing obstructive behavior of its biggest member; and a third lay in the learning curve. That is, with little meaningful experience in its primary function and without precedent in world history, it was logical to expect that with freedom to act some time would be needed for the organization to get its feet wet. The fourth reason lay in a lack of money; the United States has continued to renege on its obligations, and its dues are largest of all.

The Economist commented: "Inevitably, given the great gap between the mandates that its members ordered, and the means they allowed for fulfilling them, the results were disastrous. Such ambitions have collapsed."[3] The US government is interested in making the United Nations look weak and confused, so that in the role of world cop it will have no competition. In the perception of public officials the United States occupies the moral high ground, so logically it should call the shots.

It is hardly necessary to add that other perceptions differ. Furthermore, the United States expects a complete reformation to take place within the bureaucracy, but Chapter 7 showed that this is impractical due to vested interests and personal power seeking among bureaucrats.

The Economist continued: "America's men at the UN face their colleagues' bitterness; no longer, say America's friends as well as its foes, will the UN do what America wants, trusting in its good faith to deliver; in future it will want to see the color of American money first." When a negotiator cannot trust his counterpart across the table he will ask for the money up front.

The news media are still stuck in the cold war mentality. A 1994 article in *Time* magazine speculated that the "imperialist Russian bear has awakened from his post–cold war snooze," and was using crude tactics in an attempt to retrieve some of the republics of the old Soviet Union. It is hardly accurate to refer to a country that is desperately struggling to organize itself under a totally new and strange rubric called democracy as imperialist. Several years later there is no evidence of any return of republics; quite the contrary, places like Chechnya want to go in the opposite direction.

In the same year *The Economist* suggested that the United Nations will not always function well in crises, and therefore the West must be prepared to act on its own. This argument is shortsighted. Leaders and citizens in the more than 100 countries not subsumed under the umbrella called the "West" already perceive that group of advanced countries as a huge and overbearing presence in the world. Any unilateral actions by the West would only exacerbate feelings of resentment and alienation. The United Nations cannot function effectively in peacekeeping if any country or group of countries acts on its own, even if the United Nations is consulted in advance.

Furthermore the organization cannot do its job well when the interpretation of its primary purpose is distorted, as in the following sordid example.[4]

> *With helicopters swooping overhead, 2,000 US troops staged an amphibious practice invasion. . . The two-week exercises . . . simulate[s] a NATO-led UN* ***peacekeeping operation*** *dubbed "Unified Spirit." . . .*
>
> *Marine Commander Col. Paul Lefebvre . . . complained of the ban on using live ammunition. . . . "The goal is to fire as much as we can to gain as much proficiency as we can," he said. "That's the stress, that's the reality of* ***real combat.*** *" [emphasis added]*

A thinking citizen would ask whose spirits are being unified when a peacekeeping operation is implemented through real combat.

It is discomforting to observe that in 2001 *The Economist* had yet to learn a vital lesson.[5] "Much will depend on America. It has already played an indispensable role in peacemaking: giving Israel the weaponry to make the radical Arab states realize that destroying Israel is not a near-term option." It looks like once again it is necessary to state that weapons only perpetuate violence. The US government has been giving and selling weapons to Israel for fifty years; as this is being written Israel and Palestine are locked into a vast war zone. The tragedy is compounded when it is realized that thinking people predicted this grisly situation.

Pollsters and the news media nearly always reflect the views of the elite class in government, not those of the public (although the results may be dressed up to appear that way). Hence citizens see the United Nations as acting according to its charter: peacekeeper. But US public officials feeding off the military-industrial complex see the organization as an impediment to continuing foreign adventurism and international trafficking in weapons. It is therefore necessary that some pollsters and the media continue to deceive the public.

The United Nations was organized as an instrument of prevention. With so many of the poor countries of the world so full of weapons and accompanying temptations to use them, prevention takes on even greater importance.

Writing in August 2000, *The Economist* complained about the lack of resources for peacekeeping during the previous decade.[6] "But the one constant, throughout those ten troubled years, is that the Security Council, the world's flawed policy-maker, continues to instruct its policemen to do what needs to be done without providing them with the means to do it."

This tactic indirectly encourages warfare because it reduces the capacity of the United Nations to prevent it. Secretary-General Kofi Annan should present a budget to the Security Council that includes a prioritized list of strictly peacekeeping projects. A concise statement of its objective and a detailed list of required resources would accompany each proposal. If the news media cooperate (admittedly a big "if") the onus for most failures would then be placed on the Security Council, where it belongs.

Australia's Richard Butler served ably as the chief weapons development inspector in Iraq after the Gulf War. Shawcross was impressed:

> *Butler thought UNSCOM had an importance far beyond Iraq: it was an integral part of a 30-year struggle by the international community to create a tapestry of treaties to* ***prevent*** *the proliferation of weapons of mass destruction. At the same time a moral consensus had to be and largely was built that the use of nuclear, chemical, and biological weapons was wrong.*[7] [emphasis added]

This is a creative and forward-looking position because it relates closely to the UN charter.

Career politicians thrive on the current situation. They win votes by preaching peace and buy votes through authorizing design, construction, and international trafficking in weapons. Jobs in defense plants pay very well, and employees and their families tend to vote for incumbent politicians. Also, kickbacks from defense contractors are plentiful.

In 1990 Egypt's Boutros Boutros-Ghali was elected secretary-general of the United Nations. He, too, was not a personal power-seeking kind of man. He worked hard at making himself and his office independent of the US-dominated Security Council. This group asked him to prepare a report. Meisler noted "that he set down his proposals to improve 'the capacity of the UN for preventive diplomacy, for peacemaking, and for peacekeeping.'"[8] Every incoming secretary-general should do this.

However, there should be defined and preserved a distinction between peacemaking and peacekeeping, so that the United Nations sticks to prevention and avoids involvement in ongoing conflicts unless specifically invited by both sides. Diplomacy and prevention are major responsibilities, which would keep a United Nations with limited resources thoroughly occupied into the indefinite future and would also demonstrate more success. The latter is very important for generating faith in the organization among nations and their citizens; a strong record will induce officials to think of the United Nations first whenever a situation threatens to allow passion to displace reason.

A logical conclusion points to avoidance of any involvement in ongoing conflicts, in spite of political and humanitarian pressures. Once passion predominates, what men will do to others, especially innocent civilians, is absolutely incredible.

Somalia's clan chief, General Mohammed Siad Barre, seized power in 1969, but he was an egotist and soon discriminated against other clans. The resulting resentment erupted in civil war in the late 1980s, culminating with his ouster in January 1991. Mutual resentment and recrimination then took over, and clan chiefs became warlords as they found mountains of weapons handy and began to use them.

Predictably, the country disintegrated. Crops were destroyed, and relief workers trying to distribute food to starving people were terrorized. Gunmen demanded huge fees to protect food shipments from other gunmen, and they took food for themselves so that little reached the starving. The news media, always interested in war and tragedy, filmed these unfortunate people, focusing especially on children. These films programmed the public for a white knight role played by soldiers as they entered the country to solve the food distribution problem.

Boutros-Ghali had asked the US government to intervene and disarm the gunmen, which could have been done fairly easily. But the generals played to the media; Meisler wrote, "The US did not intend a general disarmament in Somalia. The American troops would make sure that food and medicine were distributed without interference. . . . President Bush did not want to risk even minimal casualties that might drum up public and congressional opposition to a mission that enjoyed enthusiastic approval."

A moment's reflection leads to the conclusion that the soldiers would remain for a short time only, and after they had left it would be business as usual. After having stuffed the country with weapons for decades during the cold war, apparently no top official felt the slightest moral obligation to remove them. Today it is, in fact, business as usual: warlord versus warlord, chaos, and tragedy.

The Economist observed:

> *Most countries sent their men on the understanding that they would remain neutral in Somalia's civil war. But when the Americans, who led the operation, turned it into a mission against one of the warlords, Muhamad Farah Aideed, the others were obliged, without consultation, to go along. . . . 18 American soldiers were killed. . .. That is what the world saw and remembers. What is less well known is that more [helicopter] gunships were sent in that night and circled the area firing into houses, apparently at random, with cannons and machine guns.*[9]

A thinking citizen would wonder about the presence of gunships if the original plan was to distribute food and medicines.

In peacekeeping there is no place for passions. In this instance hundreds of innocent civilians paid the ultimate price as a group of uninvited foreigners, consumed by the desire for revenge, devastated an entire neighborhood, killing indiscriminately. (The ostensibly violence-prone media did not report the massacre, and apparently saw no need to interview surviving family members.)

So the soldiers left the country and Bush's Operation Restore Hope restored very little hope. The new president, Bill Clinton, offered an explanation. Meisler summarized it: "The Clinton administration succeeded in deluding the American public into believing it was Boutros-Ghali alone who led American soldiers to disaster in Somalia." A cooperative press often comes in handy.

In Bosnia conflict was also ongoing when the United Nations was called in. This happens frequently due to its dominant member having a foreign policy which de-emphasizes diplomacy in favor of waiting until conflict has broken out. This creates a situation that suits the warlords in the Pentagon and also the rest of the huge military-industrial complex. The reality is there is very little money in peace and peacekeeping, only lives preserved and healthy, educated children.

Due to this policy and to the cold war, the same situation prevailed in Bosnia as in Somalia. The country was awash in weapons and crowded with trained warriors. Interethnic strife in this area of the world may have had its origin in a battle fought in 1221. With that kind of history it is even more difficult for an outside force, unfamiliar with the details of the region's grisly history, to bring the combatants together in a cease-fire agreement. The momentum of revenge seeking must be awesome, and this is indeed properly a task for the United nations. But allowing an incipient conflict to fester until it breaks out into open warfare is as counterproductive as it is tragic.

Since the cold war the United Nations has expanded its peacekeeping activities. Meisler: "From 1988 to 1995, the number of peacekeeping missions in the field had increased from five to 17, the numbers of troops deployed had increased from 9,600 to 73,400, and the cost—from $230 million to $3.6 billion a year. The UN needed to learn from this frenetic experience." The learning curve has been operating, even if only for a few years.

"Boutros-Ghali said that three traditional principles must guide peacekeeping operations: UN troops must have the consent of the warring parties before entering a country; UN troops must be impartial; UN troops must not use force except in self-defense." This statement is misguided, in that it blurs the distinction between peacekeeping and peacemaking. Also, when troops have been trained to make war that will be the likely result.

There has been some progress, but the learning curve needs more time. In the political arena, "consent" is an ambiguous word; it is frequently divided into explicit and implied consent. The first definition requires a definite "yes" from the giver of consent, whereas the second is often assumed in the absence of a definite "no." Therefore the first principle should require that the initiative definitely come from the warring parties, nay, **potentially** warring parties, rather than from the United Nations. In such instances it would be the United Nations that consents, not the contending parties. This distinction is important.

The most important principle is, give diplomacy total support in the interest of prevention. This institution has been in place for centuries; what is sadly lacking today and therefore much needed is support, especially from the major nations. Admittedly there is little drama and excitement in diplomacy, but its ability to use an ounce of prevention to displace a pound of cure has been proven time and again. As weapons become ever more powerful and destructive this truth takes on supreme importance.

Meisler wrote, (US secretary of state Madeleine) "Albright began a series of speeches around the country in 1995 defending the UN as an essential arm of

American policy." This is the wrong approach; no nation should dictate policy to the United Nations.

Tayeh underscored public officials' reluctance to cooperate with the UN in its efforts at peacekeeping.[10] "Late last month, the US vetoed a UN Security Council measure that would have sent an observer force to the occupied territories to protect Palestinian civilians from the Israeli army. This veto symbolizes a tacit approval of Israel's continued use of excessive force against the Palestinians." Such a team would reveal to the world the continuing maltreatment and injustice being foisted on the Palestinians by a vastly superior military force. If that veto had not been cast there would today be hundreds of residents of Nablus and Jenin still alive.

"Many Palestinians see this fight as a war of independence. They will not back down just because the US forces Arafat to utter words of retreat." The UN charter specifies that international boundaries shall not be changed through force. Israel did this in 1967, and to date its government has not returned their lands to the Palestinians.

Boutros-Ghali angered the military powers in Washington with his independence; so, flexing muscles as always, they saw to it that he was not elected to a second term as secretary-general. Today Ghana's Kofi Annan is establishing a solid track record with his soft approach to diplomacy and his ability to stay current with a variety of issues of concern.

Partially in response to atrocities in the Balkan countries, in 1998 a World Criminal Court was established with the intent of bringing perpetrators of war crimes to justice. The US government's behavior was typical; *The Economist* observed:

> *During years of discussions and five weeks of intensive talks in Rome, the US has sought to water down a treaty setting up an international criminal court. Unhappy with the outcome, America had forced a last-minute vote on the final text, hoping to block the treaty altogether. When the result of the vote was announced—120 in favor, seven against—the room erupted in jubilation.* [11]

The bully is apparently having his way less often than previously.

This country's negotiators wanted to control what cases came before the court, but other countries recognized that this would simply create a political tool for the big countries, and they refused to accept it. "So instead America's negotiators tried to create obstacles to the court's independence within the complex 200-page treaty setting it up."

The court has the potential of restraining foreign adventurism by the US government and any other that chooses not to live in the world as a citizen. Soldiers ordered to go abroad and exert overbearing force may have second thoughts (as happened in Vietnam). "Once the court is up and running, governments will have to explain to world opinion, and their own people, any reluctance to cooperate with it. . . . Most important of all, the court should stand as a reproach to countries that tolerate or shelter those who commit atrocities."

For public officials mentally dedicated to the cold war notion of superpower, the lesson is difficult to learn. In 1999 *The Economist* found it necessary to lean harder.[12]

> *But the real objection of some officials, and of opponents in Congress, is more fundamental and even less defensible: they cannot tolerate any infringement of American sovereignty by an international body over which the United States does not have direct control.*
>
> *Such an absolutist version of sovereignty is rapidly becoming an anachronism. America blew a huge hole through it by intervening in Kosovo and bombing Serbia. Its frequent denunciations of war crimes and other atrocities abroad, and its promotion of internationally enforceable rules in trade and arms control, are based on the assumption that absolute claims to sovereignty are no longer legitimate or useful. Judged in this context, America's opposition to an international court is not only hypocritical, but also misconceived. Even a superpower would be safer in a world where the rule of international law stood some chance of being applied.*

The tragedy of September 11, 2001 has amply emphasized this point.

There is a positive sign in US law, as victims are now able to bring suit in US courts for abuse committed elsewhere. This trend began in response to difficulties in bringing suits in countries with corrupt judicial systems. A case in point is a recent $150 million settlement, which may retrieve some of the billions of dollars siphoned from the Filipino economy by Ferdinand Marcos and his cronies. His twenty-year rule was rife with human rights abuses.

Other judges have awarded a total of around $2 billion in damages. Even though very little of this has actually been collected, dictators might well be thinking twice before perpetrating abuses.

General Augusto Pinochet engineered a coup in 1973 against Chile's socialist president Salvador Allende, and then proceeded to install a ruthless dictatorship during which thousands were tortured or "disappeared." Several years ago Pinochet agreed to step down, but only after having been granted lifetime immunity from prosecution.

Some of the victims of his abuse were foreign nationals, so when the general went to England for medical treatment he was served with requests for extradition to stand trial in Spain and other countries. After well over a year of legal wrangling, he was cleared to return home. To date the old dictator has yet to be brought to justice for his crimes, but the message has gone out to the world that top officials who would abuse the human rights of others can no longer do so with impunity.

With the cold war over, nongovernmental organizations (NGOs), who bring aid to mostly poor countries, have proliferated. They are supplementing and sometimes displacing government agencies organized for the same purpose. The Red Cross thinks that NGOs give out more financial aid than does the World Bank. There are instances where personnel in these organizations are working toward ending small conflicts. The United Nations may find these groups to be useful resources.

In spite of encouraging signs, dinosaurs in the oligarchy have yet to see the light. Columnist Molly Ivins wrote,

> *The USA is now out of step on some of the most obvious no-brainers in history. . . . For example, when you find yourself allied with Libya, Syria, and Iraq in refusing to comply with a global treaty to eliminate chemical weapons, this should make you think about the company you keep. When Somalia is the only country that joins you in failing to ratify the UN convention on children's rights, this is an indication that you should perhaps rethink your position. . . . And when you are odd man out on banning land mines—with countries like China, Libya, and Iraq for company . . .* [13]

These instances drmatically illustrate the need for the government to articulate a cohesive foreign policy based on citizenship rather than force.

Ivins was not yet finished:

> *[The] insane position of asking the UN for support against Iraq when we're the biggest deadbeat in the organization? . . . We may be the only superpower left, but we're starting to look like a super-jackass. . . . Compliance with the Chemical Weapons Convention is hung up in the House, which combined it with legislation aimed at punishing Russia for selling missile technology to Iran. This brilliant maneuver put us in the position of threatening to bomb Iraq over alleged chemical weapons violations when we were in violation ourselves. Shrewd move, fellas.*

In May 2002 *The Economist* elaborated on the child issue:

> *Between 1990 and 2000, conflict killed 2m[illion] children. Over 100m of primary age do not attend school, while 149m are malnourished. At the 1990 world summit for children, national leaders pledged to improve matters. On May 8th-10th, the UN general assembly will hold a special session on children to discuss what still needs to be done. The United States, as ever, is not in the mood to give the UN an easy ride. . . .*
>
> *[The] 1989 UN convention for the rights of the child. The convention—which sets standards for health care, education, social services and so on—is supported by all but two countries, the United States and Somalia.* [14]

The explanation may lie in the fact that twenty-three US states permit use of the death penalty when the defendant was under the age of eighteen at the time of the crime.

THE UNITED NATIONS IN THE NEW WORLD ORDER

In 1688 John Locke envisioned a new world order: "Reason, which is that Law . . . teaches all Mankind, who would but consult it, that being all equal and independent, no one ought to harm another in his Life, Health, Liberty, or Possessions."[15] Thomas Jefferson ranked Locke as one of the most important thinkers on liberty. These two men's writings had influence far beyond the borders of the United States.

If not reflected in impressive accomplishments in peacekeeping, its first fifty years have taught the United Nations and the world some important lessons.

1. No one can make or keep peace by waging war, because this only stimulates resentment, hatred, desire for revenge, and ultimately additional violence.
2. It is easy for a paranoid dictator to start a war, but creating a lasting peace requires courage and a protracted effort.
3. Recent successes by the United Nations indicate that the organization can play a useful role in the peace process.
4. No single nation, no matter how large and powerful, can dictate peace. There are two reasons for this truth. One is that such a nation is perceived by others as but one country among many, and therefore it lacks authority to give orders to another. The second lies in the fact that by definition peace is nonviolent, so there is no place in it for coercion.
5. Weapons, even if not used, cannot ensure peace. Their very presence is intimidating and fearful, and for peace to prevail it is absolutely essential that reason prevail over passions.

Shortly after the end of the cold war Frenchman Jacques Attali said, "The merchant is replacing the warrior on the world stage." Today the merchant is definitely present and active on that stage, but the warrior is reluctant to retire. Furthermore, the different objectives of the two constitute a trade-off: the more emphasis on the warrior, the less room for the merchant (the reverse is also true). However, this book has shown that the world's weapons merchants are gradually putting themselves out of business, and this trend opens the world stage for entrance by the Age of Reason. A United Nations organized to assume center stage during that age can and will assume a high profile.

Harris's popular book *I'm Okay; You're Okay* provided insights into why people behave as they do in their relationships.[16] Because nations are composed of people, he believed that these insights could stimulate constructive thinking in international relations. "One of the most hopeful institutions for the analysis of international transactions is the UN. It has survived many crossed transactions." The main thrust of the book emphasizes the objective of what Harris called "adult-adult" transactions; these interactions very capably illustrate the Age of Reason, in that reasoned discourse prevails over passions. On the other hand a crossed transaction such as a punitive "parent" arguing with a hurt "child" (where both people are chronologically adults and not necessarily related) arouses passions and therefore inhibits effective communication.

Harris explained,

> *But we do not have to respond with our Child. Nor do we have to respond with our sword-rattling Parent. And therein lies the possibility of change . . . by understanding the terror in our own Child in the face of rioting and war, in the people of India victimized by starvation and superstition, in the people of Russia in the memory of chains and insurrection. . . . If we can begin to see this Child as a little human being in a world full of terror, wanting only the release from pain, then perhaps our international conversations would begin to sound a little different.*

Reflection is needed to understand and appreciate the inner self of a person who comes across on the surface as a powerful and abusive dictator. If he is interacting with representatives from a big country, his Child is probably guiding his words and actions, although the rhetoric will surely be intended to distract others from seeing this truth. On the other hand if he interacts with those from a small nation it is probably the punitive, overbearing Parent that guides his use of rhetoric.

Harris concluded: "The people of the world are not things to be manipulated, but persons to know; not heathens to be proselytized but persons to be heard; not enemies to be hated but persons to be encountered; not brothers to be kept but brothers to be brothers." World brotherhood and the Age of Reason are actually one and the same.

For more than ten years the United Nations has had an opportunity to perform according to its charter. But has it really done so? There exists even today a huge impediment in the form of a lingering and outmoded cold war mentality. It is gradually fading as lack of a credible enemy taxes the ingenuity of even the most creative warrior in Washington. Ways will be found to expedite the advent of the Age of Reason, with untold benefits accruing to people everywhere.

Reflecting on this vision leads to the conclusion that there is no justification for outside interference in a country's affairs, unless it is on behalf of individual citizens. Any action against a government tends to revert back to the age of conquest and plunder in the perceptions of officials in the target government. (In Somalia, some people thought that foreign soldiers sent there to help the starving were actually there to recolonize the nation.)

Almost exclusively the main problem with individuals in many poor countries connects with basic human rights. The challenge in this area lies in the fact that soldiers and weapons don't promote human rights, they take them away. For the long term the answer lies in a coordinated worldwide moral authority, promulgated by the United Nations. But attaining and maintaining this morality requires that the organization earn a high leadership profile among its members, and this will take time and better internal organization.

It will also need better support from member nations; *The Economist* wrote, "The two American presidents who have laid most emphasis on human rights . . . were Woodrow Wilson and Jimmy Carter. Both left office disappointed men."[17] However well intentioned, their concern was premature.

> *Human rights have rarely loomed as large as they did under Jimmy Carter. When he was elected in 1976, he pledged to put concern for human rights back into the forefront of American foreign policy after the heyday of Mr. Kissinger's realism. . . . . [There was an] impression that Mr. Carter's human-rights-centered policy had merely weakened America. The election of Ronald Reagan in 1980 appeared to signal a return to hard-edged realism.*
>
> *In practice, however, far from revealing that the pursuit of human rights abroad was futile, Mr. Reagan's presidency showed that it was possible to have your cake and eat it . . . i.e., you could crusade for rights while enhancing your national power and interest.*

Both presidents could not see the whole picture, with Reagan the more disillusioned of the two.

During his administration, Carter did in fact push human rights, but he simultaneously authorized research and creation of weapons of mass destruction, which obviously doesn't promote human rights at all. Perhaps unthinkingly infused with the cold war mentality, he probably thought his policy could work to reduce rights violations, but its impact was limited.

However, President Carter's efforts toward world peace, democracy, health and economic development after he left office are utterly without precedent and more than worthy of mention here. In 1982 he and his wife Rosalynn founded the Carter Center, which has been active in at least 29 African countries, seven in Asia, four in the Caribbean, six in Central America, 11 in South America, four in Europe and five in the Middle East.

The Center's accomplishments include improving farm productivity in 16 countries, monitoring elections in 23, mediating conflicts/working toward arms sales moratoriums in 23, eliminating guinea worm infestations in 16, promoting human rights in 15, controlling river blindness/trachoma in 13, and reducing corruption in eight.

The Center helped with the birthing of East Timor, which is the first new nation of the twenty-first century. President Carter's historic visit to Cuba in May 2002 was the first by any president or former president in 74 years. He gave a major speech on state-run national radio and TV, in which he criticized the regime. Castro smiled through it all. Today El Presidente discriminates against European trade partners in his zeal to cultivate reactions with his old enemy, the USA.

In 2002, the Alfred Nobel committee in Sweden awarded its Peace Prize to Jimmy Carter. This is surely a great honor, and well deserved.

"Mr. Reagan's presidency made clear that supporting freedom could successfully be made a central tenet of American foreign policy, and that the means existed to pursue that goal. In the case of the Reagan doctrine, those means were the support of proxy wars." In this instance both Reagan's and *The Economist*'s thinking are misguided, if not just simply wrong. Freedom cannot be promoted through wars because violence is the result of the triumph of passion over reason; therefore it only causes more violence. Reagan's policy combined with that of the Soviet Union to polarize much of the world in a balance of terror; this did nothing for human rights. (The writer of the article cited on page 585 might have been taken in by Reagan's silver-tongued rhetoric. In this, he or she was not alone.)

How about promoting human rights through trade barriers, economic sanctions, or the threat of these? In view of the main objective of having every country develop its economy in the interest of improving world living standards, several arguments against this policy come forth. One is that the policy is likely to cause additional barriers to be erected in retaliation, and this often leads to a debilitating trade war that also involves other nations. A second argument is that the purpose of the World Trade Organization is to lower trade barriers and discourage economic sanctions, so the policy would probably violate its rules. A third is that the policy would tend to retard economic development in the target country, therefore it would inhibit the rise of living standards for its citizens. Living standards and human rights tend to rise in tandem.

The law of supply and demand applies to people just as it does to products, land, and money. Whenever there are too many people and too few jobs, as in China with its more than 1.3 billion souls, the value citizens and governments put on the individual person and his or her rights is seriously diminished. This explains why the officials in the Chinese government habitually imprison, torture, and occasionally murder their own citizens. Give the country a few decades of uninhibited economic growth and reasoned policies aimed at control of growth of population, and the demand will come close to matching the supply of labor, and for people in general.

The Economist showed that two different outlooks developed in the early nineteenth century (same article).

> *Liberals . . . believe that history is on the side of 'human rights.' . . . If it is wrong for an individual to do something, then it is also wrong for a state to do it. . . . Realists are more pessimistic about progress in human affairs and believe that states live by different moral rules from individuals. They see power rather than principle as the driving force of international affairs.*

This is reminiscent of the discussion in Chapter 1 of the two sides of human nature. The realists connect to the negative side, and the liberals to the positive.

Broadly speaking, the negative side connects to the age of conquest and plunder while the positive side connects to the Age of Reason. "Ask [retired president of South Africa] Nelson Mandela or [president of the Czech Republic] Vaclav Havel. In such a climate, faith in the spread of human rights and willingness to give it a helping hand may not be a liberal illusion . . . it may be realistic."

This book is concerned with replacing deception and fantasy with truth and reality. If reality can be connected to the positive side of human nature there is a bright future for humanity, and with it the United Nations.

Preventing armed conflict demands rational planning and action. Conflict occurs when passion overrules reason, and therefore stopping it becomes a towering challenge. Diplomacy is based in reason: It plods slowly and haltingly toward its objective, and it produces no dashing heroes. Therefore its importance is all too often understated and under funded, with frequently devastating and tragic results.

Today's secretary-general of the United Nations is Ghana's Kofi Annan, who said,

> *Even the costliest policy of prevention is far cheaper, in lives and in resources, than the least expensive intervention. [The] costs of prevention have to be paid in the present, while its benefits lie in the distant future. And the benefits are not tangible—when prevention succeeds, nothing happens. Taking such a political risk when there are few obvious rewards requires conviction and considerable vision.*[18]

Annan concluded: "The non-violent management of conflict is the very essence of democracy. In an era when more than 90 percent of wars take place within, not between, states, the import of this finding for conflict prevention should be obvious." Secretary-General Annan has proven himself in the job. Furthermore, he has amply demonstrated the potential of a revamped United Nations.

In an article on postcommunist poverty, *The Economist* provided useful guidelines.[19]

> *That help would have to include technical expertise and enough money to kick-start rural savings-and-loan associations, rebuild rural roads and sewers, bring in new technology and underwrite the schools. Villages would also have to play their part by rebuilding community structures, assuming responsibility for the competitiveness of their local agro-processing plants, tackling corruption and supporting cooperative efforts based not, as before, on collectivization from above, but on enterprise from below.*

This broad recommendation is reminiscent of previous discussions: people support what they help create and the bottom-up approach to solving problems. Ask local villagers to establish savings and loan institutions, build roads, and construct power lines, schools, and clinics. Ask them to make their plans detailed and explicit, including schedules of projected cash needs.

Citizens alone know the territory. Foreign experts should be resource people, to be consulted only in response to locally inspired demand. Finally, because with this approach very little money is needed and what is needed is placed under local control, there is very little opportunity for corruption to gain a toehold.

The Economist described the incredibly miserable lives of today's post-Soviet people in Moldova. Institutions built under the Soviets have vanished, and there are none available to fill the vacuum. But if new institutions were built from a top-down approach human nature will act to install another oppressive government, complete with rampant corruption. There will be no wealth created and accumulated at the grass roots. The misery would continue.

Perhaps due to serendipity, the United Nations had some success in Cambodia through utilizing the bottom-up approach, as Shawcross reported:

> *The broadcasts of Radio UNTAC helped offset the political impact of the violence of the regime and the threats of the Khmer Rouge. They became one of the most successful components of the UN's operations in Cambodia. For the first time Cambodians had a free and unbiased source of information, and nearly the entire population became avid listeners. . . . Even Khmer Rouge soldiers became loyal listeners.*[20]

Many rural and poor countries have thousands of hamlets, each of which may have only two or three radios (and no TV). Citizens by the hundreds gather around a radio to hear popular broadcasts and discuss the implications. Radio UNTAC probably went far toward undermining and ultimately neutralizing the Khmer Rouge insurgency.

Paranoid top leaders whose passions have been aroused almost invariably declare war. As Thomas Paine pointed out in Chapter 20, if the right of declaration were placed in those who must finance war and fight it, "we should hear but little more of wars." The United Nations should strongly promote this policy among all member nations. The collective wisdom of the mass of citizens is always rational, unless they are swayed by a talented paranoiac, such as Hitler. (Given time to reflect and discuss, even a situation like this poses no threat to reason, as Jefferson indicated.)

Passions can be governed by reason, but only if time is taken to allow it to enter into human thought. Once this has occurred and free and open discussion and debate have taken place, plug passion into the mix to carry out the decision(s). This process when implemented does not make reason the slave of passion. Rather, the two would work together toward a desired common objective.

Prevention must involve diplomacy, so the United Nations should provide methods of rewarding successful diplomats, just as does the Alfred Nobel committee in Sweden when it awards peace prizes. Sadly, today US ambassadorships are often purchased by rich people who fancy a soft life in a lush foreign post. Frequently they have no experience in diplomacy, and sometimes they do not even speak the language. Therefore career diplomats, far from being rewarded for dedicated service with promotion to ambassador, suffer from poor morale and performance and resentment at repeatedly having to educate their superiors.

A revamped United Nations will approach the vital issue of prevention of armed conflict as it sees fit. The final and flexible policy will be the result of experimentation and experience. Here is an outline that represents speculative thinking, but it could stimulate constructive discourse about the issue.

Any national diplomat always has an ax to grind; he will negotiate with a bias in favor of his country because he knows from whence his salary comes and he feels a natural allegiance to his native land. A UN diplomat carries with him or her a different mandate, which should be unbiased with respect to the issue being negotiated. Indeed, he will be selected as a member of a particular team primarily because he is disinterested in the outcome.

1. Diplomacy is first and foremost. Today's diplomats tend to cluster around a country's capital city, because nearly all governments are organized from a top-down perspective. But often incipient strife can be detected only in the countryside, especially with respect to domestic issues. Because these often expand into international problems, diplomats should be aware of them. This suggests a need for resources in the field, who understand the culture and are trained to be sensitive to difficulties and report them promptly to the central organization. Training should include ability to persuade local citizens to turn in or destroy any dangerous weapons in the area and to identify weapons caches. In this way, trouble could often be nipped before it sinks into passion. When an issue gets out of local control,
2. Trained international mediators would be available. If they operated free of political bias these people could accomplish much, because at this time feelings have yet to harden beyond the ability of reason to have appeal. Efforts to remove weapons from areas of tension would continue. Failing in this,
3. Arbitration panels would enter the controversy. These panels would have been organized in advance, and they would be backed by the force of international law. All member nations would have previously agreed to abide by any award that comes from arbitration. If arbitration is refused or fails,
4. The UN General Assembly would vote to impose economic sanctions. To date these have enjoyed a dubious track record because they have been imposed by one or two nations, usually the United States. When backed by the full moral weight of the United Nations the result would be different, especially if the vote were overwhelming. (If an issue should go as far as step 4, that moral force would be strong.) If this does not work,

5. Full economic sanctions and an arms embargo would be imposed through voting to isolate the potential combatants. World pressure would continue to build for a peaceful solution. The next step,
6. A total embargo on trade would probably be voted unanimously. Finally,
7. A total blockade of water, land, and air passages. This is commonly treated as an act of war, so it does not suit the purpose of the United Nations. However, such an extreme step would almost never be necessary. If the situation deteriorates further, the United Nations would proceed to step 8.
8. Once conflict has started, there is little that any outsider can do. However, there is one thing that can be done, and it is extremely important. Plans should be made in advance and carried out that are aimed at capture of those in top leadership positions who are responsible, and bringing them to the World Criminal Court for trial and punishment. The importance of this process lies in its deterrent value for future renegades who cannot or will not listen to reason.

Several large areas of land donated by countries in various parts of the world and away from densely populated areas would be selected and equipped as refugee camps. Resources would be geared for a stay of around two years or more. These camps would not be primitive, nor would they be luxurious.

In today's warfare a preponderance of casualties are noncombatants (women, children, old men). This fact would be impressed on citizens of a pair of contending countries as protracted negotiations move, say, beyond step 4. Efforts would be made to persuade them to prepare for relocation, so they would be ready on short notice if war seemed inevitable. A contingency plan would be prepared for their evacuation.

In the tragic event of war combatants would then be free to fight until they have had enough. Refugees would not be idle while they wait, as plans would be made for the return home. UN personnel would help them compile a plan of government, preferably a democracy, but they would be helped with whatever they decide to do. (The theory of democracy emphasizes free choice.)

After the conflict the United Nations would arrange for resources to help those returning to adjust to a devastated country or area and to install a government and institutions as the people request. The organization would also bring to justice the top officials who were responsible for the tragedy.

Once a strategy resembling the above is in place, there would not be many years before war will truly be a part of history. The merchant would be free to provide goods and services for people; everyone would be better off. Refugee camps could be closed or converted to other uses as appropriate.

Many countries need to prepare for the Age of Reason, the United States foremost among them. Preparation should include a return to an emphasis on individual rights instead of group rights, cleaning up corruption in Washington and in state governments, creation of an active and concerned electorate who would make the laws under which they agree to be governed, and a government based on the principle of federalism. These actions would set a constructive example for many other nations.

Along with peacekeeping the next vital effort should be education, especially at the elementary level. Pliable children could be taught tolerance, hopefully before parents can hand down prejudices to their offspring. This process has the potential to break the vicious circle of revenge seeking. They should be taught the theory of democracy; this is also vitally important because, decades of rhetoric notwithstanding, there has been precious little democracy in the world to date. Educated children would grow up with a concern about health, learning, and maintaining good government.

Attitudes of public officials are far less pliable, so they must be sold on the theory of democracy. This means a heavy emphasis on diplomacy, stroking of egos and pointing to successful examples like a revamped United States. The United Nations should organize to persuade individual national officials to divert, say, 10 percent more of their budgets each year away from the military and toward education.

The vital first emphasis should be on elementary education, because a strong system creates a trainable labor force. Multinational corporations consider this resource when deciding where to invest money in job-creating operations. Poor countries rely on foreign direct investment to build their economies and thus raise their citizens' living standards.

Institution building should be from a bottom-up perspective. This includes family, religious facilities, schools, civic organizations, clubs, and government agencies. Because people support what they help create, it is very important to involve local people at the beginning of the planning stage. They must **perceive** that what they create is their own; absent this perception, and a negative reaction to yet another top-down force is likely.

The United Nations will have available teams of trained experts; the configuration of a particular team will be adapted to the specific needs of the country that requests its assistance. Members will plan on staying in a foreign country for several years, and a member will be replaced from time to time to respond to changing needs for expertise and respite. These people will understand that they are to provide advice only; policies resulting from consultation must be perceived as owned by citizens and officials being helped. The accumulated experience of the Peace Corps, for instance, should be a useful resource.

This is as much direct involvement that the United Nations should exercise, because its primary function is peacekeeping. All fieldwork should be performed by NGOs because they have vast experience in various countries, members know how the regions within a country differ from one another, and they are willing to get their hands dirty. This suggestion applies to all field education and institution building. Democracy can be built and maintained only by citizens acting together in a common interest in good government. Another valuable function for NGOs would be to convey early warnings of incipient strife to the United Nations.

High technology can help; *The Economist* reported on the video satellite phone: "Some people see this as the beginning of a revolution in outside broadcasting. . . . If everybody can be their own reporter and camera crew, the power of the censor will fall away."[21] A journalist with a video camera could sneak into Afghanistan or any area teetering on the brink of conflict, connect with a satellite uplink, and in spite of any government attempts to control information flows (Chapter 9) truth would quickly get into newsrooms. A coding system could prevent false reporting. *The Economist* indicated that new third-generation cell phones will also have this capability soon.

The United Nations today is a stale and bloated bureaucracy that must be overhauled. In 1996 *The Economist* noted,

> *Before there can be any thought of arrears paying, say the men on Capitol Hill who control their country's purse strings, the UN must prove it has reformed itself. . . . For a start, the Americans and others insist that the UN's regular budget must show zero growth . . . [and a] painful 10 percent reduction in UN staff. . . .*
>
> *But the UN's cobwebs are in the fabric, calling for a much more radical shake-out than anything yet proposed. Right, says Mr. Boutros-Ghali, but so long as the financial crisis remains unsolved "all other efforts to cut back, reform or restructure cannot possibly succeed." Financial . . . is essential for radical restructuring: even . . . getting rid of the worst of the human dead wood, is impossible if there is no money to pay people off. And until member countries . . . pay the money they owe, there will never be enough for deep reform.*[22]

With all due apology to the then-secretary-general, this is a typical bureaucratic reaction whenever the subject of money is discussed: There is never enough. In this instance as with many others discussed in this book, providing more money simply enables a bureaucracy to go on doing what it has been doing, all the while trumpeting its efforts at deep reform. Rewarding nonproductive behavior perpetuates it. Furthermore, if a bureaucrat has produced nothing of value, why is it necessary to give more money? Just fire the rascal.

If the problem lies in the fabric (and it does) fundamental restructuring is impractical when it is attempted from within the organization. There are too many vested interests in the status quo, too many bottoms to cover, and too much political power that will weigh in against any attempt at major overhaul. The impetus must come from outside the organization, just as must happen in the case of the US government.

Therefore serious consideration should be devoted to the idea of a totally new beginning. Today there is an opportunity to create a United Nations that is oriented to the Age of Reason and to which only truly dedicated people will be attracted as public servants. This means a location outside the United States and in a place remote from areas of large population. Today and in the future there is no need to be located in a large city because research can be conducted through electronic means, and locating outside the United States will serve to reduce that government's tendency to dominate the proceedings.

The notions of a General Assembly, a Secretariat, and a World Court are sound. However, there should be no permanent member nations in the Security Council. Rather, representatives would serve in staggered terms for continuity, with the length of a term commensurate with the size of a country's economy (three months, minimum). If a developing political bias were suspected, judicial review might adjust the terms of service in order to minimize this bias.

Shawcross commented on today's UN Security Council,

> *It is a relic of World War II that the US, Russia, China, Britain, and France dominate the impossible but probably essential world body. But they do, and attempts to change the membership to reflect more accurately the world on the edge of the millennium have always foundered. None of the permanent five wishes to leave the council, and too many of the other members of the UN wish to join. So the agreements or the divisions between the victors of 1945 still determine much of the direction of the world. They can either project the power of the UN or tie its hands. That is the reality, as against the ideal.*[23]

Public servants should be paid little, and their accommodations should be spare. These conditions will put off those who are more interested in prestige than in service. Finally, the UN charter should be reworked to emphasize peacekeeping and teams of experts.

The challenge of transformation of a world encumbered by strife into the Age of Reason is indeed daunting. But there is a world full of children and grandchildren, and more generations to come, who will be eternally grateful when this task is seriously engaged. It will take enough time, so that many young people as they mature into fully functioning adults could look forward to becoming actively involved in its creation . . . **and they will support it**.

The United Nations needs to get a life, and the world needs to get with the United Nations. By logical extension the world then gets a new lease on life.

An ancient Sanskrit poem reads (edited only slightly):

> *Look to this day, for it is life; the very life of life!*
> *In its brief course lie all the realities and truths of existence:*
> *The joy of growth, the splendor of action, the glory of knowledge.*
> *For yesterday is only a memory, and tomorrow is only a vision.*
> *But today well lived makes every yesterday a memory of happiness*
> *And every tomorrow a vision of hope.*

Notes

1. Stanley Meisler, *United Nations: The First 50 Years*. Atlantic Monthly Press, 1995.
2. Eric Alterman, *Sound and Fury: The Washington Punditocracy and the Collapse of American Politics*. Harper Collins, 1992.
3. *The Economist*, "The Best World Club We Have." November 22, 1997, p. 49.
4. Associated Press, "Navy Begins Training Exercises off Disputed Vieques Island." *News and Observer* (Raleigh, NC), October 18, 2000, p. 6A.
5. *The Economist*, "Pluto Plus Tard." September 30, 2001, p. 24.
6. *The Economist*, "The UN's Missions Impossible." August 5, 2000, p. 24.
7. William Shawcross, *Deliver Us from Evil: Peacekeepers, Warlords, and a World of Endless Conflict*. Simon and Schuster, 2000.
8. Meisler, *United Nations: The First 50 Years*.
9. *The Economist*, "Good Intentions Turned to Shame." July 5, 1997, p. 48.
10. Raeed N. Tayeh, "Bush's Mideast Muddle." *News and Observer* [Raleigh, NC], April 11, 2001, p. 19A.
11. *The Economist*, "A Challenge to Impunity." July 25, 1998, p. 21.
12. *The Economist*, "A World Court for Criminals." October 9, 1999, p. 19.
13. Molly Ivins, "Time to Rethink This Rugged Individualism." March 1998 column.
14. *The Economist*, "Oh, and Somalia Too." May 4, 2002, p. 32.
15. John Locke, in Jim Powell, *The Triumph of Liberty*. Free Press, 2000, p. 22.
16. Thomas A. Harris, *I'm Okay; You're Okay*. Avon Books, 1973.
17. *The Economist*, "Human Rights and Diplomacy." January 12, 1997, p. 19.
18. Kofi Annan, "Preventing Conflict in the Next Century." *The World in 2000* [*Economist* booklet], p. 51.
19. *The Economist*, "The Land that Time Forgot." September 23, 2000, p. 27.
20. Shawcross, *Deliver Us from Evil*.
21. *The Economist*, "Picture Perfect?" October 20, 2001, page 75.
22. *The Economist*, "The United Nations Heads for Bankruptcy." February 10, 1996, p. 41.
23. Shawcross, *Deliver Us from Evil*.

CONCLUSION

Any intelligent fool can make things bigger, more complex, and more violent.
It takes a touch of genius—and a lot of courage—
to move in the opposite direction.

—E. F. Schumacher

In his 1993 book *Beautiful Losers*, Francis wrote,

Today, almost the whole of American society encourages dependency and passivity. The result is an economy that does not work, a democracy that does not vote . . . a government that passes more and more laws, a people that is more and more lawless, and a culture that neither thinks nor feels except when and what it is told or tricked to think and feel.[1]

In 1946, Phillip Wylie saw trouble ahead for his United States.[2]

The vendors of patent social medicines expect, to a man, that by deviating from the long, hard route they will uncover a short cut for everybody. The universality of the grisly battle joined on account of their error is not a lesson to them, for, having embarked upon their diagonals with great to-do, they would rather risk a millennium of doom than the exposure of their fallacies.

The emotional appeal of a shortcut to prosperity was obvious; citizens' ancestors had struggled and sweated, but after the misery of the Great Depression and the tragedy of World War II, this no longer need be so. The people had acquired an abiding faith in government as social problem solver, so they bought the vendors' snake oil.

Only when it has exhausted itself can we offer our democratic message and then only if we have clung to its meaning through holocaust. Then, the faces of two billions of exhausted people will turn toward America. Then, if we have sacrificed, worked, shared, understood, thought, talked, stripped off our luxuries, planned a world mission, prepared ourselves to give much and ask little, we can offer the world a new charter and new liberty.

More than fifty years later, socialism has exhausted itself. Concerned citizens will not dodge the question: Have Americans clung to the meaning of democracy through big government's grand vision, its paternalism, its slow movement toward socialism? Or have they been completely flimflammed over the past fifty years by the grand deception?

Wylie commented,

> *No government that is so fluid it can convert to dictatorship to meet a war emergency—or legislate partial socialization to meet a depression—and yet through both permit any man to say what he thinks—is a weak government or an unrepresentative government or an unsuccessful government. It is the mightiest government men have ever had. It is democracy.*

The government accomplished the first two, but after the big war career politicians balked at the third. They commandeered the news media, which enabled them to gradually and insidiously build a mass market for their nostrum. But democracy can thrive only when self-governing citizens enjoy free access to truth.

Jefferson recommended a major change in the system of government every twenty to thirty years. Phillips showed that an event tantamount to a nonviolent revolution happened in this country about once each generation, until 1932 when Franklin Roosevelt was elected president.[3] He presided over the Great Depression and World War II, when government grew by leaps and bounds. But after the war great mountains of money flowed into Washington, and therefore when it was time for the next revolution (the 1960s) the rebels failed to slay the monster. Citizens' efforts to retrieve representative democracy fell short. Today the situation is even worse.

Al Gore wanted citizens to believe he understood the problem, so he wrote a book called *Reinventing America*. President Clinton saw civic institutions decaying in the countryside so he created a Reinventing Citizenship project. A congressman introduced a batch of nineteen bills, calling it his Project for American Renewal.

These went nowhere, for at least three reasons. One reason is that all three men created these things while trolling for votes, so their objective was short-term whereas the nature of the task is long-term. Another reason lay in the fact that whenever a major change in any public organization is needed it must come from outside that organization. Insiders like Clinton, Gore, and members of Congress are not about to work toward real change; they and many elite friends are far too happy with the present corrupt situation. Hence the third reason: There was no real intent to push these initiatives.

An insider will react to a major change coming from outside the bureaucracy in a different way so as to distract attention from the posh nature of his or her job. "I built a historic castle, and you are trying to tell me the sands are shifting and it will tumble if I don't abandon it and build something altogether different and which I don't understand? Hell, I've spent all my life . . . !" No entrenched and ossified bureaucracy can reform itself. (This quotation anticipates the nature of the reception in Washington when this book is published.)

Written by citizens, a detailed and realistic description of the Washington of today should be securely buried in a time capsule, to be raised by their counterparts every twenty or thirty years with great fanfare to attract attention to the event. This safeguard would prevent politically inspired future historians from writing what the Soviet government called revisionism; distorting facts to suit the politics of the day. The contents of the capsule should be widely disseminated, especially among the young, so they can appreciate and guard against the inevitable resurgence of actions in government based on the negative side of human nature. This event could be timed to take place shortly before promulgation of a new constitution, as its contents could be a useful resource.

The bloated, wasteful, and corrupt oligarchy must be removed. It is equally important to punish as many guilty as possible, because then the record will show for all time that those who personally profit from a paternalistic and overbearing government will be brought to account for their dirty deeds. Public officials in the future will thus be inclined to think twice before perpetrating such deeds.

However there is no law today under which to prosecute today's looters, simply because the elite class has carefully exempted itself from the force of law. The logical recourse is therefore to political activity (which the elites used to raise themselves above the law in the first place). That is, citizens must make laws that penalize immoral behavior in public office, and they will justify making them retroactive by recourse to historical precedent: Rule of Law is contained in Article IV, section two of the Constitution, and in the Fourteenth Amendment, section one. Citizens might opt to insert Rule of Law into the new constitution (see Appendix).

To bring the needed change to today's Washington objectivity is needed, and this is not available inside the castle where even truth has been politicized. Today there is a communication revolution going on, but the action is taking place well away from Washington. The debate on the free flow of information will be resolved by engineers, not politicians. So long as information flows freely from citizen to citizen the objective of government will not be preservation into perpetuity of bureaucracy, but rather preservation of truth.

This will be a giant step forward, but by itself it is not enough. Shevardnadze in his book *The Future Belongs to Freedom*, wrote,

> *I believed that truth was all-powerful, that one need only give it a voice, and it would have its own productive effect. Now I see that I was cruelly mistaken. The productivity of truth largely depends on* ***society's readiness to demand it, and on the state of the hearts and minds of the people who find the courage*** *to disseminate the true word.*[4] [emphasis added]

The time to demand truth has arrived. Brave and thinking citizens need only generate sufficient momentum, and the media will be forced to stop being the puppets of the elite class and come over to their side. When this point is reached the media will resume their traditional function: constant and constructive criticism of government at all levels. They will help citizens determine truth and act on it. But the initiative—the courage—must be found in an aroused citizenry. No others will step forward and be counted.

There has been a long history of abuse of powers entrusted to government officials by citizens. But today there are rapidly growing squads of thinking citizens. When these groups grow beyond the stage of critical mass and members' thinking moves beyond the "tut-tut" stage, action will be taken.

What this country needs is not the Great White Father, not a faked tax cut, and not yet another smothering batch of deception and fantasy. What it does need is minimal government and a government of the people, by the people, and for the people.

Because citizens have been brainwashed for fifty years by career politicians exhorting them to "protect our precious democracy," new thinking may require some time to diffuse throughout the society. Concerned children and grandchildren who have most of their lives before them will expedite the process.

May the force be with the people, as they bend to the wheel and drive this country forward toward democracy. The supreme importance of a continuing dialog among concerned citizens cannot be overemphasized.

> *We hold these Truths to be self-evident, that all Men are created equal, that they are endowed by their Creator with certain unalienable Rights, that among these are Life, Liberty, and the Pursuit of Happiness—That to secure these Rights, Governments are instituted among Men, deriving their just Powers from the Consent of the Governed, that whenever any Form of Government becomes destructive of these Ends, it is the Right of the People to alter or to abolish it, and to institute new Government, laying its Foundation on such Principles, and organizing its Powers in such Form, as to them shall seem most likely to effect their Safety and Happiness.* (The Declaration of Independence)

Fifty years later McCullough described the last days of John Adams and Thomas Jefferson.[5] "Jefferson completed a letter to the mayor of Washington declining an invitation to the Fourth of July celebration." In 1826 only three signers were still alive; these men were two of them and neither was fit to travel.

> *May it be to the world, what I believe it will be (to some parts sooner, to others later, but finally to all) the signal of arousing men to burst the chains under which monkish ignorance and superstition had persuaded them to bind themselves, and to assume the blessings and security of self-government. . . . All eyes are opened or opening to the rights of man. The general spread of the light of science has already laid open to every view the palpable truth, that the mass*

of mankind has not been born with saddles on their backs, nor a favored few, booted and spurred, ready to ride them legitimately by the grace of God. These are the ground of hope for others; for our selves, let the annual return to this day forever refresh our recollections of these rights, and an undiminished devotion to them.

Notes

1. Samuel Francis, *Beautiful Losers: Essays on the Failure of American Conservatism*. University of Missouri Press, 1993.
2. Philip Wylie, *A Generation of Vipers*. Dalkey Archive Press, 1946.
3. Kevin Phillips, *Arrogant Capital*. Little, Brown, 1994.
4. Eduard Shevardnadze, *The Future Belongs to Freedom*. Free Press, 1991.
5. David McCullough, *John Adams*. Simon and Schuster, 2000.

APPENDIX:
PRELIMINARY DRAFT OF A CONSTITUTION OF THE UNITED STATES OF AMERICA

William Peters offered the following remark in his book, *A More Perfect Union*:

> *By his very nature, man was a mixture of good and bad qualities. By encouraging the good in man—his sociability, reasonableness, generosity, and lover of liberty—education, religion, and government might help to repress the bad—his selfishness, passion, greed, and corruptibility. And of all potentially corrupting forces, the most dangerous was political power.*

This line of thought provided for the founding fathers a framework for discussion and debate on May 25, 1787, when they finally attained a quorum in Philadelphia's Independence Hall and were thus able to open the Constitutional Convention.

The Constitution that is presumably in effect today has, in fact, been repeatedly ignored by the elite class in Washington. These people make and enforce laws to suit themselves. This practice violates several parts of the Constitution; the situation has gotten so bad that the very intent of that document has been undermined.

In addition to this important statement there is another problem. Today it is extremely difficult to accurately interpret the intent of the founding fathers, simply because tremendous changes in the culture since their time have caused changes in the meaning of words and their usage in the language. (This difficulty provided a part of Jefferson's reasoning when he recommended that a new constitution be formulated every twenty or thirty years.) Therefore at the very least the Constitution's wording needs to be updated, but it would be foolish to stop there.

This book argues for direct democracy. Therefore it is appropriate to consider a constitution that would guide lawmaking under the new precept. In 1787–88, citizens discussed the current constitution as a proposal for adoption. They compared it with the inadequate Articles of Confederation that guided lawmaking at that time, and founded the new constitution as a new precept. Publius promoted it in the *Federalist Papers*, and history shows that citizens embraced it.

Today the nation confronts a similar situation. Useful as it has been for well over 200 years, the Constitution does not meet the needs of today's citizens. A sweeping change is in order, and Publius II is promoting it on behalf of his fellow citizens through creation of the "pocket gofers" (see website in Preface, page xii).

The constitution itself should strongly emphasize the supreme importance of citizens acting on their own behalf. Persistence in this, albeit hard to accomplish, will keep personal power dispersed, and herein lies the very essence of democracy. Furthermore enlisting government assistance in the task of citizen self-improvement triggers behavior based on the positive side of human nature.

This information provides the background for the following preliminary draft. There is no intent to fashion a finished document; rather, this draft is only a basis for discussion and debate. Discussion might produce two or three well-conceived formal proposals. If this happens the resulting competition would stimulate much serious thought and debate, and the final document would probably be rendered more effective.

A careful balance should be sought between stability and dynamism. An overemphasis on the first causes centralization, overbearing government, gridlock, and eventually corruption and deception. An overemphasis on the second causes a lack of coordination and control of government institutions and functions. There is a lack of guidance for constructive change.

A Proposed Constitution of the United States of America

We the people of the United States, in order to form a more perfect union, establish justice, insure domestic tranquillity, and secure the blessings of liberty to ourselves and to our posterity, do ordain and establish this Constitution for the United States of America. It is the instrument of the people, created by the people, and for the people. Its intent is to make government the agent of the people, to help them protect their natural rights as free citizens from infringements by other individuals, groups, government itself, and nations. Furthermore the intent is to aid citizens in their pursuit of continuing, orderly change in the society.

Article I

Citizens shall create a body of federal law to guide the decisions of implementation by the president of policy making by the citizens. This body shall conform to the principles as set forth in Article VI in this document, and shall be LIMITED to those issues, national and international, which citizens deem to fall within the remit of national government, and which they find inconvenient or impossible to dispose of in other levels of government. Citizens shall create legislation intended to expedite repeals, updates, modifications or extensions of existing federal laws. Every federal law shall include a date of termination. Constant vigilance shall ensure that government does not grow beyond an absolute minimum. Citizen-made law shall put this principle into effect.

Article II

The president and vice president of the United States shall be citizens, and shall have resided within the country for at least fifteen years after age twenty. Each shall have attained age forty or more at the time of direct election by eligible citizens voting. The president and vice-president shall serve for one term of five years. For each election citizens shall select at least three candidates for president, to include the incumbent vice-president. Incumbent must capture the most votes to win the office. The second-place finisher shall serve as vice-president. Campaigns shall not commence in any way prior to sixty days before election day. Campaign resources shall be restricted to print and personal appearances.

Citizens shall determine the personal qualifications for these offices, the procedure to get on the ballot, the time and place of election, run-off elections, and the monitoring of campaigns and proceedings to ensure equal opportunity and fairness. A majority of voting citizens is required to assume office. Polling places in all states shall open and close at the same time, or the news media shall be restrained from reporting on the outcome until after the last polling place has closed.

The duties of the president shall be restricted to international relations, and providing information of his or her activities to the citizens as they shall require. He shall commit the United States to no treaties or other agreements with governments of other nations, unless they are clearly intended to make and preserve peace and goodwill among nations and enjoy the active and explicit consent of the citizenry. He shall publicly justify every position on and addition to his staff, and each employee shall receive very modest compensation and per diem for travel, and no perquisites. Increases in compensation or per diem, or any money earned from off-duty activities must be approved by the citizens. The total size of the president's paid staff shall be published at least once a year, at unannounced random times selected by citizens.

Within thirty days of assuming office the president shall either clear the incumbent among citizens for continuing service, or select at least three candidates for ambassador to the United Nations. State governors shall vote for their preferred candidates. The democratic concept of world citizenship shall guide the ambassador's arguments and recommendations before the United Nations.

The president shall have an advisory board. He shall solicit advice from this group as he sees fit. It shall be organized as follows.

There will be ten members who shall serve in rotation, such that all states will be represented equally over time. Members shall be selected from all walks of life; state governments shall strive to ensure a balance as they select members. (*Walks of life* shall be interpreted to read social status and occupations, including full-time homemaker, student and retired. Neither race nor gender nor ethnic heritage shall influence selections.) Officials of local and state governments will not be eligible.

Toward the end of a period of service, members shall elect a chairperson. This person shall serve in this capacity for one additional period. Members shall serve without compensation, except for a modest per diem allowance and transportation to and from their homes. Costs of official communications to and from home states will be covered. The advisory board shall promptly receive copies of any and all communications coming into the president's office from voters, in its discretion.

The vice president shall facilitate and coordinate interstate governmental activities, but he shall have no executive authority over these. He or she shall also help disseminate information regarding federal government activities. He shall receive inputs from citizens through other levels of government, compile these, and report results to the president. His needs for staff shall be restricted as per the president.

The president shall utilize standard accrual accounting practice in keeping the nation's books. Independent teams of auditors shall be selected by citizens according to law. The president shall provide monthly and quarterly reports of federal government expenditures to citizens through local government offices. All accounts and accounting practices shall be completely open to citizens, and no activity will take place off-budget. Extra effort shall be expended to make financial statements readable to a citizen with average intelligence. These statements shall be broadcast in accordance with law.

During his term he shall measure citizens' preferences and prepare and submit two biennial budgets for citizen approval. These shall include blanks for salary and expenses of himself and the vice president, to be filled in through citizen consent. Citizens shall have at least ninety days to discuss a budget proposal before it is due back to the president. At least thirty days shall be provided for a second submission and return if deemed necessary by citizens. There shall be no contingent obligations whatever, on or off-budget. Once the budget is approved the president shall collect citizen-authorized operating funds from state governments, pro rata by voting populations. During the biennium he shall publicize quarterly reports that directly compare actual expenses with those budgeted. He shall explain any deviations.

If approved by citizens the president may borrow money, but only for a fixed term. In no case shall obligations for interest or repayment of debt devolve on succeeding generations. He shall not tax individual incomes, nor private sector organizations' sales revenues, incomes or assets. If citizens agree to be taxed for the purpose the president may accumulate a reserve fund, to be used only for a previously specified purpose.

Citizens shall make laws. The text of every bill shall provide an explicit and direct reference to the appropriate part of the Constitution that authorizes it. A law shall be passed authorizing them to order an independent audit of the federal government's books at any time deemed appropriate.

The president shall be subject to recall or be relieved of his duties due to incapacitation, as provided by law. In such events or due to his death in office or resignation, the vice president shall assume the duties of president. When a vice president shall leave office for whatever reason, the president shall nominate at least two citizens, among whom citizens will decide at their convenience. The president shall designate one of these to serve in the interim.

The president shall convene a Cabinet of departments, consisting of a ministry of foreign relations and world peace, a ministry of interior, and a ministry of treasury. Any addition to the number of departments shall be through constitutional amendment only. All ministers shall seek guidance from citizens as well as the president, when performing the duties of office. Neither the president, the vice president, nor an employee of any department shall have authority to interfere in any way in the private sector of the economy. If the vice president is serving in lieu of the president and becomes unfit for office for any reason, the minister of foreign relations shall assume the mantle of office.

The minister of foreign relations and world peace shall be responsible for bilateral and multilateral relations with other countries, and with the United Nations. He or she shall advise the president regarding treaties to be proposed for ratification by citizens. After consultations with the president and concerned citizens, he shall set or update policies for immigration and asylum.

The minister of interior shall provide a resource for interstate relations. Except for the District of Columbia, he or she shall manage federal lands with the objective of either privatization or transfer to stewardship by state governments. He shall provide mediation in the case of disputes among states. He shall assist state governments in extradition of suspected criminals, including consideration of sentences a suspect is serving in another state. He shall adjudicate instances of cybercrime and other crimes that do not fall under the jurisdiction of one state.

The minister of the treasury shall combine with an independent central bank to manage monetary policy. The bank's primary objective shall be control over inflation. Citizens will by law determine its organization. The minister shall collect revenues from state governments and make disbursements in accordance with requests from the executive and the current budget.

All ministers shall provide information to the president and vice president as needed for sharing with the citizenry. Ministers shall coordinate their efforts and keep each other fully informed.

Citizens shall elect a shadow Cabinet, whose members shall be privy to all relevant information, and shall make decisions just as if they were in office. Results shall be disseminated to citizens. The shadow Cabinet shall meet regularly, and provide constructive criticism for the president while receiving comments from citizens. Citizens may ask the shadow Cabinet to monitor government expenditures.

Operations of all components of the federal government shall be open to public scrutiny. Information shall be carefully prepared using plain language, prior to release. The need for honesty shall pervade preparation. Citizens shall by law make requirements for dissemination, to include penalties for noncompliance or delays.

Article III

The judicial responsibility for the United States shall rest in a five-judge tribunal, members of which shall be appointed by state legislatures. The primary qualification for membership shall be familiarity with international law and the Constitution. Each tribunal shall serve for six months, in rotation, each term representing five scattered states.

It shall meet when appropriate to try cases of treason and other high crimes against the United States, as provided by law. It shall render judgment as to the conformity of a federal law with the Constitution. The tribunal shall have authority to render null and void a law that does not conform. Decisions to support or strike down a law will be accompanied by published explanations in plain language, but under no circumstances may these be construed as new law. Furthermore, the tribunal shall adjudicate disputes between state governments. The overriding purpose of the court shall be protection of individual human rights from encroachment by government.

Members shall serve without compensation other than a travel and per diem reimbursement.

Article IV

Each state government shall coordinate with all others to ensure that no state discriminates against the fundamental rights of any citizen or group of citizens of another state or states. The same applies to resident aliens. Every citizen aged eighteen or older has the right to vote except those incarcerated for felonies, and no obligation of tax shall accompany this right. There shall be no impedance of access to polling places, geographic or electronic. Cooperation shall extend to apprehension of those suspected of civil or criminal offenses, including extradition to an appropriate location for adjudication.

No federal public servant shall assume a special title or trappings or perquisites, nor shall he or she accept any gift or benefit offered to him below market cost unless specifically permitted by law. In all his dealings he shall scrupulously avoid even a suggestion of conflict of interest. Instances where this is a part of his duties and thus cannot be avoided shall be publicized and explained.

Candidates for and appointees to federal office shall demonstrate to citizens that they are public-spirited citizens who desire to serve for a limited time. Citizens shall create laws to set such limits.

Article V

This Constitution may be amended by citizen initiative as provided by law. A proposal shall be discussed and debated for at least one year. An amendment goes into full effect as part of the Constitution on the day it is ratified by three-fourths of all voting citizens. If not ratified by five years after formal presentation, a proposal becomes null and void.

Citizens may ratify an amendment to accept an additional state into the Union, or to divide or consolidate existing states. None of these actions shall be impelled by force.

Article VI

The following statement of principles shall act to preserve the freedom of individual citizens from the depredations of all levels of government. They are intended to foment morality in individual citizens, and hence a need for only minimal law. They are derived from the laws of human nature, which are also called natural law. Natural law inheres in people in light of their humanity. They preempt and are superior to any law made by man. What few laws the citizens deem to be necessary shall be guided by these principles.

1. Government shall make no law that infringes the fundamental rights to freedom of religious belief and practice, freedom of speech and writing, peaceful assembly, and petition for redress of grievance. Freedom of speech and writing shall be construed to include only criticism of government policies, laws and actions at all levels. (Any other restrictions on speech may be guided by local laws.) Legal resident aliens shall enjoy the same basic rights as citizens.
2. Government shall make no law that infringes the fundamental rights to legally and honestly acquired private property: preservation, improvement, modification, repair, transportation, inheritance, gift, and conveyance through voluntary agreement between seller and buyer. The taking of private property for the public good must be in accordance with law made by citizens within the appropriate jurisdiction, and fair compensation must be promptly provided. The same shall apply to any infringement on the full rights of private property as specified in the first statement above. Otherwise the sanctity of legal contracts freely entered into shall not be disturbed by government.

   The fundamental rights to private property shall apply as well to international trade and investment, in respect of other nations' applicable laws.

3. The Rule of Law shall prevail: Laws enacted shall apply exactly and equally to every person or group of people in the appropriate jurisdiction, with absolutely no exceptions under any conditions.
4. Citizens shall be protected from unreasonable searches of property or person, and seizure of private property.
5. Every citizen shall be protected against incursions by force or fraud on the part of government, other people, or nation-states.
6. Every citizen accused of a criminal offense is entitled to a prompt and fair trial. He may not be tried more than once for the same offense, except appeals. He or she shall not suffer cruel or unusual punishment. He shall promptly be informed of the nature of his offense, and shall have access to witnesses and competent counsel for his defense. Punishment shall be prompt, sure, fair, and fit the nature of the offense.
7. Political power shall originate in ideas, recommendations, and programs proposed, discussed, debated, and decided by citizens at the local level. With bottom-up government, citizens pass responsibility for implementation on to other levels only when they deem it necessary. Powers given to government at all levels shall be carefully specified by the citizens, and information about them thoroughly disseminated. Any powers not so delegated shall remain in the citizens. Citizens may respecify or take back powers previously granted, at their discretion. The definition of the principle of federalism includes two dimensions. The first lies in minimal government at all levels; political power remains dispersed where it originated. The second ensures a balance in powers delegated such that no one level of government gains predominance over any other.
8. State governments shall not inhibit legal goods, services, capital, and citizens from free travel and relocation between states, for employment or otherwise. In an instance of real or potential danger, information and persuasion shall guide behavior, not law. Said governments shall coordinate taxation of citizens with interests in more than one state, while guided by the objective of fairness.
9. Government shall make no law that favors one citizen or group of citizens over others, or discriminates against the same.
10. The federal government may not give or send public money to individual citizens, nor receive money from them.
11. Education shall not be subject to interference by government. Quite the contrary: the federal government shall encourage excellence in education without exerting any authority, monetary or otherwise, or any type of undue influence.

12. Government recognizes that an enlightened public can determine truth through free and open discussion and debate of relevant issues, and that the public can through these activities discover and act against any type of subterfuge or corruption on the part of government officials. These officials further recognize the vital role played by discussion among citizens, so they encourage it and listen to the results.
13. Good citizenship includes tolerance of those whose appearance, speech, and actions are perceived as different. It includes a democratic mentality, internal morality, and the desire to contribute to good government. The good citizen knows that eternal vigilance is the price of liberty.
14. By definition government is force, and therefore the principle of persuasion shall be utilized as often as practical, with reliance on force only as a last resort. The right action is that which is determined by citizens and not government officials, who shall remain public servants.
15. Every ballot for public office shall include a space called NOTA, or None of the Above. If no candidate earns more votes than NOTA, another election shall be conducted.
16. Government and affiliated organizations shall place no restriction on candidates' access to the ballot, except according to citizen-made law.
17. Members of a minority shall accept majority rule, but the latter shall respect the fundamental rights of the minority, including the right of participation in government.
18. Citizens shall make laws, first at the local level. Issues not amenable to disposition at local level shall be handed on to the next level, at which citizens shall make additional laws, etc. A body of law at national level shall address only issues left over from all previous actions.
19. A maximum proportion of money raised for government operations shall be spent where it is raised.
20. Any state or group of states retains the right to secede from the Union. Citizens shall establish the procedure by law.
21. Citizens must be formally consulted according to law whenever plans are discussed for any foreign military deployment or action whatsoever.
22. Neither national security nor any other reason shall be utilized to justify government at any level withholding information from the public. Citizen-made law shall determine punishments for any type or duration of impedance.

Article VII

This Constitution shall come into full force and effect upon ratification of three-fourths of voting citizens, at which time the original Constitution (in effect as of June 21, 1788) shall be terminated. On that date at noon thirty years hence this Constitution in its entirety, including all amendments, shall become null and void. No national debt shall be carried forward beyond this date.

Within ten days of the date of ratification, a prepared time capsule shall be securely buried. Its purpose is to describe and criticize the economic and political environments of the time, so it may provide guidance to the compilers of the new constitution thirty years hence. Its content shall be specified by citizens.

INDEX OF NAMES

— A —

— B —

— C —

— G —

— H —

— L —

— M —

— Q —

— R —

— S —

— T —

— U —

— V —

— W —

— Z —